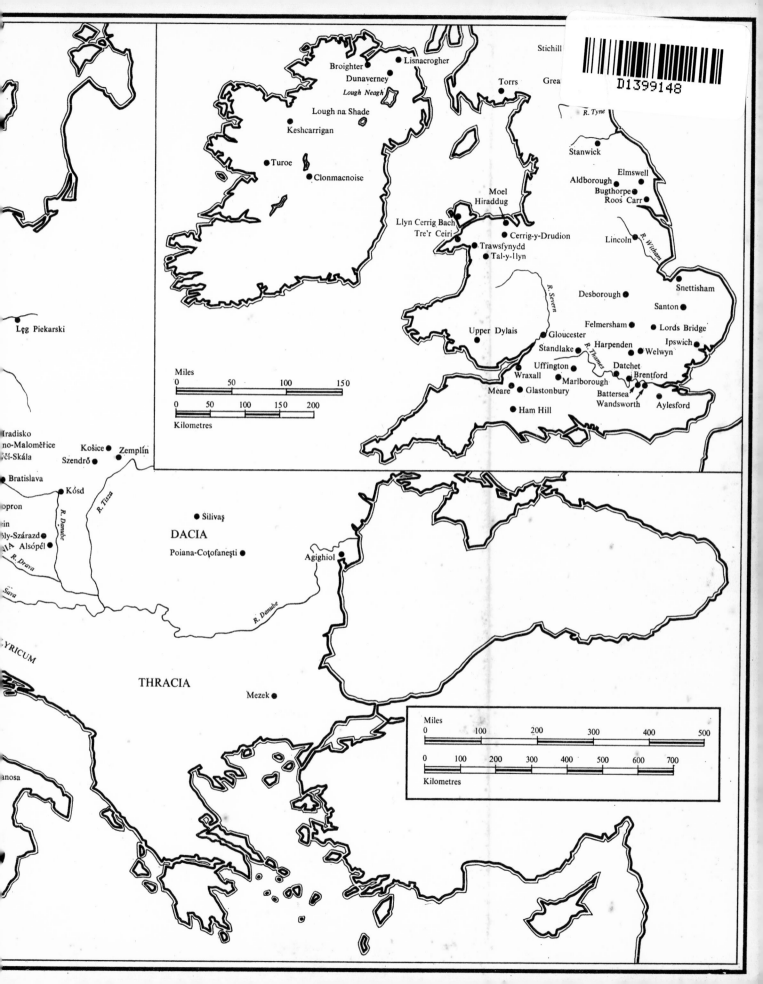

Stichill

D1399148

Broighter Lisnacrogher
Dunaverney Torrs Grea
Lough Neagh
R. Tyne
Lough na Shade
Keshcarrigan Stanwick
Elmswell
Aldborough
Bugthorpe
Turoe Roos Carr
Clonmacnoise
Moel
Hiraddug
Llyn Cerrig Bach Lincoln R. Witham
Tre'r Ceiri Cerrig-y-Drudion
Trawsfynydd
Tal-y-llyn
Snettisham
R. Severn Desborough Santon
Upper Dylais Felmersham Lords Bridge
Gloucester Harpenden Ipswich
Standlake R. Thames Welwyn
Uffington Datchet
Wraxall Marlborough Brentford
Meare Glastonbury Battersea
Wandsworth Aylesford
Ham Hill

Miles
0   50   100   150

0   50   100   150   200
Kilometres

Lęg Piekarski

Iradisko
no-Malomětice Košice
včí-Skála Szendrő Zemplín

Bratislava Kósd
opron R. Tisza
ein Silivaş
ly-Szárazd DACIA
A Alsópél R. Drava Poiana-Coţofaneşti
Agighiol
Sáva R. Danube

YRICUM

THRACIA

Mezek

Miles
0   100   200   300   400   500

0   100   200   300   400   500   600   700
Kilometres

ART OF
THE EUROPEAN
IRON AGE

ART OF
THE EUROPEAN
IRON AGE

A study of the elusive image

J. V. S. MEGAW

HARPER & ROW, PUBLISHERS
New York and Evanston

CONTENTS

Preface

EUROPEAN Iron Age art – that is, the art which flourished in barbarian Europe from about the eighth century BC to the second century AD – is still comparatively unknown to the general public and strangely is little studied today either by art historians or archaeologists. Even the art of the La Tène Celts, which was the first truly widespread European art style to emerge after the work of the nameless geniuses of the Upper Palaeolithic cave paintings, is often largely ignored in the many surveys of European art history now available. Perhaps its iconography, united in subject range but powerful and at times almost baroque in execution, no less than its often miniature scale, is out of tune with today's taste.

For any student of the Iron Age foundations of European art, the late Paul Jacobsthal's *Early Celtic Art* is an essential starting point. As Jacobsthal's title suggests, though, his survey is strictly limited in its chronological scope, while the conditions surrounding the period when the book was being compiled limited it in area also. More recently, with the aid of T. G. E. Powell's *Prehistoric Art* (London, 1966) and Nancy Sandars's *Prehistoric Art in Europe* (Harmondsworth, 1968), many English readers will have learnt for the first time that there *is* prehistoric art between the Ice Age and the coming of the Romans. In both these volumes our particular field of interest, the Iron Age, can be seen in its true artistic perspective. In the present study, however, my aim is much more limited. I am concerned with presenting the varied range of the arts of one particular period, illustrating the more mundane objects, 'folk crafts', pottery, tools, and weapons side by side with the great cult statues and the panoply of ornaments in precious metals, which were the natural accoutrements of a warrior society. To this end, the layout of my illustrations follows artistic themes rather than a strict division into types of objects; indeed, occasionally to make a particular stylistic point I have broken into a more or less strict chronological ordering. The British Isles is the one area to receive an almost exclusively regional treatment, since British Iron Age art, like many other features of British prehistory, shows a development related to, but distinct from, that of the Continent.

I should be the first to point out that my title is rather more all-embracing than the contents. With one exception, following Jacobsthal, I have omitted the arts of the Iron Age (and in fact partly Celtic) people of Iberia. Iberia in my selected period constitutes not so much a backwater as an isolated lagoon of art history and has been well served by those who have the advantage of studying its material manifestations at first hand; the same exclusion applies to the art of the Scythians. Since my theme is more precisely the art of barbarian Europe in the Iron Age, I have not discussed the strictly Iron Age antecedents of classical Greek and Roman art except of course where such classical influence may be seen in non-classical objects, nor have I included classical representations of Celts and things Celtic, however useful these may be archaeologically. Italy, then, is hardly dealt with although for the earlier part of the Iron Age a similar artistic tradition may be traced north, south, and east of the Alps. Jacobsthal's comment that Italy was a land 'where motifs grew like weeds' does, however, demand that the outward spread of some of these motifs be followed and I have chosen the art of the *situlae* for this purpose. Otherwise, the Balkans save for what is now being termed 'Istro-Pontic' art is also poorly represented; my first-hand knowledge of the fascinating East Hallstatt area is, alas, as yet only superficial.

Nowhere better than in archaeology can one find the truth of Alice's inquiry as to 'what is the use of a book without pictures?' André Malraux has pointed out in his *Museum without Walls* how photography has brought a new awareness, a new creativeness, into the study of art. Photography allows the study of detail divorced from but nevertheless strictly related to the whole. Photography, however, is itself an art, an interpretation of form, and one must realise this when glancing at the following pages. Jacobsthal's *Early Celtic Art* has the added quality of Eduard Neuffer's excellent photographs, examples of the 'visual record' or, in a non-pejorative sense, 'museum' approach to ancient art and I count myself fortunate in being able to reproduce some of Neuffer's work here. For the rest I have adhered to one simple rule for pictorial selection: to use those illustrations, from whatever source, which best illustrate the particular visual point I wish to make. This seemingly obvious premise has led over the past five years to my continually worrying a vast number of publishers, museum authorities, and colleagues, both archaeological and photographic; full acknowledgement is given elsewhere. I must note here that the University of Sydney has readily given me both the opportunity and the finance to make it possible for me to study at first hand the majority of objects illustrated on the following pages.

In conclusion, as has been well said, Jacobsthal's work is of such quality that he has made all 'his successors his commentators' and my debt to one whose absolute command of a foreign language is such as to demand frequent quotation will be obvious. Of the many others who over the years have taken great pains to discuss problems both general and in particular I must single out here Professor Dr Wolfgang Dehn, Professor Dr Jan Filip, the late Sir Cyril Fox, Professor Dr Otto-Herman Frey, Professor E. H. Gombrich, Dr F. R. Hodson, Professor Martyn Jope, Professor Dr Ole Klindt-Jensen, Professor Dr Werner Krämer, Professor Stuart Piggott, Mr T. G. E. Powell, Dr Anne Ross, Miss N. K. Sandars, and Mr M. G. Spratling. Two graduates of that great centre of Iron Age studies, the Vorgeschichtliche Seminar at Marburg, Dr Ulrich Schaaff and Dr Frank Schwappach, and my former fellow students, Dr Graham Ritchie and Dr Morna Simpson, kindly gave me access to much unpublished thesis material. While I have from time to time disagreed with such good friends and counsellors, I hope that I have presented the raw material of my study in such a way that I may be refuted from within my own pages. I hope, however, to have provoked not so much controversy as the simple enjoyment of a great period of Europe's diverse art history.

J. V. S. Megaw
Sydney – Edinburgh – London
October 1969

Introduction

A GAUNT granite figure, naked save for a pointed helmet, neck-ring, and sword-belt [12]* which once marked the last resting place of an Iron Age chieftain of South Germany; a bronze handle embellished with the head of a bull and modelled with all the cheerful abstraction of a Walt Disney cartoon [161]; scenes of military pomp and pagan mythology beaten into the silver fragments of a great eastern European cauldron placed on a Danish peat-bog [209] – these are but three aspects of the many-faced nature of the art of the European Iron Age. This art is not an art of uniformity of one style altering little in time and space. Instead it ranges in space from the mouth of the Danube to northern Denmark; in time it extends from the eighth century BC to the second century AD. We should be no more surprised to find variations within the artistic products of such a period than to observe the diversities of the same area from the Norman conquest of England to the first soft landing on the moon – to select a similar time-span. Again, we must be on our guard when observing differences in *style*, differences in that 'totality of conventions which make up the art of a particular area at a particular period of time', to borrow the definition of an American anthropologist.[1] Following on from this definition, one must remember that style in itself has no absolute chronological significance. This point may be readily illustrated by one of many examples to be observed in the following pages – the pop-eyed look of the central face of the gold armlet from a Celtic chieftain's grave at Rodenbach in the Rheinpfalz [55] has many of the features of the mask worked into the design of the twin bracelets from the Waldalgesheim chariot-burial [124–125], yet these pieces may be separated in time by upwards of a century. Equally, as Mayer Schapiro notes, 'the variation of style in a culture or group is often considerable within the same period' – a point which makes difficult any chronological ordering of ahistorical art such as that of the Iron Age. To quote another example from the context of Celtic art, we may contrast the fine, almost photographic, portraits of bronze mounts from Maloměřice, Brno [160], with the much freer abstraction of the fierce griffon from the same set [158]. It is also salutary to compare various details of the bronze flagon from a chariot burial of the later fifth century at Dürrnberg bei Hallein [72] – was this the work of one man with command of a wide stylistic repertoire or of several craftsmen-specialists? Jacobsthal was certainly right in affirming that 'the Celtic . . . Style has a firm physiognomy'[2] but it is a very varied one. Add to this statement the problems of ascribing individual pieces to localised 'hands' or even 'schools' when dealing with the products of probably no more than a handful of itinerant artists, and the difficulties of writing Iron Age art history should be all too apparent. The archaeologist's most favoured tool for assessing the origin and exchange routes of artefacts, the distribution map, is of little use in such a context. But then a distribution map of the original or present-day locations of the paintings of Albrecht Dürer, for example, would hardly give a true indication of

---

* Figures in **bold** type refer to the *Catalogue* and/or illustration numbers.
[1] M. Schapiro in A. L. Kroeber (ed.), *Anthropology Today* (1953), 287–312; see also article 'Style' in *International Dictionary of the Social Sciences* (1968), 352–61 (=E. H. Gombrich)
[2] P. Jacobsthal, *Early Celtic Art* (1944; reissue 1969), 160

the artist's origins; the study of Iron Age art is not impossible but like any other such study it must be seen in its proper context.

APPROACHES TO PREHISTORIC ART

'There really is no such thing as Art. There are only artists.'[1] With this statement Professor E. H. Gombrich has attempted to put art in its true, human perspective and to combat that common concept of art with a capital 'A' as somehow having an existence independent of its creators, independent, that is, of time and space. This human perspective is one which tries to set art against the continually changing horizons of man's experience. As an eminent architectural historian has put it, art grows with man's innate passion 'to develop a means of expression for his inner life'.[2] The precise cause and mode of this expression may alter; the basic reason for this creative passion may in fact be inexpressible or due to a simple sense of fun, of enjoyment, the creation of a 'joke motif' [59] – a common phenomenon in present-day so-called 'primitive' art – or the realm of the unconscious may be probed with a visual vocabulary of signs and symbols. A recent trend towards a psychological approach to the problems of artistic development has established the principle that an individual style is a personal expression and 'common traits in the art of a culture or nation can be matched with some features of social life, ideas, customs'[3] – a point which the next section should help to make clear.

We know the cultural perspective within which may be placed those ancient artists whose names are known to us – the great figures of Greece and Rome, who created images both of man, and, reflecting these images, of his gods. Then there are the anonymous artists of the ancient world: artists in the service of the great Pharaohs, and in Sumer and Babylon artists in the service of the temple and the priest-king. These are artists whose stylistic personalities we attempt to define through the far from infallible techniques of the art historian and his assemblage of stylistic traits. Even if physical identity cannot be achieved, we recognise that countless centuries before the flood, before the first pyramid or the first city, there was a place, a need for the artist. Amongst the art of Ice Age hunting communities from the Pyrenees to the Urals, in the earliest art in the world, we may perceive masterpieces of European painting and sculpture produced over 15,000 years ago by unknown artists living in a Europe whose climate was like that of the present-day tundra wastelands and whose coastline would have been unrecognisable to any modern European. Nevertheless the art of this far-distant period still looks strangely familiar; seeming attempts at accurate representation of natural forms ('realism' or naturalism) can often be seen side by side with apparent pure abstractions. This art was of course the work of individual artists, a palaeolithic Picasso, a Marino Marini amongst mammoth hunters. Some of the 'nature studies' of the Franco-Cantabrian caves are no less skilled in their partial formalisation (to use a less loaded word than 'abstraction') of living forms than the sketches of Dürer, Rembrandt, and Picasso, who were draftsmen before all else.

We must not, though, consider the art of yesterday entirely by the standards of mid-twentieth-century value judgements; aesthetics, after all, in the words of Henry Moore, is what you know. Twentieth-century aesthetics applied to ancient art forms may all too easily

[1] Gombrich, *Story of Art* (11 ed., 1966), 5
[2] S. Giedion, *The beginning of art* = *The Eternal Present* I (1962), 3
[3] Schapiro, *op. cit.*, 310

involve us in the concept of 'art for art's sake'. Art for art's sake can only mean art divorced from its social and historical context which may give us individual satisfaction, but this satisfaction must necessarily be totally different from the mystical and probably magical circumstances under which it may have been produced. To borrow an idea not from an art historian but from an archaeologist, the late V. Gordon Childe, only such dangerous doctrines as art for art's sake can be evoked to justify the setting up within the antiseptic walls of a London museum of such fragmented monuments as the Parthenon. The sense of beauty is a fluctuating phenomenon despite those archaeologically-biased art historians who regard art as completely subject 'to material restraint and technical determination', entirely 'susceptible to rational analysis and impartial scrutiny'.[1] Several methods of description and formal analysis have been developed, but in examining all styles of art, Classical, Gothic or Modern, we must also be prepared to admit to genuine manifestations of beauty produced by other people at other times which may be hard to grasp with our sense of values. We tend to forget that ultimately most of our definitions of art are in fact based on definitions of classical Greek and Roman art; to term an art style 'primitive' is to do little else than state that its basic vocabulary is not that of our own preconceived artistic viewpoint. In other words, a thing of beauty may not necessarily be a joy for ever.

The problem of naturalism or reality in art has already briefly been alluded to; Gombrich indeed considers that 'there is no neutral naturalism. The artist no less than the writer needs a vocabulary before he can embark upon a "copy" of reality.'[2] This view is of course not new. As long ago as 1915 Heinrich Wölfflin in his *Kunstgeschichtliche Grundbegriffe* stated that all paintings owe more to other paintings than they do to direct observation.[3] Considering that art history was predominantly a study of the development of style, Wölfflin and, after him Sir Herbert Read, has also noted that all the separate elements of a single work of art fuse into a unity which remains the expression of a certain temperament,[4] and it hardly needs emphasising that such temperaments are made up of a complex intermingling of individual idiosyncrasies and the effects of local environment. Though it might be well argued that a full understanding of any art form should lead to an understanding of the culture of which it is a part, any examination of the art style of a past, prehistoric period is rendered all the more difficult due to our inevitably incomplete knowledge of the physical and psychological characteristics of just those cultures in which such a style may have developed. Nevertheless, the attempt must be made to use what information archaeology does reveal of the past if our hypothetical ordering of style development is to have any validity at all. It is for this reason that, following the lead of Terence Powell's and Nancy Sandars's recent surveys, I have here attempted to relate art forms as artefacts to an admittedly all-too-crudely restored picture of Iron Age culture as a whole.

Some – one cannot in all honesty these days say most – art historians are content, as cultural anthropologists would not be content, to study the art of their chosen area seemingly *in vacuo*, maintaining that there are certain basic visually perceptive elements in the expression of individual styles which are susceptible of a common analytical approach. Support for this approach to art analysis is given by the often closely similar formal solutions offered by artists in

[1] Rhys Carpenter, *Art and Archaeology* (1963), 119
[2] Gombrich, *Art and Illusion: A Study in the Psychology of Pictorial Representation* (3 ed., 1968), 75
[3] H. Wölfflin, *Kunstgeschichtliche Grundbegriffe* (1915), 249; English edition: *id.*, *Principles of Art History* (1932)
[4] Sir Herbert Read, *Meaning of Art* (3 ed., 1956), 65–66

11

clearly unrelated areas to certain representational problems. For example, the *mimi* or stick-figures depicted in northern Australian rock-art are strikingly similar to those of the mesolithic paintings of the Spanish Levant or even figural representations in the Geometric phase of pre-classical Greek vase-painting. All three conventions suggest a similar use by the individual artists of limited and limiting forms concerned more with geometry than nature. Early Celtic art in this context [**6, 8, 9, 10**] is particularly susceptible to ready identification of what Gombrich calls the *schemata* or 'minimum clues' of expression.[1]

To reduce this point to a question of definitions, any single work of art is made up of a basic *theme* or *subject matter* (even if the subject is non-representational), individual *motifs* and *patterns* or repetitive units of visual expression whose recognition offers the most useful key to stylistic subdivision, and, most difficult of all to define in a few words, *form*, the stylistic impression made by the sum total of these individual traits. Expanding this interpretation of form, in much of the art we have to study in this volume, even though many of the individual pieces are strictly three-dimensional, the formal conventions used are basically linear or two-dimensional; the artist is usually concerned with the use of certain basic motifs which themselves are constructed of line rather than block masses or opposing units of light and shade. This is particularly clear in objects of Jacobsthal's so-called 'Early' style [**40, 42, 47, 56**]. In the main section of this Introduction I shall attempt to summarise the present-day impact of the varying divisions of Iron Age art style not so much by reference to our basic definitions but by use of such adjectives as 'weird', 'jolly', 'effete' and so on. Now it cannot be stressed enough that such terms are to be regarded as nothing more than a form of verbal shorthand. I have already indicated the dangers of twentieth-century value judgements; as that most sensitive of critics of insular Celtic art, the late Sir Cyril Fox, has written: 'it is, in truth, often very difficult to find secure anchorage for one's mind or sensibilities in contemplation of such creations'[2] as the intricacies of some Celtic motifs. My comments are for the most part intended to be purely descriptive and not interpretative.

'To be able to apprehend the import of a work of art, whether it is a painting or a poem, we must first learn its language', states an American art historian.[3] In most forms of later prehistoric art true realism, as generally understood, is not usually present, but, to repeat, abstraction and realism are by no means self-contradictory forms of expression. A true artist paints, models, or casts an abstract composition because he wishes to express something which he feels he cannot achieve by 'realism' – not because he is incapable of drawing. In all art 'the process of abstraction occupies a long series of gradations from one easily recognisable form to one that is, for the uninitiated, totally incomprehensible'.[4] Any student of prehistoric Europe will notice how the art of the Iron Age, a barbarian though hardly primitive art, is not concerned with the attempted perfect reproduction of natural forms or the portrayal of the human form. As such, Iron Age art is 'in aesthetic contrast to the man-centred representational and narrative arts of the civilisations of the ancient Near East, or their classical successors in the Mediterranean'.[5] For this reason if for no other, as mentioned in the *Preface*, I have omitted illustrating anything which, in this sense, can be said to be alien to the barbarian tradition. Moreover, before turning to examine in detail

[1] Gombrich, *Art and Illusion*, 126 ff.
[2] Sir Cyril Fox, *Advancement of Science* VIII (1951), 192
[3] J. Ackerman, *Art and Archaeology*, 152
[4] Giedion, *The Eternal Present* I, 10
[5] S. Piggott, *Ancient Europe: a Survey* (1965), 259

what we can perceive of stylistic development in the art of the European Iron Age, it is necessary to consider the outlines of Iron Age pre- and proto-history itself in order that we may be able to see some of the causes of this barbarian tradition.

AN OUTLINE PREHISTORY OF THE EUROPEAN IRON AGE

The most striking and most coherent barbarian art style, though by no means the only one in our period of study, is that of the Celts. Who were the Celts? There is no simple answer to this simple and obvious question. If we are to understand the cultural basis of the major part of Iron Age art we must in fact go back to about 1200 BC, the beginning of the technological period which in prehistoric Europe is termed the 'Late Bronze Age'. At this time a period of economic turmoil and folk movements, emanating at least in part from the shores of the Black Sea, brought about the downfall of the established empires of the Mycenaeans and the Hittites and threatened even Egypt. Into the later region came the invaders whom we know of from our ancient historical sources as the 'sea-peoples'. With the lessening of external demands upon local mineral resources, the metal-smiths of central and eastern Europe developed a skill, itself ultimately of east Mediterranean origin, in the production particularly of bronze vessels constructed from sheets of metal skilfully riveted together. In the eastern Alps extensive and deep shaft mining was set in hand not only for copper ores but, for the first time, for a new and valuable trading commodity, salt. From at least the twelfth century onwards an internal expansion of people from Central Europe may be traced by noting the widespread reintroduction of cremation as a burial rite, that is, ashes placed in a ritual vessel or (usually pottery) 'cinerary urn'. Celtic place names in Spain suggesting a movement there perhaps as early as the eighth century BC are amongst a series of philological and archaeological clues which support the naming of this Late Bronze Age or 'Urnfield' period as 'proto-Celtic'. Some indications of external elements which impinged upon this Central European group, perhaps indeed of a link with the 'sea-peoples' is the introduction, particularly on bronze vessels exhibiting otherwise a simple abstract repertoire of geometric forms, of sun symbols and aquatic birds [20–23], the latter to be found surviving in much later contexts [60–61].

In Greece, the eighth century sees not only the period of the Dorian invasions and the Ionian migrations but the firm establishment of the use of iron, first manufactured in some quantity by the Hittites in the fifteenth century BC but kept a jealously guarded secret until the break-up of the Hittite kingdom three centuries later. From the eighth century, in more westerly regions, we can perceive not only the first use of iron, which remained until the Middle Ages at a relatively low level amongst both civilised and barbarian peoples, but from Hungary to Switzerland and south-western Germany a whole group of novel metal types associated with bridle-bits and the bones of horses. Here for the first time in Central Europe is evidence suggestive of the use of the horse not just for traction but also for riding [10, 17]. In eastern Europe these types have a distribution which stretches back into the Pontic lands – home of the wild steppe-pony – and beyond. East or West, we have here indications of the routes followed by the nomad bands whom we know of as the 'Cimmerians', displaced from their homeland by the Scythians, who in turn are so vividly described at first hand by Herodotus. The western European distribution of the characteristic harness attachments, which in the eighth and seventh centuries ranges from Co. Durham in north-east England to the Swiss lakes, suggests not large-scale migrations but rather local contacts with the rapid movement from area to area of independent raiding parties. From about 700 BC onwards, first in Czechoslovakia and then westwards into France, we find princely burials – interments now – in wooden mortuary houses covered by round earthen mounds. This is yet another feature of Pontic burial ritual which goes back at least to the later third millennium BC. Indeed it is a moot point whether one should regard this material evidence as that of newcomers from the steppe region or simply of the taking over of new ways by the native ruling classes of Central Europe.

Under the burial mounds, the dead man (or rarely, but significantly, woman) was laid to rest on a four-wheeled waggon which was often partially dismantled. In the early Central European sites such waggons often had richly decorated yokes [8] and sometimes there were also the bones of the two-horse team – this custom was to continue in isolated examples till the coming of the Romans. The presence of not just two but three sets of harness trappings indicates the token burial of an out-rider or perhaps of the chieftain's own charger. The most usual sign of the noble warrior is, as with many later heroic societies, the sword, the long sword of iron [11]. We can see the European ancestry of the wheeled vehicle in waggons or other model carriages surmounted by metal urns. These suggest possible memories of the Ancient East and, though rarely found, extend back to the twelfth-century early Urnfield period in Central Europe the use not just of funerary cars but of more utility vehicles – not to mention the skill required to make spoked wheels. Such evidence, in its contrast to the general lack of status symbols amongst the Urnfield burials, must point to local chieftains or clan leaders. The best, although a late example, of these cult models is the famous bronze from a sixth-century grave at Strettweg near Graz [38]. Here the central female deity – she can surely be nothing less than divine – holds a bowl or cauldron emphasising the importance of ritual containers which we will also encounter in much later contexts. The goddess's mortal retainers with their helmets and shields (which, like all forms of armour in barbarian Europe, betray continued Mediterranean technological influence) demonstrate the contemporary use of mounted warriors – whatever the significance of this particular innovation may be. To repeat a point just made, the idea of a new aristocracy from the steppe introducing mounted pastoralism to proto-Celtic society has gained some support. The re-emergence of the custom of barrow burial, common in Central Europe in the first half of the second millennium, as a result of the influence of dynastic marriages, may be offered as a possible compromise. A lack in the earlier Iron Age tombs of more than a handful of grave goods of demonstrably eastern origin prevents us, however, from too readily conjuring up pictures of clan leaders from the Eastern steppe speaking the old, archetypal Celtic dialects with heavy Russian accents.

Errant knights may nevertheless have existed, to judge from the outer limits of the distributions of the typical Early Iron Age sword, with its 'Dutchman's cap' pommel [11], as well as of occasional exotic embellished vehicle parts. On a unique series of pottery vessels from burial mounds in the area of Sopron in Hungary we can make out a Celtic Helen bidding farewell to her Paris together with a funeral procession complete with four-wheeled bier and more domestic scenes of weaving and playing on the lyre [10] – activities no less evocative of Homeric epic, while the lyre points to yet further influence from the east. The Sopron pots also suggest the costume of the day, useful evidence to pad out the scanty remains of textiles and skin garments, most of the latter of which have been preserved in the flooded shafts of the Alpine salt mines.

The obvious wealth derived from such centres as the region round Hallstatt (which has lent its name to the first main period of the Celtic Iron Age) is reflected in the contents of the vast cemetery in the valley below the mountain mines [17–18, 21–22, 26, 30, 36]. Here were some 2,000 graves extending in date from the early seventh to the fifth century BC and here have been found not only the ubiquitous sign of warrior chieftains, the iron sword, but also bronze vessels whose southern point of origin we will note in the following paragraph. In 'Hallstatt' Burgundy and south Germany, the power of local rulers is indicated not only by princely graves but by fortified hill-top settlements with great wooden halls worthy of a medieval baron. The use of timber reinforcing in the walls of such forts follows a tradition old in the Aegean and perhaps introduced into mainland Europe by native Celts returning from the wars which brought about the downfall of the Mycenaean empire. Such local centres commanded the natural routes north, south, and east offered by the rivers Seine, Rhône, Rhine, and Danube.

A more complex pattern of events in Italy is indicated by vestiges of the trans-Alpine Urnfield cultures – perhaps responsible for the earlier groups of the unique carvings of the Valcamonica [1–2]. Another feature of early Iron Age Italy is contact with the first colonies of archaic Greece in the second half of the eighth century. This coincides with the beginning of the Villanovan Iron Age, so named after an extensive cemetery site on the outskirts of modern Bologna. In c. 500 BC the Bologna region was controlled by people from Central Italy, Etruscans – purveyors of that enigmatic yet historical culture strongly influenced, if nothing more, by oriental elements. Here, as with the question of the origin of our Hallstatt knights, the truth as to the origins of the Etruscans may lie in the introduction of novel ideas by a small dominant group of foreigners. Amongst the new things was the art; rich plagiarisms of Levantine craftsmen found in Etruscan tombs also remind us that Punic settlements were well established in North Africa and subsequently in Spain by 800 BC. This direct source for the oriental repertoire of Etruscan art has a counterpart in the rich Illyrian bronze-smiths at the head of the Adriatic. Here, centred on the local Venetic capital of Este, from the late seventh to the fourth century, Atestine products were marked by a strange admixture of eastern mythology and everyday scenes of peace and war [24–26]. Such are the motifs which decorate the lids and sides of bronze buckets whose basic form goes back to Central Europe Urnfield types. Certain 'orientalising' features of this so-called 'situla art' have clearly been transmitted through the agency of Greece whose first colony in the Adriatic was Apollonia, founded from Corinth in c. 600 BC; about this time Massalia, the present Marseilles, was first settled at the mouth of the Rhône by colonists from Phocis. It has also been suggested that in the eighth century BC – a period which saw Greeks in the east as well as the west – refugee craftsmen from the borders of the Assyrian empire may actually have travelled as far as Etruscan Italy, directly introducing not just individual motifs but such objects as ritual cauldrons with animal attachments. Ritual cauldrons seem to have influenced even the Central European Celts [38, 162, 164, 209, 222].

The existence of trade routes north, across or round the western end of the Alps from the end of the eighth century was established first of all by the discovery of a number of Atestine products in the Hallstatt cemetery itself. From the seventh century a steady trickle of exotic imports both Etruscan [113] and Greek [41], particularly beak-mouthed bronze wine jugs, is to be found, but tripod cauldrons and even Greek painted tableware – even if never of the best quality – passed from hand to hand until laid in such well-stocked tombs as that of the young princess of Vix near Châtillon-sur-Seine. Here, under a mound in the shadow of a local hill-top township, was found evidence of the wealth of the Celtic middleman trading in raw materials, whether slaves or minerals, with Greeks bearing gifts probably to the Phocaian entrepôt of Massalia; the rare appearance of wheel-turned native pottery in some of the local fortified trading centres can be associated with an exchange of technical ideas as well as goods, although the potter's wheel was not to come into general use in barbarian Europe until the second century. The importance of foreign objects in native contexts, however few in number, must not be underestimated for Iron Age art, since they offer the only chronological clues as to the absolute dating of the entire period until the establishment of the Roman provinces. Nevertheless, one must keep in mind that up to this period no Iron Age date can be considered as accurate to within a generation or, in other words, the working life of a craftsman. In addition, the presence of imports like those just mentioned suggests more than the perquisites of successful commercial transactions. The association with noble burials, often with pairs of drinking utensils [44], indicates the importance of the funeral banquet, which seems to have played a vital role in Celtic belief as in so many other heroic societies and of which we can read in the Old Irish tales such as the *Táin Bó Cúalnge*, 'the Cattle-raid of Cooley'.[1] Such stories are now thought to reflect a tradition first formalised some time between the second century B C and the fourth century A D and thus could be as old as the Irish Iron Age itself. It is, however, probably prudent in view of the insular background of the hero-tales to restrict their use in attempted interpretations of various aspects of continental cultures in the pre-Roman Celtic Iron Age. Nevertheless, the *Táin* does offer a unique source for the elucidation of various motifs in Celtic art and as such has been much referred to in several recent studies. The wine trade, which in fact is not directly mentioned in the hero-tales, is evidenced by the discovery in the fortified settlements not only of Attic tableware [41] but of Massaliote wine amphorae. It is also this trade which we shall shortly see as giving support for Jacobsthal's comment that 'Celtic art owed much to Celtic thirst'. Analysis has actually found the residue of ancient *retsinato* still adhering to the ancient mixing bowls and wine jugs. Jacobsthal also made the analogy between the trading patterns of the Iron Age and the eighteenth-century A D European fashion for tea-drinking and its by-products, the fine Chinese and Japanese porcelain which was for a long time imported solely as an adjunct of the essential basic product. Some Celtic exchanges for luxury products have just been hinted at; wheat from the tribes bordering on the Greek colonies of the Western Mediterranean may be added to slaves, salt, and iron ore as a staple of native primary industry while less certain, despite common belief, would have been tin, tin from the Cassiterides, the northern islands usually equated with the south-western tip of Britain but more likely to be the Isle of Wight. Similar Italo-Greek imports established the date of the beginning of the last phase of prehistoric Celtic culture no less than products of republican and early imperial Rome indicate its close. This phase is named 'La Tène' after a hoard of objects deposited in the shallows by Lake Neuchâtel [179].

The change to the La Tène period is largely a change in material culture, the result of, once more, an internal take-over bid, a shift in power against the warrior-traders aided perhaps by nomadic attacks from the east against the old Hallstatt strongholds. The change is twofold: distributional and technological. From Burgundy and the head-waters of the Danube, the

---

[1] Cecile O'Rahilly *Táin Bó Cúalnge: from the Book of Leinster* (1967)

concentration of power, as marked by chieftains' graves which continue to provide so much of the source-material for the study of Celtic art, shifts to the central Rhineland and the chalk basin of the Marne. This is in fact more or less the north-western part of the old Hallstatt zone with the addition of a few but important outliers in Bohemia and the Hallstatt Alpine mining centres. In this last region the salt workings of Hallstatt seem to have declined in favour of Dürrnberg, not far from Salzburg. In Switzerland and eastern France south of the main area of chieftains' graves, large flat cemeteries are found. These include a large number of women's graves containing richly decorated neck-, arm-, and foot-rings and extend into central Europe where they become the predominant type in succeeding centuries. The actual burial rite is usually inhumation, but cremation also occurs, if rarely, over a surprisingly wide area. Grave goods in the flat grave cemeteries are best regarded as material indicators of the dead person's station in life; Old Irish law laid particular emphasis on a strict ranking of pledges and obligations, and classical sources make reference to the Celts burying their dead together with 'those things appropriate to life'. Thus it is hardly surprising to find in the archaeological record warriors buried with their complete equipment and often the champion's joint of pork, side by side with their richly bedecked women, their cooking pots still to hand. Doctors and soothsayers can also be identified, while the preponderance in eastern Czechoslovakia of goose bones in warriors' graves may support the association of this bird with gods of war known again from historical sources. It seems likely that La Tène Celts, like their early Irish descendants, extended their concepts of obligation and duty, client and chieftain, to their gods also; the funerary feast of food and drink – evidence for which can be noted even in Britain at the time of the Roman conquest – may well have been intended not so much for the dead man himself as for those in the Otherworld to whom he would owe allegiance and service in the after-life. Other features of flat graves, such as the almost complete absence of pottery in fourth/third-century graves in Moravia and southern Germany, may on the other hand reflect economic rather than sociological factors, and it is well to keep in mind that complete conformity of burial custom is unlikely to have occurred in any part of the Celtic world any more than in later and better documented periods.

The technology of the new masters is seen in lesser things as in greater; the fibula with a built-in spring, the ancient safety-pin developed first in the Balkans and Iron Age Greece and passed thence into Italy and the North, is important in La Tène times not just for the frequent embellishment of its design but as the basic chronometer for establishing local time scales [**89–94, 135, 200–201**]. Instead of the four-wheeled waggon we now have the sometimes richly decorated two-wheeled chariot, reflecting a change not only in funerary customs but also in military tactics; the chariot was also once considered as a trans-Alpine introduction. The chief material innovation is of course La Tène art itself, a unique amalgam of earlier Iron Age non-representational forms, both the orientalised and strictly classical styles of the Mediterranean cultures, and something of the animal-dominated iconography of the eastern nomads. It is this last strain which is most difficult to trace to its source; the evidence for Scythian inroads into the West, though datable to the sixth–fourth centuries BC and probably responsible for the disruption of trans-Alpine trade, is neither of large movements nor, as to material objects, of the presence of that other classical-aided, royal, and barbarian art, that of the Royal Scythians of the Black Sea coast. Beyond the concrete manifestations of La Tène art, almost exclusively the art of the aristocrats of Celtic society probably gaining their wealth largely as the Iron Masters of

B

western Europe, there seems to be little change in the basic pattern of the society itself from late Urnfield times – basically barbarian, tribal, and stratified, with a ruling warrior-aristocracy, the beginnings of a professional class of craftsman and priest-bards, and, supporting all, a pastoral country-folk.

As evidence of the local tribal divisions within the La Tène culture are the great ditch-enclosed fortifications of upwards of a square mile in area. However, these are mostly of the last phase; similar settlements of the earliest La Tène phase are as yet surprisingly rare. The later *oppida*, as Caesar termed them, which are to be found from the eastern borders of Czecho-slovakia to the south of Britain, have revealed the evidence of iron-founders, potters' workshops, glass moulders, and moneyers. Coinage was produced in numerous local centres in the Celtic world from at least the early third century BC [**194, 217, 306, Plate IV**]; it not only aids identification of the individual local groups but presents yet another result of Celtic adaptation of classical prototypes – this time coins of Hellenistic Greece, the Greek colonies and the Roman republic. Although such a pattern of a semi-urbanised society is strictly that of the last centuries of the independence of the continental Celts, from only slightly less sophisticated centres we must imagine the setting out in the fifth–third centuries of those minor war-bands under the younger sons of local rulers, evidence of which we find in remoter and less crowded areas. So, for example, runs Livy's account of the arrival in Italy at the beginning of the fifth century of the first Celtic settlers who were to dominate the northern valleys for some two hundred years. Entering Italy by the old trans-Alpine trade routes, the Celts made for the fertile Po basin, subsequently pushing on to the region around Milan, some reaching Sicily and perhaps even Sardinia [**169**]. Celtic material culture in Italy became an amalgam of mature La Tène forms and influences from the local population – nominally under Etruscan control. Arms and armour in contemporary Celtic graves [**105–108, 137**] show this, while their association with readily datable Italo-Greek pottery establishes useful chronological coat-hangers on which to suspend at least one phase of La Tène artistic development, that named after the double chariot-grave of Waldalgesheim [**118, 124–127**]. It is this early settlement period which offered an opportunity for the Celtic absorption of classical art motifs. The earliest La Tène material in Ireland could pos-sibly belong to this stage; and if so it would support the theory of a direct settlement from north-western France. Further afield even than Italy, La Tène objects, if not La Tène people, spread to areas as far separated as the Volga and the non-Celtic tribal regions of south Scandinavia.

While Gaulish Celts were disrupting the peace of rural Italy and wakening the geese of Rome, others with a more central European homeland were following their fortunes still further to the east. In 335 BC the great Alexander gave curt audience to a deputation which contem-porary classical accounts record as including Celts from the Danube basin – in the following century the gold quarter-staters of Alexander and his father Philip were to provide some of the prototypes for the new Celtic coinage. It was one group of these slighted Celts who, in 279 BC, attacked the sacred centre of Greece, the treasures and temples of Delphi. Amongst such Celts fighting was not so much a necessary task as a way of life. It was a general sport and pastime and second nature to those who, like later artistically skilled barbarians, the Vikings, are to be found as mercenaries at the local courts of eastern Greeks. The Irish mercenaries of the last days of Royal France were only following a Celtic pattern which may extend back to the fall of Mycenae.

An oval wooden shield and an enamelled bronze harness mount found in the sands of

Fayûm is, apart from inscriptions, all the archaeological evidence for the many Celtic warriors who both fought and settled in Egypt. We may more clearly follow the journeyings of those warrior bands numbering some 20,000, including women and children, who, after the attempted sack of Delphi, were invited across the Hellespont into Asia Minor by Nicomedes, King of Bithynia. Subsequently these 'Galatae' or 'Galatians', as the Greeks called them, proved such a threat to the Hellenistic kingdom of Pergamon that Attalus I, its ruler, conducted a series of campaigns against them culminating in 240 BC with a substantial victory. The well-known 'Dying Gaul' in the Capitoline Museum is a Roman copy of a commemorative bronze group raised by Attalus. Also at Pergamon, Eumenes, Attalus' son, in honour of his father's campaigns, decorated the balustrade of a temple dedicated to Athena, bringer of victory, with relief carvings of Celtic booty. We may readily compare the carvings with actual objects from the continent of Europe; pointed helmets as found in northern Italy and the Balkans [211], yokes for paired chariot horses preserved at the type-site of La Tène (which in fact dates mainly from the second century and not from the beginning of the period to which it has given its name), and the *carnyx*, the Celtic war-trumpet with its boar-decorated bell [209, 213, 272]. The boar, we may note, is one of the most potent totemic forms in the Celtic mythological zoo [224-226, 306b]. The two-wheeled chariot was probably introduced into the Celtic world from Western Asia rather than from Etruria as once thought. Mention must be made of another chariot burial at Mezek in southern Bulgaria. Here a few years before the outbreak of the Second World War, in a rifled beehive-shaped stone tomb built probably in the fourth century, the remains of a chieftain laid out in the manner of his fifth-century ancestors were discovered [170]. He has been considered as a veteran of the raid on Delphi; the chariot fittings were decorated in a characteristic formalised style which Jacobsthal considered as later than the Waldalgesheim phase. The Mezek burial is yet another valuable clue for the absolute dating of Celtic art.

It is worth dwelling on this period of Celtic culture-contact since the widening of our sources of information allows for a fuller understanding of the nature, as well as the straight-forward material remains, of barbarian European society. In the South of France where, as in Italy, the Celts came under the influence of advanced Mediterranean culture, Massalia remained an outpost of Greek colonisation. Iberia, beyond the scope of our present survey, presented a unique admixture of Celts, Greeks and Carthaginians [37]. Britain, or rather the south-eastern part of the British Isles, had felt the backwash of La Tène settlement and society from at least the fourth century, although, as we will see with reference to Iron Age art in Britain, there were local developments not wholly dependent on Continental influence. In the same category were the eastern Celts of what is now Hungary, eastern Slovakia and the Balkan states – the meeting place of barbarians from both east and west. Celts were certainly in these parts as early as the fourth century, no doubt some acting as mercenaries. The penetration into distant areas of such tribes as the Boii, who sent offshoots from their central homeland south and west as well as east, must also have meant that those craftsmen who accompanied them would have come face to face with new artistic influences. By the same token the presence in the Balkans of the Achaemenian Persians from the end of the sixth century undoubtedly played an important part in the evolution of the earliest so-called 'Dacian' art; as has recently been suggested, the royal booty of Darius and Xerxes may well be a source of at least some of the 'orientalising' features in early Celtic art. However, despite such finds as Mezek, the middle period of La Tène culture is in fact marked archaeologically by a general levelling-off of wealth; there are no princely graves as such, and craftsmen decorated more mundane materials than gold. Also, in the South of France, we have the clearest archaeological evidence for what is but rarely archaeologically discernible – cult and religion [235–238]. Everyone knows of the Druids, the first identifiable priestly caste in early Europe whose careful training over many years was responsible for the preservation of the ancient oral traditions, but what we read of the Druids, first in Caesar's campaign notebooks, applies only to a small regional group as seen through distinctly Roman-tinted spectacles. The same is true of the many local divinities, whose animal, human or half-human forms must from the beginning have varied from region to region, from tribe to tribe. Occasionally, late inscriptions of the Gallo-Roman period allow identification, which we may only with caution project back into the prehistory of the illiterate Celts. Examples are the so-called 'Cernunnos', the cross-legged and antlered god [209b, 232], or Epona, the goddess in the form of a mare. A reliance, however, on the neat placing of the shadowy Celtic pantheon in methodical Roman or Greek pigeon-holes is certainly to misunderstand the aggressive individuality of Celtic society as a whole. On the other hand, to ignore the frequent appearance of certain iconographic or indeed totemic elements in Celtic material culture, is to ignore the obviously cultic basis of much Celtic art. The boar [222a, 224–226, 306b] and the bull are to be found on much else than just coinage; the bull seems to have been associated with running water as a particular symbol of strength and power – and both are found used as smith's stamps on later La Tène long swords [190–193], the most common emblem of heroic prowess.

Amongst the Celts the human head was venerated above all else, since the head was to the Celt the soul, centre of the emotions as well as of life itself, a symbol of divinity and of the powers of the other-world. It is this belief which most readily explains the head-hunting propensities of La Tène warriors. Sharing this predilection with the present-day Indians of the Amazon or the Dyaks of North Borneo no less than with the Scythians of their own times, the Celts depicted the severed head most spectacularly in the sacred monuments of the southern French *oppida* [76] but also, on a much smaller scale, on certain early bronzes [87]. It is the human head which, from the very beginning, predominates in La Tène art. Amongst even seemingly abstract insular designs the sacred cipher intrudes [245], while from later Celtic times and into the Roman period the Celtic veneration of the head is associated, once more, with water in local spring – or well – cults. Extensive deposits of weapons and ornaments, which lack the normal debris of every-day habitation, found at La Tène or in the vast 'cauldron of plenty' at the spring of Duchcov in Bohemia are best seen in this context as long-term ritual offerings. A third Celtic lake sanctuary and one well attested by literary references was situated at Tolosa, now Toulouse, plundered by the Romans in 106 BC when they overran the territory of the Volcae-Tectosages. Three is a significant number in Celtic symbolism and triplets abound even amongst heads of stone [286, 288]. Triplets are also to be found in examples of another borrowing from the Ancient East, the torc or sacred neck-ring [87, 143], the badge of both nobility and godhead common to both men and women. Amongst the Celts women too could gain power and riches, as archaeology not infrequently testifies [79–83].

In sum, Celtic society, as we piece it together from the patchwork results of archaeological exploration and classical (but often biased) sources, seems in the first centuries BC to have differed little from the heroic society of Old Ireland. Ireland is the one main area of the Celtic world never to have experienced the constraining influence of Roman occupation. The extant Irish hero-tales, though probably derived from not earlier than seventh-century AD written versions, give us a vivid picture of the whole gamut of pagan Celtic society from warrior prince to dishonoured captive. Descriptions of chariot fighting, head-hunting and an emphasis on local totems and tabus – these and other elements certainly strongly suggest the barbarian culture of pre-Roman Gaul. The Irish tales themselves, as we now know them, probably enshrine oral accounts handed down by local bards, father to son, remembering long-dead heroes who may have been living when other, more easterly, Celts were repulsing the first Roman onslaught on the British Isles. The Irish tales are, however, only the records of one corner of the sprawling, politically ill-defined world of the European Iron Age. Nevertheless, though we lack the details, if we put together the clues in our cultural crossword puzzle we have a clear enough picture of the ancient Celt. One can hardly improve on Professor Piggott's evocation of 'swaggering, belching, touchy chieftains and their equally impossible warrior crew, hands twitching to the sword-hilt at the imagined hint of an insult, allotted . . . the champion's portion' – of boiled pork as suggested in many a Celtic warrior's grave and yet another mark of the importance of the boar – 'wiping the greasy moustaches that were a mark of nobility'.[1]

Graves in southern Britain as well as on the continent show that the Celtic predilection for the ritual symposium or funeral feast lasted well into early Roman Imperial times. In Britain, side by side with local products, provincial Roman amphorae, imported silverware and bronze utensils take the place of Italic beaked flagons and Attic drinking cups – and the distribution of finds of those late luxury goods follows the old riverine and coastal routes first established in Urnfield times. That Celtic society, like its chariots, became obsolete in the face of growing Roman power, was due not only to the might of the Roman armies but also to the Roman capacity for political organisation and full exploitation of resources and manpower so patently lacking in even semi-urban Gaul and southern Germany. Even that last outpost of Celtdom, Ireland, ended its complete isolation from the development of post-Roman Europe as a result of the indirect influence of the Church of Rome.

It was undoubtedly the breaking down of the barbarian pattern of aristocratic patronage under Roman provincial control which brought about the decline of Celtic art – decline, not destruction, since in certain areas the later Celtic craftsmen were working for Roman patrons. Celtic artistic patronage was not that of autocratic client and subservient artisan which we associate with even the Titians and Rembrandts of the High Renaissance and later, but rather was an association, almost of equals, between chieftain and craftsman. The 'man of art' is a man of property and status as we read of him in the Irish hero-tales; in these the craftsman holds an almost sacred position. Françoise Henry, making use of the Irish evidence, considers the Celtic artist as 'a seer, a man endowed with a prophetic gift. He and the goldsmith belonged to that social class intermediary between the warring aristocracy and the common people.'[2] The evidence for belief in the near-divinity of the smith or metal-worker is widespread in primitive societies; however, again with reference to the world of the Irish hero-tales, one should also recall the evidence for a power of inventiveness, of imagination and description, together with a sense of the uncanny much more subtle than in many other areas of folk belief.

[1] Piggott, *Ancient Europe*, 229
[2] Françoise Henry, *Irish Art in the Early Christian Period (to AD 800)* (1965), 66

One most important and often analysed factor in Celtic mythology is the power of 'shape-changing' – not to be confused with metempsychosis, a power which classical writers erroneously ascribed to the Druids. Shape-changing was rather the ability to move at will between varying forms, animal, human, or inanimate, as exemplified by maidens changing into swans, the original creation of a girl from a flower, and so on. As Professor Jackson has pointed out, there is nothing mystical or esoteric in these concepts, rather 'in this world any supernatural event may occur without incongruity because, just as in the folk-tale, that distinction between natural and supernatural which is the consequence of civilised thought has not yet been clearly drawn'.[1] This seemingly ambiguous attitude towards natural forms offers at least a partial explanation for the strange beings and pseudo-faces so common in early Celtic art. In Celtic society the 'man of art' no less than the Celtic hero lives in a world saturated with magic. Despite the occasional rendering of Celtic names in Greek, and subsequently Roman characters on coins, pottery, or even on a sword of the later La Tène period [190], literacy spread only with the decline of the Celtic society. With this spread came the subsequent loss of that binding oral tradition capable of transmitting not only the legends but the whole pattern of everyday life. The artistic heritage of the Celtic world for the most part lies today under a cloak of forced nationalism and cheap tourist gimmicks. However, Iron Age art still remains as one material contribution to that barbarian element which, if subdued, nevertheless is part of European culture today.

THE RISE AND FALL OF IRON AGE ART

In writing briefly on the art history of an historical period, there are many obvious difficulties, some of which we have already discussed. With respect to Celtic art it has been stated, with some justification, that it 'has no genesis'; in other words in only a minority of examples is it possible to trace copyings or, in detail, adaptations of introduced motifs. Equally, though Celtic art has been considered to be essentially aniconic, it should also be regarded as basically religious. Again, Iron Age art is not cyclical, in the sense that it neither progresses entirely from a more linear type of representation to a more pictorial or three-dimensional style, nor is it progressively more naturalistic. It would seem that the Iron Age craftsman, altering little in his choice of themes, had a closely defined basic artistic vocabulary which allows ready perception of the 'minimum clues' of expression or *schemata*.[2] It is these clues of expression, of patterning with a bias towards freehand symmetry which is not quite symmetrical, 'in allusions to naturalistic forms within the discipline of an essentially geometric and abstract method of composition', that I shall attempt to review in the following pages.

First, however, since in any survey of Iron Age art one must inevitably refer to Paul Jacobsthal's original stylistic divisions of the earlier phases of Celtic art, it may be profitable to reiterate them here. The *Early Style*[3] is used of a period of innovation and experimentation lasting from early in the fifth century BC to some time after the middle of the fourth century (see the time chart, p. 179) and largely influenced by archaic 'orientalising' symbolism and early classical plant motifs. From the latter element of this 'style' develops the *Waldalgesheim Style*, embracing the most two-dimensional and non-representational group of all Iron Age art. Here,

[1] K. H. Jackson, *A Celtic Miscellany* (1951), 153–54
[2] Gombrich, *Art and Illusion*, 288 ff.
[3] It should be noted that Jacobsthal's use of the word 'style' is even more general a term than its use here since it may embrace more than one stylistic unit

however, the classical floral repertoire, though occasionally enriched by borrowings from contemporary provincial Greek sources, undergoes a metamorphosis which gives it a definitely alien aspect. The last of Jacobsthal's styles overlaps with that of Waldalgesheim which in certain areas – Britain for example – survives in certain forms until at least the end of the third century. Jacobsthal's third style is actually subdivided into two unrelated groups, both of which seem to have developed in the third century, in the course of which Celtic coinage – not considered by Jacobsthal in his survey – first generally appears. Of the two groups, the *Plastic Style* is concerned for once not so much with pattern but with solid masses, sometimes in human, semi-human, or animal form. The *Sword* sub-style is once more strictly two-dimensional, restricted almost entirely to engraved work which can best be expressed as a series of asymmetric variations on Waldalgesheim themes.

Our survey starts amongst the wealthy graves of the first Hallstatt trader-knights, the contents of which reveal the continuity of the skilled sheet metal-working of ultimately Late Bronze Age origin. Remembering our previous comments on the importance of the ritual feast and the general evidence for horse-riding and wheeled vehicles, it is hardly surprising that most of the art objects of the period should be harness or waggon fittings and containers of various sorts [8, 16]. The art of the Early Iron Age is usually regarded as purely abstract and geometric [7–9, 11, 22], its abstractions being of pure form, not the natural world of man and beast. Such elements as the pendant triangle or the interlocking 'Greek key' design – by no means a prerogative only of Greek art – may be seen on gold ornaments [3], textiles [7], and the red and white painted wares of local craft-potters [9, *Colour Pl.* I]. As well as abstract designs the animals basic to everyday life and the face of man do intrude from time to time. Admittedly such live motifs are almost without exception relegated to elements in design; the crude *repoussé* or beaten decoration of a gold bowl from Altstetten near Zürich has repeating sun and moon symbols above the kindergarten figures of what may be best taken as doe and buck stag [4]. The stag may seem an intruder into the predominantly cattle-raising economy of the Celts [27, 38, 209B], an animal to be revered rather by earlier hunter-fisher groups, but nevertheless this antlered form appears, if infrequently, throughout the thousand-year history of Celtic art. The horse too may stand either as partner to the sun symbol [6] or in his rightful place as the warrior's steed. Such naïvely attractive pieces as a bronze axe from one of the earlier graves of the Hallstatt cemetery [17] are not so much the results of any cultic impetus as the natural products of a horse-riding people – the very similar depictions in the round from the Black Sea area of *c.* 1000 BC, important for their archaeological significance, must represent a similar artistic situation. There is probably another source for the common juxtaposition of the sun symbol with aquatic birds, swans or crested ducks, which occurs first in early Urnfield times [21–22]. The 'duck-and-solar-disc' motif gains particular prominence on both sides of the Alps; the pre-Etruscan Villanovan Iron Age accepts it as readily as central European bronze-smiths although an ultimately eastern origin is not impossible. Not every bird, however, necessarily has ritual significance. The happy families facing each other at the end of an enigmatic object from Dunaverney in Northern Ireland [23] could equally be an example of what, following anthropological usage, I have called a 'joke-motif', rather than religious symbols.

So it is with man; the jolly triplets – however significant the number – on a pair of linch pins from the lonely Low Countries grave containing objects typical of the far-wandering Hallstatt venturers [16] also belong to the category of the 'joke motif', a category which is never completely lacking in any artistic tradition. Such heads may also be noted early on in the Scandinavian region [19], generally an artistic backwater in the later first millennium. On the other hand, statues, whether of men or gods, are not a common feature of Early Iron Age art. Instead, though the ill-preserved Stockach stone with its wide face and simple geometric design [13] need not be regarded as anything more than a local product, the recently discovered full life-size figure of Hirschlanden [12] must owe its origin to iconographic influences, if not craftsmen, from south of the Alps. The belt, short sword and neck-ring are by no means out of place in southern Württemberg, but the pointed helmet common in Etruria from the eighth century and the modelling of the nude form are wholly foreign. Even in Early La Tène times, despite the ability of local craftsmen to produce the most lifelike portraits, man in stone takes on an awesome and in many senses of the word, other-worldly aspect [14, 85]. A bronze mask from the Krollkögel, an Austrian late Hallstatt chieftain's burial [15], recalls not only near-contemporary masks from Trebenište in Jugoslav Macedonia or, at many removes, the Mycenaean gold 'mask of Agamemnon', but also stylistically a rather later Celtic piece, the Holzgerlingen cult statue [14].

Clearly not born from the artistic traditions of Central Europe, yet still part of it, is the 'art of the *situla*' [24–26], the Adriatic products of the period spanning the second half of the Hallstatt Iron Age and the first part of the La Tène culture – from the seventh to the fourth centuries BC. It is not just to be found on buckets; belt-plates [25] not unlike their Hallstatt cousins and even a typical Early La Tène scabbard can here be brought into view. This last object, a scabbard from a late grave in the Hallstatt cemetery [30], must represent something rarely noted in Iron Age art, the decoration of a native object at least under first-hand influence from a foreign craftsman. The juxtaposition of mounted warriors – no need to see foreign influence here – with a strange menagerie of winged lions and griffons must represent direct borrowings via Italy from the repertoire of the Proto-Corinthian or 'orientalising' period of archaic Greek art. On the *situlae* can be seen the formalised, almost heraldic, settings of scenes of feasting or military parades and wrestling matches. The style certainly shows something of the contemporary and, by the fifth century, adjacent, Etruscan world. This style is again not European so much as Levantine; Professor Piggott has pointed out 'the eclectic mixture of oriental styles' in the importations from Greece, Cyprus and Etruria.

It has already been noted that evidence of foreign craftsmen in northern lands is difficult to find. The local craftsman embellishing foreign products is one of the key features of the earliest aspects of La Tène art, the aristocratic innovations which Jacobsthal ranked as the 'Early Style' of his three major divisions of Celtic art. The Early Style of the fifth century BC, as we have noted, is not so much a style but rather a formative period exhibiting varying responses to various internal and external artistic influences. The area of distribution, but not necessarily manufacture, stretches from eastern Czechoslovakia to northern Germany. As again Jacobsthal was the first to note, 'Early' La Tène art has three main roots. There is an oriental contribution of strange beasts and formal human masks in which it is impossible not to see the influence of Este, all the more so because of the extreme rarity of true oriental objects in Celtic contexts. Second is the strict angular geometry and the continued archaic symbolism of bird and beast. Then there are vegetable motifs, flowers and palmette fronds which belong to the infant stage of truly classical Greek art. It is natural that such floral designs should be the first motifs to undergo those changes of artistic moods which throughout Celtic art history make it impossible to speak of the objects concerned as the work of mere copyists.

A range of finds [39–44] from the central and southern German princely graves and outliers further afield illustrate the theme of Celtic artists embellishing foreign objects. They employ classical elements, particularly the lotus bud and the palmette. The same artistic themes are applied as much to set off the native rusticism of a pair of drinking horns as to add to the value of treasured Attic drinking cups. It is obvious that these are classical motifs, but if one examines such pieces as the gold, iron, and coral inlaid disc from Auvers [42] – a French find but most probably a product of the Rhineland – there is a fullness in the freehand symmetry of the open lyres, an almost three-dimensional exuberance which is totally lacking in the ultimate Greek prototypes in monumental sculpture or vase painting. The varied nature of other 'Early' objects, with the addition of the second and third roots of Celtic art, the animal and the human aspects, is nowhere more clearly seen than in material from the Klein Aspergle and Weiskirchen barrow graves [Plate IIa]. In the first grave, side by side with the Greek drinking-cup, were found two gold embellished drinking horns, a pair as required by male Celtic custom – one for the chieftain and one for his companion in the Otherworld. The ram and ewe of the Klein Aspergle horns [44], like the rare examples of animal-terminalled neck-rings [45, 216], or even the concept of the neck-ring itself, tempt one to invoke the intermediary agency of the western Scythians in transmitting what are not so much Greek as western Asiatic artistic concepts. As so often in early Iron Age culture, however, the archaeological evidence does little to help. Again, close examination demonstrates that many of the early Celtic artistic products are related to each other despite their very different general appearances. Decorative details – the dotted bead-row, vertically broken double line or wave pattern, for example – are often more important as stylistic indicators. This is a point to keep in mind when assessing the stylistic relations of such treasure houses of Early Celtic art as the Klein Aspergle burial. Only the basal handle figure of the Klein Aspergle bronze wine flagon [50] shows that these Celtic 'copies' of the Etruscan utensils, examples of which continue to be imported for their nearly century-long life from c. 550 BC, followed foreign patterns precisely in other features than in shape. The Klein Aspergle face is almost a mirror image of the pop-eyed satyr twins on either handle of an Italic bronze bucket from the second of two Weiskirchen graves. However, this is one of a very few rule-proving exceptions. In other pieces, bracelets, ornamental plaques, finger rings or, again, other wine flagons, the Celt, though hidden by Italic fancy dress, is still clearly a Celt even down to his fine mustachios so frequently commented on by the Classical writers. The mysterious, the terrifying, is also present. The great Rodenbach bracelet [55] or the almost Aztec opulence of the torc from Besseringen [56] have much which is not just 'orientalising' but oriental – and this despite the extreme rarity so far of indisputably eastern objects in a Celtic setting. The Thracian or ultimately Persian mien of the heraldic supporters of the Rodenbach ring, mountain ibex, not just mere goats, recalls contemporary Achaemenian neck-rings. A similar oriental atmosphere is conjured up by the later, c. 400 BC, rings from the Reinheim princess's grave [79–83] – the great eagles mantling ominously over the terminal heads seem strangely at variance with the well-fed humans themselves. The almost identical flagons from Basse-Yutz [60–61, Plate III] probably just a little later than most of the material so far discussed, show something else. Springing from above yet another Celtic head based on an Etruscan prototype are two fierce canines, wolf-hounds perhaps rather than wolves themselves. As has been frequently noticed, the 'shoulder curls' which indicate the tensed muscles are exactly like those of contemporary Scythian beasts from the shores of the Black Sea; it is quite another matter to calculate how such an influence might have been transmitted. Again in the intensely catholic repertoire of this early period of experimentation it is not in the least incongruous that there should be ducks so unconcernedly swimming up the spouts of the Basse-Yutz flagons – a legacy of much earlier Iron Age iconography [21–22].

Two other pieces in what is basically a united group of products may be briefly noted. One brooch from Parsberg in Bavaria [63] is amongst the first of a whole series of safety-pin brooches found in the area of the Early La Tène chieftains' graves and whose embellishment of cast and engraved ornament makes it easy to forget their humble ancestors in earlier Iron Age Greece and Italy. The griffons with their dashed pelts are close indeed to the Basse-Yutz flagon handles, but what is really striking is the grotesque face with a fine bulbous, bibulous nose – as one might expect of any Celt, man or myth. The bronze plate from Stupava in Slovakia [64] is also similar to the flagons both as to face and griffons. This Stupava bronze is the most easterly discovered of what, to follow Jacobsthal's analogy with the development period of archaic Greek art, one may call Celtic 'orientalising' material. The similarity of the face to Parsberg is immediately apparent. Not so immediate is the impact of the inverted and incised heraldic griffon supports – griffons whom we first met amongst the orientalising 'art of the *situla*' and only recently noted on the Stupava bronze by Powell. The Stupava head has one noteworthy detail: a circle in the middle of the forehead like some Celtic caste mark, present also on the most richly embellished of all the early Celtic flagons, that found in a chariot grave at Dürrnberg [72] near Salzburg, another cemetery site beside ancient salt mines where recent excavation is revealing as great a wealth of La Tène material as that recovered for the previous phase from the type site of Hallstatt. Other finds from Czechoslovakia of probably fourth-century date and thus still within the assumed chronological limits of the Early 'style', though clearly attempting to follow more westerly patterns, seem to modern eyes at least poor pieces in comparison [68, 70–71].

To take the crystallisation of a true Celtic style, or rather, stylisation of human form a step further, we must look at some other pieces from the western centres of La Tène wealth and power. From the first Weiskirchen grave is a quadruple-faced bronze fibula with, as often in earlier material, provision for coral inlay [67], coral whose nearest source to the Rhineland would be off the south coast of France. The twin faces on the sides of the brooch with their half-moon cheeks, pronounced almond eyes and scarcely noticeable receding chin, have many of the features of much later pieces to which Jacobsthal gave the somewhat ambiguous title of 'Plastic' – the style dated tentatively by the far-away burial of Mezek [170]. A similar abstraction can be seen on the brooch from Ostheim. This brooch is linked to the example from Weiskirchen by the comma element divested of a face on the sides of the pin. The long proboscis figure of Ostheim can be matched amongst the group of no less than four decorated brooches from a burial at Oberwittighausen in Bavaria [91–92]. The odd-man-out of this particular group supports on his head a triple ball motif like a miniature pawnbroker's sign [91], a common and – possibly – mystic symbol in early Celtic art present also on fibulae from the Dürrnberg cemetery [93] and from the long-lasting fortified hilltop of the Steinsburg [94] not far from Dresden. The strange nightmare figures of Ostheim and Oberwittighausen reach their apogee in the great Dürrnberg flagon [72]. The handle monster on the rim of the flagon exhibits that tendency towards reducing realism to 'a conglomerate of protuberances', as Jacobsthal describes even as early a piece as the Klein Aspergle handle satyr [**50**]. This more advanced stage of disintegration is already far on the road to the cartoon-like treatment of natural forms which is the real trademark of the true 'Plastic' style. There is another noteworthy feature of Dürrnberg, the very devouring act itself is represented by the handle animal. The same can be seen in another Celtic but much more 'orientalising' triplet, the broken torc from Glauberg. The two smaller animals on the rim of the Dürrnberg flagon have human heads with pointed ears as on the rim of a fragmentary flagon from Borsch [**66**]. The Borsch heads do not have tails of some less fortunate and half-devoured creature protruding from their mouths as has been suggested; the 'tails' are long dwarf-like beards. The near-ritual nature of Celtic brutality can be seen in the strange sculpture from the mouth of the Rhône known as the 'Tarasque de Noves' [**76**] depicting a monster masticating in this case all too clearly on a human arm. Below the paws of this hard-to-identify and hard-to-date beast are two detached and bearded heads with a more than slight resemblance to the Klein Aspergle satyr. The Tarasque is not only clear evidence of the cultic importance of the 'severed head', but in view of its 'orientalising' monster and bearded heads probably the earliest evidence in stone of this central tenet of the harsh Celtic faith; it may even date from the fourth century.

A strange feature also of several early Celtic pieces is the so-called 'leaf-crown' which is attached like twin balloons to the temples [**48, 74, 78, 118, Plate IIb**]. Sometimes the 'crown' looks like giant ears, sometimes it suggests nothing more than yet another piece of Celtic adaptation, this time of the fill-in eye-shaped features to be seen on the handle attachments of just such Italic bronze buckets as we were earlier comparing with the Klein Aspergle flagon satyr – indeed this feature may best be seen in an import from the Klein Aspergle grave itself. The appearance of such leaf-crowns on several of a group of stone pillar-statues [**14, 75**], the ancestry of which is now well established in Early Iron Age times by the Hirschlanden figure, and also attached to some of the most naturalistic of Celtic faces, suggests some deeper reason for this mystical embellishment. One such statue is the Holzgerlingen figure with, as we have already noted, some early features [**14**]. A second is a much more sophisticated piece, the pillar from Pfalzfeld [**75**]. Probably surmounted originally with a head like that from Heidelberg [**49**], the Pfalzfeld stone with its cord-like beading ornament, phallic base and running spiral design indicates continued contact with Etruria and Etruscan monuments – especially those Etruscan *cippi* depicting battles with the local Celts and to be found around Bologna *c.* 400 B C in the old Atestine region. Pfalzfeld, though, if one compares its purely decorative elements with local material, also exhibits the same repertoire of palmette stacks which one can see, for example, on the Dürrnberg flagon; one other possible Etruscan borrowing is the oval pop-eyed feature so characteristic of Celtic faces, small or large, stone or bronze.

The key, then, to material of the Early, formative period of La Tène art is variety, as one might expect amongst experimenters and innovators. It is necessary to consider carefully the range of this variety since from it stem almost all the more readily defined stages in the later artistic development of the Celts. We may notice here one other decorated brooch, that from Schwieberdingen in Germany [**89**], provided yet again with once ruby-red coral inlay. The brooch is decorated with two heads; opposed to the pensive-looking individual on the catch-plate is a sharp-featured creature crowned with comma-like horns which again recall the Dürrnberg flagon [**72**] – here the devouring handle monster. The fibula no less than the flagon exhibits the use of those 'protuberances' whose grotesqueness is set side by side with almost portrait-like naturalism. This is the sort of juxtaposition which is so confusing to the orderly mind of the twentieth-century-conditioned archaeologist, that significant and clearly intentional juxtaposition by one and the same craftsman of not only the image of man but also the raw material for 'a mythology preceding shaped myth of an age to come'.[1] The Dürrnberg monster finds his proper place at the end of a progressive *stylistic* development whose progenitors are, in reverse order, the Schwieberdingen fibula, a gold armlet from Dürkheim, Klein Aspergle and the Schwarzenbach armlet, all of which retain the satyr's characteristic pointed ears [**89, 54, 50, 53**]. Two other groups of objects must close our survey of the artistic birth pangs of La Tène style; first from both sides of the Alps, Switzerland, Austria, and the early Celtic cemeteries of northern Italy come a number of belt-hooks [**95–99**] whose delicate open-work binds into a pyramidal shape birds, naked men, strange horse-like creatures, as well as the eastern and backward-looking griffon, in a Celtic version of that much later and even more intricate interlace which is a key feature of the earliest Anglo-Saxon metalwork. These belt-hooks represent probably the earliest objects which we can relate to the settlement of *c.* 400 BC and they embrace motifs which we will see recurring elsewhere. Second is a pair of objects, the ring from Pössneck [**100**] and the fibula with twin humans and ram's head from Niederschönhausen, a Berlin suburb [**101**]. These two pieces are the most striking of a small group, obviously products of one crafts centre made to the order of a local La Tène enclave well to the north of the main Rhineland complex, a community attracted doubtless by the mineral wealth of the Saale region. The ring, which is in fact not actually twisted but cast, is little different from many others of earlier La Tène date, but the disembodied face, schematic ram's head and indeterminate spiral feature present a fine mystical Celtic triumvirate of the human, the animal and the ambiguous.

To sum up finally these notes on the early stages of La Tène art, the problem of the exact relationship between imports and that elusive blending process which is at the very roots of Early Celtic art, is akin to the questions which may be asked about the manner in which the closely related and contemporary Atestine metal-workers abstracted and adapted 'orientalising' features from Greece and even further East. It is, I think, reasonable to state that such objects as the Celtic wine flagons [**50, 60–61, 66, 72–73, 78, Plate III**] may have derived their form from Italic models but that their embellishment only reflects that interest in the decorative possibilities of the human figure and its parts which was exploited by the Greeks and perpetuated to an extent in neighbouring and subsequent civilisations. As to physiognomy itself, unlike much of Italic iconography, in Celtic representations beards are in the minority. In the place of beards, as one would expect and as we have already seen, the luxuriant moustaches of the typical Gaulish warrior are well represented in a style which is wholly native. In short, even if one accepts the 'eastern' character of the range of early La Tène masks it is perhaps neither necessary nor possible to look for precise external parallels; the human faces of the Celtic 'orientalising' style are truly part of a new innovation.

A further innovation still which introduces maturity into the stylistic development of La Tène art can be seen on the flagon from the Waldalgesheim chariot grave [**78**]. Old when buried, and with a close artistic cousin in the gilt-bronze flagon from Reinheim [**73**], the Waldalgesheim piece shows a strikingly naturalistic and really talented example of miniaturist casting in the head

[1] Jacobsthal, *Early Celtic Art*, 24

above an open-work base to the handle. A similar severe rendering of the earliest vegetable designs to this open-work can be noted on other objects also [111–112]. Engraved round the bodies of both the Waldalgesheim and the Reinheim jugs, however, is also a complex interlacing palmette pattern. Here no less than on two very disparate objects, an Etruscan flagon locally decorated to the order of its Celtic owner [113] and a fragmentary bronze bowl from South Wales [114], one can discern various stages in the evolution of a new free interpretation of the old classical motifs. On the basis of other objects in the Waldalgesheim grave [118, 124–127], which contained one of the latest Italic imports in the Celtic hinterland, Jacobsthal borrowed the name 'Waldalgesheim' for this new style. Several pieces decorated in this style come once more from the North Italian cemeteries, and from the non-Celtic grave goods at these sites we are able to set the beginning of the mature Waldalgesheim phase late in the fourth century. The human mask no longer dominates but is far from absent, particularly on a new and long-living class of neck-rings, those with buffer-shaped terminals. The strictly patterned forms of the Waldalgesheim Style appear to reach west from their southern Rhineland origins to influence local craftsmen in Brittany [156–157]. It has been claimed that subsequent immigration of these latter craftsmen may have represented the advance guards of La Tène culture to reach Ireland as well as the Thames valley. Certainly an immigration of style rather than craftsmen must account, if only at long range, for the few but striking objects which, as we will see, set the foundations for a truly British Iron Age art [244–252].

The key feature of the new 'mature' continental Waldalgesheim style is its uniquely blended patterning. A good example is the fragmentary bronze scabbard found in a Gaulish cemetery at Filottrano in northern Italy [137]. Here can be made out a series of partial lyres linked in a running palmette chain based on the decorative elements of fourth-century Italo-Greek pottery such as occur in the Italo-Celtic settlement areas. The new style often decorates cast bronze fibulae with coral-decorated feet, the so-called 'Münsingen' type, named after one of the large flat inhumation cemeteries in which women were occasionally buried with more than a dozen brooches. A characteristic plastic 'cross-over' of the palmette design allows one to identify the work of what one may term the 'Waldalgesheim master' [124–125, 137]. This palmette chain is just the sort of pattern which one requires as a first stage in the transformation into the bulging eyes, bulbous noses, and curl-fringed brows of a western group of torcs [119–121] which link the formalisation of Waldalgesheim with the good-humoured floridness of the full 'Plastic Style' [158 ff.]. Once more it is difficult to follow precisely the mechanics of such motif transplantings. Only a helmet reputedly found in Umbria [108], with its faces peering out from the foliage above the ear-flaps and the chain of palmette lyres round the base of the cap, suggests so direct an influence as the result of collaboration between Etruscan and Celtic artisans in an Italian workshop. Elusive images began to appear with this free handling of classical floral motifs in patterns artistically if not mathematically precise. One is attracted by the inborn human propensity to see faces into such objects as the buffer-torcs and a group of disc-termi-nalled neck-rings, the latter found particularly in the flat cemeteries of south Germany and the Swiss plateau [145–147]. These rings have red enamel instead of coral set in their terminals – a technique which was to become more common with the development of glass for ornaments from the second century on. By the subtle Celtic artist's love of ambiguity, of the visual *double entendre* as seen on the Filottrano scabbard, we are drawn 'into the mechanism of dreams where things have floating contours and pass into other things'.[1] The ambiguity of this 'Cheshire Cat Style', to borrow with Jacobsthal a term from Lewis Carroll's fantasy, adds to the difficulties of the modern art critic, who is certainly interested in abstractions, but abstractions altered so radically in background and purpose by two and a half thousand years of artistic development.

There is no ambiguity, however, about one of the most attractive groups in all Celtic art, represented by the baroque fancies of a Central European school whose products coincided with the most widespread extent of Celtic migration. This school is dominated by what Jacobsthal termed the 'Plastic Style'. 'Plastic', though, as we have already commented, is none too happy a discriminating adjective since plasticity or three-dimensionalism is present in a partially abstracted form even in the early 'formative period' pieces. In attempting to describe succinctly the essence of the products of the third century BC school one might call it rather the 'Disney Style' [161–162, 164–170]. The manner in which, in this style, a face is broken down into a number of curvilinear geometric forms – crescents, ovals, circles, and the like – is close to the twentieth-century film cartoonist's process of creation. In the modern cartoon as with its three-dimensional prehistoric predecessors, no single detail is academically representational, but the total image is brilliantly evoked with a great economy of form which is nevertheless immediately recognisable. The partial abstraction of the Celtic style – very often of animal rather than human forms – seems to be striving towards a typical Celtising of motifs in which human, floral and abstract elements fuse.

It is from Moravia that the largest group of objects of the Plastic Style comes. The mounts from Maloměřice, a flat cemetery site on the outskirts of modern Brno, show considerable artistic variety [158–160, 165]. The griffon-terminalled ring of this set, which perhaps we can see as a last descendant of the Stupava heraldic pair, shares many details with the bronze mountings of the cauldron from Brå [162, 164], an export to distant, non-Celtic, Scandinavia. In parenthesis, though the latter can hardly be anything other than a product of Central Europe, its animal decoration of a clearly ritual cauldron harks back to the Italian and Greek products of provincial Assyrian-inspired manufacture. The remarkable pseudo-portraiture of the Maloměřice twin-faced open-work fragment on the other hand [158] is, as previously hinted, in its confrontation of realism and abstraction, the most telling warning against generalised statements on the rigid conventionalisation of any phase of Celtic art.

Statuary, at least as it has survived from this, the peak of Celtic artistic production, is somewhat surprisingly rare, although we noted at the outset that most of Celtic art is basically two-dimensional. As with the early pillar-stones, the usually isolated occurrences of several of the later key pieces of stone sculpture makes any sort of dating totally reliant on stylistic analysis and comparison. The ragstone head of a Celtic warrior found in a pit near a triple-divided rectangular enclosure at Mšecké Žehrovice, Bohemia [171], is generally considered to belong to the Middle La Tène period. The enclosure, however, is a characteristic and apparently ritual structure of the later Celtic period as found in an area stretching north and west into the central Rhineland, and the most recent view of the head is that it may date to late in the second century BC. It is instructive to compare this buffer-torc-wearing individual, with his fine sergeant-major moustaches, with the Hellenistic 'Dying Gaul' from Pergamon known from a Roman copy now in the Capitoline Museum, a nearly contemporary but very different evocation of the essential

[1] Jacobsthal, *Proc. British Acad.* XXVII (1941), 308

features of the Celtic character. Mšecké Žehrovice is indeed 'an excellent instance of the counter-attractions of nature and abstraction in Celtic portrayal'.[1]

We have briefly noted the appearance of horse- and griffon-terminalled spirals in the Alpine group of Early Style belt-hooks [95–99]. The same feature appears with a series of engraved scabbards [179–183], delicate by-products of the swordsmith's skill of several individual 'schools' in Switzerland and further east and as found in considerable numbers at the type-site of La Tène. Some of these scabbards date from much the same period as the putative beginning of our 'Disney Style' objects though most cannot be earlier than the second century B C. These and certain allied objects such as a bronze plaque from Kelheim [178], site of one of the great south German *oppida*, exhibit this strange iconography with the same selective cartoonist's skill. The assured line of the engraver's burin seen in the scabbard decoration – an assurance which disguises its freehand application – incidentally sets a continental precedent for the absorption in engraved vegetable designs which are the staple motifs of (?) second-century British fine metal work [247–249, 251]. The 'Sword Style' is in many ways simply a continuation of many of the elements to be seen in the pattern-books of Waldalgesheim artists, as may be most clearly seen in the occasional low-cast relief ornament of various scabbard belt staples. Punch marks found on the actual iron sword blades, on the other hand, clearly copy the totemistic repertoire of the first local coinage. The horse comes into his own in the later phase of Celtic art where, to anticipate, his frequent appearance is again a direct product of the evolution of Celtic coinage [194]. The bronze-mounted wooden bucket from a cremation grave at Aylesford in Kent [187], though found in a late first century B C context, harks back to earlier things in its crested twin heads with their half-forgotten memories of the 'leaf-crown', its backward-looking, feather-tailed equines and its effete spiral designs. Both Aylesford and the mounts from a somewhat similar though larger and probably later bucket found at Marlborough in Wiltshire [186, 188] possibly were made on the continent, perhaps in northern France rather than in Britain itself, where there was a lack of interest in animal depiction. Both buckets are also to be associated with the settlement in south-east England of the latest of the Celtic newcomers to arrive in Britain.

The adoption of coinage by the continental Celts [194, 217, Plate IV] is a clear indication of the gradual failing of the old patterns of barbarian barter economy. It is also the most important innovation amongst the art of the closing centuries of La Tène culture. Celtic numismatics, however, despite more than a hundred years of sporadic research, is still a much neglected field. A complete and up-to-date survey of the styles, let alone of the distribution, of continental coinage still remains to be written. For this reason, if for no other, our brief survey is concerned with coins solely in the wider context of Celtic art. The most obvious feature of Celtic coinage, both continental and British, is that it owes most of its varying forms to a limited number of Hellenistic prototypes – coins not only of Macedonia but of southern Italy and Massalia. The most common forms are the adoption and adaptation of the Apollo or Hercules head on the obverse, and the horse and rider or charioteer and quadriga on the reverse, of issues of Philip II and Alexander III of Macedon [194A–B, Plate IVa]. The well-fed contours of the animals on eastern Celtic silver coinage – in contrast to the free abstraction of some French gold pieces where, as so often, natural form is wholly subordinate to design [194F, Plate IVc] – result in folksy cart horses which no ancient Greek would have recognised as a copy of the sleek

[1] T. G. E. Powell, *The Celts* (1958), 255

mount of one of Alexander's auxiliary cavalry. As to the commencement date for the production of local Celtic coin issues, associations with Roman republican coins in hoards in northern Italy indicate at least the middle or the first half of the third century. A recent find in Romania points to a date as early as the second half of the fourth century for the eastern coinage – or within a generation of the reign of Philip II of Macedon, whose coins were being imitated. These early coins are all silver, however; we are as yet less certain of the precise beginnings of the more westerly gold Celtic coins.

The lack of any great unifying style amongst the art of the later Celts, reflected clearly in their coinage, is, like the coins themselves, a direct expression of the fragmented, or rather localised, nature of contemporary Celtic society. The local centres were the tribal *oppida*, which by the first century BC would have been artistic as well as geographical landmarks in a barbarian Europe stretching from the mouth of the Danube to the lowlands of Scotland [**184, 196–199, 207, 213, Plate Vb**]. In some small pieces the general concern with the human head is continued, even if in this later period the head may take on the aspect of a Roman actor's mask or a latter-day Silenus [**195–197, 200**]. Again, the head, like much earlier objects, may be adorned with a helmet of clearly Italian provenance [**201**]. From later Swiss cemeteries come a number of coral-decorated brooches which in basic form follow an archaic pattern devised at a time when the Waldalgesheim Style was being ordered; the helmeted heads have a close parallel in several of a cache of bronze figures found in Liechtenstein [**202**]. More in the main stream of Celtic tradition are the mustachioed faces from two widely separated areas. First are the mounts on a pair of four-wheeled funerary waggons from Dejbjerg in Denmark [**203**], the latest evidence for the old Hallstatt rites which first introduced us to human embellishment of vehicle fittings. Second is a group of silver discs and other objects, including probable torc fragments and horse or waggon decorations, from Manerbio sul Mella in northern Italy [**204–206**]. These are difficult to date in view of their employment of such long-followed conventions as the ridged almond eyes and the juxtaposing of ram and man [**206**]. However, the slack version of the triskel roundel suggests a late date, no less than the comparisons one can make with other decorative sheet metal fragments found in late contexts [**207**]; several of these offer a comparison with the well-combed locks of the chieftain of Mšecké Žehrovice [**171**].

Mention of silver, common only in Spain and the eastern Celtic area where the local supplies of Transylvania would have answered a need reflected in the common use of this metal for coinage [**194A, D**], brings us to one small and until recently little-known school of Iron Age metal craft. Centred on the lower Danube and the imperial Roman province of Dacia and thus strictly beyond the confines of true Celtic settlement, extending in time from at least the fifth to the first century [**219–221**], this 'Dacian' art exhibits something of the range of weird oriental borrowing which we have seen amongst products of the Atestine region [**24–26**] and which in fact has a very similar time-span. In gold, not silver, the helmet from Poiana in Romania [**221**] exhibits similar hoofed beasts to those Persian-looking supporters on the great Rodenbach bracelet [**55**], while the first-century silver coinage of the Bratislava district [**217**] sports the old orientalising winged griffon, a figure we have seen on a much earlier piece from Slovakia [**64**]. Greatest of all these eastern pieces is the imposing silver cauldron found dismantled in a northern Danish peat bog at Gundestrup [**209, Plate VI**]. Here, as the gaunt figure dipping its victim in a tall bucket hints, is a scene which reminds one not only of the ritual importance of the 'cauldron of plenty' in the Celtic world but of the association of sacrifice, cauldrons, and the god Dagda recounted in the legends of the old Welsh tradition.

The rectangular internal panels offer a valuable visual commentary on those aspects of Celtic belief which we have already considered. The Gundestrup cauldron exemplifies a style which is again not so much Celtic as Atestine. The marching figures certainly recall the *situlae* [24], although the weapons carried, the great boar-decorated horns blown and sacred buffer-terminal torcs so proudly displayed, indicate a date not earlier than the second century [209A]. The griffons occur not only on the first-century coins we have just mentioned, but also as western Greek survivals in southern France. A similar source can be found for the winged Pegasus figures, while the single heads can be seen as descendants of such 'orientalising' pieces as the Glauberg torc [87]. The cross-legged 'Cernunnos' figure is, as its distribution confirms, mainly a south and central French deity [212, 232]. Even the elephant was not unknown to the Celts either in life or in art, since it is found on late Etruscan pots as well as on south French sculpture. The almond eyes of the stag and the boar beside Cernunnos introduces us to another foreign piece on Danish soil, the bronze cauldron from Rynkeby on Funen [222]. This is a poor thing when compared with the vigorous zoology of the 'Plastic' or 'Disney' style [161–162]. The half-hearted triskel, like that on the Manerbio discs [204–206, 222B], shows its late date, while the dull formalism of the central and still torc-wearing head points once more southwards, to the same area which probably produced the Aylesford and Marlborough buckets. The bull torsos of Rynkeby likewise are but shadows of the vital religious heraldry of Brå [162, 164], earliest of the three decorated cauldrons from Denmark. The bull on the central disc of the Gundestrup bowl is a much more awesome creature [214], strong even in his last agony fought out in the centre of a great hunting pack, a barbarous version of the Calydonian boar and of equal ritual significance. We have also our own Celtic version of the epic boar hunt in a Spanish wheeled cult model of probably second century BC date [37]. On Gundestrup, the central disc and its several pendants [215] establish, as clearly as the detailed execution of the individual scenes on the sides, its eastern origin.

The frequent mention in the last paragraph of the later art of the South of France leads us to glance briefly at the products of another region where the Celtic world not only met that of Greece and Italy but was heavily influenced by it. It is perhaps significant that the *oppida* of this area are those which most clearly have claim to the description of the Celtic tribal centres as 'hilltop towns'. The largest body of sculpture of this region comes from the sanctuaries of Entremont and Roquepertuse [212, 235, 236], local rallying points destroyed in the formation of the first Roman *provincia*, Provence, in 124 BC. Some figures, despite such 'Celtic' elements as formalised facial features and neat vertically combed hair, clearly display their classically derived origins [231], as also do the few attempts at architectural ornamentation [236]. Occasionally there is something which proclaims more clearly its barbaric purpose. Such is the pillar-statue of Euffigneix [226] from, not the South of France, the chief artistic centre for the period, but the Marne. In France the conspicuous heraldic emblem of the boar continues the tradition laid down in material evidence by our earlier cult models [37, 224–226, 238]. The style of the boars is sometimes not unlike the emaciated creature on the Rynkeby fragments. Bronzes are fewer and apart from the ubiquitous tribal emblems few require more than a passing glance, though there is a Mediterranean lightness and gaiety in the little male and female dancers from yet another sanctuary site, Neuvy-en-Sullias on the south bank of the Loire [237]. In contrast, the 'Cernunnos' figure in bronze from Bouray [232] with the feet, not horns, of a stag and a torso set off by the sacred torc, is classed by Powell with other bronzes as the handiwork of craftsmen coming from across the Rhine during the increasingly troubled times of the early first century BC. But Bouray and other (probably male rather than female) masks from the Paris basin region [239–240], with pierced eye-holes and nominal but clearly discernible torcs, must owe all but their ritual purpose to the growing hybridisation of what is no longer Celtic but Gallo-Roman art. This feature can be noticed in such minor objects as the anthropomorphic hilts of Late La Tène swords, which in the late second or first century alternate between rigidly Celtic and effeminately provincial Roman [229, 241]. The granite head recovered by chance from Roman Gloucester [243] is also provincial, but certainly Celtic, and by no means effeminate. In its wholly Celtic transformation of the conventions of Roman portrait sculpture here is a suitable piece to introduce our last field of study, the later, Iron Age art of the British Isles.

There are other, non-Celtic, elements in the British Iron Age but these are not to be our concern here. Pre-Roman Celtic art in Britain shows in its development a partial parallelism to continental styles and contemporary classical influences. From its outset, probably in the third century BC, British art exhibits an individuality which, because of its limited distribution and physical insularity, allows individual ascriptions to local schools or craft-centres more readily than on the continent. British art, whether linear or plastic – that is, modelled – is primarily based on swirling, rhythmic circular patterns often grouped in triple repeating units. The linking or terminal features are much in evidence: the stylised bird head, the eye-comma, and curved sided triangle or 'trumpet spiral' [244, 254, 270]. In contrast with the continent and the general trend of Celtic religion, British Iron Age art seems at a first glance to be essentially aniconic, although on close examination certain elusive images of faces-which-are-no-faces begin to obtrude. Animal ornaments [273–277] certainly increase in the later period while definitely human forms are generally absent save for late or even sub-Roman stone heads of obviously votive importance [283, 285–286]. Earlier instances, for example a face peering out of an abstracted floral design [245], look back to Italo-Celtic forms such as we have already noted [108].

The late fourth-century Waldalgesheim phase is usually considered the key stage of continental stylistic development from which the roots of British La Tène art sprang. It is, however, difficult to ascertain with certainty many objects found in Britain as being of definite continental workmanship, though British Iron Age craftsmen seem continually to be fishing in a reservoir of continental motifs. Indeed, until shortly before the Roman conquest, one cannot even be certain of dating any single British piece to within a century either way. If anything, the similarity of the putative early British material is to the developed continental 'sword' – or, as termed here, the 'advanced Waldalgesheim' – style of the third and second centuries BC. It would in fact be possible to suggest that true British Iron Age art developed only with the coming of the Belgae and the resulting virtual population explosion. The fragments of a bronze bowl from Cerrig-y-Drudion in South Wales [114], generally but not necessarily correctly dated to the late fourth century, have sometimes been considered to be from northern France, an area colonised from the Rhineland probably in the search for tin and for control of the Atlantic trade route. The engraved design of the bowl, however, has an asymmetry and feeling for extemporisation which only reflects at a distance the basic Italo-Greek patterns, and the whole does not precisely match the general run of Breton decorated pottery [**157**]. On the other hand Cerrig-y-Drudion shares certain features visible on engraved and open-work bronzes of the immediately pre-Waldalgesheim style [**112–113**]. In Ireland we may perhaps see more clearly the direct immigration from the continent of Celtic craftsmen in the wake of Celtic chieftains. There is, however, no clear evidence of La Tène inspired art in Ireland before the second century, despite frequent claims. Most famous of a small group of carved stones from the south of Ireland is that which stands at Turoe, Co. Galway, originally close to the site of a local fortified settlement [**129**]. The stone is carved all over in what might be called again the 'advanced Waldalgesheim style' but, as has already been hinted in connection with swords, this 'style', if it can be so termed, had a very long life; coins of the first century BC continue the motifs. Indisputably early is the gold torc from Clonmacnoise, a product of the continental 'Plastic' style [**174**]. From eastern Britain is a cast armlet found in a typical warrior's grave at Newnham Croft [**131**] and bearing at many removes a low-relief version of motifs of not so much the true Waldalgesheim style but rather the derived art of the third and second centuries [**124–127**]. The use of incised cross-hatching or 'basketry' on the ring suggests much later and definitely insular work. This local adherence to a simple basic repertoire is reflected in a bronze mount from the Thames at Brentford [**130**] with its thrice repeated and truncated palmette forms and adaptation of Hellenistic-type scroll leaves. This skilful casting has, again, been taken as a late extension of the Waldalgesheim Style contemporary with the 'Sword Styles' and compared with some of the first definitely local products [**246**]. Much more likely, the Brentford cap should be considered to be as late as the end of the first century BC.

A first movement towards undoubtedly mature native schools can be observed in the decorative bronze mounts of a sword found by the Thames at Standlake – a find spot which offers yet another hint of the local continuity of the water cults and sacred hoards already noted. One mounting has a pelta design [**250**] which can certainly be seen in continental material from the late fourth–second centuries but, once more, comparisons are too general to offer any sound stylistic or chronological affinities. In north-east Ireland the skill of related local princely swordsmiths [**248–249**] shows an exploitation of the free-running engraved pattern favoured by the scabbard engravers of Switzerland and Hungary of certainly not earlier than the second century [**179–183**]. Probably contemporary with these Irish scabbards are three bronzes found at Torrs in south-west Scotland and formerly in the private collection of Sir Walter Scott, antiquary as well as novelist and poet. The Torrs bronzes [**244–245**], a pony cap and a pair of tubular terminals for Nordic-type drinking horns show the two main features already alluded to; the feeling for free plastic asymmetry with the bird-terminal clearly discernible, and the linear patterns of the swordsmiths. Torrs and other objects, mainly sword or shield fittings [**246–247, 251–252, Plate VII**], show the range of this eastern British art which finds its final expression in the careful symmetry of the well-known bronze and glass inlaid parade shield from Battersea [**253**]. This is certainly of the early first century A D and anthropomorphic masks intrude in a characteristically ambiguous Celtic manner. Of other second or, more probably, first century B C pieces we may note two – a shield mounting from Llyn Cerrig Bach in Anglesey [**254**], a lakeside sacred hoard deposited over at least a century, and yet another engraved scabbard, this time from Bugthorpe in eastern Yorkshire [**259**]. The former demonstrates the growth of feeling for plastic trumpet or bird scrolls building up a free moving triquetra or triskel. In addition to this plasticity seen also on the latter bronze, the asymmetrical engraved pattern reveals the vogue *c.* 50 BC for matting or basketry patterns [257] which later in the century were to be built up with geometric precision.

The acme of this incised tradition is reached in a group of bronze mirrors produced between the latter half of the first century BC and the middle of the first century AD. These mirrors, whose form was probably adapted from provincial Roman patterns, were mainly manufactured for Belgic overlords in the south-east. As Sir Cyril Fox, the first to study and identify the main stages of development of the 'mirror style', has written, the method of engraving the mirror reverses was by means of a chaser which 'is used to make (sometimes with a rocking motion) tiny dents – parallel rows of short strokes filling or framing the design previously drafted by fine incision on the metal'.[1] The basic pattern of the mirror is a triskel set against a roundel. Experimental work with the engraver's tracer rocked from side to side is occasionally discernible in early pieces [250] or in free-hand attempts at mirror decorations in the early first century AD [261]. Once more the presumed earliest in this class of objects [260] shows a brilliant combination of asymmetry of detailing developed within a balanced whole; the elaboration of the mirror handle here illustrated on a rare British export to the continent [263], is a later feature.

As has already been remarked, in British art, save for coinage and a few cult figures of uncertain date, man is almost a stranger. Exceptions are a few pieces from the stock-breeding, non-Belgic, Brigantian area of north-east England in which it is possible to see both the textbook mustachioed Celt and the horned 'Cernunnos' [264–265]. The bronze buckets from Aylesford and Marlborough [186–188] have already been alluded to in their continental context. Here we may note that the Aylesford bucket, old when buried *c.* 10 BC, shares with objects found on the other side of the Channel a poor and remarkably stiff version of the triskel. There is a long-remarked affinity between the Aylesford bucket, the early uninscribed series of British gold coins, and the great White Horse beside the hill-fort of Uffington on the Berkshire downlands – though there are reasonable grounds for thinking that this last may be of Saxon date [184]. Notwithstanding, these similarities may also be taken to illustrate the transmission of north or central French 'Belgic' motifs into native British contexts. In its human decorative elements, however, Aylesford contrasts strongly with Marlborough, which, at upwards of half a century later, whatever its origin, compares well with continental Roman-influenced masks [232]. Further skilled work of south-western manufacture and a similar time-span to the mirrors is marked by a series of bronze bowls finished and cleaned on a rotary lathe [273, 276–277] – a suggestion this time of Roman technological rather than artistic influence. Linked by a general use of tremolo decoration around the rim – a western stylistic trick – the handles of these bowls illustrate what is often absent elsewhere, the usual holy menagerie of the Celtic world, a duck or the wild boar. The latter is to be seen on another rare British export found across the Iron Age curtain between Celt and non-Celt [277]. Again, the enamel enrichment of several of the bowls shows the progressive popularity of inlay which under the Roman occupation adds yellow and blue to the original red [Plate VIIIb]. Bucket handle mounts follow the old continental tradition of adding a bull's head [274]. The ram [275] is also found, while iron bull- or ox-decorated 'fire dogs', witness to the skill of first-century AD native blacksmiths, are found not only in British Belgic

---

[1] Fox, *Pattern and Purpose: a Survey of Early Celtic Art in Britain* (1958), 84

chieftains' graves but in a wide area across the whole of the Late La Tène world [278–279]. These accessories for the funeral symposium were either used as spits against which rested the joints of pork or provided support for the great imported amphorae of Mediterranean wine.

The last phase of what may be regarded as main-stream British Iron Age art commences in fact at the end of the first century BC. In eastern England fine gold and bronze work [290–294] continues the style established by the Llyn Cerrig mounts but now various roundels are set against the basketry background. A helmet dredged from the Thames – another product of eastern England – has a plastic but somewhat stringy stalk pattern enriched with enamel studs, the 'stalks' matching those on an Irish gold torc from Broighter [289], although this latter piece has also been quoted as an imported pendant to a continental ring from Frasnes-lez-Buissenal [173]. In both the northern and south-western British provinces collars [297–298] decorated with the latest versions of the spiral ornament of the Torrs horns begin to follow Roman forms and formalism. The old cross-hatching is replaced by stippling as a fill-in. The magnificent bronze-covered wooden tankard from Trawsfynydd [296] reflects not so much what has been termed the 'rococo' as the 'art nouveau' phase of Celtic art in Britain. The swirling triskels are seen there for the first time in full open-work three-dimensional relief. In Ireland, unaffected by Roman invasion or settlement, the later use of bird scroll and trumpet spiral, as seen on skilfully cast bronze objects whose purpose can only be the subject of surmise [270–271], extends at least as late as the third century AD. These products made for some of the last great Celtic warrior chieftains act as a bridge between the art of the pre-Roman Iron Age and the non-representational ornament of the gospel books of the sixth–ninth century AD, the Golden Age of the Christian West.

The last century of British independence of Roman rule saw the introduction of the berried rosette motif. It occurs on furniture fittings or on the metal work of the refugee workshops in north-eastern England [299ff.]. It also decorates such alien objects as a helmet neckguard of typical Roman auxiliary form, echoing the over-elaborate plastic handle ornaments of the contemporary late mirror series. Even a brief glance at this material demonstrates the artistic decline of the years preceding and following the Claudian conquest. British coinage [306], inscribed with the first names of British history, as on the continent reflects the gradual numbing influence of Mediterranean culture as well as government, though with the political break-up of the native tribal system the impetus and demand was only partially denied the native artist. On the bronze plaque from Elmswell in Yorkshire [303] one can see on the blue enamelled rectangle a vine scroll thinly disguised from its provincial Roman antecedents by the addition of Celtic trumpet terminals. The great central lyre palmette on the other hand has an ancestry which stretches through the British mirror series to Cerrig-y-Drudion and beyond to the gold work of Waldalgesheim itself, which, despite the later dating suggested here, is the ultimate starting point of all British Celtic art.

*   *   *

Our survey both on the continent and in the British Isles closes with the coming of the Romans, but this is not a true closing point for Celtic art any more than for Celtic culture. In Ireland, and through Ireland back into continental Europe, revitalised by the continued animalistic traditions of northern nomads, we have the Celtic or at least native art of both the Roman and post-Roman period, the art which paradoxically owed much of its impetus to the spread of a Mediterranean- or indeed Roman-based religion, Christianity. If in a sense 'Celtic art has no genesis',[1] one cannot say that with the decline of Roman power in the fourth century 'the stream is dry which had so much to say'. Unlike the Delphic oracle, whose last words these were, Celtic art was long to survive the fall of great cities.

As to the main lines of the development of Iron Age art, more detailed study will doubtless show the growing importance of local styles over and against, for example, the three main divisions offered by Jacobsthal for art of the La Tène culture. Running throughout the Iron Age in whatever area we may choose there is clear evidence of a close relationship between man and beast not even entirely altered by a change in social conditions or by the hybrid nature of the new society which followed in the wake of Roman conquest. As Celtic culture in France was closest to the classical world, so was it furthest from the spirit of Iron Age art, lacking that vital spark conjoining representation and creation. Thus with the introduction of Mediterranean civilisation came the snapping of that cord between man and the world of myth and symbol around him which survived in British pagan religion and even in some crude forms of art [283–286].

In offering a few comments by way of conclusion I want to refer to the general principles which I have attempted to follow in this study. Firstly, it would be foolish to pretend that any survey of Iron Age art is ever likely to be definitive. As with all archaeological materials, the fragmentary and often ambiguous nature of the basic evidence will always present an insuperable barrier. For example, the valuable information which might result from the discovery of an early continental Iron Age artists' workshop is at the moment denied to us – and if we are correct as to the peripatetic nature of such artists in contrast to those of classical Greece and Rome, such information is unlikely to be discovered. Nevertheless, this lack in itself offers a challenge to reconsider what should be our basic approach to so varied and ill-defined art styles as those of the European Iron Age. For this reason I have tried to make use of new attitudes towards art analysis to make up for the cultural *lacunae* in the study of Iron Age archaeology as a whole.

Secondly, it should be clear that Iron Age and particularly La Tène art is predominantly a religious art, though of course not in the more strictly didactic sense of Early Christian art. La Tène art employs an iconography which imbues even the simplest objects with a degree of the mysterious or indeed the divine. It also uses a kind of visual overstatement which, to modern eyes at least, often seems to border on the grotesque. Nancy Sandars, in her examination of the nature of La Tène art style, acknowledges the key position held by the Celts' view of divinity – though one must admit that we are still far from understanding the full significance of Celtic myth or symbolism. Miss Sandars makes use of the metaphor of the triskel or triple whirligig, one of the most common motifs in Celtic design of both the pre- and post-Roman period. This 'triskel of style' is composed first of *tension*, an artistic tension in which symmetry and asymmetry, balance and imbalance, are continually being played off against each other in a kind of visual counterpoint. The second element is *ambiguity*, while the third is *the ideal*, or the close adherence to what I have termed here the *schemata* or readily definable basic artistic vocabulary of the La Tène craftsman. Certainly, the seemingly ambiguous nature of Celtic beliefs and customs should not prevent one from probing, however tentatively, into the possible meaning of

[1] Jacobsthal, *Early Celtic Art*, 158

varying individual elements or motifs in Iron Age art. This leads to a third feature noted at the outset of our discussion: the fact that Iron Age art seems at many points in its evolution to have a direct formal relationship with the 'developed' roots of the contemporary arts of the Mediterranean world. It can, however, only be grossly misleading to attempt to reconstruct either the form or purpose of Iron Age art in terms of classical art history, a trap into which even Jacobsthal may have fallen, for all his unsurpassable powers of evocation of the background to Celtic art. A concentration on attempts to establish an ordered 'classical' development for Iron Age art must tend to ignore the existence of sharply individual yet contemporary styles. Equally dangerous or futile is the following through of certain foreign or 'oriental' figural elements to their supposed source of origin. To adapt Jacobsthal's description of contemporary Italy, Central and Western Europe was an area where motifs grew like weeds. Such were the varied sources for the original transplanting of these motifs, that it must be regarded now as impossible to establish with any certainty the precise seeds from which these motifs sprang. Itinerant artists of Jacobsthal's 'Early Style' are more than likely to have picked up the same foreign elements and combined and developed them in characteristically individual ways, unaware of other contemporary experiments; the comparative lack of interacting artistic influences within the Celtic sphere is one possible reason for the co-existence of disparate styles.

A more valuable point to make is that a study of the entire range of material here presented indicates that details of pattern in the widest sense rather than figural decoration may offer the best clues as to individual attributions in Iron Age art. To quote a few examples of early date, it is pattern rather than the over-all design which allows one to distinguish as products of one crafts centre the rings from Reinheim [79–83], Zerf – not illustrated here – and perhaps Rodenbach [55], as well as at least one of the fine pieces from the as yet incompletely published Swiss hoard of Erstfeld [84]. Details of patterning suggest a relationship, despite very different areas of discovery, of the decorated brooches from Chýnov [90] and Oberwittighausen [92], no less than those from Panenský Týnec [65] and Parsberg [63], the Borsch Aue flagon fragment [66], and the Stupava plaque [64]. Additions to the all-too-few technical analyses should also aid attributions.

Finally, though we have attempted to follow through a hypothetical development of certain long-lasting motifs or artistic conventions, many of which may be regarded as ciphers, elusive images of the human head so vital in Celtic belief, it will be readily noted that there is a complete lack of a firm chronological framework. To suggest exact dates is a very different matter from pointing out those affinities in style which have been set out as aids in constructing the products of a single artist or workshop. However, as with my occasional exercises in extracting individual identities from the all-embracing anonymity of Iron Age art, a chronological framework has been set up if only to offer a basis for future discussion (see also the chart on p. 179).

Few would deny the claim to universal recognition of the major works of Iron Age creative spirit. As in all art, however transcendental in quality, the objects to be illustrated on the following pages reflect not only the time and taste of the period in which they were made, but also contain the fruit of past styles and the seeds of the forms which were to follow. To take one last quotation from Nancy Sandars's brilliant analysis of the nature of prehistoric art, it is possible to see it in terms of two poles at either end of a tightrope; 'sometimes [the poles] stand for natural observation and ideal construction, or for that European abstract curvilinear style and the representational style that grew up in the Mediterranean world . . . there is between [the poles] a permanent tension which . . . the student of European art of any period ignores at his peril'.[1]

Iron Age art did not have to suffer total 'submergence beneath the tide of the dreary mediocrity of Roman provincial art',[2] as some scholars would have it. Rather, like the phoenix, pre-Roman Celtic art dies to rise again and take its place as a major contribution to the formation of a truly European artistic heritage. If great art is to be acknowledged as a reality – and much of our Iron Age art, however elusive, is undeniably great – there can never really be an end; only continually, a beginning.

NOTES ON ABBREVIATIONS AND REFERENCES USED

The purpose of the *Catalogue* (on the following pages) is twofold; first, to place the individual pieces in their precise archaeological setting with particular emphasis on find conditions and associations where present, and secondly to discuss each object as an individual work of art and to suggest stylistic comparisons. With a few particular exceptions, detailed descriptions are not given since in most cases these are readily to be found in such sources as Jacobsthal's *Early Celtic Art*. The individual bibliographies make no claim to being complete; key references containing further indications for source works are cited wherever possible, earlier works being largely omitted save where these contain material of particular importance and, since this is predominantly a volume of illustrations, references are also given to good alternative views of individual objects.

Abbreviations in the *Catalogue* should be self-explanatory with the following exceptions:

ABA	S. Piggott and G. E. Daniel, *A Picture Book of Ancient British Art* (1951)
ArtG	A. Varagnac and G. Fabre, *et. al.*, *L'Art Gaulois* (1956)
Aú ČSAV	Archeologický ústav, Československá Akademie Věd
AuhV	*Die Altertümer unserer heidnischen Vorzeit*
Aú SAV	Archeologický ústav, Slovenská Akadémia Vied
Ber.R-GK	*Bericht der Römisch-Germanischen Kommission*
Besançon	O.-H. Frey, 'Eine Etruskische Bronzeschnabelkanne', *Ann. Littéraires de l'Université de Besançon* 5 = *Au Musée de Besançon* 1 (1955)
Brå	O. Klindt-Jensen, 'Bronzekedelen fra Brå', *Jysk Arkæologisk Selskabs Skrifter* III (1953)
CCH	J. Filip, *Celtic Civilization and its Heritage* (1960)
Celts	T. G. E. Powell, *The Celts* (1958)
ECA	P. Jacobsthal, *Early Celtic Art* (1944; reissue with corrections 1969) – P and PP refer to Jacobsthal's 'List of Patterns'
Espérandieu	E. Espérandieu and R. Lantier, *Recueil général des bas-reliefs, statues et bustes de la Gaule romaine* I–XIV (1907–55)
EV	W. Torbrügge, *Europäische Vorzeit* (1968); English edition with identical pagination: *Prehistoric European Art* (n.d.)
FbS	*Fundberichte aus Schwaben*
Festschr. Dehn	O.-H. Frey (ed.), *Marburger Beiträge zur Archäologie der Kelten: Festschr. für Wolfgang Dehn* = *Fundber. aus Hessen* Beiheft 1 (1969)
Festschr. R-GZM	*Festschrift des Römisch-Germanischen Zentralmuseums Mainz*
IPEK	*Jahrbuch für Prähistorische u. Ethnographische Kunst*

---

[1] Nancy K. Sandars, *Prehistoric Art in Europe* (1968), 293
[2] Piggott and G. E. Daniel, *A Picture Book of Ancient British Art* (1951), 11

JL	P. Jacobsthal and A. Langsdorf, 'Die Bronzeschnabelkannen', *Römisch-Germanische Forschungen* 14 (1929)
JR-GZM	*Jahrbuch des Römisch-Germanischen Zentralmuseums Mainz*
JSGU	*Jahrbuch der Schweiz. Gesellschaft für Ur- u. Frühgeschichte*
KvsE	J. Filip, *Keltové v střední Evropě = Monumenta Arch.* V (1956)
LPA	J. W. Brailsford, *Later Prehistoric Antiquities of the British Isles in the British Museum* (1953)
Manuel	J. Déchelette, *Manuel d'Archéologie préhistorique, celtique et gallo-romaine* II–IV (2 ed. 1924–27)
PAE	Nancy K. Sandars, *Prehistoric Art in Europe = Pelican History of Art* 30 (1968)
PCB	Anne Ross, *Pagan Celtic Britain: Studies in Iconography and Tradition* (1967)
PP	Sir Cyril Fox, *Pattern and Purpose: A Survey of Early Celtic Art in Britain* (1958)
PPS	*Proceedings of the Prehistoric Society*
PRB	S. E. Thomas, *Pre-Roman Britain* (1965)
PreA	T. G. E. Powell, *Prehistoric Art* (1966)
Problems	S. S. Frere (ed.), 'Problems of the Iron Age in Southern Britain', *Institute of Archaeology Univ. of London Occ. Papers* 11 (n.d.)
R-G Forsch.	*Römisch-Germanische Forschungen*
R-GK	*Römisch-Germanische Kommission*
V and A	J. V. S. Megaw, 'Two La Tène finger rings in the Victoria and Albert Museum, London: an essay on the human face and Early Celtic art' in *Praehist. Zeitschr.* XLIII/XLIV (1965–66), 96–166.
VE	H. Müller-Karpe, *Das Vorgeschichtliche Europa = Kunst der Welt* (1968)
VRD	W. Kimmig and H. Hell, *Vorzeit an Rhein und Donau* (1958)
WK	J. Moreau, *Die Welt der Kelten* (1956)

The following additional abbreviations are used: d. – diameter, Ha – Hallstatt, ht. – height, l. – length, LT – La Tène, w. – width.

Centuries are indicated by Roman numerals thus: III BC, I AD and cross-references to other object and/or illustration numbers thus: **[28, 306C]**. Cultural periods where given follow the nomenclature most commonly used for the particular region concerned.

The dates quoted in the plate captions have been added for general ease of reference, and in view of the present imprecise state of Iron Age absolute chronology most should be regarded in the nature of educated, but in many cases personal, guesses (see also the chart on p. 179).

The question mark before certain dates indicates that even such guesses may be suspect in view of the lack of associations and/or stylistic parallels.

Where the source of the illustration differs from that of the object concerned, this is indicated in *italics* at the head of the note.

The following references, though not necessarily referred to in the *Catalogue*, contain material of general relevance to the present study.

M. Dillon and Nora K. Chadwick, *The Celtic Realms* (1967), esp. chap. 12 – an illustrated volume on pre- and post-Roman Celts particularly in the British Isles by two acknowledged experts of insular Celtic studies; stimulating if not always archaeologically reliable.

W. Dehn and O.-H. Frey, 'Die absolute Chronologie der Hallstatt- und Frühlatènezeit Mitteleuropas auf Grund des Südimports', in *Atti del VI Congr. Intern. delle Sci. Preist. e Protostoriche* I (1962), 197–208 – an invaluable summary with full bibliography.

M. Ebert (ed.), *Reallexikon der Vorgeschichte* 1–15 (1924–32).

J. Filip (ed.), *Enzyklopädisches Handbuch zur Ur- u. Frühgeschichte. Europas* I (1966), II (1969) – useful brief accounts with bibliographies on many sites and topics mentioned in the present study, though does not entirely replace the older and much larger *Reallexikon* cited above.

H. Hubert, *Les Celtes et l'expansion celtique jusqu'à l'époque de la Tène* and *Les Celtes depuis l'époque de la Tène et la civilisation celtique* (rev. ed. 1950) – though archaeologically out of date, still useful for its historical perspective. An English edition of these two volumes was published as *Rise of the Celts and Greatness and Decline of the Celts* (1934).

K. H. Jackson, *The Oldest Irish Tradition: a Window on the Iron Age* (1964) – an essay on the combination of archaeological, historical, and linguistic evidence to reconstruct the society of the later Iron Age in Ireland.

R. Lantier and H. Hubert, *Les origines de l'art français* I = *L'art préhistorique, l'art celtique, l'art gallo-romain* (1947).

Cecile O'Rahilly, *Táin Bó Cúalnge: from the Book of Leinster* (1967) – a recent edition and translation of the most important of the Old Irish hero-tales.

K. Schefold, 'Die Stilgeschichte der frühen keltischen Kunst', in *Praehist. Zeitschr.* XXXIV–XXXV (1949–50), 11–17 – a critique of Jacobsthal's *Early Celtic Art* with suggested new terminology.

J. J. Tierney, 'The Celtic Ethnography of Poseidonius', in *Proc. Roy. Irish Academy* 60C2 (1960), 189–275 – a commentary on classical references to the Celts.

E. Vogt (ed.), *Kunst und Kultur der Kelten*, Mus. zu Allerheiligen, Schaffhausen (1957) – a museum catalogue of a special loan exhibition of Celtic art in Western Europe.

Note

Although it has been possible to add a few recent references in proof I have unfortunately not been able to make use of one important new source, the catalogue prepared by Stuart Piggott for the Exhibition of Early Celtic Art held at the Royal Scottish Museum as part of the 1970 Edinburgh Festival of the Arts, and subsequently at the Hayward Gallery, London – the most comprehensive exhibition of European and insular Iron Age Art so far assembled.

J.V.S.M.
June 1970

Catalogue to the Plates

1 Sura Naquane, rock no. 98, Valcamonica, Brescia. Rock engraving. L. c. 50 cm. Anati Middle Period IVb, ?VII BC. *Photo courtesy Dr E. Anati.*

Rock art is known from many areas of the world. Apart from the well-known Upper Palaeolithic groups, the rock engravings of Scandinavia are certainly the oldest in Europe[1] – the earliest of these are assigned to the immediate post-glacial period. From the later Bronze Age or first millennium BC, as well as in Scandinavia, the rock engravings of Spain, the Alpes Maritimes, and northern Italy are also of the greatest importance. First discovered in 1916, the rock engravings of the Valcamonica, near Lake Garda in Lombardy, are concentrated in some thirteen separate areas, the sloping face of the Great Rock of Naquane alone being covered with some 876 figures produced by a dotted or pecked line.[2] Analysis of superimpositions of various scenes and the comparison of objects depicted with actual archaeological artefacts has suggested that the engravings of Valcamonica were executed during two main periods: XVII–IX BC and VIII–III BC.[3] The actual subject matter ranges from single symbols to vast congregations of animals, processions of warriors, views of whole villages with their fields, ploughmen and their teams, and scenes of unknown but clearly cultic significance. Some resemblance has been claimed to the so-called '*situla* art' of the head of the Adriatic [24–26] and the latest phase of rock art seems to reflect Graeco-Etruscan or even La Tène influence from the Celtic settled regions of the Po valley.[4]

The scene here depicted is one of many showing four-wheeled waggons, the characteristic vehicle of the princely graves of the Hallstatt Iron Age which was occasionally depicted on contemporary pottery from central Europe.[5] The manner in which the Valcamonica engravings show the waggons in a flattened-out child-like perspective is again not unknown north of the Alps, and waggons can be found carved on the rocks at Bohuslän, south Sweden (?500 BC). Nearer in time and space to Valcamonica is the scene carved on a bone knife from Dobrčice in Moravia, a piece belonging to the so-called 'Platěnice' culture[6] where, as in Lombardy, the evidence of actual four-wheeled vehicles is iconographic as well as archaeological, as evidenced in the latter area by the famous HaD four-wheeled waggon of Como.[7] Most recently an important group of rock-carvings of probable Iron Age date has been studied on the Adriatic Coast south of Dubrovnik.[8]

P. Graziosi, *Archivo per l'Anthrop. e l'Etnologia* 1929 (1931), 105 ff.; E. Anati, *Camonica Valley* (1964), esp. ill. p. 146

[1] H. Kühn, *Die Felsbilder Europas* (1952), esp. Taf. 76 ff.; P. Gelling and H. R. Ellis Davidson, *The Chariot of the Sun* (1968); P. V. Glob, *Helleristninger i Danmark = Jysk Arkæologisk Selskabs Skr.* VII (1969)

[2] E. Anati, 'La grande roche de Naquane', *Archives de l'Inst. Paléontologie humaine: Mémoire* 31 (1961)
[3] E. Anati, 'La datazione dell' arte preistorica Camuna', *Studi Camuni* II (2 ed., 1966)
[4] E. Schumacher, *JR-GZM*, 13 (1966), 37–43; see also [185]
[5] W. La Baume, *IPEK* (1928), 25 ff.; see also [10]
[6] E. and J. Neustupný, *Czechoslovakia before the Slavs* (1960); 133 and Pl. 60 (incorrectly listed as East Bohemia)
[7] E. Ghislanzoni, *Riv. Arch. Como fasc.* 99 (1930), 3–25
[8] M. V. Garašanin, *Germania* 46 (1968), 213–24

2 Sura Naquane, rock no. 96, Valcamonica, Brescia. Rock engraving. L. c. 65 cm. Anati Middle Period IVb, ?VII BC. *Photo courtesy Dr E. Anati.*

In this stag-hunt scene may be detected hints of the ritual purpose which must have been the stimulus behind the art of Valcamonica. Ritual hunts are not infrequent in Iron Age iconography, the most famous being that depicted on the Strettweg model waggon [38]. The clearly phallic nature of the hunter on the left is to be noted as well as the central figure, half-man, half-stag. If this is not just another primitive attempt at perspective – which seems unlikely, to judge from other rider figures – it may offer a foretaste of the later importance of an antlered male deity, found particularly in central France but also occurring as far afield as a I BC Dacian fortification at Popeşti, Romania,[1] and even in a late engraving at Valcamonica itself.[2]

E. Anati, *Camonica Valley* (1964), ill. p. 171

[1] R. Vulpe, *Materiale şi Cercetări arh.* III (1957), 227 ff. and fig. 23; *PCB*, 131, n. 5 and fig. 91
[2] *ECA*, 3, 11, Pl. 217a; *WK*, Taf. 13 right; Anati, *Camonica Valley*, ill. p. 172

3 Stuttgart—Bad Cannstatt, Württ. grave I. Gold bowl. D. 16·5 cm. Ha D2, late VI/early V BC. Württ. Landesmuseum, Stuttgart. *Atlantis Verlag, Zürich.*

This gold bowl hammered out of a single sheet and decorated with the aid of various punches follows a technique which has its origins in the Early Bronze Age. The bowl is part of the drinking set associated with the burial of a warrior in one of two of the typical *Fürstengräber* or princely graves of the later Hallstatt Iron Age found in the Cannstatt region. Discovered during building operations in 1934, the Bad Cannstatt grave had originally been marked by a burial mound under which a square timber-lined burial chamber had been constructed. A four-wheeled waggon had been placed intact along the west side of the grave, and parallel to the waggon, which was probably constructed especially for the burial rites, the dead chieftain had originally lain with his head to the north; the bones had not survived.

The Cannstatt drinking set, which comprises two bronze bowls as well as the gold cup, marks the importance of the funerary symposium in the Celtic world which, though it may have been introduced from central Italy or southern France in late Hallstatt times, has reflections in certain local Late Bronze Age practices.[1] Apart from the drinking set and the various waggon fittings including the iron tyres, hubs and bronze decorative strips for the sides of the vehicle, were found three iron spears and several brooches, useful for establishing the grave's relative chronology. Other gold objects included armrings and one of the circular gold ornaments as found in other princely graves including the second Cannstatt *Fürstengrab* and illustrated here by an example from France [5]. The absolute chronology of these graves is assisted by the finding of occasional imports from Italy such as the so-called 'Rhodian' bronze jugs as discovered in the gold-rich tomb of Kappel-am-Rhein, Baden.[2] The strictly geometric decoration of the Bad Cannstatt bowl, particularly the concentric circles and parallel lines, recall contemporary funerary pottery [9].

O. Paret, 'Das Fürstengrab von Bad Cannstatt', *FbS* VIII (1933–35), Anhang I, esp. Taf. IV; *id.*, *IPEK*, 15–16 (1941–42), 76–85; *VRD*, ill. 99 – with gold finds from Kappel; *Celts*, Pls. 11–13; *WK*, Taf. 22 below; *PreA*, 180 and ill. 178

[1] S. Piggott, *Antiquity* LIII (1959), 122–23; J. V. S. Megaw, *Antiquity* XL (1966), 40–41
[2] W. Kimmig and W. Rest, *JR-GZM* 1 (1954), 179–216, esp. 208 ff.; O.-H. Frey, *Marburger Winckelmann-Programm 1963* (1964), 18–20

4 Altstetten, Zürich. Gold bowl. D. 25 cm. Late VI BC. Schweiz. Landesmuseum, Zürich. *Landesbildstelle Baden u. Württ.* (*Dr Helmut Hell*)

The Zürich gold bowl, like that from Cannstatt beaten from a single gold sheet and decorated from the inner surface by *repoussé* technique, has long been the subject of discussion because of its twin sun and moon symbols and attendant beasts of which only a stag is clearly identifiable. Sun and moon symbols are common in the contemporary art of the area south of the Alps, while animal figures occur not only in rock art but also in other forms of the east Alpine Late Bronze Age, but precise parallels are hard to find.[1] Recently a flat bronze dish embossed with horses and sun symbols in the manner of the Zürich bowl was found in a Hallstatt D burial chamber under one of four burial mounds at Donauwörth, Bavaria, associated with typical Schwabian painted pottery[2] [compare **Plate I**]. The bossing effect of the Zürich bowl occurs, however, on contemporary Spanish gold work, and as Iberia was certainly a source for gold and, in later times, probably also goldsmiths for much of south-west Europe, it is not impossible that the bowl may be an import into central Europe from the Iberian peninsula.[3] A detail to note is the small area of concentric stamp decoration on the Zürich stag's antlers.

J. Hierli, *Anz. f. schweiz. Altertumskde.* IX (1907), 1–7; *Manuel* III, 280 and fig. 312; W. Kimmig and W. Rest, *JR-GZM* 1 (1954), 204 f.; *VRD*, ill. 106; *WK*, Taf. 16 below; *PreA*, 180–81 and ill. 179; *EV*, 114–15 and ill.

[1] W. Schulz in P. Grimm (ed.), *Varia Archaeologica*=

Schriften d. Sektion f. vor- u. frühg., Deutsch. Akademie d. Wiss. zu Berlin 16 (1964), 435–39, esp. Taf. 74
[2] K. Schwarz, *Jahresber. d. bayer. Bodendenkmalpflege* 1 (1960), 64 and Abb. 3–5; W. Torbrügge and H. P. Uenze, *Bilder zur Vorg. Bayerns* (1968), 217–18 and ill. 244
[3] W. Schule, *FbS* 12 (1965), 173–80; E. Sangmeister, *Germania* 33 (1955), 424

5 ?'Brittany', France. Fragment of sheet gold ring. W. c. 4 cm., ht. of human heads c. 2 mm. Ha D, VI BC. Musée des Antiquités Nat., St-Germain-en-Laye.

Originally purchased in Paris in 1880 as two separate fragments and alleged to have been found in Brittany, this gold ring with its decoration produced by a combination of stamped and incised *repoussé* ornamentation, belongs to a group of similar ornaments found in later Hallstatt princely graves in western Switzerland and Germany such as Bad Cannstatt and Kappel.[1] Once considered as hair ornaments or diadems (*Goldreifen*), these rings may have originally formed the outer covering of a special class of funerary torc with an inner core of pitch or resin in the manner of much later pieces [173, 289].[2] The geometric decoration of the Brittany fragments, the imitation twisted wire design and the simplified interlocking 'Greek key' patterns are common motifs for *repoussé* metalwork of the period; the two rows of minute clean-shaven faces are, on the other hand, unique and foreshadow the strange human or semi-human three-dimensional heads of early La Tène art constructed as they are of a conglomeration of raised curved planes or 'protuberances'. A somewhat similar frieze of human faces occurs on a gold diadem from Valle Pega, tomb 136, grave A in Etruria, but as this is dated to the later fifth century[3] it can hardly be used to suggest a direct trans-Alpine influence for the Brittany ring although this is not impossible.

H. de Villefosse, *Bull. Soc. nat. antiq. de France* (1880), 60; W. Kimmig and W. Rest, *JR-GZM* 1 (1954), 214, 216 and Abb. 6; *V and A*, 103, n. 27; R. Joffroy, *Bull. des Antiquités nat.* 1 (1969), 7–13; F. Schwappach, *Festschr. Dehn* 251 and Abb. 2

[1] Kimmig and Rest, *op. cit.*, 196 ff., Abb. 5, Taf. 13–15
[2] O. Paret, *Germania*, 32 (1954), 322–24; *PreA*, 179–80; see also notes to [12]
[3] *Mostra dell' Etruria Padana e della Città di Spina* I (1961), no. 1125 and Pl. LXXIII

6 'Gemeinmerker Hof', Kaltbrunn, Kr. Konstanz. Sheet bronze belt plate. Total dim. c. 60×17·5 cm., ht. of detail c. 15 cm. Ha D1, early VI BC. Badisches Landesmus., Karlsruhe. *Landesbildstelle Baden u. Württ.* (*Dr Helmut Hell*)

Contemporary with the later Hallstatt gold work of [3–5] and sharing with it many of the simple geometric motifs which are the characteristic feature of the art of the period, are a series of belt-plates not infrequently found with fragments of their original leather backing still riveted to them. The Kaltbrunn plate comes from one of eighteen skeleton burials discovered in 1864 with fragments of a cremation pyre under a large barrow mound; the old report makes reference to the discovery of big fibulae but it is difficult to be certain of the precise associations of the various objects. The horse and sun symbols recall the Donauwörth dish[1] but occur on several other belt-plates. Recent studies note their concentration in south-west Germany and west Switzerland;[2] at Kappel the galloping horse frieze occupies two rows of a design which also incorporates tiny amulet-like human figures with outstretched arms while one of the outliers from the Austrian Hallstatt cemetery, urn-grave 404, contains the horse with a chorus of dancing figures.[3]

Once more it is tempting to cite the metopic layout of contemporary Mediterranean art but once more also – as with the '*situla*' style' – it is difficult to lay down the precise routes by which such influences might have been transmitted.

E. Wagner, *Hügelgräber u. Urnfriedhöfe in Baden* (1885), 9 ff.; F. Maier, *39. Ber.R-GK 1958* (1959), 242–44, Taf. 66: 3, 67; *VRD*, ill. 104

[1] See notes to [4]
[2] F. Maier, *op. cit.*, 131–249; W. Drack, *JSGU* 54 (1968–69), 13–59
[3] Kappel: W. Kimmig and W. Rest, *JR-GZM* 1 (1954), 189 f. and Abb. 3; Hallstatt: K. Kromer, *Hallstatt, prähist. Kunst: Naturhist. Mus. Wien* (1963), Taf. 14

7 'Hohmichele', Hundersingen, Kr. Saulgau, grave VI. Wool and ?silk textile fragment. L. 11 cm. Ha D1, early VI BC. R-G Zentralmuseum Mainz.

The great Hohmichele barrow which, even at its present dimension of some 13 m. high and 80 m. in diameter, is one of the largest burial mounds in Europe, lies in a group of some 21 other mounds 2 km. from the fortified hill-top chieftain's residence of the Heuneburg high above the north bank of the Danube. The Heuneburg is a strategically placed fortification whose very construction, let alone contents, shows evidence of trading contacts with the Greek world particularly through the *entrepôt* of Massalia (the present Marseilles). The largest Hundersingen barrows, those nearest to the Heuneburg being constructed over an earlier settlement, probably mark the last resting place of the local trader-chieftain dynasty; the Hohmichele, which was excavated during 1936–38, contained not one but two adjacent wooden chambers (robbed while under construction), the larger of which was a waggon grave with the remains of a woman's body as in the famous and slightly later burial at Vix beside the fortified Mont Lassois settlement near Châtillon-sur-Seine.[1] In a somewhat smaller chamber with the remains of another funerary waggon and attendant harness for a pair of horses, a man was laid out on a bull's hide with, beside him, a second woman. Amongst a whole range of bronze vessels, fibulae, glass and amber beads, the man's quiver, with its 51 iron arrows and the fittings for probably not one but a pair of bows, suggests contact with Scythian or other steppe nomads, evidence for whose presence in western Europe can be traced back to the seventh century. In the surrounding barrow mound were some ten other burials, four of them cremation graves. Both men and women are represented, all are with attendant grave goods, some being of comparative wealth and accompanied by fine 'Alb-Salem' ware [9]. As in several other late Hallstatt burials in France and Germany – including Vix – the Hohmichele produced fragments of rich textiles both as clothing and for draperies on the walls of the burial

chambers and the four-wheeled waggons. The use of true Chinese silk thread, the first recorded in central Europe, is an indication of even more widespread trade contacts than are demonstrated by the Greek imports of the Heuneburg, since the silk probably travelled via Thrace and Scythia rather than Greece.

The present textile fragment from the second burial chamber was found inside the woman's left ankle. It is of weft-faced woollen cloth, now a uniform brown in colour. The warp is of double yarns, each yarn Z-spun and S-plied, 6–7 doubles per cm.; the weft is of single yarns, Z-spun and S-plied, 30 per cm. Four shots of silk, separated by one shot of wool, were woven into the weft at the edge of the cloth. The embroidery is in S-plied wool, which survives. It was probably originally dyed, but is now brown. The silk embroidery is now missing, but is reconstructed in black stitching in the illustration. The design incorporates once more strictly geometric patterns, lozenges, 'Greek key' derivatives, and the swastika, another common Hallstatt take-over from the trans-Alpine repertoire and one which occasionally appears in certain backward-looking La Tène pieces.[2]

G. Riek and H. J. Hundt, 'Der Hohmichele', *R-G Forsch.* 25 (1962), esp. 206 ff. and Taf. 37; W. Kimmig, *Die Heuneburg an der Oberen-Donau=Führer z. vor- u. frühg. Denkmälern* I (1968), esp. 96–100; S. Piggott, *Ancient Europe* (1965), 183 ff., fig. 101

[1] R. Joffroy, 'Le Trésor de Vix (Côte-d'Or)', *Monuments et Mém. Piot* XLVIII: 1 (1954); id., *Le trésor de Vix: histoire et portrée d'une grande découverte* (1962); J. V. S. Megaw, *Antiquity* XL (1966), 38–44
[2] *ECA*, PP. 216, 261 =[115]

8 Hradenín, Kolín, grave XLVI. Wooden yoke covered with leather and studded with bronze nails. L. 1.20 m. Ha C, VII BC. Dvořákovo Muz., Kolín. *Aú CSAV Prague.*

The Bylaný culture of central Bohemia, including the area east of Prague, seems to have evolved in the course of the seventh–fifth centuries from local groups of the late Bronze Age which were strongly influenced by the general development of a wealthy warrior society concerned with horse riding. This latter equestrian group developed probably as a result of contact with eastern nomads from whom also may have been borrowed at least some features of the characteristic mounded waggon burials.[1] Of the sixty-odd graves at Hradenín excavated in the mid-twenties by a local doctor and founder of the Kolín collections, František Dvořák, grave XLVI is typical of the finest examples in the group which are clearly related to the Swiss, east French and German early *Fürstengräber*.

This, third of three waggon graves, contained the body of an elderly man lying in the middle of the waggon, whose four wheels with their iron tyres each had a diameter of some 80 cm. At the side of the man, point upwards, was the iron blade of a typical Ha C long sword. Apart from two large storage jars there were no less than 40 fine pots either painted in simple geometric patterns or with stylised human figures; both styles recall south German vessels. Some pots were coated with graphite. Also of pottery was a head rest or portable altar in half-moon shape recalling the crescentic 'moons' of south-western Hallstatt decorative metalwork. Apart from the storage jars the remains of a pig's skeleton – also found in the first waggon grave XXIV – point once more to the funerary symposium and the warrior's share of pork of later Iron Age contexts.[2]

At the southern, head, end of the low timber-lined chamber lay the yoke and harness mounts for an out-rider as well as the twin horses which would have provided the traction for the waggon, though the horses them-selves were presumably to be provided in the Other-world – perhaps in exchange for the pork. The simple lozenge pattern of the nail-studded yoke is again in the mainstream of early Iron Age non-representational art; similar yokes have been found in Switzerland and southern Germany and, most recently, at Stadtwald in Hesse, where a single yoke was found buried, presumably as a token deposit for the whole vehicle.[3]

Fr. Dvořák, *Knížecí pohřby na vozech ze starší doby železné=Praehistoria 1* (1938), esp. pp. 23, 39–48 and obr. 21; *KvsE*, 265 and obr. 74:1; W. Drack, *Zeitschr. f. schweiz. Arch. u. Kunstgeschte.* 18 (1958), 17, Abb. 11, 53, Taf. 1:2b; *CCH*, 30 ff. and Pl. I above

[1] D. Koutecký, *Památky Arch.* LIX (1968), 400–87
[2] See notes to [224–226]
[3] Drack, *op. cit.*, 14 ff.; Frankfurt: U. Fischer, *Fundber. aus Hessen* 8 (1968), 118

9 Sternberg, Gomadingen, barrow 1. Kr. Münsingen. Incised and painted pot. D. 55 cm., ht. c. 9 cm. Ha C1, early VII BC. Württ. Landesmus., Stuttgart, *Landes-bildstelle Baden u. Württ.* (*Dr Helmut Hell*)

This bowl was one of five fine decorated vessels found with an iron longsword with gold inlaid hilt and wooden sheath [11]. The bowl is made from a reddish-brown clay, painted in parts and decorated with a series of motifs produced by a combination of lines incised probably with a metal blade, finger-tip impressions, and a series of stamps of different types. Apart from the ubiquitous concentric circles, the latter produced on the rim a kind of false-relief effect recalling the so-called 'Kerbschnitt' pottery of western Europe in the preceding Late Bronze Age period, a style of pottery considered to have its origins in wood-carving techniques.

The use on the Gomadingen plates of natural colours – in this case black and red – is common in pottery of the 'Alb-Salem' type, one of several regional styles in south-west Germany and a form concentrated in the Hallstatt graves of Schwabia and found in the Hohmichele burials [7].[1]

P. Goessler, *Beschreibung d. OA. Münsingen* (1921), 221; O. Paret, *IPEK* (1930), 31–37 esp. Taf. 1; F. J. Keller, 'Die Alb-Hegau-Keramik der älteren Eisenzeit', *Tübingen Forsch.* XVIII (1939), 20, 50–51, 65–66, 76 and Taf. VIII below; *VRD*, ill. 90; *PAE*, 216, Pl. 221; *EV*, ill. on p. 104

[1] H. Zürn, *Germania* 35 (1957), 224 ff.

10 Sopron-Várhely (Burgstall), barrow 3. Incised pot originally filled with white paste. Ht. c. 38 cm. Ha C2, late VII BC. Ferenc Liszt Múz., Sopron. *Belzeaux-Zodiaque* (photographed from a replica).

Representational art in the earlier Iron Age is never common and for this reason the incised and stamp-decorated urns from a group of barrows close to a large fortified settlement in the neighbourhood of Sopron, the contents of which are divided between that town and the Naturhistorisches Museum in Vienna, are justly famous. The scenes of women weaving on vertical looms, playing lyres, following the funerary bier or, as here, with a figure like some Celtic Helen bidding farewell to her Paris – one of the few representations in Celtic Iron Age art of a mounted warrior – have, once again and perhaps more justifiably than usual, been ascribed to the influence of Greece possibly through the medium of colonies at the head of the Adriatic. Both waggons and weaving scenes occur in the art of Valcamonica [1],[1] but perhaps more comparable, since the form of the Sopron urns is basically Hallstatt, are a small number of Ha D pots from Bavaria with decoration produced by a toothed wheel; the decoration of these pots includes not only animals but standing or dancing figures and riders on horseback.[2] On the Sopron pot one can not only reconstruct still further than is allowed by actual textile fragments [7] the nature of Hallstatt fashion, modern-looking tent dresses and all; another feature is perhaps the influence of textiles themselves on the geometric designs of the pot[3] – the use of concentric stamps is also a point to notice. The 'face' urns of eastern Pomerania of c. 500 BC and later exhibit a similar use of 'opened out' perspective.[4] More apposite here is material from the recently published Hallstatt culture barrow cemetery site of Nové Košariská in eastern Czechoslovakia; painted pottery with figural decoration and similar in profile to the Sopron urns is dated to Ha C2-D1 and is related to pottery from the Austrian Gemeinlebarn group [see notes to 17].[5]

S. Gallus, 'A Soproni Burgstall alakos urnái', *Arch. Hungarica* XIII (1934), esp. 15–17, Taf. XVI–XVIII; *ArtG*, 240, Pl. 46; *WK*, Taf. 10 below; S. Piggott, *Ancient Europe* (1965), 181, 199, figs. 110–111

[1] E. Anati, 'La grande roche de Naquane', *Archives de l'Inst. Paléontologie humaine: Mémoire* 31 (1961), 60 ff., figs. 20, 30, Pl. IX
[2] W. Torbrügge, 'Die Hallstatt in der Oberpfalz', *Materialheft. z. Bayer. Vorg.* 20 (1965), 72, 85–86, Taf. 33, 63:3, *id.* and H.P. Uenze, *Bilder zur Vorg. Bayerns* (1968), 218 and ill. 246–48; *EV*, ill. on p. 180
[3] *PAE*, 216
[4] W. La Baume, *Praehist. Zeitschr.* XXXIV–XXXV (1949–50), 158–78, here esp. Abb. 10; T. Malinowski, *Archaeology* 19 (1966), 120–27
[5] Magda Pichlerová, *Nové Košariská=Fontes Slov. Národného Muz. v Bratislave* III (1969), esp. p. 189 ff. and Tab. IV–V, XX

Plate I 'Burrenhof', Marking-Erkenbrechtsweiler, Kr. Nürt-lingen, barrow 2, grave 1. Painted pot. Ht. 22 cm. Ha D, late VII/early VI BC. Württ. Landesmus., Stuttgart.

In the so-called 'Batik' style of late Hallstatt painted pottery – named 'Batik' because of the stencilling effect of the red and white body colouring which recalls south-east Asian vegetable cloth patterns – it seems difficult to deny at least a degree of southern influence, even though the shape of the biconical pot with its tiny foot and low waist-line is typically central European. The Burrenhof pot is handmade without the aid even of a slow wheel, as with all but a few specialised fabrics of the period, again made under Mediterranean influence and as found in such centres of cultural interchange as the Heuneburg.[1] The abstract face of the Burrenhof pot is a strange foretaste of the shape of faces to come.

The Burrenhof grave 1 contained, as well as the painted vessel, an antennae-hilted dagger and an iron spearhead, both types characteristic of the later Hallstatt period when the iron longsword temporarily went out of fashion.

O. Paret, *IPEK* (1930), Taf. 4 above; F. J. Keller, 'Die Alb-Hegau-Keramik der älteren Eisenzeit', *Tübingen Forsch.* XVIII (1939), 23, 79, 93–94, Taf. XIV below; *VRD*, ill. 105 below; *VE*, 13 f. and ill. p. 12; *EV*, ill. p. 103

[1] W. Dehn, *Alt-Thüringen* VI (1962–63), 372–82; see also notes to [154]

11 Sternberg, Gomadingen, Kr. Münsingen. Hilt of iron sword inlaid with gold and ivory and covered with gold leaf. Total l. 1·06 m., w. of pommel c. 8·6 cm. Ha C1, late VIII/early VII BC. Württ. Landesmus., Stuttgart. *Landesbildstelle Baden u. Württ.* (*Dr Helmut Hell*)

This sword, an iron version of the so-called 'Mindelheim' bronze type,[1] with its long heavy iron blade and its 'cocked hat' pommel found with fine funerary ware [9] in a burial at the foot of the Sternberg, is typical of the warlike gear of the knights of the expansion period of the earliest phase of the Hallstatt Iron Age; a similar sword from the type-site of Hallstatt has a zigzag of ivory set in an amber hilt.[2] The warrior burials of the period often contained not the entire panoply of weapons and horse gear but sometimes only a partial selection. Such a 'selective burial' was that found inside a bronze bucket containing cremated bone recovered from a barrow at Oss in the Dutch province of Nord Brabant, possibly the remains of some pioneering Hallstatt warrior from central Europe or the result of an adventurous local trader's southern foray.[3] The Oss bucket had placed in it, apart from other weapons and harness fittings, an iron sword closely paralleling Gomadingen even down to zigzag gold inlay, but the Oss blade was bent almost into a circle, not just to fit it into the bucket but almost certainly as a kind of ritual 'killing' of the dead man's weapon, a feature well established in archaeology and ethnology.[4]

L. Lindenschmidt, *AuhV* IV (1900), Taf. XXXI; F. J. Keller, 'Die Alb-Hegau-Keramik der älteren Eisenzeit', *Tübingen Forsch.* XVIII (1939), 22, 65–66; *Celts*, Pl. 7; *VRD*, ill. 101

[1] J. D. Cowen, *PPS* XXXIII (1967), 377–454
[2] G. Kossack, 'Südbayern während der Hallstattzeit', *R-G Forsch.* 24 (1959), 48 ff. and Abb. 12:A; Hallstatt, grave 573: K. Kromer *et al.*, *Das Gräberfeld von Hallstatt* (1959), Taf. 108–9 esp. 108:6a
[3] P. J. Moddermann, *Bull. v.d. Vereeniging . . . v.d. Antieke Besch.* XXXIX (1964), 57–62
[4] L. V. Grinsell, *Folklore* LXXII (1961), 475 ff.

12 Hirschlanden, Kr. Leonberg. Statue, Stuben sandstone. Present ht. 1·5 m. Ha D3, late VI/early VBC. Württ.

Landesmus., Stuttgart. *Staatl. Amtf. Denkmalpflege, Stuttgart.*

The remarkable Hirschlanden statue was found in 1963 lying broken at the perimeter of a partially destroyed barrow with stone cairn and carefully constructed stone kerb. Originally the statue must have stood atop the barrow mound[1] which contained some sixteen inhumation burials including two central and superimposed graves contained in wooden coffins. The finds associated with one of these central burials, though scanty, included a fragmentary fibula of late Hallstatt form and a simple openwork belt-hook of equally clearly early La Tène type related to the 'Ticino' class of hooks [95–99]; the construction of the barrow, then, must coincide with the period marked archaeologically by the new types of the second Iron Age, but marked historically and socially by either a gradual shift of power or by the rapid and devastating occupation of key trading positions, as occurred in the case of the Heuneburg.

The change-over in local economic conditions in central and western Europe coincided with the growth of Etruscan power in the north of Italy and a subsequently greater use of the trans-Alpine than of the western Mediterranean routes for commerce between the classical and barbarian worlds. There can certainly be no doubt that the Hirschlanden statue, though carved of sandstone quarried west of Stuttgart and with the accoutrements of a late Hallstatt warrior, is the artistic outcome of such a change in local cultural patterns. The dagger which the warrior holds with his right hand is a representation of a typical late antennae-hilted dagger, the neck ring may be intended as a representation of a fine *Goldreifen* [5], and the double-loop belt has a parallel not only in the Vix tomb but amongst the actual Hirschlanden grave goods. Even the original height of the figure corresponds with the calculated average height of the contemporary male population.[2] On the other hand the pointed helmet is more proper to the southeast Alpine area [see also 24] and the whole concept of a standing nude figure with exaggerated musculature and even the hunched shoulders recall such sixth-century central Italian Etruscan sculpture as the Capestrano warrior.[3] From farther north, from the ancient Nesactium in Istria comes a similarly fragmentary ithyphallic figure dated to the sixth century BC;[4] however, although such obvious symbols of potency are rare in later La Tène art there are a number of equally phallic but tiny nude pendants and finger rings in the form of men from sites in Germany and France which, like Hirschlanden, date from the transition between the end of the Hallstatt and the beginning of the La Tène Iron Age [see 18.]

As to who carved the Hirschlanden figure – a local craftsman trained in or at least conversant with transAlpine styles or an immigrant sculptor trying to adapt his skills to local needs – both alternatives are possible. But in view of the period of artistic experimentation which was to last throughout the fifth century, there is perhaps little need to look for too exotic a source for this remarkable and as yet unique figure north of the Alps.

H. Zürn, *Antiquity* XXXVIII (1964), 224–26; id., *Germania* 42 (1964), 27–36; W. Kimmig in P. Demargue (ed.), *Le rayonnement des civilisations grecque et romaine sur les cultures péripheriques* = *Actes du VIIIᵉ. Congr. Intern. d'Arch. classique* (1965), 94–101; *VE*, ill. p. 184; *EV*, 8, 135 and ill.; Zürn, *IPEK* 22 (1966–69), 62–65

[1] W. Kimmig and H. Hell, *Schätze der Vorzeit: Funde aus Deutschland, Frankreich u. d. Schweiz* (1965), ill. 108–09 = *VRD* (2 ed.)

[2] R. M. Rowlett, *Science* 161 (1968), 131 and fig. 6

[3] G. Moretti, 'Il Guerriero italico di Capestrano', *Opera d'arte* 6 (1936); N. K. Sandars, *Antiquity* XXXVIII (1964), 306

[4] A. Puschi, *Nesazio Pola* 22 (1905), 57–58, fig. 18; F. von Duhn and F. Messerschmidt, *Italische Gräberkunde* 2 (1939), 142 ff.; J. Mladin, *Umjetnički spomenici prahistorijskog Nezakcija = Kulturno-Povijesni spomenici Istre* V (1966), esp. Tab. IV:2

13 Stockach, Kr. Tübingen, barrow grave 8. Stone *stele*. Ht. 75 cm. Ha C1, early VII BC. Württ. Landesmus., Stuttgart.

There is little representational sculpture closely datable from the earlier pre-Roman Iron Age of central Europe, and certainly nothing of the artistic standard or archaeological interest of Hirschlanden [12]. There are, however, a number of cruder figures of more or less indisputable antiquity from the Rhineland and Schwabian Alb region. The Stockach stone – like Hirschlanden, carved from local Stuben sandstone – has unfortunately lost most of the human face (or perhaps twin faces) with which it was originally crowned, but the simple triangular nose and dot-eyes on the better preserved side no less than the zigzag 'bib' belong rather to the pictorial vocabulary of the 'Burrenhof' pot than Hirschlanden. A somewhat similar but elongated and 'phallic' *stele* found in the neighbourhood of a late Hallstatt grave comes from Stammheim, Kr. Calw.[1]

The Stockach stone originally stood on the top of the grave mound, one of twelve in the Forest of Hechelhart, a stone cairn covering the remains of a funeral pyre including cremated bone. Amongst the associated pottery was a small urn decorated with stamped and incised geometric designs [see 9].

G. Riek, *Germania* 25 (1941), 85–89; *FbS* 11 (1938–50), 81 and Abb. 22; *EV*, 134–135 and ill.; H. Zürn, *IPEK* 22 (1966–69), 65 and Taf. 42:7

[1] R. Ströbel, *FbS* 12 (1938–51), 41–43 and Abb. 16; Zürn, *op. cit.*, Taf. 42:8

14 Holzgerlingen, Kr. Böblingen. Stone *stele*. Ht. without horns 2·3 m. ?VI/V BC. Württ. Landesmus., Stuttgart. *J. V. S. Megaw* (left), *Landesbildstelle Baden u. Württ.* (*Dr H. Hell*) (right)

Certainly the most archaic in aspect of the handful of sculptured figures ascribed to the earlier La Tène period, the isolated find of the Holzgerlingen 'Janus' *stele* is very obviously a cult figure. The four-square form of the main sandstone pillar and the carefully rebated base – hidden by its modern footing – for a separate setting-block have suggested to more than one commentator that this type of pillar statue has its source in a direct translation into stone of the long-lasting Celtic tradition of wooden tree-trunk images [234][1] in contrast to more obviously 'sculptured' heads [171]. The most obvious feature, the twin-horned crown – reconstructed as shown in the detail of the reverse face – is an example of the variously termed 'Astarte', 'Hathor', 'leaf-crown' or '*Fischblasenmüster*'. Although an oriental or more

particularly Phoenician source has often been claimed for this strange motif, pottery half-moons are found in the Late Bronze Age Swiss lakeside villages no less than in the Hradenín Bylaný culture graves;[2] as so often with Celtic Iron Age symbols, no single source can be claimed to the exclusion of all others. The comma-like features of other La Tène stone heads [49, 75] may have yet another explanation. The belt, rigidly crossed arms and raised thumb of Holzgerlingen recall the Hirschlanden figure and its presumed Italian prototypes, but yet another sandstone statue from Raibreitenbach, Kr. Starkenburg, despite the Slav date given it by Jacobsthal, has also very similar features.[3] The face of Holzgerlingen with the T-shaped construction of conjoined nose and eyebrows and slit mouth follows a formulation seen on many objects of the so-called Early 'style' of the fifth century in the Rhineland area, while those who have considered a later, even Middle La Tène date (not before the third century BC) have seen the influence of the sculptures of the southern French sanctuary, sites and even Spain;[4] a Janus head from Hungary, which should not be earlier than the second century, has a somewhat similar flat-featured aspect.[5]

R. Knorr, *Germania* 5 (1921), 11 ff., Abb. 4; *ECA*, no. 13; *Celts*, 270, fig. 26, Pl. 63; *VRD*, ill. 142; *CCH*, 162 and fig. 4; *PreA*, 206 and ill. 202; *PAE*, 247–48, fig. 95c, Pl. 269; *EV*, 240 and ill.

[1] M. Szabó, *Acta Arch. Hung.* XVII (1965), 238–40

[2] W. Kimmig, *Praehist. Zeitschr.* XXV (1934), 52 ff.; see also notes to [8]

[3] E. Anthes, *Germania* 4 (1920), 37; *id.*, *Germania* 5 (1921), 9; A. Koch, *Frühgeschichte Starkenburgs* (1937), 68, Abb. 193, Taf. 40; *ECA*, 10, n. 3. See also J. Rosen-Przeworska, *Archéocivilisation* IV: 14–16 (1963), 65–69, Pls. 7–10

[4] P. Lambrechts, 'L'exaltation de la tête dans la pensée et dans l'art des Celtes', *Diss. Arch. Gandenses* II (1954), 72 and Pl. 60

[5] J. Csemegi, *Arch. Értesítö* 88 (1961), 52–65; see also notes to [235]

15 'Kröllkogel', Kleinklein, Steiermark. Bronze mask. W. 23 cm. VI BC. Landesmus. Joanneum, Graz.

At the foot of the Burgstall in Austrian Steiermark near Leibnitz originally stood a group of five rich barrow burials, the contents of which demonstrate the Alpine, trans-Alpine, and even Balkan connections of a local version of the late Hallstatt culture. Although certain features of the finds reveal a continuity with the previous Late Bronze Age 'Urnfield' culture,[1] the number of bronze vessels and particularly parallel-sided *ciste* or pails decorated with friezes of animal, human and geometric motifs are in some ways similar in subject but separate in style from the finer products of the Atestine '*situla*' artists of the head of the Adriatic[2] and also form a local parallel to the south German belt plates [6].

The fourth barrow, the Kröllkogel, first opened in 1905 and excavated in 1917, contained, apart from a considerable amount of pottery and bronze vessels including a *situla* of native 'Kurd' bucket form with geometric and representational motifs, three axes, six spears and, once more demonstrating the influence of the higher cultures across the Alps and in the colonial settlements of the Adriatic, a ridged bronze helmet, as found in the Hallstatt cemetery,[3] and breastplate. The bronze *repoussé* decorated mask, here illustrated for its similarity to the Holzgerlingen faces, was found attached to the remains of a coffin which, like several of the other burials, contained cremated bone. The dot technique of the mask is similar to that of the figures on the Kleinklein *cista* but the face as a whole with its overtones of the Mycenaean shaft-grave 'death masks' has a closer parallel in a series of gold masks from a Jugoslav cemetery at Trebenište near Lake Ohrid.[4] The Trebenište cemetery, which includes material traded north from Greece, has been variously dated but the masks have been placed within Phase IIIb or not much before 425 BC on the latest assessment of the site.[5]

W. Schmid, *Praehist. Zeitschr.* XXIV (1933), 219–82, esp. 253 ff. and Abb. 32; R. Pittioni, *Urgeschichte des österreich. Raumes* (1954), 612 ff. and Abb. 436 right; K. Kromer, *Von frühem Eisen und reichen Salzherren* (1964), 154 ff.; *VE*, 144 ff. and figs. 94–99; *EV*, 129, 131 and ills.

[1] W. Mondrijan, *Praehist. Zeitschr.* XLIII–XLIV (1965–66), 329–30
[2] O.-H. Frey, 'Die Enstehung der Situlenkunst', *R-G Forsch.* 31 (1968), 68 ff. *contra* Pittioni in *Civiltà del Ferro=Documenti e Studi* VI (1960), 393–404
[3] Kromer, *Hallstatt. prähist. Kunst: Naturhist. Mus. Wien* (1963), no. 12, Taf. 54; S. Gabrovec, *Arh. Vestnik* XIII–XIV (1962–63), 293–325
[4] V. Popović, *Arch. Iugoslavica* V (1964), 33–46
[5] V. Lahtov, *Problem Trebeniške Kulture* (1965), 76–78

16 Wijchen, Wezelsche Berg, Gelderland. Bronze linch pin. L. c. 8 cm. Ha C1, early VII BC. Rijksmuseum van Oudheiden, Leiden. *Rijksdienst voor het Oudheidkundig Bodemonderzoek.*

In 1897 the remains of a grave was found in the Dutch province of Gelderland. The grave, which still awaits full publication, though partially disturbed, contained some of the fittings of a four-wheeled waggon including the iron tyres and harness for a pair of horses as well as the handle for a bucket of the type found at Oss. Like Oss, the Wijchen grave marks one of the farthest outliers of the early Hallstatt empire, although the Hallstatt objects may have come as a result of trade or barter rather than settlement. A pair of linch pins used to keep the free-running wheels in position on the axles are decorated in a unique manner. As the detail shows, apart from a series of rings – such jangles are not an uncommon feature of Hallstatt harness and waggon-fittings – the trio of little heads with their sharp features and almost leprechaun-like ears and neatly parted hair-do's running down into an abstract zigzag have an accomplished sense of caricature unusual in early Iron Age art. Only somewhat earlier first-millennium material from the Nordic Bronze Age is really comparable [19], though an artistic link here is unlikely; for, like all the finds from Wijchen, the linch pins must have been made by a central European craftsman. Jacobsthal considers the linch-pins to have affinities with seventh-century 'orientalising' Etruscan girdle clasps, and even considers the possibility that they may have been Italic imports also,[1] an unlikely alternative. Such seemingly unique decoration looks forward to the human head terminals of certain late La Tène knives and swords, in particular

that from Salon, Aube, with similar almost pigtail-like hair-do [198, 228–229].

Verslag der commissie . . . van gedenkstukken van geschiedenis en Kunst te Nijmegen 1897 (1898), 3–4, 12 and Pl. II; S. De Laet and W. Glasbergen, *De Voorgeschiedenis der Lage Landen* (1959), 162 and Pl. 37

[1] *ECA*, 159, n. 2

17 Hallstatt, Salzkammergut, grave 641. Bronze axe with rider figure. L. 10·9 cm. Ha C, c. 600 BC. Naturhist. Mus., Vienna.

The present small town of Hallstatt is situated at the south-east end of the lake of that name, right in the heart of the Salzkammergut some 30 miles from Salzburg; above the village rises the Salzbergtal, which has been mined for its salt since the beginning of the Iron Age. The immediate proximity of this major source of rock salt, no less than the copper deposits of the region, particularly that of the Kelchalpe, and the natural trading routes south across the Alps to Italy and the Adriatic and to such sites as Kleinklein [15] explain the reason for Hallstatt's wealth in prehistoric times.[1] Although little remains of the contemporary dwellings beyond a few miners' log cabins, a mass of material has been recovered from the extensive cemetery discovered on the flat bottom of the narrow alluvial valley below the salt mines. Between 1824 and 1939 some 2,000 graves had been uncovered, though more than half of these were robbed rather than excavated. The original division by Hoernes of the cemetery's use into two phases is still followed. The phases are roughly equivalent to Ha C and D: Phase I 700/650–600/550, Phase II 600/550–500/450. Only a few graves can be placed firmly in the early La Tène period [30], at which time Hallstatt seems to have lost its economic importance to Dürrnberg near Hallein [see notes to **32, 48, 72, 93, 163**]. Though sexing of the graves is unreliable the cemetery has been considered mainly male[2] though three-quarters of the graves were without weapons of any kind; both cremation and inhumation were practised to an almost equal degree, the few 'warriors' graves' being almost exclusively cremations: those with swords containing a very high proportion of the cemetery's fine sheet-bronze work [21–22: 26].

The bronze rider figure cast on to the axe blade – a not inconsiderable technical feat, indicating the skill of the Hallstatt craftsmen – was found in 1858 in a cremation grave together with a straight-shanked cloak-pin; the axe is presumably a ritual piece with no practical purpose. The crude modelling of the horse and man which has the unsophisticated charm of a child's plasticine figure recalls certain features of the Wijchen faces, particularly the simple eyes and beak-like nose. Apart from an unprovenanced bronze rider figure from Hungary,[3] the closest early Hallstatt parallels are simple nude and sometimes phallic figures such as that mounted on a large pot decorated with other anthropomorphic models and found with an iron longsword from Gemeinlebarn barrow 1, Lower Austria, and a free-standing figure from a Bavarian barrow cemetery at Speikern, Ldkr. Lauf an der Pegnitz;[4] also from Hallstatt is a similar axe to that from grave 641 decorated with a pony of possible steppe type – another hint of contacts with eastern nomads.[5] The zigzag decoration and 'ground

D

lines' on the side of the present Hallstatt axe as well as the horse's bridle and halter are executed in a close-set herring-bone or 'tremolo' line making use of the so-called 'rocked-tracer' technique. The tracer, presumably of tempered steel – yet another indication of advanced metallurgy – is a chisel-like cutting tool which is held at an angle of 45° and rocked from side to side while scribing along a fixed line. The technique was often used in the decoration of the late Hallstatt belt plates and was adopted by early La Tène craftsmen [see **71, 73, 93**]. The Hallstatt rider may, like the Hungarian piece mentioned above, have once carried a weapon, while the modelling of the lower part of the body seems to represent a short tunic or, indeed, trousers.

M. Hoernes, *Das Gräberfeld von Hallstatt* (1921), esp. Fig. 1:13; K. Kromer et al., *Das Gräberfeld von Hallstatt* (1959), Taf. 137:3; Kromer, *Hallstatt, prähist. Kunst: Naturhist. Mus. Wien* (1963), 56, Taf. 42–43; *id.*, *Von frühem Eisen und reichen Salzherren* (1964), 53, 77, Abb. 18; *VE*, ill., p. 175; *EV*, 179 and ill.

[1] Kromer, *Spina e l'Etruria Padana=Studi Etruschi* XXV: suppl. (1959), 151–54
[2] A Häusler, *Ethnog.-Arch. Zeitschr.* 9 (1968), 1–30.
[3] E.-B. Thomas (ed.), *Arch. Funde in Ungarn* (1956), 132 and ill.
[4] Gemeinlebarn: *Inventaria Arch.: Österreich* 2 (1958), A 11 esp. K 56; Speikern: F. Vollrath, *Germania* 40 (1962), 402–4; W. Torbrügge and H. P. Uenze, *Bilder zur Vorg. Bayerns* (1968), 218 and ill. 250
[5] Kromer, *Hallstatt: prähist. Kunst*, Taf. 51; *PreA*, 176 and ill. 171

18 Hallstatt, Salzkammergut, grave 585. Bronze figurine. Ht. 2·9 cm. Ha D, VI BC. Naturhist. Mus., Vienna

This fragment of a tiny bronze figurine found in 1857 together with part of a bronze mount comes from a cremation grave. The face is clearly male and its features follow the basic formula of the Holzgerlingen pillar-statue [**14**]. On the man's arms are two armlets such as are frequently found in the Hallstatt graves, but what he carries is difficult to make out – possibly some sort of drinking vessel. In general the formulation of the little figure is similar to the naked amulet figures of some final Hallstatt and early La Tène sites in France and south-west Germany;[1] to these may be added a curious bronze mount probably from France and usually but somewhat fancifully considered as a mirror-handle.[2]

K. Kromer et al., *Das Gräberfeld von Hallstatt* (1959), Taf. 115: 13; Kromer, *Hallstatt, prähist. Kunst: Naturhist. Mus. Wien* (1963), 56, Taf. 39; *id.*, *Von frühem Eisen und reichen Salzherren* (1964), 78, Abb. 17

[1] P. Goessler, *Préhistoire* I (1932), 260–70; R. Joffroy, 'L'oppidum de Vix', *Publ. de l'Université de Dijon* XX (1960), 53–56 and Pl. 11: 5–7; E. Penninger, *Mitt. Ges. Salzburger Ldskde.* 100 (1960), 4–7, Abb. 4–5
[2] O. Schwabe and G. Behrens, *Germania* 17 (1933), 85 and Taf. 11:3

19 Gjerdrup, Sømme Herred, grave 216. Bronze razor handle. L. of total blade 8·5 cm.; ht. of head 1·3 cm. Nordic Bronze Age, Montelius III, early first millennium BC. National Mus., Copenhagen.

Although strictly outside the chronological and cultural limits of this study, this little decorative cast-bronze handle is a reminder that for a brief time the bronze-smiths of southern Scandinavia and northern Germany – gaining their skill and presumably much of their raw material from the Late Bronze Age centres of central Europe – were concerned with the use of the human head or indeed the human form for the decoration of razors, pins or as individual miniature figures for attaching to ritual models of various sorts [compare **38**].[1] The Gjerdrup razor, found with a characteristic Montelius III riveted hilted longsword, a fragmentary bronze pin and a pair of tweezers, is one of a group of later single-edged razors perhaps concerned in some way with a local version of the common primitive belief in the sacred use of hair cutting. Such razors, where not isolated finds, are invariably found in graves; earlier examples bear on their sides versions of the solar boat and water-bird theme found not only on the Nordic rock carvings but often considered to show a link with the symbolism of the southern 'Urnfield' culture and even farther afield.[2]

The style of the Gjerdrup head with its pin-point eyes and straight hair worn long at the back not only looks forward to certain early La Tène heads [**63, 64**] but also finds close parallels in a number of standing figures forming the handles of single-edged knives or, in one case, the head of a long pin.[3] These figures, more or less contemporary with the central European Hallstatt Iron Age, all wear a neck-ring and some more than one, and their distribution, which is similar to that of actual hoards of two or more such rings,[4] points to a northern version of that veneration of the sacred torc which seems to be so universal a feature of barbarian Europe in the first millennium BC.

The upper edge of the Gjerdrup knife is decorated with an incised band of false relief in 'chip-carving' style; the 'naturalist style' of the Gjerdrup head is, however, an early example of a growing feature in prehistoric European art – professionalism. The hair style also compares with that of the young girl found in the Egtved bog-coffin of much the same period.

H. C. Broholm, *Aarbøger* (1935), 263–64, figs. 10–11; *id.*, *Danmarks Bronzealder* II (1944), 201, fig. 75, Pl. 18:10; J. Brønsted, *Danmarks Oltid* II (2 ed., 1958), ill. pp. 149, 56,d; Broholm, *Bronzealders Dragt* (1961), 66 and fig. 51; *PAE*, 196–99, Pl. 195 top; *VE*, 118 and ill. p. 119 top

[1] *PAE*, 204 ff.
[2] E. Sprockhoff, *JR-GZM* 1 (1954), 28–110; P. V. Glob, *Kuml* 1961 (1962), 9–18; *id.*, *Helleristninger i Danmark=Jysk Arkæologisk Selskabs Skr.* VII (1969), 15 ff.; see also notes to [**20–23**]
[3] C. Engelhardt, *Aarbøger* (1871), 451 ff., Pl. IX; Broholm, *Acta Arch.* XVIII (1947), 196–202
[4] T. Capelle, *Acta Arch.* XXXVIII (1967), 209–14

20 Lezoux, Puy-de-Dôme. Bronze rims with cast rattle plates. L. 28·5, 35·5 cm. Villanovan II, VIII BC. Ashmolean Mus., Oxford.

These two fragments of four presented by Sir Arthur Evans to the Ashmolean Museum in 1898 introduce the first examples of aquatic birds, the 'Hallstatt ducks' – which may in fact be swans [see **23**] – which link the symbolism of the latest stages of the central European and Alpine Bronze Age and its offshoots south of the

Alps with contemporary northern Europe. Although water birds swim on through the Hallstatt Iron Age and survive in early La Tène art [61],[1] the main spread of this particular symbolism seems inextricably linked with the development of skilled 'Urnfield' culture sheet-bronze metal-making centres in the mineral-rich zones of the eastern Alps and Hungary;[2] birds also occur on Alpine equivalents of the Nordic single-edge razors.[3]

If the find spot of these fragments is genuine, they must represent one of the rare instances of imports across the Alps from the pre-Etruscan Villanovan Iron Age cultures of north and central Italy, since the Lezoux pieces are probably from the sides of one of the rectangular 'offering tables', usually with dished centres and sometimes provided with wheels as found in graves from the centre of Italy; close parallels occur at such sites as Veii.[4] Although the little anthropomorphic pendant rattle-plates are fairly widespread throughout the whole area of the Hallstatt Iron Age culture and stem from early 'Urnfield' prototypes, birds in the round are rare in south-east France and have no 'Urnfield' background – though from Pépinville near Marseilles comes the only three-dimensional early Urnfield bird north of the Alps.[5]

Inv. nos. Pr. 329, 331

[1] A. Roes, *IPEK* 13–14 (1939–40), 57–84; E. Sprockhoff, *PPS* XXI (1955), 257 ff.
[2] G. von Merhart, *Festschr. R-GZM* (1952) II, 1 ff.; G. Kossack, 'Studien zum Symbolgut der Urnen-felder- und Hallstattzeit Mitteleuropas', *R-G Forsch.* 20 (1954)
[3] H. Dolenz, *Arch. Austriaca* 44 (1968), 88–93
[4] R. V. Garucci, *Archaeologia* XLI (1867), 187 ff. and Pl. IV:2
[5] N. K. Sandars, *Bronze Age Cultures in France* (1957), 127–29, Pl. VII:8

21 Hallstatt, Salzkammergut. Bronze pail. Ht. 30·5 cm. Ha D, VII/VI BC. British Mus., London. (*Courtesy Trustees of the British Museum.*)

In about 1869 a number of graves at Hallstatt were opened at the instigation of Sir John Lubbock (later Lord Avebury), whose *Pre-historic Times* (1865) was one of the first and most popular of archaeological text-books. Little is known of the find conditions of any of the material recovered, much of which was purchased by Lord Avebury and presented to the British Museum in 1916, since such notes as were kept at the time were lost. However, the pail, of Dr Stjernquist's '*Hallstatt-Gruppe*', which consists of two riveted sheets of bronze with a separate convex disc with central boss or 'ompha-los' as the base, has a close parallel in a *repoussé* decorated bucket found with an iron long sword in grave 271. Somewhat similar vessels come from, for example, the Vače cemetery in Slovenia and Słupca in Poland.[1] The 'ducks' and suns – important symbols of healing powers in later Celtic belief – are applied with stamps. Their crests are characteristic of several other pieces from the cemetery [22] as well as those on the rims of three bronze dishes – one only now surviving – from a Ha C barrow grave at Oberwisenacker, Kr. Parsberg, somewhat beyond the main distribution area of the Alpine bronzes;[2] the same motifs were also in use by the contemporary Villanovan Iron Age smiths of

central and northern Italy and crested birds suvive into the iconography of late Iron Age Ireland [270].

C. Hercules Read and R. A. Smith, *Archaeologia* LXVII (1916), 145–62 and Pl. XXVI; R. A. Smith, *B.M. Guide to the Antiquities of the Early Iron Age* (2 ed., 1925), 30 and fig. 25; Berta Stjernquist, *Ciste a Cordoni (Rippenzisten)*=*Acta Arch. Lundensia* ser. 4°, no. 6 (1967) I, 57 ff. esp. no. 9:2

[1] Hallstatt: K. Kromer *et al.*, *Das Gräberfeld von Hallstatt* (1959), Taf. 50:16; Kromer, *Hallstatt, prähist. Kunst: Naturhist. Mus. Wien* (1963), 54, Taf. 46; Vače: *id.*, *Von frühem Eisen und reichen Salzherren* (1964), Abb. 48; see also, for Vače and Słupca, Stjernquist, *op. cit.*, II, nos. 6 and 13
[2] N. Åberg, *Bronzezeitl. und früheisenzeitl. Chronologie* 2 (1931), 47, Abb. 88; W. Torbrügge and H.P. Uenze, *Bilder zur Vorg. Bayerns* (1968), ill. 242

22 Hallstatt, Salzkammergut, grave 507. Bronze container and stand. Ht. 36 cm. Ha C, VII/VI BC. Naturhist. Mus., Vienna.

One of the more elaborate examples of local sheet-bronze working in the cemetery, this stand-cum-container from a cremation grave combines the central European stamped 'duck' and solar symbols, birds in the round with up-curved beaks like those from Lezoux [20] and provision for rattle-plates with the idea of the ritual stand or 'offering table' borrowed from the 'orientalising' influenced grave goods of the Italic Iron Age as exemplified by bronzes from the ancient cemetery of Veii [see notes to 20]. A somewhat similar stand from Strettweg [see notes to 38], again used as a cremation container, is another Alpine example of this uncommon form.

Other finds in the grave included a free-standing figure of a bull [see also 36], part of an iron longsword with ivory inlay, three bronze buckets without decoration and part of a bowl and a belt-plate decorated with crested birds.

K. Kromer *et al.*, *Das Gräberfeld von Hallstatt* (1959) Taf. 98–101, esp. 101:3; Kromer, *Hallstatt, prähist. Kunst: Naturhist. Mus. Wien* (1963), 46–47, Taf. 22–23; *PreA*, 172 and ill. 170; *VE*, ill. p. 149; *EV*, 96–97 and ill.

23 Dunaverney Bog, Co. Antrim. Bronze 'flesh hook'. L. 60·7 cm. ?VI BC. British Mus., London. (*Courtesy Trustees of the British Museum.*)

This isolated find from a Northern Ireland peat-bog with its separately cast double hook and riveted bird figures was clearly originally mounted on a long wooden shaft. Variously considered a charioteer's or waggon-driver's goad or a hook for selecting pieces of broiling meat for the hero's feast, the archaeologist's much over-laboured let-out adjective, 'ritual', seems for once amply justified. The water birds, identified as two swans and their cygnets facing a pair of ravens, as well as the provision of rattle-plates, place Dunaverney firmly in the traditions of the central European early Iron Age; although most Irish continental links of the period are with northern Europe, an import from the main Hallstatt area would not be out of the question. Water birds and particularly swans certainly play an important part in late Irish mythology where swans occur frequently in incidents involving 'shape changing'.[1] Another 'flesh-hook' – again more probably a goad and a continental Ha C import – comes from Kintyre, Argyll.[2]

R. A. Smith, *B.M. Guide to the Antiquities of the Bronze Age* (2 ed., 1920), 103 and fig. 109; *ABA*, Pl. 36; *LPA*, Pl. IV:4; *PreA*, 172 and ill. 168; *PCB*, 257, Pl. 75a; T. G. E. Powell, *Antiq. J.* XLIX (1969), 125 and n. 3

[1] *PCB*, 242–43
[2] J. M. Coles, *Proc. Soc. Antiq. Scot.* XCIII (1959–60), 25 and fig. 3; for continental goads see M. E. Mariën, *Trouvailles du champ d'urnes et des tombelles hall-stattiennes de Court-Saint-Étienne = Monographie d'Arch. nat.* 1 (1958), 115–17

24 Certosa di Bologna, grave 68. Bronze *situla*. Total ht. 32·7 cm., ht. of individual panels c. 7 cm. Early V BC. Mus. Civico, Bologna. *Thames and Hudson Ltd.*

The Iron Age cemetery site of Certosa is one of several in the region of Bologna marking the importance of the ancient town, placed strategically as it is in the centre of the Po valley commanding the natural routes north across the Alps, east to the Adriatic and southwards into Etruria. 'Certosa' has been used as the type-name for the last phase of the local northern branch of the native Villanovan culture, a phase which begins at the end of the sixth century just before the period of intensive connections between the north and the Etruscans of central Italy. This phase lasted until about the time of the Celtic incursions towards the end of the fifth century.

The Certosa cemetery as excavated contained some 287 skeleton graves and 130 cremations; grave 68 contained the *situla* which had been used as a cremation urn with, in the ashes, an Attic black-figure *lekythos* (c. 490–480 BC), a small dish and two fibulae with knobbed feet turned up at a right angle to the catch plate, a form to which the cemetery has given its name and a type with a long life [see notes to **63**].

The *situla* is decorated in four separate zones: (1) a procession of soldiers, (2) a second procession with offering-bearers, a ploughman and cattle (clearly borrowed from the repertoire of contemporary black-figure Attic pottery), (3) a banqueting scene with boxers [not visible; see also **30**] and musicians – as in the second procession scene, *situlae* of the type of Certosa can be seen – (4) a row with lions and other animals. This is in fact one of the finest examples of the so-called 'situla' style which has been the subject of considerable study in recent years.[1] Basically the art of the *situla* is formed of an amalgam of elements: the forms – but little of the iconography – and boss-decorating techniques of the bronze-smiths of the Alpine regions, scenes of ritual as evidenced in Etruscan culture, and a strange menagerie of oriental looking beasts probably inherited more or less direct from the 'orientalising' phase of Greek art, probably again through the intermediary of Etruria, though Corinth had colonies such as Apollonia at the head of the Adriatic established by c. 600 BC.[2]

Situla art was produced in three main areas: Upper Slovenia between the rivers Sava and Drava, Carinthia and the Alpine foot-hills, and the Po region centred on the ancient towns of Bologna and Este. As has already been noted [**21, 22**], the Alpine region has a series of mainly animal-decorated bronze vessels and the eastern branch of the Hallstatt culture was responsible for a related series of *situlae*. The larger and more spectacular series of bronze vessels and other objects produced particularly by the non-Celtic Illyrian community of the Atestine region has mixed scenes as on the Certosa *situla*; the first of these is usually dated to the later seventh century and the last to the earlier fourth with the major period of production within the fifth century, although most recently it has been suggested that all 'situla art' is more or less contemporary and differences in style are purely local and not chronological indicators.

The main artistic influence is ultimately that of Greece, though probably more was transmitted through the intermediary of Etruria than through direct contact with the Greek colonies of the Adriatic. There are difficulties, however; there is, for example, no Etruscan material in the Certosa cemetery, and no Etruscan imports in the east Hallstatt region unlike the west, despite representations of spouted Etruscan flagons in *situla* art. The range of scenes on the *situlae*, however, do have many links with Etruscan tomb painting and sarcophagi, particularly the art of the seventh century – even in such details as the winged 'Corinthian' lions. The presumably funerary symposium scenes may have something of the art of the bronze-smiths of Urartu on the borders of the Assyrian empire who, displaced by nomadic incursions in the late eighth and early seventh centuries, filtered into Greece and the western Mediterranean as refugees;[3] such motifs certainly also belong to the world of the Etruscans. Nonetheless, though the division into three basic units of subject matter – war, peace and mythological or 'heraldic' beasts – has a long oriental background, both the subjects and the arrangement in zones are followed by Greek artists of the archaic period, as for example by the painter of the famous 'François' vase of the early sixth century found in an Etruscan tomb at Chiusi,[4] and there can be little doubt that the figures of pacing and grazing animals often found on the *situlae* no less than the original lions strongly indicate the influence of Corinth.

Like so much of barbarian Iron Age art, its eclectic nature and tendency to re-employ old motifs makes it difficult to analyse with certainty, but even so 'oriental' a piece as the Bologna *situla* or its closest parallels of the late sixth century, the *situla* from the Vače cemetery or that now in the School of Design at Providence (Rhode Island)[5] exhibit signs of the native sub-stratum of the eastern Alpine early Iron Age such as the swans decorating the central table flanked by two musicians on the Certosa *situla*; the buckets carried in the procession are clearly of the early Hallstatt 'Kurd' type and the warriors have east Alpine 'bowl' helmets. The musicians themselves, who are to be found on other *situlae*, are not likely to represent typical guests at an Illyrian or Atestine banquet; the pan-pipe player – recalling the muse Kalliope on the François vase – and the lyre are probably no more than half-understood representations of archaic Greek instruments; even cruder lyres appear on the incised vases from the Sopron barrows [**10**] and on a 'Kurd' type *situla* from the Krollkögel [**15**].[6] Although a hard judgement, it is probably a fair one to conclude, as has been done recently, that 'situla art' 'is in essence not of Europe'; truly provincial, it lacks 'the humanistic spirit behind natural representation'.[7]

P. Ducati, *Mem. della R. Accad. dell' Ist. di Bologna: Cl. di Sci. Mor.* 2 ser., 5–7 (1923), 23–94; *Mostra dell' arte delle situle dal Po al Danubio* (1961), no. 17; G. A. Mansuelli, *Ill. London News* (24 Feb. 1962), 295–97 and fig. 5–6; W. Lucke and O.-H. Frey, 'Die Situla in Providence (Rhode Island)', *R-G Forsch.* 26 (1962), no. 4; J. Kastelic *et al.*, *Situla Art* (1965), Pl. 13; Frey, 'Die Entstehung der Situlenkunst', *R-G Forsch.* 31 (1968), 88–91

[1] Lucke and Frey, *op. cit.*; Frey, *Germania* 40 (1962), 56–72; *id.*, *Germania* 44 (1966), 48–73, esp. pp. 65 ff., Taf. 6–7; *id.*, 'Die Entstehung der Situlenkunst', *R-G Forsch.* 31, esp. 2 ff. and *loc. cit.*

[2] D. Rendić-Miocević in *Preistoria dell' Emilia e Romagna* II = *Doc. e Studi* VII (1963), 109–16

[3] R. K. Maxwell-Hyslop, *Iraq* XVII (1956), 150–67

[4] S. Piggott, *PPS* XXX (1964), 438–39 = review of Lucke and Frey, *op. cit.*

[5] Vače: Lucke and Frey, *op. cit.*, no. 33; Kastelic, *Das Situla von Vače* (1956); Providence: Lucke and Frey, *op. cit.*, no. 1

[6] J. V. S. Megaw in J. M. Coles and D. D. A. Simpson (edd.), *Studies in Ancient Europe* (1968), 340 ff., esp. Pl. XIVb

[7] *PAE*, 223–25

25 Vače, Litija, Slovenia. Bronze belt-hook. L. 28·5 cm. V B C. Naturhist. Mus., Vienna.

The great cremation barrow cemetery of Vače marks one of the major centres of the east Hallstatt culture, the contents of which span the seventh–fourth centuries.[1] Occasional early La Tène material such as swords and girdle-hooks occur as evidence of sporadic contacts with the true central and western European Celtic world in what otherwise is a cultural backwater. The belt-hook here illustrated was found in the Austrian excavations of the last century and is one of a number of pieces showing the continuity in the Vače region of the old 'situla' art motifs. It is related in style to the contemporary Certosa *situla* [24] but though the right-hand figure with his 'pilgrim's hat' looks like an intruder copied from another model from that of the main composition, the combatants in the battle-scene are equipped in just the manner one would expect from the grave goods of such sites as Vače and Stična [28]; note the helmets, the waisted axes, the shield bosses, and the horse's crescentic cheek-pieces. Similar belt-plates occur elsewhere in the Tyrol and Craiova as well as Este and south at Bologna.

Mostra dell'arte delle situle dal Po al Danubio (1961), no. 43; W. Lucke and O.-H. Frey, 'Die Situla in Providence (Rhode Island)', *R-G Forsch.* 26 (1962), no. 35; A. Stipčević, *Art of the Illyrians* (1963), ill. 24–25; K. Kromer, *Von frühem Eisen und reichen Salzherren* (1964), 76 and Abb. 14; J. Kastelic *et al.*, *Situla Art* (1965), Pl. 64–65.

[1] F. Starè, *Vače* = *Arh. Kat. Slovenije* I (1955)

26 Hallstatt, Salzkammergut, grave 696. Bronze *situla* lid. D. 23·7 cm. Ha D, early VI B C. Naturhist. Mus., Vienna.

This lid, a product of Este and clear evidence of the cultural exchange across the Alps during the later phase of the use of the Hallstatt cemetery,[1] exhibits the common use of animal forms which is a feature of earlier Atestine *situla* art. Similar lids come from Stična, another east Hallstatt cemetery in Slovenia[2] [see 28] in a cremation grave with pottery including two pots made in imitation of bronze buckets as well as a pair of buckets themselves and from Rebato grave 187 at Este itself.[3] Similar processions occur on Etruscan *bucchero* ware and on pottery from the Veii cemetery of about 600 B C. The lion with the hind quarters of an animal protruding from his jaws occurs on the Rebato lid and also on the Certosa *situla* [24], while a lion with a human hand in its teeth has a long history in Iron Age art [76]; both, again, are borrowings from Etruria. The Hallstatt stag with raised head and antlers running parallel with its back, the 'sphinx', and the animals with plants hanging from their mouths all point to Etruria and to motifs of the early Corinthian phase.

The Hallstatt lid came from a rich cremation grave with a fine gold-ornamented iron antennae-hilted dagger and sheath, several bronze vessels of central European form including buckets as found with the Stična lid, and decorated sheet-bronze fragments.

K. Kromer *et al.*, *Das Gräberfeld von Hallstatt* (1959) Taf. 124–26, esp. 126:1; *Mostra dell' arte delle situle dal Po al Danubio* (1961), no. 14; Kromer, *Hallstatt, prähist. Kunst: Naturhist. Mus. Wien* (1963), 48–50, Taf. 26–27; *id.*, *Von frühem Eisen und reichen Salzherren* (1964), 72–73 and Abb. 13; O.-H. Frey, *Germania* 44 (1966), 58 ff. and Taf. 5; *id.*, 'Die Entstehung der Situlenkunst', *R-G Forsch.* 31 (1968), no. 7

[1] Kromer, *Spina e l'Etruria Padana* = *Studi Etruschi* XXV: suppl. (1959), 151–54

[2] *Mostra dell' arte delle situle dal Po al Danubio*, no. 12; *Inventaria Arch.: Jugoslavija* 5 (1962), Y4:1; Frey, 'Die Entstehung der Situlenkunst', *R-G Forsch.* 31 (1968), no. 6

[3] *Mostra dell' arte . . .*, no. 13; Frey, *Germania* 44, 56 ff. and Abb. 8; *id.*, 'Die Entstehung der Situlenkunst', no. 1

27 Matzhausen, Burglengenfeld, Ldkr. Parsberg. Detail of pottery flask. Total h. 23·8 cm., l. of stag c. 9 cm. L.T. A2/B1, early IV B C. Mus. f. Vor- u. Frühgeschichte, Staatl. Museen, Berlin. *R–GK* (*E. Neuffer*).

This is a detail from a slender flask with wide-flared base, the La Tène type known as '*Linsenflaschen*', carefully wheel-turned pottery, which is in contrast with the ornate but hand-made earlier Hallstatt wares. The present flask was found in one of a group of about 50 barrows with, under a stone cairn, the bodies of a man, woman and child; the flask lay by the woman's right shoulder. From the arm-rings, a simple neck-ring with eye-terminals, a single-edged knife, and four fibulae of the developed 'Certosa' form, as well as from the flask shape itself (but ignoring some late Bronze Age material confused by the excavators with the Iron Age burials), the barrow can be dated to the transition to, or beginning of, the second main phase of the early La Tène period.

The flask's decoration, however, restricted to a circular frieze running round the shoulder of the squat base, like the Vače belt-hook [25] and its parallels marks a later survival of the animal friezes of Este. The entire frieze arranged in antithetic pairs like the archetypal Greek

Fig. 1 [27] Matzhausen, Germany. Incised and stamped decoration on *Linsenflasche*. Scale c. 1:4
After Reinecke

material of the seventh–sixth centuries, consists of a grazing stag – again in the attitude of Archaic art – a hare being pursued by a wolf or dog, a roebuck and his mate, front legs facing forwards but with heads turned over their shoulders, a pair of boars, a long-necked bird of a type found elsewhere in early La Tène art [56], a second grazing deer and another long-necked bird.

The style of the frieze, in contrast to its subject matter, is, like another object illustrated here [30], an example of local Celtic craftsmen adapting ancient and trans-Alpine motifs to a purely central European technique which has a long life – in this case, incised animal scenes on otherwise geometrically decorated pots [see also 10, 223]. Here, however, Italy provides the best models.[1] The ground-line of the frieze incorporates the use of two different toothed stamps while a third, of double circles in the old Hallstatt C tradition, runs round below the neck of this flask. The use of these particular stamps is a feature of north-east Bavaria[2] but stamp-decorated pottery runs through into the middle La Tène period and has a number of important regional variants [116, 133, 156–57];[3] stamped '*Linsenflaschen*' – which seem to fall into two main forms – are a feature also of the important Austrian and Bohemian early La Tène cemeteries.[4]

A. Nagel, *Zeitschr. f. Ethnologie* XX (1888), 25–28 and fig. 2; P. Reinecke, *AuhV*, V (1911), 282, Abb. 2 and Taf. 50: 892–95; *ECA*, no. 201; *WK*, Taf. 31; *CCH*, 147; W. Torbrügge and H. P. Uenze, *Bilder zur Vorg. Bayerns* (1968), 219–20, ill. 260–61; *EV*, 12, 207 and ill.; F. Schwappach in *Festschr. Dehn*, 256 and Taf. 21:3; Th. Voigt, *Jahresschr. f. mitteldt. Vorg.* 53 (1969), 415–36 esp. Taf. 41

[1] W. Lucke and O.-H. Frey, 'Die Situla in Providence (Rhode Island)', *R-G Forsch.* 26 (1962), 61 and Abb. 6:2–3
[2] Reinecke, *op. cit.*, Abb. 1; Torbrügge and Uenze, *op. cit.*, ill. 87, 91
[3] W. Dehn, *Bonner Jhrb.*, 151 (1951), 83–95; Schwappach, *op. cit.*, 252 ff
[4] R. Pittioni, *Urgeschichte des österreich. Raumes* (1954), Abb. 456, 458–59

28 Stična, Slovenia. Bronze earring W. 2 cm. V/IV BC. R-G Zentralmus. Mainz.

The site of Stična, a circular fortified settlement and attendant barrow cemetery of some hundred barrow mounds dating to much the same period as Vače (seventh–fifth centuries), though first excavated in the second half of the nineteenth century,[1] is currently being re-examined by a joint Jugoslav, American, and German team, whose work is confirming the site's occupation also by Celtic settlers of the Middle La Tène period.[2]

The contents of the burials excavated in the nineteenth and earlier twentieth centuries, which included rich barrow graves with helmets, breastplates, axes and spears, as well as fine jewellery and other objects recalling not only other Slovene cemeteries of the east Hallstatt culture overlapping with western early La Tène, but such Austrian cemeteries as Kleinklein [15], is now widely dispersed. The punched dot, *repoussé* and scribed line ornament of this little earring is in the continuing tradition of Alpine bronze metal-work and there is little reason to consider it as anything other than an east Hallstatt product; two similar earrings are known from Vače. The motif of the hare seen in profile with its long flattened pointed ears, however, is often found on *situlae* and other material of the fifth century, especially at Este,[3] both, then, on objects presumably made in Este and those from the Alpine regions; a belt-hook from Vače has four hares, all with tendrils falling from their mouths and two with heads turned. As in other areas bordering on the Alpine regions, one must not forget the interchange not only of artistic ideas but of actual craftsmen.

O.-H. Frey, *JR-GZM* 13 (1966), 44–48, Abb. 1 and Taf. 3:1; *id.*, 'Die Entstehung der Situlenkunst', *R-G Forsch.* 31 (1968), no. 43

[1] J. Kastelic, *Situla* I (1960), 3 ff.
[2] Frey in *Festschr. Dehn*, 7–20
[3] W. Lucke and Frey, 'Die Situla in Providence (Rhode Island)', *R-G Forsch.* 26 (1962), nos. 4, 15, 44; Frey, 'Die Entstehung der Situlenkunst', Taf. 70, no. 23 ff.

29 Libkovice, Duchcov. Stamped sherd. c. 4·5×5 cm., hares c. 2 cm. long. LT A, early IV BC. Formerly Mus. Teplice. *Aú ČSAV Prague.*

This unique sherd, unfortunately stolen, a surface find from an early La Tène occupation site, demonstrates the extension into eastern Bohemia of the use of stamps in pottery making [see also notes to 27, 115, 133]; in this instance the main stamp is obviously based on the hares of the later '*situla* style' and, like the Matzhausen vase [27] and the sword from Hallstatt, grave 994 [30], clearly shows Celtic craftsmen's familiarity with the motifs of that style. The half-moon stamp with circular terminations is common on other examples of Bohemian stamped pottery.

KvsE, 178 ff., esp. 183, obr. 8:1 and Tab. CVI:11; O.-H. Frey, *JR-GZM* 13 (1966), 46 and n. 17

30 Hallstatt, Salzkammergut, grave 994. Details of iron and bronze sword scabbard with remains of coral studs. L.

68 cm., w. c. 5 cm. LT A, c. 400 BC. Naturhist. Mus. Vienna. *J. V. S. Megaw* (lower detail).

This bronze scabbard, with its slender bladed iron sword decorated on the pommel with two simple bird's heads, and rounded cast bronze chape, is typical in its basic form of the standard weapon of the early La Tène warrior; in the fifth century the long sword came back into fashion, although the short dirk of the preceding late Hallstatt period was not entirely superseded. The sword was found in 1875 in one of the latest of the

Fig. 2 [30] Hallstatt, Austria, grave 994. Incised decoration on front of scabbard. Scale c. 1:3
After Kromer

Hallstatt graves with the body of a warrior. The body was aligned east–west and laid out on an oval stone platform with the sword lying high on the right side – the Celts seem to have slung their swords over the shoulder rather than from a belt around the waist. Also in the grave was a knife by the skeleton's left hand, two iron spearheads, part of a bronze cap and a carefully constructed pouring spout with fine-meshed bronze sieve. It is, however, the engraved ornamentation on the bronze front plate of the iron scabbard which makes this sword one of the best-known pieces in the early La Tène armoury.

At the outset it should be stated that, whatever the immediate source of the scenes depicted, there is no reason to doubt that the engraving was the work of a Celtic craftsman, probably an itinerant like so many others of his trade, and possibly, to judge from some of the artistic parallels which may be cited, originally trained amongst the local centres of the early La Tène chieftains of the Rhineland. The figural decoration, now much worn, falls into four unequal areas: (1) the central battle-scene with three foot-soldiers and four cavalry men, the second of whom is despatching a fallen enemy – clearly based on the battle scenes of such pieces as the Vače belt-hook even down to the weapons and decorated shields with their interlocking rim designs [25] – (2, 3) two flanking pairs of men are in the stance of the boxers of the *situlae* but hold between them a spoked wheel, a symbol of considerable importance in later Iron Age times [209a]—(4) towards the tip of the blade where the design is particularly poorly preserved a man with a long floral tendril growing from the middle of his back

watches a fight between two other men. Although the basic iconography of the Hallstatt sword follows that of the art of the *situlae* – the cavalry may be intended to be those of contemporary eastern Scythians – even such details as the clothing of the men and the harness of the horses betray their Celtic origin. The long Celtic trews and shoes with upturned points – a fashion apparently borrowed from Etruria possibly via Este – can be paralleled in some remarkable fibulae from Austria and Czechoslovakia [31, 32].[1] The helmet is not only possibly represented by the fragment from grave 994 but is also portrayed on another Czech fibula (from Kšice in Bohemia) and the Kärlich bronze mount [104, 33] as well as by more ornate pieces from the contemporary Celtic cemeteries in northern Italy; four helmets, now lost, from burials at Ogmore Down, Glamorganshire, are of this type and amongst the earliest evidence for the La Tène culture in Britain.[2] The little round discs or *phalerae* decorating the horses' bridles are a common feature of early La Tène graves with horse-gear sometimes being elaborately decorated [47, 111]. Details of the horses' physiognomy no less than those of the men's have parallels in yet more early La Tène fibulae: one from the Dürrnberg cemetery [93], and a couple found with two human-headed fibulae from Parsberg [63] and Schwieberdingen [89]. The incised decoration on the horses' haunches and the coils of the strange man-plant at the tip of the scabbard have close similarities not only with the Alice-through-the-Looking-Glass engraving on a bronze from Stupava, Slovakia [64] but also with the fragmentary design on a strainer-cum-funnel from a rich barrow grave in the Hunsrück-Eifel, Hoppstädten, Kr. Birkenfeld, barrow 2.[3] The sieve, like that from the Hallstatt grave, was probably needed to drain off at least some of the additives which the Celts seem to have regarded as essential for civilised drinking;[4] it embodies also some of the geometric elements of the Hallstatt scabbard including the interlocking key – yet another indication of the origins at least of the scabbard's engraver. The 'feathering' of the Hallstatt horses' haunches can also be seen as a motif on another group of engraved ornaments [110] related to Hoppstädten and has something of the nomadic 'shoulder curls' of the Basse-Yutz flagons [60–61]. The Hallstatt men's faces with their long slicked-back hair, sharp features and jug-handle ears can be found on many pieces associated with not so much the very earliest period of La Tène fine metal work in the west but with that of the first phase of Celtic expansion to the east and south of the close of the fifth century and beginning of the fourth [31, 54, 73, 79–81].

Other aspects of the Hallstatt scabbard's non-representational decoration are worth brief comment; the 'plated' zigzag running towards the tip occurs again on the Basse-Yutz flagons – this time on their rims – as well as on a contemporary decorated scabbard from Vert-la-Gravelle in the Marne.[5] The same design can be seen on a circular bronze harness disc allegedly found in the near vicinity of Prague and of the type illustrated on the Hallstatt scabbard.[6] The decoration of Vert-la-Gravelle is executed with a rocked tracer as is the line at the top and bottom of the main Hallstatt frieze. Finally the two cast 'dragons' which form the terminals of the scabbard chape are of a type which also have pendants on German fibulae [69].

ECA, no. 96; R. Pittioni, *Urgeschichte des österr. Raumes*

(1954), 679 ff., Abb. 464 below; *WK*, Taf. 8; K. Kromer et al., *Das Gräberfeld von Hallstatt* (1959), 182 and Taf. 201–2; *Mostra dell'arte delle situle dal Po al Danubio* (1961), no. 63; O.-H. Frey, *JR–GZM* 13 (1966) 48, n.28; W. Dehn, *Sborník Národního Muz. Praze* A XX: 1/2 (1966), 137–39, 147, Abb. 13

[1] F. Schwappach, *Památky Arch.* LVIII (1967), 322–23 and Abb. 1:4; Frey, *R-G Forsch.* 31 (1968), 22, Abb. 9:1 and Raf. 34:1.

[2] *Archaeologia* XLIII (1873), 553–55 and Pl. XXXVI: 1–4; P. Ashbee, *Bronze Age round barrow in Britain* (1960), 104, 143 and fig. 52

[3] L. Kilian, *Trierer Zeitschr.* 24–26 (1956–58), 86 ff. and Taf. 19; see also notes to [42, 78]

[4] Pliny, *Nat. Hist.* XIV, 24

[5] *ECA*, no. 90

[6] Dehn, *op. cit.*, 137 ff. and Abb. 7

31 Manětín-Hrádek, Plzeň-sever, grave 74. Bronze fibula. L. 8·8 cm. LT A V/IV BC. Západočeské muz., Plzeň. *Aú ČSAV Prague.*

This remarkable fibula was found in 1967 in a grave under a low stone cairn, one of a number of graves aligned roughly north–south from which the original inhumations had not survived. The associated grave goods included, apart from pottery and the remains of a wooden platter, a number of embossed gold discs similar to those found in the second Hoppstädten, Kr. Birkenfeld barrow [see notes to 30], Dürrnberg grave 44, the Reinheim 'princess's' grave, and other sites in the western part of the early La Tène culture.[1]

The form of the brooch is considered by its excavator to be a sort of anthropomorphism of the 'Certosa' type of fibula with the head taking the place of the usual upstanding knob above the catch-plate; however that may be, a fibula whose bow is formed of an entire human being is without parallel, though a somewhat similar human form, likewise with tiny arms, is incorporated in the brooch from the Niederschönhausen district of Berlin [101]. The punch marks and cast sockets for (probably) coral inlays do have parallels on Rhineland fibulae such as that from Budenheim as well as a disc from Königsheim, Kr. Tutlingen.[2] The emphasised ridging in the area of the figure's 'midriff' recalls that on a 'Certosa' brooch from Markt-Forst in Bavaria,[3] something possibly reflecting the influence of Etruscan craftsmanship as, in the last analysis, do the pointed-toed shoes whose representation in the Celtic world is restricted to finds north-east of the Alps [see notes to 32]. The face of the Manětín fibula with its jug ears, straight-brushed hair, emphasised jaw and protruding eyes with well-delineated pupils has a number of fairly close parallels in fibulae such as, again, that from Budenheim or those from Parsberg [63] and Schwieberdingen [89] illustrated here; the Stupava plaque [64], cited like Parsberg in connection with the Hallstatt sword scabbard [30] is also close. Somewhat similar, but probably later than most of the material considered here, is a bronze head, a surface find from Dürrnberg.[4] On the rear of the Manětín catch-plate and running down the figure's chest is an area of hatched and incised ornament to be seen again on the Parsberg fibula and on another Bohemian find of undoubted German origin, the brooch from Panenský Týnec [65]. Despite this apparently respectable artistic pedigree sketched out for the Manětín brooch, like other brooches from the area of

Plzeň [68, 70] it is certainly not of the first quality; indeed, like these last brooches, it is probably best to regard Manětín either as a product of an inferior German-trained craftsman, or, more likely in view of the distribution of the pointed shoes, the work of a local or east Alpine artist, influenced by the style of inlaid brooches found in the region of Este[5] aiming to produce the acceptable thing in what was very likely a style of brooch made for and given only to the dead.

E. Soudská, *Arch. roz.* XX (1968), 451–69, obr. 3, 5–6 and Tab. II–IV

[1] F. J. Keller, *JSGU*, 52 (1965), 42–57; *Keltische Kunst: Bodemschatten uit Salzburg*, Frans Halsmuseum, Haarlem (1963), no. 18

[2] Budenheim, nr. Mainz: *ECA*, no. 295; Königsheim: *ECA*, no. 201; F. Fischer, *FbS* 18 (1967), List 1: 76

[3] H. P. Uenze in *Bayer. Vorg.* 29 (1964), 83, Abb. 1:1

[4] M. Hell, *Germania* 18 (1934), 258–62; *Keltische Kunst . . .*, no. 38

[5] O.-H. Frey, 'Die Entstehung der Situlenkunst', *R-G Forsch.* 31 (1968), Taf. 31:2, 5, 39 and Abb. 9:4

32 Dürrnberg, Hallein. Bronze fibula. L. 2·7 cm. LT A, c. 400 BC. Stadtmus., Hallein. *Ing. E. Penninger.*

The modern town of Hallein south of Salzburg is still an important salt-mining centre as it was at the close of the Hallstatt period when it gradually took over from Hallstatt as the centre of local salt production, a position which it held for much of the early and middle La Tène period, to judge from material recovered from a number of burials, both flat and barrow graves, of which over 50 have been carefully excavated since the 1930s [see also notes to 48, 72, 138, 163]. The graves lie on the high pastures close to the ancient salt workings and overlooked by a fortified hill-top, the Ramsaukopf, as yet unexcavated but certainly occupied in later La Tène times.

The present tiny fibula discovered by Ing. Ernst Penninger in his most important but as yet only partly published post-war series of excavations in the cemetery, is one of five in the form of pointed-toe shoes so far known from north-east of the Alps – the most recently discovered of these fibulae is an as yet unpublished brooch, again from the Dürrnberg cemetery, found in 1968. Shoes of this type are known from Etruscan tomb-paintings of the sixth and fifth centuries from Chiusi and Tarquinia, and their best-known Celtic representation is on the Hallstatt grave 994 sword scabbard [30]. On the Hallstatt scabbard, as on the illustrated Dürrnberg fibula and one from a sword grave in the Leopoldau cemetery on the outskirts of Vienna (Wien-Leopoldau grave 8), the square tongue of the shoe is clearly indicated – the Leopoldau fibula has in fact a pair of still smaller pointed shoes loosely swivelling from its own heel!

Other features of this first Dürrnberg shoe fibula can be noted; most obvious is the little dog face protruding seemingly incongruously from the heel of the fibula. This has a close parallel on another brooch from Dürrnberg, one from grave 2 of which as yet no illustration has been published.[1] The dog's 'ruff' and the zigzag ornament cast in to the side of the shoe can be seen on the originally coral inlaid brooch with human head from the Reinheim 'princess's' grave; this human head has been compared not very convincingly with the head of the Manětín man.[2] A similar collar or ruff runs round the neck of the sheep of the Panenský Týnec brooch [65] although it is unlikely that this last comes from the same crafts centre as the Dürrnberg fibula, even making allowances for Celtic versatility. The large dumb-bell-like balls, either side of the Dürrnberg brooch spring, are a characteristic of other brooches from the cemetery as well as of a group from Bavaria and of a third group centred on the fortified hill-top of the Kleiner Gleichberg in Thüringia [94]; all these may be products of a south German centre specialising in the production of ornate brooches.

Keltische Kunst: Bodemschatten uit Salzburg, Frans Halsmus., Haarlem (1963), no. 31; F. Schwappach, *Památky Arch.* LVIII (1967), 320–24

[1] E. Penninger, *Mitt. Ges. Salzburger Ldskde.* 100 (1960), 3
[2] *ECA*, nos. 29–31; F. J. Keller, *Das Keltische Fürstengrab von Reinheim* I (1965), no. 13; E. Soudská, *Arch. roz.* XX (1968), obr. 11:3

33 Kärlich, Ldkr. Koblenz, grave 3. Bronze appliqué figure. L. 5 cm. LT A, early V BC. Städt. Mus., Koblenz. *Rhein. Landesmus., Bonn.*

This tiny curved piece of sheet-bronze provided with seven long-shanked square rivets was recovered during the 1928 excavation of one of a group of no less than eight barrows containing remains of two-wheeled chariots. Together with another fragment of bronze representing the hind quarters of a horse, this silhouette figure of an armed cavalryman just like those on the Hallstatt grave 994 scabbard [30], was probably part of the decorative frieze of a wooden vessel. The fragments look like a local attempt to copy the '*situla* art' type of mounted procession more successfully handled by the decorator of the Hallstatt scabbard. The plain sheet-bronze *situlae* from another of the Karlich chariot graves, like the imports found in the richer Hunsrück-Eifel princely barrow burials, offer a hint of a continuing northern spread of southern techniques and artistic ideas.[1] The details of the Kärlich figure are executed in a series of freehand punched dots, a technique which can be seen in use on pieces from other early La Tène chariot graves and some similar silhouette figures from the Tyrol,[2] as well as in the representational friezes of late Hallstatt pots [see notes to **10**]. The rider, who may or may not be intended to have a cap helmet with side-flaps like the riders on the Hallstatt scabbard, shows himself as a typical early La Tène warrior by the short sword he wears by his side with its pointed-oval openwork chape.[3] The musculature of the shoulder is executed in such an ambiguous way – probably in a botched attempt to show perspective – that it is again difficult to decide whether the man is intended to be wearing a breatplate, something certainly unknown in the early La Tène contexts but possible if one assumes the figure to be based at least partially on a southern model. A third enigmatic detail is the circular object hanging from the rider's left hand. Two explanations of this are possible. It could be intended as a representation of one of the so-called 'pilgrim-flasks', flat-sided bronze containers like a modern water-bottle known both from an import of c. 500 BC in the Rodenbach, Rheinpfalz

grave and as a local Celtic copy from the second Dürrnberg chariot burial, grave 44.[4] More likely, if more gruesome, the roundel may be intended as a human skull, a reminder of the head-hunting aspect of Celtic warfare and the central position taken in Celtic belief by the cult of the severed head; several classical writers comment on Celts riding off from the battlefield with the skulls of their victims hanging from their horses.[5]

There is some confusion over the associations of the various Kärlich graves, but grave 3 seems certainly to have included a plain arm ring and a number of disc fibulae fragments similar to those found in the upper Hirschlanden central burial [12]. This brooch type is placed in a final, overlapping, phase of the Hallstatt Iron Age and would not be out of place in the later 'Hunsrück-Eifel' culture to which the Kärlich cemetery belongs, since this is a native, Hallstatt-based culture which seems to have given gradual rise to a local wealthy La Tène community gaining its riches probably as a result of the working of local iron ore deposits. One final detail: like Hirschlanden and, more comparable, like the little naked figurines of other final Hallstatt or early La Tène sites [see notes to **18**], the Kärlich rider appears to be phallic.

J. Driehaus, *Bonner Jahrb.* 165 (1965), 58–71; H.-E. Joachim, 'Die Hunsrück-Eifel-Kultur', *Bonner Jahrb.* Beiheft 29 (1968), esp. 110 and Taf. 31A; *EV*, 10 and Abb. 6

[1] W. Kimmig, *42–44. Ber. R-GK 1962–63* (1964), esp. 102–06; Joachim, 'Hunsrück-Eifel-Kultur', 106
[2] *ECA*, nos. 166, 168; *EV*, ill. on p. 229 below
[3] *Manuel* IV, figs. 457–58
[4] Rodenbach: *ECA*, 140–41, Pl. 254–55; Dürrnberg: see notes to [48]
[5] Livy, *Histories* XXIII, 24; Diodorus Siculus V, 29; Strabo, IV, 4, 5

34 Este, Fondo Baratela. Bronze plaque. L. 15·7 cm. IV–III BC. Mus. Nazionale Atestino, Este.

This incised and *repoussé* decorated fragment was found in a local shrine or *stipe* dedicated to the Etruscan goddess Reitia together with a number of votive figures, model shields and the like. The mounted warriors, executed in a style which follows the traditions of the region's '*situla* art' and continued in contemporary *stele*, may be intended as representations of local Celts, settled in northern Italy from at least the beginning of the fourth century; more probably the figures represent locals armed in a Celtic manner. The shields, with their rectangular bosses covering a central spine, are a type introduced only in the middle stages of the La Tène culture as marked by several examples from the type-site itself. In many ways the Baratela plaque is as much an adaptation of old artistic themes to local models as the slightly earlier Hallstatt grave 994 scabbard [30]. A grave *stele* from Padua with palaeovenetic inscription and dated to the fourth–third century BC has a somewhat similar galloping rider with shield, spear and simple 'jockey cap' helmet[1] [see also **104** below].

O. Klindt-Jensen, *Acta Arch.* XX (1949), 133–36 and figs. 88–90; *Mostra dell' arte delle situle dal Po al Danubio* (1961), no. 60; O.-H. Frey, 'Die Entstehung der Situlenkunst', *R-G Forsch.* 31 (1968), no. 38

[1] A. Prosdocimi, *Atti e Mem. Accad. Patavina di Sci., Lettere ed Arti* LXXVIII: III (1965–66), 196–205, esp. 204 and fig. 4

35 Býčí Skála, Adamova. Bronze bull with iron inlay. Ht. 11·4 cm. ? VI BC. Naturhist. Mus., Vienna.

This cast bronze figurine found in 1869 in a pottery vessel containing carbonised millet grains comes from a big limestone cave in the Moravian karst land north of Brno. The site seems to have been a cult centre of considerable importance, possibly owing to its proximity to local iron workings. Although the majority of material recovered from nineteenth-century investigations belongs to the later Hallstatt Iron Age, a number of hollow knobbed foot-rings of a type characteristic of the middle La Tène phase [see **175**] indicates a considerable period of use.

Two main areas within the cave seem to have been used as great funeral pyres, included in which were the fittings for four-wheeled waggons, harness fittings, bronze vessels, pottery and jewellery. Amongst the bronze vessels was a parallel-sided cordoned bucket, an import from northern Italy as found in several early La Tène chieftains' graves.[1] Offerings of grain, beasts and humans also seem to have been made; some forty skeletons were found, mostly of women, and many missing heads, hands, or feet; near by were the quartered carcasses of a pair of horses while within a cauldron was a human skull. Elsewhere, surrounded by pottery vessels, another skull had been made into a drinking cup.

Amidst all this grim evidence of ancient Celtic belief in the importance of rites concerned with the Otherworld, the little bronze bull, cast by the *cire perdue* method, stands out as a masterpiece of miniature modelling; inlaid into the shoulders and the forehead are three triangular 'brands' of iron, and originally the eyes must have been filled with glass or amber. Free-standing figures of bulls – second only to the boar in cultic importance – occur right the way through to late La Tène times[2] but this figure, with its feeling almost of caricature despite the well-observed realism of such details as the hooves, has its closest parallels not in fact amongst the rather childlike zoo figures of the later Hallstatt period but rather in the accomplished cartoon characters of the (?) early third-century 'Disney style' [**160–162**]. In view of the disturbed nature of the Býčí Skála deposits a La Tène date for the bull figure might well be a possibility.

H. Wankel, *Mitt. d. Anthrop. Ges. Wien* VII (1878), 125 ff.; E. Benninger, *IPEK* 8 (1932–33), 80–99; W. and B. Forman and J. Poulík, *Prehistoric Art* (n.d. but 1956), ill. 118; K. Kromer, *Von frühem Eisen und reichen Salzherren* (1964), 78 f., 147 ff., Abb. 39; *PAE*, 215 and Pl. 219; *EV*, 108–109 and ill.; *VE*, ill. P. 161; *Hallstatt a Býčí Skála*, Brno-Bratislava-Praha (1969), 38–49, 85–86 and Tab. 10–12

[1] B. Stjernquist, *Ciste a cordoni (Rippenzisten)*=*Acta Arch. Lundensia* ser. 4°, 6 (1967) II, esp. no. 50; see also notes to [**40–41**].
[2] W. Krämer, *Germania* 28 (1944–50), 210–13; J. V. S. Megaw, *Antiq. J.* XLII (1962), 26 ff.; W. Torbrügge and H. P. Uenze, *Bilder zur Vorg. Bayerns* (1968), 221, ill. 272–73

36 Hallstatt, Salzkammergut, grave 671. Detail of handle of bronze bowl. D. of bowl 30 cm., l. of cow 14·4 cm. Ha D, VI BC. Naturhist. Mus., Vienna.

This cast bronze figure of a cow and her calf forming part of the handle of a shallow bowl decorated below the rim with incised geometric ornament, was discovered in 1858 in a cremation grave together with fragments of belt-plates. These last have the normal punched and incised ornament including both stags and shaggy horses looking rather like the 'steppe pony' in the round from grave 697 [see notes to **17**]. The cow has provision for triangular inlay in the forehead like the Býčí Skála bull [**35**]; it has been compared with pottery figures such as those from Kleinklein and Gemeinlebarn.[1] Two other late Hallstatt bronze vessels with similar ox mounts come from a barrow burial at Au, Ldkr. Aichach where the vessel copies urns like that from Burrenhof [**Plate I**] and from the Bachbauernköpfl at Dürrnberg.[2]

E. Benninger, *IPEK* 8 (1932–33), 87 f.; K. Kromer *et al.*, *Das Gräberfeld von Hallstatt* (1959), Taf. 130–31, esp. 130:2; Kromer, *Hallstatt, prähist. Kunst: Naturhist. Mus. Wien* (1963), 56–57, Taf. 48–49, *id.*, *Von frühem Eisen und reichen Salzherren* (1964), 57–58 and Abb. 11; *PreA*, 175 and ill. 173; *EV*, 105, 107, 109 and ill.; *VE*, ill. p. 166

[1] L. Franz, *Arch. Austriaca* 40 (1966), 99 ff.
[2] Au: F. Wagner, *Germania* 30 (1952), 203–4; Dürrnberg: M. Hell, *Mitt. d. Anthrop. Ges. Wien* LXIX (1929), 156 f. and Abb. 2:1

37 Mérida, Badajoz. Bronze cult model. L. c. 25 cm., ht. of horse 13 cm. ? II/I BC. Mus. des Antiquités nat., St-Germain-en-Laye. *Belzeaux-Zodiaque*.

The Celtiberians of the period of the Roman occupation of Spain and Portugal were the descendants of a late branch of the central European 'Urnfield' communities, retaining much of their language and basic way of life which clearly show their connection with the Iron Age communities to the north and east. One piece must stand for their own characteristic art, some small examples of which even made their way to the British Isles.[1]

The Mérida cult cart, purchased in 1913 from an antique dealer in Madrid, is supposed to have been found in a Roman drainage system in the so-called 'Casa de Meleagro', a town house in Roman Emerita Augusta, capital of the province of Lusitania. The piece seems to have gone through several stages of construction; originally there was only the figure of the mounted huntsman with his spear to which was added a pair of dogs (one only surviving) and the boar; other details such as the wire harness are even later additions. Similar Celto-Iberian depictions of riders can be seen for example on fibulae of about the last two centuries BC.[2]

A very similar mounted warrior, also complete with greaves, comes from Cabeza del Buey in the same (modern) province of Badajoz[3] while, despite connections cited with Meleager and the Calydonian boar hunt, the symbolism of this Celtic cult animal *par excellence* is marked by a number of large stone statues of boars found in central Spain and northern Portugal usually in the vicinity of the local Celtiberian defended hill-top settlements.[4] The idea of the four-wheeled cult waggon, not to mention the attaching of rattle-plates – transformed on Mérida into bells – is basically a survival from the earlier world of Hallstatt.

M. Lafuente and J. Valera, *Historia general de España* I (1887), 247; R. Lantier, *Bull. des Musées de France* (1931), 28–29; R. Forrer, *Préhistoire* I (1932), 19–123; A. García y Bellido in *Ars Hispaniæ* I=*Historia Universal del Arte Hispanica* (1946), 337 and fig. 410; R. M. Pidal (ed.), *Historia de España* I:III (1954), 173, 777, and fig. 98; J. M. Blazquez, *Zephyrus* 6 (1955), 41–60; *ArtG*, 96, Pl. 51; *WK*, Taf. 46

[1] *LPA*, 70 and Pl. XXII:3
[2] K. Raddatz, 'Die Schatzfunde der Iberischen Halbinsel', *Madrider Forsch.* 5 (1969), 145–46 and Taf. 2:17
[3] J. Ramón Mélida, *Catálogo monumental de España: Provincia de Badajoz (1907–10)* (1925), no. 625, figs. 54–55
[4] *Celts*, 146 f. and fig. 29

38 Strettweg, Jüdenburg. Bronze cult model. 35×18 cm. at base, ht. of goddess figure 22·6 cm. Ha C, VII BC. Landesmus. Joanneum, Graz.

Under a barrow the cremation grave of Strettweg contained, in addition to the famous cult model, an iron-socketed axe and a spear head, horse bits, belt-plates, a gold bead and painted pottery and, as cremation container, a bronze urn on a stand related to that from Hallstatt gr. 507 [22] – the typical grave goods of an east Alpine chieftain of the earlier Hallstatt period.

The use of the four-wheeled model cult waggon as a substitute for the burial of an actual vehicle goes back to the last stages of the Late Bronze Age in central Europe, while bronze vessels used as cremation urns mounted on a platform with four spoked wheels can be found in sites in Czechoslovakia, northern Germany and southern Scandinavia.[1] There may in fact be some recollection of this custom in the shallow basin supported by the central figure of the Strettweg model. From a barrow burial at Frög in Carinthia is another Hallstatt cult waggon made largely of lead.[2]

Apart from the 'goddess' figure, which is naked save for a belt, the symmetrical arrangement of figures front and back – separately cast and riveted on to the platform as on the much later Mérida model [37] – consists of (1) a pair of mounted spearmen, each with pointed trans-Alpine helmets and circular shields, (2) between them stand two ithyphallic axemen each accompanied by a woman with (3) in front of them a stag, presumably object of the hunt, standing between a pair of (probably female) figures; at each corner of the platform is a bull's head. The crude modelling of the features of the humans with detailing limited to some punched dot ornamentation is similar to that of the few modelled humans from the Hallstatt cemetery [17–18], and the combination of riders, cattle, and wild beasts must reflect the same evocation of the basic components of Hallstatt society as found in the pottery figurines from the great ornamented urn in the Gemeinlebarn first barrow [see notes to 17].

Nonetheless, as has been recently observed, there could be something of archaic Greek art if not also Greek legend in what at first seems typically Hallstatt imagery. A seventh-century figure of Zeus from Olympia is very similar to the goddess.[3] The idea of a cauldron on a stand, though it may reflect the influence of Italy as does the strange object from Hallstatt grave 507 [22], is an 'orientalising' feature also introduced through Greece. Finally, the horses of Strettweg have been compared with those on Greek cauldron-tripods,[4] though whether all this adds up to the model's production by a Greek-trained, let alone an actual Greek, craftsman is perhaps another matter. An Italic model cart from Bisenzio with a woman holding a jug, a warrior, a dog and an unidentified wild beast offers a nearer source.[5]

W. Schmid, 'Der Kultwagen von Strettweg', *Führer zur Urg.* 12 (1925); R. Pittioni, *Urg. des österreich. Raumes* (1954), 620 ff. and Abb. 438–39; W. Modrijan, *Das Aichfeld=Jüdenburger Museumsschriften* III (1962), 18 ff. and Abb. 16–18; K. Kromer, *Von frühem Eisen und reichen Salzherren* (1964) 154 ff.; *PAE*, 215–16, fig. 96B and Pl. 218; *VE*, 164 and ill. p. 159; *EV*, 147–48 and ill.

[1] E. Sprockhoff, 'Zur Handelgeschichte der germanischen Bronzezeit', *Vorg. Forsch.* 7 (1930), 124 ff.; T. G. E. Powell, *PPS* XXIX (1963), 216 ff.
[2] F. Kanitz, *Mitt. d. Anthrop. Ges. Wien* XIV (1884), 141 ff. and Taf. III; *EV*, 122 and ill.
[3] *PAE*, fig. 96A; H. Lorimer, *Homer and the Monuments* (1950), 246 and Pl. XXII:4
[4] S. Benton, *Ann. Brit. School at Athens* XXXV (1934–35), 85 and Pl. 18–19, 21
[5] *Not. Scavi* (1928), 440 ff., Tav. VIII

39 Schwarzenbach, Kr. St Wendel barrow I. Gold openwork over bronze backing. D. 12·6 cm., ht. 8·5 cm., LT A, later V BC. Antikenabt., Stiftung Preussischer Kulturbesitz, Staatl. Museen, Berlin. *Jutta Tietz-Glagow*.

The two barrows of Schwarzenbach form part of a group of more than a dozen Saarland princely graves of the late 'Hunsrück-Eifel' culture on the southern edge of the Hunsrück with the huge defences of the 'Hunnenring' of Otzenhausen perhaps making the ancient focal point;[1] these graves form only one of several regional or dynastic groups of princely burials.[2] The first Schwarzenbach grave, discovered by ploughing in 1849, contained a two-handled bronze amphora of the second quarter of the fifth century imported from the big Etruscan workshops at Vulci,[3] part of a beaked flagon, again probably of Italic workmanship but now lost, and this openwork mounting for a wooden or pottery bowl (the present is a modern reconstruction).

The production of fine gold leaf decoration ornamented with a combination of slight *repoussé* tooling, with punch work and sometimes cut-out patterns in which the spaces or voids are an essential part of the over-all design, as they are in insular Celtic art, is a particular feature of craftsmen based on the Rhineland. Products of these Rhineland artisans appear in princely graves over a widespread area from Eigenbilzen in the Low Countries [40] to the c. 400 BC grave at Chlum in central Bohemia, both also found with imported beaked flagons, the new mark of the funerary symposium.[4] The basic features of this gold work, which belongs to an already fully individual 'school' of early La Tène art, are the variations played on a number of classical themes which would have been transmitted north through knowledge of the decorative repertoire of Etruscan and Italo-Greek bronzes and painted wares. This Celtic variation, this fluctuation of motif, is a characteristic of early La Tène art especially in its borrowing of southern themes. Three separate elements, basically plant motifs, of considerable importance in early La Tène art, can be seen on the Schwarzenbach gold mounting: (1) in the upper register are triple-leafed half-palmettes with (2) below them, a pair of 'commas' depending from an 'eye' composed of a concentric circle stamp and (3) between the comma pairs and touching the base of the mounting, a simplified 'lotus bud' in the form of a three-limbed droplet. Each motif is capable of more than one reading; like a piece of programme music, several allusions can be imagined for the one theme. This extracting of separate but recognisable parts of classical motifs and recombination in new and varying forms results in forms whose roots are clear but whose meaning or representational intent is not.

Gold leaf covers a large number of other fragments from Schwarzenbach, some for decorating vessels and probably others for native drinking horns like those from Klein Aspergle [44]. Some pieces, presumably for decorating rims, have versions of the simplified Greek key or stepped design seen on the Hallstatt scabbard [30] while six other pieces, a group of four and a pair, are human faces flanked by comma-leaves [see also notes to **40, 57, 59, 104**].[5] A somewhat similar and rather crude openwork strip comes from Waldgallschied, Ldkr. St. Goar.[6]

H. Gerhard, *Bonner Jahrb.* 23 (1856), 131 and 194; H. Baldes and G. Behrens, *Katalog Birkenfeld* (1914), 52 ff.; P. Jacobsthal, *Die Antike*, X (1934), 24 ff., Abb. 6 and Taf. 3; *JL*, 27, n. 36; *ECA*, no. 18; *WK*, Taf. 30; P.-M. Duval, *Art de France* IV (1964), 10, ill., 37, fig. 20; R. Schindler in *Saarland=Führer zu vor- u. frühg. Denkmälern* 5 (1966), 216–18 and ill.; *EV*, ill. p. 199

[1] H. Lehner, *Der Ring bei Otzenhausen* (1894); *Celts*, pl. 58–59; Schindler in *Saarland* . . . 219–20
[2] U. Schaaff in *Festschr. Dehn*, 187–202
[3] P. J. Riis, *Acta Arch.* XXX (1959), 36–50, esp. p. 38
[4] *ECA*, 92, PP 391–92; *KvsE*, 272 f., obr. 76 and Tab. I:4, II:5; H. P. Uenze, *Bayer. Vorg.* 29 (1964), 103, n. 92, 112
[5] *ECA*, no. 34, esp. [21-26]
[6] *ECA*, no. 26; see also notes to [41]

40 Eigenbilzen, Limburg. Gold band. L. 22 cm. LT A, c. 400 BC. Mus. Royaux d'Art et d'Histoire, Brussels.

This gold band comes from a grave discovered in the north of Belgium in 1871. It is the memorial of a pioneering and perhaps younger chieftain going west from the central area of Iron Age power, in this case the Rhineland; it is in fact the farthest north as well as the westernmost of all the early La Tène *Fürstengräber*. The grave contained an imported Italic cordoned bucket, used as a cremation container,[1] and a beaked Italic flagon. In the grave were also a sword, a fragment of a gold-covered bronze ring, some unidentifiable pieces of iron and a (probably native) bronze vessel with incised decoration. This gold band, together with another gold mount from Eigenbilzen, was probably intended by its local Celtic owner to be enrichment for a drinking horn like those from Klein Aspergle [44]. Another important find in the grave was the lower part of a Celtic biconical copy of an Italic flagon with carefully scribed geometric ornamentation, including stepped or key patterning and paired lobes, which relates it to, amongst other pieces,

another Celtic copy of a foreign type, the 'pilgrim flask' from Dürrnberg grave 44 as well as the Hallstatt scabbard [see notes to **30, 48**].

Two armlets from the Reinheim 'princess's' barrow grave in the Saarland[2] are closely related to the Eigenbilzen mount with its rather more rounded leaves and freer design than Schwarzenbach [39]; Eigenbilzen and its parallels probably mark a slightly more developed but contemporary style than that represented by Schwarzenbach.

JL, 32–33; *ECA*, no. 24; S. J. De Laet, *The Low Countries* (1956), 100–1, Pl. 56; *Inventaria Arch.: Belge* I (1956), B6; M. E. Mariën in M. Renard (ed.), 'Hommages à Albert Grenier', *Coll. Latomus* LVIII (1962), 1113–16

[1] B. Stjernquist, *Ciste a Cordoni (Rippenzisten)=Acta Arch. Lundensia* ser. 4°; 6 (1967), no. 50
[2] *WK*, Taf. 39 below; F. J. Keller, *Das keltische Fürstengrab von Reinheim* I (1965), nos. 7–8

41 Klein Aspergle, Ldkr. Ludwigsburg. Attic red-figure stemless cup with gold LT A embellishment. W. including handles 22 cm. Date of cup c. 450 BC. Württ. Landesmus., Stuttgart.

This cup, decorated on its inside surface with the figure of a priestess before an altar, was painted in a mid-fifth-century Athenian workshop by the 'Amphitrite' painter (formerly named the 'Amymone' painter).[1] Together with a second plain black glaze cup found with it, also with later Celtic embellishment, it forms a most important peg on which to hang at least one corner of early Celtic art, several other important pieces of which come from the same grave [43, 44, 50]. The Klein Aspergle barrow grave, which recent examination shows originally had a large encircling ditch,[2] included two burial chambers, of which the main chamber was plundered in the Middle Ages. The side chamber, unsystematically excavated in 1879, contained a cremation, probably that of a woman. Klein Aspergle lies close to a number of other barrows and a hill-fort, the Hohenasperg, from which LT A sherds have been picked up.[3] Recently another barrow grave in the area, at Markung Asperg – again robbed but like the Hohmichele [see notes to **7**] probably in the Iron Age – was excavated and shown to belong to the final Hallstatt phase, Ha D3, contemporary with nearby Hirschlanden [12] and the Vix burial and overlapping with the first La Tène communities; the Markung Asperg grave contained a fantastic wealth of Mediterranean imports including not only products of Italy and mainland Greece but an ivory Syro-Phoenician mirror handle.[4] A similar situation to that at Vix and Mont Lassois or the Hohmichele and the Heuneburg must be envisaged for this area with the ruling family being buried close to their fortified citadel.

Like the late Hallstatt graves just mentioned, there were imports from Italy in the Klein Aspergle barrow, a cordoned bucket[5] like that from Eigenbilzen and a two-handled bronze *stamnos* probably made at Vulci [see notes to **50**]. A bronze cauldron also may have been imported and, like most other objects in the grave, was obviously part of the preparations for the Otherworld feast.

The originally complete net of open-work gold with its triple-leaf 'lotus blooms' is very similar to Schwarzenbach [39] and was fixed to the body of the cups by small bronze rivets; such enrichment of exotic objects almost amounts to enshrinement. A large number of other fragments was also recovered including strips probably for running round the rims of the cups; similar strips were found at Schwarzenbach [see notes to **39**]. Small discs from Klein Aspergle – probably dress ornaments – have their closest parallels amongst the contents of the 'Hunsrück-Eifel' barrow grave 2 at Hoppstädten, Kr. Birkenfeld [see also notes to **30, 42**] as well as at other Rhineland princely graves.[6] The date of the burial must obviously be a little later than the actual date of manufacture of the Greek cups but perhaps within less than a generation of 450 BC. The poor quality of the cups has been remarked; it seems that if Greeks came bearing gifts they never gave of their best. The distribution of Greek pottery in the Celtic area is more southerly than that of the Italic imports, suggesting that most of it was imported by way of the Greek colony of Massalia at the mouth of the Rhône, though products of the 'Amphitrite' painter are found at Bologna and at the head of the Adriatic.[7]

L. Lindenschmidt, *AuhV* III:12 (1881), Taf. 4–6; H. Baldes and G. Behrens, *Katalog Birkenfeld* (1914), 51; P. Jacobsthal, *Die Antike*, X (1934), 19, Abb. 1; *JL*, 30–31; *ECA*, no. 32; O. Paret, *IPEK*, 17 (1943–48), 47–51; *WK*, Taf. 24; *VRD*, ill. 119; *Celts*, Pls. 16–17; Paret, *Württemburg in vor- u. frühg. Zeit* (1961), 231 ff.; *PAE*, 235; *EV*, 198 and ill.

[1] J. D. Beazley, *Attic red-figure vase-painters*, II (2 ed., 1963), 830–31, no. 25
[2] F. Fischer, *FbS* 18:1 (1967), 81–82; W. Kimmig in 'Siedlung, Berg, und Stadt', *Deutsch. Akad. der Wiss. zu Berlin: Schriften der Sektion f. Vor- u. Frühg.* 25 (1969), 102 ff.
[3] H. Zürn, *FbS* 17 (1965), 194 ff.
[4] Zürn and H.-V. Hermann, *Germania* 44 (1966), 74–102
[5] B. Stjernquist, *Ciste a Cordoni (Rippenzisten)=Acta Arch. Lundensia* ser. 4°, 6 (1967) no. 60
[6] Hoppstädten: L. Kilian, *Trierer Zeitschr.* 24–26 (1956–58), Taf. 20; Waldgallschied: *ECA*, no. 29; Remmesweiler: *ECA*, no. 31
[7] P. Jacobsthal, *Germania* 18 (1934), 14–19, and see also [**111**] below; H. Reim, *Germania* 46 (1968), 274–85

42 Auvers-sur-Oise (Seine-et-Oise). Gold sheet over two bronze discs with ? coral inlay. D. 10 cm. LT A, end of V/beginning of IV BC. Cabinet des Médailles, Bibliothèque Nationale, Paris.

This disc, possibly a harness ornament like those represented on the Hallstatt scabbard [**30**], came from a barrow excavated in 1882 without record of further finds. Here half-palmettes reduced to swashbuckling 'S' pairs form a continuous lyre pattern divided by a dissected lotus bud – a central droplet and two comma-leaves. All the elements of the 'academic' Schwarzenbach open-work [**39**] are present but are executed here with considerably more freedom and feeling for modelling and for light and shade, aided not only by the slight relief but, originally, also by the complete pattern of bright red inlay – usually identified as coral, but which may in fact be a vitreous paste. The 'cable' edging is executed with a goldsmith's hammer working on an anvil.

There is another visual illusion; in each 'S' pair, when read as a lyre pattern with touching tightly spiralling bases, there is a hint of a human face such as those of torcs of the following half-century [**119–121**] whose anthropomorphic intent cannot be doubted. For similar employment of the 'swash-buckling S' one may cite again the Eigenbilzen openwork gold-mount [see notes to **40**] and yet another piece from Hoppstadten barrow 2 [see notes to **30, 41**], this time a bronze girdle-hook not from the main timber-lined grave, but from the barrow covering.[1] Another piece with ? coral inlay offsetting the main design of 'S' spirals is a bronze terret from a chariot grave at Laumersheim, Kr. Frankental.[2]

There are parallels, however, to Auvers from other French finds. Four bronze crescentic plaques from an inhumation grave in the Marne, 'Le Mont Blanc', Étrechy, Vertus, following some discussion recently shown to be shield mounts, and a small bronze fragment in the form of a double palmette from Mairy, grave 47, again in the Marne, exhibit the same plump curves which are the hallmark of the gold disc and which separate it from the flatter, more precisely geometric lay-out of, for example, gold leaf discs from the first Schwarzenbach burial.[3] The Auvers disc and its closest parallels belong to a more individual, but not necessarily later hand than the craftsman – or men – responsible for Schwarzenbach, Eigenbilzen and Klein Aspergle. The 'master of the Auvers disc' clearly had a clientèle largely to the west of the Rhine.

P. Jacobsthal, *Die Antike* X (1934), 22 f. and Abb. 5; *ECA*, no. 19; *Art G*, 240, Pl. 15; *WK*, Taf. 78; *CCE*, 145–46; *PreA*, 188, ill. 181; *EV*, ill. p. 201

[1] L. Kilian, *Trierer Zeitschr.* 24–26 (1956–58), 92–93, Taf. 21:1
[2] W. Kimmig, *Germania* 28 (1944–50), 38 ff. esp. Abb. 1
[3] Étrechy: P. du Chatellier, *Rev. Arch.* XXXIV (1877), 212–16 and Pl. XX:1; *ECA*, no. 376; I. M. Stead, *PPS* XXXIV (1968), 176 and fig. 17:4; Mairy: *ECA*, no. 379; Schwarzenbach I: *ECA*, no. 345–46

43 Klein Aspergle, Kr. Ludwigsburg. Gold open-work on iron plate. W. 6·8 cm. LT A, mid V BC. Württ. Landesmus., Stuttgart. *Landesbildstelle Baden u. Württ.*

This fragment still has parts of bronze rivets for attachment to coral or other inlay on the front. It may be a belt ornament. The deposition of the ornament – another variation of the comma-leaf/lotus bud pattern with, this time, the buds formed by one of the most common motifs in Celtic visual symbolism, the triple circle – is close to a plaque from the Chlum, Bohemia barrow grave with its warrior's sword, spear, and axe and imported Italic beaked flagon. On the Chlum plaque, however, the design is 'on the flat', the whole design embossed on a sheet without the cut-out voids.[1]

P. Jacobsthal, *Die Antike* X (1934), 22 f. and Abb. 3; *ECA*, no. 22; *WK*, Taf. 26 below; *VRD*, ill. 116; *EV*, ill. p. 200 below

[1] *KvsE*, Obr. 76, esp. 76:6; see also notes to [**39**]

44 Klein Aspergle, Kr. Ludwigsburg. Details of gold sheet drinking-horn mounts. Total l. 14·5 and 17·5 cm., l. of lower head 1·8 cm. LT A, mid-V BC. Württ. Landesmus., Stuttgart. *Landesbildstelle Baden u. Württ.* (*Dr H. Hell*).

Most of the drinking equipment of early La Tène graves is either imported or modelled on forms known from actual imports. It is quite likely that the humble drinking-horn of wood or actual horn continued side by side with the more exotic funerary table ware, although we have no material evidence - with the exception of the present example - until the Roman Iron Age of Scandinavia when drinking-horns with animal head terminals are found in graves accompanied not by Etruscan, but by Augustan bronzes.[1]

These horn mounts were possibly made by a group of craftsmen responsible not only for other gold work in the Klein Aspergle barrow grave but also for gold finds in other sites like Schwarzenbach I [39] and Eigenbilzen [40]. They are the only pair preserved in anything like their entirety. The decoration is not identical on the two horns although both make use of the common cable design. The larger horn cap also shares with the Eigenbilzen mount - recently identified as part of another drinking-horn - dot-arcading and a sinuous wave pattern. The ribbing between the four collars (originally inlaid), the smallest of which forms a 'ruff' for the animal terminal, is a 'bead-and-reel' motif which may be seen on other early La Tène pieces [54, 63]; these are decorative features common in the contemporary pattern-books of Greek and Graeco-Etruscan art.

Apart from another Schwarzenbach mount, other horn mounts - with arcading or 'scale' design and use of the bead-and-reel - have been found in a barrow-burial at Gross Rohrheim near Darmstadt. Here, as on the Klein Aspergle pair, the gold covers a bronze sheet base.[2] The actual animal heads of Klein Aspergle are riveted on to iron rods which would have been pushed into the base of the horns.

Although the idea of animal terminals on drinking-horns may have been inspired by the much more ornate classical or Thraco-Scythian *rhyta* of the fifth century, found particularly in the Black Sea area, where in turn the influence of Achaemenian Persia may have been felt,[3] the use of the sheep or, here, perhaps a ram and his ewe, is not unknown in early La Tène iconography [65], although caprids more frequently are found with humans [55, 73, 92, 206]. The male and female pair perhaps hints at the hoped-for Otherworld companion whose presence is clearly always expected, to judge from the pairs of objects found in the early *Fürstengräber* - at Klein Aspergle even a couple of imported Greek drinking cups [41].

P. Jacobsthal, *Die Antike* X (1934), 19 ff. and Taf. 1; *ECA*, nos. 16–17, esp. pp. 111–14; *Celts*, Pl. 18; *WK*, Taf. 25; *VRD*, ill. 117–18; M. E. Mariën in (ed.) M. Renard 'Hommages à Albert Grenier', *Coll. Latomus* LVIII (1962), 1113–14 and Pl. CCXII; *EV*, 196–97 and ills.

[1] M. Ørsnes-Christiansen, *Acta Arch.* XIX (1948), 231–43; F. Tischler, *Praehist. Zeitschr.* XXXIV–XXXV (1949–50), 374–84
[2] W. Jorns, *Fundber. aus Hessen* 4 (1964), 187–89 and Abb. 4–7
[3] W. Culican, *The Medes and Persians* (1965), 120–24 and Pl. 57

45 Vieille Toulouse, Haute Garonne. Detail of bronze torc.

D. 14 cm., l. of heads c. 2·5 cm. LT A, late V/early IV BC. British Mus., London. *J. V. S. Megaw.*

The only details of the finding of this ring are those contained in the first published description by Léon Morel, from whom it was purchased by the British Museum in 1901 together with the rest of his highly important collection for the sum of £2,500 [see also **111**]; the ring, Morel writes, was found 'dans un étang sacré où il avait été jeté par les Gaulois au retour d'une expedition'! There may well be some truth in the theory of ritual deposit for which there is widespread evidence in Iron Age Europe [see notes to **179**].[1]

Animal-terminalled torcs are far from common in La Tène art; there is a fragment of a gold-covered ring in the form of a lion dredged from the Rhine[2] and, amongst later and not strictly La Tène Iron Age art, the great silver ring from Trichtingen [**216**]. Again one can cite ultimately Achaemenian parallels; the figure of Darius fleeing from Alexander on the mosaic of the Battle of the Issus from the 'House of the Faun' at Pompeii - a copy of a fourth/third century BC Hellenistic painting - is shown wearing an animal-headed torc. Contacts through the Balkans with Graeco-Iranian art could have taken place in the later stages of the early La Tène period, but despite such equally 'oriental'-looking pieces as the Klein Aspergle horn mounts [**44**], Vieille Toulouse has no feature, beyond the basic idea of an animal-headed torc, which need be regarded as non-Celtic.

The Klein Aspergle ewe and ram and the mild-looking sheep on a contemporary brooch from Panenský Týnec [**65**] offer close parallels to the French animals - Panenský Týnec wears a similar hatched collar. Other details of the ring, its ridged form, the triangular area between the ears and the blank knobs behind them all have parallels on early La Tène torcs and armrings from the Rhineland, the most probable source for Vieille Toulouse.

As to the actual animals themselves, there seems little reason to differ from the usual attribution of a pair of horse's heads even though, apart from a number of fibulae formed of freestanding horses[3] and those in profile on the Hallstatt scabbard [**30**], equines are not frequent animals in the Celtic zoo; a rather jollier horse-head balanced by that of a sheep - with a collar - forms the catch plate head of a fibula from Dürrnberg [**93**].

L. Morel, *La Champagne souterraine* (1898), 151–52 and Pl. 37:1; *ECA*, no. 123, n. 1; *KvsE*. 156; J. V. S. Megaw, *Antiq. J.* XLVII (1967), 209–13

[1] *PCB*, 19 ff.
[2] *ECA*, no. 61
[3] W. Kersten, *Praehist. Zeitschr.* XXIV (1933), 134

46 and Plate IIa Weiskirchen a.d. Saar, Kr. Merzig-Wadern, barrow I. Gold plaque on ?bronze and iron base for ornamental brooch. W. 8 cm. LT A, early IV BC. Rhein. Landesmus., Trier.

Originally there were no less than three barrow graves in the vicinity of Weiskirchen, but only two have produced grave goods. This plaque - possibly part of a large decorative brooch - was found in 1851 with a group of objects in a wooden chamber, contents of a warrior's grave. Apart from the triple-headed bronze brooch [**67**], girdlehook [62] and short iron sword in its decorated bronze sheath [109], two originally inlaid discs, part of a fibula in the form of an owl or just possibly a lion, spearheads and an iron knife, the grave contained an imported Italic beaked flagon with ornate animal-decorated handles; the Celtic owner of the flagon had caused the neck and body to be embellished with rocked-tracer engraving combining arcaded or 'scale' decoration, zigzags, bead-and-reel and half-moon motifs. Such subsequent ornamentation – finding its most extreme form in the Klein Aspergle Greek cups [41] – is known on other imported beaked flagons [113].[1]

The lobed or drooping bud ornament with its punched cable edging relates this piece at once to the gold-decorated sheet ornaments of other early La Tène princely graves. Particularly close is the mount from Eigenbilzen [40] and another possible disc fibula mount from a skeleton grave at 'Reitzegalge', Schwabsburg in Rheinhessen[2] which has the same unequal-armed-cross lay-out and lacks only the human faces; the associated grave goods of 'Reitzegalge' – two brooches (one with coral inlay), an iron ring and an openwork girdle-hook – are characteristic of the same early phase as Weiskirchen.

The four faces of the Weiskirchen plaque have no absolutely similar relations although the faces of the Czech disc [47] come closest; somewhat similar are the owl-like pair on a gold bracelet from another Saarland grave, in Reinheim [80]. Large disc brooches are known from such sites as Reinheim and Dürnberg [see 73, 138].

P. Jacobsthal, *Die Antike* X (1934), 24 ff. and Taf. 2; *JL*, 28–29; *ECA*, no. 20; *WK*, Farbtaf. II right; *CCH*, 146; *V and A*, 111; A. Haffner in *Saarland-Führer zu ur- u. frühg.* Denkmälern 5 (1966), 212–16; *EV*, ill. p. 200 above

[1] W. Kimmig, *Germania* 28 (1944–50), 46 and Abb. 2:1–2
[2] G. Behrens, *Bodenurkunden aus Rheinhessen* I (1927), 49, no. 172; *ECA*, no. 21

47 Hořovičky, Podbořany. Bronze *phalera* with iron binding strip. D. 12 cm. LT A, late V/early IV BC. Národní Muz., Prague.

This disc, the better preserved of a pair, comes from one of a number of early La Tène graves in Bohemia marked by barrows and containing evidence for the settlement of a pioneering group of horse-riding and chariot-using warriors from the west in what was otherwise an area of flat grave burial. The Hořovičky barrow with its stone cairn seems to have covered a cremation grave; on excavation in 1881 the remains of a two-wheeled chariot, a pair of bits and ten small discs, as well as the two large ones, were found; one of the latter has textile impressions still adhering to it. The discs certainly seem best explained as *phalerae* or decorative harness plaques as seen on the bridles of the Hallstatt scabbard horses [30]; other finds in the grave included two flat bronze dishes, possibly Italic imports, decorated gold sheet mounts and an iron fire-dog of Etruscan type, ancestor of a regular companion of many late La Tène burials [278–279].

The idea of *phalerae* decorated with human heads has a long history running down to the Gallo-Roman period [204–205]; art of the Black Sea region can provide a similar lay-out.[1] Here one sees the separation from the

surrounding foliage of the human face flanked by two comma-leaves which one comes across in many different Iron Age contexts including full-scale sculpture [49]. The plump clean-shaven faces with eyebrows and nose conjoined in one curved side 'T' feature and 'D'-shaped mouth are all very close to the four faces of the Weiskirchen gold plaque [46]; the only facial detail which differs is that the eyes of Hořovičky are more carefully delineated and lentoid rather than the simple button eyes of the German piece. The curious twin droplets or horns which sprout from the centre of the Hořovičky heads do crop up in even more bud-like form on material from other early graves [58]; this may be nothing more than a purely decorative treatment of the Italic satyr ears which are more explicitly copied in other early pieces [50, 54].

J. L. Píč, *Památky Arch.* XXI (1906), 162 ff., Tab. IV; *ECA*, 16, 18, 21; *KvsE*, 159, 272–73, Tab. VI; E. and J. Neustupný, *Czechoslovakia before the Slavs* (1961), Pl. 69; *CCH*, 58, 144, Pl. VIII:3; *V and A*, 111 and Taf. 3:3; W. Dehn, *Sborník Národního Muz. Praze* A XX: 1/2 (1966), 142–43; J. V. S. Megaw, *Mankind* 6 (1967), 399–400 and fig. 4

[1] *ECA, loc. cit.*; J. A. H. Potratz, *Die Skythen in Südrussland* (1963), 123 and Taf. 55

48 Dürrnberg, Hallein, grave 44, skeleton burial 2. Bronze mount. Ht. 8·3 cm. LT A, c. 400 BC. Stadtmus. Hallein. (Jacket cover) *Archaeologie Bild Berlin;* (black-and-white) *Ing. E. Penninger.*

This bronze mount formed part of the decoration of a wooden flagon together with two cut-out lobes ending in lotus buds in the manner of the Eigenbilzen gold openwork [40] or the low relief decoration of the famous Dürrnberg grave XVI bronze flagon [72]. This second of two apparently contemporary warrior's inhumation graves covered by a stone cairn lay above a main burial, which was in fact, like grave XVI, a chariot grave. The most important objects associated with the present burial, apart from the warrior's long sword, were: a late fifth-century Attic stemless black-glaze cup somewhat similar to that found at Klein Aspergle [see notes to 41] and discovered inside a great local bronze bucket; a tall pointed bronze helmet with close parallels in graves from the Marne region of France, several with chariot remains;[1] a Mediterranean cowrie shell found near the helmet; a Celtic version of the Greek or Italian 'pilgrim flask' or flat-sided bronze drinking vessel provided with four little human feet wearing pointed shoes [see notes to 32] and carefully laid-out geometric ornament executed with compasses in the manner of the fragmentary bronze jug from Eigenbilzen and a bronze mount from the early La Tène grave of Chlum in western Czechoslovakia[2] [see notes to 40]; an openwork beltplate is again decorated in a manner which recalls objects from Marnian chariot graves [112], and its central design of open S's is even more clearly anthropomorphic than the Auvers disc [42] – indeed it follows the same archetype as the flagon mount.

The actual face is based on an Italic prototype seen on imports in early La Tène graves [see notes to 50] despite its very Celtic features: the great lentoid eyes, the conjoined eyebrow curls like those of the great Rodenbach ring [55] – not intended in lieu of ears, as has sometimes been considered, since these are clearly represented – fine moustache, and the ambiguity of the tightly clinging outward and inward curving comma-leaves which may or may not be intended as hair and forked beard. The 'bib' effect can be found on the clean-shaven Schwarzenbach I mounts[3] and on the rings from the Reinheim princess's grave [79–80] and in fact another gold leaf face mount from Ferschweiler in the Rhineland Pfalz is even closer [57]. One significant detail of the construction of the Dürrnberg mount is the fine dotting of the main surfaces, giving almost the effect of etching. Similar freehand dotting is employed not only to lend light and shade to purely geometric designs such as those on the Dürrnberg pilgrim flask and the Eigenbilzen bronze but also on the anthropomorphic spout for another wooden flagon, that from Dürrnberg grave 46 [163].

The contents of Dürrnberg grave 44 with its indications of far-flung artistic no less than trading links is a fair indication of the key position the site must have held in early La Tène culture.

K. Willvonseder, *Keltische Kunst in Salzburg=Schriftreihe d. Salzburger Mus. C.A.* 2 (1960), 27 and Abb. 8; E. Penninger, *Mitt. Ges. Salzburger Ldskde.* 100 (1960), 11 and Abb. 6; id., *Germania* 38 (1960), 358–62 and Taf. 46:1; *Keltische Kunst: Bodemschatten uit Salzburg*, Frans Halsmus., Haarlem (1963), no. 21; *V and A*, 100 ff., 117, n. 9 and Taf. 3:2; W. Dehn, *Památky Arch.* LX (1969), 130f.

[1] *ECA*, 116, nos. 135–36
[2] *KvsE*, obr. 76:1; see also notes to [39]
[3] *ECA*, no. 34, [24–26]

49 Heidelberg. Fragmentary stone head. Ht. 31 cm. LT A, late V/early IV BC. Badisches Landesmus., Karlsruhe. *Landesbildstelle Baden u. Württ.* (above).

This fragment of reddish sandstone was probably originally the capping for a pillar statue such as those from Holzgerlingen [14] and Pfalzfeld [75]; it is in fact a 'Janus' or double-headed piece, but without the explicitness of Holzgerlingen whose pronounced half-moon horns have become clinging comma-leaves of precisely the type we find on the Hořovičky discs [47].

On the upper illustration the triple-lobed lotus-bud, doubtless a sacred sign like the 'hero's light' of the Irish tales, rises from the heavily emphasised eyebrows; the button eyes are double circles, a formulation found on several pieces from the early La Tène princely graves [72, 81]; the face stares as if in a state of ecstasy. The other side of the stone, by means of four carefully laid out arcs, offers a reversible face construction which, taken with the repeated comma-leaves, can hardly be intended as mere patterning; this counterpoint between the explicit and the illusory is typical Celtic visual punning.

Other clean-shaven faces crowned with comma-leaves can be found; the bronze and iron disc from a later burial in a Hallstatt barrow at Königsheim [see also notes to 31][1] and a mirror-handle from the Reinheim princess's grave in the form of the upper part of a human with upward stretched arms[2] are two examples. Parallels with brooches considered to be contemporary are not so close [91].

The Heidelberg stone may once have been associated with a cemetery since there are reports of two inhumations and one cremation grave near by. It should also be noted that clean-shaven faces such as Heidelberg and its

pendants may just as well be intended as female, rather than male, representations.

E. Wagner, *Fundstätten u. Funde im Grossherzogtum Baden* 2 (1911), 295; A. Schober, *Österr. Jahreshfte.* 26 (1930), 42 ff.; *ECA*, no. 14: *Celts*, 135, fig. 24; *VRD*, ill. 122; *CCH*, 111–12, fig. 40; *PreA* 208–09, ill. 203–04; *PAE*, 247 and Pl. 266

[1] *ECA*, no. 201
[2] F. J. Keller, *Das Keltische Fürstengrab von Reinheim* I (1965), no. 15

50 Klein Aspergle, Ldkr. Ludwigsburg. Bronze flagon. Total ht. 37 cm., ht. of handle base c. 7 cm. LT A, mid-V BC. Württ. Landesmus., Stuttgart.

The bronze flagon from the Klein Aspergle ?female cremation grave [see also notes to **41**] is the most striking and probably the earliest surviving example of the ability of Celtic craftsmen to transmute imported forms and styles, in this case, the imported Italic bronze vessels (mainly made in the workshops of Vulci) as found in early La Tène *Fürstengräber*. Here the basic model is a beaked wine flagon, as found in nearly 60 Celtic graves including those of the final Hallstatt phase and produced in Italy over a period of about a hundred years from the middle of the sixth century BC on. The distribution of imported flagons in the Celtic area overlaps with, but is more northerly than, that of imported Greek pottery; they are however absent at Este.[1]

Here, of the four faces decorating the terminal points of the squatly cast handle, the key feature is the basal unit, a face built up of a number of protuberances, with pointed ears and a forked beard resting on a stack of down-pointing leaves like a massive budding lotus in reverse. The face, for all its exploitation of the Celtic gift for caricature, is that of an Italic satyr as found decorating the shield-shaped handle mounts of the *stamnoi* made in Vulci in the first quarter of the fifth century BC and as recovered from Klein Aspergle itself, from the Marnian barrow grave of La Motte de Saint Valentin, Courcelles-en-Montagne and from the second Weiskirchen barrow burial.[2] The satyr type continues to play a key rôle in the development of a certain Celtic facial type, but the Weiskirchen *stamnos* faces with their bulging cheeks, bottle noses and lentoid eyes – not to mention crowning 'S' spirals which strongly recall at least certain versions of the Celtic comma-leaf head pieces – are so close to Celtic Klein Aspergle as to suggest that here are both the originals and the copy. The comma 'stack' is found elsewhere on early La Tène pieces [73, 75, 71].

The two smaller faces on the rim of the flagon are obviously intended as dogs and, like those on the rim of the Basse-Yutz flagons [60–61], must have been suggested by the feral terminals commonly found on such Italic flagons as that from the Weiskirchen first grave [see notes to 46]. They similarly belong to what one might term the 'protuberance' class of early La Tène facial representations; another 'protuberance' dog decorates one end of a brooch from the as yet unpublished Dürrnberg grave 2 and similar but human faces occur on another Celtic flagon from Germany [66]. It is perhaps a bit much to suggest these pudgy-jawed individuals as 'the hall-mark of sapient man'; the beetling brows, particularly that of the large upper handle face (again with satyr ears) certainly look forward to later things [164] but equally there is more than a hint of closely fitting comma-leaves.

The Klein Aspergle flagon – certainly the product of a different crafts centre to that producing the gold mounts – may well be the oldest native piece in the grave.

ECA, no. 385; *Celts*, Pl. 19; *VRD*, ill. 120–21; *V and A*, 100, 107 ff., Abb. 2, Taf. 6:1; *PAE*, 235, 241, fig. 88A, Pls. 241–2; *EV*, 202–03 and ill.

[1] *Manuel* IV, 1110–13; K. A. Neugebauer, *Jahrb. d. Deutsch. Arch. Inst.* LVIII (1943), 206–78; J. G. Szilágyi, *Acta Antiqua* I (1951–52), 419–57; O.-H. Frey in *Mostra dell' Etruria Padana e della città di Spina* II (1960), 147–52; *id.*, 'Die Enstehung der Situlenkunst', *R-G Forsch.* 31 (1968), 115–17; H. Reim, *Germania* 46 (1968), 274–85, esp. Abb. 1

[2] *ECA*, 21–22, 136–38 and Pl. 220; J. D. Beazley, *Etruscan Vase Painting* (1947), 248–49; P. J. Riis, *Acta Arch.* XXX (1959), 38; U. Schaaff, in *Festschr. Dehn*, Abb. 4 and List 3

51 Andernach, Kr. Mayen. Detail of bronze neck-ring with enamel inlay. Internal d. 14·1 cm., ht. of face 2 cm. Late LT A, IV BC. Rhein. Landesmus., Bonn. *J. V. S. Megaw.*

This hollow sheet bronze neck-ring was found in a female inhumation burial together with a pair of armlets each with two similar faces flanking a single knob and a third armlet with simple stamped circle ornament and rounded terminals. The face-decorated rings belong to one of two related classes of rings with human faces which seem to have been a speciality of the simpler women's graves of the early La Tène period Hunsrück-Eifel culture in the wooded heights between Saarbrücken, Bonn and Trier. Although faces of the type represented by the Andernach objects and the related 'Horchheim' class – in which the faces cast on to solid bronze are composed of a number of more or less triangular features with heavy ridging of the eyebrows – are usually found on rings, they occasionally appear as the catch-plates of simple belt-hooks.[1] Rings of both classes or their makers travelled south to eastern France and Switzerland and even into central Germany, an area of only sparse Celtic settlement; an old find from Bavaria recently illustrated for the first time has a pair of armlets with triple pairs of grotesque 'Andernach' faces.[2]

The closest parallel to the Andernach faces are those flanking the hood-shaped terminals of a pair of arm-rings from barrow D3 of the important 'Königsfeld', Rascheid, group near Hermeskeil, Kr. Trier.[3] The red enamel inlaid cast bronze knob has a crude palmette spiral which relates it to a number of enamelled disc terminalled rings of LT B date from southern Germany, some of which also have the lobing and diamond-shaped lozenges with stamped circles of the 'Andernach' class.[4] This women's jewellery of the later Hunsrück-Eifel culture may overlap with the period marked by the rich princely graves with their connections more towards the eastern Rhineland.

C. Koenen, *Bonner Jahrb.* 86 (1888), 150–51 and Taf. 4:3–5; J. V. S. Megaw, *Germania* 45 (1967), 50–59, esp. pp. 57–58 and Taf. 12:7; H.-E. Joachim, 'Die Hunsrück-Eifel-Kultur', *Bonner Jahrb.*, Beiheft 29 (1968), 107, 121 and Taf. 32B

[1] W. Dehn. *Trierer Zeitschr.* 20 (1952) 44, n. 67
[2] W. Torbrügge and H. P. Uenze, *Bilder zur Vorg. Bayerns* (1968), ill. 171
[3] H. Lehner, *Jahresber. Ges. f. nüztliche Forsch. zu Trier 1882–1893* (1894), 31–32 and Taf. VI:1; Dehn, *op. cit.* 45, n. 14 and 50; Megaw, *Germania* 45, *loc. cit.*
[4] *ECA*, nos. 226, 229, 232; see also notes to [145–47]

52 Spiez-Schönegg, Kt. Bern, grave 2. Detail of bronze torc. Maximum d. 15·6 cm., ht. of faces c. 1·5 cm. Early LT Ib, IV BC. Bern. Hist. Mus., Bern.

This detail of one of the two faces decorating the lower part of a neck-ring found in 1853 with a number of bracelets and amber beads in one of a series of pit graves containing sherds and cremated bone is clearly in the tradition of the 'Andernach' class rings of the Hunsrück-Eifel culture, a number of which have been found in western Switzerland although the face recalls other objects as well [54, 101].

The Spiez ring ends in ridged horse-hoof-ended terminals, a type of terminal characteristic of many rings from the Marne and eastern France; one example, one of several head-decorated rings recently published from a barrow group at Losheim, Kr. Merzig-Waldern near Saarbrücken, is that from barrow 9, a large neck-ring with plain hoof terminals and outward-looking masks of the 'Horchheim' type.[1]

The setting of three knobs between terminal and face on each half of the Spiez ring and the half-palmette ornamentation built up of 'S's – not visible in the illustration – recalls the unique silver torc allegedly found at Mâcon [77] and the combination of this type of long-chinned face with spiral motifs on a torc from Cernay-les-Reims in the Marne destroyed in World War II[2] underlines the trading in artistic motifs which seems to have been a feature of the decoration of women's ornaments in the more advanced stages of the early La Tène period.

From grave 6 of the great flat cemetery at Münsingen-Rain, Kt. Bern is a very similar hoof-ended torc which seems to be by the same craftsman as a pair of armrings from grave 9 which by association should date between LT Ia/b of the local sequence [see also notes to **56**].[3] The German 'Horchheim' class of rings like these come from women's graves and may represent a local Hunsrück-Eifel group's attempt to copy the Italian-influenced style of human representation developed by the craftsmen of the Rhineland princely graves.

The association of a 'Certosa'-derived brooch with the Spiez torc, a type not well dated in Switzerland until LT Ib, no less than the decoration of a Jugoslav sword, one of several from Srijemska Mitrovica on the Sava with a similar half-palmette design,[4] suggests the torc's fairly late position in early La Tène. The common double-punched circles can also be seen.

D. Viollier, *Les sépultures du second âge du fer sur le plateau suisse* (1916), 120 and Pl. 12, 21; J. V. S. Megaw, *Germania* 45 (1967), 52 ff. and Taf. 9:1–3

[1] A. Haffner in *Saarland=Führer zu vor- u. frühg. Denkmälern* 5 (1966), 33; *id.*, 16. *Ber. d. Staatl. Denkmalpflege im Saarland=Beiträge zur saarländ. Arch. u. Kunstgeschichte* (1969), 79–82 and Abb. 17:2
[2] P.-M. Favret, *Bull. Soc. Préhist. Française* XLVII (1950), fig. 12:8

E

[3] F. R. Hodson, *The La Tène cemetery at Münsingen-Rain* = *Acta Bernensia* V (1968), 31 and Pl. 1:666 (grave 6); Pl. 9:651–52 (grave 9)

[4] *ECA*, no. 126; Ksenija Vinski-Gasparini, *Arheološki radovi i rasprave* I (1959), 285 ff. and Tab. IV:20

53 Schwarzenbach, Kr. St Wendel, barrow II. Detail of gold armring. D. 7·2 cm.; l. of pair of faces c. 2·5 cm. LT A, mid-V BC. Formerly private collection, copy in Rhein. Landesmus, Trier. *R-G K* (*E. Neuffer*).

This hollow gold armring, the original of which was lost in the course of World War II, has its decoration arranged in a triple setting of which the illustration shows one unit; the original was much worn and had been repaired in antiquity.

The second Schwarzenbach grave [see also notes to **39**], excavated in 1849, was a warrior's burial with iron sword, spears and arrow-heads – all also now lost. An imported Vulcian beaked flagon does, however, still exist; this is of an early fifth-century type with handle in the form of a naked youth.[1]

The faces clearly belong to the Italic satyr-derived 'protuberances' type of physiognomy of the Klein Aspergle Celtic flagon [**50**] though the forked beard and pointed satyr ears are reduced almost to details of ornament; despite the damage the original piece suffered during excavation it looks, however like the work of either an apprentice or someone not used to working in gold sheet. Simpler bronze rings with triple pairs of human faces are to be found elsewhere in the Hunsrück-Eifel area.

H. Baldes and G. Behrens, *Katalog Birkenfeld* (1914), 51 ff. and Taf. 5:24; *JL*, 26–27; *ECA*, no. 58; *V and A*, 99 ff. and Taf. 6:3; H.-E. Joachim, 'Die Hunsrück-Eifel-Kultur', *Bonner Jahrb.*, Beiheft 29 (1968), 121

[1] D. K. Hill, *Am. J. Arch.* 62 (1958), 200

54 Bad Dürkheim, Kr. Neustadt, Rheinland-Pfalz. Detail of gold armring. D. 5·7 cm., l. of pair of faces c. 2·8 cm. LT A, late V/early IV BC. Hist. Mus. der Pfalz, Speyer. *Dr Carl Albiker, Karlsruhe.*

The Dürkheim barrow grave was excavated in 1864; one of several burial mounds in the area, it contained the body of a woman and no less than three imported Italic bronzes – a beaked flagon, a *stamnos* claimed to be of the early fifth century like that from Klein Aspergle, and another Vulcian piece, a complex tripod stand with lion's feet, dated in Italy by examples such as that from a c. 420 BC grave at Spina.[1] Reports of the finding of the wheels of a chariot from the Dürkheim grave, if correct, would be unusual since there are few other well-attested *female* Celtic chariot burials.

The ring has the same sharp chin and great exophthalmic eyes of the Spiez torc; similar faces peer out of the heraldic crest of the Erstfeld rings [**84**] which also have the same buffer-like junctions which remind one of the rings on such drinking horn mounts as those from Klein Aspergle [see notes to **44**]. The hair with its pointed nape is like that of the human faces of the Reinheim and Dürrnberg jug handles [**72–73**] as well as the cruder but otherwise basically similar Schwarzenbach ring illustrated above; the latter's satyr ears are also more explicitly repeated and, for its rather podgy 'bead

row' back-bone, Dürkheim substitutes a raised row of circles repeated on a piece which must be from the same workshop, the Besseringen torc [**56**].

L. Lindenschmidt, *AuhV* II:II (1870), Taf. 1–2; F. Sprater, 'Die Urgeschichte der Pfalz', *Veröffentl. d. Pfälz. Ges. z. Förderung d. Wiss.* 5 (1928), 110, 115, Abb. 122–24; *JL*, 22; *ECA*, no. 57; J. V. S. Megaw, *Germania* 45 (1967), 52 and Taf. 8:5; H.-J. Engels, 'Die Hallstatt- und Latènekultur in der Pfalz', *Veröffentl. d. Pfälz. Ges. z. Förderung d. Wiss.* 55 (1967), 50 ff.

[1] K. A. Neugebauer, *Jahrb. d. Deutsch. Arch. Inst.* LVIII (1943), 222 ff.; P. J. Riis, *Acta Arch.* XXX (1959), 38; J. G. Szilágyi, *Acta Antiqua* I (1951–52), 427–28

55 Rodenbach, Kr. Kaiserslautern, Rhineland-Pfalz. Gold armring. D. 6·7 cm. LT A, later V BC. Hist. Mus. der Pfalz, Speyer.

This spectacular gold sheet ring comes from another warrior's burial under a stone cairn in a mound first used as a Hallstatt grave contained also in a stone cairn. In the later grave there were, together with the local gold work which includes a gold finger ring [**58**], weapons including an iron sword and spears; imports included a beaked flagon, a 'pilgrim flask' with animal frieze related to the '*situla* style',[1] two bronze basins and the handle for a third. Finally there was an Attic pottery *kantharos* with geometric decoration, the 'Motte St Valentin' type named after another western barbarian grave, a barrow burial with chariot in the Marne.[2] There may also have been a decorated bronze belt hook.

The ring is again related to the gold finds from Reinheim and Erstfeld [**79–84**] as well as to a ring with three areas of palmette decoration from Zerf in the Saarland, products of a craftsman or craftsmen of considerable technical skill, let alone wide artistic range. The 'fence' of separately soldered-on balusters is only closely paralleled by the Besseringen ring illustrated below, but similar balusters crown the comparable heads on the sides of the Reinheim rings. The central human faces – both sides of the Rodenbach ring are more or less mirror images – are a simplification of the developed Celtic versions of the satyr type in which the beard has disappeared and the outline become triangular in shape; the neat fringed hair and the eyebrow-cum-nose curl formulation is still present. The button eyes and nose are not far, though, from the gold and iron plaque from Weiskirchen I [**46**]; they also have something of the south German 'mask' brooches [**91–92**].

Other details of the Rodenbach ring's ornamentation are 'orientalising' if not Etruscan. The technique of imitation plaited gold wire as used for the horns of the caprid (probably ram) supporters – not griffons as has been suggested – recalls the drop-soldering or filigree work of Etruscan jewellery. The motif of the backward-looking beast also has a long life in the Mediterranean region, although it did not reach Este and the art of the *situlae* until the fifth century [**24–26**];[3] despite the 'contouring' of the animals and their pointed ears – again found on the Erstfeld rings – looking like Scythian or even the Luristanian animal art of Persia,[4] it was probably once more northern Italy which provided the main sources; one must not forget, however, the backward-looking animals of the almost contemporary art of the Dacians [219–221]. A pin with human head and horns surmounted by the head of a ram from a hoard found at Rovalls in Gotland, south Sweden – dated to the Montelius V phase of the Nordic Bronze Age or eighth–seventh century BC – shows how universal this motif of the ram surmounting the human head is [73, 92, 206].[5]

L. Lindenschmidt, *AuhV* III: V (1881), Taf. 1–3; F. Sprater, 'Die Urgeschichte der Pfalz', *Veröffentl. d. Pfälz. Ges. z. Förderung d. Wiss.* 5 (1928), 115 and Abb. 125–30; *JL*, 25–26; *ECA*, no. 59; *V and A*, 99 ff., 114, n. 81; *PreA*, 190, ill. 184; *PAE*, 234 and Pl. 236; H.-J. Engels, 'Die Hallstatt- u. Latènezeit in der Pfalz', *Veröffentl. d. Pfälz. Ges. z. Förderung d. Wiss.* 55 (1967), 49 ff.

[1] *ECA*, 135–36, 140 and Pl. 254e, see [24] ff. esp. [27]
[2] S. Howard and F. P. Johnson, *Am. J. Arch.* 58 (1954), 191–207='Class I'; see also notes to [50]
[3] G. Behrens in *Festschr. R–GZM* I (1952), 28–30
[4] R. Ghirshman, *Artibus Asiae* XXI (1958), 37 f.; see also notes to [59]
[5] H. Hansson, *Gotlands Bronsalder* (1927), 46, fig. 30; E. Sprockhoff, *PPS* XXI (1955), 274, fig. 10:6

56 Besseringen, Kr. Merzig-Wadern. Detail of gold neck-ring. Total d. 20·5 cm., w. of centre feature 3·9 cm. LT A, V BC. Formerly Mus. f. Vor- u. Frühg., Berlin. *Dr O. Doppelfeld.*

This ring, constructed on a putty core, comes from a female cremation grave found in 1851 under a barrow apparently together with fittings for some kind of funerary car (similar to those from Kärlich), although these may be from another grave;[1] the grave also contained an Italic beaked flagon which had been used as a cremation container as in several other early La Tène graves [see also notes to **113**].

The balusters are more elegantly made than those of the great Rodenbach armlet illustrated left; the pair of pointed lotus buds relate to the early gold openwork [**39–40**, see also note to **57**]. Similar balusters can be seen on a mount from a chariot grave at Rappenau, Kr. Sinsheim.[2] The backward-looking birds, however, again have a 'foreign' look – they are certainly from a grander aviary than the homely Hallstatt 'ducks'. The birds on Protocorinthian *aryballoi* have been cited as antecedents; so at considerable distance they may be. Nearer in time and space are the long-necked birds of the Matzhausen *Linsenflasche* [see note to **27**], even down to the formalised feathers in parallel bands. Other birds executed perhaps in the same workshop tradition are those decorating the spring of the Panenský Týnec brooch [**65**], and, as one might expect, on the Erstfeld rings [**84**]. As to species, the birds look like geese, the regular companions of the war-gods in much later Celtic belief,[3] and whose bones sometimes replace those of the more common boar in central European graves.

A brooch without provenance but supposed to be from northern Italy has a similar pair of ducks or geese – Jacobsthal prefers eagles for Besseringen – with heads resting on their backs but without feet. This brooch, though one of the few pieces claimed to be of the earliest phase of La Tène art from Italy, has many features, not least its basic form, which suggest that, if it is indeed an example of 'orientalising' Celtic art, it is very much an imitation of local products.[4] Closer to Besseringen are the backward-looking birds incised on a probable belt-plaque from a woman's grave at Münsingen-Rain, Kt. Bern, grave 6, with a torc closely related to that from Spiez-Schönegg [**52**].[5] The multiple bead-row decoration of Besseringen also ends in a lotus bud element incised above two comma-leaves like an isolated leaf crown, each leaf being hatched in the centre [see notes to **49**]. The ring was lost in World War II.

L. Lindenschmidt, *AuhV* II : II (1870), Taf. 1 :3; *JL*, 21–22; W. von Jenny, *Keltische Metallarbeiten aus heidnischer und christl. Zeit* (1935), Taf. 1; *ECA*, no. 41, *WK*, Taf. 30 below; A. Haffner in *Saarland=Führer zu vor- u. frühg. Denkmälern* 5 (1966), 170–72 and ill. p. 171

[1] Besseringen: *ECA*, no. 154; Kärlich: *ECA*, no. 167 [see also notes to **33**]
[2] *ECA*, no. 76 and Pl. 243c; see also notes to [**101**]
[3] *PCB*, 272–73
[4] *ECA*, no. 297
[5] *ECA*, no. 365; F. R. Hodson, *The La Tène cemetery at Münsingen-Rain=Acta Bernensia* V (1968), Pl. I, esp. no. 678; for birds see also Jacobsthal, *Greek Pins* (1956), 118, n. 1

57 Ferschweiler, Kr. Bitburg. Gold leaf mount. Ht. 4 cm. LT A, later V BC. Rhein. Landesmus., Trier.

The Ferschweiler barrow grave contained not only a beaked flagon but, also imported, a flat-based bronze solid cast beaker, a type which dates the deposition of goods in the burial not before the middle of the century.[1]

The gold mount with signs of bronze patina and a slight convex cross-section suggesting its having been mounted on a bronze fitting of some sort, is roughly cut around the edge of the *repoussé* design. The face itself, with tiny satyr ears placed at the side of the temples, is of the triangular format which, now without any clear indication of a beard at all but retaining a good fulsome moustache, is the type of a number of other related pieces from princely graves with fifth/fourth-century imports [**58–62**]; a bronze fibula from Dürrnberg, an old and isolated find discovered in 1886, has a very similar face above the provision for the spring.[2] An important feature is the closely clinging hatched 'S' curls, something which recalls the patterning of the Eigenbilzen and Klein Aspergle mounts [**40–41**]. The triple-pronged 'crowning' feature of the Ferschweiler face might be seen as a parallel to Rodenbach [**55**]; both, but particularly the mount, are in fact close to the face on an Etruscan earring from the district of Parma.[3]

P. Steurer in *Schumacher-Festschr.* (1930), 166–68 and Abb. 2; *ECA*, no. 30; *WK*, Farbtafel II; *V and A*, 100 and Taf. 3:1

[1] *ECA*, 139 and Pl. 254c
[2] M. Hell, *Germania* 27 (1943), 65–68 and Abb. 1; *ECA*, no. 307
[3] O. Montelius, *La Civilisation Primitive en Italie* I ser. B (1895), Pl. 98 :4; E. Soudská, *Arch. roz.* XX (1968), 464

58 Rodenbach, Kr. Kaiserslautern, Rheinland-Pfalz. Gold finger ring. D. 2·1 cm. LT A, later V BC. Hist. Mus. der Pfalz, Speyer. *Dr Carl Albiker, Karlsruhe.*

This finger ring is one of the very few Celtic finger rings with figural decoration [see also **88, 169**]; only one other ring, contemporary, and with the unlikely provenance 'Sardinia', is, as Jacobsthal describes the present ring, 'a Janus head in flat projection',[1] though of course adjoining heads are not uncommon elsewhere in Celtic art [53–54, 70]. Jacobsthal again may be correct in seeing an ultimate origin for this type of ring in Etruria – one of two silver rings from grave 40 in the cemetery of the Celtic Senones at Montefortino dated to some time in the fourth century has a double portrait of an old Senon with a beard. There is little, however, which is not Celtic in this so-called 'orientalising' ring from Rodenbach, despite the formal similarities which this type of material may call to mind – similarities which include the late eighth-century art of Luristan[2] no less than jewellery from Graeco-Etruscan Spina.

The Rodenbach faces, with clean-shaven chins but full Celtic moustaches such as even classical artists depicted them wearing, are closely related to the triangular form of the Ferschweiler fragment, the Weiskirchen I girdle-hook, or the Basse-Yutz flagons [57, 60–62]. The tightly clinging leaves terminating in the ubiquitous triple circle motif are, as might be expected, found in other gold work from the princely graves, including the Sardinian finger ring and that from Zerf, Kr. Saarburg, found with Etruscan imports[3] as well as the Klein Aspergle open-work [41]; the upward-slanting eyes, though not common, again can be found elsewhere in early La Tène art [149]. The unit of 'S' spirals and central lotus bud motif dividing the two heads – an economical plant in which one bud does duty for both aspects – is hardly anything other than a decorative 'fill-in' device related to the general horticultural vocabulary of the Celtic gold-smith's pattern-book.

JL, 25; *ECA*, no. 72, esp. pp. 124–26; *V and A*, 98 ff., Abb. 2H and Taf. 2:1–4; *PAE*, 234 and n. 22, Pl. 236 inset

[1] *V and A*, loc. cit., Abb. 1:1 and Taf. 1:1–4
[2] M. E. Mariën in (ed.) H. Reykers, *Analecta Arch.: Festschr. Fritz Fremersdorf* (1960), 265–67 and Taf. 69–70
[3] *ECA*, no. 73; *V and A*, 98–99 and Taf. 2:5–6

59 Bad Dürkheim, Kr. Neustadt, Rhineland-Pfalz. Gold openwork fragment. LT A, late V/early IV BC. Ht. of face c. 1·7 cm. Hist. Mus. der Pfalz, Speyer.

This is a detail from a section of rectangular-shaped gold openwork rather crudely executed with a combination of scallops, hatched leaves and cut out swastika-like elements. What is not immediately apparent is that two fragments have a face substituted for the normal central bud of the lotus bloom; one only of these is illustrated here. This is in fact the most remarkable example of visual punning or 'shape changing' in the entire repertoire of early Celtic art. As viewed normally, the face, with tight clinging side curls and surmounted by a palmette stack in the manner of the somewhat later upper face of the Reinheim flagon handle [73] seems a fairly straightforward clean-shaven Celt of the 'protuberances' class as on the lost ring from Schwarzenbach II [53] or the heavy-browed individual at the top of the Klein Aspergle flagon handle [50]. When the illustration is reversed, however, the shape changes into that of an old bearded man, just like those on Italic rings, usually considered as the prototypes for the 'Janus' finger

ring from Rodenbach illustrated above. An unstratified girdle-hook with huge lobed 'crown' from the Kleiner Gleichberg at Steinsburg in Central Germany again seems to show the same dumb-bell nose feature.[1]

There is no precise parallel for this kind of visual *double entendre* in La Tène art, though other kinds of trick images can be perceived from time to time [158, 163]; the throat decoration of the Basse-Yutz flagons [60–61] could also be read as a reversible image based on the palmette.[2] The source for the Rodenbach 'funny face' – an artistic formula still followed by New Guinea wood carvers, poster designers and the illustrators of children's magazines – must again be Italic. The 'Silen' version with, literally for a change, a leaf crown, is of course common enough, but clean-shaven faces protrude as ornamental features on Apulian red-figure vases of c. 350 BC like that related to the work of the Iliupersis painter and cited by Jacobsthal in connection with the fourth-century Italo-Celtic helmet from Umbria [108].[3] It is more difficult to decide whether the Dürkheim 'funny face' is intended as two significant alternatives, such as male and female, youth and old age, sorrow and happiness – or just a 'joke motif'; but then it is just this – probably – unconscious ambiguity which is so much a keynote of Celtic art.

ECA, no. 28; J. V. S. Megaw, *Mankind* 6 (1967), 395, fig. 1a; id., *Pfälzer Heimat* 20 (1969), 85–86

[1] G. Neumann 'Das Gleichberggebiet', *Werte der deutsch. Heimat* 6 (1963), 14 ff. and Abb. 13: 30; H. Kauffmann, *Jahresschr. mitteldt. Vorg.* 50 (1966), 215–16 and Abb. 4a
[2] *ECA*, P 425
[3] P. Jacobsthal, *Ornamente griechischer Vasen* (1927), Pl. 117c; *ECA*, 16 and Pl. 219a

60–61 and Plate III Basse-Yutz, Thionville-Est, Moselle. Pair of bronze flagons with ?coral and enamel inlay. Total ht. [60], 39·4 cm. [61], 40·4 cm., w. of shoulder c. 19 cm. LT A late V/early IV BC. British Mus., London. [Plate III, 60] *courtesy Trustees of the British Museum*; [61] *J. V. S. Megaw*.

These two not quite identical Celtic imitations of Italic beaked flagons were found in 1927 by workmen, together with a pair of imported *stamnoi*, simpler and rather later than those in the Klein Aspergle and Weiskirchen graves [see notes to 50]. It seems likely that all four objects originally formed part of the contents of yet another *Fürstengrab* and although no other site has ever produced a pair of flagons, pairing of objects is a common feature of the Celtic funerary symposium.

The flagons, products of some Rhineland-based workshop, have been frequently illustrated, but, beyond Jacobsthal's discussion of various details of their decoration, and Smith's original publication, really still await a full stylistic analysis. Technically they are most accomplished pieces; the main body is hammered out of a single sheet of bronze now finely patinated. The slightly concave profile and sharp shoulders are shared by another local flagon [72] and by one recently recovered from a barrow burial at St Geneviève-des-Bois (Loiret)[1] as well as by contemporary wheel-made pottery from the Marne and elsewhere; the closest parallel is a pottery imitation of a beaked flagon – one of several – from the Hallstatt cemetery.[2] The handle and rim fittings are separate castings attached to the body and, at the rim, to one of three separate plates – the other two being the 'collar' round the base and a shield-shaped plate riveted to the throat. Each plate has been provided with spaces cut to take coral inlays, the whole then being attached to the main body and the engraved ornament being added last of all. A stopper attached by a chain to the mouth and also the decorative areas on the curve of the handle of each flagon have provision for enamel inlay;[3] the eyes of the faces at the base of the handle, like the settings of the rim and base mounts, were probably originally of coral, possibly of east Mediterranean origin – only one 'eye' survives [Plate IIIa].

The faces, despite the great circular eyes, are closely related to the triangular 'satyr'-derived faces with tightly clinging 'S' curls of the type represented by Ferschweiler, Rodenbach, and the Dürrnberg 1886 fibula [57–58]; one can also add the rather crude human faces on the rim of the flagon from Borsch [66] which Jacobsthal maintained was by the same hand as Basse-Yutz. The handle beasts, dogs rather than wolves, are the most nomadic of all the animals in early Celtic art; the pointed and scrolled ears and emphasised shoulder curls in lieu of musculature can be readily paralleled in the contemporary Scythian animal style where the influence of wood-carving techniques amongst metal-workers is clearly strong.[4] Very close are the heads on the only La Tène double-dog-headed fibula – that from the Leopoldau, Vienna, cemetery [see also notes to 32];[5] the backward-looking griffons on the catch-plate of the Parsberg fibula, another piece considered to be by the Basse-Yutz master, have similar pelts produced by freehand incised dashes as well as shoulder curls [63]. An unprovenanced handle in the British Museum and a bronze mould for a fibula of the Dürrnberg 1886 type from Louny in Bohemia again show the 'nomadic' element, perhaps the most elusive component in early Celtic art to trace to its immediate source.[6]

The ducks swimming unconcernedly up the spouts of the flagons have good parallels in the standing pair on a bronze comb from Aigle, Lausanne;[7] the origins of this bird lie in the aquatic birds of the Hallstatt period,[8] but here there can be little cultic intention but rather the simple expression of a neatly observed bit of nature.

The non-representational decorative elements include several variations on the palmette motif. It has been suggested that the classical date of the supposed prototypes of the throat palmette [here illustrated on Plate IIIb, a detail from 61] make it impossible to place its imitation north of the Alps earlier than the fourth century. Certainly the split palmettes executed freehand on Basse-Yutz have parallels on other native material of presumed fourth-century date [see notes to 52], and the ending of the individual lines of the incised fronds with a dot is an engraver's trick which extends even to British insular La Tène art [114, 252]; the crude palmettes originally inlaid with enamel on the handles could also be compared with similar features on disc-ornamented torcs of definitely La Tène B type.[9] On the other hand the punched concentric circles, plaited zigzag – with dotted background – and maze- or meander-filled squares are all within the repertoire of such scabbard engravers as those responsible for the ornamentation of the swords from Hallstatt [30] and Vert-la-Gravelle,[10] whose date can hardly be later than 400 BC; though the throat palmette is similar to details of the 'Comacchio' bronzes [117], where the design is built up entirely of punched stippling, stippling also occurs on the belt-hook from Hoppstädten barrow 2 [see notes to 42], and so once more a date at least early in the fourth century can be advanced. Despite the fourth-century date generally assumed for the *stamnoi* (largely on the supposed date of the flagons!) if all four objects did come from a single grave, there is certainly evidence for the burying of heirlooms [see notes to 78].

R. A. Smith, *Archaeologia* LXXIX (1929), 1–12; P. Jacobsthal, *Jahrb. d. Deutsch. Arch. Inst.* XLIV (1929), 198–223; R. Forrer and H. Linckenheld, *Cahiers d'Arch. et d'Hist. d'Alsace* (1933), 101 ff.; Jacobsthal, *Die Antike* X (1934), 28 ff., Abb. 9 and Taf. 5; *ECA*, no. 381 a–b; *PP*, XXIII and Pl. I; *Besançon*, 20–21, 30n. 49, and Abb. 7; *WK*, Taf. 81; J.-P. Millotte, 'Carte archéologique de la Lorraine (Ages du Bronze et du Fer)', *Ann. Litt. Univ. de Besançon* 73=*Arch.* 18 (1965), 58, no. 26; *V and A*, 100 ff., 119–22 and Abb. 2F; *PreA*, 192–93, ill. 187–90; *PAE*, 235 ff., Pl. 246

[1] *Gallia* XVII (1959), 318–22
[2] *ECA*, no. 406
[3] F. Henry, *Préhistoire* II (1933), 65 ff. and fig. 2:4
[4] T. Talbot Rice, *The Scythians* (1957), 188, 191 and Pl. 45; I. Venedikov, *Arkheologia* (Sofia) VIII (1966), 7–15 and obr. 6
[5] *ECA*, no. 315A; R. Pittioni, *Urg. des österreich. Raumes* (1954), Abb. 468 below
[6] British Museum: *ECA*, no. 384; Louny: *KvsE*, 232, 364 and Tab. CXXV:3
[7] *ECA*, no. 375
[8] E. Sprockhoff, *PPS* XXI (1955), 259 ff; G. Cordier, *Rev. Arch.* (1966:1), 79–88
[9] *ECA*, nos. 229, 234
[10] *ECA*, no. 90 17; U. Osterhaus in *Festschr. Dehn*, 134 ff.

62 Weiskirchen, Kr. Merzig-Wadern, barrow I. Bronze belt-plaque with coral inlay. W. 6·6 cm. LT A, late V BC. Rhein. Landesmus., Trier.

This girdle or belt-hook plate is the piece most closely related in style to the twin flagons from Basse-Yutz illustrated above. Certainly it is the product of a different and probably later workshop than the gold mount from the same grave [46] which has a more archaic appearance than any other object associated with the burial.

The ground line for the Siamese-twin sphinx-griffons is provided for by alternate rows of 'bead-and-reel' inlay and diagonally hatched cable ornament, while the damaged area of coral inlay forming the central platform appears to be built up from a series of interlocking comma-leaves. Another, rather cruder belt-plaque from Schwabsburg, Ldkr. Mainz has a similar deposition of ornament.[1] The central face with its pronounced cheeks and its lantern jaw surmounted by scrolled eyebrows is clearly related to the basal handle faces of Basse-Yutz and to their parallels. The hatched 'S' curls which crown the head and which like everything else in this subtly balanced design do double duty – in this case as tails of the inner griffon pair – are in fact the tight-clinging curls of the Basse-Yutz split palmette pushed up through a right angle; the whole facial unit recalls the openwork triangular plaque found with the Dürrnberg grave 44 bronze mount [48].

As to the male sphinxes, these are certainly 'orientalising' in form, but it is not necessary, as one writer has

69

done, to go as far afield as Achaemenian reliefs such as those at Persepolis which show similar horned beasts. There is, in the second Weiskirchen barrow, in addition to the fifth-century *stamnos* compared with the Klein Aspergle flagon [50], a thin gold band decorated with ten seated sphinxes with horned helmets.[2] Such sixth-century Etruscan pieces – as this is generally now considered to be – could well have formed the basis for the peculiar Celtic horned hybrids, usually with backward-turning heads,[3] which can be seen on objects other than the Weiskirchen I girdle plate [63–64]. Such backward-looking heads are unknown in Etruscan art though not in the art of the *situlae*. Other pieces also have human heads surmounted with knobbed horns or crests, these examples being the Parsberg brooch [63], the upper handle animal of the Dürrnberg flagon [72], and a brooch from a barrow cemetery at Riekofen, Ldkr. Regensburg, in Bavaria.[4] One detail of the outer pair of Weiskirchen sphinx-griffons is that they appear to be wearing pointed shoes of the Hallstatt-Manětín-Dürrnberg type [30–32]. For a special Celticised class of true griffons of late fifth-century date there are the girdle-hooks of the cemeteries of Italy and immediately north of the Alps [95–99].

ECA, no. 350; A. Haffner in *Saarland=Führer zu vor- u. frühg. Denkmälern* 5 (1966), ill. p. 213 below; *PAE*, 235 and Pl. 240

[1] *ECA*, no. 351
[2] *ECA*, 136, 140 and Pl. 254d
[3] G. Behrens in *Festschr. R–GZM* I (1952), 28–30
[4] L. Lindenschmidt, *AuhV* V (1911), Taf. 20:320; P. Reinecke, *Festschr. R-GZM* (1902), 73 ff. and Taf. VI:2; *ECA*, 128, n. 8; W. Torbrügge and H.P. Uenze *Bilder zur Vorg. Bayerns* (1968) 219 and ill. 258; see also notes to [65, 68]

63 Kleinmittersdorf, Ldkr. Parsberg, Oberpfalz. Bronze brooch. L. 8·8 cm. LT A, c. 400 B.C. Germanisches Nationalmus., Nürnberg (detail). *Dr Carl Albiker, Karlsruhe.*

It is unfortunate that precise details are not known of the discovery of this fine brooch from a Bavarian barrow. The original account indicates that there was at least one skeleton grave under the barrow associated with some seven other brooches, an iron single-edged knife characteristic of many early La Tène barrow burials, and a belt-hook and clasp, part only of which now survives. These fibulae include one 'Certosa'-derived brooch and two in the form of standing horses. Horse fibulae, a north Bavarian speciality, have been found with another human face brooch at Schwieberdingen [89] and at the Staffelberg fortified settlement site near Lichtenfels.[1] These brooches can be compared with the horses on the Hallstatt scabbard [30]. All three brooches have the large knobs at the spring end which seem to be a special feature of brooches made by a Bavarian-based work-shop. The belt-hook has a clean-shaven head which is in general form a simplified version of the Dürrnberg grave 44 mount [48] and the Holzgerlingen pillar statue [14].

The present brooch would certainly fit well into such a context although its stylistic eclecticism makes it difficult to decide which are its closest artistic relatives. The human face, a fine Celtic grotesque with bulbous, bibulous nose, its pronounced widow's peak coming down to a central 'caste mark', fine long mustachios and dot eyes and nostrils (probably for enamel enrich-ment) has a near twin from eastern Czechoslovakia illustrated below. The jug-handle ears – seen earlier on the Manětín brooch [31] and the Dürrnberg grave 44 mount – link the face with the upper handle face on the Dürrnberg flagon [72]; two flattened horns are placed above the temples somewhat in the manner of the basal handle head on the Dürrnberg flagon. The great lower face, with its crowning palmette terminating in a lotus bud and partially incised on the body of the brooch after the casting of the main form, is really another Celticised satyr complete with pointed ears, a more horrendous and individual interpretation than that based on the same archetype by the maker of the Dürrkheim ring [54]. Closer in fact are the Schwarzenbach faces [53]; traces of enamel remain in the left eye. The pair of griffons of the spring plate – so different in style to the human faces that, if versatility were not the keynote of early La Tène art, it would be tempting to suggest they were the work of a different craftsman to the one respon-sible for the original model from which the brooch was cast – are precisely in the manner of the Basse-Yutz wild beasts, 'shoulder curls' and all; the griffons' tails form two parts of the common triple circle motif.

The incised decoration on the sides of the brooch in-cludes a comma-leaf and two linked 'S' curls forming a leaf collar rather than leaf crown which curls down from behind the ears of the upper face; similar comma-leaves incised or in the round occur on other ornate brooches [65, 69]. The cast ornament of the upper surface – some-thing like that of the Besseringen gold torc [see notes to 56] – includes, as a literal tie between the chin of the upper face and the palmette-lotus bud, a short length of 'bead-and-reel' decoration [see notes to 44, 86]. In general, despite those various parallels, it seems difficult to ascribe any other piece with certainty to the manufac-turer of the Parsberg brooch with the exception of the Stupava plaque [64]; the development of individualism and individual styles owing nothing directly to outside influences is a feature of later art associated with graves.

J. Naue, *Prähist. Blätter* XIV (1902), 1–8 and Taf. 1; W. Kersten, *Praehist. Zeitschr.* XXIV (1933), 133; *ECA*, no. 316; *WK*, Taf. 31; *V and A*, 113–14, 117; *PreA*, 192 and ill. 186; *PAE*, 237 and Pl. 248; W. Torbrügge and H.P. Uenze, *Bilder zur Vorg. Bayerns* (1968), 219 and ill. 259; *EV*, 193 and ill.

[1] Schwieberdingen: *ECA*, no. 321; Staffelberg: Kersten, *Praehist. Zeitschr.* XXIV, 133 and Abb. 8:10. On the 'Certosa' brooch type see now Margarita Primas, *JR-GZM* 14 (1967), 99–123, esp. p. 121ff.

64 Stupava, okr. Teplice. Bronze plaque 6·6 × 3·3 cm. LT A, c. 400 B.C. Slovenské Národné Múz., Brati-slava. *W. and B. Forman (Artia, Prague).*

This plaque is the easternmost find of the earliest phase of La Tène art; it was found in 1929 in a disturbed grave, one of some ten forming a flat cemetery in the vicinity of Bratislava,[1] capital of Slovakia, an area which in the Iron Age had a mixed population of eastern nomads, western Celts and a local population virtually unchanged since earlier Bronze Age times. Although there are no certain associations with the plaque, the presence of typical early La Tène warrior's equipment suggests that the site, in what otherwise was part of the late East Hallstatt culture, marks a pioneering extension from the main Austrian La Tène centres [see notes to **30, 32**].

The face on the plaque, cast in one with the main rectangle of what may have been an ornamental lid, shows that this piece must have been brought from somewhere in the general Rhineland region; indeed it may be fairly claimed to be by the same hand or hands as the Parsberg brooch illustrated above. Like Parsberg, the plaque bears subsequent incised ornamentation, the upper border consisting of a series of running waves with filled-in hatching such as may be seen on another western import, the Panenský Týnec brooch [**65**], as well as other slightly later bronzes.[2] A cruder face in a similar position on a bronze plaque with signs of gilding and crude flanking ornament with pseudo-leaf crowns comes from Rainberg, Salzburg.[3]

Flanking the face and not readily recognisable for what they are until the plaque is reversed, is a pair of supporting griffons with long, almost equine rather than aquiline beaks such as are found in the round decorating other German brooches [**69**]. In view of the 'orientalising' supporters of such obviously western pieces as the Weiskirchen I belt-plaque [**62**], not too much should be made of Stupava's find-spot being close to areas where such features might be artistically more at home. Indeed the technique with which the griffons are delineated – hatching, curls at the joints and stipple shading – recall the plant scroll on the tip of the Hallstatt sword and the fragmentary design on the rim of the sieve from the Hoppstädten barrow 2 main grave [see notes to **30**]; the Boldù-Dolfin I *situla* from Este does, however, have very similar griffons so, as with Hallstatt, the influence of other styles, however transmitted, is certainly present[4] [see also notes to **221**].

J. Eisner, *Časopis spol. přátel staro. v Praze* XXXVIII (1930)=*V. Šimák Festschr.*, 12–20; id., *Slovensko v Pravěku* (1933), 168 ff. and Tab. LII–III; L. Franz, *Praehist. Zeitschr.* XXVIII–XXIX (1937–38), 406 ff. and Abb. 2:1; *KvsE*, 269, 284, 421–22, obr. 79; W. and B. Forman and J. Poulík, *Prehistoric Art* (1956), ill. 123; *CCH*, 55–58 and fig. 23; J. Paulík et al., *Život a umenie doby železnej na Slovensku* (1962), 167 and obr. 47; T. G. E. Powell, *Antiquity* XXXIX (1965), 69; id., *Sborník Národního Muz. v Praze* A XX: 1/2 (1966), 133–36 and Tab. XVIIIa; *EV*, 194–95 and ill.

[1] B. Benadík, *Slov. Arch.* XI (1963), 372–73
[2] *ECA*, nos. 140, 401 and PP 129–31, 133
[3] M. Hell, *Arch. Austriaca* 36 (1964) 50–56
[4] G. Ghirardini, *Mon. Antichi* X (1900), 71–94 and Tav. IV; *Mostra dell'arte delle situle del Po al Danubio* (1961), no. 25; O.-H. Frey, 'Die Enstehung der Situlenkunst', *R–G Forsch.* 31 (1968), no. 36; see also notes to [**76, 90**]

65 Panenský Týnec, Louny. Bronze brooch. Total l. 10·2 cm., l. of sheep's head c. 1·3 cm. LT A, V BC. Národní Muz., Prague.

This brooch was found in the course of the last century in a flat grave near Louny in Bohemia and, together with the Hořovičky *phalerae* [**47**] and Stupava plaque [**64**], is part of the evidence of the penetration of Czechoslovakia in the LT A period by numbers of warrior chieftains of western origin.

Unlike that of the Parsberg fibula [**63**] which may be a somewhat later piece, the decoration of the Czech brooch seems to be wholly cast; the sheep head, with its crest looking like a character from *Alice through the Looking Glass*, may be compared with the more realistic Klein Aspergle drinking-horn animals [**44**] or the animal heads on the Erstfeld rings [**84**]; the crest, however, is also paralleled on a local series of brooches from the east Hallstatt region of Croatia, a region which may have been instrumental in introducing the idea of animal- and human-decorated fibulae into the Celtic world.[1] Like Erstfeld, too, is the general form of the bird of prey mantling its wings above the spring of the brooch. Even closer is an unprovenanced bird-decorated girdle-hook in the Rheinisches Landesmuseum, Trier;[2] the hook has provision for large circular insets like those on the Manětín fibula [**31**]. Brooches made in the shape of birds on the wing are known from other early La Tène burials; no less than four were found at Dürrnberg in a disturbed grave which probably contained the bodies of both a man and a woman.[3] The occurrence of birds on ornate local brooches, again from the east Hallstatt area, especially the Vače cemetery, may point to a source in contemporary Greek art as with the birds which actually appear on the decorated *situlae* [see notes to **24**].

Of the decorative elements on the Panenský Týnec brooch, the wave-like fleece is adapted from a fairly common classically derived motif [see notes to **64**], and the linked curved lobes at the apex of the bridge are found both on bronzes and sheet gold work. The 'basketry' or hatched ornament not only decorates the bow but also forms the feathers of the bird – for which, like the Besseringen birds [**56**], it is again possible but not necessary to find eastern parallels amongst contemporary Graeco-Scythian art of the mid-fifth century BC.[4] Both bird and sheep wear collars in the manner of the Vieille Toulouse torc [**45**]. The basketry is an important feature in linking Panenský Týnec with Erstfeld [**84**], Reinheim [**80**] and the Borsch flagon fragments (illustrated below); it is thus another piece considerably east of at least its artistic pendants. Another brooch whose decoration has certain points of similarity is that from Riekhofen, Ldkr. Regensburg [see also notes to **62**] with both hatching and scrolled ornament like the Hoppstädten, barrow 2 sieve.[5]

ECA, no. 318; *KvsE*, 81–82, 371 and Tab. IV:3–V; J. V. S. Megaw, *Antiq. J.* XLVII (1967), 209 and Pl. XLIb; *PreA*, 192 and ill. 185; *EV*, 196–97 and ill.

[1] (Ed.) A. Mahr, *Treasures of Carniola: The Mecklenburg Collection* (1934), 34–35, 55–56, Pl. XII ff.; S. Gabrovec, *Arheološki Vestnik* XVII (1966) 185 ff.
[2] W. Dehn, *Praehist. Zeitschr.* XXXIV–XXXV:1 (1949–50), 329–35
[3] M. Hell, *Mitt. d. Anthrop. Ges. Wien* LVIX (1929), 161 ff. and Abb. 4:4–7
[4] P. Jacobsthal, *Proc. British Acad.* XXVII (1941), 309 n. 2
[5] L. Kilian, *Trierer Zeitschr.* 24–26 (1956–58), Taf. 19:5

66 Borsch, Kr. Bad Salzungen. Fragmentary bronze flagon (body modern). Ht. handle 17 cm. LT A, late V BC. Vorg. Mus., Friedrich-Schiller-Universität, Jena.

This flagon was found acting not as part of the normal

setting of the funerary feast but as a cremation container for a burial under one of a group of barrows. Together with a local geometric decorated pot was a single-edged iron knife with curved handle grip, a type found frequently in more southerly and westerly early La Tène graves. The early accounts also mention a fragment of a bronze plaque with *repoussé* decoration in the form of a long-legged stork-like bird.

There can be little doubt that the flagon is a product of the same crafts-centre which produced the Panenský Týnec brooch – but perhaps not the Basse-Yutz flagons as Jacobsthal claims, despite their having such features in common as the nomadic style 'shoulder curls'. It also seems best to regard the find-spot of the flagon as the result of local barter for salt by the non-Celtic communities of Thuringia [see also notes to **94**]. Handles in the shape of animals are common enough in the classical world, but in Celtic art there is only the unprovenanced handle in the British Museum [see notes to **60–61**] and the devouring beast crouching on the upper part of the Dürrnberg flagon [**72**]. Both the hatching of the Borsch beast's pelt and its slender claws may be compared with Panenský Týnec; the lower end of the animal terminates in outspread feet which do double duty as the front paws of a little pointed-eared face which in turn grows out of the handle animal's tail. The pointed ears with their horizontal hatching look very like the little grotesque on the catch-plate of a brooch found on the outskirts of Prague [**90**] as well as a very different-looking piece, the strap end from Herrnsheim, Kr. Worms, where the 'ears' are part of a 'leaf crown' [see also notes to **77–78**]. Hatched commas-within-commas can be seen also incised on the Besseringen ring [**56**] and the gold leaf faces from Schwarzenbach.[1]

The two more or less human faces on the rim of the flagon also have feline ears. These faces, with their bulbous noses, neatly fringed hair and circles delineating the pupils, have a number of fairly close parallels amongst material from the general area of Bavaria – the Parsberg brooch [**63**] and one of four decorated fibulae from Oberwittighausen [**91–92**]. Although they have something of the Klein Aspergle prototype of the 'protuberance' class [**50**], even down to the pod-shaped beards, the Borsch faces do seem more at home with rather later material such as the very similar dwarf-headed twin animals of the Dürrnberg flagon and a belt-hook from Schwabsburg near Mainz.[2]

P. Reinecke in *Festschr. R-GZM* (1902), 72 and Taf. VI:1; G. Eichhorn, *Thüringen* 2 (1926), 85 ff.; R. A. Smith, *Archaeologia* LXXIX (1929), 6, Pl. IV:13; *JL*, 30; L. Franz, *Der Spatenforscher* 8 (1943), 12 ff.; *ECA*, no. 383; *V and A*, 114–15 and Taf. 7:5; H. Kaufmann, *Jahresschr. mitteldt. Vorg.* 50 (1966), 211 and Abb. 6; *PAE*, 235 and Pl. 243

[1] Herrnsheim: *ECA*, no. 366; Schwarzenbach: *ECA*, no. 34²¹⁻²⁶; see also notes to [**48**]

[2] *ECA*, no. 351

67 Weiskirchen, Kr. Merzig-Wadern, barrow I. Details of bronze fibula with provision for ? coral setting. Total l. 4 cm.; l. of central face (right), c. 1·5 cm.; catch-plate face (left), c. 1 cm. LT A/B1, early IV BC. Rhein. Landesmus., Trier.

This brooch together with the short sword [**109**] are probably the latest objects in the grave [see also notes to **46, 62**]. It is one of three fibulae with no less than four human faces worked into the design; the other two brooches are also from barrow burials: Butzbach, Kr. Friedberg, and Rüdesheim, Kr. Rheingau (now lost).[1] Details of two of the Weiskirchen faces are shown here – the face above the catch-plate (left) and one of the two central faces which take up most of the bow, the top of which has a pointed oval socket originally filled with some viscous substance to hold a setting of coral or enamel as with the lost but very similar, if cruder, Rüdesheim brooch.

The two central faces are of the utmost interest for the elucidation of the subsequent, third-century development of La Tène art [**158** ff.] since they are patterned constructions rather than attempts at true representations of human physiognomy. The cheeks, for example, are peltas or hollow-sided triangles and the brows single comma-leaves meeting at their narrow ends – a feature which, devoid of any representational hints, can be seen on the brooch from Ostheim, Ldkr. Mellrichstadt [**69**]. The tiny mouth and chin also look forward to the shape of things to come [**167, 169**], although the later pieces are even more strictly 'patterned', being based on a break-down of the old classical palmette-lyre motif.

The faces above the spring and catch-plate also have 'comma' brows forming a sort of widow's peak in the style of Parsberg [**63**] and Stupava [**64**]; the inward-instead of outward-looking faces of the Butzbach brooch are similar, if again cruder. Several features recall the fragmentary brooch from the Reinheim princess's grave[2] – perhaps once provided with two heads since the spring end has not survived. As on the Reinheim brooch, the catch-plate of the Weiskirchen fibula does duty as an arm upon which one head rests his clean-shaven, jutting chin, in profile also like the triple pairs of the Dürkheim ring [**54**]. The same feature can be seen on the now destroyed brooch in the form of a human-headed beast from Langenlonsheim, Kr. Kreuzenach.[3] A simple double-lined zigzag joining the terminal heads with those in the centre (not clear in the detailed views) also runs on either side of the Reinheim brooch bow, and the simple cable patterning framing the central faces not only runs down the 'body' of the Reinheim fibula but frames the 'owls' on the larger armring from the same site [**80**]. Another brooch which links both Weiskirchen and Reinheim is a brooch with single head at the catch-plate end with the body of the brooch acting as a neck rather than arm as is the case with the Weiskirchen rear head; this brooch came from Zerf, Kr. Saarburg, and was found with Etruscan imports, as well as a gold finger ring [see notes to **58**] and hollow armring with palmette decoration precisely paralleled by the large Rodenbach ring [**55**] and one of the smaller rings in the Erstfeld, Kr. Uri gold find [see notes to **84**].[4]

All these clues seem to indicate an advanced date in the earliest La Tène phase for the Weiskirchen brooch which none the less belongs to the main stream of fibulae decorated with human and animal faces which seems to have been a speciality of craftsmen based on the princely centres of the Middle Rhineland.

ECA, no. 290; A. Haffner in *Saarland=Führer zu vor- u. frühg. Denkmälern* 5 (1966), ill. p. 214 (top left); *V and A*, 128 and Taf. 10:2

[1] Butzbach: *ECA*, no. 296; Rüdesheim: *ECA*, no. 294

[2] F. J. Keller, *Das keltische Fürstengrab von Reinheim* I (1965), no. 13
[3] *ECA*, no. 319
[4] *ECA*, no. 301; *V and A*, 99, 111

68 Kyšice, Dýšina, okr. Plzeň. Bronze fibula. L. 5·6 cm. Late LT A, early IV BC. Západočeské Muz., Plzeň. *Aú ČSAV, Prague.*

Not all La Tène art, any more than that of any other culture, is always of the highest quality; in addition to the present brooch and the anthropomorphic example from Manětín [31], two other Bohemian finds are illustrated here which have some claim to being local, native Czech, products and not the work of western-based craftsmen [see also notes to 70–71].

The Kyšice brooch was excavated at the turn of this century by a local archaeologist, F. X. Franc, whose meticulous notes record its association in a grave with a ritually bent anthropoid hilted sword – a type ancestral to late La Tène sword handles[1] [228–229] and descended from late Hallstatt dirks. A number of bronze rings, a set of three comprising a simple neck-ring and two open-ended armrings, made of sheet bronze with incised and cross-hatched lozenges and concentric rings forming the simple decoration, were also found. These last are types not uncommon in western Switzerland and the Rhineland at the end of La Tène A or the beginning of La Tène B1.

As to the brooch itself, like that from Nová Hut' [70], it might be described as a crude version of ornate fibulae such as Parsberg [63]. There are in fact three faces on Kyšice. Above the catch-plate a long-jawed moustache-wearing face follows the 'satyr'-derived prototype of the Basse-Yutz flagons and their pendants [60–62]. The apex of the bar has a human face with satyr ears, large nose, eyes delineated by concentric circles and only a tooth-brush moustache to differentiate it much from the head in a similar position on the Parsberg brooch. The stylised hair is neatly parted along a central ridge rather like the hair of an unassociated brooch from a barrow cemetery at Riekhofen, Ldkr. Regensburg [see notes to 62]; the lower face on one of the four famous brooches from Oberwittighausen in Bavaria also has several points of similarity [91–92].

What is not immediately apparent with the Kyšice bow face is that what looks at first like nothing more than a version of the tightly clinging 'S' curls of Basse-Yutz type double as the upswept horns of a now rather damaged face with down-curling moustaches and square cut – can it be? – beard. This pseudo-face complete again with pointed ears seems to be yet another version of the Basse-Yutz Celticised satyrs whose complete naturalisation into the native world of ambiguity can be seen again on the Oberwittighausen brooches. Other crude versions made by unskilled craftsmen are the Dürrnberg 1886 brooch – where Jacobsthal mistook the moustache for teeth – and a belt-hook from a barrow burial at Langenlonsheim, Kr. Kreuznach.[2]

F. X. Franc, *Věstnik čs. musei* I (1896), 91–93; A. Stocký *La Bohème à l'âge du fer* (1933), Pl. XX: 6, 10; *ECA*, 14, 16, 128 n. 8; *KvsE*, 83 and Tab. VIII:6; *V and A*, 117 and Taf. 7:2; E. Soudská, *Arch. roz.* XX (1968), 464 and obr. 10:2

[1] C. F. C. Hawkes, *PPS* XXI (1955), 203–04, 206, 221 and fig. 2:1–2=no. 11

[2] Dürrnberg: *ECA*, no. 307 – see also notes to [57]; Langenlonsheim: W. Dehn, *Katalog Kreuznach* I= *Kat. west- u. süddeutscher Altertumsslg.* 7 (1941), Abb. 72; *ECA*, no. 353

69 Ostheim, Ldkr. Mellrichstadt. Bronze brooch. L. 8·8 cm. LT A, late V BC. Vorg. Mus., Friedrich-Schiller-Universität, Jena.

It is the catch-plate head of this stray find from a sand-pit in lower Franconia which first catches one's attention on this highly individual product of Celtic distorting imagery. The head, with its great rounded beak, although often referred to as a 'dragon', is really a Celticised griffon complete with horn, other versions of which may be seen in the round on one of the Oberwittighausen fibulae[1] or even more clearly, though in two dimensions, on the Stupava plaque [64] and on an openwork fitting from the Dürkheim chariot grave which is a piece from the same workshop as the Schwabsburg, Ldkr. Mainz, belt-hook.[2] The face at the other end of the Ostheim brooch has a single griffon horn and, grotesque though it is, may be a variant on the horned sphinx-griffon heads one sees on the Weiskirchen I belt-plaque [62] or, much altered, on another Bavarian brooch from a barrow grave at Kümmersbruck, Landkr. Amberg.[3] Immediately above the actual spring mounting of Ostheim is what appears in the illustrated view as an upward curling comma-leaf; this is one half of a curved 'V' feature probably best read as stylised moustaches, but this motif elsewhere may have other interpretations [100].

The cast ornament on the side of the Ostheim brooch is not unlike the incised ornament of Parsberg [63]; the double intertwined comma-leaves flanking either side of the main curve of the bow are the eyebrows of the Weiskirchen I brooch faces without the faces [67]. Even more plastic eye-commas (which are not necessarily Celtic symbols of strength as they have recently been interpreted) appear on the side of a twin-headed brooch from Heidenheim. It was found with two other bird-headed fibulae and one with a ram's head as well as with an anthropoid hilted sword more or less like that from Kyšice [68]. It is one of a class of eastern double bird-headed fibulae, another example of which has a vaguely similar 'griffon' catch-plate head with curling beak.[4] This is related to an unlocated brooch in the Museum für Vor- und Frühgeschichte, Frankfurt, which Jacobsthal unconvincingly considers to be a product of the same craftsman as Ostheim.[5] Isolated double comma-leaves also appear on the spring-plate of the Oberwittighausen fibula already referred to.

Finally, another brooch from Taschendorf, Ldkr. Steinfeld, also in Lower Franconia, has a variation of the Heidenheim double-beaked fibula found with a simple iron version of the Bavarian large knobbed brooch type [see notes to 91].[6]

All these brooches suggest a source south and east of the Rhine for the Ostheim fibula.

ECA, no. 315; Ch. Pescheck, *Mainfränkisches Jahrb. f. Ges. u. Kunst* 11 (1959), 7–10 and Abb. 3; *id.* in *Fulda, Rhön, Amöneburg, Giessen=Führer zu vor- u. frühg. Denkmälern* 1 (1959), 25 and ill. p. 26; G. Neumann, *Ethnog.-Arch. Zeitschr.* 5 (1964), 89; *V and A*, 128; H. Kaufmann, *Jahresschr. mitteldt. Vorg.* 50 (1966), 209–10 and Abb. 8

[1] *ECA*, no. 313; *VRD*, ill. 129; *V and A*, 128–29, 114

[2] Dürkheim: *ECA*, no. 166; *PAE*, 237 and fig. 89A; see also notes to [112]; Schwabsburg: *ECA*, no. 351

[3] W. Torbrügge and H.-P. Uenze, *Bilder zur Vorg. Bayerns* (1968), 219 and ill. 162, 257

[4] W. Dehn in (ed.) R. Degen *et al.*, *Helvetia Antiqua: Festschr. Emil Vogt* (1966), 137 ff. and Abb. 5, esp. figs. 4–5; Heidenheim: K. Bittel, 'Die Kelten in Württemberg'=*R-G Forsch*. 14 (1934), 9, 92–96 and Taf. I; C. F. C. Hawkes, *PPS* XXI (1955), 222

[5] *ECA*, 129, n. 1: *V and A*, 128, n. 131

[6] Peschek, *Mainfränkische Jahrb.*, Abb. 2:3, 8

70 Nová Hut', Plzen. Bronze brooch. L. 3·5 cm. LT A, c. 400 BC. Západočeské Muz., Plzeň. *Aú ČSAV, Prague.*

Even poorer in quality than the brooch from Kyšice [68], this tiny cast brooch, probably from a barrow burial, looks like a piece made to the acknowledged formula for decorated brooches for funerary use by a second-rate craftsman far from the main artistic centres of the Rhine; the miniature scale of the piece must, however, be kept in mind.

The catch-plate is a long-jawed version of the 'cat' faces one finds on more accomplished but equally miniature brooches [90, 94] with something of the 'dragon'-griffons cited in connection with the Ostheim brooch illustrated just above. The double faces of the lower part of the brooch, like those on the Langenlonsheim belt-hook [see notes to 68], the upper Kyšice brooch face, or the Želkovice plaque [71], are little understood copies of the type of head seen on the Rodenbach finger ring [58]; even the miniature faces on the rim of the Borsch flagon [66] are superior members of the same family. One detail which seems to have been remembered from contemporary western motifs is the square 'caste' mark set between the eyes as seen also on both Parsberg heads [63].

A. Stocký, *La Bohème à l'âge du fer* (1933), Pl. XX: 4, 8; *KvsE*, 83 and Tab. IV:1; K. Ludikovský, *Sborník ČSSA* (*Brno*) 2 (1962), 265 ff., Obr. 46:8; *Vand A*, 117, Taf. 7:4

71 and Plate IIb Želkovice, Hořovice, okr. Beroun. Bronze belt-plaque. L. 7·3 cm. LT A, c. 400 BC. Národní Muz., Prague.

This cast belt-plaque with incised ornament executed in rocked tracer technique, though an isolated find, comes from near one of the early Bohemian chariot burials like that at Hořovičky [47]. This grave contained cremated bone, harness fittings for two horses and a number of *phalerae* one of which bore a carefully laid out compass-drawn design of intersecting arcs alternately filled in with dots; this geometric ornament is precisely that found on the Eigenbilzen fragmentary jug and the Dürrnberg grave 46 'pilgrim flask'[1] and must represent a western import. This is not necessarily so with the plaque even though the use of a rocked tracer to produce a simplified 'Greek key' or step pattern reminds one of the Hallstatt sword [30] and other accomplished early pieces.[2]

The Želkovice face again follows the Basse-Yutz/Rodenbach finger ring prototype even to the latter's crowning 'calyx' or lotus bud motif; the square 'caste' mark of Nová Hut' and Parsberg [70, 63] is also present. If the plaque really does come from the chariot grave –

another doubtful find is a sherd of early stamp-decorated pottery [see notes to 27] – it can only be assumed that it must represent a local and recent acquisition on the part of its probably Rhineland-born owner.

A. Stocký, *La Bohème à l'âge du fer* (1933), Pl. XV:4; W. A. von Jenny, *Keltische Metallarbeiten aus heidnischer und christl. Zeit* (1935) Taf. 3:3; L. Franz, *Praehist. Zeitschr.* XXVIII–XXIX (1937–38), 406 ff., Abb. 1:1, 2:2; *ECA*, 119; *KvsE*, 268, 284 and obr. 79:1; (ed.) J. Neustupný, *The Prehistory of Czechoslovakia* (1958), Pl. XX; *V and A*, 118–19 and Taf. 3:4; T. G. E. Powell, *Sborník Národního Muz. v Praze* A, XX:1–2 (1966), 133–34

[1] Želkovice: W. Dehn, *Sborník Národního Muz. v Praze* A, XX, 141 and Abb. 11; Eigenbilzen and Dürrnberg: M. E. Mariën in (ed.) M. Renard, 'Hommages à Albert Grenier'=*Coll. Latomus* LVIII (1962), 1113–16; see also notes to [40, 48]

72 Dürrnberg, Hallein, barrow grave XVI. Bronze flagon. Total ht. 46·7 cm., ht. neck 12·2 cm., w. at shoulder 18 cm. LT A, late V/early IV BC. Salzburger Mus. Carolino-Augusteum, Salzburg. (Details) *Ing. E. Penninger; R-G Zentralmus., Mainz.*

If one were to select a single piece from the range of early La Tène material known to us to exemplify the technical mastery and stylistic virtuosity of the major craftsmen of the Celtic Iron Age, it would surely be the flagon from the first of the two barrow-covered chariot graves from the Dürrnberg salt-mining centre.

It was in 1932 that the site was investigated; apart from the flagon and the remains of the fittings for a two-wheeled vehicle including the iron tires, there were no signs of particular wealth. Parts of two pots were found, one being of the *Linsenflasche* form like that from Matzhausen [27], several other examples being known from the Dürrnberg cemetery. Together with part of an early disc-footed fibula of the so-called 'Münsingen' type, this suggests a date for the burial right at the end of the La Tène A phase or in the transition between LT Ia–b of the Swiss sequence.

Since recent restoration of the flagon has resulted in a detailed technical analysis of its construction,[1] it will suffice to note here that, like the Basse-Yutz jugs [60–61], which, despite Jacobsthal's claim of an 'insuperable connection' with Dürrnberg, are stylistically linked to it only by their generally similar profile, the body of the Austrian piece has been beaten up from a single sheet of bronze. The handle and rim unit are cast and soldered on as a single unit, certain details such as pupils and shoulder-joints being added afterwards with an engraving tool, concentric circles with a punch. The base-plate seems to have been finished on a lathe or turntable before being joined to the bottom of the flagon body.

It is impossible to do justice in a few sentences to the bafflingly eclectic imagery of the maker(s) of the Dürrnberg flagon – either the work of a single master-craftsman completely at home in all the various 'styles' of his day, representational and non-representational, or perhaps of two men, one being responsible for the body and one for making the mould from which the handle and rim mounting was cast. Nevertheless, purely as a pointer to the directions in which further study may take one, a few notes may be added on, first, the representational features and, second, some of the abstract motifs used.

First, then, the clearly human heads at either extremity of the handle proper: clean-shaven, oval ridged eyes with punched central 'caste' mark and neatly fringed page-boy hair-do. The upper face has a cleft chin and what appears to be a neck-ring; he also has well-defined ears, a comparatively rare feature on any Celtic 'portrait' but with something of the Parsberg human head [63] or the Manětín figure [31]. The lower face has only vestigial ears but there are two up-swinging horns or commas again recalling Parsberg or, closer, another Bavarian find, the brooch from Riekhofen, Ldkr. Regensburg;[2] another brooch with similar human head is that from Schwieberdingen, Kr. Ludwigsburg near Stüttgart [89]. The 'commas' on the hair of the lower face, though not as definitely comma-like as those on the side of the Ostheim brooch [69], may be related to the horns between the leaf-crowns of the Hořovičky plaques [47] – with similar eyes and hair to Dürrnberg and, like Dürrnberg, following the same 'protuberances' physiognomy of the undoubtedly earlier Klein Aspergle flagon [50]. The horizontal division of the hair of the lower face is present in two other pieces illustrated here: the Schwarzenbach II gold armring [53] and the nail head from Dürkheim [74], the latter again with central 'caste' mark. The upper part of the Dürrnberg flagon handle is in the form of a strange carnivorous monster, with a thick tail and bird's claws like those of the equally fierce animals on the rings from Erstfeld, Kt. Uri [84]; pronounced 'shoulder-curls' may vaguely recall Basse-Yutz or the Borsch flagon handle [66] but here the face with its great staring concentric eyes – eyes as big as saucers, like the dog in Hans Andersen's story of *The Tinder Box* – is constructed of protuberances, a fierce version of the rather more whimsical faces on the Oberwittighausen brooches [see notes to 92]. Again it is Schwieberdingen which provides the closest parallel, this time the face above the spring, although there is also something similar in the Ostheim grotesque. The decapitated head is a reminder that not everything in Celtic society is a matter of skilled artistry; the gruesome aspects of the cult of the head obtrude in many different forms [see notes to 76]. There are two other little monsters on the rim of the Dürrnberg flagon. Despite their talons and leonine tails, they are certainly far from the heraldic lions of the Etruscan prototypes; they are perhaps also more in the class of the Oberwittighausen grotesques than part of that cultic chamber of horrors which has given artistic birth to the handle animal itself. Despite those who maintain that the rim pair are busy devouring a human limb, even though the ultimate prototype may be the devouring beasts of '*situla*' art' and other Mediterranean-influenced pieces [see notes to 24], the long 'tongues' are in fact beards and the faces with their pointed ears as much based on the old Italic satyr or silen prototypes as are the not dissimilar disembodied faces which act as terminals on the Borsch rim mount; the 'tongues' may also be in some way related to the tendrils which can be seen growing from the mouths of some of the *situlae* animals.

Of the non-representational motifs on the Dürrnberg flagon, the 'running dog' or wave pattern on the rim of the spout is not particularly common in Celtic art, although it can be found in several variations on material from the Marne chariot burials and it borders the sheath of the short sword from Weiskirchen I [109].[3] The backbone of the devouring handle-beast is a stack of curved 'V's – like those which form the 'body' of the Riekhofen fibula. The 'tail', which ends above the basal head, is a 'bead-and-reel' design like that found on the Parsberg brooch, the Erstfeld rings, or, closer to its classical prototype, on one of the gold horn mounts from Klein Aspergle [see notes to 44]. The open work forming the basal plate of the handle is composed of a series of linked full-bodied 'S' curls edged with simple cable ornament and ending in a triple leaf palmette, all reminiscent of more westerly gold work such as the Eigenbilzen ?horn mount [40] or the Auvers disc [42]. The use of the leaf or 'comma-spiral' stack can also be found on the handle of the Reinheim flagon [73], which is in many ways the closest piece to Dürrnberg despite its seemingly different form. The handle of the Reinheim flagon, like the upper part of Dürrnberg, has flanking lines of punched circle ornament – but this is a common feature on many different pieces of the later part of the early La Tène phase, for example a chariot mount from La Bouvandeau in the Marne[4] and a silver torc allegedly from Mâcon [77]. Finally the *repoussé* decoration of the body of the flagon again makes use of common motifs based on the lotus bud, while the twin-pointed leaves on the shoulder of the flagon occur frequently amongst contemporary early La Tène stamped pottery including sherds from the Dürrnberg cemetery.[5] The long-lobed elements running down the body and ending in triple leaves may be compared with openwork ornaments – in the round – from the contemporary chariot grave of 'La Gorge Meillet', Somme-Tourbe, again in the Marne,[6] or, nearer at hand, the two attachments found with the flagon mount in the shape of a human face from the second Dürrnberg chariot burial, grave 44 [see notes to 48].

In trying to sum up these numerous stylistic allusions, the two most pressing questions concerning any archaeological or artistic artefact, 'where' and precisely 'when', must remain largely unanswered. There is no doubt that the wealth of the Dürrnberg salt tycoons could have commanded the services of several craftsmen and that indeed they did becomes clear if one looks at the contents of just one single rich grave such as grave 44. The general run of artistic parallels, however, does indicate that the Rhineland Pfalz is as likely an area as any other in which the maker(s) of the Dürrnberg flagon at least had their artistic training. As to date, in a review of Jacobsthal's *Early Celtic Art*, Karl Schefold placed the flagon in his 'contrast' style, a useful if not very precise term for products of the period following after such early princely burials as Klein Aspergle. Dürrnberg is certainly a more mature-*looking* work than the Basse-Yutz flagons, and a case can be made out that it fits better with such material as that associated with the graves of Reinheim and Dürkheim and the Erstfeld hoard.

O. Klose, *Wiener Prähist. Zeitschr.* 21 (1934), 83–107; *ECA*, no. 382; R. Pittioni, *Urgeschichte des österreich. Raumes* (1954), 660, Abb. 451–52; *Keltische kunst: Bodemschatten uit Salzburg*, Frans Halsmus., Haarlem (1963), nos. 2–6; *V and A*, 106 ff. Abb. 2G and Taf. 6:4; *PreA*, 197–98 and ill. 191–92; *PAE*, 235–36, 280, fig. 88B and Pl. 244–45

[1] H.-J. Hundt, *Jahresschr. Salzburger Mus. C. A. 1960* 6 (1961), 39–49

[2] W. Torbrügge and H.P. Uenze, *Bilder zur Vorg. Bayerns* (1968), ill. 258; see also notes to [62]

[3] *ECA*, PP 113–16; see also Jacobsthal, *Greek Pins* (1956) 74, no. 2

[4] *ECA*, n. 168; see also notes to [112]

[5] E.g. H.P. Uenze, *Bayer. Vorg.* 29 (1964), 95 and Abb. 8:5; Dürrnberg: M. Hell, *Mitt. d. Anthrop. Ges. Wien* LXIX (1929), 165 f. and Abb. 5:3; see also notes to [65]

[6] *ECA*, nos. 196–97

73 Reinheim, Kr. St Ingbert, barrow 'A'. Gilt-bronze spouted flagon. Ht. to tip of spout 50·4 cm., max. d. 23·2 cm. Late LT A, first half IV B C. Saarland Landesmus. f. Vor- u. Frühg., Saarbrücken; (left) *R-G Zentralmus., Mainz*; (right) *Staatl. Konservatoramt, Saarbrücken*.

One of the richest finds of the post-World War II period was the discovery and partial destruction in 1954, in the course of sandpit operations, of the princess's grave overlooking the river Blies above the village of Reinheim. Originally the burial, covered with a mound and surrounded by a narrow ditch, formed part of a group of barrows, only one other of which has been examined. This second barrow, also surrounded by a ditch, was of somewhat earlier date and contained the body of a man in his 50s.

Although no sign of the actual body had survived it was quite clear that the burial of barrow 'A', placed within an oak-lined chamber, was of a woman of considerable importance although, unlike the woman laid to rest at Besseringen not far away [see notes to 56], she was not accompanied by a funerary vehicle. The Reinheim princess seems to have been placed on her back, head to the north and arms crossed over the stomach. Owing to the acid nature of the soil many of the 200 or more separate objects recovered were in a delicate state of preservation; nonetheless, the presence even of textiles could be deduced from fragments adhering to the various bronze objects. Necklaces of glass and amber beads were worn by the dead woman – the amber beads including one in the shape of a pointed boot [see notes to 31–32] – as well as a great gold torc, armrings and a pair of finger rings [79–83]; there was a brooch in the form of a domestic chicken with coral and bone mounting, and another fibula with human head terminal [see notes to 67] together with gold disc brooches which lay on her chest. Close at hand was a bronze circular mirror – a rare type in Celtic contexts – with its handle in the shape of a naked, clean-shaven man with 'comma-leaf' headdress. Also of gold was a pair of openwork circular gold mounts probably for drinking cups and related to the style of the Eigenbilzen and Schwarzenbach II mounts [see notes to 39–40]; a pair of bronze bowls was also provided to underline the practice of the deceased providing for a drinking companion in the Otherworld.

First of all, however, amongst evidence for the funerary symposium was the tubular-spouted jug found with the bowls on the eastern side of the burial chamber; the vessel is carefully gilded from top to bottom. One other fine tubular-spouted jug with the same wide flaring belly and narrow base is known from the later Waldalgesheim chariot burial [78]; there are other bronze examples however, including one from France and one from Switzerland,[1] while it is likely that the wooden jugs with bronze fittings from Dürrnberg graves 44 and 46 were also of this type [see notes to 48 and 163]. The form of

these vessels seems wholly Celtic and owes little save the basic idea of a wine pourer to the Italic imports which served as models for Klein Aspergle and Basse-Yutz [50, 60–61]; the profile is much closer to that of contemporary pedestalled pots like those of the Marne with painted curvilinear ornament [154].

Curvilinear decoration does in fact appear in a fantastic profusion of intricately laid out and mathematically

Fig. 3 [73] Reinheim, Germany. Details of incised decoration on body of gilt flagon. Scale c. 1:7
After Keller

precise incised ornament covering much of the body of the Reinheim jug. The design, which really can only be fully appreciated in a carefully reconstructed drawing, has developed a long way in skill if not in time from the crude embellishment of the imported jug in the first Weiskirchen grave.[2] Carefully executed designs involving the use of compasses and the rocked, chisel-ended, cutting tool or tracer (first encountered in these pages when discussing the La Tène scabbard from the Hallstatt cemetery [30]) seem to have been the speciality of a master-craftsman working up and down the Rhine. He was undoubtedly the inspiration for, if not the maker of, the decoration on the strange wine-strainer from the late Hunsrück-Eifel culture burial at Hoppstädten, Kr. Birkenfeld, barrow 2,[3] as well as of the Waldalgesheim jug. An isolated find of a heavily decorated sword scabbard from Bavilliers in the territory of Belfort just west of the Rhine, and a bronze mount found further north in a barrow in the Forest of Haguenau,[4] also almost certainly came from the same hand. The same master-engraver seems to have had a pupil responsible for the decoration of a number of belt-plaques found in western Switzerland.[5]

This engraver, in order to execute the details of his design, must have developed ultra-near-sightedness as it is thought the illuminators of the Celtic gospels did, unless he used a fragment of rock crystal as a lens. The motifs he employs are those found in low relief in the gold work of the early La Tène princely burials (as represented in the twin gold mounts from Reinheim itself) repeated in two dimensions – the linked 'S' or comma-leaf, the triple-leafed palmette or lotus bud, the zigzag or 'dragon's tooth' design, and the concentric circle. This is undoubtedly specialist work, so specialised that, as with the Dürrnberg flagon [72], it would seem logical, if nothing else, to separate the personality of the engraver from that of the individual responsible for the cast decoration of the flagon handle and the Celtic 'centaur' riveted to the lid.

The fulsome 'S' stack of the shield-shaped, Borsch-type [66] basal plate, simple, subsequently inscribed, circle decoration on the sides of the handle, and the triple-lobed 'bib' springing from the chin of the ram's head – all these are features which may be matched to some degree either by the gold work from Reinheim itself or by another actual flagon handle, that from Dürrnberg; this, however, may represent nothing more than a common artistic vocabulary. The human faces, on the other hand, are three versions of the old bearded Italic prototype. The basal face has a long pod beard with small moustache and tight-clinging horns rather than comma-leaves; basically this character, whose foreboding look may be due as much as anything to the need to construct him out of a very narrow area, has sound affinities with other contemporary pieces [78, 104]. The upper face, chin resting on the ram's horns rather in the manner of the Kyšice brooch [68] and a particularly common Celtic marriage of man and beast, has a more cheerful expression, a trimmer beard and a palmette crest like one aspect of the Dürkheim 'trick' faces [59]. The lid figure in the form of a human-headed horse is unique but only in basic conception; brooches in the form of standing horses come from further south [see notes to 63], and a somewhat similar 'humanisation' forms the sphinx-griffons of the Weis-kirchen I belt-plate [62] and of a girdle-hook from the Somme-Bionne chariot grave [see also notes to 111],[6] while from a nearby Hunsrück-Eifel chariot grave at Freisen comes a miniature bronze horse of very similar appearance and perhaps use.[7] The bearded face of the Reinheim 'centaur' – for which Celtic ingenuity rather than classical influence is probably to be credited – forms the third of the three variations on the bearded silen or satyr theme. With typical ambiguity the craftsman has made animal ears which may also be crowning leaf-commas, as seems more explicitly intended on such miniature but related pieces as a belt fastening from a grave at Herrnsheim, Kr. Worms,[8] and the chariot fitting from Dürkheim illustrated to the right [74].

The heavily emphasised lines of the hair and beards and the ridging of the eyes relates the maker of the Reinheim handle and lid figures to a group of rings and belt-hooks, the 'Horchheim' class, predominantly from the Hunsrück-Eifel [see notes to 51] and it is probable that at least the final touches to the great Reinheim jug were executed comparatively close to its find-spot.

WK, Taf. 38; F. J. Keller, *Das keltische Fürstengrab von Reinheim I* (1965), esp. no. 12, Taf. 19–25; *V and A*, 115–16 and Taf. 6:5; Keller in *Saarland=Führer zu vor-u. frühg. Denkmälern* 5 (1966), 154–58, esp. ill. p. 157; *EV*, 205 and ill.

[1] *ECA*, nos. 389, 395; see now also W. Dehn, *Památky Arch.* LX (1969), 125–33
[2] *Besançon*, 15; see also [113] and A. Haffner in *Saarland* . . ., 216 and ill. p. 214 (left)
[3] L. Kilian, *Trierer Zeitschr.* 24–26 (1956-58), 88 ff. and Taf. 19

[4] Bavilliers: J. V. S. Megaw, *Rev. arch. de l'Est et du Centre-Est* XIX (1968), 129–44; Haguenau: F. A. Schaeffer, *Les Tertres funéraires préhist. dans la Forêt de Haguenau* 2 (1930), 96–97 and fig. 88 f; *ECA*, P 284
[5] W. Drack in (ed.) R. Degen *et al.*, *Helvetia Antiqua: Festschr. Emil Vogt* (1966), 129–36, esp. 134 and Abb. 8
[6] *ECA*, no. 359
[7] *ECA*, no. 370; *WK*, Taf. 44 above; A. Haffner in *Saarland* . . ., 39 and ill. p. 36
[8] *ECA*, no. 366; Megaw in *Germania* 45 (1967), 52 and Taf. 8:4

74 Bad Dürkheim, Kr. Neustadt, Rhineland-Pfalz. Chariot fitting, iron with bronze veneer. Ht. 3·5 cm., LT A, late V/early IV BC. Hist. Mus. der Pfalz, Speyer.

This detail of a bronze-coated iron pin, usually presumed to be a linch pin or other fitting associated with the chariot from the Dürkheim princely burial, shows a human, bearded face set against an outline version of the sacred 'leaf-crown' motif.

The face, now much rubbed, with its ridged eyes, horizontal band across the hair and central 'caste mark', has many of the features of the lower Dürrnberg flagon handle face [72]. The cruder, more 'geometric' formula used for the Dürkheim nail relates it more closely to the Hunsrück-Eifel group of rings and to other objects of the 'Horchheim' class. One example, though clearly not by a master craftsman, is complete with simplified leaf-crown and comes from the 'Königsfeld' barrow D1 burial at Hermeskeil, Kr. Trier; it is compared by Jacobsthal with the very much finer Heidelberg stone head [49].[1]

ECA, no. 165; *V and A*, 116

[1] *ECA*, 118; W. Dehn, *Trierer Zeitschr.* 20 (1951), 19 ff., 43–44, Abb. 22 and Taf. 2:1

75 Pfalzfeld, Ldkr. St Goar. Sandstone pillar. Ht. 1·48 m. Late LT A, V/IV BC. Rhein. Landesmus., Bonn.

This pillar statue from the territory of the Treveri, with design repeated on all four faces, was once surmounted by a head, possibly a double 'Janus' face like the Heidelberg fragment [49] with which it has several similarities. Already, however, when the first drawing was made of the stone in 1608–09, the terminal fitting was recorded as missing; there is no indication of the stone's original siting.

The cable pattern forming the 'edging' of the main shaft has been remarked upon as having affinities with fifth-century *cippi* from the Etruscan-occupied Venetic region of north-eastern Italy, but beyond this there is little that is 'foreign' about the stone's decoration. The lantern-jawed faces, with their great balloon-like 'leaf-crowns' and simple button-eyes, can be found on small things as well as large [91], but, although the Pfalzfeld faces seem to have moustaches, they are closest perhaps to those pendants cited for the more refined Heidelberg head, to the Reinheim mirror-handle mannikin and to the lost ?brooch disc from Königsheim.[1] Like Heidelberg, the Pfalzfeld faces have on their foreheads a double-leafed emblem; while the triple-lobed 'bibs' and background of fat-bodied 'S' curls linked at the top with a large 'lotus bud' both recall the decoration of the Reinheim flagon or that from Dürrnberg [72–73].

The shape of the pillar has given rise to the suggestion that this and similar pieces may be phallic in intent;[2] however, despite Hirschlanden [12] and one other piece illustrated below [101], sex plays but a minor rôle in most Celtic art.

ECA, no. 11; *Celts*, 134–35, fig. 23 and Pl. 60; *WK*, Taf. 43; *CCH*, 161 and figs. 22, 39; *PreA*, 208–09 and ill. 201; *PAE*, 246 ff., Pl. 267; *EV*, 236, 238 and ill.

[1] Reinheim: F. J. Keller, *Das keltische Fürstengrab von Reinheim* I (1965), no. 15; Königsheim: *ECA*, no. 201; see also notes to [31] and [49]

[2] *PCB*, 62 f. and fig. 23; Anne Ross, *Proc. Soc. Antiq. Scot.* XCI (1957–58), 21 ff.

76 Noves, Bouches-du-Rhône. Limestone statue. Total ht. 1·12 m., ht. of human heads c. 30 cm. ?III BC. Musée Calvet, Avignon, Vaucluse. *Franceschi-Zodiaque*.

This awesome statue, the so-called 'Tarasque-de-Noves' from one of the native sanctuary sites of Provence which were overrun by the Romans in the second century BC, belongs to the group of Mediterranean-influenced art of Southern France represented here in a later section [231 ff.]. It is instructive, however, to compare the art of the early La Tène *Fürstengräber* with this great ithyphallic carnivore with human arm – complete with bracelet – protruding from his mouth, clawed front paws resting on the decapitated heads of two other victims.

The concept of the 'devouring beast' was known to the makers of the decorated *situlae*, for example the Boldù-Dolfin examples[1] [see also notes to 24 and 64]; it can be seen on the Dürrnberg flagon [72] and runs through to later continental and even insular pieces [209, 285]. The long-faced – as well they might be – heads with their forked beards, emphasised features and well-pronounced widow's peaks, moreover, look like another version of the Etruscan prototypes for the Klein Aspergle flagon mounts [50]. The Tarasque itself may be not an attempt at an archaic lion such as is seen devouring a warrior in a fragmentary group from the Col de la Vayrède, Baux (also now in the Musée Calvet), but rather a wolf as the handle animals of Basse-Yutz may possibly be [60–61] or, more appositely, like a granite sculpture at St-Germain-en-Laye.[2] Certainly the influence of Italy is strong; fourth-century statues from Vulci and similar figures from the Greek colonies of south-east Spain offer the most obvious sources, but the concept of the severed head cult is wholly native. The great fortified *oppidum* of Entremont, which was totally destroyed by the Romans in 123 BC during the establishment of their first extra-Italian colony, contained within its sanctuary two cross-legged figures holding human heads and similar figures – not to mention an almost Aztec-like skull-rack which was found at Roquepertuse [see notes to 212].

Dates for the Tarasque have varied from the first to the third centuries BC; in view of the Roman occupation it is unlikely to be later than the end of the second century, and in view of the general exchange of ideas no less than goods between Italy and southern France from the sixth on, an early date is quite possible.

Espérandieu, I (1907), no. 121; F. Benoit, *L'art primitif méditerranéen de la Vallée du Rhône*=*Publ. des Ann. de la Faculté des Lettres, Aix-en-Provence* 9 (1955), 36 ff. and esp. Pl. XVIII below, XIX; *ArtG*, 96, Pls. 24–25, 27,

colour pl. opp. p. 81; *WK*, Taf. 52–53; *CCH*, 157 and fig. 37, M. Pobé and J. Roubier, *Art of Roman Gaul* (1961), Pl. 31, 33; *PreA*, 210 and ill. 206; J.-J. Hatt, *Sculptures gauloises: 600 av. J.C.–40 apr. J.C.* (1966), 28 and fig. 12a, b; *PAE*, 250, 281 and Pl. 275

[1] G. Ghirardini, *Mon. Antichi* X (1900), 71–94 and Tav. IV; *Mostra dell'arte delle situle dal Po al Danubio* (1961), no. 25–26; O.-H. Frey, 'Die Enstehung der Situlenkunst', *R-G Forsch.* 31 (1968), no. 34–36

[2] Col de la Vayrède: Benoit, *op. cit.*, 30 and Pl. XV:1; *ArtG*, 96, Pl. 40; St-Germain: *ArtG*, 96, Pl. 34

77 ?Mâcon, Saône-et-Loire. Silver torc. D. 15·2 cm., ht. of heads c. 1·7 cm., LT A/B, first half IV BC. Metropolitan Mus. of Art, New York (Fletcher Fund, 1947).

Silver was little used in the western Celtic areas; indeed, apart from some minor pieces [136, 204–206], it is a speciality of the naturally silver-rich eastern Iron Age groups [209, 215 ff.]. The only other silver torc even comparatively near the present ring's find-spot – which is poorly authenticated – is a globe-headed example from Pallon au Val Freissinières, Hautes-Alpes.[1]

There is, however, little which is eastern in the torc's form. It is wrought from at least three separate pieces of silver – a join is clearly visible towards the base of the two outward-facing heads which act as 'supporters' for the main decorative areas – and belongs to a class of disc-terminalled rings common in western Germany and the Marne region as well as the Swiss plateau; two close parallels of this particular form are in the museum at Darmstadt.[2] Such rings bridge the first and second sub-phases of La Tène and a detail which suggests at first a date not too early in this period are the countersunk discs with fastening pins still visible on either side of the Mâcon torc. Such areas filled with enamel are a feature of another group of neck-rings found mainly in Germany and Switzerland and all dateable within LT B [145–47].

There are several features, however, which recall the Spiez torc [52] which is considered to be somewhat earlier in the relative sequence; these include not only the general placing of the ornament but also the relative position of the heads, the fat-bodied 'S's, and the punched circles on the otherwise plain section of the ring. Fat 'S's and punched-dot ornament are also a feature of the Reinheim flagon [73], while the raised circles just visible in the detail above the circular knobs recall those on another piece from a princely burial, the Dürkheim gold armlet [54].

The faces are fine-featured yet hardly portraits. Their rather downcast expression and full set of moustache and beard, have two close parallels, one, a belt-hook from a grave – there is nothing known of the associated finds – from Herrnsheim, Kr. Worms, and the other is the basal face of the Waldalgesheim double chariot grave illustrated on the right. All in all, despite the use of silver, the craftsman who fashioned the Mâcon torc most probably plied his trade in the central Rhineland area and not further east.

ECA, 123, n. 1 (probably this piece); J. V. S. Megaw, *Germania* 45 (1967), 50 ff., Taf. 7:1–2, 8:1–2

[1] *ECA*, no. 85
[2] *ECA*, nos. 220–21

78 Waldalgesheim, Kr. Kreuznach. Bronze spouted jug.

Total ht. 35 cm., l. of lid animal 4·9 cm., ht. of basal head with beard c. 4 cm. Late LT A/early LT B1, first half IV BC. Rhein. Landesmus., Bonn. *J. V. S. Megaw* (right and below).

The chariot grave of Waldalgesheim, a chance find of which the precise details are unknown, appears to have been a double burial covered by a stone cairn in the manner of the Dürrnberg chariot graves [see notes to 48 and 72]. The upper burial was that of a woman associated with the fine gold ornaments executed in the well-dated style to which the grave has given its name [124–26]; the lower grave with the remains of a chariot, harness, other ornaments and the now carefully restored jug, was that of a man though without any weapons. That this grave is indeed the latest in date of such graves in the area is established not only on stylistic grounds but also by the finding of a two-handled pail with cast palmette decoration, a type now established as a 'bell-*situla*' imported from Tarentum in southern Italy where it would have been made not before c. 325 BC.[1]

In this context the flagon could have been anything up to a generation-and-a-half old when buried. The spout and separate body hammered out of a single sheet of bronze is close in shape to that from the Reinheim princess's grave [73], the animal handle, an attempt at a more domestic beast than that on the Reinheim lid, was originally attached by a chain to the main body like that surviving on the Le Catillon or Basse-Yutz jugs [60–61]; even closer is a plain bronze jug found somewhere in the Rheinpfalz.[2] Again it seems likely that the making and decoration of the main part of the jug was by a specialist craftsman, separate from the man responsible for the handle and lid mount, in the same way as in Etruscan metal workshops different craftsmen seem to

have made different parts of *Schnabelkanne*. Certainly the fine ornament round the body of the jug (just visible in the detailed illustrations) looks like the work of the decorator of the Reinheim jug and the Hoppstädten sieve,[3] although this time the closely intertwined design of 'S' curls has been executed over a prepared lay-out in a series of fine punched dots and not with a *tremolo* line.

The handle is simpler than those of many of the other flagons depicted in earlier illustrations, but the elderly man with long pod-shaped beard forming the base of the mount is a masterpiece of miniaturist modelling though, like its twins on the Mâcon ring illustrated on the left, not a true portrait; the jug ears, rather ill-positioned, 'leaf-crown', conjoined eyebrows and nose, and oval eyes with dotted pupils, all have affinities with more grotesque variations on the Italic satyr prototype. Yet there is something so individual in this face and its few pendants – which might be extended to include the unique little helmeted fibula terminal from Kšice in Bohemia [104] – that one is indeed tempted to see a craftsman leaving his physical signature as a medieval stone-carver might include his own caricature on a cathedral corbel end. But then how many Celts wore such splendid beards?

The openwork plate out of which the head grows has its affinities amongst chariot- and belt-fittings of earlier Marnian graves and the ? belt-mount from the second Dürrnberg chariot burial[4] [see also notes to 62 and 112]. The horse – or possibly sheep – now fixed to a modern lid comes complete with Basse-Yutz-like 'nomadic' shoulder-curl and, like the stylised ram's head at the upper end of the handle, is a surprisingly primitive piece in contrast to the brilliant workmanship of the human 'portrait'.

The Waldalgesheim jug, then, old when buried – a valuable heirloom – to judge from its pendants, is a product probably of craftsmen based on the area west of the Rhine and on the edge of the Hunsrück-Eifel. Though some authorities consider that of the two flagons Waldalgesheim is later than Reinheim, the affinity of the non-representational ornament seems too close for this to be the case; a date shortly after 400 BC would seem reasonable as far as our present knowledge goes.

E. Aus'm Werth, 'Der Grabfund von Wald-Algesheim', *Bonner Winkelmannsprogramm* (1870), esp. Taf. 4; L. Lindenschmidt, *AuhV* III:1 (1881), Taf. 1–2; W. Dehn, *Katalog Kreuznach=Kataloge west- u. süddeutscher Altertumssammlungen* 7 (1941), I, 117 ff., Taf. 13–15, esp. 14:3; II, 63–64; *ECA*, no. 387; *Celts*, Pls. 26–27; *WK*, Taf. 34 below; *PreA*, 198–99, ill. 194; J. V. S. Megaw, *Germania* 45 (1967), 52 and Taf. 8:3; U. Schaaff in *Nördl. Rheinhessen=Führer zur vor- u. frühg. Denkmälern* 12 (1969), 37–41; Dehn, Památky Arch. LX (1969), 126ff.

[1] P. J. Riis, *Acta Arch.* XXX (1959), 21 and 24
[2] Le Câtillon: *ECA*, no. 389; 'Rheinpfalz': *ECA*, no. 388
[3] L. Kilian, *Trierer Zeitschr.* 24–26 (1956–58), 88 ff., Abb. 2 and Taf. 19
[4] Marne: *ECA*, nos. 171 and 200; Dürrnberg, grave 44: *Keltische Kunst: Bodemschatten uit Salzburg*, Frans Halsmus., Haarlem (1963), no. 16

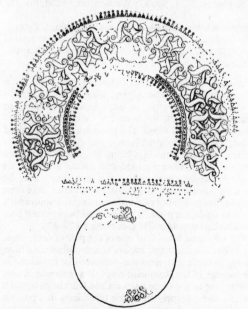

Fig. 4 [78] Waldalgesheim, Germany. Details of incised decoration on body of spouted flagon. Scale c. 1:4 *After Jacobsthal*

79–83 Reinheim, Kr. St Ingbert. Gold rings. 79, gold torc, d. 17·2 cm.; 80, larger gold armring, d. 8·1 cm.; 81, smaller armring, d. 6·7 cm.; **82,** small finger ring, d. 2·0 cm.; **83,** large finger ring d. 2·1 cm. Late LT A, V/early IV BC. Saarland. Landesmus. f. Vor- u. Frühg., Saarbrücken. *Staat. Konservatoramt, Saarbrücken.*

Two pieces may be selected for special mention from the gold finds of the Reinheim princess's grave [see notes to **73**]: the neck-ring and armring with figural ornamentation. Of the other objects, the smaller armring [**81**] has palmette decoration either side of a smooth knob, the palmettes, like so many other features of the Reinheim gold work, suggesting that it was made by the same workshop as was responsible for a ring from the Zerf barrow grave,[1] for the great Rodenbach armring [**55**], and for the Erstfeld treasure [**84**]. The ornamental finger ring found in position in the area of the right hand [**83**] uses undulating twisted gold wire soldered between three plain hoops. The use of undulating wire ornaments is a feature of later women's jewellery [see also **174**] but a gold ring of somewhat similar form was found in a male barrow burial in the Forest of Haguenau at Weitbruch (Bas-Rhin) together with the bronze fitting engraved in a style comparable to the Reinheim and Waldalgesheim flagons.[2]

Turning to the neck-ring, imitation hollow twisted or cast rings in twisted form [**100**] are not common in early La Tène metal work, though the type has a considerable ancestry in the later Bronze Age. Despite the hollow ring, the Reinheim torc still has a considerable weight (187·2 grm.). The outward-staring, beardless human face may well be intended as a woman in view of its close resemblance to the armring from the Dürkheim chariot grave, almost certainly also a woman's grave [**54**]; the Reinheim fibula with human terminal also looks like the same craftsman's work as the Reinheim torc and the Erstfeld rings also are similar. Both pairs of human faces on the torc and on the armlet have the pointed 'satyr' ears of the Dürkheim ring, while the 'bibs' hanging down from the chin of the human face on the torc and flanking faces on the armring are really a version of the triple-lobed palmette feature of the Pfalzfeld pillar [**75**] or of the ram at the top end of the Reinheim flagon-handle [**73**]. Both Pfalzfeld and the Reinheim flagon are almost certainly the work of different hands from what, following the laws of priority in typological nomenclature, might well be called the 'Dürkheim goldsmith'. The 'scarf' round the neck of the, dare one say, goddesses has the alternate hatching not infrequently found as a 'fill-in' motif on early La Tène gold and bronze work. Hatching appears on the Erstfeld rings and it forms the plumage of the wings of the Panenský Týnec bird, whose tail is simply a quadruple version of the Reinheim 'scarf' [**65**].

The mantling birds perched on the 'goddesses'' heads on the neck-ring are fierce relatives of the heraldic pair on the Besseringen torc [**56**], another product of the Dürkheim goldsmith's workshop. The concept is certainly that of a *potnia theron*, a Celtic Artemis, or 'mistress of the wild beasts', but to consider the idea as entirely a borrowed one is perhaps again to underestimate the power of the Celtic imagination. The down-curved beaks of the birds appear disembodied on more southerly but more or less contemporary finds [**91, 96–98**].

The great cushioned balusters of both torc and armring are key features of the Dürkheim goldsmith's most ornate work; Rodenbach, Besseringen, and Erstfeld all exhibit variations on this theme. But what of the round-eyed faces beneath each terminal baluster? The clue is given by the single outstretched wings of the faces on the armlet; these are owls such as may be seen in later work [**164**], and which appear at either end of a gold strip from the Dürkheim grave as well as forming the only surviving part of a bronze brooch from the first Weiskirchen barrow,[3] both, one may suggest, also products of the Dürkheim workshop. The semi-circular tooling under the wings and leading up to the 'goddess's' bracelet-wearing arms may be an attempt at double perspective – showing the body of the 'owls' from the side which strictly would be hidden behind the wings in a front-on view. One further detail of the armring 'owls' requires comment: the tooled dots on the part of the throat immediately below the beaks. These may be representations of the bearded tufts of feathers of the tawny owl or, since their position is similar to the punched circle 'tattoos' on the basal Reinheim flagon handle face, these may be half-human owls – note the neat fringed 'hair'. Jacobsthal considered the Weiskirchen brooch 'owls' as representing a conjoined pair of lions with one head and two bodies, which shows how dangerous it is to be too assertive in identifying the details of Celtic imagery.

Celts, Pl. 32–33; *WK,* Taf. 40–41, Farbtafel III below; R. Joffroy in *Kelten und Germanen=Kunst der Welt* (1964), 143, colour ill. p. 141; F. J. Keller, *Das keltische Fürstengrab von Reinheim* I (1965), nos. 1 [=**79**], 2 [=**80**], 3 [=**81**], 5 [=**83**], 6 [=**82**]; *V and A,* 100, 128, 158, and Taf. 5:5–6; *PreA,* 112, ill. 188–89; *PAE,* 234 ff., Pl. 237–38; *EV,* 208–09 and ills.

[1] *ECA,* no. 53
[2] F. A. Schaeffer, *Les Tertres funéraires préhist. dans la Forêt de Haguenau* 2 (1930), 96–101 and fig. 88; see also notes to [**73**]
[3] Dürkheim: *ECA,* no. 27; Weiskirchen: *ECA,* no. 317

84 Erstfeld, Kt. Uri. Detail of two gold neck-rings. Total d. (left) 14·5 cm. (right) 15·5 cm.; l. of right-hand animal face c. 2 cm. Late LT A, V/early IV BC. Schweiz. Landesmus., Zurich.

In August 1962 a bulldozer clearing the slopes of a valley moraine near the Alpine town of Erstfeld north of the St Gothard pass, in the course of building an avalanche revetment uncovered a cache of gold rings lying under a small stone. The treasure, for such indeed it was, comprised four neck-rings and three armlets, two armlets and two neck-rings being obvious, but not quite identical, pairs. Since Erstfeld still awaits a more than summary description, only a few comments may be made on this unique find, consisting as it must have done not of grave goods but of an itinerant craftsman-trader's stock-in-trade, the product of what has been termed here the 'Dürkheim goldsmith' [see notes to **79–83**].

The left-hand detail is of one of the pair of neck-rings, one half of the decorated zone of which is illustrated here. Facing inwards with a central baluster-like headdress in the manner of the Reinheim rings, is a man with a very similar face to the three pairs on the Dürkheim bracelet [**54**]; he has a shapely leg which terminates in a pointed shoe like those shown on the Hallstatt sword scabbard and the Austrian shoe fibulae [**30, 32**]. The representation of such shoes on the Erstfeld ring as well as the

Manětín fibula [31] and the Weiskirchen belt-plaque [62]–all save Manětín are pieces probably made by craftsmen based on the Rhineland–indicates how such 'foreign' details gained artistic currency. A strange Siamese twin, who wears a bracelet on his wrist like one of the Reinheim 'goddesses' [80], faces away from the ring. His ears and single horn give the 'twin' a griffon-like aspect [compare 62–63], while his body and hind legs are covered with what, in comparison with the Panenský Týnec brooch [65], we may interpret as feathers. He in turn stands on the neck of a backward-looking beast which, with horn and beard, seems in its upper details a mountain goat but otherwise a bird. The lowest figure is either a caprid or, more likely, a bovine with enormous upcurling horns. Furthermore, just visible at the top of the main and otherwise undecorated hoop of the ring which forms a separate unit joined by two catches, is the eye and beak of a predatory bird, below which a multiple palmette figure acts as plumage.

The second ring, shown on the right, has the same basic construction; the ends of the decorated arc form a tenon which fits into the hollow main tube. The central feature this time is a waisted knob, like those of the Dürkheim bracelet. The large backward-looking soft-eyed creature with short curling horns resembles in its stylisation the lowest figure on the other ring; both are obviously caprids in the style of the catch-plate sheep on the Panenský Týnec brooch, and all three contrast rather than compare with the presumably somewhat earlier terminal animals on the Klein Aspergle drinking-horn mounts [44]. The body of the second ring of Erstfeld is, however, that of a great bird with talons. The wings of this bird are in the down-beat position and the huge grasping talons are rather in the manner of the clawed feet of the rim animals of the Dürrnberg flagon [72]; a domesticated version of the same bird is the hen or, more probably, cock fibula from Reinheim with coral inlay and similar long hatched tail feathers.[1] A long drooping tail-palmette in the style of the Reinheim 'bibs' [79–80] completes the design. One feature which is shared with Klein Aspergle is the 'bead-and-reel' backbone on the outer edge of the Erstfeld ring; this appears also on other pieces of more comparable date [63, 72, 86] than Klein Aspergle.

This incomprehensible mixture of observed nature and calculated fantasy, of whimsy and nightmare with a characteristic quality of Celtic elusiveness and lack of direct statement, is without parallel – save perhaps for a later group of objects which again can be considered as the work of at least a single crafts 'school' [158–161]. To our modern taste it may seem strange adornment for a wealthy woman – for from the grave finds it seems that ornamental neck-rings of the earlier La Tène phases were almost always for female use. Why these fine pieces should have been stacked away in the Swiss Alps never to be recovered is a matter for surmise. Their position so far from the main distribution of the other works of the 'Dürkheim goldsmith' but so close to one of the oldest transalpine passes suggests that, as with other La Tène objects of about the end of the fourth century [128, 137], an enterprising craftsman-trader of a century earlier (earlier dates still have been suggested)[2] may have been attempting to try a new market amongst the first Celtic settlers of northern Italy.

E. Vogt, *Neue Zürcher Zeitung*, no. 4290 (4 Nov. 1962); *id.*, *Ill. London News* 242:6441 (12 Jan. 1963), 48–49, esp.

figs. 6–7; *Schweiz. Landesmus. Zürich* 75 (1966), 6, 14–15, colour Pl. on p. 2; E. Soudská, *Arch. roz.* XX (1968), 464 and obr. 10:3

[1] F. J. Keller, *Das keltische Fürstengrab von Reinheim* I (1965), no. 14; *PAE*, 234 and Pl. 239
[2] H.P. Uenze, *Bayer. Vorg.* 29 (1964), 110

85 Leichlingen, Kr. Rhein-Wupper. Stone head. Ht. 12 cm. ?Late LT A, IV BC. Rhein. Landesmus., Bonn. *J. V. S. Megaw.*

This double or 'Janus' head carved from basaltic lava quarried in the Eifel district is a simpler piece than the Heidelberg fragment [49], though like it probably a finial for a pillar-statue. The face, with its saucer eyes, button nose and highly stylised ears, has the same general aspect as other works of less than top quality craftsmanship like the Manětín anthropomorphic brooch [31]; somewhat similar faces are illustrated in other objects on this page.

The concept of the 'Janus' face has a long and widespread distribution in the Celtic world as other pieces show [235]. The 'collar' around the Leichlingen head may possibly be intended as a representation of a torc.

ECA, no. 10 (= 'Solingen'); *Celts*, Pls. 64–66; M. Szabó, *Acta Arch. Hungarica* XVII (1965), 238 and fig. 4

86 Marson, Marne, grave 22. Bronze scabbard mount on iron sheath. Total l. sword, 54 cm., ht. mount 4·5 cm. LT A, late V BC. British Mus., London. *J. V. S. Megaw.*

In 1873 a group of more than 25 inhumation graves cut into the solid chalk was excavated at Marson near Châlons-sur-Marne; the total number of graves in the area was something in excess of 200. Grave 22 was a warrior's burial, the body placed with head towards the west. An openwork belt-hook with large terminal knob of a type common in the Marne[1] was found with four flat rings (also commonly found in early La Tène graves in eastern France), and the sword, whose iron sheath terminates in a trefoil-shaped clasp with three circular settings in two of which corals still remain; the type is that of the sword scabbard from the Somme-Bionne chariot burial [see notes to 111].

The embossed shield-shaped plaque worked up from the back in normal *repoussé* technique has on its margins two common early bordering motifs: the 'bead-and-reel' and the simple cable ornament. The faces have compressed leaf-commas [compare 63] and in aspect belong to the 'protuberance' class of the Hořovičky *phalerae*; Jacobsthal called them 'negroes'. Though presumably earlier than the other objects illustrated on the same page, the Marson mount is worth comparing with the only other anthropomorphic manifestation of the sacred Celtic trinity. The mount has no parallel in France and the style suggests the work of a German-based rather than local craftsman.

L. Morel, *Mém. de la Soc. d'Agric., Science, Commerce et Arts de la Marne* (1873–74), 174–95; *id.*, *La Champagne souterraine* (1898), 5–20, esp. 14–15 and Pl. 2:9; P. Reinecke, *Festschr. R-GZM* (1902), 81; *ECA*, no. 93; *KvsE*, 159, 192, 262 and obr. 4:2; *WK*, Taf. 86 above

[1] *ECA*, no. 355; see further notes to [95ff.]

F

87 Glauberg bei Stockheim, Kr. Büchingen. Detail of fragmentary bronze neck-ring. L. of surviving chord 12 cm., ht. of heads c. 1·5 cm. ?LT A, late V/early IV BC. Wetterau Mus., Friedberg, Hessen. *Dept. of Illustration, University of Sydney* (from an electrotype).

This fragment with ends filed down in antiquity is a stray find from the neighbourhood of a large fortified hill-top settlement. It is a single, solid casting with the moulding seam still clearly visible. Each of the three faces is a 'Janus' head, the central head resting between the jaws of what are only clearly recognisable as lions when the whole is literally stood on its heads, the lions' bodies and outstretched rear legs forming part of the curvature of the ring. Such inversion is a typical example of Celtic 'tricksiness' or shape-changing [see notes to **59**].

Although Jacobsthal considered this fragment as 'probably the work of an artisan from the East employed by the Celts', there are several points of comparison with other native pieces. The basic idea of the devouring beast and the severed head has been noted with the handle beast of the Dürrnberg flagon [**72**], while the representation of the human faces is a crude version of the 'protuberance' class also illustrated by the Marson trio above. Another crude but similar face is that of a little naked man with upstretched arms, a pointed chin and (possibly) helmet; this, again unfortunately a chance find, comes from Ilsfeld, Kr. Heilbronn,[1] and may also be compared with the central face of the Weiskirchen belt-plaque [**62**]. Other examples of crude faces of this general class are those at the ends of the Borsch handle mount [**66**]. The flat caps of the three Glauberg faces are certainly difficult to parallel, but the appearance of lions is not enough in itself to postulate a foreign craftsman working for new masters as the contemporary east Greek artisans did for the Royal Scythians; one has only to examine the 'foreign' imagery of such pieces as the Hallstatt scabbard [**30**] or the Erstfeld rings shown opposite, to observe what various elements could be decked out in Celtic garb.

R. Knorr, *Germania* 5 (1921), 14 ff.; G. Behrens, *Germania* 17 (1933), 86–87 and Abb. 2; O. Kunkel, *Oberhessens vorg. Altertümer* (1926), 198 and Abb. 186; *ECA*, no. 246

[1] P. Goessler, *Préhistoire* I (1932), 265–67 and fig. 4; K. Bittel, 'Die Kelten in Württemberg', *R-G Forsch.* 8 (1934), 41 and Taf. 8:2

88 Lahošt', Duchcov. Bronze finger ring. Internal d. 2·2 cm. ?IV/III BC. Muz. Ústí, Lahošt'–Trmice. *Aú ČSAV, Prague.*

This stray find wrongly described by Jacobsthal as gold – the bronze casting seam is clear in the illustrations – is difficult to date [see also notes to **229**] though it does have two features shared by several pieces of undoubtedly early La Tène date: 'satyr' ears pointed at the tip and comma-like knobs on the forehead, perhaps intended as vestigial ram's horns, the emblem of the Celtic war-god. The 'naturalism' of the face is certainly at variance with the general stylisation of most Celtic physiognomy, though there are exceptions [**78, 158**]; nevertheless the shouting mouth and upswept mane of hair look more like a classical representation of a Celt than the work of

a Celt himself – one may compare the representation of Vercingetorix on Celtic coins to that [see notes to **Plate IVe**] on a *denarius* of L. Hostilius Saserna, c. 48 BC.[1] The habit of stiffening the hair with limewash is recorded by the first-century Greek writer, Diodorus Siculus, as a common version of Celtic 'war-paint'.[2]

ECA, 125; *KvsE*, 83 and Tab. IV:2; *CCH*, 82, 169 and Pl. VIII:1; *V and A*, 115 and Taf. 8:4–5

[1] E. A. Sydenham, *Coinage of the Roman Republic* (1952), no. 952; *Celts*, Pl. 5a
[2] Diodorus Siculus V, 28; M.-L. Sjoestedt, *Études Celtiques* I (1938), 21 ff.; J. J. Tierney, *Proc. Roy. Irish Academy* 60 C 2 (1960), 249; *PCB*, 69

89 Schwieberdingen, Kr. Ludwigsburg. Bronze brooch with coral inlay. Total l. 4·5 cm. LT A, late V/early IV BC. Württ. Landesmus., Stuttgart. *Landesbildstelle Baden u. Württ. (Dr H. Hell).*

The brooch, of which two details are shown here, comes from a skeleton grave (probably female) and was found with a pot and four other brooches, one in the form of a little standing horse[1] and one, also with coral inlay along the bow, with both ends decorated with stylised duck heads, a type recently established as being a product of the central Rhineland.[2] There was also a pair of armlets decorated with very formalised human faces, of the 'Horchheim' type with a distribution mainly in the Hunsrück-Eifel.[3] It is probably from the edge of this area that the present brooch also came; the Reinheim and Zerf graves both have somewhat comparable brooches while the human face, rather crude in detail though it is, is not unlike the head on a poorly preserved brooch from an unlocated barrow burial at Urexweiler, Kr. St Wendel.[4]

The face above the spring is a sharp-nosed little creature with great curling horns which may be compared both with those of the handle monster of the Dürrnberg flagon [**72**] and the enigmatic figures on the Erstfeld rings [**84**]; the same feature, repeated several times and only in low relief, forms the back of the sheep on the Panenský Týnec brooch [**65**]. This face, really much more competently modelled than that at the other end of the brooch, is in fact related to the general class of 'protuberance' heads; similar but as yet unpublished heads are found on some of the many decorated fibulae from the post-World War II excavations at Dürrnberg.

A. Stroh, *Germania* 19 (1935), 290–95, esp. Abb. 2:5 and Taf. 39:1; O. Paret, *FbS* 8 (1933–35), 92–94 and Taf. XIX–XX; *ECA*, no. 310; *VRD*, ill. 127; H.P. Uenze, *Bayer. Vorg.* 29 (1964), 97, 110, n. 151; *V and A*, 111, 114–15 and Taf. 8: 4–5

[1] *ECA*, no. 321; see also notes to [**30, 63, 73, 78**]
[2] W. Dehn in (ed.) R. Degen *et al.*, *Helvetia Antiqua: Festschr. Emil Vogt* (1966), 140 ff. and Abb. 3:2
[3] J. V. S. Megaw, *Germania* 45 (1967), 56 f.; see also notes to [**51**]
[4] Reinheim: F. J. Keller, *Das keltische Fürstengrab von Reinheim* I (1965), no. 13; Zerf: *ECA*, no. 301; Urexweiler; L. Lindenschmidt, *Auh V* III:IX (1881), Taf. 1:1

90 Chýnovský Háj, Libčice, Prague. Bronze brooch with inlay. L. 7 cm. LT A, late V/early IV BC. Národní Muz., Prague. *W. and B. Forman (courtesy Artia, Prague).*

This brooch from a barrow burial outside Prague is another indication of the original homeland of the first barrow-burying La Tène Celtic colonists in Bohemia. With its coral inlay it is of the same class as Schwieberdingen illustrated above; the lower face with sharp pointed ears is in fact close to that in a similar position on the German brooch. The face at the catch-plate end with its great bulbous nose, staring eyes and cat-like ears can be traced back to 'situla art' prototypes and to the old east Hallstatt area where the double griffons of Boldù Dolfin[1] also do duty for a frontal 'cat face' in an Atestine example of 'shape-changing'. On Chýnov with a twist of Celtic whimsy, a 'joke motif' if ever there was one, the artist has added a neatly squared-off beard with side curls like rather flatter versions of the Schwieberdingen horns. The total effect of this little head is like a profane version of the Waldalgesheim 'old man' and his counterparts [see notes to 78]. A brooch from Bavaria however, offers the closest parallel [92].

J. Felcman, *Pam. Arch.* XX (1900), 41–44; P. Reinecke in *Festschr. R-GZM* (1902), 74 and Abb. 4; A. Stocký, *La Bohème à l'âge du fer* (1933), Pl. XX:5; *ECA*, 128, n. 8; *KvsE*, 82 and Tab. III:16; *CCH*, 174 and Pl. VIII:2; *V and A*, 114–15

[1] O.-H. Frey, 'Die Enstehung der Situlenkunst', *R-G Forsch.* 31 (1968), no. 36; see also notes to [64] and [76]

91 Oberwittighausen, Kr. Tauberbischofsheim. Bronze brooch. Total l. 10·5 cm., ht. of head c. 1·2 cm. LT A, late V/early IV BC. Badisches Landesmus., Karlsruhe, *Landesbildstelle Baden u. Württ.* (*Dr. H. Hell*).

The large brooch of which a detail is shown here was found with three others, all produced by the 'lost wax' or *cire perdue* method in which the original mould was broken after casting [see also 92]. It had been buried with a north-south oriented skeleton laid out on a central sandstone pavement and covered with a barrow mound; the only other recorded finds were a pottery vessel and the bones of a small domestic pig, and it is likely that it was a woman's grave.

This brooch is basically a development of the Italian 'Certosa' type with long bow and turned-up knobbed foot. The foot in this case is in the shape of a curved-beaked bird as occasionally found not only on other brooches including two from the early 'colonist's' graves in Bohemia[1] but also on a special Alpine group of belt-hooks [95–99]. The face, with its saucer eyes and wedge-shaped nose, is in the same general style as the Reinheim 'owls' [79–80]; even closer is the head on one of the three decorated knobs of an armring from Thuringia [100]. The great swirling hollow bow is also a feature of two other Bavarian brooches, one the 'Certosa' type possibly associated with the Parsberg brooch illustrated earlier [63] and another from Pottenstein[2] with catch-plate decorated with a very stylised horse head with coral-set eyes. Both these share with the Oberwittighausen brooch the addition of a great dumb-bell-like pair of knobs which on the present example is augmented by a third to form a three-dimensional version of the common Celtic triple circle motif.

This use of large decorative knobs seems to be a characteristic of a workshop based in Southern Germany whose products were exported not only to the Dürrnberg salt-working centre not far to the south but to a Celtic

outpost in Thuringia also concerned with salt trading [93–94]; one of the Bohemian brooches cited above is also of this type.

E. Wahle, *Bad. Fundber.* I (1925–28), 7⁓ ⁓ and Abb. 3–5; *ECA*, no. 303; *VRD*, ill. 125–26; *V a A*, 128 ff.

[1] *KvsE*, obr. 78:2, 5
[2] Kleinmittersdorf, Ldkr. Parsberg: W. Kersten, *Praehist. Zeitschr.* XXIV (1933), Abb. 8:1; Pottenstein: W. A. von Jenny, *Keltische Metallarbeiten aus heidnischer u. christl. Zeit* (1935), Taf. 3:4

92 Oberwittighausen, Kr. Tauberbischofsheim. Bronze brooch. L. 4·4 cm. Late LT A, late V/early IV BC. Badisches Landesmus., Karlsruhe, *Landesbildstelle Baden u. Württ.* (*Dr H. Hell*).

The three smaller fibulae from Oberwittighausen are all decorated in more or less the same manner; a human caricature of a face above the spring over which is a second head curving back from the catch-plate; originally all three may have had ball terminals to the springs. The human faces with saucer eyes and circles marking the pupils have exaggerated scroll eyebrows, bulbous noses and, what appears most clearly on the example illustrated here, a squared-off beard precisely in the manner of the Chýnov grotesque illustrated on the opposite page. Indeed, except for the eyes, the catch-plate head of the present brooch, which also has a squared beard, is almost a copy of the head in similar position on the Czech piece; another brooch with a combination of bottle-nosed bearded face, griffon and beaked bird spiral comes from Criesbach, Kr. Künzelsau, Württemberg.[1]

Of the two Oberwittighausen brooches not illustrated here, one – with dumb-bell spring terminals still surviving – has a ram's head above the catch-plate; the other a griffon-cum-dragon like the incised supporters of the Stupava plaque [64], both characteristically ambivalent Celtic images. The beaded back-bone of the present brooch is in a similar position to that on the Parsberg brooch with human head which, like the possibly local Bohemian brooches found near Plzeň [68, 70], has the same circled pupils. Indeed it seems possible that the Bohemian pair may be intended as imitations of the Oberwittighausen class of fibulae. Despite the differences of detailing of the four Oberwittighausen brooches it seems highly probable that all were made in the same crafts centre; whether variations in quality represent the work of master and pupil or simply good and less good products of the same hand is much more difficult to determine.

ECA, no. 312; *VRD*, ill. 129; R. Joffroy in *Kelten und Germanen* = *Kunst der Welt* (1964), 142, colour ill. p. 145; *V and A*, 114 ff. and Abb. 4 D; *PAE*, 237, 281 and Pl. 247

[1] K. Bittel, 'Die Kelten in Württemberg', *R-G Forsch.* 8 (1934), Taf. 10:7; *ECA*, no. 311

93 Dürrnberg, Hallein, grave 37. Silver-bronze brooch. L. 4 cm. Late LT A, late V/early IV BC. Stadtmus. Hallein. *Ing. Ernst Penninger.*

Found in a grave with a brooch in the form of a boar

with triple knobs[1] in the manner of the largest Ober-wittighausen example [91], this brooch with ram- and horse-head terminals, like several others from the post-World War II excavations at Dürrnberg, must be the result of trading with south German Celts or, perhaps no less likely, the result of a visit from a south German craftsman. Apart from the knobs on the spring plate, the eyes of this brooch are a clear trade-mark. The 'eye-lashes' round the horse's eye are a convention also found on Bavarian brooches although here it has been executed by a rocked tracer after the original casting. There is also some sign of silvering, perhaps the product of eastern rather than western technical know-how. A third brooch from grave 37 has a sharp-featured face with 'cat' ears, chin linked to the bow with the same tongue as the horse head, and dumb-bell spring ornaments.

E. Penninger, *Mitt. Ges. Salzburger Landeskde.* 100 (1960), 4; *Keltische Kunst: Bodemschatten uit Salzburg,* Frans Halsmus., Haarlem (1963), no. 17

[1] Penninger, *op. cit.,* Abb. 7 ('Grab 39'); K. Willvon-seder, *Keltische Kunst in Salzburg* = Schriftreihe d. S.M.C.A. 2 (1960), Abb. 11; *Keltische Kunst . . . ,* no. 20

94 'Kleiner Gleichberg', Steinsburg, Kr. Meiningen. Bronze brooch L. 3 cm. Late LT A, late V/early IV BC. Steinsburgmus., Römhild.

The fortified hill-top site of the Kleiner Gleichberg commands the main valley route between the mountains of Rhön and the Thuringian Forest. Occupied more or less continuously from Late Bronze Age times to the end of the La Tène period, it seems to have owed its import-ance as a local outpost regularly strengthened by the more southerly and westerly Celtic tribes to its proximity to the salt supplies of the Wirra valley near Bad Salzun-gen – the find spot of the Borsch flagon mount [66].

A considerable quantity of material with imported La Tène pottery as well as bronzes has been recovered from the area of the Steinsburg as the result of modern quarrying, although no large-scale scientific excavation has taken place. Amongst the large scatter of early La Tène objects from the Gleichberg are almost a dozen miniature brooches with terminal spring knobs and faces in the manner of those found at Dürrnberg – another salt-trading centre – and south Germany. In fact, such a collection of fibulae in an occupation rather than burial site must indicate the stock of a craftsman-trader, perhaps from the same workshop group as was exploiting the needs of the rich Austrian centre of Dürrnberg. It is noticeable that with few exceptions the Steinsburg is the only area where such ornate brooches were not found in a grave; such human face-, animal- or bird-decorated brooches may have been intended for funerary and female use only.[1]

The present example is a rather crude piece, but one must remember its miniature size. The swollen, hollow bow is a particularly south German form [91]. Apart from a second brooch by the same hand and with a similar crude lower face and upper ram's head from the Gleichberg,[2] a find from a barrow grave at Grafrath, Kr. Bruck an Amper in Upper Bavaria has the same profile and a similar catch-plate head.[3]

G. Neumann, 'Das Gleichberggebiet', *Werte der deutsch. Heimat* 6 (1963), Abb. 13:2; H. Kaufmann, *Jahresschr. mittld. Vorg.* 50 (1966), 209 and Abb. 4c

[1] G. Jacob, *Die Gleichberge bei Römhild als Culturstätten der La Tènezeit Mitteldeutschlands* = *Vorg. Altertümer Prov. Sachsen* 5–8 (1887); A. Götze, *Praehist. Zeitschr.* XIII–XIV (1921–22), 19–83; *Manuel* IV, 479, 869 ff.; H.P. Uenze, *Bayer. Vorg.* 29 (1964) 114 ff.; P. Donat, *Die Steinsburg: Besiedlungsgeschichte des Kleinen Gleichbergs* (1965), esp. Taf. 5; see also the finds from Staffelberg, Kr. Lichtenfels: W. Kersten, *Praehist. Zeitschr.* XXIV (1934), 133f.; K. Schwarz, *Germania* 41 (1963), 108–14
[2] Kaufmann, *Jahresschr. mitteldt. Vorg.* 50, 209, 215 and Abb. 4b–c
[3] L. Lindenschmidt, *AuhV* V (1911), Taf. 20:322

95 Hölzelsau, Kufstein, Unterinntal. Bronze belt-hook. L. 16·2 cm. Late LT A, early IV BC. Prähist. Staatssamm-lung, Munich. R-GK (*E. Neuffer*).

Openwork belt-hooks, particularly those based on the palmette, are a not uncommon feature of the Marnian cemeteries of France including the Somme–Bionne chariot grave [see notes to **111**].[1] There is one ornate variant of this basic form of which more than a dozen examples are known from the area centred on the Celtic flat cemeteries of northern Italy and the Ticino valley in the Alps north of Lake Maggiore, an area which seems to have been settled, to judge from such things as sword types, in the latter part of the fifth century by Celts with strong links with the Marne [see also notes to **96**]; there are extensions of this general type into the Adriatic and across to south-east France. Of the four outliers to this distribution this belt-hook from the Tyrol is the finest of all. These belt-hooks from their distribution seem to be the only definite local art product which may be associated with the first Celts south of the Alps.

The basic design consists of a cast openwork mount (in this case riveted to a bronze backing plate with a crude *graffito* in the form of the letter 'W') built up of a maze of beast and birds impinging upon either a central naked figure or a simple 'cross of Lorraine' device; there is often provision for coral or enamel settings, though these have not survived. This particular Celtic version of the old oriental motif of 'master' (or mistress) 'of the beasts' has an Italian background in openwork pendants of the eighth and seventh centuries particularly from Chiusi and Vetulonia.[2] A closer contemporary is an openwork pendant from Viniča, grave 358, in Carniola, now north Jugoslavia, a region where early La Tène Celts came in contact with a retarded Hallstatt culture owing much to its proximity to both northern Italy and the more southerly Balkans [see also notes to **64**].[3]

The Viniča pendant has one feature which appears prominently on the Hölzelsau plaque and crops up also in engraved sword scabbards of La Tène Ic/II date [**179–183**][4] – what for want of a better name might be termed a maze of sea-horses. The horses of the Tyrol piece indeed are not unlike the horse on the brooch from Dürrnberg, grave 37 [**93**]. The whole layout of the belt plaque shows an admixture of La Tène and Hallstatt elements, the little naked man with outstretched arms harking back to the miniature figures of the transitional period between the end of Hallstatt and beginning of La Tène [**17–19**], while the intermingling of man and beast stems from a similar type of conception to that behind the Erstfeld rings [**84**].

P. Reinecke, *Wiener Prähist. Zeitschr.* X (1923), 28 ff.

and Abb. 1; *ECA*, no. 360, esp. p. 53 ff.; R. Pittioni, *Urgeschichte des österreich. Raumes* (1954), 680 and Abb. 469; *WK*, Taf. 9 below; *PreA*, 188, 190 and ill. 183; W. Torbrügge and H.P. Uenze, *Bilder zur Vorg. Bayerns* (1968), ill. 251

1 *ECA*, no. 355
2 *ECA*, 56–57 and Pl. 237a; G. Kossack 'Studien zum Symbolgut der Urnenfelder- u. Hallstattzeit Mittel-europas', *R-G Forsch.* 20 (1952), 56 ff. and Taf. 13:1–2
3 (Ed.) A. Mahr, *Treasures of Carniola: The Mecklen-burg Collection* (1934), no. 102; *ECA*, Pl. 230:g
4 J. M. de Navarro, *Germania* 37 (1959), 134–35; see also notes to [178]

96 Campo di Servirola, S. Polo d'Enza, Reggio Emilia. Bronze belt-hook. L. 8·1 cm. Late LT A/early IV BC. Mus. Civico 'G. Chierici', Reggio Emilia.

On this plaque the struggling man's opponents are pre-datory birds and backward-looking griffons, the heads of which occasionally decorate fibulae and other objects [see notes 62 and 92]; indeed an unpublished brooch in Vienna, a stray find from Hallstatt, has the backward-turned head of these 'orientalised' early La Tène pieces[1] set on the body of a short-tailed dog or perhaps horse;[2] this brooch must be added to Hölzelsau as a product of the belt-plaque craftsmen based on the area south of the Alps. The Hallstatt brooch is not unlike a strap-end from Somme–Bionne and another from Hauviné in the Ardennes with two backward-look-ing griffons chest to chest and provision for inset eyes. The tradition of such bird-beasts continues into the later fourth century in a chariot mount from the Waldalgesheim double grave.[3]

This present piece is one of four[4] which one can pre-sume were traded across the Alps into north-east Italy; other scattered finds from the same site included local 'Certosa' brooches and a later La Tène import from the Marne, a fragment of a torc with triple ball settings [see notes to 143]. What is really exceptional about the Campo di Servirola plaque is that it has a precise pendant cast from the same mould and illustrated right [97].

E. Magagnini, *Emilia Preromana* 4 (1953–55), 45–67 and Tav. IV:7; *V and A*, 132 and n. 139

1 G. Behrens in *Festschr. R-GZM* I (1952), 28–30
2 Naturhist. Mus. Vienna, Prähist. Abteilung inv. no. 35746
3 Somme–Bionne: *ECA*, no. 359 [see also notes to 111]; Hauviné: *Manuel* IV, 617, 743 and fig. 524:2; *ECA*, 42 and Pl. 230b; Waldalgesheim: *ECA*, no 156b
4 An unpublished belt-hook from Lagole di Calalzo in the Mus. Pieve di Cadore looks like a companion for [96–97]

97 Castaneda, Kt. Grisons, grave 75. Bronze belt-hook. L. 11·2 cm. Late LT A/early B1, early IV BC. Rätisches Mus., Chur. *Schweiz. Landesmus., Zürich.*

This plaque, an obvious twin to [96] and proof of the latter's immediate source, comes from a man's grave excavated in 1941 from a large cemetery and settlement bordering on the Ticino valley. In some of the 100

inhumation burials were inscriptions in a northern form of Etruscan – one on an imported beaked flagon and evidence of the continuing contacts of what must have been a very mixed population with northern Italy, contacts which brought not only trade to the Celtic west but probably also part of the artistic inspiration for the very form of the 'Ticino' belt plaques [see also notes to 30]. A new grave find, numbered 76, includes a LT A sword probably made in France together with one of the locally made beaked flagons.[1]

Other finds from Castaneda grave 75 included a wooden bucket, a decorated armring, Alpine-type 'Certosa' brooch and a number of other openwork fittings for the same belt. These included a strap end with horse-head terminals in the style of the Hölzelsau plaque [95] and similar to a recent find from St Denis-de-Palin (Cher).[2] One of the other mounts is in the form of an ivy-leaf rather than palmette, a type well dated by association at two other sites from which complex openwork plaques of the 'Ticino' class have been found [see notes to 98–99].

One other related Swiss find is a loose openwork plaque with highly stylised backward-looking griffon-birds, their beaks touching a triple circle setting for coral inlay. This plaque, similar to one of the St Denis-de-Palin mounts, was almost certainly added locally to a complex brooch with tiny human masks, an isolated find made at Champ du Moulin, Val-de-Travers, Ct. Neuchâtel,[3] though the brooch itself is decorated in a style which recalls the 'Horchheim' class of neck- and armrings [see notes to 51].

JSGU, 32 (1940–41), 103 and Taf. XXVI:2; B. Frei in (ed.) W. Drack, 'Die Eisenzeit der Schweiz', *Reportium d. Ur- u. Frühg. der Schweiz* 3 (1957), 31 and Taf. 16:16

1 Margarita Primas, *JSGU* 54 (1968–69), 61–68
2 J. Favière *et al.*, *Gallia* 22 (1964), 224 ff. and figs. 21–22
3 *ECA*, no. 293; J. M. de Navarro, *40. Ber. R-GK 1959* (1960), 105 and Taf. 18:2a–b; W. Dehn in (ed.) R. Degen *et al.*, *Helvetia Antiqua: Festschr. Emil Vogt* (1966), 137 ff. and Abb. 1–2

98 Este, Villa Benvenuti, grave 116. Bronze belt-hook. L. 11 cm. Late Este period III, early IV BC. Mus. Nazionale Atestino, Este. *Soprintendenza alle Antichità delle Venezie-Este.*

That the Celts were closely in touch with Este, centre of 'situla' art, is clear from several objects here illustrated [see notes to 30]. The present belt-hook, the most com-plex of a number from Este, was found in a native grave with cremation urn and a large number of local pots, as well as a number of other bronzes including a local 'Certosa' brooch. The remains of two belts were also in the grave.

In the place of the 'master of the beasts' or the simple 'cross of Lorraine' [99], the central feature is an ivy-leaf, like that from Castaneda [97]; two other somewhat simpler iron mounts were found in another Este grave, Capodaglio grave 31, together with a late V/early IV BC Italic red-figure *skyphos*, and two Attic pots, a stemless cup like that from Dürrnberg grave 44 [see notes to 48], and a *kantharos* of the St Valentin type related to that found at Rodenbach [see notes to 55].[1] Capodaglio grave 31 also contained a low 'fire dog' of a type found in grave 38 with another Celtic piece, this time an early LT short sword and single-edged knife;[2] the converse of these Celtic finds in native Atestine contexts is exemplified north of the Alps by finds of very similar fire dogs [see notes to 47].

The open-beaked birds-cum-griffons on the Villa Benvenuti girdle-hook again resemble the openwork mount from the Waldalgesheim chariot burial [see notes to 96].

ECA, no. 363a

[1] G. Fogolari and O.-H. Frey, *Studi Etruschi* 33 (1965), 237 ff. and Tav. XXXIII:31–33; Frey, 'Die Entstehung der Situlenkunst', *R-G Forsch.* 31 (1968), 26, 99 and Taf. 33:31, 33
[2] Frey, *op. cit.*, Taf. 31:17–19

99 Giubiasco, Ct. Ticino, grave 29. Bronze belt-hook. L. 11·7 cm. Late LT A, early IV BC. Schweiz. Landesmus., Zürich.

The cemetery of Giubiasco comprises more than 500 graves and must have been in use for upwards of two centuries. The present plaque was found with a fragment of a bronze bucket, an urn, and an archaic type of serpentine brooch more usually found in Ha D contexts like, for example, period IV of the Heuneburg hill-fort.[1] The 'master of the beasts' is highly stylised and the representation of what look like more peaceable water-birds relates this plaque to one – again only the most ornate of a series – found in the cemetery of the southern French settlement site of Ensérune (Hérault) west of the old Greek colony and *entrepôt* of Massilia. The Ensérune plaque came from grave 41 in which was found an Attic red-figure cup (by the Jena painter) of early IV BC date.[2] There seems little doubt that this French piece, together with the mounts from the other French sites noted above [96–97], which include Somme-Bionne, found with a later fifth-century Attic cup [see notes to 111], must have come either in the course of trade across the Alps or more likely round the coast-line to the mouth of the Rhône and thence north and west. Both these routes were used by the importers of Italic drinking-vessels and tableware, such as have been found not only in the western princely graves but also in the Ticino valley flat cemeteries including Giubiasco.

R. Ulrich, *Die Gräberfelder in der Umgebung von Bellinzona* (*Kt. Tessin*) (1914), 547 and Taf. XLII:3; *ECA*, no. 361a

[1] W. Dehn *et al.*, *Germania* 32 (1954), 53 and Taf. 11: 19–20; see also notes to [7]
[2] F. Mouret, *Monuments Piot* 27 (1924), 51 and fig. 4; Ph. Héléna, *Les origines de Narbonne* (1937), 272 and fig. 166; *ECA*, no. 362; J. Jannoray, 'Ensérune . . .', *Bibl. des Écoles françaises d'Athènes et de Rome* 181 (1955), 394–96; fig. 40 and Pl. LVII:1; *V and A*, 132 and n. 139; see also J. D. Beazley, *Attic red-figure vase-painters* II (2ed. 1963), 1512

100 Pössneck, Kr. Saalfeld, grave 4/5. Bronze armring. D. 7·9 cm., ht. of each decorated knob c. 1·5 cm. ?Early La Tène B1, IV BC. Landesmus. f. Vorgeschichte, Dresden.

This, like the great neck-ring from Reinheim [79] or a simpler ring from the upper Waldalgesheim grave [126],

is a rare example of the twisted ring form in earlier La Tène metal work. The ring, a solid casting, was discovered in 1874 together with a number of other graves at the east foot of the Altenburg in Thuringia. Together with it was a brooch and a plain armring (both now lost) and a ritually bent iron sword – fairly typical contents for a La Tène grave but in this case probably a grave of a Celt far from his normal homeland, a Celt probably concerned with trading for raw materials in what was in fact a largely non-Celtic area [see notes to 94].

The decoration of an armring at three separate points is a common feature of many early La Tène rings from superb gold examples like that from the Dürkheim chariot grave [54] to much simpler non-figural ornament on rings of the later Hunsrück–Eifel culture. In this case the three areas of decoration form a mystical Celtic triumvirate of the human, the animal and the ambiguous. The face, showing considerable wear, indicating that this ring at least was not just produced for the funerary rites, is in the simple stylisation of the large Oberwittighausen brooch [91] and not unlike the two faces on the other central German find illustrated on this page. The stylised ram's head can be compared with that at the top of the Reinheim flagon handle [73]; a ring from Pierre Morains in the Marne, now unfortunately stolen but related to some of those illustrated below [see notes to 120–121] has a pseudo ram's head as one point in a triple division of decoration.[1] Another rather similar pseudo-face forms the central part of the design on a linch pin from Niederweis, Kr. Bitburg, but this is probably a later piece.[2] The third element of the Pössneck ring is a triple spiral which again foreshadows later forms [132–133].

It is difficult to be dogmatic about the general area where this armring may have been made; somewhere in the central Rhineland might be a fair guess.

ECA, no. 249; H. Kaufmann, *Die Vorg. Besiedlung des Orlagaues: Katalog* (1959), 97 and Taf. 57–58:13; *ibid.*, *Text* (1963), 137; *V and A*, 131; Kaufmann, *Jahresschr. Mitteldt. Vorg.* 50 (1966), 205 ff., Taf. 12–15

[1] =Mus. Épernay inv. no. 1792; L. Coutier, R. Duval and A. Brisson, *Bull. de la Soc. Arch. Champenoise* 4 (1928), 115–18; *V and A*, 131, n. 135
[2] *ECA*, no. 161; *V and A*, 129–30 and Taf. 10:4

101 Berlin–Niederschönhausen, Bez. Pankow. Bronze brooch. L. 9 cm. Late LT A, early IV BC. Staatl. Museen zu Berlin (former Mus. f. Vor- u. Frühgeschichte).

Like the Pössneck ring and the Ostheim brooch [69], this single find must be regarded as a stray from some central or southern Rhineland workshop. The decoration of this brooch consists of the head over the now missing spring back-to-back with a similar head complete with tooth-brush moustache but with an elongated chin rather than a beard. This second head, very much out of scale, is attached to a tiny naked male body not unlike the 'master of the beasts' of the 'Ticino' class of belt-hooks [95–97]. Apart from the (clothed) full-length figure of the Manětín brooch [31], this is the only example of such a complete representation, and – clear only in profile – the only example of sexual 'indecency' in early La Tène art.

The culprit is a ram's head stylised again like the upper Reinheim handle figure compared to the Pössneck ring; the elongated ram on one of the Kleiner Gleichberg brooches is also comparable [see notes to **94**]. The addorsed human heads are similar to the pair on a miniature brooch from barrow B at Rappenau, Kr. Sinsheim,[1] adjacent to a chariot grave [see notes to **56**]. Rappenau also has the emphasised jaws-cum-beard of the Berlin heads, and is another hint as to the source from which the latter piece was originally brought. The deep ridges between the Niederschönhausen heads were probably originally filled with enamel.

W. A. von Jenny, *Keltische Metallarbeiten aus heidnischer u. christl. Zeit* (1935), Taf. 9:3; C. Schuchhardt, *Vorg. von Deutschland* (5 ed. 1943), 231 and Abb. 210d; *ECA*, no. 308, esp. p. 3, n. 4 and 194; H. Kaufmann, *Jahresschr. mitteldt. Vorg.* 50 (1960), 213–15 and Abb. 8; E. Soudská *Arch. roz.* XX (1968), 462 f. and obr. 9:6

[1] E. Wagner, *Fundstätten u. Funde aus dem Grossherzogtum Baden* II (1911), 350 and Abb. 238d; *ECA*, no. 309

102 Via Ognissanti – Vicolo San Massimo, Padua. Grave *stele*. 79×69 cm. IV/III BC. Museo Civico, Padua.

Mention has already been made of the local carving of northern Italy in connection with later '*situla* art' [**34**] and Celtic pillar statues [**75**]. The present example of palaeovenetic art is a recent find and bears an inscription running round two margins which seems to follow a fixed dedicatory formula for such grave monuments. The greatest interest of this slab of local limestone is of course in the main figures of warrior and driver standing in a chariot pulled by two horses. Although except for a few coins [**103**] we have no representation by the Celts themselves of their own war vehicles, other archaeological evidence[1] allows one to be fairly certain of at least some details of their construction. On this and another grave *stele* from Padua now in Verona we have evidence, as on the votive deposit figures of Baratela at Este, that the indigenous population borrowed the subject matter for their art from, in this case, later Celtic settlers in the north of Italy. Celtic settlement continued even after the Roman defeat of the Cisalpine Gauls at the battle of Telamon in 225 BC.

The shield lying in the chariot has the long central mid-rib, oval shape and central rectangular boss typical of Middle La Tène forms. One other such metal boss was found in a later Celtic grave at Este, Benvenuti grave 123, together with a glass armlet and a La Tène brooch; this is the shield form of the Baratela votive models [see notes to **34**]. The warrior driving to the Otherworld and either carrying his spear or holding a goad has a companion, perhaps a woman, crouching on the narrow platform. This matches what is known from classical authorities of the warrior chieftain and his companion as well as being confirmed by the layout of the earlier Marnian graves. The curved sides of the low chariot body, the spoked wheels, great hub caps, and outer tires are also true to Celtic pattern. The method of yoking and haltering the paired horses is also compatible with archaeological evidence. The clearly delineated omega-shaped bridle-bits are a type first introduced in the fourth century; they have been found in a third-century chariot grave at Adria and occur north of the Alps at the great Bavarian *oppidum* of Manching [see notes to **189**]. Other details such as the bird in flight above the chariot, the plant between the horses' legs and the dot-in-circle ornament belong more to the local artistic tradition

based on the '*situla* style' of some two centuries earlier. An even more recently published *stele* from Padua showing a rider with helmet and spear rather in the manner of the Baratela plaque also has a bird in flight.[2]

All in all, this *stele* is as clear a representation of the intermingling of cultural traditions in the middle La Tène phase as the Hallstatt scabbard is for the early phase [**30**].

A. Prosdocimi, *Atti e Memorie Accad. Patavina di Scienze, Lettere ed Arti* LXXVI:III (1963–64), 2–15; O.-H. Frey, *Germania* 46 (1968), 317–20

[1] I. M. Stead, *Antiquity* XXXIX (1965), 259–65; P. Harbison in *Festschr. Dehn*, 34–58
[2] Prosdocimi, *Atti e Memorie Accad. Patavina di Scienze, Lettere ed Arti* LXXVIII:III (1965–66), 196–205

103 N.E. France, 'Remi'. Bronze coin (reverse). D. 1·5 cm. Mid I BC. Cabinet des Médailles, Bibliothèque Nationale, Paris.

This coin bears on the obverse a holy trinity of Celtic heads which possibly copy a coin of the Triumvirs, Octavian, Antony and Lepidus [see notes to **286**]. The reverse, though based on a classical prototype as indicated by the partially obliterated winged figure, represents a Belgic chariot of the time of Julius Caesar. The low curved framework, similar to the Padua *stele* representation, is on the evidence of the Padua *stelae* surely not intended to show in flat perspective the front and one side but simply a side view of a chariot with double bowed hand-rail; there is the usual pair of horses.

E. Muret and M. A. Chabouillet, *Catalogue des monnaies gauloises de la Bibliothèque Nationale* (1889), no. 8406. Sir Cyril Fox, *Antiq. J.* XXVII (1947), 118 and Pl. XVIIIa; L. Lengyel, *L'art gaulois dans les médailles* (1954), no. 433; *Celts*, Pl. 47b; I. M. Stead, *Antiquity* XXXIX (1965), 264; P. Harbison in *Festschr. Dehn*, 47–49

104 'Čertův Kámen', Kšice, Stříbro, okr. Tachov. Fragment of bronze brooch. Ht. c. 1·5 cm. LT A, mid-IV BC. Mus. Stříbro. *Aú ČSAV*, Prague.

This terminal from a brooch was found with a disturbed grave under one of a group of forty-two barrows in central Bohemia. Pottery including both early La Tène sherds and some in the earlier Hallstatt tradition was found in an area of considerable burning.

The long bearded face with its clipped moustache has been compared to the 'old man' of the Waldalgesheim flagon [**78**], but the general form is in fact closer to the face in a similar position on the Reinheim jug [**73**].

The discovery of two bronze balls attached to part of the spring mechanism suggests that the complete Kšice brooch would have been of the Oberwittighausen 'dumb-bell' form [see notes to **91**]. The most interesting feature, however, of what is quite clearly a western import brought by the pioneering La Tène settlers of Bohemia, is the simple helmet with its carefully scalloped border like that fringing the gold leaf heads from the first Schwarzenbach grave[1] or the Klein Aspergle horn mounts [**44**]. Helmeted fibulae occur in a later context [**200–202**], but here the form is that of the simple helmets on the cavalrymen of the Hallstatt sword scabbard [30]. It is a suitable enough, if early, piece to introduce a series of objects associated with the established Celtic settlements of fourth-century Italy.

O. Eichhorn, *Sudeta* XI (1935), 33–47 and Abb. 18; *KvsE*, 82 and obr. 12:2; *V and A*, 116; E. Soudská, *Arch. roz.* XX (1968), 463–64 and obr. 12:1

[1] *ECA*, no. 34, [21-26]; see also notes to [57]

105 Canosa di Puglia, Bari, tomb 'A'. Iron helmet with bronze overlay and coral mounts. Ht. 25 cm., d. 23·3 cm. Second half IV BC. Antikenabteilung, Stiftung Preussischer Kulturbesitz, Staatl. Museen, Berlin. *R-GK* (E. Neuffer).

This helmet, originally with cheek pieces like that illustrated below [107], was found in 1895 in a six-chambered *hypogea* or underground tomb complex built during the last quarter of the fourth century at the ancient town of Canusium (flourishing in the fourth/third century BC).

Of the two main chambers tomb 'A' – the second tomb was that of a woman – also contained a fine bronze cuirass, a horse-bit and a number of south Italian vases as exported to the Celts of the north of Italy. A third chamber contained an important collection of glass of Alexandrine origin.[1]

The helmet itself, originally gilt at least in part, is a type adopted by the Celts from contemporary Italic fashions and distributed on both sides of the Alps. In view of another helmet illustrated here [110], it has been suggested that the Canosa example might be an import from the Marne, but the distribution of this particular 'jockey-cap' type of head-gear is very much concentrated in the transalpine cemeteries with an outlier in Slovenia.[2] The decoration – which includes half-way down the scalloped pattern of Kšice – is a return to the fashions of non-representational early La Tène goldwork with a repertoire drawn at first hand from the plant-motifs of contemporary Graeco-Italic art, examples of which in the form of pottery and metal work are abundant in the Celtic settled regions of northern Italy. With such pieces as the Canosa helmet it is possible also to invoke the actual participation of native, non-Celtic, craftsmen to explain the rigidity and 'academic' quality of the designs, designs nonetheless which north of the Alps were to inspire a master workshop of major importance for the later development of La Tène art [124 ff.]. But even here on the Canosa helmet the main palmette design bordered by half-palmette fronds can be read as a pseudo-face anticipating later and less indefinite allusions to the human form.

Various explanations have been offered for the presence of this Cisalpine Gaulish helmet in an Apulian grave: that it belonged to a Celtic mercenary seeking his fortune in the armies of Dionysius of Syracuse (369 BC) or of Agathocles (c. 310 BC), to a refugee from Roman repulses in the north (c. 348 BC), to an even earlier stray adventurer following the sack of Rome in 387 BC – all these theories have been advanced, though the last must be rejected on a number of counts. There is certainly evidence for later Celtic use of local tombs in another context [see notes to **170**] but since the helmet is the only 'foreign' piece in the Canosa grave – the cuirass for example can be matched by two others from

the ancient town cemetery – it is equally likely that tomb 'A' marks the last resting place of an Apulian mercenary – not a Celt – who gained a trophy while serving in Sicily in the Greek army of Timoleon against the Carthaginians who certainly recruited barbarians from the north. As it is now preserved, the helmet is without the plume mountings and part of the brim shown in this pre-World War II photograph.

P. Reinecke, *Wiener Prähist. Zeitschr.* XXVII (1940), 50 ff.; *ECA*, no. 143; *Besançon*, 29 ff. and Abb. 3f; *PAE*, 259; A. J. Oliver Jnr., 'Reconstruction of two Apulian grave groups', *Antike Kunst*, Beiheft. 5 (1968), esp. 15 f. and Taf. 2:1

[1] D. B. Harden, *J. Glass Studies* X (1968), 21–47; *id.*, *Arch. J.* CXXV (1968), 62–63
[2] *Manuel* IV, 666 ff. and fig. 488:1

106–107 Gottolengo, Brescia. Bronze cheek-piece and helmet mount on iron base. Ht. [106] 13 cm., [107] 10·5 cm. Later IV BC. Mus. Civico Romano, Brescia.

These recent finds from a Celtic grave disturbed during building works comprised both cheek-pieces (only one shown here) – of the type which would have originally been attached to the Canosa helmet illustrated above – and one of a matching pair of mounts which would have decorated the iron cap of a helmet very similar to that illustrated overleaf from Umbria [108]. The cheek-piece of this helmet from the territory once occupied by the Cenomani is decorated with a simple leaf pattern and three roundels, while the upper fitting to which the cheek-piece would have been hinged has a lyre composed of 'S' scrolls enclosing the roundel. The terminals of the lyre-scrolls form pseudo bird's heads with long down-curving beaks, more like pelicans or storks than ducks, the eyes being formed by the rivet holes for attachment of the plaque to the iron cap. Both the lyre and curl features are copied on the helmet from Amfreville in northern France [110].

This is the most northerly of the decorated helmets so far found in Italy, though it is closely paralleled not only by that from Umbria [108] but by helmets from the Celtic cemeteries at Montefortino and Filottrano,[1] the second with a great anthropomorphic crest.

Mostra dell'Arte e Civiltà romana nell'Italia settentrionale Mus. Civico, Bologna (1964), no. 57; A. Rampinelli, *Sibrium* 8 (1964–66), 61–63

[1] *ECA*, nos. 146 and 147

108 'Umbria.' Iron helmet with bronze covering. Ht. of cap 19·5 cm., ht. of cheek-pieces 13 cm. Later IV BC. Antikenabteilung, Stiftung Preussischer Kulturbesitz, Staatl. Museen, Berlin.

This helmet, supposedly found in Umbria, has traces of textile still adhering to the iron bosses as on other helmets. It is the most flamboyantly decorated of all those which Jacobsthal considered as 'the result of collaboration between Etruscan and Celtic artists in an Italian workshop'.[1]

The most clearly 'Italic' feature is the palmette chain round the edge of the cap mentioned below, but this also occurs on the helmet from Montefortino cited in connection with the Gottolengo mounts [106–107], and whatever the precise find conditions of the present helmet may have been, it certainly comes from an area where decorated helmets which were at least worn by Celts have been found.

As on the Gottolengo helmet [106–107], the bosses to which the winged cheek-pieces are attached form the base for a great flamboyant lyre with swollen tips and beaded edging which recall the decoration of the Auvers disc [42]. The round faces which 'grow' out of the lyre-palmettes with their crowning 'S' curls must, however, reflect the decorative tricks of later fourth-century Apulian vase painters;[2] it is to be seen as a strangely archaic artistic memory in a Scottish bronze mount at least a century and a half later in date [245]. The palmette chain of the now only fragmentary strip at the base of the Umbria cap again is closely paralleled by south Italian and earlier classical motifs; the fringe of tongue-and-groove ornament is similar to that on the Canosa helmet [105].

P. Reinecke, *Wiener Prähist. Zeitschr.* XXVII (1940), 51 ff. and ill.; *ECA*, no. 144; *V and A*, 127–28

[1] *ECA*, 118
[2] *ECA*, Pl. 219a (='Darius' painter); P. Jacobsthal, *Ornamente griechischer Vasen* (1927), Taf. 117c (=related to 'Iliupersis' painter)

109 Weiskirchen, Kr. Merzig–Wadern, barrow I. Iron short sword in bronze scabbard with coral enrichment. L. of scabbard 32·5 cm. LT A/B1, IV B C. Rhein. Landesmus., Trier.

This scabbard, probably the latest piece stylistically from the first Weiskirchen grave [see notes to **46**, **62** and **67**], has a morphologically early openwork chape with tips in the form of open-beaked birds – close to those of the Ticino belt-plates [95–99]; only one of the coral 'eyes' survives.

The decoration of the front of the actual scabbard plate is, like that on the sides of the Reinheim jug [73], produced by a rocked tracer following the lines of an originally lightly scribed design; a rocked tracer was also used by a native craftsman to decorate the imported Italic jug found with the scabbard.[1] The wave-like fronds of the running pattern of unlinked 'S's, however, do not follow the strict geometric constructions of the earlier engraved ornament but are closer to the ornamented repertoire of the Italo-Celtic helmets. At the mouth of the scabbard and half-way down were apparently once two openwork plaques. The rear of the scabbard has a double band of the so-called 'running dog' or wave pattern supporting an open leaf pattern not unlike those on the upper and lower sections of the Canosa helmet [105]; the 'running dog' can also be seen on the rim of the Dürrnberg flagon [72].[2] The overlapping heart-shaped leaves or scales visible just inside the binding strip have no close parallels save in an enamel and coral inlaid circular mount from a chariot burial with conical helmet at Berru in the Marne [see also notes to **113**].[3]

There seems little doubt that the Weiskirchen sheath indicates that the majority of other objects from the grave must have been old when buried – a not surprising conclusion since many of the rich finds recovered from the earlier princely graves can hardly be considered as made solely for the purposes of burial.

ECA, no. 100; A. Haffner in *Saarland=Führer zu vor- u. frühg. Denkmälern* 5 (1966), 212; *Besançon*, 30, n. 49

[1] Haffner, *op cit.*, ill. on p. 214, left
[2] See also *V and A*, 145 ff.
[3] *ECA*, no. 186

110 Amfreville sous-les-Monts, Eure. Bronze helmet with iron bands and gold and enamel enrichment. Ht. 17·5 cm., d. 23 cm. LT A/B1, later IV B C. Mus. des Antiquités Nat., St-Germain-en-Laye, Paris.[1] *R-GK* (*E. Neuffer*).

Found in an old stream bed of the Seine in 1861, this helmet is of complex construction and must originally been an object of great brilliance. Of a type nicknamed 'jockey-cap' because of the jutting-out neck-guard, Amfreville and its parallels are based on prototypes again found in the early Celtic cemeteries of northern Italy such as those cited in connection with the Gottolengo fragments [see notes to **106–107**]. The cap is beaten bronze – the original top knob has not survived; the remains of openwork iron bands once enriched with enamel inlay cover the apex, base and neck-guard of the cap divided by a *repoussé* or embossed decorated bronze strip over which has been placed a sheet of gold leaf. Tiny gold rosettes survive on the upper and lower rim bands.

The decorative motifs of the Amfreville helmet are a combination of the old and the new; the piece stands artistically on the threshold of a new stage in the development of La Tène art marked by the growing use of free-flowing patterns based on the non-representational repertoire of contemporary Italian art and introduced north of the Alps through the intermediary of the Celts who, like a much later group of barbarians, 'came first to plunder and then to settle'.

One motif is certainly of some antiquity in Celtic art – the twin rows of hooked and hatched waves; these can be seen on later fifth-century material [40, 64] including the engraved sword scabbard from Somme–Bionne,[2] although such decoration also occurs on the terminals and central band of the twin gold armlets from the upper, woman's, burial from Waldalgesheim which may be upwards of a century later [124–125]. The gold rosettes and rather spindly three-legged or triskel motif of the central band is likewise not far from the decoration of the torc from Waldalgesheim [127], although the dot-in-circle 'eyes' have a more archaic look. Much more clearly part of the literally 'new wave' is the assured irrationality of the lower cap and neck-guard enamel-filled iron mounts; the fleshy interlocking 'S' scrolls with dependent tendrils or rather shoots, with their curved triangle or trumpet-mouth terminals – such a key feature of later insular art – are very different from the tentative unlinked 'S's of the Weiskirchen scabbard [109]; the most easterly of the 'jockey-cap' helmets found with a sword typologically of Middle La Tène type in a burial at Silivaş near Cluj in Romania[3] has the same 'irrational' or asymmetric plant design with trumpet joints on the neck-guard but executed more in the manner of the spindly central band of Amfreville; a fully developed but purely linear version of this 'Waldalgesheim' version of the classical vine scroll or 'running dog' can be seen on a fragmentary scabbard mount from Sanzeno dell' Anaunia in the Alto Adige region of the Dolomites.[4] The top of this scabbard, found with no less than three helmets, has a lyre design; two areas on either side of the Amfreville helmet have a similar empty lyre-shaped opening originally filled by two S scrolls back to back with a triple leaf at the top and single central droplet, to judge from the marks left by the missing design. The most obvious purpose for these panels would be as the upper half of twin cheek-piece units like those of the presumably somewhat earlier Gottolengo and Umbria helmets [106–108].

Despite its northern find-spot – significantly enough as a deposit in a river – Amfreville, like Canosa [105], was either a trophy of campaigns in the Italian peninsula or the work of a craftsman who had his training in the transalpine region; the influence of pieces such as the Gottolengo fragments, where once more curls appear as the crowning element of the side ornament, is clear. Other decorated 'jockey-cap' helmets have certainly been found in northern France, but even those closest in form to Amfreville have incised decoration which, although more or less contemporary, belongs to a rather different stylistic group [see notes to 113].

P. Jacobsthal, *Die Antike* X (1934), 26 ff. and Taf. 4; *ECA*, no. 140, esp. p. 100–02; *Besançon*, 20 ff.; *ArtG*, 240, Pl. 16; *Celts*, Pl. 20; *WK*, Taf. 84; H. P. Eydoux, *La France antique* (1962) 16, colour pl.; R. Joffroy in *Kelten und Germanen* (1964), colour ill. p. 135; *EV*, 220–21 and ill.

[1] Some fragments are in the Mus. Rouen
[2] *ECA* no. 94
[3] *ECA* no. 142; D. Berciu, *Romania* (1967), 152 and fig. 67; *PAE*, 240
[4] *ECA*, no. 104

111 'L'Homme Mort', Somme–Bionne, Marne. Bronze open-work disc. D. 6·9 cm. LT A, last quarter V BC. British Mus., London. *Belzeaux–Zodiaque*.

This is one find from one of the best known of the early La Tène chariot barrow graves of the chalk region of the Marne whose position amongst the simpler flat graves must mark the last resting places of members of a particular warrior élite. These chariot graves, cut into the solid chalk with slots to take the wheels, chariot pole and yoke, form the sole source of helmets from France with the exception of Amfreville [110], and are usually accompanied by a standard armoury of at least three light throwing spears, a sword and single-edged iron knife. In France women were also buried in, or rather, as recently suggested, under chariots, as for example at the Berru cemetery [see notes to 54, 113]. Evidence for funerary meals was extensive with pig predominating – a burial at Châlons-sur-Marne closest in plan to Somme–Bionne had the remains of no less than a hundred animals.[1]

The associated objects from Somme–Bionne excavated by Léon Morel in 1837, included gold ornaments, a sword, and a local wheel-made vessel with pedestal foot. The most important items for dating purposes are a girdle-hook which, on the basis of comparative typology, *could* be as late as early LT B1 but certainly no later, and two imports, a beaked Italic flagon – whose distribution in French graves is almost entirely restricted to chariot burials – and an Attic red-figure stemless cup showing a discus thrower in action. This cup, which has given its site name to a group with only one other assigned example, is dated to about 420 BC.[2] It is of the same

basic form as the plain cup from Dürrnberg grave 44 found with a conical helmet of a type almost exclusively represented in the Marnian graves [see notes to **48**]. In view of the Attic import the date of the actual burial, but not necessarily the date of the *manufacture* of the native contents, would probably not have been before c. 400 BC if not later.

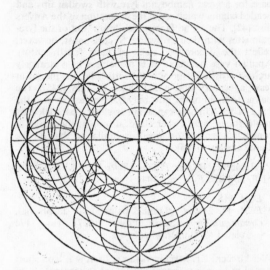

Fig. 5 [**111**] Somme-Bionne, Marne, France. Construction diagram of lay-out of ornamental bronze disc. Scale 1 : 1 *After Frey*

The cast disc illustrated here, with a central rear loop and provision on its frontal boss for inlay, presumably formed part of the harness mounts, a less ornate *phalera* than those from France and Czechoslovakia illustrated on earlier pages [**42, 47**]. It is also one of the most striking examples of the use of the strict geometrical pattern in early Celtic art, the whole design being built of compass-drawn circles and arcs laid out on a framework of nine concentric rings radiating out from the mathematical centre, certain arcs forming the typical curve-sided triangle or 'trumpet' motif. The subsequent dot ornamentation is a feature of several bronzes from the French chariot graves, as can be seen on the illustration below. Similar discs of triple form came from as far apart as the Rhine at Mainz[3] and from Anloo in the Netherlands.[4]

L. Morel, *La Champagne souterraine* (1898), 23–82, 139–40, esp. Pl. 11:10; *Manuel* IV, 528 ff., fig. 424 and *App.* VI, no. 554; *JL*, 36–37; *ECA*, no. 180; *Besançon*, 22 ff. and Abb. 8–9; *ArtG*, 240, Pl. 13; *WK*, Taf. 79; *EV*, 252 and ill.

[1] R. Joffroy and D. Bretz-Mahler, *Gallia* XVII (1959), 5–36, esp. 17 and fig. 14; I. M. Stead, *Antiquity* XXXIX (1965), 259 ff., esp. 260 and fig. 1
[2] J. D. Beazley, *Attic red-figure vase-painters* II (2ed. 1963), 1299
[3] *ECA*, no. 190
[4] S. J. De Laet and W. Glasbergen, *De Voorgeschiedenis der Lage Landen* (1959), 185 and Pl. 44

112 'La Bouvandeau', Somme-Tourbe, Marne. Detail of bronze openwork ?hame mount. Total l. 18·5 cm., ht. of detail c. 2 cm. LT A, late V BC. Mus. des Antiquités Nat., St-Germain-en-Laye. *Belzeaux–Zodiaque.*

This detail is of one of a pair of coral-decorated curved mounts which came from another of the Marnian chariot graves. Various uses have been suggested for the bronzes with their semicircular cross-section and tapering form, most recently the horns of a helmet,[1] but in the absence of any supporting evidence, mounts for a hame, a horse collar or, on evidence from Somme–Bionne, mounts for the ends of the chariot double-yoke, are all possible guesses.

The chief feature of this ornament is an openwork design built up of linked 'S's emphasised by freehand incised lines following the curves and filled in turn with dots. This rough infilling of a design with dots is used on another mounting from La Bouvandeau, a so-called chariot 'horn' with a rough palmette design related to the decoration of the beaked flagon in Besançon, illustrated on the opposite page [113]; the horn[2] also has dot-in-circles either side of a median line in the manner of the Reinheim jug handle and other pieces, but quite lacks the latter's precise layout of incised decoration [see notes to 73]. Other pieces from French chariot graves make use of similar openwork designs, sometimes in semi-representational form as on the Ticino class of girdle plaques [95–99]; a coral-studded mount from La Gorge Meillet[3] – found with a conical helmet – and an openwork plaque with dragon-like faces from the chariot grave with conical helmet at Cuperly, are two such.[4] There are also comparable pieces from Germany; a mount from Dürkheim and the openwork plate on a girdle-hook with human head from Schwabsburg, Ldkr. Mainz,[5] and the openwork basal handle mount of the Waldalgesheim jug [78]. Two finds from the Dürrnberg cemetery, an openwork disc brooch from grave 42 – almost as much a geometry exercise as the Somme–Bionne *phalera* – and the girdle-plaque from the second skeleton burial in chariot grave 44,[6] further underline the connections which the Austrian salt-mining centre had with the Marne; it was also Dürrnberg grave 44 which contained a conical helmet.

ECA, no. 171; *ArtG*, 240, Pl. 12; R. Joffroy and D. Bretz-Mahler, *Gallia* XVII (1959), 20 and fig. 16; *PAE*, 237–38

[1] *PAE*, 254, n. 79
[2] *ECA*, no. 168, esp. P 200
[3] *ArtG*, 240, Pl. 31
[4] *ECA*, no. 200
[5] *ECA*, no. 351
[6] *Keltische Kunst: Bodemschatten uit Salzburg*, Frans Halsmus., Haarlem (1963), no. 13=gr. 42; no. 16=gr. 44

113 Unprovenanced. Detail of incised decoration on zone 'C' of bronze beaked jug. Total ht. 25·3 cm., d. of circular motif illustrated c. 6·5 cm. LT A, first half IV BC. Mus. de Besançon.

The gold leaf 'lace work' of the Attic cups found at Klein Aspergle [41] shows how native craftsmen occasionally embellished their treasured imported drinking vessels; some decoration was added to the imported beaked flagons from Vulci found at Armsheim, Rheinhessen and in the first Weiskirchen grave.[1] There is, however, nothing to compare with the total patterning of an Italic beaked flagon now in the Museum at Besançon.

It is without details as to its place of discovery but, like the flagon from Besseringen [see notes to 56],[2] it was originally used as a cremation container. Here almost every available part of the vessel, including the base, has become the ground upon which five separate zones of decoration have been laid out and subsequently filled in with a combination of dotted edging – like the La Bouvandeau 'hame mounts' illustrated above – or closely pecked dotted areas or sinuous lines.

Fig. 6 [113] Unprovenanced. Incised decoration on bronze flagon; (b) basal decoration. Scale 1:4
After Frey

The ultimate source of the decoration must be the Etruscan metal-work itself; the ornamental motif under the neck (zone 'A'), a palmette with flanking 'S' scrolls can be found in a precisely similar position on an Italic flagon now in the British Museum,[3] the *interpretatio Celtica* of Besançon has its immediate parallel in the incised and dot-infilled ornament of a conical helmet from a Marnian chariot burial at Berru.[4] The large central zone 'C' of the Besançon flagon, which takes up the greater part of the vessel's body, is a loose version of a motif which appears not infrequently in later art of the third and second centuries, the Celtic version of the Chinese *yin-yang* or two comma-leaves revolving in opposite directions within an enclosing circle; one of these elements is illustrated here. The feeling of movement round a central point is particularly clear on the base with its four elements, dismembered tendrils, linked by 'trumpets' to the central circle. A triskel version of this design occurs in the centre of a incised, decorated bronze bowl from the chariot barrow known as 'Mont Renard' at Les Saulces-Champenoises in the Ardennes,[5] and a simpler version on the smaller pair of four *phalerae* from yet another chariot grave in the Marne in the cemetery of Écury-sur-Coole.[6] Both finds use the random-dot infill, while bordering the larger pair of Marnian *phalerae* is the sinuous line flanked by single dots used to divide the zones on the Besançon flagon. A four-limbed pattern forms the main part of a sieve mount from the Marne, though this piece is closer to the full 'Waldalgesheim' style.[7]

It is difficult to be precise as to the dating of the Besançon decoration; certain motifs such as the quadrilobe or triskel are probably just ancestral to the decoration on the gilded bronze band of the Amfreville helmet [110], while the disjointed elements of the bordering zones 'B' and 'D' look forward to the closely entwined 'Waldalgesheim' scrolls [124 ff.] which should date to the end of the fourth century. Chariot graves like Berru are probably upwards of a century earlier than this date. As so often, precision in the dating of this particular example of Celtic art is impossible. Notwithstanding, Besançon – which may well be a product of the region where it is now located – and its eastern French counterparts cited here may be taken as a group already influenced by Italic plant motifs and paving the way for the fully developed Waldalgesheim 'school' and its related groups of more eastern and southerly regions.

Besançon: S. Piggott, *Ancient Europe* (1965), 242 and fig. 135; F. Schwappach in *Festschr. Dehn*, 258 ff. and Abb. 24:3

[1] *JL*, Taf. 15:3, 20 and 37:3; see also notes to [109]
[2] J. Driehaus, *Bonner Jahrb.* 166 (1966), 31 ff., 47
[3] *JL*, Taf. 14a and 37a; *Besançon*, 7 f. and Abb. 1
[4] *ECA*, no. 136, esp. P 464; *Besançon*, Abb. 5
[5] *Manuel* IV, 961, fig. 655; *ECA*, P468; *Besançon*, Abb. 19
[6] *ECA*, no. 189, esp. Pl. 117 above
[7] *ECA*, no. 400

114 Cerrig-y-Drudion, Denbighshire. Fragment of rim of bronze bowl. Total d. c. 24 cm., w. of fragment 3 cm. ?IV/III BC. National Mus. of Wales, Cardiff.

Fig. 7 [114] Cerrig-y-Drudion, Wales. Incised decoration on bronze bowl. Scale c. 1 : 3 *After Smith*

Few objects found in the British Isles can now be assigned to continental earlier La Tène workmanship with certainty save for a handful of decorated fibulae and daggers. The fragments of an engraved bronze bowl with suspension chain found in 1924 in a stone cist are no exception. The common view, recently supported by a detailed study of stamp-decorated pottery in Brittany [see notes to 156–157], has been to ascribe it to a Gaulish craftsman of the late fourth century, one perhaps working in the Marne following the style of the Besançon 'school' and related to, if later than, the decorators of such Breton pots as those from Hénon, Le Flavet[1] and Pol-de-Léon [157]. The rather crude lyre-palmettes with their split fronds curving out like fans, each 'rib' of the fan ending in a punched dot, go back to the throat

ornament of the Basse-Yutz flagons [60–61]; details of the Canosa helmet could also be cited [105]. Counterparts for the hatched and dotted filling-in of the lyres and lobes no less than for the undulating 'edging' which appears at various points of the design of Cerrig-y-Drudion can certainly be found on the pre-Waldalgesheim-style Besançon flagon, though the bowl is not, as often claimed, related to the later true Waldalgesheim style [124 ff.]. Cross-hatching is certainly to be found on continental early La Tène objects [65ff.] and if an early date for the Welsh bowl is to be preferred this offers a useful bridge with the use of the cross-hatching or rather alternating hatching or basketry background to offset the main design – a characteristic of undoubted British metal-work of probably no earlier than the late third or even second century [245, 247–248]; the dot termination of the fan ribs also occurs on the shield from the River Witham [252]. Again the large rivet bosses also have an insular air about them, and, in the absence of other fine metal-work from north-western France, it is perhaps prudent to maintain an open verdict on the date and precise place of origin of this unique piece in Britain.

R. A. Smith, *Antiq. J.* VI (1926), 276–80; *ECA*, 95, 211, 471 and P471; W. F. Grimes, *Prehistory of Wales* (1951), 119, no. 699 and fig. 38; *Besançon*, 29 ff.; *PP* 1 and fig. 1; *Problems*, 74, 80 and Pl. IVb; *PAE*, 259 and fig. 98; H. N. Savory, *Early Iron Age art in Wales* (1968), 12 ff. and fig. 1–2; F. Schwappach in *Festschr. Dehn*, 271 ff. and Abb. 28

[1] Schwappach, *op. cit.*, no. 35

115 Alsópél, Kom. Tolna. Detail of ornament on shoulder of pot. Total ht. 40 cm., d. at mouth 19·8 cm., detail as illustrated c. 2 cm. high. LT B1, late IV BC. Magyar Nem. Múz., Budapest. *R-GK* (*E. Neuffer*).

The incised decoration on this dark burnished wheel-turned pot has been applied before firing and consists of two units thrice repeated in the area between the neck and a cordon. The cordon marks the flaring out of the body of the vessel which then curves in to a comparatively narrow foot. One element of the design is a rough maze or swastika similar to that incised on a flat ring from the Waldalgesheim chariot burial.[1] The other element is the tendril design filled with dots and set within a roughly triangular scallop-edged frame, the points of the scallops marked by stacks of multiple dots. The general layout of the design looks like a local imitation of the motifs of Waldalgesheim by a potter without the skill or the wherewithal to produce the stamped ornamentation exemplified below [116, 133]; the multiple stacks of dots on curved points are a particular feature of stamped pottery of the LT B1 phase.

Another piece which is sometimes compared with the Alsópél curvilinear design is a gold torc found on the banks of the Danube at Zibar in Bulgaria; this has a similar scallop edging and random dotted background, but in fact the Zibar torc is obviously a stray from much further west, and belongs rather to a class of arm- and neck-rings from eastern France and western Switzerland.[2] A silver finger ring from a female grave found at Dietikon, Kt. Zürich, in 1951 and associated with no less than fourteen brooches which establish a relative date more or less approximating to the beginning of LT B1 has a spindly series of leaf-commas against a reserved ground which is not unlike Alsópél.[3] Alsópél itself is only one of several pieces from Hungary related to or actually in the Waldalgesheim style whose development corresponded with an expansion of La Tène Celts into Slovakia and Transylvania.

L. Márton, 'Die Frühlatènezeit in Ungarn', *Arch. Hungarica* XI (1933), 63 ff., Abb. 9, Taf. XVIII; 1, 4 and XIX; I. Hunyady 'Kelták a Kárpátmedencében', *Diss. Pann.*, ser. II:18, I (1944), 135–36; II (1942), T. LXIII:6; *ECA*, no. 414; *KvsE*, 188

[1] *ECA*, no. 156f
[2] *ECA*, no. 46; E. Vogt, *60. Jahresber. Schweiz. Landesmus. 1951* (1952), 57 and Abb. 32
[3] Vogt, *op. cit.*, 62–63 and Abb. 33 and 36; *V and A*, no. 22

116 Komjatice, Šurany, grave 1. Detail of stamped decoration on pot. Length of lozenge stamp c. 10 cm. LT B1/B2, late IV/early III BC. Aú SAV Nitra. *Dr Frank Schwappach.*

The use of single or multiple stamps of various types to build up often complex designs on pottery first commenced in the La Tène A phase in a fairly concentrated area of the Oberpfalz in north-east Bavaria, south Bohemia, and Austria, with the Dürrnberg cemetery a key site. Stamped ware, particularly the so-called 'Braubach' bowls with decoration restricted to the inside of the bowls, may have had its starting point in stamped and rouletted or rilled black burnished ware of the late fifth and fourth centuries imported into Italy from mainland Greece, although the evidence is not strong.[1] The simplest Celtic designs are certainly very close to the presumed Greek prototypes – curved garlands produced by a toothed wheel or single curved stamp with dots within circles at the apex of the garlands; a similar pattern in metal-work occurs on the La Bouvandeau 'chariot horn' [see notes to 112]. Other more complex patterns copy contemporary La Tène motifs; another sherd from Slovakia recalls the Auvers disc and its parallels as well as the later buffer torcs illustrated on the next page [see notes to 42].[2]

Three separate stamps are used on the sherd here illustrated which comes from a disturbed grave in a Slovakian flat cemetery site:[3] a double circle used to build up a pyramid of five circles – a characteristic of stamped pottery of LT B1 – a lozenge made from four impressions of a single-toothed stamp or comb, and the central square double 'S' unit. This double 'S' is a common element in La Tène art, and Braubach bowls and, as here, the outer surface of larger flasks or urns often incorporate stamps of this type;[4] its use should belong to a phase contemporary with or just before the development of the Waldalgesheim style which was to be reproduced also on stamped pottery including vessels from Hungary [see also notes to 133]. Stamped pottery in eastern Czechoslovakia and Hungary is amongst the most useful material for plotting the western origins and connections of the Celts who settled in what was mainly a non-Celtic region.

Inv. no. 14. xii. 1955

[1] W. Dehn, *Bonner Jahrb.* 151 (1951), 83–95; *KvsE*, 178

ff.; F. Schwappach in *Festschr. Dehn*, esp. 241 ff.; H. Kaufmann, *Arb.- u. Forsch.-Ber. sächs. Bodendenkmalpflege* 16–17 (1967), 277–305
[2] M. Hell, *Germania* 33 (1955), 410–13; B. Benadík, *Slov. Arch.* IX (1961), 193, 195, 202 and obr. 21
[3] L'udmila Kraskovska, *Slov. Arch.* V (1957), 347–49
[4] K. Willvonseder, *Jahresschr. Salzburger Mus. C.A.* 9 (1963), 27–34

117 ?Comacchio, Emilia. Bronze mount. L. 12·5 cm. LT B1, late IV BC. Staatl. Museen zu Berlin (former Mus. f. Vor- u. Frühg.). *R-GK (E. Neuffer).*

This is one of some 30 bronze mounts purchased in Rome but probably from Comacchio on the Adriatic, north of Ravenna – in what would have been the territory of the Celtic Lingones. The 'Comacchio' bronzes appear to have been originally mounts for wooden vessels but complete reconstruction is not now possible. The ornament is produced by a punch giving a dotted false relief effect; the dot-and-circles bordering the main pattern are made with a single die and repeat this common motif illustrated above as a pottery stamp. The pattern is in the free-flowing 'Waldalgesheim' style and the find as a whole demonstrates further the close relationship this style seems to have had with the Celtic settlement of northern Italy.

The false relief technique used on other pieces to build up a balanced palmette design occurs also – and perhaps earliest – on the actual hook of the belt plaque from Hoppstädten, Kr. Birkenfeld, compared previously with the Auvers disc [see notes to 42];[1] this palmette belongs indeed to the period of the La Bouvandeau 'horn'[2] and the Basse-Yutz flagons where it appears on the throat plate. Split palmettes or 'fans' also appear on other Comacchio bronzes. A link with the Amfreville helmet [110], a piece which also bridges early motifs with those of the Waldalgesheim style, is a strip from the Comacchio fragments with single curled waves.[3]

P. Jacobsthal, *Prähist. Zeitschr.* XXV (1934), 62–104, esp. Abb. 6–8; *ECA*, no. 401b; *Besançon*, 8 ff. and Abb. 3d, 7a

[1] L. Kilian, *Trierer Zeitschr.* 24–26 (1956–58), Taf. 21:1
[2] *ECA*, no. 168; see also notes to [112]
[3] *ECA*, no. 401h

118 Waldalgesheim, Ldkr. Kreuznach. Bronze mount (one of a pair). Ht. 8·9 cm. LT B1, late IV BC. Rhein. Landesmus., Bonn. *J. V. S. Megaw.*

From the lower (male) grave of the Waldalgesheim double grave [see notes to 78] are a number of pieces probably originally forming part of the harness trappings or chariot mounts; of those whose definite purpose can now be ascertained, only the remains of one wheel and an iron bit now remain; two chariot 'horns' – most probably yoke terminals, like that from La Bouvandeau [112] – also survive. The pair of *repoussé* mounts, of which the better preserved is illustrated here, are usually considered to have decorated the sides of the chariot; their curvature forms one-fifth of a complete circle and their precise intention must in fact remain a matter of guesswork.

The figure represented on both plaques with its disproportionate head, buffer-terminalled torc or neck-ring (a representation of the type found in the upper burial [127]) probably cross-legged attitude and tiny upraised hands like some early Christian devotee, can hardly be intended for anything less than a god; a goddess is also possible, to judge from sockets for inlay in the centre of each breast, since women wore torcs as frequently as men, to judge from the grave finds. These Waldalgesheim figures look both backwards and forwards in Iron Age iconography. The cross-legged position, not necessarily oriental, since it is the natural way of sitting for a people of at least partially nomadic stock, is that of the so-called 'Cernunnos' or antlered god of the last two centuries BC [209, 212]. 'Cernunnos' appears not only on coinage of the Somme [194g] but also on the great Gundestrup cauldron, as do half figures with upraised arms. The Waldalgesheim face, with its tiny mouth, conjoined eyebrows and wedge nose, recalls the largest of the Bavarian Oberwittig-hausen brooches [91] and in general aspect the mirror-handle figure from Reinheim.[1] The Waldalgesheim heads have oval eyes, not circular ones as on the faces on the gold armlets from the upper burial [124–125]. Like Reinheim and the stone heads such as Heidelberg [49], these faces have a 'leaf crown'. The lobes of this crown are separate down-curling comma 'S's recalling the Dürrnberg grave 44 mount [48] and the Weiskirchen barrow I belt-hook [62]; the fleshy lobes have something even of those of the pseudo-faces of the Auvers disc [42]. The key feature stylistically of the Waldalgesheim mounts is the tattoo-like tendrils on the chest of each figure. These motifs, with their tortuous swirling and twisting movements and 'trumpet' joints which seem almost to move over the surface of the figure like snakes over a Celtic Laocoön, are the hall-mark of what might well be termed the 'Waldalgesheim Master' whose *floruit* on the dating evidence of the Waldalgesheim grave itself and of the association of his works with finds in northern Italy [see notes to 128] should lie within the last decades of the fourth century.

R. Knorr, *Germania* 5 (1921), 11 ff. and Abb. 4; *ECA*, no. 156d [1-2]; W. Dehn, *Katalog Kreuznach=Kataloge west- u. süddeutscher Altertumssammlg.* 7 (1941), I, Taf. 14: 1 and II, 64; *WK*, Taf. 32 below; *CCH*, fig. 22; *PreA*, 201–02 and ill. 195; *PAE*, 238–39 and Pl. 253

[1] F. J. Keller, *Das keltische Fürstengrab von Reinheim* I (1965), no. 15

119 'Des Closeaux de la Couche', Courtisols, Marne, grave 11. Bronze torc. D. 13 cm. LT I b–c, late IV/early III BC. British Mus., London. (Whole torc) *courtesy Trustees of the British Museum*, (detail) *J. V. S. Megaw.*

One speciality of the later flat cemeteries of the Marne is a group of rings and cast bronze torcs with large buffer-like terminals sometimes decorated with human faces.[1] Where associated with other objects or when the skeleton has survived, these usually indicate a female grave.

The present example, from the second of two flat cemeteries in the region of Courtisols, was found with two armlets, one of lignite and a second in bronze with simple ridged decoration. The figural decoration of Courtisols consists of not one but two pairs of heads set chin to chin with the buffers acting like a sort of pasha's turban for the upper heads of each pair. The faces, with

their tiny mouths, hollow cheeks and long eyebrow curls, stand mid-way in the development of the construction of recognisable human features from what has been termed 'an intermittent wave-tendril'; what goes before are the almost chinless faces of such pieces as the Basse-Yutz flagons [60–61] or the gold finger ring from Rodenbach [58], and what follows is what is termed here the 'Disney' style of the third century [159 ff.]. The non-figural decoration of the buffers is in a series of comma-spirals and stacks of palmette-derived lyre patterns, more plastic than the more or less contemporary Waldalgesheim motifs but drawing upon the same basic repertoire. The general deposition of decoration on Courtisols has its closest parallels on buffer torcs from the large cemetery of Les Jogasses[2] and from the barrow burial of Mont Desclus at Bussy-le-Château[3] of which the unpublished associated finds include a 'Dux'-type brooch [see notes to 134], a fragmentary bridle-bit and a pot decorated in a curvilinear style illustrated below [154]. Associations for these torcs, where present, are never earlier than LT Ib (or B1 in southern Germany) and Jacobsthal's description of these torcs as belonging to his Early 'Style' – that is, the styles represented in the fifth- and early fourth-century princely burials – seems hard to substantiate either typologically or on his own stylistic criteria.

L. Morel, *La Champagne souterraine* (1898), 135–36 and Pl. 37:4 (wrongly cited as Pl. 27:4); *ECA*, no. 208; *KvsE*, 154, 197, 212 and obr. 3:8; *CCH*, fig. 12:3; K. Ludikovský, *Sborník ČSSA* (*Brno*) 2 (1962), 265 ff. and obr. 4b–5; *V and A*, 116–17, 134 ff., Abb. 2J, 4G and Taf. 12:3–4; *PreA*, 218 and ill. 212

[1] P.-M. Favret, *Bull. soc. préhist. de France* XLVII (1950), 433–48, esp. fig. 12:7
[2] *ECA*, no. 211
[3] J. de Baye, *Mém. Soc. Antiq. de France* 44 (1885), 113–14 and fig. 2; *V and A*, 136 f. and Taf. 12:5

120 ?Champagne. Bronze torc. Total d. 13·2 cm., d. of terminals c. 3·2 cm. LT Ib/c, late IV/early III BC. Mus. Lorrain, Nancy.

This torc, about the finding of which little is known, is probably the best preserved of the buffer torcs with human faces. On the terminals directly above the heads is a palmette construction which, when reversed, may be 'read' as another pseudo-face in the precise manner of the 'Disney' style [compare 169]. As it is seen here the terminal decoration is clearly related to such Waldagels-heim pieces as the gold torc and two bronze rings from the type-site [127 and 132] and a silver finger ring from Deisswil, Kt. Bern [139]. The plastic spirals and ridging of the encircling lines dividing the buffers from the rest of the ring are close to the torcs from Les Jogasses and Mont Desclus cited above in connection with the Courtisols torc. As to the actual faces, again Mont Desclus offers the closest parallel, though there the eyes are round and not pointed ovals. The formulation of the Champagne face is, however, an old one and its apparent resemblance to the faces of the largest Oberwittighausen brooch [91] or that from Berlin–Niederschönhausen [101] shows how unreliable such likenesses are for dating purposes. Seemingly incidental or decorative fill-in motifs in La Tène art are much more certain chronological indicators. Above the foreheads of the Champagne faces may be incipient 'leaf-crowns'.

94

ECA, no. 208 B ('Vitry-les-Reims'); *V and A*, 136 and Taf. 12:6

121 'La Barbière', Villeseneux, Vertus, Marne, grave 3. Detail of bronze neck-ring. Total d. 15·2 cm., ht. of central face c. 1·8 cm. LT Ib–c, IV–III BC. Mus. de Préhistoire et d'Arch. régionale, Épernay.

This cast bronze ring fastened by a tenon-catch and with its ornament laid out in three identical units at equidistant points around the circumference following the pattern of several pieces from the early princely graves [53–54], underlines the sacred triple element in Celtic belief with a unique setting of three faces. A large outward-looking head takes the place of the buffers on the Courtisols and Champagne torcs as a supporter for two flanking heads with long 'pig-tails' or tightly clinging spirals; the decoration is 'one-sided', that is, not repeated on the under surface.

The associated objects in the grave, apart from some sherds, were a jet bracelet repaired with an iron pin, two iron rings, and a bronze bracelet with cast decoration consisting of pairs of plastic 'S' spirals such as have been found in several Marnian graves of LT Ib–c date. A ring from grave 2 at Villeseneux cited in note [122] below is clearly by the same craftsman.

P.-M. Favret, *Bull. soc. préhist. de France* XLVII (1950), fig. 10:2; *V and A*, 138

122 Avon-Fontenay, Aube. Bronze neck-ring. D. 13 cm. LT Ib–c, IV–III BC. British Museum, London. *J. V. S. Megaw*.

This ring fastened by a tenon-catch has its decoration divided into three zones with knobs marking the voids between the zones. This and a very comparable ring found in Villeseneux grave 2,[1] with the burial of an old woman and brooches which should, if anything, belong to the end of La Tène Ic, have faces peering out of either end of a spiralling plant motif. Like the larger Villeseneux ring illustrated on the opposite page, they represent a French variation on the Waldalgesheim themes represented by the twin gold bracelets from the type-site [124–125]. The knobs, however, (not illustrated in this detailed view) have plastic spirals like two associated but greatly separated pieces. These are torcs with conjoined terminals, one the gold torc from Clonmacnoise in Ireland [174], the other a bronze torc from Praunheim near Frankfurt[2] with associated finds which would suggest a relative date not before LT B2 in Germany. It seems thus all the more difficult to follow Jacobsthal's description of the present ring as 'definitely . . . of the Early Style', though he does subsequently imply a connection with Waldalgesheim.

ECA, no. 241, esp. pp. 19 and 153; P.-M. Favret, *Bull. soc. préhist. de France* XLVII (1950), 446 and fig. 11:3; *V and A*, 139 f. and Taf. 11:4

[1] Favret, *op. cit.*, 438 and fig. 10:3; *V and A*, 136, 139 and Taf. 11:6

[2] *ECA*, no. 210

123 Criesbach, Kr. Künzelsau. Bronze fibula. L. 4·7 cm. LT A, early IV BC. Württ. Landesmus., Stuttgart. *Landesbildstelle Baden u. Württ.* (Dr H. Hell).

This little cast bronze brooch is related to those from the Oberwittighausen, Bavaria, grave [91–92], and is inserted at this stage to act as a visual reminder of the artistic antecedents of the faces of the late fourth or early third century. Above both the catch-plate and the spring mounting are similar outward-looking heads with upward-scrolling eyebrows which, particularly in the case of the catch-plate face, may be intended to double as the eyes of a down-curving dragon face like those that animate the 'S' curve which clings to the back of the brooch. The great saucer eyes, pencil moustache and lantern jaw of the undoubtedly human aspect of the brooch are similar to the lower face on the Nová Hut' brooch [70] or the 'owl' faces of the Reinheim rings [79–80], but they are also very close to the faces inserted into the foliage of the Waldalgesheim gold bracelets, also illustrated on this page. Comparisons with the Dürrnberg 1886 fibula are not convincing [see notes to 57] for this piece from a simple flat grave.

ECA, no. 311; M. Hell, *Germania* 27 (1943), 67; *V and A*, 129 n. 133

124–127 Waldalgesheim, Ldkr. Kreuznach. **124–125.** Pair of hollow gold bracelets. D. 6·5 cm.; **126** Wrought gold armring with imitation twist. D. 8·2 cm.; **127** Gold torc. D. 19·9 cm. LT B1, late IV BC. Rhein. Landesmus., Bonn. [124] *R-GK* (E. *Neuffer*). [Detail of 125] *J. V. S. Megaw*.

Such is the distribution of the products of the true Waldalgesheim style, as represented by the find at the type-site, that the association with an imported Italic bucket may be regarded as supporting the theory that the craftsman responsible for this style had his chief market in the Celtic settled areas of northern Italy and western Switzerland [see also notes 78, 128 and 134–139].

124–125. Within a complex fold-over band the rear-decorated portion of the twin bracelets from Waldalgesheim, which, like all the gold work from the chariot burial, come from the upper, woman's, grave, encloses writhing and asymmetric plant spirals. These spirals are the hall-mark of the work of what has been termed the 'Waldalgesheim Master'. It has already been illustrated on the chest of the twin ?chariot mounts from the lower grave [118] and a version can be seen on one of the 'Comacchio' bronzes [117]. Divided by the fold-over band of decoration but facing each other are two glum-faced individuals with tiny mouths and exuberantly scrolling eyebrows; the faces are really archaisms in the general context of the later fourth century as other objects illustrated beside them show [120–123]. Resting on each head like the buffers of the buffer torcs with figural decoration, and like the torcs marked off by a horizontal cable design, is a row of broken waves or drooping curls as discussed in connection with the Amfreville helmet [110]; the same motif is repeated on the actual miniature buffer terminals of the bracelets. The last unit of decoration of both the rear and terminal features is a more plastic version of the lyre-palmette discussed above in connection with the 'Comacchio' bronzes and a motif which is seen on both the gold torcs illustrated on this page. The detailed photograph clearly shows the marks of the tooling of the 0·08 cm. thick gold. Two armlets in the British Museum purchased in Belgium have much the same basic form but a more flamboyant and, to modern taste, less successful style of decoration.[1] Of the Waldalgesheim pair, one is very much more worn than the other, suggesting that the other may have been retained for use only on special occasions.

ECA, no. 55; *Celts*, Pl. 30; *WK*, Taf. 33; *V and A*, 127, 133 ff., Abb. 4D and Taf. 11:5; *PreA*, 202 and ill. 196–97; *PAE*, fig. 89B

[1] *ECA*, no. 56; see also notes on [127] below

126. This mock-twisted gold ring, with its tooling between the ridges and no visible join, is without precise parallel in gold work of the later Iron Age; the Reinheim gold torc [79] is perhaps the nearest piece in its basic form.

ECA, no. 54

127. The gold torc from the Waldalgesheim find is wrought from no less than ten separate sections, the two discs used to close the actual buffers bearing a small hole dead centre, indicating the use of a turntable for executing at least part of the decoration. The motifs are more soberly balanced than those on the bracelets; indeed, if one did not know the ability of Celtic craftsmen seemingly to move at will between almost opposing styles, one might be tempted to assign the torc to another hand than that responsible for the bracelets, 'chariot mount' and so forth. The main decoration on the hoop of the torc is, like that on the Italian ring illustrated below, based once more on the palmette-lyre and once more harks back to the Basse-Yutz flagons – a reason for the late date some authorities would ascribe to the flagons [see notes to 60–61]. The star-shaped flowers growing from the side-shoots of the main stem of the lyre recall the gold studs on the Amfreville helmet [110], but the over-all pattern can be seen in an even more classical guise decorating the bows of the two fibulae with coral disc feet from graves 49 and 50 of the great Münsingen-Rain flat cemetery near Bern; these two graves fall respectively in the earlier and later part of LT Ib as recently defined.[1] The gold torc and pair of armlets purchased in Belgium and now in the British Museum exhibit a much more flamboyant and 'botanical' version of this floral element; these, one may be fairly certain, are not by the 'Waldalgesheim Master'.[2] The fronds or concentric arcs filling in details of the Waldalgesheim lyre occur at one point on the decoration of a bronze torc from a double burial at Thuizy in the Marne, where the balanced lyre collapses into a compressed mass of sinuous curves, an unsuccessful attempt to produce the ordered asymmetry of the true 'Waldalgesheim Master's' style and one which looks as if the French craftsman had been copying a model the separate elements of which all of a sudden had fallen in a heap at his feet.[3] The ornamentation of the Waldalgesheim terminal buffers uses the 'intermittent wave tendril' motif noticed already on the bronze torc from the Champagne [120], while in their centre four detached commas – like those from a 'Waldalgesheim' school mount from Upper Austria[4] – revolve round a central boss.

ECA, no. 43; *KvsE*, 153–54, obr. 3:2 and Tab. III: 2–3; *CCH*, fig. 12 and Pl. XIV; *V and A*, 128, 134 ff. and 141; *PAE*, 238 and Pl. 254

[1] *ECA*, nos. 332–33; F. R. Hodson, *The La Tène Cemetery at Münsingen-Rain* = *Acta Bernensia* V (1968), Pls. 22–23, esp. nos. 797, 839

[2] *ECA*, nos. 45 and 56

[3] *ECA*, no. 206

[4] *ECA*, no. 377 and P 450a; *Besançon*, 8, 21 ff. and Abb. 3a; see also notes on [137]

128 Filottrano, S. Paolino, grave N.2. Detail of gold torc. Total d. 14·9 cm., d. of terminals c. 2·5 cm. LT Ib, late IV BC. Mus. Nazionale delle Marche, Ancona. *Soprintendenza alle Antichità delle Marche.*

The Celtic cemetery of Filottrano in the tribal area of the Senones (who were defeated by the Romans in 283–82 BC) is invaluable for the association of the Celtic objects from north of the Alps – or at least decorated in styles which reached north of the Alps [see also notes to 137]—with well-dated Etruscan, Italo-Greek and mainland Greek imports. From their first settlement in the eastern Po area in the late fifth century BC, the Celts gradually adopted more and more the accoutrements and even the way of life of their involuntary hosts, even though this settlement may have led initially to a break in the flow of Greek imports into the area in the middle of the century.

Grave 2 at Filottrano is a rich male inhumation grave containing a bronze stamnoid *situla* of the early fourth century, three red-figure bell-kraters, two Attic and one Apulian (the last to be dated not earlier than the middle of the fourth century), and an Etruscan mirror which Jacobsthal, it is now thought erroneously, regarded as of post-300 BC date. Also in the grave was a gold finger ring with, on the beazel, a horse or griffon rampant facing left, its feet ending in triple balls. Although this ring may, like one from the Montefortino cemetery,[1] have been engraved for its Celtic owner by a second-rate Italian craftsman, the animal certainly has affinities with east Celtic silver coinage, which, on the latest evidence, is well established by the last decades of the fourth century [see notes to **194a**]. Lastly, two gold beads, one with eight mustachio'd heads and one with a series of Medusas set between palmettes, offer the sort of source material which late fourth-century Celtic artists would be drawing upon for devising the particular relationship between human features and plant motifs which is the key feature of the central period of development of La Tène art.

The torc itself is clearly close to the style of the 'Waldalgesheim Master'; the detail shows the same swirling movement and trumpet joints and also the arcaded fill-ins and palmette-lyre of the Waldalgesheim torc [127]. Not visible in the present view is the way in which the base of the palmette-lyre is capped by the terminal buffers – each with some indication of a turntable chuck or central hole as on the terminals of the Waldalgesheim torc. Each lyre forms a 'Cheshire Cat' or pseudo-face; the torc from Les Jogasses is somewhat similar.[2] The decoration of the buffers themselves is a version of the old tongue-and-groove motif which reappears on two of the Celtic helmets [105, 108]. From the weight of the torc it can be deduced that it has a clay or base metal core.

E. Baumgärtel, *J. Roy. Anthrop. Inst.* LXVII (1937), 236–37 and Pl. XXIV:1–2; *ECA*, no. 44; *Ori e argenti dell'Italia antica*, Palazzo Chiablese, Turin (1961), no.

133 and Tav. XVI; C. Carducci, *Antique Italian gold and silver* (1964), 22 and Pl. 23b; *V and A*, 136 f., 103, 150 and no. 17

[1] *ECA*, 125; see notes to [58]
[2] *ECA*, no. 211

129 Turoe, Loughrea, Co. Galway. Carved granite boulder (view from south-west). Present ht. 1·20 m. ?III–I BC. *Green Studios, Dublin.*

The first account of what many would still regard as the clearest evidence of direct continental La Tène settlement in Ireland appeared in 1902. The carefully pre-shaped stone – phallic in outline to those who would see it that way – with its unequal quartering of pelta designs by separate tendrils looking like some prehistoric ancestor of a Joan Miró painted pebble, now stands on the lawn of Turoe House. Originally its position was on the north side of the first century BC circular fortified settlement or 'rath' of Feewore, opposite its entrance.

At first sight the decoration of the stone, with its swirling movement and 'trumpet' or pelta junctions, recalls the fourth-century art of Waldalgesheim and contemporary styles; the 'step' or simplified Greek key design running around the base of the stone has even earlier parallels, the Želkovice plaque for example [71]. Other, though simpler, carved stones with curvilinear and rectilinear patterns both from Ireland and from Brittany, at Mullagmast, Co. Kildare, Castlestrange, Co. Roscommon, and Kermaria in Finistère[1] can hardly fit into this archaic framework, but when they are taken together with coinage of the local Breton tribe of the Coriosolites of the period just before the Roman conquest [194f], there is certainly a respectable continental background for Turoe although it is of at least some two centuries later date than that usually advanced for the stone. It is, after all, important to keep in mind that certain basic motifs, first developed in the later fourth century, have – particularly in Britain [see notes to **130**] – a very long life. For example, the multiple-armed whirligig or triskel, which commences as the disjointed element on the base of the Besançon flagon [113], survives even on the continent to decorate long-bowed brooches of developed La Tène II form – or around the second century in date.[2] Other elements on the stone such as the fat commas and peltas or curved-sided triangles are certainly key features of later British art [see notes to **254**].

Britain in the Iron Age is an anthology of archaisms, so it should come as no surprise that the step pattern on the base of Turoe also occurs on native Irish metal-work – again of possibly no earlier than second-century date [248–249]. Turoe is a unique example of skilled stonemason's work in the British Isles; perhaps if contemporary woodwork had survived, its uniqueness might be somewhat diminished.

E. C. Armstrong, *J. Royal Soc. Antiq. Ireland* LIII (1923), 30–31 and Pl. VI; J. Raftery, *J. Royal Soc. Antiq. Ireland* LXXIV (1944), 23–52, esp. fig. 5; *Problems*, 69, n. 2 and 80; E. Rynne in *Ber. V Intern. Kongr. f. Vor- u. Frühg.* (1961), 706; *PreA*, 209, ill. 205; F. Henry, *Irish Art (to AD 800)* (1965), 5 ff., fig. 1

[1] *Manuel* IV, 1029 and fig. 700:2; P.-M. Duval, *Art de France* IV (1964), ill. p. 38; F. Schwappach in *Festschr. Dehn*, 265 f. and Taf. 22:1

[2] *ECA*, 207, 210 and P 286; *ArtG*, 240, Pl. 23 (=Conflans, Marne); F. R. Hodson, *The La Tène Cemetery at Münsingen-Rain=Acta Bernensia* V (1968), Pl. 88 nos. 199, 201 (=gr. 184); see also notes to [136] and (for Britain) [262]

130 Lower Thames at Brentford, Middlesex. Bronze 'chariot horn' with traces of red enamel inlay. D. 7·3 cm. ?I BC–I AD. London Museum.

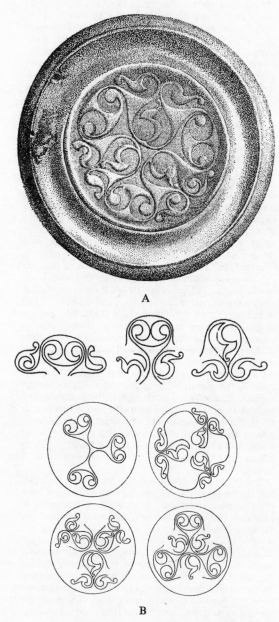

A

B

Fig. 8 [130] R. Thames at Brentford, England. (a) Top view and (b) four separate readings of cast design on bronze chariot 'horn'. Scale of (a) c. 1:1 (a) *After Fox*; (b) *After Duval*

G

This elegant though heavy casting was recovered during the construction of Brentford Dock and comes from an area of the Thames which seems to have included a later Iron Age settlement.[1] Despite Sir Cyril Fox's description of the mount as a balanced three-way design 'in the Waldalgesheim style', the very strictness of balance of the palmette units, linked to peltas or hollow-sided triangles terminating in pseudo-birds' heads, is an indication of its insular nature; the contrast with the free-flowing considered asymmetry of actual continental material, such as those pieces illustrated on the opposite page, is immediately apparent. In fact the influence on native British art of those fourth- and early third-century styles more or less closely related to the school of the 'Waldalgesheim Master' has been much over-emphasised in recent years. The Brentford bronze has little in either general layout or detail which can divide it from the common use of trumpet ornament in provincial Roman metal-work of the period around the Claudian conquest of Britain.[2] The details of the ornament of the Brentford mount have parallels amongst native material of the same period; tendril variants occur on enamelled harness mounts[3] and the actual palmettes, with their double ball terminals, recall not only the strange crests of the helmeted faces on the Aylesford bucket [178] but occur in a more ornate, spindly, and even more strictly symmetrical version on the famous Battersea shield [253]. For an asymmetrical version of the Brentford pattern in which scroll-like leaves sprout forth elements as the stem for the growth of another unit, two of a series of enigmatic flat spoon-shaped bronzes which seem undoubtedly no earlier than the first century BC may be cited. This pair, from Weston in Somerset, like Brentford—which is capable of multiple but always symmetrical readings of its basic motifs—it has low-relief and probably tooled-down rather than cast ornament, but unlike Brentford and closer in feeling to the carving on the Turoe stone [129]. The pattern of the spoons has an unpredictable element of construction from the same artistic vocabulary of palmette tendrils, peltas and pseudo-bird finials.[4] Although nearly all traces have disappeared, the sunk areas of the Brentford mount were once filled with red enamel – again in the manner of Battersea and the later harness mounts. Enamelling was recognised by later classical authors to be a skill peculiar to the native inhabitants of the Atlantic seaboard. Philostratus of Lemnos, writing in the third century AD and describing what seems to be a suitably Celtic bronze panel depicting a boar hunt, comments on the pouring of enamel on to heated 'brass'.[5]

The purpose of the mount has been much debated, but, on the basis of not dissimilar capped bronzes from the continent, including La Bouvandeau [see notes to 112] and Waldalgesheim itself, and even the Hallstatt Iron Age barrow cemetery of Hradenín [8], terminals for waggon or chariot double-yokes seems preferable to the 'hand-grip' suggestion put forward by earlier writers.[6] Some ten 'horn caps' are known from Britain, and the fact that those closest in form to Brentford come from late levels of native hill-forts at High Rocks in Leicestershire and Maiden Castle, Dorset, tend to support the late dating suggested here for the Brentford ornamentation.[7]

R. A. Smith, *Archaeologia* LXIX (1918), 22 and fig. 22; E. T. Leeds, *Celtic Ornament* (1933), 58–59 and fig. 23b;

J. M. de Navarro in (ed.) M. Charlesworth, *Heritage of Early Britain* (1952), 73–74; *PP*, 3 ff., Pl. 3a–c and 4; *Problems*, 78; *PRB*, Pl. 246; *PreA*, 202–04 and ill. 198; P.-M. Duval, *Art de France* IV (1964), ill. on p. 12

[1] R. E. M. Wheeler, *Antiquity* III (1929), 20–32
[2] W. von Jenny, *IPEK*, 1935 (1936), 31–48
[3] E. g. H. Harrod, *Archaeologia* XXXVI (1856), 454–56, Pl. XXXVII:3–4 (Westhall, Suffolk); see also notes to **Plate VIIIa**
[4] *Manuel* IV, 781–83; J. H. Craw, *Proc. Soc. Antiq. Scot.* LVIII (1923–24), 143–51; *PP*, 36–37, 111 and fig. 22
[5] *Iconographia* I, 1, XXVIII
[6] M. E. Mariën, 'Le Groupe de la Haine', *La Période de la Tène en Belgique=Monographies d'Archéologie Nat.* 2 (1961), 176 and fig. 66; I. M. Stead, *Antiquity* XXXIX (1965), 261–62
[7] Sir Cyril Fox, *A find of the Early Iron Age from Llyn Cerrig Bach, Anglesey* (1947), 15–19

131 Newnham Croft, Cambridgeshire. Cast bronze armring. Total d. 7·9 cm., W. 0·8 cm. ?II/I BC. University Museum of Archaeology and Ethnology, Cambridge. *J. V. S. Megaw.*

This solid bronze armring with hinged tenon joint was found in 1903 with the remains of what may possibly have been a chariot burial associated with a contracted male skeleton. Amongst the accompanying objects was a cast bronze *phalera* or harness mount with a profile somewhat similar to the 'chariot horns' [see notes to 130]. There was also an ornate coral-studded fibula of local manufacture as the cast 'hair-spring' spirals show [see notes to 255], which has cast decoration not unlike that found on Middle La Tène II brooches of c. 200 BC and later [see notes to 129],[1] but whose profile is in fact Late La Tène. Finally there were the remains of two penannular brooches – the prototype of the modern kilt pin. These last, though considered by one authority to be introduced into British Iron Age fashions by the third century BC, certainly do not become common until after the Roman conquest.[2]

As to the decoration on the armlet, together with part of a tubular bit-ring probably from West Coker in Somerset,[3] it has been claimed that this derives from second century BC Marnian work or indeed represents an import. In fact the design is a rather more spindly version of that on the Torrs mounts from Kirkcudbrightshire [245]. Together with the use as a background of matting or gridded basketry – a particularly British feature already noted on the Cerrig-y-Drudion bowl [114] and only rarely occurring on continental material [65, 84] – the armlet is best regarded as a typical piece of insular artistic archaism in which a local interpretation is given to a pattern only loosely based on Waldalgesheim elements. Comparisons which have been made with plastic ornament on Middle La Tène bracelets[4] indicate at the most a parallel but unconnected development, and the decoration of the Brentford 'horn cap' [130] is surely more apposite.

C. C. G. Clarke, *Antiq. J.* VI (1926), 176 ff.; (ed.) L. F. Salzman, *Victoria County History: Cambridgeshire* I (1938), 293 and fig. 26; Sir Cyril Fox, *Archaeology of the Cambridge region* (reissue 1948), 81, 118 and Pl. XV:5; R. J. C. Atkinson and S. Piggott, *Archaeologia* XCVI

(1955), 228–9 and fig. 5; *PP*, 11 and fig. 6; *Problems*, 76

[1] P. Jacobsthal, *Antiq. J.* XXIV (1944), 123
[2] E. Fowler, *PPS* XXVI (1960), 155 ff. and fig. 3
[3] *PP*, 14 and fig. 10
[4] E.g. *ECA*, no. 252; *KvsE*, Tab. XXXVI:8–9; J. Déchelette, *Le Collection Millon* (1913), 98 f. and fig. 12

132 Waldalgesheim, Kr. Kreuznach. Detail of bronze bracelet. Total d. 8·1 cm. W. c. 0·7 cm. LT B1, late IV BC. Rhein. Landesmus., Bonn. *J. V. S. Megaw.*

This bracelet was cast as one of a pair and originally fastened by means of a flexible catch joint. It has no precise parallel, though a pair of armlets from a small La Tène B1–2 cemetery at Nebringen, Kr. Böblingen, has a similar series of knobs with cast decoration separated by blank waisted joints.[1]

The decoration is a combination of two separate variations on the 'intermittent wave tendril' which forms the terminal decoration of a torc from the Champagne already illustrated [120] and a 'tendrilised' version of a horizontal 'S' spiral which shows the armlets' relationship to the gold pair from the upper, female, grave at Waldalgesheim. A repeating version of the intermittent tendril is illustrated below [139] and its pseudo-anthropomorphism is made explicit on a British piece of some three centuries later, an enamelled terret from Westhall in Suffolk.[2] These German bracelets have been considered to show a combination of plastic 'Waldalgesheim' elements with those of the two-dimensional 'sword style'.[3]

ECA, no. 247; *V and A*, 131 and Abb. 6:2

[1] W. Kramer, 'Das keltische Gräberfeld von Nebringen (Kr. Böblingen)', *Veröffentl. d. Staatl. Amtes f. Denkmalpflege Stuttgart*, Reihe A:8 (1964), Taf. 8:6–7; see also notes to [146]
[2] H. Harrod, *Archaeologia* XXXVI (1856), Pl. XXXVII:4; *PP*, fig. 82:B14
[3] J. M. de Navarro, *PPS* XXI (1955), 240; see also notes to [179–183]

133 'Wienerhügel', Sopron. Detail of stamped decoration on pot. Ht. of lozenges c. 1·5 cm. LT B1, late IV BC. Ferenc Liszt Múz., Sopron. *Dr Frank Schwappach.*

From a barrow grave at Sopron on the western edge of the great Hungarian plateau was recovered a decorated sword and spear-head, a bracelet,[1] a brooch and a long-necked pottery flask with stamped decoration. The flask – of the same type as that from Matzausen whose stamped and incised decoration has been illustrated above [27] – is wheel-turned with an *omphalos* or dimpled base and is of a blackish-grey colour. Like the other objects from the grave, it dates from the period of the first stages of the consolidation of the eastern spread of La Tène Celts whose settlement is marked by large-scale flat rather than barrow cemeteries.

Two stamps are used in building up the over-all design, a dot-in-circle – commonest of all motifs in stamped pottery decoration [see notes to 116] – and, within a lozenge border, sinuous 'Waldalgesheim' tails related to the 'S's on the bronze bracelet from the type-site illustrated to the left [132]. It is likely that the pot, like at least the brooch in the grave, was imported from

as far afield as the western Alps. The lozenge stamp is at the moment a unique example of the transference of the basic motifs of the 'Waldalgesheim Master' into media other than metal-work – fine wood-carving for which in the earlier La Tène phases pottery stamps remain the only possible clue.

L. Marton, *Dolgazatok* IX–X (1933–34), 93 ff., esp. Taf. 34:11; *ECA*, no. 419; *KvsE*, 186 ff.; Th. Voigt, *Jahresschr. mitteldt. Vorg.* 53 (1969), 416 ff., no. 9

[1] *ECA*, P 263 (spear-head) and no. 258 (bracelet)

134 Duchcov spring, Lahošt'. Bronze brooch. L. c. 6·4 cm. LT Ib, late IV BC. Mus. Duchcov. *Aú ČSAV, Prague.*

In 1882 one of the most striking Iron Age and presumably ritual deposits associated with water was found in the vicinity of a spring at the foot of the Krušné Hory range in north-west Bohemia. Some 2,000 bronzes, mostly brooches and bracelets, were found, the majority being contained within a great bronze cauldron. The finds were distributed shortly after discovery and so it is difficult to make a precise assessment of the totals involved – pieces from the Duchcov hoard are to be seen in no less than eight Czechoslovak museums as well as in Vienna and in several major German collections. Thus an estimate of the total number of brooches involved, which undoubtedly formed the major type represented by the hoard, varies between 400 and 1,500. The find has given its name to one particular shape of brooch with pointed knob or vase-shaped foot which is a particular cultural marker for the first extensive flat cemeteries of central Europe and their satellites in the Carpathian basin. The appearance of this 'Dux' fibula – like all such brooches, chiefly found in women's graves – in Swiss flat cemeteries such as those at Münsingen near Bern, underlines the interconnections between east and west indicated by such objects in the Duchcov hoard as the present brooch.

The cast decoration on the bow of this and of the brooch shown by its side [135] has already been illustrated in these pages; it appears at the base of the ? chariot mount from Waldalgesheim [118] and may be compared to the openwork 'waves' at the base of the Amfreville helmet [110]. Jacobsthal, considering the key features of the Waldalgesheim Master, in whose workshop this brooch was probably made, and preferring an aquatic to a botanical metaphor, has written of 'a winding stream flowing into banked-up lakes and out again'.[1] The design occurs not only on the re-used sword scabbard from Sanzeno[2] in Celtic northern Italy but also along both edges of a sword and scabbard from an as yet only partially published warrior's grave at Moscano di Fabriano near Ancona. Here were found a bronze *stamnos* and Vulcian tripod, both probably heirlooms and the latter close to that found in the Dürkheim princely grave, as well as a Greek *krater* and *kylix-krater* of the last quarter of the fourth century; the warrior was accompanied by not only the sword but also an Italo-Celtic helmet like that from Umbria illustrated above [see notes to 106–108].[3] It is finds like Moscano which not only serve to emphasise the popularity of the Waldalgesheim style in the regions immediately north and south of the Alps but also help to establish its absolute chronology.

Originally the foot of the Duchcov brooch would

have held a coral or enamel stud, such circular disc-footed brooches being called the 'Münsingen' type [see notes to **135**], the actual terminal of the foot here being in fact in the form of a miniature human head. Such brooches with miniature heads are known from flat grave cemeteries in France[4] and Hungary; there is also a second Czechoslovak example from Moravia, while a contemporary 'Certosa'-type fibula from Münsingen-Rain has what appears to be a much-worn mask.[5] These may possibly form the archetype for much later brooches with human head terminals concentrated in the Ticino region of Switzerland [see notes to **200–201**].

The much-rubbed nature of this and of the pieces from the Duchcov find suggests that an alternative to the theory of ritual deposition may be the cache left behind by an itinerant trader-smith with particular connections in western Switzerland.

S. Berger, *Památky Arch.* XII (1882), 71–79, 109–22; *KvsE*, 90 ff. and Tab. XXIII:5; *V and A*, 133–34

[1] *ECA*, 93
[2] *ECA*, no. 104; see also notes to [**110**]
[3] G. Annibaldi, *Il Museo nazionale delle Marche in Ancona* (n.d.), ill. on p. 23; W. Dehn and O.-H. Frey in *Atti del VI Congr. Intern. delle Sci. Preist. e Protostoriche* I (1962), 205; for tripods *Manuel* IV, 572 and fig. 437; 942 ff. and fig. 643; see also notes to [**54**]
[4] C. Coyon, *Travaux de l'Acad. nat. de Reims* CV (1898–1899), 299–301
[5] F. R. Hodson, *The La Tène cemetery at Münsingen-Rain = Acta Bernensia* V (1968), Pl. 19:783 (= gr. 46)
[6] *V and A, loc. cit.*

135 Rickenbach, Kt. Solothurn. Bronze fibula with coral mounted foot. L. 9·2 cm. LT Ib, late IV BC. Bern. Historisches Mus., Bern.

The brooch from Duchcov just described is the easternmost example of a fibula with cast decoration in the manner of the 'Waldalgesheim Master' – a brooch from Pleurs in the Marne[1] is the westernmost. A small number came from south-west Germany,[2] but by far the largest group have been found in western Switzerland, in particular in the canton of Bern. Four fibulae with disc feet, the Münsingen type as illustrated here, and with varying forms of cast 'Waldalgesheim' ornament came from the type-site where the decoration also occurs on brooches of the 'Certosa'-derived form.[3]

The brooch from Rickenbach was found in a flat grave with two knobbed penannular bronze bracelets, one with plastic decoration paralleled by a ring from Echaudans, Ct. Vaud.[4]

D. Viollier, *Les sépultures du second âge du fer sur le plateau suisse* (1916), 134 and Pl. 2:5; *ECA*, no. 336 ('Yverdon, Ct. Vaud')

[1] L. Morel, *La Champagne souterraine* (1898), Pl. 27
[2] Christa Liebschwager, *Bad. Fundber.* 23 (1967), 76–77 and Taf. 34:2
[3] P. Reinecke, *AuhV* V (1911), 335 and Abb. 3:a, c–e, g–i; *ECA*, nos. 332 ff.; F. R. Hodson, *The La Tène cemetery at Münsingen-Rain = Acta Bernensia* V (1968), Pls. 21:787; 22: 797; 23: 839; 28:851; 47:575
[4] Viollier, *op. cit.*, Pl. 22:123

136 Schosshalde, Kt. Bern. Silver brooch. L. 6·3 cm. LT Ib, late IV BC. Bern. Historisches Mus., Bern.

Silver was rarely used in the west Celtic world [see notes to **77, 204–206**], but occasionally finger rings both plain and ornamented [see notes to **139**] of the La Tène Ib–c period are made in this metal. The elongated 'Münsingen' brooch from Schosshalde is a unique example of a silver brooch. It was found, not in a woman's but in a man's grave, together with a sword, two iron spears, three bracelets – two of hollow bronze sheet with *repoussé* zigzag ornament, a common form in Swiss graves of the La Tène Ib phase – and two glass beads.

Though the brooch lacks its original, presumably coral-inlaid, foot decoration, the pattern on the bow is much lighter in feeling than that on the two bronze examples illustrated on this page; it is closer to the spirit of classical and in particular Hellenistic plant motifs suggesting a continuing familiarity amongst at least some native craftsmen with the ultimate sources of their stylistic repertoire. The incised fronds of the palmettes hark back to the split forms on the Basse-Yutz flagon ornament [**60–61**] but, in this split form, occur on a later La Tène Ib brooch with 'Waldalgesheim' derived ornament from Münsingen and the considerably later sword from Dickenhof, Kt. Thürgau [**181**]. The peaked trumpet spiral tendrils springing from the main stem of Schosshalde, which some see as playing a key rôle in British insular art, look forward to decorated Middle La Tène fibulae from France, Switzerland, Jugoslavia and Poland. The Polish example was found with a spear decorated in the 'advanced Waldalgesheim style' as found on some decorated swords of the early part of the same period[1] – which in fact offer more likely, if more widely distributed, counterparts to the plant motifs of early Celtic art in Britain. Here again the revitalising influence of Hellenistic art may be a point to keep in mind.

D. Viollier, *Les sépultures du second âge du fer sur le plateau suisse* (1916), 106–07 and Pl. 2:53; *ECA*, no. 331; O. Tschumi, *Urg. des Kantons Bern* (1953), 204 and Abb. 8, bottom right; H. N. Savory, *Bull. Board of Celtic Studies* XXII (1966), 88 and fig. 1:1

[1] L. Le Clert *Musée de Troyes: Catalogue des Bronzes* (1898), no. 232; *ECA*, 207, 210 and P110 and 286= *ArtG*, 240, Pl. 23; F. R. Hodson, *The La Tène cemetery at Münsingen-Rain = Acta Bernensia* V (1968) Pl. 88:199; L. Bolta, *Arheološki Vestnik* XVII (1966), 380–81 and T.5:2; J. Rosen-Przeworska, *Swiatowit* XIX (1948), 189–90 and ryc. 13–15; see also notes to [**142**] below

137 Filottrano, S. Paolino, grave 22. Fragment of bronze scabbard on iron backing. Total l. 67·5 cm., l. of fragment c. 20 cm. LT Ib, late IV BC. Museo nazionale delle Marche, Ancona. *R-GK (E. Neuffer).*

This scabbard, with its ritually bent iron sword [see notes to **11** and **190**] was found in one of the simpler flat graves from the large Celtic cemetery of Filottrano in the territory of the Senones [see notes to **128**]. With it were an iron spear and two iron rings – probably for slinging the sword from the shoulder;[1] there is evidence that the Celts did not usually wear their swords at their sides in the classical manner [but see **30, 33**]. A fragment of textile is rusted on to the scabbard towards the mouth and forms a dark, slightly diagonal band.

Like that on the gold torc from grave N.2, the very

slightly raised decoration of the bronze plate shows clearly that here is a work closely related to the school of the 'Waldalgesheim Master', a key feature being the intertwining or 'plaiting' of the running palmette motif. Even more certainly than on the 'Canosa' helmet [105] and despite Jacobsthal's denial, one can guess at the anthropomorphic intent behind the individual lyres with their 'Cheshire Cat'-like faces. These one can trace from the purely floral elements of Apulian vase painting of the fourth century through to the unambiguous faces of the Waldalgesheim armlets and perhaps slightly later pieces such as the neck-ring from Barbuise in the Aube [143]. The raised circle ornament of the mouth is similar to that on a mount with *repoussé* lyre-palmettes from Brunn an der Schneebergbahn, Upper Austria.[2]

E. Baumgärtel, *J. Roy. Anthrop. Inst.* LXVII (1937), 266; P. Jacobsthal, *J. Roman Stud.* XXIX (1939), 98 ff.; P. Reinecke, *Wiener Prähist. Zeitschr.* XXVII (1940), 44ff.; *ECA*, no. 103; *V and A*, 126 ff., Abb. 4B and Taf. 10:1

[1] L. Lepage and F. Claisse, *Rev. Arch. de l'Est et du Centre-Est* XVIII (1967), 294 ff. and fig. 1
[2] *ECA*, no. 377 and P450b ('Brunn am Steinfeld'); *Besançon*, 8, 21 ff. and Abb. 3a; see also notes to [127, 138]

138 Dürrnberg, Hallein, grave 28. Gold finger ring. D. c. 2·4 cm. LT Ib, late IV BC. Stadtmus. Hallein. *Ing. E. Peninnger.*

Although finger rings of gold, bronze, or occasionally silver wire are not uncommon, particularly in women's graves of the western flat cemeteries of La Tène Ib–c, more ornate examples are comparatively rare. Two examples have already been illustrated [58, 88] but the present ring with its *repoussé* decoration of a repeating and intertwining palmette chain unlike these earlier pieces, is clearly a piece from the school of the 'Waldalgesheim Master'. It demonstrates the difference between this style and that of objects closer to classical archetypes such as the helmet from Umbria [108] where, as Jacobsthal comments, 'lyres subordinate to palmettes . . . [while] in Celtic ornaments the lyres, even if sprouting, are all and everything'.[1] The lyre chain of the Dürrnberg ring is not far from the frieze running round the buffer terminal of the Waldalgesheim gold torc [127] or the central element of the Brunn an der Schneebergbahn mounts.[2]

The relationship which exists between the Dürrnberg ring and that illustrated on the right from western Switzerland shows the connections the salt-traders had with the Waldalgesheim 'school' craftsmen trading and working in the latter area; the connection is strengthened by Ernst Penninger's comparison of the decoration of the ring from grave 28 with the open-work form of a disc-shaped brooch from grave 42.[3]

This finger ring was associated with a second plain electrum example and an amber bead girdle.

E. Penninger, *Mitt. Ges. Salzburger Landeskde.* 100 (1960), 4; *Keltische Kunst: Bodemschatten uit Salzburg*, Frans Halsmus., Haarlem (1963), no. 8; *V and A*, 155–56 and Taf. 14:1=no. 1

[1] *ECA*, 84

[2] *ECA*, no. 377
[3] =*Keltische Kunst*, no. 13

139 Deisswil, Stettlen, Kt. Bern, graves 8–15. Silver finger ring. D. 2·4 cm. LT Ib, late IV BC. Bern. Historisches Mus., Bern.

This ring is made of silver, the rarest metal in the Celtic west, like the brooch from Schosshalde illustrated above [136]. Though related in form to the Dürrnberg ring, it exhibits the use of a different motif from the Waldalgesheim repertoire – the basic unit is a lyre with central diamond precisely in the manner of the twin bronze armlets from the Waldalgesheim grave itself and with the same hint of a human face as the torc from the Champagne [120].

The flat cemetery from which the ring was recovered was unfortunately unsystematically excavated and no certain associations can now be worked out; comparison with Münsingen-Rain suggests, however, that nothing from it should be later than late La Tène Ib.

O. Tschumi, *Urg. des Kantons Bern* (1953), 356, 358 and Abb. 214; *V and A*, 125, 131 ff., 161 and Taf. 14:2–3= no. 21

140 La Charme, Troyes, Aube. Cast bronze armring. External d. 5·7 cm. ? Early III BC. Musées de Troyes. (left) *Belzeaux-Zodiaque*; (right) *J. Bienaimé, Troyes.*

This single find from the Champagne consists of a triple repeat design with addorsed clean-shaven heads; the style is, however, very different from the Dürkheim and Schwarzenbach armlets from the early La Tène princely grave groups [53–54] which have only a roughly similar layout. The La Charme faces have something of the Marson 'negroes' [86] or the La Tène Ib–c Courtisols buffer torc [119], although the great cauliflower ears are not so easy to parallel. The twin 'horns' sprouting from the chins of each head may be compared with those on the Panenský Týnec brooch [65], the Dürrnberg grave 44 mount [48], or, more apposite as equally 'provincial' – which means no more in the context of Iron Age art than idiosyncratic – the Kyšice brooch [68]. With the exception of Courtisols, all this material must be earlier in date than La Charme. Between each pair of heads a spiral fill-in design looks more like the Waldalgesheim-derived style of the Middle La Tène fibulae discussed in connection with the Schosshalde brooch [see notes to 136]. Certainly the heavy stylisation has similarities to the full 'Plastic Style' of the third century BC [158 ff.].

L. Le Clert, *Musée de Troyes: Catalogue des Bronzes* (1898), no. 602; *ArtG*, 240, Pl. 20; *V and A*, 148; *PreA*, 218 and ill. 213

141 Křinec, Nymburk, grave I. Cast bronze bracelet. D. 8 cm. LT Ic–II, III BC. Národní Muz., Prague.

In one of two skeleton graves recovered during rescue excavations in 1957 was found a warrior with iron spear, longsword in scabbard, and iron chain clearly, from its position, slung from the right shoulder [see notes to 137]. On the right wrist the warrior was wearing the bracelet with hinge and spring-catch illustrated here.

In general the bracelet is related to a group of rather heavy cast armrings usually with hinged catches and crude loop and spiral ornament found, with one exception, within the borders of Czechoslovakia.[1] The exception is an armlet from the Celtic cemetery at Fondo Benacci outside Bologna – an undoubted import from central Europe and one which establishes at least some degree of continuing Celtic settlement well into the third century.[2] The striking feature of the Křinec bracelet is the two rows of fishes swimming in opposite directions between a raised wavy margin and divided by raised dot-and-circles. Apart from coinage, there is only one parallel in Celtic art for such fishes, and this is a bronze armring from the Duchcov deposit where the fishes have simpler paddle-like tails and are set face to face.[3] Although Scythian material has been cited as a source for the Křinec fishes with their great webbed tails, coinage[4] does in fact form a more possible source, since coinage introduces into the Celtic world a range of Hellenistic motifs no less important for the later development of La Tène art than Italic metal-work is for the earlier period [see also notes to **194**].

(Ed.) J. Neustupný, *The Prehistory of Czechoslovakia* (1958), Pl. XXI below; J. Břeň, *Časopis Národního musea. Praha* CXXXIV (1965), 146–54; *V and A*, 148, n. 182 and Taf. 14:7

[1] *KvsE*, Tab. XXXVI:8–10, LXXIV:6; K. Ludikovský, *Sborník Č.S.S.A.* (*Brno*) 2 (1962), 270 and obr. 5:1, 4 and 6:4–5
[2] *ECA*, no. 252
[3] S. Berger, *Památky Arch.* XII (1882), 109 and Tab. V:67; *KvsE*, obr. 26:20; *V and A, loc. cit.* and 156 and Taf. 14:6 (wrongly described as a finger ring)
[4] A. Blanchet, *Traité des Monnaies gauloises* II (1905), 379 and nos. 401, 427, 554

142 Steinenbronn (Waldenbuch), Kr. Böblingen. Stuben sandstone pillar-statue. Ht. 1·25 m. IV–III BC. Württ. Landesmus., Stuttgart. *Landesbildstelle Baden u. Württ.* (*Dr H. Hell*).

The fragmentary rectangular pillar-statue, lacking its head, was found in the forest of Greuten in 1864 not far from the find-spot of the Holzgerlingen statue [**14**]. Three of the four faces of the Waldenbuch stone bear within the lower rectangular panels a false-relief lyre design which also extends under the (single) left arm. The fourth face on the short side, not visible in the present illustration, has a slender tendril not unlike those on certain of the cast bracelets from Czechoslovakia discussed above [see notes to **141**] and certainly related in a general way to the tendril designs of the Waldalgesheim 'school' [**134–136**]. An early publication of the Waldenbuch stone compares the lyre designs on the three sides to the decoration on a sword scabbard from northern Jugoslavia,[1] where the layout recalls that on certain Middle La Tène fibulae, but a girdle-hook plate of undoubtedly early La Tène date from Schwabsburg, Kr. Mainz, has very similar incised decoration.[2] The 'step' pattern on the upper part of the stone may be compared with the coral-filled compartments on the Basse-Yutz flagons [**60–61**], the bronze comb from Aigle, Ct. Lausanne, or a spear from Neuchâtel, but these are all again early pieces.[3] The vertical lines, it has been suggested, are a breastplate, but though chain-mail is known from La Tène contexts, no breastplates of the early La Tène period have been found north of the Alps [see notes to **202**].

It is difficult to be dogmatic about the dating of the Waldenbuch statue; however, it seems by no means obligatory to assign it as early as the La Tène Ib *floruit* of the Waldalgesheim school, the more especially since it would thereby constitute a unique piece for the period.

R. Knorr, *Germania* 5 (1921), 11 ff. and Abb. 1–2; K. Bittel, *R-G Forsch.* 8 (1934), 79; *ECA*, no. 15; *Celts*, pls. 61–62; *WK*, Taf. 23; *VRD*, ill. 123; *CCH*, 162 and fig. 42; *PreA*, 208 and ill. 200; *PAE*, 247–48 and fig. 95A; *EV*, 238–39 and ill.; H. Zürn, *IPEK* 22 (1966–69), Taf. 42:9

[1] P. Reinecke, *Mainzer Zeitschr.* II (1907), 46 and Abb. 9a; *ECA*, Pl. 247b; J. M. de Navarro, *Germania* 37 (1959), 136 and Abb. 1; Ksenija Vinski-Gasparini, *Arheološki radovi i rasprave* I (1959), 287 and Tab. IV: 21; Jacobsthal and Vinski-Gasparini wrongly ascribe this sword to Mitrovica [see note to **52**]
[2] *ECA*, no. 351; see also notes to [**112**]
[3] Aigle: *ECA*, no. 375; Neuchâtel: *ECA*, no. 129; *PAE*, fig. 94B

143 Barbuise, Villenauxe, Aube. Bronze neck-ring. Internal d. 12·7 cm. LT Ib, late IV/early III BC. Musées de Troyes. *J. Bienaimé, Troyes.*

The *torques ternaires* or neck-rings with triple knob decoration either, as here, three times repeated in a series of miniature 'pawnbrokers' signs' or as a single unit or, again, with a more ornate openwork setting, are almost exclusively types associated with the flat cemeteries of the Marne region.[1] Two outliers of this distribution are one of the ornate type from a flat-grave cemetery in Bohemia[2] and one fragment with 'pawnbroker's sign' from the Reggio Emilia cemetery of San Polo d'Enza[3] which also contained a 'Ticino'-class girdle-plate [**96**]. This last find strengthens the connection between the Celts of north-central and eastern France and those of northern Italy suggested by such pieces as the Amfreville helmet [**110**]. One feature of the construction of these *torques ternaires*, which is clear on the right of the upper, general view of Barbuise, is the way in which one-third of the circumference of the ring is detachable by means of a long pegged male and female joint.

The most striking feature of the Barbuise ring is of course the triple setting of heads, each head being what Jacobsthal termed 'a Janus in flat projection', since the faces with their great scrolling curls have each a Siamese twin joined at the chin on the under surface – an unusual example of a reversible garment in La Tène neck-wear. The faces set against a pounced background somewhat in the manner of the bronze flagon mount from Dürrnberg [**48**], or, closer in date and style, a linch-pin from Niederweis, Kr. Bitburg,[4] are an unambiguous construction of human features stemming literally from the 'Cheshire Cat'-faces of the Filottrano scabbard [**137**] with their pseudo 'leaf crowns'. Barbuise stands midway between the stylisation of the tiny Weiskirchen brooch faces [**67**] and those of what is termed here the 'Disney Style' [see notes to **164, 167–169**].

Two other *torques ternaires* from France have much simpler trios of human faces; a ring from Aulnizeux[5] – now missing its removable section – has three pairs of crude faces separated by ridging and plain knobs which relates it in general to the 'Andernach' and 'Horchheim' class of rings [see notes to **51**], while the crude faces on another ring from the Troyes region, Rouillerot,[6] has the faces actually superimposed on the triple ball settings.

From associations as well as styles, the *torques ternaires* should bracket the period of production of objects in the more southerly and eastern 'Waldalgesheim' manner.

L. Le Clert, *Musée de Troyes: Catalogue des Bronzes* (1898), 52–53 and fig. with Pl. XVI=no. 132; *ECA*, no. 245 (confusing with Rouillerot); E. Sprockhoff, *PPS* XXI (1955), 268–70, fig. 5, 7a–c; *ArtG*, 240, Pl. 32; *V and A*, 131–32, 141, Abb. 4C and Taf. 10:3

[1] P.-M. Favret and J. Prieur, *Rev. Arch. de l'Est et du Centre-Est* I (1950), 11–21
[2] *KvsE*, Tab. LVI:4
[3] E. Magagnini, *Emilia Preromana* 4 (1953–55), 55 and Tav. IV:4
[4] *ECA*, no. 161; see also notes to [100]
[5] J. de Baye, *Mém. de Soc. Antiq. de France* 44 (1883), 126 and ill.; J. V. S. Megaw, *Germania* 45 (1967), 36 f. and Taf. 10:4
[6] Le Clert, *op. cit.*, no. 512; *ECA*, P45 (confuses location with Barbuise following A. Blanchet, *Bull. de la Soc. Nat. des Antiquaires de France* [1901], 165 and n. 4); Sprockhoff, *op. cit.*, fig. 8:2

144 Eschersheim, Ldkr. Frankfurt, grave IV. Bronze fibula with remains of coral setting on foot. L. 7·3 cm. LT B2, III BC. Mus. f. Vor- u. Frühg., Frankfurt. *J. V. S. Megaw.*

This cast bronze brooch, on which the centre section of the bow has been filed down in probably fairly recent times, was found in 1899 in a skeleton grave with an iron sword and armring. The form of the ring is derived from the classic Swiss 'Münsingen' brooches [see notes to **134–136**], but both the exaggerated foot-disc and the general layout of the decoration suggest a later date than these. The over-all patterning, in fact, only slightly anticipates the 'advanced Waldalgesheim' decoration on the swollen bows of the archaising brooches of LT C date with large discs and human head terminals produced in the Ticino region and exported from there into south Germany and the Tyrol.[1] Amongst earlier material the ornate decoration spreading as with Eschersheim on to the outer coils of the spring of a brooch from Münsingen-Rain, grave 50,[2] should date to the end of La Tène B1 in Germany. Decoration of 'advanced Waldalgesheim' type also curls round the spring of the two iron fibulae from Conflans, Marne – again, however, of La Tène C or Middle La Tène date.[3]

The 'pseudo-face' seen in the right-hand detail appearing above the spring is a common construction on armrings contemporary with later La Tène B both from France and from Switzerland, and it is more than likely that Eschersheim represents an export from the latter area. The unique brooch from Newnham Croft, Cambridgeshire, whatever its source, must have a similar artistic background.[4]

ECA, no. 325

[1] W. Krämer, *Germania* 38 (1960), 20 ff. and Taf. 1 and 5:1; see also notes to [201]

[2] *ECA*, no. 333; F. R. Hodson, *The La Tène cemetery at Münsingen-Rain=Acta Bernensia* V (1968), Pl. 23:839
[3] *ArtG*, 240, Pl. 23; see also notes to [136]
[4] *PP*, 11 and fig. 6b; see also notes to [131]

145 Andelfingen, Kt. Zürich, grave 1. Bronze neck-ring with enamel inlay. D. 14·7 cm. LT B2, III BC. Schweiz. Landesmus., Zurich.

The disc-terminalled neck-ring or *Scheibenhalsring* was developed as a woman's ornament in the Upper Rhine;[1] its distribution overlaps with the more westerly buffer torcs [see notes to **119–120**] though, like these, it has outliers far to the east in Hungary. A subsidiary group found their way into northern Switzerland, though surprisingly none has been found at Münsingen; several came from the extensive flat cemetery of Andelfingen. The distribution pattern, like the similar spread of much later Merovingian women's jewellery, seems to mark the results of migration rather than of trade. As can be seen here, sometimes the disc-terminalled rings can be decorated in a style which recalls that of the buffer torcs and, indeed, a hybrid of both types has been found both at Laumersheim in the Pfalz and Rácalmás in Hungary.[2] The ornamentation of the Andelfingen ring is on the whole in very low relief – a more 'plastic' version of the same 'Waldalgesheim'-derived motif can be seen on the ring from Nebringen [147]. Basically the three areas of incised decoration on the main ring consist of an elaborated 'S' curl terminated at either end by a small and highly stylised pointed-chin face – similar to the tiny heads occasionally found on 'Münsingen' and related fibulae of the earlier La Tène B phase [134]; closest to this very low relief is perhaps the neck-ring from Unteriflingen near Stuttgart.[3] Actual enamelling is still to be made out surrounding the low relief and is concentrated on the disc-decorated arc which, by means of tenon joints at either end, can be detached from the main ring. The rosette-like disc can certainly be compared with some of the large disc fibulae of the later 'Münsingen'-derived type dated to the end of La Tène Ic in Switzerland.

The associated fibulae found in grave 1 at Andelfingen establish it as belonging to the later phase of La Tène B.

D. Viollier, *Les sépultures du second âge du fer sur le plateau suisse* (1916), 41, 135 and Pl. 14:28; *ECA*, no. 234

[1] R. Giessler and G. Kraft, *32. Ber. R-GK 1942* (1950), 79 Abb. 15; W. Krämer, 'Das keltische Gräberfeld von Nebringen (Kr. Böblingen)', *Veröffentl. d. Staatl. Amtes f. Denkmalpflege Stuttgart*, Reihe A:8 (1964), esp. 18 f.; *V and A*, 139 ff.
[2] *ECA*, nos. 226–27
[3] *ECA*, no. 229, esp. P 94–95

146 Nebringen, Kr. Böblingen, grave 14. Bronze neck-ring with enamel inlay and mounts. D. 15·2 cm. LT B2, III BC. Württ. Landesmus., Stuttgart.

The small and recently excavated flat cemetery of Nebringen near Stuttgart is important for the light it throws on the burial customs of what must have been the well-to-do members of Celtic society in the southern part of Germany during the closing years of the Early La

Tène period. The *Scheibenhalsring* here illustrated is one of several from the cemetery, traces of red enamel being present in the knobs – with 'S' spirals in the manner of Andelfingen [145] – and longitudinal grooves. The three areas of relief decoration on the main ring are in effect a non-representational version of the anthropomorphic 'intermittent wave tendril' as developed on the Barbuise ring [143].

Grave 14 at Nebringen contained the remains of a woman between 35 and 50 years of age together with a 'Münsingen'-derived fibula, a spiral wire armlet and two laterally twisted and ridged rings – which, like the gold and silver finger rings in the other female graves in the cemetery, underline the cultural connections of this area with the Swiss plateau in the later La Tène B phase.

W. Krämer, 'Das keltische Gräberfeld von Nebringen (Kr. Böblingen)', *Veröffentl. d. Staatl. Amtes f. Denkmalpflege Stuttgart*, Reihe A:8 (1964), esp. Taf. 4:2, 13:1; *PreA*, 218, 220 and ill. 209

147 Michelbach, Kr. Brackenheim. Bronze neck-ring with enamel inlay. D. 12·5 cm. LT B2, III BC. Württ. Landesmus., Stuttgart. *R-GK* (*E. Neuffer*).

The decoration – 'one-sided' as is usual with La Tène neck-rings – on the rear portion of this rather poorly preserved *Scheibenhalsring* serves to illustrate the wide dissemination of motifs no less than of objects and people in the later part of the early La Tène period from the Swiss plateau to the Rhineland and further west. Three interjoined reversible faces with staring eyes employ the usual topsy-turvy trickery seen in much more academic form in the gold leaf fragment from Dürkheim [59]. Here the faces are built up of 'a spiral ribbon with a double pelta in the involutions', as Jacobsthal wrote of a different but closely related *Scheibenhalsring* from Beine grave 22 in the Marne found with two 'Dux' fibulae with vase-shaped feet.[1] Similar faces are to be found on armlets and fibulae from Switzerland and central Czechoslovakia[2] as well as on the easternmost tubular torc, that from Zibar in Bulgaria[3] where, as on Beine, the trick-faces are set against a dotted background recalling that of the Barbuise neck-ring [143]. Part of another *Scheibenhalsring* from a grave at Bodersweier, Kr. Kehl in South Baden, combines the pelta pseudo-faces with an isolated and clearly human bottle-nosed face[4] like that on the combined *Scheibenhalsring* and buffer torc from Dammelberg illustrated on the following page [148]. One other French piece, an armring from somewhere in the Marne,[5] fills up the gap between twisted pseudo-faces in the Michelbach manner with split palmettes and fans, first seen on the Basse-Yutz flagons but which continue on the Waldalgesheim torc [127] and in the more or less contemporary products of the 'sword style' [181].

These elusive elements of design show the continuing evolution of that most intriguing but baffling element in Celtic art, the adaptation of plant motifs to the main features of the human face.

ECA, no. 230; *V and A*, 141–42

[1] C. Bosteaux—Paris, *Ass. française pour l'avancement des Sci.19* (1890), 592 ff. and fig. 2; *ECA*, no.228 *ArtG*, 240, Pl. 35
[2] E. Vogt, *60. Jahresber. Schweiz. Landesmus. Zürich*

1951 (1952), 56–57 and Abb. 30, 32; K. Ludikovský, *Sborník ČSSA (Brno)*, 2 (1962), 257 ff. and obr. 4b:3, 5:2
[3] *ECA*, no. 46
[4] G. Fingerlin, *Arch. Nachrichten aus Baden* (Oct. 1968), 13 and Abb. 4:2
[5] *ArtG*, 240, Pl. 36

148 Dammelberg, Trebur, Kr. Gross-Gerau, Bronze torc with traces of enamel and bronze armlet. D. of torc 14 cm. LT B2, III BC. Formerly Hessisches Landesmus., Darmstadt, (details) *R-GK* (*E. Neuffer*).

This find from a grave, destroyed in World War II, with buffers curving into the main arc of the ring is a combination of two neck-ring types, the disc-terminalled rings illustrated on the previous page [145–147] and the more northern and westerly buffer torcs. Here, as in another hybrid torc from Pfaffenschwabenheim, which is, however, closer to the *Scheibenhalsring* form,[1] the disc section incorporates a tenon-catch; a socket for one fastening pin for the joint is clearly visible on the left. As usual, the rear of the neck-ring is flat and free from ornament.

The emphatic spiral decoration of the twin knobs between the flat discs, with their central pins for keying the enamel inlay and the fused buffers, is to be seen on several other pieces of the later La Tène B phase including two other torcs with fused buffers, one from Praunheim near Frankfurt[2] and one, in gold, from Clonmacnoise in Ireland, a unique continental export [174]. Praunheim was found with a stamp-decorated pot and a number of armlets including a pair similar to the one associated with the Dammelberg ring and is securely dated to La Tène B2. The Niederweis linch-pin, a single find already noted in connection with Barbuise [see notes to 143], also has a plastic spiral on the knob at the base of the actual pin, and its use of dot background or rather edging ornament caused Jacobsthal to suggest a link with Dammelberg, where dotting emphasises the tendril curling up away from the large discs. These tendrils on Dammelberg have in turn been compared with the vine scrolls on the back of the 'Disney Style' owl heads on the great Brå cauldron [164], but in fact the decoration has rather the discipline of the Brunn an der Schneebergbahn mounts (again with dotted ornament)[3] or of two fibulae from later La Tène I contexts at Münsingen-Rain.[4] Closest of all to the Dammelberg tendril pattern is the cast decoration either side of a 'Münsingen'-derived brooch from Ebreichsdorf in lower Austria.[5] This brooch has a human head capping the enlarged enamelled disc foot and an elongated spring which gives the type the name of the 'cross-bow' brooch; such brooches are dated right at the close of La Tène Ic in Switzerland. The Ebreichsdorf brooch ornament, like that of Dammelberg, is based on a simple 'S' spiral with tailing-out tendrils fitting into the narrowing curve of the bow; as on a neck-ring, the pattern follows the narrowing of the ring. Ebreichsdorf was found with a ridged armlet and a torc with fused hoof-ended terminals.

As to the decoration at the rear of Dammelberg, the face is unusually turned inwards, that is toward the wearer's neck. Like Barbuise, it is based on the wave tendril. While it has certain archaic features such as the vertically 'combed widow's peak' to be seen on the Parsberg brooch [63], the great staring circular eyes, squared-off rather than bulbous nose, and thin-lipped mouth are more in the manner of the faces on the Waldalgesheim gold bracelets [124–125] or, more apposite in view of its emphatic, almost rococo, spiral ornament, the Avon-Fontenay ring and its related pieces from the Champagne [see notes to 122]. The triskel detail moulded in the triangle behind the Dammelberg head and forming the flanking elements of the main wave tendril is really a development of the basic triple circle feature so common in early Celtic art; in its present form it can be seen once more on the contemporary decorated sword scabbards from Hungary and Switzerland.[6]

Dammelberg with its 'plasticisation' of certain Waldalgesheim themes is too individual a piece to tie down to a precise style or even school. It is best regarded as a local product reflecting various common elements of the contemporary artistic vocabulary but without the mastery of such readily defined groups as the 'Disney Style'.

P. Reinecke, *AuhV* V (1911), 331=nos. 1052–55; *ECA*, no. 224; *Brå*, 70; *V and A*, 142–45 and Taf. 11:1–3

[1] *ECA*, no. 225; K. Dielmann, *Hanauer Geschichtsbl.* 17 (1960), 19
[2] R. Welcker, *Festschr. Frankfurt (Anthropologie)* XXXIX (1908), 25–36; *AuhV* V, nos. 1049–51; *ECA*, no. 210; Dielmann, *loc. cit.* and Abb. 5:1
[3] *ECA*, no. 377; see also notes to [127]
[4] F. R. Hodson, *The La Tène cemetery at Münsingen-Rain=Acta Bernensia* V (1968), Pl. 35:533 (=*ECA*, no. 335), 59:318
[5] F. Berg, *Arch. Austriaca* 28 (1960), 44–49 and Abb. 1–2; W. Krämer, *Germania* 39 (1961), 309; see also notes to [200]
[6] C. F. C. Hawkes, *PPS* XXI (1955), 226, fig. 2:3 and Pl. XXV:1; *KvsE*, obr. 5:7; J. M. de Navarro, *40. Ber. R-GK 1959* (1960), 109–10 and Taf. 21

149 La Courte, Hainaut. Detail of linch-pin with iron shank and bronze head. Total l. 9 cm., w. of head 5 cm. ?LT Ib, IV BC. Mus. royeaux d'Art et d'Histoire, Brussels. *M. E. Mariën.*

This chariot linch-pin, one of a pair from a grave in an early La Tène cemetery marking a definite Celtic expansion from probably the Marne, if not also Switzerland, into the southern part of what is now Belgium, has been compared by Jacobsthal to the face on the Dammelberg torc [148]. In fact once more it is not easy to assign it precisely to any particular style. The great bushy eyebrows and slanting eyes certainly have much of the appearance of the 'Disney' Brå owl and Brno griffon [159, 164]. The isolated central horns, however – inlaid, as recent analysis shows, not with enamel but with Baltic amber – though less like ears than those on a later and even more unusual Belgian find [173], hark back to the satyr or 'Acheloös' prototypes behind the faces of the Hořovičky discs [47] or Rodenbach finger ring [58]. The flanking curls on the linch-pin heads have become subsidiary horns and, as Monsieur Mariën has pointed out, there is an inexplicable resemblance to eighth-century Luristanian bronzes from Persia, where flourished a style with a very similar ambiguity of the animal and the human.

The outline of the La Courte pins and the flanking curls are not dissimilar to another pin, now lost, from Grossdraxdorf, Kr. Greiz, an import into central Germany with tiny human head, dotted background and knobbed terminal in the manner of the Niederweis linch-pin.[1]

ECA, no. 162 (=Leval-Trahegnies); M. E. Mariën in (ed.) H. Reykers, *Analecta Archaeologica: Festschr. Fritz Fremersdorf* (1960), 265–67, esp. Taf. 69:10, 70:10; *id.*, 'Le Groupe de la Haine' *La Période de la Tène en Belgique=Monographies d'Archéologie nat.* 2 (1961), 40–44 and Pl. 1=nos. 54–55; *V and A*, 125; *PreA*, 220 and ill. 218

[1] Grossdraxdorf: H. Kaufmann, *Jahresschr. mitteldt. Vorg.* 50 (1966), 209 and Abb. 3; Niederweis: *ECA*, no. 161

150 Urach, Kr. Reutlingen. Iron linch-pin with bronze flashing. L. 11·1 cm. ?IV/II BC. Württ. Landesmus., Stuttgart. (general view) *R-GK* (E. Neuffer); (detail) *J. V. S. Megaw.*

This pin, like that from Grossdraxdorf mentioned in connection with La Courte illustrated above, was found close to a Celtic fortified settlement site, in this case the great 'Heidengraben', the largest presumed *oppidum* in Germany.[1] Urach's precise find-spot is by the river Erms. It has a menacing look which is not entirely due to the loss of inlay for the eyes and the general crudity of the workmanship. Usually it is considered as La Tène A in date; the simple St Andrew's cross-design on the lower part of the pin can certainly be paralleled on early La Tène objects of around 400 BC.[2] But the massive head itself, with the heavily-ridged hair and the wings of the pin forming shoulder and arms, also looks forward to anthropoid-hilted swords of no earlier than La Tène C date [228–229]. Another difficult-to-date piece in which the arms have a practical use to perform and with a similar, almost simian cast to the head, is an unprovenanced mirror-handle possibly from France and now in the Römisch-Germanisches Zentralmuseum in Mainz.[3] Yet another find, from Württemberg, always presumed to be of early date, is the bronze mannikin from Ilsfeld, Kr. Heilbronn,[4] which has been compared with the rim 'Father Christmas' heads of the Borsch Aue flagon fragment [see notes to 66].

All in all, Urach has the appearance of what might be regarded as more the product of a local blacksmith's workshop rather than the handiwork of some highly considered skilled artisan much patronised by wealthy chieftains as the purveyors of the art of the princely burials must have been.

P. Goessler, *Préhistoire* I (1932), 268–69; K. Bittel, 'Die Kelten in Württemberg', *R-G Forsch.* 8 (1934), 63–64 and Taf. 8:4; *ECA*, no. 160; *VRD*, ill. 141; F. Fischer, *FbS*, 18:1 (1967), List 1, no. 82; *EV*, ill. p. 194

[1] W. Dehn, *Celticum* III=suppl. *Ogam: Tradition Celtique* 79–81 (1962), 351 ff. and Pl. 106
[2] *ECA*, nos. 184 and 358
[3] Goessler, *op. cit.*, 265–67 and fig. 4; Bittel, *op. cit.*, 41 and Taf. 8:2
[4] O. Schwabe and G. Behrens, *Germania* 17 (1933), 85 and Taf. 11:3

151 Gašić, Vojvodina (formerly Hercegmárok, Kom. Baranya). Gold torc. D. 10 cm. ?LT Ic, III BC. Magyar Nem. Múz., Budapest.

Made up of two separate sheets of gold and fastening at the terminals, though now fractured at five different places, and with six fragments missing, this gold torc is one of the most remarkable pieces of west Celtic craftsmanship to reach eastern Europe, since, despite claims for Balkans influence in its style, all its known parallels came from France [152–153]. The rich rosette-like style is applied to the outline of what is basically a standard Marnian buffer-terminalled torc.

L. Éber, *Arch. Értesítő* 23 (1903), 22 ff.; P. Jacobsthal in *Epitymbion Chrestou Tsounta=Arch. tou Thrakikou Laograph. kai Gloss. Thesaurou* 6 (1940), 397 and Abb. 6; I. Hunyady 'Kelták a Kárpátmedencében', *Diss. Pannonicae*, ser. II:18 (1942), T. XXVI:1–2 (1944), 91; *ECA*, no. 62

152 Fenouillet, Haute-Garonne. Gold torc. D. 13·5 cm. ?LT Ic, III BC. Mus. St-Raymond, Toulouse. *Yan-Zodiaque*.

This is one of six gold torcs (one very fragmentary) discovered during canal construction in 1841. The similarity with the Gašić example even to tenon-catch has long been commented on. The piece here illustrated is that comparatively rare thing in continental Celtic neck-rings, a torc with twisted cross-section in the manner of that depicted round the neck of the 'Dying Gaul' [see also notes to **126**]; it may be compared to a multi-strand torc from Montans, Tarn.[1] If one has to look for outside influences on the decoration of this buffer-terminalled torc, Iberia is both distributionally and stylistically a safer bet than Hungary, which Jacobsthal suggested, since Iberia was not only a source for gold and silver but also a centre for skilled fine metal-smiths influenced by the mixed traditions of Carthaginians, Greeks and, at long range, even Etruscans.[2]

Manuel IV, 845–49 and fig. 588; *ECA*, no. 67; *ArtG*, 240, Pls. 25, 28 (=caption 26); *WK*, Taf. 71 below; H. P. Eydoux, *La France antique* (1962), ill. 7; *PreA*, 214 and ill. 207

[1] *Manuel* IV, fig. 589
[2] A. Arribas, *The Iberians* (n.d.), Pl. 67

153 Aurillac, Cantal. Gold armlet. Total d. 7·9 cm., ht. 3 cm. ?LT Ic, III BC. Bibliothèque Nationale, Cabinet des Médailles, Paris. *Belzeaux–Zodiaque*.

This ring and two others found with 'pre-Roman Celtic pottery' at Lasgraïsses, Tarn, composed of gold with almost 25 per cent. silver content,[1] can best be described in Miss Nancy Sandars's words:

> By a form of *legerdemain* the artist has hoodwinked us into believing we see a nature that is not there. The impression of acorns, buds, leaves, and the conventional concomitants of a classical wreath turns out on analysis to be nothing of the sort; it has nothing at all to do with organic forms.

This visual trickery exploited by the goldsmiths of south-western France takes abstraction a stage further than the work of the 'Waldalgesheim Master', though there is a link with the gold mock-twisted bracelet from the upper Waldalgesheim grave in the beaded strand which weaves its way in and out of the pseudo-jungle of the Aurillac ring. The use, however, of stylistic terms such as 'Plastic' or 'Waldalgesheim' in connection with

such pieces as Aurillac gives a falsely limiting impression of a period when, even for Celtic art, style seems to have been a remarkably fluid concept.[2]

ECA, no. 63; *Art G*, 240, Pl. 24 ('St Leu-d'Essereut, Oise'); *WK*, Taf. 71 above; *PAE*, 244, 283 and Pls. 264–65 ('Tarn')

[1] *Manuel* IV, fig. 587; *ECA*, nos. 68–69; *ArtG*, 240, Pl. 26 (=caption 28); H. P. Eydoux, *La France antique* (1962), ill. 8
[2] *V and A*, 150 ff.; *PAE*, 240

154 Prunay, Cher. Painted pedestalled urn. Ht. 31 cm. LT Ib–c, IV/III BC. British Mus., London. (*Courtesy Trustees of the British Museum.*)

It has already been suggested when discussing the engraved ornament of the imported bronze flagon now in Besançon [**113**], that the centre and eastern part of France had its own rôle to play in the developing art of the later part of the early La Tène phase. In much the same period, skilled potters in the Champagne basin were transforming motifs otherwise known only from metal-work on to the surface of elegant funerary vessels of undoubtedly local manufacture.

As to the shape of the urn, here illustrated from a large cemetery with several mounded chariot burials, despite some controversy on the matter, it has certainly been made with the aid of a turntable. The making of wheel-turned pottery in southern Germany and in France dates back to at least the fifth century when it was probably influenced by the export of so-called 'Phocaian' ware through the intermediary of Massaliote traders from the south of France.[1] The actual profile first occurs in the early Marnian princely graves such as Somme-Bionne [see notes to **111**]. The connections of the Marne region with central Europe in the fourth/third centuries are, however, underlined by the appearance of urns of this pedestalled profile at Dürrnberg[2] and used as cremation containers in the Moravian flat grave cemetery of Maloměřice outside Brno where, unlike Switzerland, pottery was not uncommonly found in graves [see notes to **158–160**].[3] Several features of this vessel with its purple-brown design on red slip painted before firing – hardly a glaze as sometimes described – recall the 'Waldalgesheim' Waldenbuch pillar-statue [**142**], not only because of the loose flowing spirals and curved-sided triangles or peltas but also, just visible, the old step pattern painted below the rim on the narrow neck-band. The lower bordering design, however, a sinuous line like the main pattern, recalls the immediately pre-'Waldalgesheim' Besançon and Les Saulces-Champenoises engraved motifs as do the lobe-shaped terminal features; indeed from the Les Saulces-Champenoises cemetery comes a pedestalled vase with a somewhat freer painted design of the same general class as Prunay.[4]

Statements that this vessel was associated with a warrior chariot burial are incorrect. That pottery with this style of decoration should be ascribed to the transition between LT Ib–c seems borne out by the association of a similar vessel with a decorated buffer-terminal torc from Bussy-le-Château [see notes to **119**].

C. Bosteaux-Paris, *Ass. française pour l'avancement des Sci.* 16 (1887), 743–46; L. Morel, *La Champagne souterraine* (1898), Frontispiece; *Manuel* IV, 966 ff., esp. fig. 660:2; R. A. Smith, *Guide to the early Iron Age antiquities in the British Museum* (2 ed., 1925), 71 and Pl. VI:5; *ECA*, no. 408, *Besançon*, 18; *PAE*, Pl. 295

[1] W. Dehn, *Alt-Thüringen* VI (1962–63), 372–82
[2] E. Penninger, *Germania* 38 (1960), 375; *Keltische Kunst: Bodemschatten uit Salzburg*, Frans Halsmus., Haarlem (1960), no. 23
[3] *KvsE*, 197–98, obr. 61 and Tab. LXXVI:9; E. and J. Neustupný, *Czechoslovakia before the Slavs* (1961), Pl. 72=*CCH*, Pl. XXXIII:4
[4] *Manuel* IV, fig. 661:2

155 Prunay, Cher. Painted pot. Ht. 19 cm. LT Ib–c, IV/III BC. British Mus., London. (*Courtesy Trustees of the British Museum.*)

This squat vessel is usually considered to come from the cemetery at Beine but, according to the notes of Léon Morel, in whose collections it formerly was, it comes from Prunay as does the pedestalled urn illustrated on the left. The design is even closer to the layout of the Besançon flagon ornament [113]; the dark painted pattern appears once more over a slipped body colour contained within a horizontal, basically rectangular layout demarcated, as on both the bronze flagon and the pedestalled urn, by an undulating line. The shape, no less than the design, looks forward to painted wheel-turned pottery of the late La Tène period such as the well-known pot from the Basle gas-works site [*Colour Pl.* **Vb**], although here later classical influences may also have their part to play.

L. Morel, *La Champagne souterraine* (1898), Frontispiece; R. A. Smith, *Guide to the early Iron Age antiquities in the British Museum* (2 ed., 1925), Pl. VI:4

156 Kélouer (Kerbrut en Plouyé), Plouhinec, Finistère. Pot with stamped decoration. Ht. 31 cm. ? early LT Ib, IV BC. Mus. des Antiquités nat., St-Germain-en-Laye. *Belzeaux-Zodiaque.*

The development of stamp-decorated pottery in southern Germany and further east during the early La Tène period has already been briefly noted [see notes to **27, 116** and **133**]. A small group of pots from north-western France employ this technique for producing designs closely related to the painted pottery and incised metal-work of the Marne and further east, perhaps as a result of migration from these areas in search of iron ore supplies.

The Plouhinec pot, one of Dr Schwappach's newly-defined '*Metallstil*', employs not less than half-a-dozen circular and toothed stamps to build up a pattern, the margins of which are applied by a thin cut-out line executed free hand. The main design, with its dotted fill-in and lower margin pattern of sinuous line-and-circle ornament, once more closely echoes the Besançon flagon [113], while the upper arcading or garland motif and lower overlapping 'S's or 'running dog' pattern are both common features of the 'Braubach' bowls and related stamp-ornamented vessels of early La Tène B[1] also to be seen on the Basse-Yutz flagons [**60–61**].

The Plouhinec pot was found in a barrow with three skeletons, an iron axe, a whetstone and two pendants,

and seems to have been used as a cremation container.

J. Déchelette, *Rev. arch.* XXVI (1895), 196–212, Pl. V–VI; id., *Rev. arch.* XXXIX (1901), 51–61; *Manuel* IV, 973 ff., esp. fig. 663:2; R. E. M. Wheeler, *Maiden Castle, Dorset=Soc. Antiq. London Research Rep.* XII (1943), 216 and Pl. XXVII; W. F. Grimes, *PPS* XVIII (1952), fig. 12 right; *ArtG*, 240, Pl. 52; R. E. M. Wheeler and K. M. Richardson, *Hill-Forts of Northern France=Soc. Antiq. London, Research Rep.* XIX (1957), 98 and fig. 30; P. R. Giot *et al.*, *Brittany* (1960), 190 ff. and Pl. 64; P.-M. Duval, *Art de France* IV (1964), ill. p. 28 top; F. Schwappach in *Festschr. Dehn*, no. 18, esp. 233 ff. and Taf. 18

[1] P. Reinecke, *AuhV* V (1911), 281–82 and Abb. 1; W. Dehn, *Bonner Jahrb.* 151 (1951), 88, Abb. 1; *KvsE*, obr. 54

157 St-Pol-de-Léon, Finistère. Incised and stamp-ornamented pot. Ht. 26 cm. ? early LT Ib, IV BC. Mus. Morlaix. *M. B. Cookson.* (*Courtesy Sir Mortimer Wheeler.*)

Fig. 9 [**157**] Pol-de-Léon, France. Incised and stamped decoration on pot. Scale c. 1:7

After Déchelette

This vessel was discovered in 1882, like Plouhinec, in a barrow. Though less sophisticated in style than the latter's decoration, it has no less than Plouhinec been much commented on by students of early Iron Age art in Britain in view of the Gaulish origin often claimed for the Cerrig-y-Drudion bronze bowl with which it has certain points of resemblance [114]. However that may be (and stamped ornament is also present on a sherd from Merthyr Mawr, Glamorganshire),[1] the main simplified palmette design – partially repeated on the base – harks back to what must be not only earlier but Rhineland and non-local products like the throat decoration of the Basse-Yutz flagons [**Plate IIIb**]. Otherwise the long flowing comb-stamped ribbons and undulating marginal patterns point to the same eastern sources as those which must have influenced the Plouhinec urn.

The rather heavy profile of both vessels, no less than the meagre proportions of the St-Pol-de-Léon design, may be ascribed to their provincial source; once more we are probably looking at products of local craftsmen rather than artists with an international reputation.

P. du Chatellier, *La poterie aux époques préhistorique et gauloise en Armorique* (1897), 22 and Pl. 14:1–2; *Manuel* IV, fig. 663:1; *ECA*, 95 and P 470; *Besançon*, 16 ff.; R. E. M. Wheeler, *Antiquity* XXXIV (1960), 58 and Pls. VI–VII; P. R. Giot *et al.*, *Brittany* (1960), 192 ff.; F. Schwappach, *Festschr. Dehn*, no. 32, esp. p. 258 ff. and Taf. 18

[1] H. N. Savory, *Bull. Board of Celtic Studies* XIV (1950), 171 and Pl. II:1; *id.*, *Bull. Board of Celtic Studies* XXII (1966), 91 and fig. 1:5; *id.*, *Early Iron Age Art in Wales* (1968), 13 and fig. 12:5

158 Maloměřice, Brno. Bronze mount. Two fragments, (upper) 5×4·4 cm.; (lower) 6·2×3 cm. ? LT Ic, early III BC. Moravské Muz., Brno.

In 1941 a number of intricately cast openwork bronzes, variously interpreted as chariot yoke fittings[1] or as (more likely) mounts for a wooden-spouted flagon like that from Dürrnberg grave 46 [see notes to **163**], were recovered from a disturbed grave in an extensive flat cemetery, containing some 75 graves of LT Ic–II date outside Brno, the capital of Moravia in central Czechoslovakia [see also **159–160, 165**]. The lack of definite association is all the more unfortunate since the mounts belong to a small, distinctive but widely scattered group of objects which, though mostly poorly dated, in all likelihood bridge the end of the Early and beginning of the Middle La Tène phase.

All the mounts belong to what Jacobsthal loosely termed the 'Plastic style' with roots which undoubtedly go back to the fifth century. The present pair of faces in the context of the other Maloměřice mounts offer as striking a confrontation of near-realism and abstraction as for example the basal handle face of the Waldalgesheim spouted flagon [**78**] compared to that from Reinheim [**73**].

The faces are not too far from the sharp-featured individuals on the Dürkheim gold bracelet [**54**], and the openwork attachments sprouting from each head are indeed in the same tradition as the clean-shaven aspect of the Dürkheim trick faces [**59**]. As with the Dürkheim 'funny-faces', it is possible to read the Maloměřice mounts as portraits of two opposing humours, the sardonic and the genial. The openwork lobes themselves also have roots in motifs employed on earlier material – a chariot mount from La Gorge Meillet[2] and, in flat, two-dimensional form, the basal mount on the Dürrnberg flagon [**72**]. Comparisons with the unique British double heads from the Tal-y-llyn hoard are not convincing [see notes to **265**], while claims that the centre of the style represented by the Maloměřice mounts must lie within the territory of the far-wandering Boii [see notes to **168**] rest almost entirely on this single find.

K. Hucke, *Zeitschr. des Mähr. Landesmus.* II (1942), 87–96, esp. Taf. 3:4; *Brå*, 68–70, esp. Pl. VIId; *KvsE*, 400–01, obr. 14–15 and Tab. LXXVII–LXXVIII, esp. Tab. LXXVIII:1; *CCH*, 149 and Pl. XXIII; *V and A*, 101, 125 and Taf. 7:3; *PAE*, 241 and Pl. 260

[1] A. Radnóti, *Germania* 36 (1958), 28–35

159 Maloměřice, Brno. Bronze handle mount. Maximum d. of ring 11·8 cm. ? LT Ic, early III BC. Moravské Muz., Brno. *W. and B. Forman.* (*Courtesy Artia, Prague.*)

There are two predatory birds cast into the outer form of this mount from the Maloměřice set; one, with vicious, pointed beak and body cleverly hinted at by the main curve of the ring and back-swept knobbed horn running into the great crest, has a clear ancestry in the Persian-looking griffons of the Weiskirchen belt-plate [**62**] and the Erstfeld rings [**84**] which reappear as undoubted

horned heads on another Maloměřice openwork piece.[1] Here the 'tail' of the main bird when reversed turns into another curved-beaked bird with more elongated, almost pelican shaped, bill. The eyes and heavy fringed brow can be used to claim a later stylistic association than that of Waldalgesheim for the La Courte linch-pin also with heavy brow ridges [**149**]; one of a set of chariot mounts from the region of Paris translates the same expression into more congenial human form [**168**]. The emphasis on the staring eye, constructed basically of a comma outline, gives support to the claim for seeing an apotropaic eye on such early pieces as the brooch from Ostheim [**69**].

The circle of the Maloměřice ring is not perfect; the overlapping lip can be seen on another French example [**161**] of what in view of the sophisticated use of almost a modern cartoonist's method of abstraction of natural forms and its reduction to a number of standard curvilinear geometric shapes, may be termed the 'Disney style' after the great American pioneer of the animated film, a context in which that most modern of mythical Celts, Asterix the Gaul, might well feel at home.

Brå, Pl. IV; *KvsE*, Tab. LXXVII:7; W. and B. Forman and J. Poulík, *Prehistoric Art* (n.d.), ill. 131; *PAE*, 242–43 and fig. 91

[1] *KvsE*, Tab. LXXVII, 3–4

160 Maloměřice, Brno. Bronze mount. Total ht. c. 18 cm., ht. of central animal head 6 cm. ? LT Ic, early III BC. Moravské Muz., Brno. *W. and B. Forman.* (*Courtesy Artia, Prague.*)

Considered by some as the spout mount for a jug or similar vessel, the third mount illustrated from the Maloměřice series has, like the griffon handle [**159**], a distinctly frightening aspect. The great upswept horns are not sufficient evidence to claim the animal as an orientalised ibex instead of, as the heavy brows and full muzzle indicate, that great totemic beast of the Iron Age, a bull. Here in any case is an interpretation of nature rather than a case of stylised observation such as the other two much more domesticated bovines illustrated on this page [**161–162**]. It is surely significant that when looked at from above and to the rear a second, reversed, but still horned head appears with tiny, not bulging eyes, with the 'horns' of the main beast forming open jaws. There can be little doubt that for the most part the Maloměřice mounts exhibit the horrific and the intangible aspects of Celtic imagery.

KvsE, Tab. LXXVIII, 2–3; W. and B. Forman and J. Poulík, *Prehistoric Art* (n.d.), ill. 130; (ed.) J. Neustupný, *Pravěk Československa* (1960), Tab. 70; *PreA*, 220 and ill. 219; *PAE*, 241–42 and fig. 90 left

161 ? Mâcon, Saône-et-Loire. Bronze ?cup handle. L. 7·1 cm. ?LT Ic, III BC. British Mus., London. *J. V. S. Megaw.*

This, the second miniature masterpiece of early Celtic art supposedly from the region of Mâcon to be illustrated in these pages [see notes to **77**], was purchased for the British Museum in 1872 from a locally assembled private collection. Plastic bull mounts have a long prehistory in Europe commencing with the handles of Neolithic pots and continuing through such forward-looking pieces as the free-standing bull from Byčí Skala [35]. Here, this tiny casting with an angled slot with rolled over rim at the top of the head suggests, not a mirror-handle for which the ring would also be rather curiously aligned, but possibly the handle for a small drinking cup. The heavy but unridged brows of this placid-looking beast and its literally cow-like eyes, though contrasting in expression, may be compared with not only one of the Malomĕřice mounts [165] but with the handle-fitting owls on the great Brå cauldron [164]. The general hour-glass formulation of the Mâcon face when viewed from the front, the spiralling nostrils, and dot-ending to the mouth-line all recall a later and insular formulation of an animal head, the 'bulls' of the oval Witham shield [252].

The lipped joints of the main stem of the mount with its ring are very much in the manner of the Malomĕřice handle illustrated on the opposite page [159] while the rear lip has almost a duck-like aspect like an armring from Nový Bydzov in Bohemia.[1]

As to the validity or otherwise of the find-spot, in view of the presumed provenance of the 'Paris' mounts illustrated below [166–168], Mâcon may also owe its deposition to trade or other contact with the far-wandering Boii of Central Europe [see also notes to 169–170].

W. Watson, *Antiq. J.* XXIX (1949), 48 and Pl. VIIIb; J. V. S. Megaw, *Antiq. J.* XLII (1962), 24–29 and Pl. XIV

[1] *ECA*, no. 279

162 Brå, Horsens, Jutland. Bronze bull mount from cauldron. W. between horns c. 5·2 cm. ? LT Ic, early III BC. Forhistorisk Mus., Moesgaard, Højbjerg. *L. Larsen.* (*Courtesy National Mus., Copenhagen.*)

The most northerly find of the 'Disney style' was made in 1952 when, from a pit under a stone cairn on the edge of a peat bog, were recovered the dismantled remains of a great bronze cauldron originally measuring about 2 metres across the mouth and with a capacity of at least 600 litres. An iron ring ran round the rim and three bronze-coated iron rings ran freely in bronze castings in the shape of owls' heads [164]. On the outer edge, on either side of the handles, were originally a pair of bull's head mounts, four smaller and one larger mount (illustrated here) surviving, the larger mount being also the best modelled and perhaps used as the base from which the smaller versions were copied by a less skilful apprentice.

The fashion for ornamenting clearly ceremonial cauldrons with bulls' heads was introduced into the Mediterranean world, and in particular Greece and Italy, by trade and subsequent refugee settlement in the eighth century BC from the kingdom of Urartu on the borders of the old Assyrian Empire near Lake Van on what is now the eastern Turkish border. It was also from Italy that the technique of beating cauldrons out of a single sheet of bronze – like the Brå cauldron – was first transmitted north of the Alps during the earlier part of the Iron Age. The long-standing Celtic tradition of the cauldron of plenty, a kind of barbarian *cornucopia* with the added powers of rejuvenation as recorded by later classical authors, must also stem from this period.[1]

Though in comparison with the fierce creature of Malomĕřice illustrated above, the Brå bulls are veritable ancestors of Munro Leaf's Ferdinand, smelling not the blood of sacrifice but flowers, they are just as much part of the close-knit 'Disney style'; both the neatly groomed cow-licks and great eyes with ridged borders compare with the style of the Moravian mounts.

The only associated finds with the Brå cauldron fragments were an iron axe, some leather fragments and a strange bronze hook in the shape of a long-tailed bird somewhat like the predatory birds of Erstfeld [84]. There can be no doubt that the Brå cauldron marks an import into the non-Celtic territory of the Cimbri, who in the second century were to threaten the Alpine borders of the Republican empire. What particular trading exploit or war-like campaign was the cause of the cauldron's transportation from Central Europe must, in the absence of comparative Scandinavian finds, remain a matter for speculation.

Brå, 64 ff., Frontispiece and Pl. II; *PreA*, 221–23, ill. 221; *PAE*, 241 and Pl. 255; *PCB*, 94 and 273

[1] Strabo, *Geographia* IV, 2, 1; scholiast on Lucan, *Civil War* I, 443; C. F. C. Hawkes and M. A. Smith, *Antiq. J.* XXXVII (1957), 176–78; see also notes to [209]

163 Dürrnberg, Hallein, grave 46. Bronze spout. Total l. 14·3 cm., l. of 'crocodile' head c. 4 cm. LT A–B1, IV BC. Stadtmus. Hallein. *Ing. E. Penninger.*

Although there are many instances of archaisms in Celtic and particularly insular Celtic art, every now and again one finds a piece which has an uncanny element of stylistic prophecy in its layout. The present spout from the second wooden flagon to be found in the post-World War II excavations at Dürrnberg is a case in point. At first sight it would seem to have many of the features of the presumed third-century 'Disney' or, in Jacobsthal's sense, 'Plastic' style, and as such it has been published – by the present writer and others. In fact the spout was recovered from beside the third of three skeleton burials found in a stone cairn under a barrow mound. The skeleton was associated with five pottery vessels including two Linsenflaschen [see notes to 27], a spear and an iron armring. There were two crude little naked figures, one male and one female, also mounts from the wooden flagon.[1] The last named are in the style of other miniature figures from early La Tène contexts discussed in connection with [16] above. Other objects in the graves included slender-spouted pottery flasks like that from Matzhausen [27] and gold-leaf rosettes like those found at Manĕtín [31] and Reinheim [73]. Thus the Dürrnberg mount should be not later than the end of the LT A phase or the very beginning of LT B1.

Turning to the actual ornamentation of the piece, it offers a sort of descending escalator into that artistic underground 'where things have floating contours and pass into other things'.[2] The spout-mouth itself is the clearest figure in what is, on close examination, an intertwined triumvirate of three heads even more difficult to delimit than the Erstfeld menageries [84] or the Malomĕřice double mounts illustrated above and to the left. The excavator calls the spout-head a 'crocodile', and while exotic animals are far from unknown even in early Celtic art, a boar with flaring nostrils is a possibility which appears certainly in a later and hardly less peculiar context [277]. The outlined almond eyes and dot-punched surface of the boar-crocodile face relate it to the mask mount from the other wooden flagon in Dürrnberg grave 44 [48], whose attendant mounts terminate, as on the grave 46 spout, with crude lotus blossoms pierced for nails (not visible in this view).

Below the spout-head, forehead to forehead, is the second face, the one which has given rise to comparisons with the so-called 'Plastic style' – it is a great bull's head with flaring nostrils. Here, however, the third personality intrudes; looking along the line of the spout instead of from one side, one realises that the 'nostrils' of the bull are in fact the almond eyes of a crude semi-human face for which admittedly the only parallel is a pair of rings from a third-century grave at Steinhausen, Kt. Zug, wrongly compared by Jacobsthal on the basis of poor illustrations with the great torc from Frasnes-lez-Buissenal in Belgium [173].[3]

Such a combination of animal, human and the ambiguous is typically Celtic and has already been illustrated in another early piece [100].

K. Willvonseder, *Keltische Kunst in Salzburg* (1960), 27–28 and Abb. 9; E. Penninger, *Mitt. Ges. Salzburger Landeskde.*, 100 (1960), 4–7 and Abb. 3; *id.*, *Germania* 30 (1960), 356–57; *Keltische Kunst: Bodemschatten uit Salzburg*, Frans Halsmus., Haarlem (1960), no. 28; J. V. S. Megaw, *Antiq. J.* XLII (1962), 25–26; *PAE*, 241 and Pl. 257; W. Dehn, *Památky Arch.* LX (1969), 130 ff.

[1] Penninger, *Mitt. Ges. Salzburger Landeskde.* 100, Abb. 4–5; *Keltische Kunst*, Haarlem, nos. 26–27
[2] P. Jacobsthal, *Proc. British Acad.* XXVII (1941), 308
[3] D. Viollier, *Les sépultures du second âge du fer sur le plateau suisse* (1916), 134=no. 133; *ECA*, 211

164 Brå, Horsens, Jutland. Bronze handle mount from cauldron. W. c. 4·2 cm. LT Ic, early III BC. Forhistorisk Mus., Moesgaard, Højbjerg. *L. Larsen. (Courtesy National Mus., Copenhagen.)*

This illustration of a massive casting weighing about 1,000 grm. shows the inward-facing aspect of one of the three ring-handle mounts which were attached to the lip of the great Brå cauldron. There are minor differences on all three mounts showing that they were cast in separate and probably closed clay moulds by the so-called *cire perdue* method which only allows one casting per mould.

The great malevolent owl face–no cosy companion of the goddess of wisdom this, but rather the fierce eagle owl (*Bubo bubo* Linn.), like the more domesticated pairs on the Reinheim rings [79–80]–reminds us that this bird also has a minor part to play in Celtic belief.[1] Stylistically, the Brå owl is very much a cartoonist's construction, semi-circles, half-moons, triangles and the like. The close comparison of detail with the little Mâcon handle [161] should suffice to demonstrate that both pieces are the work of the same craftsman. The thin tendril spiralling up the 'backbone' of the owl though hardly 'pure Waldalgesheim style' or really close to such more or less contemporary pieces as the Dammelberg torc [148], certainly does have elements of Waldalgesheim-derived patterns – the scrolls of the Newnham Croft armlet, for example [131]. Closer parallels for the Brå tendril, however, are the heavy-hinged bracelets compared here with the Křinec armring [see notes to **141**], another point possibly suggesting a Moravian centre for the craftsman or craftsmen of the 'Disney style'. Best of all, though, is the loose tendril at the top of a sword scabbard from the type site of La Tène itself which should date from La Tène II.[2] Some indication of just how late the basic features of the representational Disney style survived can be seen from a bronze and iron linch-pin from the late La Tène *oppidum* of Manching [see notes to **196**]. The head of this pin is an eagle with just the same beak, staring eyes, and heavy brows as the Brå owl.[3]

Brå, 69, fig. 10 and Pl. I, III; *V and A*, 125 and Taf. 9:1: *PreA*, 223, ill. 221–22; *PAE*, 241 and Pl. 256

[1] *PCB*, 273–75 and Pl. 76b
[2] *ECA*, no. 106; see also notes to [**179**]
[3] *Deutsches Archäologisches Institut: Ausgrabungen-Forschungen seit 1950* (1969), Abb. 1

165 Maloměřice, Brno. Bronze mount (incomplete as illustrated). Total l. 10·5 cm., w. 4·6 cm. ? LT Ic, III BC. Moravské Muz., Brno. *W. and B. Forman (courtesy Artia, Prague).*

Here, with a studied asymmetry which is a characteristic of the so-called 'Plastic style' of the end of the early and beginning of middle La Tène phases, and in prehistoric garb, is the bottle-nosed 'Chad' figure of twentieth-century folk art and mass advertising. His ancestry can be traced back to the cat-like creatures on the Chýnov and Oberwittighausen brooches [90, 92] and even beyond to our archetypal Klein Aspergle satyr face [50]. The brows and rimmed eyes relate this face to other pieces of the 'Disney' style illustrated on the previous page and the face, despite its tipsy joviality, is based on the intermittent wave tendril construction as already seen in an advanced stage of development on the Barbuise neck-ring [143]. The 'wings' sprouting from the brows can be read either as some last memory of the old leaf-comma as seen on the La Courte linch-pins [149] or as horns like those on the great bull head [162]. More than likely, however, the mount is nothing more than an artistic *jeu d'esprit* in which the artist leaves each individual beholder to give his own personal interpretation.

KvsE, Tab. LXXVII:1; W. and B. Forman and J. Poulík, *Prehistoric Art* (n.d.), ill. 128; *V and A*, Taf. 9:2

166 ? Paris, Seine. Linch-pin, bronze-covered iron. W. 8·5 cm. LT Ic, III BC. Mus. des Antiquités nat., St-Germain-en-Laye. *Belzeaux-Zodiaque.*

In 1907 a collection of bronzes was purchased for the French nation for the not inconsiderable sum in those days of 4,000 francs. Included were a number of chariot fittings (three of which are illustrated here), a tiny mount in the form of a sharp-featured human head with great protruding pointed oval eyes – a linear descendant of the Dürkheim armlet pairs [54][1] – a triangular cross-section spear, and a fragmentary sword in its scabbard. The scabbard was strengthened by a so-called 'pseudo-bird bridge' such as appear with swords from the type site of La Tène; swords of this type are not uncommon in France though more usually considered as products of a specialised Swiss school of swordsmiths.² Despite doubts which have been cast on the supposed provenance of the Paris bronzes ever since their acquisition, it is not impossible that they could have come from a later warrior chariot burial within the territory of the Parisii – chariot fittings in the 'Disney style' as here have been found in even stranger contexts [170].

The face here shows the culmination of the constructional series based on an intermittent wave tendril, the face being the centre of a double lyre formed above by the scrolling eyebrows-cum-leaf-curls, more anatomical perhaps than the 'horns' of the La Courte linch-pin heads [149] but not so far from the crowning features of the Courtisols torc faces [119]. In between the brows of the Paris face is a single 'lotus bud' whose history may be traced back through another buffer torc [120] to the Heidelberg head [49] and the Rodenbach finger ring [58]; a comic detail is the large wart on the end of the creature's nose.

J. D. Cowen, *Proc. Soc. Antiq. Scot.* LXIX (1934–35), 456; P. Jacobsthal, *Proc. British Acad.* XXVII (1941), 307–08; *ECA*, no. 163, esp. pp. 120, 184; *ArtG*, 240, Pl. 22; *WK*, Taf. 72 top, P.-M. Duval, *Paris antique des origines au troisième siècle* (1961), 66–74, 296; J. V. S. Megaw, *Antiq. J.* XLII (1962) 26; *V and A*, 125 f., 152, Abb. 4H and Taf. 9:3; *PAE*, 243 and Pl. 261

¹ *ECA*, Pl. 175c
² E.g. *Manuel* IV, fig. 435:1; see also [182]

167 ? Paris, Seine. Bronze terret with iron core. Ht. 8·5 cm. LT Ic, III BC. Mus. des Antiquités nat., St-Germain-en-Laye. *Belzeaux-Zodiaque.*

The face of the lower part of this terret or rein-ring from the Paris collection of bronzes is one of a pair cast on a saddle-shaped curve either side of the main ring, the curve being presumably to fit the chariot rail or yoke. In style the face is very close to the linch-pin from the same set [166] and with the addition of the small rounded chin even closer to the presumably contemporary Courtisols torc [119]. Round the ring is a chain of three medallions, each with a stylised human face constructed from a lyre spiral – complete with wart on the end of each nose just like the linch-pin face. Both the form of the ring and the high relief knobs recall the heavy decorated cast bronze anklets found in LT Ic–II flat grave cemeteries in Central Europe [see notes to 176] – another pointer to the possible origin of the 'Disney style'.

J. D. Cowen, *Proc. Soc. Antiq. Scot.* LXIX (1934–35), 456 and fig. 2; *ECA*, no. 175a (Pl. 111 top left has '175b'), esp. P 475; *ArtG*, 240, Pl. 19; *WK*, Taf. 73; P.-M. Duval, *Art de France* IV (1964), ill. p. 16 centre

168 ? Paris, Seine. Ring, bronze over iron core. D. c. 7 cm. LT Ic, III BC. Mus. des Antiquités nat., St-Germain-en-Laye. *Belzeaux-Zodiaque.*

On this ring the pseudo-faces of the ring illustrated above are made explicit in three sharp-nosed human heads, arty types with slicked-back hair and side-boards curling down one side of each face almost to meet a twisted and tiny pursed-lipped mouth. With the heavy fringe recalling the Brå and Malomĕřice mounts of the previous two pages, one eye half-closed and one eye opened, the

construction, fitting into a neat *tondo*, offers a prehistoric antecedent for the long history of the circular composition in Western art.¹ The planned asymmetry of the faces which, as it were, hold a distorting mirror up to the human face as represented by the miniature mount from the Paris set,² takes the twisted form of the winged 'Chad' face from Malomĕřice one stage further [165]; in between each head is an elongated double comma-spiral rather in the manner of the Étoy, Switzerland, finger ring.³ It has been suggested that this trio of Paris faces may represent a central European version of the Irish hero Cú Chulainn, with his power of pulling in one eye and expanding the other until it was as big as a cauldron; with the warts of the Paris mounts in mind [166–167], one may recall that Cú Chulainn had no less than four warts, which were considered as marks of great beauty. Certainly some such apotropaic exploitation of the decoration for a Celtic chariot would be in keeping with the basic Celtic use of satirical representation.

J. D. Cowen, *Proc. Soc. Antiq. Scot.* LXIX (1934–35), 456 f. and fig. 3; P. Jacobsthal, *Proc. British Acad.* XXVII (1941), 307–08; *ECA*, no. 175b; *ArtG*, 240, Pl. 22; J. V. S. Megaw, *Antiq. J.* XLII (1962), 26; P.-M. Duval, *Art de France* IV (1964), ill. p. 16 below; *PAE*, 243–44 and Pl. 262

¹ E. H. Gombrich, *Norm and Form: studies in the art of the Renaissance* (1966), 64 ff., esp. fig. 126–27
² *ECA*, no. 175c
³ *ECA*, no. 74; see also notes to [169]

169 ? Sardinia. Gold finger ring. D. 2·5 cm. ? LT Ic, III BC. Victoria and Albert Mus., London. (*Crown copyright reserved.*)

In 1871 the then South Kensington Museum purchased for the sum of one thousand pounds sterling a large collection of European finger-rings of all ages. The owner had been Edmund Waterton, son of Charles Waterton, the eccentric naturalist and patron of taxidermy. Amongst the rings, but unnoticed until a few years ago, were two gold rings of undoubtedly La Tène workmanship, one related to the Rodenbach finger ring [see notes to **58**] and the present example, originally catalogued as 'ninth century sub-Mycenean'.

Here, however, is perhaps the masterpiece amongst 'Disney style' faces constructed from a wave tendril, the key stages of the evolution for which are provided by the Weiskirchen brooch [67], the Waldalgesheim gold armlets [124–125] and the Barbuise ring [143]. The general construction of the face follows the Brå owl [164], while the actual scrolling of the eyebrows, the bulbous nose, and the tiny glum mouth are closer to the Paris mounts [166–167]. The ring, with its tapering cross-section from front to rear and its *repoussé* pattern contained within raised borders, has a general resemblance to another gold ring, a single find from Étoy, Ct. Vaud, whose decorative layout consists of heavy 'S' spirals such as occur on central European La Tène II brooches and armrings, making Jacobsthal's description of the Swiss piece as 'a forerunner of the [Plastic] style' a bit hard to substantiate.¹

As to the plausibility of a Sardinian location for not one but two Celtic finger rings, while there seems little reason to doubt the fact that they were *purchased* on the island, the simplest solution would be to regard them as fairly modern importations from the mainland of Italy. Celts with contacts north of the Alps were settled there from the latter part of the fifth century; in the early second century the Boii, who had occupied the area round Bologna and in whose central European homeland the centre of the 'Disney style' is presumed to be, were defeated by P. Cornelius (Scipio) Nasica. Sardinia in the third century was Carthaginian territory, and Carthaginians had undoubted contacts with the Celts. Not only is a Carthaginian glass 'face bead' of the sixth/fourth century known from Narbonne, where it may have been traded through Spain, but a pair have been found also in a La Téne Ic context in a flat grave cemetery at St Sulpice, Ct. Vaud – not far from Étoy – while a fourth comes from the cemetery of Witry-les-Reims in the Marne.[2] Other evidence of central and eastern European contacts with Carthaginian trade exists, while Celts from Italy served as Carthaginian mercenaries first in 393 BC – together with Sardinians – and later in the Punic wars.[3] Thus it must remain an open question as to just where and when this splendid example of the high baroque of La Tène Iron Age art found its last resting place before being placed on public view together with Victorian mourning lockets and Renaissance enamels, forgotten and unremarked for almost a century.

C. C. Oman, *Catalogue of rings: Victoria and Albert Museum* (1930), 46 and Pl. II=no. 17; C. M. Guido, *Sardinia* (1963), 180 and fig. 56 below; *V and A*, 122 ff., 153–55, Abb. 1:2, 4I and Taf. 1:5–8=no. 20

[1] *ECA*, no. 74, esp. p. 97; *V and A*, 145 ff. and Taf. 13; *Praehist. Zeitschr.* XLIII–XLIV (1965–66), 406

[2] Narbonne: P. Héléna, *Les origines de Narbonne* (1937), 267 ff. and fig. 163; St Sulpice, grave 22: D. Trumpler, in (ed.) W. Drack 'Die Eisenzeit der Schweiz', *Reportium der Ur- u. Frühg. der Schweiz* 3 (1957), Taf. 8:39; *V and A*, Taf. 4:7; Witry-les-Reims: C. Bosteaux-Paris, *Ass. française pour l'avancement des Sci.* 21 (1892), 616

[3] Diodorus XIV, 95, 1; Livy XXVII, 36, 2; Polybius IX, 91, 3; G. T. Griffith, *Mercenaries of the Hellenistic World* (1935), 252 f.

170 Mal-Tepe, Mezek, Bulgaria. Detail of bronze-covered iron terret. W. 7·5 cm. ? LT Ic, III BC. Nat. Mus., Sofia.

Just before the outbreak of World War II excavations took place in one of a number of local beehive-shaped stone-built *tholoi* or chamber tombs built on the slopes of Mount Rhodope in southern Bulgaria (ancient Thrace). Originally constructed in the first half of the fourth century, the tomb had contained within its great bronze doors several burials of presumably a local ruling class: the grave goods included numerous Greek objects of the Hellenistic period including a silver coin of Alexander II of Macedon. The graves had been extensively disturbed following the original interments. Included amongst the grave goods were what may be interpreted either as the remains of a Celtic chariot burial, the bones of horses having been found in the long entrance or *dromos* of the tomb, or, like Canosa [see notes to **105**], trophies of local contact with Celtic warriors. Apart from two linch-pins decorated in a crude bossed version of the basic lyre pattern, some five terret rings – our illustration is a detail of one of these – show yet another variant on the wave-tendril face construc-

tion. Though detailing is not clear owing to the uncleaned state of the Mezek terret faces, they form a cross between the lyre pseudo-faces around the ring of the larger Paris terret [**167**] and the bulbous-nosed, tiny-mouthed, Sardinian finger ring [**169**]. Here undoubtedly the accoutrements of a Celtic chieftain had become a funerary magpie in a Thracian nest, accompanied suitably enough by a local bronze figure of a great boar and a third-century imported Italic bucket. A series of gold beads found amongst the Celtic pieces is compared by Jacobsthal to the gold 'berried' torc from Jugoslavia illustrated above [**151**].

It is not unreasonable to expect third-century Celtic material in the southern Balkans, and other La Tène objects are known from Greece proper.[1] During the end of the fourth and early part of the third century BC considerable numbers of Celts moved east and south from central Europe. In 335 BC Alexander the Great, campaigning in Bulgaria, received local deputations including Celts, and Celtic warriors are depicted on a fifth- or fourth-century tomb painting at Kazanlĭk in Bulgaria.[2] In 298 BC Celts, including members of the tribe of the Boii, moved into present-day Bulgaria, and in 279 BC under their leader (or is it a classical author's misunderstanding of the name of a god?) Brennus, one large body reached into Aetolia and allegedly sacked the holy precincts of Delphi, their subsequent defeat being recorded by the trophies shown on local coinage;[3] some of the survivors retired to settle in Thrace. Another group, refused permission to settle in the north, laid waste parts of Macedonia and subsequently several thousands were invited by Nicomedes of Bithynia to settle in Asia Minor, where they soon became a major threat to the stability of the local Hellenistic kingdoms [see also notes to **211**]. Against this background, the chieftain of Mezek could have been a Celtic veteran of Delphi or as one who answered the call to go east but died on the way. Despite the lack of any other standard material such as fibulae or weapon types for establishing a relative chronology for the style marked by the Mezek 'Chad' faces, and despite the rifling of the tomb which makes it difficult to prove any precise association with the Greek manufactured objects, the general historical picture supports a date around the end of the first quarter of the third century for the chariot fittings which compares well with the LT Ic date suggested for the other presumed chariot burial with 'Disney style' mounts, that supposedly from the region of Paris.

B. Filov, 'Die Kuppelgräber von Mezek', *Bull. de l'Inst. arch. bulgare* XI (1937), esp. 107 ff., p. 63 and no. 31; id., *Antiquity* XI (1937), 300–05; P. Jacobsthal, in *Epitymbion Chrestou Tsounta=Archeion tou Thrakikou Laographikou kai Gloss. Thes.* 6 (1940), 391–400; *ECA*, no. 176b, esp. 151–52; Filov, *Actas y Memorias de la Sociedad Española* XXII (1947), 21–33; *V and A*, 131 and Taf. 9:4; *PreA*, 220 and ill. 217; *PAE*, 230, 244

[1] J. V. S. Megaw in (ed.) K. Jażdżewski, *Liber Iosepho Kostrzewski octogenario a veneratoribus dicatus* (1968), 185–93; M. Szabó, *Acta Antiqua* XVI (1968), 173–7

[2] V. Mikov, *Le tombeau antique près de Kazanlak* (1934), Pl. III–IV; E. Condurachi in (ed.) P. Demargne, *Le rayonnement des civilisations grecque et romaine....= VIIIᵉ Congrès Int. d'Arch. class.* (1965), 324 and Pl. 64:2

[3] *Celts*, Pl. 47a

171 Mšecké Žehrovice, Nové Strašeci. Ragstone head. Ht. 23·5 cm. ?III/II BC. Národní Muz., Prague. *Aú ČSAV, Prague.*

Since its accidental discovery in 1943 not far from Prague, this head has been frequently published and much discussion has taken place as to its date and stylistic affinities. The head was found just outside the south-west corner of a square enclosure or *Viereck-schanze*.[1] Such square enclosures, sometimes associated with deep shafts containing offerings of various sorts, have been the subject of considerable investigation in recent years. With a concentration in southern Germany and an outlying group in western Bohemia they seem to mark local late La Tène cult places. At Mšecké Žehrovice there were not only a number of graves in the vicinity of the enclosure but also evidence of iron working and of the manufacture of lignite bracelets of a type dated to around the end of the second century;[2] graphite and stroke-ornamented pottery also indicate the site's use in this period. In the same area as the supposed find-spot of the head were a number of pits containing the bones of horse, pig, and cattle which may have been offering places.

As to the head itself, to comment that this is the nearest thing to portraiture in pre-Roman Celtic sculpture is to give a false impression of the Iron Age artist's approach to the human form; there is in fact no true portraiture in Celtic art, a point which becomes immediately clear if one examines inscribed native coinage [**Plate IVe**] or compares Mšecké with more or less contemporary Roman and Hellenistic depictions of Celts, moustaches and all.[3] Even Romano-British craftsmen with the model of Julio-Claudian portrait busts available to them, still clung to the old Celtic 'ideal' formulations [see notes to **243**].

Looking at the flattened features of the Czech head, it is certainly pattern not portraiture that is to the forefront. The spiralling eyebrows and outlined almond eyes follow traditional formulations extending back into the art of the early princely graves, for example the mount from Dürrnberg, grave 44 [**48**]. The bud-like ears again recall the Dürrnberg mount or amongst other, presumably earlier, sculpture, the Leichlingen 'Janus' head [**85**]. The moustaches are not a common feature in this highly stylised form save on coinage;[4] moustaches certainly occur in later Iron Age art but are not of this type [**203, 206**]. The hair *en brosse* is a common feature in all periods of La Tène; the difficult-to-date Urach linch-pin [**150**] is a comparably stylised piece. As to the torc, worn both by noble men and women and certainly by gods as well as humans, of itself it is only the most general of chronological indicators. Buffer-terminal torcs commence at the end of the early La Tène phase and last until the time of the Roman conquest of Gaul. Certain similarities with the even harder-to-date but allegedly pagan stone heads of Ireland include the small hole in the centre of the mouth of the Czech piece.

On general stylistic grounds an earlier rather than later date for Mšecké seems likely and, in view of the uncertain nature of its precise association with the *Viereck-schanze*, little chronological importance should be placed on its location. On the other hand that such a head would have been a much venerated and long preserved object seems more than likely.

I. Borkovský, *Umění* 16 (1944–45), 51–54; *id., Obzor*

Prehistorický XIII (1946), 16–22; J. Filip, *Praha Pravěka* (1949), 101 and obr. 72; J. Frel, *Časopis Národního Mus. v Praze* XXII (1953), 30–46; *KvsE*, 145, 188, 314 and Tab. LXX; *Celts*, Pl. 2; E. and J. Neustupný, *Czechoslovakia before the Slavs* (1960), 148, 156–57 and Pl. 74; *CCH*, 162 ff. and Pl. XX; E. Rynne, *Sborník Národního Muz. v Praze* A XX:1/2 (1966), 151–54; *PAE*, 250 and Pl. 274; L. Jansová, *Arch. roz.* XX (1968), 470 ff.; *EV*, 236–37 and ill.

[1] K. Schwarz. *20, Jahresber. d. Bayer. Landesamtes für Denkmalpflege 1962* (1963), 22–77; Schwarz and A. Dauber in *Miltenberg-Amorbach-Obernburg-Aschaffenburg-Seligenstadt=Führer zu vor-u. frühg. Denkmälern* 8 (1967), 50–51, 118–27

[2] J. Břeň, *Sborník Národního Muz. v Praze* A IX:1 (1955), 18 ff.

[3] *Celts*, Pls. 1, 3–4

[4] L. Lengyel, *L'art gaulois dans les médailles* (1954), Pl. XII, no. 429; *Celts*, Pl. 5c

172 Kamenné Žehrovice, Rakovník. Iron mask. Ht. 22 cm. ?II BC. Národní Muz., Prague. *Aú ČSAV, Prague.*

Found in a quarry and ascribed to several periods including the Middle Ages, this unique example of early iron smithing, considering the flamboyant up-curling moustaches and the oval eyes, has a distinctly Celtic look about it. Iron Age Celts were skilled ironmasters from early Hallstatt times, and by the La Tène period were producing over 70 different types of iron.

The Kamenné mask was attached to some sort of backing, to judge from the surviving nail holes, and as such also continues a tradition which extends back to the bronze mask of Kleinklein [**15**].

I. Borkovský, *Obzor Prehistorický* XIII (1946), 21; R. Pleiner, *Archaeology* 16 (1963), ill. on p. 234; *id., Staré Evropské Kovařství* (1962), 89–90, 216 and Tab. IV; L. Jansová, *Arch. roz.* XVIII (1966), 261 ff.

173 Frasnes-lez-Buissenal, Hainaut. Gold torc. Max. d. 20·3 cm., d. of tube 2·7 cm. ?II/IBC. Metropolitan Mus., New York (Guennol Coll. Loan). *Charles Uht.*

This *repoussé* decorated tubular torc, found in a wood near Tournai in 1864, was associated with a second, much plainer, gold torc with large terminals – which could have well been the model for the torc around the neck of the Mšecké Žehrovice stone head [**171**] – and some 52 coins of the Morini and Nervii[1] contained within a pot; these local coins date from 70–50 BC.

The larger Frasnes torc here illustrated was constructed over an iron core with the addition of beeswax and resin packing; the covering of sheet metal approx. 0·23 mm. thick is composed of an alloy of gold with some 10 per cent. silver, the plain torc having upwards of 20 per cent. silver. The main features of the decoration of this ring are the outward-facing beasts placed just below the pseudo-buffer terminals which incorporate a tenon-catch at the left-hand end. The beasts, constructed of a basic lyre and flanked in the old manner with florid 'S' spirals, have been variously interpreted as bulls, or, in view of the pricked-up ears, as horses in the manner of the early Vieille Toulouse torc [**45**], but the great curling horns suggest rather rams [see also notes to **206**]. British material in fast supplies good analogies both for similar stylised caprids [275] as well as the 'hour-glass' or lyre-constructed faces themselves [252]. On the torc is a sliding, loose circular band, now placed at the rear of the collar. The slender, high-ridged 'S's, which appear as a linked series of broken-backed curves on this loose band, have given rise to the opinion that the torc belongs to Jacobsthal's 'Plastic style'. Similar 'S's appear on French buffer torcs of not earlier than La Tène Ic date[2] and linked slender 'S's on an unlocated late Marnian pot.[3] Parallels could also be cited for the slanting almond eyes of the 'rams' from similar dated material such as that other example of La Tène metal-working skill from Hainaut, the La Courte linch-pin heads [149], and this material would tend to suggest that the Frasnes torcs on the coin evidence at least would have been of some considerable age when buried. One detail shared by both Frasnes rings is that the inside of each ring is decorated in the region of the terminals with a number of rows of punched dot-and-circles; on the plain torc the mid-point of the rear of the ring has a fine band of twisted cross-sectioned gold wire. On the lower part of the relief decoration of the larger ring can clearly be made out a pair of remarkably Hallstatt-looking waddling ducks [see notes to 21 – 23].

There are a small number of parallels to the general form represented by the Frasnes torcs, one of which, with a similar tenon-catch, is illustrated below. This is the great torc found under an old umbrella in 1895 at Broighter, Co. Derry [289]. Another British find which, whatever the origins of Broighter, must be regarded as an import, is the tubular torc with similar dot-and-circle punch marks found with two other smaller examples in Hoard 'A' of the Snettisham, Norfolk, series of dis-coveries [see notes to 291].[4] A fragmentary torc from the type site of La Tène may also belong to the group,[5] while two others are known from north and eastern France, one from Alsace, discovered in 1883, and one recently unearthed by chance at Mailly-le-Champ, Aube, of gold with only a 4 per cent. silver content.[6]

It seems more than likely that northern Gaul, an area closely in touch with Britain in the later Iron Age, must have been the centre for the production of these tubular torcs, and it must be admitted that the dating evidence for both the Snettisham finds and Frasnes would suggest the very end of the second or the first rather than the later third or second centuries for their manufacture. But then, as often commented in this study, style in Iron Age art is a most unsure chronological indicator.

ECA, no. 70; R. Rainbird Clarke, *PPS* XX (1954), 42–45 and Pls. V–VII above; S. De Laet, *The Low Countries* (1958), 165–66 and Pls. 58–59; De Laet and W. Glasbergen, *De Voorgeschiedenis der Lage Landen* (1959), 188 and Pl. 45; J. M. de Navarro, *Germania* 37 (1959), 135; *V and A*, 123, n. 121 and 138, n. 155

[1] J. A. Blanchet, *Traité des monnaies gauloises II* (1905), 605 and Pl. 151
[2] E.g. *ECA*, no. 222; see also notes to [174]
[3] *ECA*, no. 412
[4] Clarke, *op. cit.*, 38–41 and Pls. I–II
[5] P. Vouga, *La Tène* (1923), 67–68 and fig. 8
[6] Mailly-le-Champ: R. Joffroy, *Comptes rendus de l'Acad. des Inscr. et Belles-Lettres: Juillet-Oct. 1967* (1968), 479–83; Alsace: Rainbird Clarke, *op. cit.*, 44 and Pl. VII; Joffroy, *op. cit.*, fig. 3 (after reconstruction)

174 Clonmacnoise, Co. Offaly. Details of front and rear sections of gold torc. Total d. 13 cm., d. of terminals 3·8 cm. LT Ic, III BC. National Mus. of Ireland, Dublin.

Associated with a spatulate-ended gold torc of a type more proper to the native Irish later Bronze Age, this torc is, apart from some brooches, probably the only undisputed example of imported early La Tène art to be found in the British Isles. The hollow gold torc, with one half fitting in to the other by means of a long tenon joint fastened by a pin clearly visible on the right of the lower detail, has been variously described as in the 'Waldalges-heim' style and as 'continental work in the Plastic style'. In fact the torc belongs to the same class of torcs with 'fused' buffer or hoof-shaped terminals as the hybrid disc-ornamented ring from Dammelberg [148]. Other examples come from a skeleton grave at Praun-heim near Frankfurt, from the Vosges, and from Laim-bach in Thuringia,[1] and the torc is probably an import from the central Rhine region where the type seems to have evolved. Dammelberg and Praunheim share with Clonmacnoise the 'S'-decorated knobs with bossed terminals to the spirals which may be compared in turn with the gold finger ring from Étoy, Ct. Vaud.[2] All the comparable torcs have the more elongated spirals visible on the actual buffer(s) of Clonmacnoise – either ancestral to or contemporary with the same elongated spirals we have just examined on the Frasnes torc, another link being the soldered spiral wires either side of the Clon-macnoise knobs. The rough dotted 'background', like the median ridged line, is a feature of the more westerly human-head-decorated buffer-torcs [120] as well as of a ring with loose tendril design from a female grave of late La Tène Ib date in Dietikon, Kt. Zürich,[2] or the Tarn armring – also with ridged cable design – illustrated below [175].

The rear box feature, with its neat *repoussé* meander and dotted background, may be compared with the more complex designs of the La Tène B1 ring from Dürrnberg [138]; certainly there is no reason to consider it as a later, Irish, addition. What is not so simple is to decide by what route Clonmacnoise may have reached the British Isles; and it can in any case have little weight in deciding such disputed issues as the origins of the carver no less than of the style of the Turoe stone [129].

W. Wilde, *Descriptive catalogue of antiquities in the Royal Irish Academy* (1861), 74 and fig. 603–07; E. C. Armstrong, *J. Roy. Soc. Antiq. Ireland*, LIII (1923), 14–16 and fig. 9; H. H. Maryon, *Proc. Roy. Irish Acad.* 44 C 7 (1938), 210; *ECA*, no. 49; J. Raftery, *Prehistoric Ireland* (1951), 198 and fig. 234; *Problems*, 76, 80; E. Rynne in *Ber. V. Intern. Kongress f. Vor- u. Frühg.* (1961), 705 f.

[1] Praunheim: *ECA*, no. 210: K. Dielmann, *Hanauer Geschitsbl.* 17 (1960), 19ff., and Abb. 5:1–4; Vosges: L. Lindenschmidt, *AuhV* II:12 (1870), Taf. 4·3; Laim-bach: T. Voigt, *Jahresschr. mitteldt. Vorg.* 52 (1968), 159 and Abb. 7:a–b
[2] *ECA*, no. 74; see also notes to [169]
[3] *V and A*, 161, Abb. 9:2 and Taf. 14:5; see also [113]

175 R. Tarn, Tarn. Bronze ? bracelet. Internal d. 5 cm. ? Late LT Ib–early Ic, III BC. Mus. des Antiquités nat., St-Germain-en-Laye. *Belzeaux-Zodiaque.*

This cast ring, with its single removable joint visible top right and its decoration placed in alternating small and large oval enclosed areas, is considered by Jacobsthal to be ancestral in style to the knobbed anklets of the class discussed below. Certainly its linked twin triskel spirals on the larger four knobs and double 'S' spirals with large central boss and dotted background recall both the art of the Marnian buffer torcs [119–120] and such pieces as the Dammelberg ring [148]; another cast ring from Montsaugeon, Hte. Marne,[1] with the same slender cable bordering element, bridges the two groups. One more backward-looking feature on the ring from the River Tarn – unfortunately not particularly well-illustrated in the present illustration – is the central boss on the smaller knobs. This, like all the bosses, has punched circle decoration, here around a double curved-sided triangle. Jacobsthal illustrates but does not comment on this motif as it appears on an unprovenanced helmet.[2] Similar motifs occur on the enamelled knobs of 'Münsingen' brooches and related material of later La Tène Ib/c date from Switzerland in particular;[3] another, insular, example is the decoration on the spring of the Newnham Croft brooch, which is more probably an import than is the armlet from the same grave [131]. Indeed the punched circles on the smaller Tarn knobs probably copy the riveted enamels of such brooches – another argument to support the comparatively early date suggested for the Tarn ring.

ECA, no. 275, esp. P 432–33; ArtG, 240, Pl. 21; WK, Taf. 70 below; PAE, 242, fig. 92a and Pl. 263

[1] ECA, no. 250
[2] ECA, P 433a
[3] ECA, nos. 235, 256, 337, 334; F. R. Hodson, The La Tène cemetery at Münsingen-Rain=Acta Bernensia V (1968), types 28–29 passim.

176 Klettham, Ldkr. Erding. Bronze hinged anklet. D. 13·5 cm. Late LT B2, later III BC. Prähist. Staatssammlung, Munich. R-GK (E. Neuffer).

This anklet is one of a pair; with its florid rococo-like protuberances it represents the high point of Jacobsthal's 'Plastic style'. Its antecedents can be seen in the triple pattern round the ring of the complete Paris terret [167], an example of the 'Disney style' supposedly emanating from central Czechoslovakia. It is in fact the flat grave cemeteries of Moravia and Bohemia which contain the largest number of this type of ornamented anklets with extensions west into Bavaria and east into Hungary.[1] Plain examples with, as here, six to ten knobs and a hinged section incorporating two knobs have an even wider distribution, and a pair found in a well at Corinth may be connected with the supposed Celtic sack of Delphi in 279 BC [see also notes to 169].[2]

ECA, no. 267; Brå, 80, 85 and Pl. IX top; W. Torbrügge and H.P. Uenze, Bilder zur Vorg. Bayerns (1968), ill. 264–65

[1] E.g. ECA, nos. 266, 268–70; KvsE, Tab. XXXVII:5; XLI:12, 14; XLV:13; LX:8–9; LXXIV:7–8
[2] W. Krämer, Germania 39 (1961), 32–42; J. V. S. Megaw in (ed.) K. Jażdżewski, Liber Iosepho Kostrzewski octogenario a veneratoribus dicatus (1968), 189–90; M. Szabó, Acta Antiqua XVI (1968), 173–7

177 La Cheppe, Marne. Detail of incised decorated pot. Total ht. 34·5 cm., d. at rim 20 cm. ?LT I, IV BC. Mus. des Antiquités nat., St-Germain-en-Laye. Belzeaux-Zodiaque.

The decoration of this dark, burnished pot with narrow pedestalled foot is arranged in two registers of which a detail of the upper register is shown here. The freehand incised decoration – perhaps once filled with red – shows at both levels antithetical pairs of 'sea-horses', basically lyre patterns with the addition of downward drooping muzzles whose beak-like appearance recalls the griffon figures no less than the actual horse heads of the early La Tène 'Ticino' class of girdle-plates [95–99]. The 'horsy' nature of the present pot seems borne out by the decoration of a second vessel, a bi-conical urn, possibly from the same site with four incised quadrupeds with raised tails and backward-looking drooping muzzles,[1] the backward glance following the old orientalising stance encountered previously in the decoration of the Weiskirchen belt-hook [62].

The present vessel, which survives only in a much restored version, is reputed to have been discovered in a chariot grave in 1883; an early LT sword with decorated scabbard from the Suippes district has a somewhat similar simple version of the so-called 'dragon pair'.[2]

A. Nicaise, Bull. de la Soc. Anthrop. de France 5 (1884), Pl. 5:3; id., L'Époque gauloise (1884), 11 f. and Pl. 3:3; ECA, no. 411; ArtG, 240, Pl. 59; J. M. de Navarro, Germania 37 (1959), 134; U. Osterhaus, in Festschr. Dehn, 141

[1] ECA, no. 410
[2] Osterhaus, loc. cit.; see also notes to [178] ff.

178 Kelheim, Kr. Kelheim. Bronze ? box mount. Ht. 6·1 cm. ?LT C/D, II/I BC. Mus. Kelheim. Prähist. Staatssammlung, Munich.

The bronze repoussé plaque from Kelheim was found in 1937 buried in a pit together with a purple glass bead with yellow ribbon decoration [see notes on Plate Va], a socketed iron chisel and some late La Tène comb-decorated graphite ware at the east end of the great oppidum centred on the site of the Michelsberg near Kelheim on the north bank of the Danube. Kelheim lies some 30 kilometres north-east of the capital of the Vindelici at Manching [see notes on 189, 194h and 196] and can be identified with 'Alkimoennis' of Ptolemy's Geography. The oppidum area was vast, some 2,000 by 3,000 metres and containing an area of nearly 1,000 acres. The oppidum, with a satellite citadel on the south bank of the Danube, the Frauenberg near Weltenburg, was a great centre for iron working.[1]

The plaque, like the La Cheppe 'sea-horses' above [178], is an example of the 'zoomorphic lyre' but, in comparison with these stylised creatures let alone the supposed equines of Frasnes-lez-Buissenal [175], these are much more 'horsy' horses. The form is related to the 'dragon pairs' or double-headed lyres of what have been termed Type II decorated sword scabbards of La Tène Ic–II[2] [see also notes to 179] and must be more or less contemporary with the sources for the double horses of the Marlborough bucket [186]. First-century Armorican coins and those of the Arverni[3] [see also notes to Plate IVe] have similar 'realistic' horse's heads and there is no doubt of the horse's cultic as well as practical significance to later Celts.[4] The 'tails' of the Kelheim horses – the left-hand horse with a mane, the right seemingly without–form a yin-yang design or 'two intensely revolving comma-leaves closely clinging together within a circle'[5] such as may be found on the Besançon flagon [113] or, more apposite here, on a sword scabbard from La Tène.[6]

All in all, the plaque most reasonably may be seen as a local artistic response to the developed 'sword style' of the Swiss bronze-smiths of not earlier than the second century whose experiments with zoomorphic spirals are illustrated below [181–183]; de Navarro cites an imported Swiss sword from cremation grave 7 at Obermenzing near Munich with zoomorphic terminals to a triskel—the grave apparently of a Celtic surgeon.[7] Even despite its association with Late La Tène material, a date in the latter part of the Middle La Tène period is not impossible for the Kelheim plaque.

J. M. de Navarro, *Germania* 37 (1959), 131–40; Taf. 20:1; *PAE*, 269 ff. and Pl. 297 ('scabbard')

[1] P. Reinecke, *24–25. Ber. R-GK 1934–35* (1937), 167 ff.; K. Schwarz, *Jahresber. d. Bayer. Bodendenkmalpflege* 6–7 (1965–66), 35 ff.
[2] *ECA*, no. 121
[3] L. Lengyel, *L'art gaulois dans les médailles* (1954), Pl. VII:72, Pl. VIII:84
[4] J. De Vries, *Keltische Religion* (1961), 180–81; *PCB*, 321 ff.
[5] *ECA*, 78
[6] *ECA*, P 312; de Navarro, *op. cit.*, Taf. 21:1
[7] De Navarro, *PPS* XXI (1955), 231 ff., esp. Pl. XXX:2

179 La Tène, Ct. Neuchâtel. Detail of iron sword scabbard. W. 5·1 cm. Late LT II, II BC. Schweiz. Landesmus., Zürich.

The type site of La Tène lies on the east side of Lake Neuchâtel at the mouth of the old course of the River Thièle. Although Iron Age finds were recorded there as early as 1858, the major discoveries arose as a by-product of the rectification of the Jura waterways from 1868 when the level of the lake was considerably lowered. Between 1907 and 1917 excavations in the old stream bed revealed a mass of wooden piles spread over a roughly triangular area of nearly 150 metres. To the north and south were two causeways, constructed of jointed sleeper beams, iron nails and clamps, and covered with horizontal planks. From within this area came a mass of finds, over 2,500 in all, wood as well as metal having been preserved by the waterlogged nature of the site. There were some 400 brooches, 270 spears and 27 oval wooden shields, the material mainly dating from the later Middle La Tène period with a central point around 100 BC and continuing into the first century. Amongst the handful of coins found at the site one was a north Italian issue [194c].

The purpose of the La Tène site has been disputed since its discovery; the most likely explanation is that it was a sanctuary for the ritual deposition of objects; two isolated human skulls and a handful of complete skeletons were also recovered from the shallows. The Celtic use of peat bogs, lakes and running water for depositions is well attested both archaeologically [see also notes to **190, 209, 251–253, 254**] and in classical

sources, including the account of the Roman victory over the Boii of northern Italy in 191 BC [see also notes to **169**].[1] It is in fact from La Tène that one can match certain objects – such as wooden yokes and shields – on the famous series of trophy reliefs erected at Pergamon in Asia Minor around 181 BC by Eumenes II on the balustrade of the shrine of Athena Polias Nikephoros, a shrine built to celebrate his father's victory over the immigrant Celts a generation earlier.[2] Evidence for partial horse burials—a rite common to a number of more northerly and non-Celtic Iron Age sites—adds to the Celtic significance of La Tène.[3]

The present illustration shows one of some 170 swords and their scabbards from La Tène, the scabbards being constructed of thin iron sheets welded together. The incised decoration is in de Navarro's later Type III variation of the zoomorphic lyre, a variation restricted almost entirely to Switzerland, especially La Tène and the neighbouring Port deposit [see notes to **190**], and the proliferation and wide distribution of such decorated scabbards point to a period of unrest and general mobility within the Celtic world [see also **192**].

P. Vouga, *La Tène* (1923), 75–76 and Pl. VI:1; R. Wyss, *Funde der jüngeren Eisenzeit=Aus dem Schweiz. Landesmus.* 8 (1957), 13 and Taf. 9b centre; J. M. de Navarro, *40. Ber. R-GK 1959* (1960), 79–119, esp. 99 ff. and Taf. 13:1

[1] Diodorus Siculus, V, 27; Livy, *Histories* XXXVI, 40; Strabo IV, 1, 13; J. M. de Navarro, *40. Ber. R-GK 1959* (1960), 111; W. Torbrügge, *Bayer. Vorg.* 25 (1960), 16 ff.; S. Piggott, *Ancient Europe* (1965), 230–32; *PCB*, 19 ff. and 303 ff.; see also notes to [190]
[2] *ECA*, nos. 172–73; *Celts*, Pl. 49; P. Jaeckel, *Waffen-u. Kostümkde.* VII (1965), 94–122; see also notes to [211]
[3] H. Jankuhn in (ed.) R. Degen *et al.*, *Helvetia Antiqua: Festschr. Emil Vogt* (1966), 155–58

180 Groitzsch, Kr. Borna. Detail of fragmentary bronze sword scabbard. W. 5·3 cm. LT II, late III/II BC. Landesmus. f. Vorg., Dresden.

This is a detail of the scabbard of a ritually bent iron sword found in a cremation grave with a spear and shield boss of a type common in the Middle La Tène phase.[1] The loose tendril design is a distant descendant of the old Waldalgesheim motif; it is common on decorated sword scabbards from the type site of La Tène as well as from eastern Europe which seems to have been a subsidiary market for the production of, or, more likely, trade in, decorated sword scabbards. A disturbed grave at Batina in Jugoslavia, also with shield boss – and shield grip – and spear seems to have contained a ritually bent sword with scabbard decorated in this tendril design as well as a helmet of precisely the form illustrated on the Pergamon balustrade reliefs [see notes to **179**]; this offers a useful chronological clue to just how early this 'sword style' may have commenced.[2] Actual decorated Celtic swords are depicted also in classical representations; one, again probably from Pergamon, though surviving only in a Roman copy, and another from the trophy reliefs erected by the Romans at Entremont, Bouches-du-Rhône, after their defeat of the Germanic tribes in the last quarter of the second century.[3] Another

Middle La Tène warrior's cremation grave with bent sword from Geislingen, Kr. Göppingen, in Württemberg, whose scabbard decoration may be compared both with Groitzsch and with the scabbard from Dickenhof illustrated on the right [181], has, however, a narrowing, pointed chape which indicates a late-ish date in the sequence of swords at La Tène.[4] The sword scabbards of the Middle La Tène period in fact mark a continuation of what has been termed here the 'advanced Waldalgesheim style' with an emphasis on low relief or incised ornament. These techniques are more suited to the motifs of the late Waldalgesheim style proper than to those of the contemporary 'Plastic' style for which such techniques are also sometimes employed. It should also be clear, if only from the few sword scabbard details here illustrated, that many variants and doubtless many hands were involved in what therefore should strictly not be named the 'sword *style*' since on any chronological analysis this must have had a life of at least a century. The decorated sword scabbards produced at La Tène itself may well represent the latest in the series.

W. Radig, *Sachsens Vorzeit* (1936), 46 and Abb. 27, 29; *Ausgrabungen u. Funde* 11:2 (1966), cover ill.; W. Coblenz, *Arbeits- u. Forschungsber. zur sächs. Bodendenkmalpflege* 19 (1970), 69–103

[1] *Manuel* IV, 676 ff.
[2] La Tène: *ECA*, no. 106; Jugoslavia: Ksenija Vinski-Gasparini, *Arheološki radovi i rasprave* I (1959), 281–97 (=Batina); J. Todorović, *Arch. Jugoslavica* VI (1965), 71–75; id., *Kelti u jugoistočnoj Evropi=Dissertationes* (Belgrade) VII (1968), 64 ff.
[3] ? Pergamon: B. Forlati-Tamaro, *Il museo archeologico del Palazzo reale di Venezia* (1953), 19 f., Vinski-Gasparini, *op. cit.*, Tab. VI (see also Conflans fibula, *ECA*, P 286); Entremont: O. Klindt-Jensen, *Acta Arch.* XX (1959), 132 and fig. 88b below
[4] F. Fischer, *FbS* 18:1 (1967), 69 ff. and Abb. 6:1

181 Dickenhof, Basadingen, Kt. Thürgau. Detail of iron sword scabbard. W. 5·2 cm. LT II, II BC. Schweiz. Landesmus., Zürich.

Found during quarrying operations in 1848, this scabbard probably marked yet another warrior's grave since a spear and iron ring were found on the same spot. The sword blade is one of about 10 to bear a 'smith's mark' in the form of a boar stamped into the iron [see notes to 190–193] while the surface of the scabbard has a pitted surface in the so-called *chagrinage* technique, a Swiss speciality produced probably by multiple punch work from the back of the scabbard plate and not by etching as has been suggested.[1] The central spindly design with its split palmettes harks back to the Basse-Yutz throat mounts [60–61] and, as previously commented, occurs on British work of presumably much the same period as the present sword [114, 252]. Split palmettes are particularly common on Swiss swords and on presumed exports from Switzerland; Groitzsch [180] has one version while others may be found on the Geislingen scabbard – another example of *chagrinage* – and on one associated with several decorated scabbards from Srijemska Mitrovica.[2] The bird-like terminals – or are they latter-day griffons or even bearded 'funny faces'? [see notes to 59] – obviously are related to the 'dragon pairs' or zoomorphic lyre heads which Jacobsthal illus-

trates exclusively from Hungary and which may represent an eastern 'school';[3] a late example from La Tène is illustrated here [179]. Bird-like terminals also occur on the Obermenzing sword cited in connection with the Kelheim mount [178] as well as, reversed, at the top of the scabbard of another sword from La Tène which also has the undulating bordering ornament seen on Dickenhof, though here the decoration dips down either side of the apex of a triangle.[4] A similar triangle, undulating border line and upper spiral ornament with inturned bird terminals whose heads are formed of split palmettes comes from a warrior's grave at Brüttisellen, Kt. Zürich – the scabbard again decorated in *chagrinage*.[5] A real outsider to this distribution is a Middle La Tène sword with scabbard crudely decorated with a balanced split palmette design from a Bulgarian barrow-grave at Kopana Mogila, Pavolce; this is only one of several Middle La Tène sword finds from strictly Thracian contexts.[6]

All in all, Dickenhof is a typical example of the Swiss Middle La Tène swordsmith's art.

W. Drack, *Zeitschr. f. Schweiz. Arch. u. Kunstgeschichte* 15 (1954–55), 197 ff. and Taf. 61=cat. no. 4; R. Wyss, *Funde der jüngeren Eisenzeit=Aus dem Schweiz. Landesmus.* 8 (1957), 8, 13, Abb. 2 and Taf. 9b left

[1] J. M. de Navarro, *40. Ber. R-GK 1959* (1960), 91 ff.; *PAE*, 244–45
[2] *ECA*, no. 126; J. Todorović, *Kelti u jugoistočnoj Evropi=Dissertationes* (Belgrade) VII (1968), 65 and S1.15:1; see also notes to [52]
[3] *ECA*, nos. 120–25
[4] P. Vouga, *La Tène* (1923), Pl. II, 1; *ECA*, no. 108
[5] Wyss, *op. cit.*, Taf. 9b right
[6] B. Nikolov, *Izvestia na Arkh. Inst.* (Sofia) XXVIII (1965), 163 ff. esp. obr. 21

182 Drňa, Rimavská Sobota, Slovakia. Detail of iron sword scabbard. W. c. 5 cm. Early LT II, III/II BC. Mus. Rimavská Sobota. *J. V. S. Megaw.*

This sword was discovered in 1963 in a disturbed cremation cemetery from which had previously been recovered typical remains of Middle La Tène warrior graves including a shield boss and the second example of a Type II 'dragon pair' decorated sword scabbard to have been found in Czechoslovakia, the first coming from Bohemia far to the west [see 178–179].[1] It represents one extreme limit of the products of a master swordsmith, the western limit being the well-known sword from Cernon-sur-Coole [183].

The Drňa sword, probably associated with an iron suspension chain and spear, has a simplified 'bird-bridge' strengthening the lower part of the scabbard.[2] It is decorated both rear (illustrated here) and front with a number of curved-beaked birds' heads, not less than six such heads being incorporated on the front which has the folded-over 'wings' of metal somewhat similar to those on the Jugoslav scabbard referred to in discussing the Waldenbuch stone [142]. The design incorporates the split palmettes and peaked triangle motif discussed in connection with Dickenhof [181].

The oval eyes and heavy 'plumage' of the 'dragon-birds' on the suspension loop remind one of features of the Malomĕřice mounts [158–160].[3]

Inv. no. 73/1963

[1] G. Balaša, *Arch. roz.* X (1963), 687–93
[2] J. M. de Navarro, *40. Ber. R-GK 1959* (1960), 88 ff. and Taf. 5
[3] *KvsE*, Tab. LXXVII:3–4

183 Cernon-sur-Coole, Marne. Detail of iron sword scabbard. W. c. 5·2 cm. Early LT II, III/II BC. Mus. de Châlons-sur-Marne (*courtesy M. P.-M. Duval*).

In 1892 a cremation grave was found at Cernon-sur-Coole, the bones contained within a pit and associated with a spear and two iron chain belts, a typical Middle La Tène warrior's grave in which, as so often, cremation rather than inhumation was the preferred rite – a reflection perhaps of some particular custom associated with the death of a warrior and particularly those far from home. The most notable object in this grave was the iron sword in its decorated scabbard, a detail of the reverse of which is illustrated here.

The suspension loop has a neatly balanced Waldalgesheim-derived tendril pattern which, though one can note a version on the apex of the bow of a LT Ib 'Certosa'-type decorated brooch from Münsingen-Rain, grave 62,[1] can be paralleled more closely with the decoration loop of a scabbard from Rábatamási in Hungary and a second, also Middle La Tène, scabbard from Formín in Jugoslavia;[2] Jacobsthal, not very helpfully, claims the scabbard to be thus a combination of Waldalgesheim and sword 'styles'. As to the engraved design on the scabbard proper, with its minute detailing of curved cross-hatching and rocked-tracer filled lines, Jacobsthal compares the beaked and crested birddragon or griffon with the sinuous five-headed beaked serpent tendril on a sword from La Tène.[3] This piece is again executed with the aid of a rocked tracer. The analogy with the scabbard from Drňa [182] is much more immediate and seems to offer one of those rare instances in later La Tène art when one is safe in presuming a common work-centre, if not indeed craftsman, for two pieces. The loose asymmetrical palmette and split palmette vine show the origin of Cernon-sur-Coole to be once more Switzerland; the chape (not illustrated here) is typical of the Middle La Tène swords there.

A. Nicaise, *Mém. de la Soc. d'Agric., Commerce, Sci. et Arts de la Marne* (1897), 143–48; *Manuel* IV, 543 and fig. 463:2; *ECA*, no. 113; J. M. de Navarro, *PPS* XXI (1955), 240 f. ; P.-M. Duval, *Art de France* IV (1964), ills. p. 14; Ann Birchall, *PPS* XXXI (1965), 272–73 and fig. 28=no. 234

[1] *ECA*, no. 339; F. R. Hodson, *The La Tène cemetery at Münsingen-Rain=Acta Bernensia* V (1968), Pl. 28:851
[2] Hungary: I. Hunyady, 'Kelták a Kárpátmedencében', *Diss. Pannonicae* ser. II:18 (1942), T. XLII:5; Jugoslavia: S. Pahič, *Arheološki Vestnik* XVII (1966), Tab. 4:5
[3] *ECA*, Pl. 233d; see also notes to [30]

184 'White Horse', Uffington, Berkshire. L. c. 110 metres. ? AD I–VI. *Committee for Aerial Photography, University of Cambridge* (*Dr J. K. St Joseph*).

The significance of the horse in later Celtic art has already been touched on [see notes to 178]. The great White Horse of Uffington hewn through the turf into the upper chalk of the Berkshire Downs in the near vicinity of an Iron Age single ditch-and-rampart fort, has for many years been considered part of the iconography of the later prehistory of the British Isles, the more especially since its dissected form recalls the abstractions of later continental and British coinage [see **Plate IVc**].[1]

The first recorded account of the White Horse – only one of some nine chalk-cut figures known to be of at least some antiquity in England – is in a twelfth-century AD manuscript, *The Wonders of Britain*, where it was considered to be a Saxon emblem cut by Alfred the Great after the Battle of Ashdown in AD 871. It is only fair to comment that this tradition may well be far from incorrect, for recent study of the White Horse indicates that the figure, as we see it today, owes much of its 'Celtic' form to subsequent recuttings down the centuries following natural weathering lines. Its original form, as reconstructed, suggests a standard of the pagan Saxon period rather than a coin of the ancient Britons.

S. Piggott, *Antiquity* V (1931), 42–46; *ABA*, Pl. 60; *WK*, Taf. 99; *PP*, 70 and Pl. 42; *PRB*, Pls. 307–08; D. Woolner, *Folklore* 78 (1967), 90–111; *PAE*, 271

[1] E. A. Sydenham, *Numis. Chron.* 6 ser., VI (1944), 65–76

185 Coren del Valento, rock no. 59, Valcamonica, Brescia. Rock engraving. L. c. 20 cm. ? IV BC. (*Courtesy Dr E. Anati.*)

Reference has already been made to Celtic occupation in the area of Brescia [see **106–107**], so it is not surprising that part of the great series of rock engravings in the Camonica Valley should long have been considered to reflect La Tène influence no less than others should be related to the 'art of the *situlae*' [see also notes to **1–2**]. The present figure of a well-fed and aggressively male horse probably has its closest analogies in East Celtic silver coinage [**194a**], but it also has certain points of similarity with the backward-looking horses of the pot supposedly from Suippes.[1]

P. Jacobsthal, *J. Roman Studies* XXVIII (1938), 65–67 and Pl. 10:3; F. Altheim and E. Trautmann, *Mitt. d. Deutsches Arch. Inst.* (*Röm. Abt.*) 54 (1939), 1–15, esp. p. 9 ff. and Abb. 4; *ECA*, 3 and Pl. 217d; E. Anati, *Camonica Valley* (1964), ill. p. 149; E. Schumacher, *JR-GZM* 13 (1966), 40 and Abb. 2:8

[1] *ECA*, no. 410; see also [177]

186 St Margaret's Mead, Marlborough, Wiltshire. Detail of bronze ornamental sheet from wooden bucket. L. 18·5 cm. ? I BC/I AD. Devizes Mus. *F. K. M. Carver* (*courtesy Wilts. Arch. and Nat. Hist. Soc.*).

This detail of the third register (as reconstructed) of the bronze bucket found near Marlborough [see **188**] with its heraldic facing horses with tendrils sprouting from their mouths and forming pseudo-lyres has its parallels on presumably contemporary Armenian coins, as Sir Arthur Evans was the first to note. It also reflects the continuity of the zoomorphic lyre horse-pairs of the sword 'style' and, even further back in time, the flower-eating beasts of the *situla* style [26]. The flowing manes certainly may be compared with the Kelheim plaque [178] and one of the free-standing horses on the middle register of Marlborough serves to associate it with continental and probably central Gaulish metal-work such as the fragmentary disc from Levroux, Indre,[1] of around the period of the Roman conquest. Even here, though, there is a link with much earlier material–the pronounced 'shoulder curl' harks back to the 'nomadic' handle animals of Basse-Yutz [60–61].

A. J. Evans, *Archaeologia* LII:2 (1890), Pl. XVII:4; *PP*, Pl. 35b; J. M. de Navarro, *Germania* 37 (1959), 138–39 and Taf. 21:4; *PRB*, Pl. 309

[1] J. V. S. Megaw, *Gallia* XXVI (1968), 33–41, esp. fig. 5

187 Aylesford, Kent, grave 'Y'. Details of bronze-covered wooden bucket. D. 26·7 cm. Ht. of human head c. 4 cm. Later I BC. British Museum, London. (Above) *J. V. S. Megaw*; (below) *Courtesy Trustees of the British Museum.*

In 1890 Arthur Evans published the results of his father's and his own excavations carried out in the same year at the cremation cemetery of Aylesford. In this cemetery, with its evidence of settlement from the northern French territory of the Belgae, were a number of richer graves with imported Roman drinking vessels – replacing the Etruscan and Greek luxury goods of early La Tène graves [41, 113] – as well as the characteristic Belgic pedestalled urns thrown on a fast wheel. Grave 'Y' at Aylesford, of what has now been termed the 'Aylesford-Swarling Culture', was a circular pit cut into the chalk to a depth of just over a metre in which the present bronze-covered parallel-sided stave-bucket had been placed as the cremation container. Also in the bucket were three iron brooches, one of a type identifiable as common in the final La Tène cemeteries of north Italy contemporary with the early Augustan period.[1] A bronze jug and *patella* similar to that found in both of the vault graves at Welwyn [see notes to 230] should date to the second half of the first century BC.[2]

Such bucket burials are known from at least two other graves, one each from Aylesford and Swarling; Marlborough may have been a third [186, 188] and Harpenden a fourth [see notes to 275]. The rite of bucket burial can also be inferred, if not proved, from La Tène sites in Aisne, Normandy and Picardy though, with the exception of the Levroux plaque mentioned above in connection with the Marlborough bucket, there is little evidence for sheet bronze work either in Britain or on the continent.

On the bucket from Aylesford as it is reconstructed at the moment apart from the twin cast handle mounts the decoration is restricted to one upper, complete, band of *repoussé* ornament with a median and lower band of undecorated bronze; there are, however, other fragments of ornamental bronze suggesting that there was probably a second *repoussé* band placed between the two plain bands. The most striking features are the two lantern-jawed, almond-eyed and helmeted faces, fine examples of the *tête coupée* [see notes to 76], guarding both aspects as on the early La Tène jugs [66, 72–73]. These 'split' Janus or identical twins have elongated features which can be traced back through the Courtisols pairs [119] to the Pfalzfeld pillar [75]; two

faces on the fragmentary and unfortunately unassociated Levroux plaque, though with circular and not almond eyes and without the great crested helmet – perhaps a latter-day leaf-crown – again emphasise the cross-Channel background of the Aylesford bucket.[3] The heads also have certain features in common with the late La Tène anthropomorphic sword hilts [229]. On the other hand the reversible pseudo-faces on the late Battersea shield have similar crests [253] and the ridged 'edging' of the crest appears on one of the bronzes from the Seven Sisters, Glamorganshire, hoard of probably immediately post-conquest date and the 'ram' mount of the Youlton, Cornwall, bowl mentioned below [see notes to 273].[4] Neither of these analogies, however, need be pushed too far. The decoration of the *repoussé* band as illustrated here shows one of a pair of spindly quadrupeds in the archaic backward-glancing pose; once more it is possible to see a similarity with the native coinage of northern France. Evans in his original publication cited coins of the Remi, but the beaked mouths, pointed ears and split-palmette-like tails also suggest the influence of the Swiss swordmakers [179–183]. It is of course unfortunate that the White Horse of Uffington should no longer seem to be in so strong a position to offer a contemporary British example of the 'dissected' equine of later Celtic coinage, since stylistically it would otherwise offer useful evidence for the argument that the Aylesford bucket is an insular product [184]; the hind legs of each Aylesford quadruped look almost human – are these intended for Celtic hobby-horses?

The central feature is a loosely constructed triskel within a circle supported top and bottom by what appear to be misunderstood and therefore poorly executed versions of the wave tendril, each arm curling round into a pseudo-bird's head, something which again suggests the sword 'style' but which also appears in late Irish metal-work [270–271]. On the continent the 'yin-yang' and occasionally true triskel are a feature of the sword style[5] but later versions of them appear both on the Levroux disc fragments[6] and the Rynkeby cauldron plates and in Britain on the Battersea shield. Rynkeby also has antithetically placed beasts and, to anticipate, is also probably a north or central Gaulish product [222]. Closest, however, to the triskel motif of Aylesford is the low relief decoration on a bronze box from Ölberg, Kr. Wöllstein in Rheinhessen, found with a sword, Middle La Tène brooch, chain, and girdle-hook.[7]

There have been opposing views as to the actual place of manufacture of the Aylesford bucket: Evans suggested north-western France, while more recent authorities have preferred an insular origin. About the date of the grave there is fortunately less dispute and, even if the bucket was old when buried, it is not likely to have been deposited more than a generation before the last three decades of the first century BC. The recent discovery of a rich burial at the suitably-named site of The Tene, Baldock, Hertfordshire, has resurrected the pros and cons of the origin of Aylesford.[8] This grave, with all the accoutrements for the Belgic chieftain's journey to the Otherworld – whole pig, bull's-head-decorated iron fire-dogs [see 278–279], imported bronze bowls and wine amphora as in the Welwyn burials [see notes to 230] – also had the remains of probably two stave buckets with sheet bronze *repoussé* decorated bands and three handle mounts in the form of human heads. The heads, all cast from different moulds, are poor versions of the Aylesford helmeted twins with down-turning horns not unlike those on the handle mount of a bronze drinking bowl at Youlton in south-west England,[9] while the *repoussé* sheet has a series of dot-in-circle motifs and diagonal lines looking like a misunderstood attempt to produce a linked 'S' or wave motif. It certainly seems possible that the maker or makers of the Baldock bucket(s) may have actually seen Aylesford, but such poor art craftsmanship can hardly be used one way or the other for supporting an insular source for the Kentish piece. On balance it seems most reasonable to link Aylesford with the still all-too-little understood native elements in the art of Gaul at the beginning of the rule of Rome, although it still remains open to consider the bucket's maker as trained on the continent but resident in Britain.

A. J. Evans, *Archaeologia* LII (1890), 317–88, esp. figs. 11–19 and Pl. XII; S. Piggott, *Antiquity* V (1931), 42 ff.; E. T. Leeds, *Celtic ornament* (1933), 38 ff. and fig. 16; *PP*, 68 and Pl. 38a; Anne Ross, *Proc. Soc. Antiq. Scot.* XCI (1957–58), 31; Ann Birchall, *British Mus. Quarterly* XXVIII (1964), 21–29; *id.*, *PPS* XXXI (1965), 243–49, 302 and fig. 7; *PRB*, Pls. 298–300; *PreA*, 225 and ill. 224–26, *PAE*, 252, 269 ff. and Pl. 301; J. V. S. Megaw, *Gallia* XXVI (1968), 34 ff., esp. figs. 3, 6

[1] C. A. Moberg, *Acta Arch.* XXI (1950), 88 ff.
[2] H. J. Eggers, *JR-GZM* 13 (1966), 68–69 and Abb. A and 1=no. 2
[3] Megaw, *op. cit.*, esp. figs. 1–2
[4] *PP*, fig. 78:6; see also [301]
[5] J. M. de Navarro, *PPS* XXI (1955), 237 ff.; *id.*, *40. Ber. R-GK 1959* (1960), Taf. 6:1, 21:1; 22:2
[6] Megaw, *loc. cit.*
[7] G. Behrens, *Bodenurkunde aus Rheinhessen* I (1927), 59, nos. 213–17
[8] I. M. Stead, *Antiq. J.* XLVIII (1968), 306 and Pl. LXXVII
[9] *PP*. Pl. 51; see notes to [273]

188 St Margaret's Mead, Marlborough, Wiltshire. Reconstructed bronze and iron-covered wooden stave bucket. Ht. 52 cm. d. 60 cm. ?I BC/I AD. Devizes Mus. F. K. M. Carver (*courtesy Wilts. Arch. and Nat. Hist. Soc.*).

The remains of the Marlborough bucket were found in 1807 with what appeared to be a cremation burial; the report that 'skeletons and Roman pottery [lay] in its neighbourhood' unfortunately cannot be used as evidence of the date or nature of the find-spot, but it seems most likely that the bucket formed part of a 'bucket burial' like that from Aylesford [187]. The bucket, shown here as reassembled in 1967, was originally bound with iron hoops; the two drop handles are of iron, and an iron bar was slotted through the two projecting staves to hold down the lid. Of the *repoussé* decoration on the three registers of bronze bands, the horse figures have already been briefly discussed [186]; they, even more than those on the Aylesford bucket, seem to be in the tradition of later continental metalwork. As to the human heads, these are shown both in profile and full face, Sir Cyril Fox suggesting on the grounds of coinage and of the Gundestrup cauldron [209] that profiles must represent mortals, and full-face busts, gods – perhaps too hard and fast a distinction for the ambiguous iconography and beliefs of the later Celts. Provision for inlay in the almond-shaped eyes

certainly has parallels, however, in the manufacture of frontal-facing bronze figures of deities from the continent [222b, 232, 239–240] and inlay can also be seen on certain northern British pieces [264–265]. The influence of coinage certainly seems indisputable, though again, as with Aylesford, a link with central rather than north-western France seems more likely; the coinage of certain Belgic tribes or of the area between the Seine and the Loire provides particularly close analogies for the profiled heads with their flourishing moustaches.[1]

The exuberance of Marlborough compared with the tense hieratical lines of Aylesford may indicate nothing more than that it is a product of a separate workshop or just a more extroverted craftsman. The tendency has usually been to place the Wiltshire bucket somewhat later than Aylesford, perhaps within the first half of the first century AD although all the coinage parallels are earlier than this date.

The size of the Marlborough bucket suggests ritual use in accordance with the considerable importance that washing and ritual bathing had in Celtic society.[2]

Sir Richard Colt Hoare, *Ancient Wiltshire II* (1822), 33 and Pl. VI; A. J. Evans, *Archaeologia* LII (1890), 360 ff. and Pl. XIII; W. Cunnington and E. H. Goddard, *Devizes Mus. Catalogue* I (1896), no. 387; *Manuel* IV, 962–63 and fig. 658:1; S. Piggott, *Antiquity* V (1931), 42–43 and Pl. II:4, III:6; *PP*, 68–70 and Pls. 34–36; E. Nylén, *Acta Arch.* XXIX (1958), 1–20; Morna MacGregor (Simpson), *PPS* XXVIII (1962), 27; J. M. C. Toynbee, *Art in Britain under the Romans* (1964), 23 and Pl. Ie; *PRB*, Pls. 309–10, 312; H. J. Eggers, *JR-GZM* 13 (1966), 69 and Abb. 2=no. 8; *PCB*, 69 ff. and fig. 34; *PAE*, 252, 269 ff. and Pls. 297–99

[1] *Celts*, Pl. 5c; *ArtG*, 192, Pl. VI, 3; see also notes to [171]
[2] A. T. Lucas, *J. Roy. Soc. Antiq. Ireland* 95 (1965), 65–114

189 Manching, Ldkr. Ingolstadt. Bronze ?rein-ring or yoke mount. Ht. 9 cm. LT D, II/I BC. Prähist. Staatssammlung, Munich. *Bayer. Landesamt. f. Denkmalpflege.*

Manching was probably the site of the *oppidum* of the Vindelici, who controlled the area between the Alps and the Danube until their defeat by the Romans in 15 BC, following the victorious campaigns in Switzerland of Drusus and Tiberius. Originally it covered an area of some 380 hectares or about 900 acres and had fortifications over 7 kilometres in circumference. Large-scale excavations have been in progress for a number of years, though much of the area is now a military airfield;[1] within the ramparts remains of a well laid out township of timber buildings have been found. Two large, flat cemeteries of the LT B and C periods are in the neighbourhood – although none surprisingly of the late, LT D, phase – while within and around the ramparts a spread of broken shield bosses, swords and spearheads testify to the centre's later troubled history. The *oppidum*, as is usual for such tribal capitals, contained an industrial complex with plain and painted wheel-turned pottery [see notes to **Plate Vb**], glass works [see notes to **Plate Va**], evidence for iron smithing and a local mint, analysis of residual metal in the moulds of which match the composition of the so-called *Regenbogenschüsselschen* gold coins [194h]. Extensive trade clearly took place both with the Alpine regions [see notes to **200–201**] and with the non-Celtic north German area.

The present casting, probably a chariot mount of some description, was discovered in 1957; chariots and chariot burials are not unknown even in Middle and Late La Tène contexts.[2] Like the pendant illustrated below [**196**], it is one of the few pieces of fine decorative metal-work which, with the growth of village industrialisation – the word 'urbanisation' gives too settled an impression of later Celtic society – seems to have been in much less demand than in earlier times, although a detailed study of fine late La Tène metal-work still remains to be undertaken. The double bulls with their heraldic knobs[3] follow the old tradition of bovine terminals, while the junction of the upper lyre form with the lower ring has two pseudo-birds' heads in the manner of the junctions of one of the Maloměřice mounts [**159**] and the Mâcon bull handle [**161**]. This is an 'archaic' piece and here the stylistic affinities seem to be with the true 'Plastic' style of the last stages of the Early and beginning of the Middle La Tène phase, although it is difficult to be dogmatic about the Manching mount's precise dating or stylistic analogies [but see also notes to **164**].

W. Krämer in *Neue Ausgrabungen in Deutschland* (1958), 192 and Abb. 14; *id.*, *Antiquity* XXXIV (1960), 197 and fig. 6:2; W. Torbrügge and H.P. Uenze, *Bilder zur Vorg. Bayerns* (1968), ill. 274; *EV*, 228–29 and ill.

[1] Interim reports: *Germania* 35 (1957), 32–45; 39 (1961), 299–383; 40 (1962), 292–317; 43 (1965), 49–62
[2] H.-E. Joachim in *Festschr. Dehn*, 84–111
[3] O. Jansé, *IPEK* 10 (1935), 66–72; see also [**274, 279**]

Plate Va Wallertheim, Kr. Alzey, grave 31. Miniature glass dog. L. 2·1 cm. LT D, late I BC. Mittelrhein. Landesmus., Mainz.

Although glass in the form of beads or simple armlets is known from Hallstatt and Early La Tène contexts – the Reinheim princess's grave, for example [see notes to **73 ff.**] – it was not until about the middle of the second century BC that glass working became a major industry, the chief evidence for which is to be found in the *oppida* of the final stages of the pre-Roman Iron Age.[1] One particular technique was the production of complex multi-strand glass rings by spinning on a rod ribbons of various coloured glass while in a semi-molten state.

This miniature member of some Celtic glass menagerie was found in 1958 with a circular shield boss and heavy Late La Tène iron sword; a number of offering pits containing animal bones surrounded the area. The body is of spiral-moulded blue glass with additional pieces for the tip of the nose, ears, legs, and tail, followed by white and then yellow 'piping'. There are in fact no similar glass animals known and indeed dogs are rare in any period of Celtic art though they have their place in Celtic belief,[2] usually as hounds or hunting dogs. Some miniature dogs in bronze are known from late native and provincial Roman contexts in Britain,[3] including an 'Aberdeen terrier' very similar in outline to the Wallertheim dog, but there is still no good continental parallel[4] for this charming talisman of some stocky native hunting dog of the terrier breed, a type known in Europe from at least the third century BC.[5]

H. Schermer, *Germania* 29 (1951), 250–52; *PreA*, 246 and ill. 252; *EV*, 213 and ill.

[1] Thea E. Haevernick, *Die Glasarmringe u. Ringperlen der Mittel- u. Spätlatènezeit* (1960)
[2] *PCB*, 239–41
[3] J. M. C. Toynbee, *Art in Roman Britain* (1962), no. 59; *id.*, *Art in Britain under the Romans* (1964), 126–27; see also notes to [**224**]
[4] Compare G. Behrens, *Denkmäler des Wangionengebietes* (1923), 55–56 and Abb. 53
[5] C. L. B. Hubbard, *Dogs in Britain* (1948), 284 f.

190 Port, Nidau, Kt. Bern. Detail of sword stamp on iron sword. L. of inscription and stamp 2·7 cm. LT III, I BC Bern. Historisches Mus., Bern.

This sword was found in the Nidau-Büren canal during the rectification of the Jura waterways (1868–75). It bears the name 'Korisios' in Greek characters and, at right angles, a stamp with an oriental-looking 'tree of life' supported by two goats. Originally the sword formed part of a large votive deposit – also suggested by some as a customs control-post – laid down in water like La Tène but of later date than the type site [see notes to **179**].[1] The blade, with fine welded cutting edges, was of the typical heavy Late La Tène form with more or less parallel sides, fairly blunted tip, and well-marked 'blood grooves' either side of the mid-rib; it had been sharply bent almost into a right angle, a ritual breaking or 'killing' of the sword which extends back to the earlier Hallstatt period [see notes to **11, 137**] but which has a widespread distribution in time and space.[2]

The use of stamps of human heads, bulls and boars on swords, already noted on a sword of Middle La Tène date [**181**], probably served a talismanic purpose like the sword-rings on Scandinavian swords of the Migration period. Some 50 and more stamps are known almost exclusively on swords from Switzerland, although several come from the district of Sombor in Jugoslavia, in an area which, together with parts of Hungary, seems to have proved a ready market for the Swiss swordsmiths; there are also sword stamps known from Hungary.[3] The actual Port stamp is without parallel, but it may have been copied from an imported classical intaglio or through the intermediary of one of the later Bologna grave *stelae*.[4] As to the inscription, although Latin names are found on some late swords, this is the only example in Greek script. The name itself is Celtic and 'Corisius' occurs in local Roman dedications, and as a potter's name; the word is made up probably of two roots and, if reconstructed as *Corisi(oritum)*, means a 'war host'+'ford'. Greek inscriptions certainly occur on imported amphorae in the southern and central Gaulish *oppida* and Caesar records how the Helvetii used Greek to draw up their census lists.[5] The most probable date for Port is between the incursions of the Cimbri and Teutones in 103–01 BC and the final destruction of the Helvetii by Julius Caesar in 58 BC.

R. Wyss, *Jahrb. des Bern. Historisches Mus.* XXXIV (1955), 201–22; W. Drack, *Zeitschr. f. Schweiz. Arch. u. Kunstgeschichte* 15 (1954–55), 210 ff., Taf. 59:7, 60:18= no. 18; Wyss, *Antiquity* XXX (1956), 27–28; *WK*, Taf. 21 above and centre left

[1] Wyss, *Germania* 33 (1955), 349–54

121

[2] L. V. Grinsell, *Folklore* LXXII (1961), 475 ff.

[3] Jugoslavia: J. Todorović, *Kelti u jugoistočnoj Evropi* = *Dissertationes* (Belgrade) VII, Tab. XXXVII:6–9; Hungary: É. F. Petres, *Alba Regia* VIII–IX (1967–68), 35–42

[4] O. Klindt-Jensen, *Gundestrupkedelen* (1961), 44, 46 and fig. 61–63

[5] *De bello Gallico* I, 29, 1

191 Heiligenstein, Kr. Speyer. Detail of sword stamp on iron sword. W. of stamp 0·9 cm. LT C, II BC. R-G Zentralmus., Mainz.

This detail is from a sword erroneously thought to have come from the area of Speyer Cathedral and was the first stamp to be recognised in print as such; it has a pattern-welded or 'damascened' blade. The frontal aspect of the face, without its lunate setting, suggests a link with contemporary coinage, although the size, let alone shape, of the sword stamps precludes the re-use of actual coin dies. For such well-fed frontal faces coins of either the Boii[1] or the so-called 'potin' coins of the Catuvellauni [194g] (as found at La Tène) could have formed suitable and available models. The hatched 'moon' setting looks almost like a latter-day leaf-crown, and stamps of this type are distributed as far east as Jugoslavia [see notes to **190**].

L. Lindenschmidt, *AuhV* II:VII (1870), Taf. VI:3; W. Drack, *Zeitschr. f. Schweiz. Arch. u. Kunstgeschichte* 15 (1954–55), 212 ff., 220 ff., Taf. 60 and Abb. 8:24ff= no. 28

[1] J. A. Blanchet, *Traité des monnaies gauloises* II (1905), fig. 503; *ECA*, Pl. 218c; see also notes to [204–205]

192 La Tène, Kt. Neuchâtel. Detail of sword stamp on iron blade. W. of stamp c. 1 cm. LT II, II BC. Mus. d'Art et d'Histoire, Geneva. (*Courtesy Dr J. M. de Navarro.*)

This unpublished sword stamp from the type-site may be added to the 35 or so sword stamps, including some dozen of this type previously published by Drack from La Tène and, though lacking the usual vertical hatched background, is a member of the same class of stamps as that represented by Heiligenstein [**191**].

Inv. no. M. 464

193 Ilbesheim, Kt. Kirchheimbolanden. Detail of stamps on iron sword. D. of left stamp c. 0·8 cm. LT C, II BC. Historisches Mus. der Pfalz, Speyer.

This rare instance of two stamps on the one sword blade comes from a grave found in 1954. The sword scabbard has a spindly spiral *repoussé* pattern at the mouth and dot-punched *chagrinage* extending down the front [see **181**]. Other typical finds including cremated bone, a spear, and two Middle La Tène fibulae would suggest a La Tène II date for the grave; however, amongst the seven pots also discovered were several late or La Tène D1 shape, two with geometric painted designs [see notes to **Plate Vb**]. This suggests that the actual *burial* must date around the first half of the first century BC.

As to the stamps themselves, very similar profile heads occur on two of the swords from Sombor in

Fig. 10 [**193**] Ilbesheim, Germany. Stamps on iron sword. Scale 3 : 1   *After Fischer*

Jugoslavia,[1] and a cruder version is one of the few French sword stamps so far recorded – from Courgenay, Yonne. The profile head, here, as always on the swords, facing left, is the most common aspect of the human head shown on coins, and here one may cite in particular coins of the Arverni and Mediomatrici. For the fierce bird (?an eagle) clasping a ball in its talons coin parallels again can be found, this time on coins of the Carnutes,[4] although the distribution of these tribes is admittedly well west of the Swiss swordsmiths.

O. Roller, *Pfälzer Heimat* 7 (1956), 138–42; J. M. de Navarro, *40. Ber. R-GK* 1959 (1960), 110; F. Fischer, *FbS* 18:I (1967), 77–80 and Abb. 8

[1] J. Todorović, *Kelti u jugoistočnoj Evropi* = *Dissertationes* (Belgrade) VII (1968), Tab. XXXVII:6–7; see also notes to [**190**]

[2] W. Drack, *Zeitschr. f. Schweiz. Arch. u. Kunstgeschichte* 15 (1954–55), Abb. 8:46

[3] Arverni: L. Lengyel, *L'art gaulois dans les médailles* (1954), Pl. VIII:87; Mediomatrici: *ibid.*, Pl. 5:55

[4] Lengyel, *op. cit.*, Pl. XII:138–42

194 and Plate IV Various continental Iron Age coins

In the absence of a really comprehensive and up-to-date survey of the stylistic range and distribution of continental Iron Age coins, the following selection has been made merely to indicate something of the variety which the numismatics of barbarian Europe has to offer.

All Iron Age coinage is based ultimately on classical and mainly Hellenistic prototypes. Thus for the eastern silver issues the models included silver tetradrachms of Philip II of Macedon (382–336 BC), father of Alexander the Great. These tetradrachms had the head of Zeus on the obverse and an Olympic rider carrying a palm frond on the reverse, or the head of Hercules and the seated Zeus with his eagle [see **194a, d**]. The gold stater of Philip II, with the wreathed Apollo on the obverse and a *biga* or two-horse chariot on the reverse, became the archetype for the majority of the western Celtic gold issues about whose earliest beginnings we know less than for the eastern silver coins. Gold staters of both Alexander (336–323 BC) and his successor, the bastard son of Philip, Philip III Arrhidaeus (323–317 BC) sharing on the obverse the helmeted head of Athena and on the reverse a winged victory, became the models for central European coinage, in particular that of the Boii who later based their coinage on the modified 'Athene Alkis' stater of Philip V (220–179 BC). In Italy issues of Massilia (Marseilles) with Artemis and, on the reverse, a lion [**194c**] or those of Rhoda Emporium on the south-east coast of Spain with the punning symbol of a rose on the reverse, were the chief sources from about 200 BC on; the so-called 'monnaies à la croix' or native imitations probably date from as early as the third century. In later times Roman republican issues including those of Julius Caesar and L. Cornelius Sulla were copied by the Celts of northern Italy and France.[1]

The distribution of these prototypes began with the expansionist policies of Philip II from 339 BC on, and imitations were already in circulation in some areas early in the third century. Massiliote coinage starts appearing in Roman republican contexts by the middle of the third century. The Philip II gold stater is believed to have begun to become familiar in the west from the third century on, probably being introduced by way of Romania, the Danube, and through Switzerland. A theory that during the Macedonian wars of the first half of the second century BC the Philippic stater was in use as the common coin for payment of mercenaries – amongst whose number Celts were often included [see notes to **169, 170**] – is now largely discounted.

Celtic coins, like other ancient coins, were produced by a common method; a series of flans or blanks were cast off in open clay moulds which have been found only in Celtic contexts, as for example in most of the main central European *oppida* so far excavated. The obverse was engraved on a metal die capable of producing several thousand impressions, the reverse die was mounted on a block and impressions were struck on the blank or flan which was set between the two dies. Dies have been found, though rarely, both for west and east Celtic coinage,[2] one discovered near the amphitheatre of Avranches being for a pre-58 BC issue of the Helvetii. Celtic coins of each separate type conform more or less to a standard weight.

The following references are intended as a guide to the still standard, though now often much dated, earlier source books and also to brief but usefully illustrated and more recent accounts.

E. Muret and M. A. Chabouillet, *Catalogue des monnaies gauloises de la Bibliothèque Nationale* (1889); H. de la Tour, *Atlas des monnaies gauloises de la Bibliothèque Nationale* (1892; reprint 1965); J. A. Blanchet, *Traité des monnaies gauloises* I–II (1905); R. Forrer, *Keltische Numismatik der Rhein- u. Donaulande* (1908; reprint ed. K. Castelin 1968-); K. Pink, 'Die Münzprägung der Ostkelten und ihrer Nachbarn', *Diss. Pannonicae* II ser., 15 (1939); H. Behrens, *Keltische Goldmünzen= Bilderhfte. des R-GZM* (1955); L. Lengyel, *L'art gaulois dans les médailles* (1954); *ArtG*, 151–212; *KvsE*, 224–48; K. Christ, *Historia* VI (1957), 215–53; *WK*, Taf. 87–93; Pink, 'Einführung in die keltische Münzkunde', *Arch. Austriaca*, Beiheft 4 (2 ed.), 1960); P. La Baume, *Keltische Münzen: ein Brevier* (1960); M. E. P. König, *IPEK* 21 (1964–65), 65–77; *id.*, *Archaeology* 19 (1966), 24–30; L. R. Laing, *Coins and Archaeology* (1969), esp. 145 ff.

[1] *ArtG*, 192, Pl. XVI
[2] Blanchet, *op. cit.*, 47 ff.

194a Scărişoara, Oltenia. Silver coin, obverse and reverse. D. 2·6 cm. Late IV BC. Mus. Olteniţta. (Photo from a cast; *courtesy Dr C. Preda*.)

Much work has been done in recent years on the native silver coinage of the Balkans since this region offers frequent opportunities for the possible association of native copies and Hellenistic prototypes. In about 1950 a hoard was found at Scărişoara in the plain of Oltenia south of Bucarest. Amongst a collection of coins of the Greek commercial centre of Histria on the Black Sea – which was destroyed at the end of the fourth century BC – was this single imitation of a silver tetradrachm of Philip II which could date to within the last decades of the fourth century or just the period when Philip's expansion campaigns were making his coinage known to the barbarians of the northern Balkans. This coin is at the moment the earliest securely dated native coin, though the discovery of another Romanian coin inscribed with the name of Moskon has been associated with a historical figure of the late fourth to early third century BC.[1]

C. Preda, *Dacia* X (1966), 223–35, esp. Pl. I:8

[1] D. Berciu, *Romania before Burebista* (1967), 142

Plate IVa ?Transylvania. Silver coin, obverse and reverse D. 2·5 cm. III BC. Coll. M. E. P. König, Güdingen. *Dip. W. Ing. Rainer König.*

The distribution of native silver coinage based on the tetradrachms of Philip II[1] is concentrated in Oltenia and Transylvania and into the Burgenland, but with examples as far west as Bohemia.

The fat well-fed horse on the reverse looks more like a Suffolk Punch than a sleek thoroughbred, and as such may have more than a little to do with horse figures such as that from the Camonica Valley illustrated above [**185**]; the style is really the eastern low relief counterpart of the 'Disney style' [**159** ff.]. A die for producing this type was found in 1961 with a hoard of actual coins at Tilişca in Romania.[2] A further interesting example of the influence of coinage on other forms of native art already inferred when discussing La Tène sword stamps [**190–193**] is the rider stamp used in the decoration of what might be termed 'Thraco-Getic' rather than La Tène pottery from Zimnicea also in Romania.[3]

De la Tour, *op. cit.*, no. 9870; Forrer, *op. cit.*, 17, nos. 25, 146, 266 and Taf. XXX; Pink, 'Die Münzprägung der Ostkelten . . .', 78 f., nos. 296–99; C. Preda, *Jahrb. f. Numismatik u. Geldges.* XVI (1966), 68–82, esp. Taf. 4:3–4; König, *IPEK* 21, Taf. 50:20, 55:26; *id.*, *Symbolon* 5 (1965), 159 and Abb. 28

[1] K. Castelin, *Jahrb. f. Numismatik u. Geldgeschichte* XII (1962), 199–208
[2] D. Berciu, *Neue Forschungs. zur Vorg. Rum.* (1966), Taf. 22 below
[3] D. Berciu, *Zorile istorei în Carpaţi şi la Dunăre* (1966), Pl. XXVII:2, XXVIII; *id.*, *Neue Forschungs.*, Taf. 22 top; *id.*, *Romania before Burebista*, 142 and Pl. 68

194b North-west France, 'Redones'. 'Billon stater', obverse. D. 2·3 cm. Late II/I BC. Coll. Colbert de Beaulieu, Paris. *L. Lengyel (courtesy Editions Corvina, Montrouge.)*

Base coins of the so-called 'billon stater' form are a feature of Celtic coinage of the time of Caesar's conquests of Gaul. The bearded head, comparatively rare, is influenced by Roman types and not by the Philippic stater.

Blanchet, *op. cit.*, fig. 221 ('Ambrincatui'); Lengyel, *op. cit.*, Pl. XVIII:202; *ArtG*, 192, Pl. X:23

194c Northern Italy. Silver coin, reverse. D. 1·5 cm. ?later III BC. Cabinet des Médailles, Bibliothèque Nationale, Paris.

The silver coinage of the Celtic tribes of the Ticino and Po Valley, including the area around Milan, is based on Massaliote coinage. In this example the lion is just recognisable as such, though already the native moneyer is more concerned with his model as a theme for abstract variations with, as usual in Celtic coinage, the legs being the first to suffer the change [see also **194e**]; the inscription 'Massal(ia)' has been reduced to a series of 'V's which one can only just equate with the original Greek letters. Later native versions of this coin see a return to almost realistic depiction.

Although these coins were in circulation until the first century AD, since they occur in finds with issues of Augustus and Tiberius, a recent complete study has shown that they were certainly being struck in the third century BC. A hoard found on the Capitoline Hill in Rome, by the north side of the *tabularium* in the Piazza del Campidoglio, contained a number of these native coins. There were four examples of the sub-type illustrated here – class 3 – and on the evidence of Greek coins of Neapolis and Tarentum further to the south, as well as so-called 'Romano-Campanian' issues, the deposition of the hoard may be dated to before 212 BC.[1]

The furthest distributed examples of north Italian silver coins come from Paul, near Penzance, in southwest Cornwall, where they may reflect some by-product of the Greek tin trade or perhaps more likely indirect exchange over the Alps and through Germany.[2] A poor example of class 3 is known from the type site of La Tène.[3]

Muret and Chabouillet, *op. cit.*, no. 2131; Lengyel, *op. cit.*, Pl. II:6; La Baume, *op. cit.*, Taf. III: 28–30; A. Pautasso, 'La moneta preromana dell'Italia settentrionale'=*Sibrium* VII (1962–63), esp. 8 and Tav. LXXIX

[1] M. H. Crawford, 'Roman republican coin hoards'= *Roy. Numismatic Soc. Special Pub.* 4 (1969), no. 60
[2] D. F. Allen, *Numis. Chron.* 7 ser. I (1961), 91–106; L. R. Laing, *Cornish Arch.* 7 (1968), 15–21; *id.*, *Coins and Archaeology* (1969), 119–20
[3] Pautasso, *op. cit.*, Tav. LXV, fig. 34:1; see also notes to [179]

194d Lower Danube. Silver coin, reverse. D. c. 2·8 cm. III BC. Cabinet des Médailles, Bibliothèque Nat., Paris.

This coin follows the pattern of the silver tetradrachm of Philip III, bearing the head of Herakles dressed in his lion's skin on the obverse. As with the north Italian series [**194c**] the process of abstraction, of breaking down natural forms into geometric shapes rather than anatomical details, does not take long to develop. The turned-up shoes of the seated figure of Zeus have more than a memory of the transalpine sartorial borrowings of the Early La Tène Celts [**30–32**].

Muret and Chabouillet, *op. cit.*, no. 9635; Pink, 'Die Münzprägung der Ostkelten . . .', 117–18 and Taf.

XXVIII:579–83; Lengyel, *op. cit.*, Pl. XLV:538; La Baume, *op. cit.*, Taf. XXVII:162

Plate IVb Belgium, 'Ambiani'. Gold coin, obverse and reverse. D. 1·5 cm. ?Late III BC. Coll. M. E. P. König, Güdingen. *Dipl. W. Ing. Rainer König.*

Though not a common version, this coin shows a variant on the famous Philippic stater in which the details of the reverse still remain fairly close to the original; the immediate source of the bearded head on the obverse is probably issues of Tarentum with which it has been suggested the Ambiani had indirect contact owing to their strategic position on the old north–south tin route. As might, however, be expected, the Greek inscription 'Philippou' on the reverse has been the first thing to suffer the disintegration process. Occasionally a severed head or standard appears by the chariot, and these attributes rather than the over-all design must have been the tribal distinguishing features.

Gold coins of the Philippic type in the Celtic west after a certain time maintained a more or less standard weight of 7·6 gm. until the later first century BC when troubled conditions disrupted the local ore supplies.

Several examples of this general type have been found in Kent, while the original tribal mint may have been in the area of Amiens.

Blanchet, *op. cit.*, 62; *ArtG*, 192, Pls. XI:4, XV:2; König, *Archaeology* 19, figs. 4, 6; Simone Scheers, *Rev. belge de Numismatique* CXIV (1968), 45–73, esp. Pl. XII (='Série II, classe 1')

Plate IVc Seine basin, 'Parisii'. Gold coin, obverse and reverse. D. 2·5 cm. I BC. Coll. M. E. P. König, Güdingen. *Dipl. W. Ing. Rainer König.*

Here the process of disintegration is well advanced; individual elements such as the half-moon features on the obverse – where once were the leaves of Apollo's wreath – or the hair in almost leaf-like fronds are obviously the artist's main concern; the eyes, however, are always prominent.

The hair fronds and the horse on the reverse, bereft of his companion and with the chariot lost in a net-like pelta shape, recall the Aylesford bucket [**187**]. Here is the barbaric 'will to form' or rather 'will to make conform' where the Celtic artist, coping with the unfamiliar in a surprisingly successful manner, builds up an image from shapes which belong to his normal artistic repertoire.[1]

Coins of this general type are well attested in the central basin area of France.

De la Tour, *op. cit.*, Pl. XXXI:7777; Blanchet, *op. cit.*, 367 and fig. 343; Forrer, *op. cit.*, 253, fig. 444; *ArtG*, Col. Pl. opp. p. 160; 192, Pl. IX; König, *IPEK* 21, Taf. 46:11, 53:23; *EV*, 216–17 and ill.

[1] A. Malraux, *Voices of Silence* (1954), 132 ff.; R. Bianchi Badinelli, *Organicità e astrazione* (1956), 17–40; E. M. Gombrich, *Art and Illusion* (3 ed. 1968), 65–66

194e Brittany, 'Redones'. Gold coin, reverse. D. 2·2 cm. Late II/early I BC. Cabinet des Médailles, Bibliothèque

Nationale, Paris. *L. Lengyel (courtesy Editions Corvina, Montrouge).*

There is little that is Macedonian in this very Celtic scene except the basic idea of a chariot. The human-headed horse has a long history in Iron Age art extending back to the Reinheim jug lid [73]. Such 'hippocamps' can be seen sprouting out of the hair of heads on coins from the Finistère territory of the Veneti;[1] the head of the horse here has the same features as the profile heads on the Marlborough bucket [188].

Under the horse, where sometimes one finds boar- or lyre-like emblems like those on coins of the Coriosolites [194f], is what can only be described as a fox-headed or perhaps rather dog-headed hippocamp. This has a rather later parallel in English metal-work, a bronze disc-brooch mount from Lancing, Sussex, where the dog has become the forequarters of a horse;[2] the sources must be classical but it is impossible to offer any convincing models.

In 1969 a coin of this Armorican type was found on the foreshore at Barton-on-Sea, Hampshire.

Muret and Chabouillet, *op. cit.*, no. 6804; Lengyel, *op. cit.*, Pl. XVII:198; *ArtG*, 192, Pl. X:12, 21, 23

[1] J.-B. Colbert de Beaulieu, *Gallia* XII (1954), 55–72 and fig. 8:1–3; *Art G*, 192, Pl. X:5, 11–16
[2] E. T. Leeds, *Celtic ornament* (1933), 95–96 and fig. 30a

194f Brittany, 'Coriosolites'. 'Billon stater', obverse and reverse. D. 2 cm. Late I BC. Cabinet des Médailles, Bibliothèque Nationale, Paris.

This coin, with the now completely Celticised Apollo head, has the long, pointed oval eyes which recall once more the Aylesford bucket horses [187]. The spiralling and trumpet terminal tendrils which grow from the mouth and nose are details which suggest that a Breton home for the carver of the Turoe stone is indeed a plausible proposition [129].

Coins of this type were being struck by the Coriosolites, neighbours of the Veneti, at the time of Caesar's conquest of north-western Gaul in 56 BC. They occur in the important Le Catillon hoard from Jersey in the Channel Islands, a hoard deposited presumably in advance of the Roman threat and including uninscribed British coins – an important fixed point in working out the chronology of insular coinage.[1] The reverse shows, below a very abstracted horse, one of the simplified lyre symbols which, however, should not be taken as an indication of Celtic musicianship.[2]

Muret and Chabouillet, *op. cit.*, no. 6692; Blanchet, *op. cit.*, fig. 211; J.-B. Colbert de Beaulieu, *Numismatic Circular* 59 (1951), 321–24; Lengyel, *op. cit.*, Pl. XXV: 263, 268

[1] Colbert de Beaulieu, *PPS* XXIV (1958), 201–10, esp. Pl. XXIV; see also [306]
[2] J. V. S. Megaw in (ed.) J. M. Coles and D. D. A. Simpson, *Studies in Ancient Europe* (1968), 352 and fig. 76:2; *id.*, *Archaeology* 21 (1968), 132 and ill. top

194g Somme basin. 'Potin' coin, obverse and reverse. D. 2 cm. I BC. Cabinet des Médailles, Bibliothèque Nationale, Paris.

Coins of 'potin' – in fact a tin-bronze with about 25 per cent. tin and a trace of silver – are common in the Celtic *oppida* from Bibracte (Mont Beauvray) in the west to Stradonice in the east. On the reverse of this type of coin, found in north and eastern Gaul, is a boar and what often looks very like a La Tène fibula. The face, with its pigtails [see notes to 228], has been compared to the later sword stamps [191–192][1] while the cross-legged figure holding the sacred torc seems to have wide currency in the late Celtic world; it appears on the Gundestrup cauldron [209b], on a statue from Rodez, Aveyron and on a small bronze figurine from the *oppidum* site of Bonnan (Indre).[2]

The 'tag' at the top of the coin, with part of the circumference of another coin, shows how such coins were produced in strips. The reverse shows yet another example of the heraldic boar with what may be intended as a war trumpet above [see notes to 209, 272].

Muret and Chabouillet, *op. cit.*, no. 8147; Lengyel, *op. cit.*, Pl. XLI:454; *ArtG*, 192, Pl. VIII:2; Pink, *Arch. Austriaca*, Beiheft 4, 20 and Taf. II:31; La Baume, *op. cit.*, Taf. VIII:83 ('Remi')

[1] W. Drack, *Zeitschr. f. Schweiz. Arch. u. Kunstgeschichte* 15 (1954–55), Taf. 70:10
[2] Rodez: *Espérandieu* XIII (1949), no. 8187; *ArtG*, 96, Pls. 35–36; Bonnan: H. Bonstetten, *Receuil d'Antiquités Suisses* 2e suppl. (1847), Pl. IX:10; J. A. Blanchet, *Bull. de la Soc. nat. des Antiq. de France* (1901), fig. on p. 161

Plate IVd Brittany, 'Namnetes'. Gold coin, reverse. D. 1·2 cm. II/I BC. Coll. M. E. P. König, Güdingen. *Dipl. W. Ing. Rainer König.*

The little dancing figure is as Gallic as the head on the obverse is almost academically classical. Though it is a northern piece, this Armorican coin has the Mediterranean gaiety of the dancing figures from Neuvy-en-Sullias [237]. Various symbols repeated on other coins can also be made out on the reverse: an axe, a ball – or is it another torc? – and a barred cross looking like the folding-stool symbol to be seen on earlier Danubian coins [194d]. Coins of the Veliocasses are very similar and the single figure can be shown to have developed from isolation of the charioteer of the old Hellenistic prototypes.

De la Tour, *op. cit.*, Pl. XX:6722; Blanchet, *op. cit.*, 153, fig. 4; Lengyel, *op. cit.*, Pl. XXX; *ArtG*, 192, Pl. X: 8–9; König, *IPEK*, 21, Taf. 56:29

194h Goldberg bei Mardorf, Hesse. Gold coins, obverse. D. c. 1·8 cm. I BC. Universitätsmus., Jubiläumsbau, Marburg/Lahn. *Bildarchiv Foto Marburg.*

These five examples are derived from the so-called *Regenbogenschüsselschen* or *guttae iridis* types of the Vindelici with their *oppidum* at Manching in south Bavaria [see notes to 189]. They were found in 1880 near the local *oppidum* of the Amöneburg[1] as part of a hoard of some 200 coins, and represent two of the three main types found. The reverses consist either of dot-in-circle pyramids or – the form which gives the coins their German name – of a curved arc containing three or more balls. Like the hatched edging ornament on the obverse of the coins, the arcs probably represent torcs and in particular the twisted type which is little found outside the British Isles [291] except in representations [209b]. The beaked bird's heads pointing inwards can also be read, when turned through a right angle, as a blob-nosed twisted face, a sort of latter-day version of the Maloměřice 'Chad' mount [165]; the triskels once more recall the central motif of the upper Aylesford bucket hoop [187], and the large Manerbio discs may also be cited [204].

Coins of this general form have been found inside the Manching *oppidum* together with moulds and a blank unstamped series.[2] Two large hoards have been found in the area of Manching, presumably buried during Tiberius' campaigns, the Irsching, Kr. Ingolstadt, hoard having more than 1,000 coins.[3] Though concentrated in southern Bavaria, the coin type has an extended distribution[4] up the Neckar into the non-Celtic region of what is now Poland, south to Switzerland and east into Bohemia, where it appears at the great *oppidum* site of the Hradiště at Stradonice; indeed, the coins may be based on late coins of the Boii.[5]

De la Tour, *op. cit.*, Pl. XXXIX; Blanchet, *op. cit.*, 474; Forrer, *op. cit.*, 15 and fig. 20, 221 and figs. 396–97; H. Schaafhausen, *Bonner Jahrb.* LXXVI (1888), 64 ff.; Pink, *Arch. Austriaca*, Beiheft 4, 22, and Taf. II:37–39; La Baume, *op. cit.*, 38 and Taf. XVI; König, *IPEK*, 21, 70 and Taf. 44:8

[1] R. Gensen in *Festschr. Dehn*, esp. 25 and Taf. 4:2
[2] K. Castelin, *Germania* 28 (1960), 32–42; *id.*, and H.-J. Kellner, *Jahrb. f. Numismatik u. Geldgeschichte* XIII (1963), 105–30
[3] Blanchet, *op. cit.*, 446 and figs. 491–92; W. Torbrügge and H.P. Uenze, *Bilder zur Vorg. Bayerns* (1968), ill. 267; *EV*, 217 and ill. top row
[4] C. Peschek, *Mainfränkisches Jahrb. f. Ges. u. Kunst* 11 (1959), 16 and Taf. III:6; Castelin, *Numismatické Listy* X (1955), 33–50
[5] *KvsE*, obr. 69:12–13

Plate IVe 'Poinsat' hoard, 'Arverni'. Gold coin, obverse. D. 1·8 cm. Mid-I BC. Cabinet des Médailles, Bibliothèque Nationale, Paris (Fonds Bestegui). *Ina Bandy.*

Together with coins bearing the name of Epadnactus, the twenty-odd gold and two bronze coins so far known with the name of Vercingetorix are the only issues which can be certainly associated with the six chieftains of the confederation who, under Vercingetorix, 'Great-King-of-Warriors', unsuccessfully challenged Julius Caesar in 52 BC.[1] The site of this last-ditch stand, the *oppidum* of Alesia Mandubiorum, is usually considered to lie under the Gallo-Roman settlement (with its evidence of a sanctuary to the mare-goddess Epona) on Mt Auxois, Alise-Ste.-Reine (Côte-d'Or); the site was investigated first in 1839 at the instigation of Napoleon III and claimed as Alesia though only a single coin inscribed with the name of Vercingetorix, a bronze, was found there (associated with an uninscribed coin type, however, which also seems to have been issued by Vercingetorix); with one exception the balance have been found in the territory of the Arverni which was centred on the Puy-de-Dôme.

The present example belongs to class I of the ten different classes which have been worked out – allowing

for an original minting of perhaps 7,500 coins! The reverse shows a riderless horse leaping over an amphora, evidence perhaps of the importance of the wine trade between the central Gaulish *oppida* and the southern Graeco-Roman colonies. The heads on the obverse of the Vercingetorix staters – the influence of Rome seen in the alphabet used – are, it should be noted, by no means portraits of the chieftain or indeed of any Celt, but simply a late version of the Philippic Apollo heads minus their wreaths. Even here, portraiture has no part in Iron Age iconography any more than in the inscribed coins of the contemporary figures of the beginning of Britain's written history [306b]. One as yet unpublished coin of Vercingetorix from the 'Poinsat' hoard is in the Lewis Collection of Corpus Christi College, Cambridge.

Celts, Pl. 5e; J.-B. Colbert de Beaulieu and G. Lefèvre, *Gallia* XXI (1963), 11–75, esp. 24, 37 and fig. 16 (=A10); Colbert de Beaulieu, *Bull. Soc. Française de la Numismatique* (1964), 365–66; *Archéologia* (Paris) 24 (1968), ill. on cover

[1] Caesar, *De Bello Gallico* VII

195 Unprovenanced. Bronze girdle-hook. Ht. 4·4 cm. ?I BC/I AD. British Mus., London. *J. V. S. Megaw.*

This unprovenanced ?belt-hook fitting, formerly in the Franks collection, has the bust raised on a right angle stem bent up from the ring. This forms a hook round which the strap of a belt could have been fixed – a pattern which, complete with human head, goes back to Early La Tène times and the Herrnsheim, Mainz, hook.[1]

The grinning face is no longer an Italo-Greek satyr but rather a Roman Silenus, and as such the piece has analogies with three finger rings also in the British Museum with bezels in the shape of actors' masks, one found near the amphitheatre of Lyons.[2] The face also has much of the character of the basal handle faces on provincial bronze wine jugs of the so-called 'Kelheim' type as found in Late La Tène graves on the continent and in Britain.[3] It is difficult to be certain, in the absence of evidence as to location or association, whether we have here a late Celtic piece or not, though the eyes, eyebrows and hair-line have a distinctly native look. The wedge-shaped notches probably had enamel inlay, and recall similar enamel-filled areas on southern British harness fittings of the period around the time of the Claudian invasion.[4]

Inv. no. Æ 436

[1] *ECA*, no. 366; J. V. S. Megaw, *Germania* 45 (1967), 52 and Taf. 8:4; see also notes to [78]
[2] F. H. Marshall, *Catalogue of Greek, Etruscan and Roman finger-rings in the British Museum* (1907), nos. 1621, 1624, 1629
[3] J. Werner, *Bayer. Vorg.* XX (1954), 43–72; F. Fischer, 'Der spätlatènezeitl. Depot-Fund von Kappel', *Urkunde zur Vor- u. Frühg. aus Südwürtt.-Hohenzollern* I (1959), 16–18; J. M. C. Toynbee, *Art in Britain under the Romans* (1964), 41–42 and Pl. III:C
[4] *PP*, Pls. 70c, 72a, c

196 Manching, Kr. Ingolstadt. Bronze pendant, lower part of face restored. Ht. 4·4 cm. LT D1, I BC. Prähist. Staatssammlung, Munich. *R-GK, Frankfurt.*

This and the almost identical pendant from Bad Nauheim shown on the right [197] are the best justification for ascribing a Celtic origin to the British Museum belt-hook illustrated to the left [195]. The Manching pendant, a hollow casting without its suspension ring, was found during the excavations of the East Gate of the Vindelician *oppidum* in 1962–63 [see notes to 189]. The ridged almond eyes, large nose and exaggerated brows remind one of the slick-haired trio on one of the Paris terret rings [168] or even more perhaps the pendant from the same set;[1] the lips have nonetheless the upturned twist of a Roman actor's mask. A miniature version of such a Celtic Silenus head occurs on three Late La Tène fibulae, one from Switzerland illustrated on the opposite page [200], the brooch from Ebreichsdorf, lower Austria, quoted in connection with the Dammelberg torc [see notes to 148], and one from the *oppidum* site of Ste-Blandine, Isère, capital of the Allobroges, sacked in 60 BC.[2] Another similar pendant is illustrated by Gensen from the Museum at Calais.

R. Gensen, *Germania* 43 (1965), 55 and Taf. 10

[1] *ECA*, no. 175c
[2] G. Chapotat, *Actes 89e congrès nat. des soc. savantes: Lyon, 1964*, Section d'Arch. (1965), 18 and fig. 2

197 Bad Nauheim, Kr. Friedberg, Hessen. Bronze pendant. Total ht. as illustrated, 5·3 cm. LT D1, I BC. Hessisches Landesmus., Darmstadt. *R-GK* (*E. Neuffer*).

This cast bronze pendant originally had a ring through one of the two hoops, both of which are now broken, on the crown of the head. It comes from a flat grave cemetery of La Tène C–D date. Associated with the pendant were three brooches with feet cast in one with the flattened bow – rather like a modern string player's bow – a type to which the cemetery has given its name. The first appearance of the Nauheim fibula is usually associated with the beginning of La Tène D but, despite its importance as a chronological indicator, it is difficult at the moment to be precise as to the absolute date for its introduction though this must lie some time before the middle of the first century BC.[1] Other objects discovered with the pendant were a silver chain, a triple pot, a bowl and an iron ring. The original description of the grave as 'La Tène C' is incorrect.

The face pendant is in fact a Janus head, since it has two identical aspects joined about the median line. The nose is even more Cyrano de Bergerac-esque than that of the Manching pendant, but the eyes and great grinning mouth are very similar.

The area of Bad Nauheim seems to have contained import salt works and was taken over in Augustan times, as recent rescue excavations have confirmed.[2]

E. Quilling, *Die Nauheimer Funde in den Museen zu Frankfurt a.M. und Darmstadt* (1903), 47–48, no. 176; O. Schwabe and G. Behrens, *Germania* 17 (1933), 85 and Taf. 11:2

[1] Jiří Břeň, *Třísov: a Celtic oppidum=Guides to Prehistory* 2 (1966), 69 ff.
[2] W. Jorns, *Germania* 38 (1960), 178 ff.; L. Süss, *Fundber. aus Hessen* 5–6 (1965–66), 26–39; *id.*, *Festschr. Dehn*, 288–338

198 Basle, Gasworks site, Kt. Basle. Detail of bronze knife. Total l. 18·3 cm., l. of handle c. 7·5 cm. LT D2, I BC/IAD. Historisches Mus., Basle.

This well-groomed head wears a twisted torc. The single-edged knife to which it forms the terminal comes from what has been identified as the site of the *oppidum* of the Raurici, reoccupied by the Helvetii who, according to Caesar, had no less than 400 settlements and twelve major *oppida*.[1] The site was examined during the construction of the Basle Gasworks and material was recovered during 1913–38, finds of the La Tène C–D periods coming from what was clearly a cemetery as well as an occupation site. These included Nauheim fibulae [see notes to 197], pottery [Plate Vb], multi-coloured glass armrings [see notes to Plate Va], and 'potin' or tin-bronze coinage [194g].

The tradition of human-headed knives starts in the later Scandinavian Bronze Age [19]. From Late La Tène contexts one can cite, apart from the Slovakian 'Janus' knife illustrated on the right, a similar single-edged knife from Monsheim in Rheinhessen, a bronze nail head from Křivoklat not far from the famous Bohemian *oppidum*, Hradiště, near Stradonice;[2] the so-called 'head of Vercingetorix' in the Museum at Peronne is also similar.[3]

E. Major, *Gallische Ansiedlung mit Gräberfeld bei Basel* (1940), 24–25 and Taf. 1; R. Wyss in (ed.) W. Drack, *Die Eisenzeit in der Schweiz=Reportium der Ur- u. Frühg. der Schweiz* 3 (1957), 22 ff. and Taf. 12:3

[1] K. Schumacher, *Praehist. Zeitschr.* VI (1914), 240; J. Caesar, *De Bello Gallico* I, 5, 2
[2] Monsheim: G. Behrens, *Bodenurkunden aus Rheinhessen* I (1927), 50, no. 176:2; Křivoklat, J. L. Píč, 'Hradiště u Stradonic jako historické Marobudum', *Starožitnosti země České* II:2 (1903), 67 and obr. 9 – trans. J. Déchelette, *Le Hradischt de Stradonitz en Bohème* (1906)
[3] R. Forrer, *Urgeschichte des Europas* (1908), 506 and Taf. 173:1

199 Zemplín, Trebišov. Detail of iron knife handle. L. 9·0 cm., ht. of head c. 1·8 cm. LT III, I BC. Aú SAV, Nitra-Hrad.

The defended settlement – not an *oppidum* – of Zemplín, in eastern Slovakia, was placed right on the eastern periphery of the Celtic area; as the pottery from the site showed, there was considerable contact with the Dacians of the northern Balkans. The fortifications of the site, occupied between the second half of the first century BC and the first half of the first century AD, were probably set up at the time of the Roman campaigns in Pannonia; a Roman silver *denarius* was found within the site.

The faces, a crude Janus pair, on this single-edged knife are not identical. The one shown here looks a typical long-moustached Celt; on the other side is a more slender-faced head, possibly meant as a woman. This, though, is not the work of a specialist artist-craftsman; similar crude faces can be seen on the foot of a 'Certosa'-derived brooch from grave 8 of the Welzelach cemetery in the Tyrol.[1] Even closer, right down to the simple punched-circle eyes and dot-and-circle ornament, is the head at the base of the handle of a native beaked bronze flagon from grave 32 of the Giubiasco cemetery in the Ticino, seemingly associated with both a republican bronze *patella* and a Middle La Tène sword[2] [see also notes to **99** and **200–201**]. Another early example of what might be termed Celtic 'folk' art is the group of Early La Tène neck- and arm-rings in the 'Horchheim' style.[3] A knife handle with human head and apparently late example of a Negau helmet [see **201**], comes from Oškobrh, Poděbrad in Bohemia.[4]

K. Andel, *Arch. roz.* VII (1955), 795–99 and Obr. 359; J. Paulík *et al.*, *Život a umenie doby železnej na Slovensku* (1962), 187 ff. and obr. 48; B. Benadík, *Germania* 43 (1965), 63–91 esp. Abb. 17; *id.*, 'Die Besiedlung von Zemplín an der Wende der Zeitrechnung', *Excursion en Slovaquie: VIIe Congr. Intern. des Sci. prehist. et protohist.* (1966), esp. Abb. 9

[1] G. von Merhart, *Wiener Prähist. Zeitschr.* XIV (1927), 105 and Abb. XIV:5
[2] *JL*, 19–20; *ECA*, no. 393d
[3] J. V. S. Megaw, *Germania* 45 (1967), 55 ff.; see also notes to [**51**]
[4] J. Hellich, *Památky Arch.* XIX (1900–01), 388–89 and obr. 3

Plate Vb Basle, Gasworks site. Painted wheel-turned pot. Ht. 37 cm. LT III, second half I BC. Historisches Mus., Basle. (*Photo courtesy Sandoz AG, Basle.*)

Painted pottery in Iron Age Europe north of the Alps is known from HaD2 times when influence from the south was strong.[1] The growth of painted wheel-turned ware dates, however, from the later La Tène C phase in Germany and has already been mentioned in connection with the stamped sword from Ilbesheim [**193**]. In the east central area, where the standard decoration of late painted pottery associated with the territory of the Boii was limited to geometric patterns or bands of colour in the manner of most vessels from *oppida* sites like Manching [see notes to **196**], such pottery is almost entirely late second or first century in date.

With a rough division into two stylistic groups but with many local variants – plant motifs in the west, geometric in the east – Late La Tène painted pottery seems best regarded as stemming from several sources. For the west, influences may have included not only the curvilinear decorated pottery of the Marne [**154–155**] but also the pottery of Gallia Narbonensis and the Spanish so-called 'Merida' pottery based on local Ionian wares. The closest contemporary parallels to this much-restored Basle pot come from the Loire region, from Manching and – the only sherd in the western style from the region – from Stradonice in Bohemia.[2]

E. Major, *Gallische Ansiedlung mit Gräberfeld bei Basel* (1940), 91 ff., Vorsatztafel and Taf. 18; *ECA*, 95ff.; R. Wyss in (ed.) W. Drack, *Die Eisenzeit in der Schweiz= Reportium der Ur- u. Frühg. der Schweiz* 3 (1957), 22 ff. and Taf. 12:8; R. Laur-Belart, *Zur Geschichte der ältesten Basler Siedlung* (n.d.), Frontispiece; *VRD*, ill. 136; F. Maier, *Germania* 39 (1961), 363; *id.*, *Germania* 41 (1963), 259–68; *EV*, ill. p. 214

[1] W. Dehn, *Alt-Thüringen* VI (1962–63), 272 ff.
[2] Loire: *Manuel* IV, 994 ff. and fig. 682; Manching: Maier, *Germania* 39, Beilage 4:7; Stradonice: J. L.

Píč, 'Hradiště u Stradonic jako historické Marobudum', *Starožitnosti země České* II:2 (1903), Tab. 49:18

200 Giubiasco, Ct. Ticino, grave 221. Bronze brooch with provision for inlay. L. 6·8 cm. LT C–D1, II BC. Schweiz. Landesmus., Zürich.

The idea of disc-decorated brooches terminating in little human heads has already been encountered amongst 'Münsingen' fibulae of LT Ib date [**134**]. In Middle and Late La Tène contexts some 100 examples of fibulae based on this type have been found; these are spread over upwards of thirty sites north and south of the Alps. The concentration is within the large flat cemeteries of Ticino with extensions into the Tyrol and, despite the male and usually helmeted appearance [**201**] of the terminal heads, these brooches seem to be the exclusive property of women and are usually found in pairs sometimes linked with a chain.

In the present example, one of several from Giubiasco, the head has a crude little silen mask and the punched-dot eyes recall those of the Giubiasco grave 32 flagon [see notes to **199**]. A skeleton grave at Přemyšlení on the outskirts of Prague, with two late Duchcov-type brooches and a plastic, decorated knobbed armring, also contained an unusual fibula. Its heavy spring case was decorated in cast tendril ornament which relates it to the hinged armlets of the Křinec type [see **141**]. From the centre of the bow grows a crude little human head, while the foot is in the shape of a horse's head, the 'muzzle' of which is in fact a crude little silen in the precise manner of the present Giubiasco brooch.[1]

The slot on the Giubiasco brooch to take ?enamel inlay is another archaic feature going back to the Early La Tène Schwieberdingen and Reinheim fibulae [see **89**].

The other grave goods in grave 221 consisted of a plain silver finger ring, two plain bronze rings with amber beads, and a pair of fibulae of related form with even simpler human head terminals.

R. Ulrich, *Die Gräberfelder in der Umgebung von Bellinzona, Kt. Tessin* (1914), 601; W. Krämer, *Germania* 39 (1961), esp. 314, 320–21, Abb. 2 and Taf. 42:1

[1] *KvsE*, 95–96, 106, 377 and Tab. XXII:3; *V and A*, 134, n. 144

201 Giubiasco, Ct. Ticino, grave 450. Pair of bronze brooches with enamel inlay. L. 11·4 cm. LT C/D1, II BC. Schweiz. Landesmus., Zürich.

This pair of brooches was found in a woman's grave with another pair of helmeted head-terminalled brooches – but minus their disc inlay – two plain rings like those from grave 22 [**200**]with amber beads attached, and an iron ring possibly from a belt. The helmets of the miniature heads, which rise to a central ridge [see **202**], appear to copy the so-called 'Negau' type probably first adopted by the Celts from Etruscan fourth century BC models.[1] Two actual examples of 'Negau' helmets, though, found at Giubiasco, come from Late La Tène graves, probably of mid-first century BC date.[2]

The helmeted type of disc-ornamented fibula has also been found at Manching [see notes to **189**] where it may have been introduced by women from the southern Alps before the Roman campaigns against the Raeti and the

Vindelici. In support of this sort of tribal intercourse may be quoted Caesar's account of how Ariovistus, chief of the Suebi, married the king of Noricum's (=Austria) daughter.[3]

R. Ulrich, *Die Gräberfelder in der Umgebung von Bellinzona, Kt. Tessin* (1914), 660–61; W. Krämer, *Germania* 39 (1961), 313 ff. and Taf. 42:2

[1] P. Reinecke, *32. Ber. R-GK 1942* (1950), 117 ff.; S. Gabrovec in *Atti del III° Congr. Intern. d. Sci. Preist. e Protostoriche* III (1966), 114–20
[2] Grave 119: Ulrich, *op. cit.*, 585 and Taf. LXXII:1; grave 262: *id.*, 295 and Taf. LXXX:2
[3] Krämer, *Antiquity* XXXIV (1960), 197 and fig. 5:8, J. Caesar, *De Bello Gallico* I, 53

202 Balzers, Gutenberg, Liechtenstein. Bronze figurine. Ht. 12·7 cm. ?LT D1, II/I BC. Historische Sammlung, Vaduz. *R-G Zentralmus., Mainz.*

This cast bronze figure was found with six smaller bronze figures, all with location pegs under their feet; two have helmets, as here, of the 'Negau' type [see notes to **201**], and one of them also carries a spear. There were also two animal figurines, a stag and a boar, the latter looking in fact as if it could have decorated a helmet and in profile not unlike the boar stamps on later La Tène swords [see **181**].[1] The site was a cult place within an *oppidum*, a suitable place for such warrior's votive offerings which recall the armed figurines from the temple site at Baratela, Este [see **34**].[2] Like the Baratela figures, the Balzers warrior probably held a shield and, in the upraised hand, a spear. The classical-looking cuirass, its neck indicated by a line executed with a rocked tracer, is the only garment. The figure's ithyphallic stance reminds one of that much earlier representation clearly influenced by the classical world, the Hirschlanden stone statue [**12**], as well as of accounts like that of Polybius of the battle of Telamon in 225 BC describing the Celt's ritual nakedness in combat.[3] The crude modelling of the face does appear to show a drooping un-Celtic beard and there are at least two other figurines of probably Late La Tène date from the general Alpine region, one from Vild, Sargans, Kt. St Gallen, with a Negau-type helmet and torc, and another, also with helmet and naked save for shield and cuirass, from the Rheintal by the Bodensee.[4]

The figures have been classified as 'Veneto-Illyrian', a usefully imprecise portmanteau label; all that may be said definitely is that such figures demonstrate the continuing trans-Alpine influences in the later Iron Age.

G. von Merhart, *Mannus* 24 (1932), 56–63; A. Hild and G. von Merhart, *Jahrb. Hist. Ver. Fürstentum Liechtenstein* 33 (1932–33), 27 ff.; Von Merhart, *Marburger Jahrb. f. Kunstwissenschaft* XIII (1944), 8; W. Drack and K. Schib, *Illustrierte Geschichte der Schweiz* I (1958), 65 and Taf. 14a; W. Krämer, *Germania* 38 (1960), 31 and Taf. 5; *EV*, 206 and ill.

[1] R. Wyss in (ed.) Drack, *Die Eisenzeit in der Schweiz = Reportium der Ur- u. Frühg. der Schweiz* 3 (1957), 24 ff. and Taf. 11: 22–23; *WK*, Taf. 16 above
[2] O. Klindt-Jensen, *Acta Arch.* XX (1949), 136 and fig. 90
[3] Polybius, II, 23 ff.
[4] Von Merhart, *Marburger Jahrb. f. Kunstwissenschaft*

XIII, 6–11 and Abb. 2–3; B. Frei in (ed.) Drack, *op. cit.*, 13 and Taf. 14:53 (=Vild)

203 Dejbjerg Mose, West Jutland. Ritual waggon with (above) details of left front and right rear hand-grips. D. of wheels c. 95 cm.; masks on hand grips 6·5 × 7·6 cm. I BC. National Mus., Copenhagen.

During 1881–83 peat digging near the presbytery of Dejbjerg uncovered two dismantled four-wheeled waggons placed on a low mound and associated with a cremation burial, the whole being contained within a staked enclosure; the pots shown in the lower illustration may or may not have been directly associated with the burial. This, the most famous of the three late waggon graves so far known in Denmark [see also **223**], continues the old central European Hallstatt custom of waggon burial into the later non-Celtic north. Late waggon graves of this type are in any case not common; there is one recorded from the Aisne and one from Transylvania in eastern Europe, while from Württemberg a great ritual deposit at Kappel near Dürnau contained waggon fittings.[1] The skilled workmanship of the waggons' construction can hardly have been Scandinavian, though it is not possible to offer much in the way of detailed comparison. The iron tires were carefully sweated on to the oak wheels with, on the waggon here illustrated, fourteen carefully turned spokes, the second waggon having twelve spokes. Skilled lathe turning had also been employed to produce the bronze hubs with their roller-bearings. The shaft, intended for paired draft, had once been provided with a double yoke. A throne-like construction in the centre of the actual waggon may have been intended for a lay-figure of a god or goddess and reminds one of Tacitus' description of the Teutonic rites to the goddess Nerthus [see notes to **281**], or, much earlier, the goddess of Strettweg [**38**].

The openwork fittings and decorated nail heads – not unlike some from the first century BC Hradiště at Stradonice – recall the early tradition of such chariot fittings as those from Le Bouvandeau [**112**]. As to the mustachio'd human heads, the three mounts from one of the two Belgic chieftains' graves at Welwyn offer the closest parallels [**230**], while other objects of Late La Tène date illustrated on this page give somewhat similar clean-shaven impressions of the same face; one may note particularly the tubular fragments from Manerbio [**206**]. A series of bronze plates from Öland in south Sweden of perhaps rather later date can also be added to the list, though these have the look not of imported pieces but of local attempts at the Celtic idiom.[2]

A source somewhere in Gaul may be offered as an uninspired guess as to the origins of the style represented by the Dejbjerg waggon mounts.

H. Petersen, *Vognfundene i Dejbjerg Præstegaardsmose* (1888); O. Klindt-Jensen, *Acta Arch.* XX (1949), 87–100, esp. figs. 62, 64; *WK*, Taf. 94; Klindt-Jensen, *Denmark before the Vikings* (1957), 88–89; J. Brønsted, *Danmarks Oltid* III (1960), 68–73; H. R. Ellis-Davidson, *Pagan Scandinavia* (1967), 73 ff.; *EV*, 218–19 and ills.; P. V. Glob, *The bog people* (1969), 168 ff. and ill. 63

[1] F. Fischer, 'Der spätlatènezeitl. Depot-Fund von Kappel (Kr. Salgau)', *Urkunden zur Ur- u. Frühg. aus Südwürtt.-Hohenzollern* I (1959)
[2] Louise Halbert, *Medd. från Lunds Univ. Historiska Mus.* (1961), 107–22, here esp. fig. 9

I

204 Villa Vecchia, Manerbio sul Mella. Large silver disc. D. 19·2 cm. ? III/II BC. Mus. Civico, Brescia.

In 1928 a quantity of turned and *repoussé* decorated silver discs and other objects were found together with a plain bronze torc in the territory formerly occupied by the Celtic Insubres. Silver was little used in the Celtic west and, like silver coinage, is more proper to the highly individual and strictly non-Celtic art of Dacia and further east [**209** ff.]. Jacobsthal regarded these silver discs as products of the territory of the Boii buried in the second century following the defeat of the Celts in 191 BC by the Romans under Scipio. With earlier material such as Hořovičky in mind [**47**], the discs might be termed harness decoration or, more likely, clothing ornaments in view of the small fixing holes which Jacobsthal considered to be for attaching to leather backing.

However that may be, the twenty heads around the circumference of this, the largest of three large discs and, to judge from the lack of rim, an unfinished piece, have certain similarities to Celtic coins, including both those of the Boii and silver issues of Noricum.[1] The ridged eyes and fringed hair follow old conventions [see **72**]. The central triple-legged motif can be compared with the Aylesford triskel [**187**] or again with coins such as those of the Vindelici – found within the central European territory of the Boii [**194h**] – of the Volcae Tectosages, or of the Carnutes.[2] A source north of the Alps seems to be demanded for the Manerbio pieces, though their date is not so easy to decide.

P. Jacobsthal, *Praehist Zeitschr.* XXV (1934), 104; *id.*, *Am. J. Arch.* 47 (1943), 306–12; *ECA*, no. 84(A), esp. pp. 122, 130 (quotes wrong totals for various types from find); W. Deonna, *Rev. arch.* XXXV (1950), 37–40; *Arte e civiltà romana nell'Italia settentrionale* (1954), Mus. Civico, Bologna, no. 63 and Tav. V:10; R. Chevalier, *Latomus* XXI (1962), 267 and Pl. XLIII:5; C. Carducci, *Antique Italian gold and silver* (1964), 22

[1] Boii: H. de la Tour, *Atlas des monnaies gauloises de la Bibliothèque Nationale* (1892), Pl. LI:9925; *ECA*, 12 and Pl. 218e; K. Pink, 'Einführung in die Keltische Münzkunde', *Arch. Austriaca*, Beiheft 4 (2 ed., 1960), Taf. VIII:111a; Noricum: Pink, 'Die Münzprägung der Ostkelten und ihrer Nachbarn', *Diss. Pannonicae* II ser., 15 (1939), 112 and Taf. XXVI:529–35
[2] De la Tour, *op. cit.*, Pl. X: 3560–63, XVIII:6017

205 Villa Vecchia, Manerbio sul Mella. Small silver disc. D. c. 9 cm. ? III/II BC. Mus. Civico, Brescia.

The Manerbio find included 14 smaller discs or portions of discs, each, when complete, with eight clean-shaven heads of the same type as on the larger discs and, like them, produced after the turning and raising of the main disc. One of the small discs still has one of three surviving pendants.

ECA, no. 84(A); C. Carducci, *Antique Italian gold and silver* (1964), Pl. 23a

206 Villa Vecchia, Manerbio sul Mella. Silver fragment of semi-circular cross-section. L. 10·2 cm. ? III/II BC. Mus. Civico, Brescia.

This is one of a series of fragments which must have made up at least five separate tubes each with the *repoussé* decoration showing an apparently helmeted and mustachio'd male head above that of a ram and flanked by two simple 'S' curls.

Despite the faint resemblance of the helmeted heads to those on later native coins based on republican prototypes like those from France of the Atrebates, Aedui, or Vocontii,[1] and the general form of simplified ram and 'S' curls reminding one of the Frasnes-lez-Buissenal torc [**173**], the combination of man and ram is more common in the Early La Tène period [see **73**, **101**].

As to the actual human face, amongst classical or classicising material this may be compared in the first place with a gold diadem from Vale Pega grave 136A with four Attic fish-plates and a *krater* of the first quarter of the fourth century BC by the South Italian 'Iliupersis' painter.[2] More apposite may be the frieze of mustachio'd heads from Nages[3] with plaits rather like those on the coins of the Somme [**194g**], and, closest of all, the Dejbjerg heads [**203**] and the head on an anthropomorphic sword from Gampelen, Kt. Bern[4] – parallels which tend to support a late-ish date for Manerbio.

ECA, no. 84(B); *KvsE*, 28 ff.; *V and A*, 154, n. 212

[1] *ArtG*, 192, Pl. XVI:2, 4, 31
[2] *Ori e argenti dell'Emilia antica*, Mus. Civico, Bologna (1958), no. 83
[3] *Espérandieu* I, no. 515
[4] O. Tschumi, *Urg. des Kantons Bern* (1953), Abb. 76 centre; C. F. C. Hawkes, *PPS* XXI (1955), 222 and fig. 5:1=no. 22; W. Torbrügge and H.P. Uenze, *Bilder zur Vorg. Bayerns* (1968), ill. 253 left

207 Staré Hradisko, Prostějov. Sheet bronze fragment. 6·3 × 7·7 cm. LT D1, I BC. Muz. Města, Boskovice. Aú ČSAV, Brno.

The first mention of the *oppidum* site of Staré Hradisko in central Moravia was made by Bishop Blahoslav in the sixteenth century AD. Excavations began just before the outbreak of World War II and are continuing at present. The contents of the site, painted and graphite pottery, ironwork, and gold coins including imitations of Alexander's tetradrachms with the head of Athena [see notes to **194**], are typical of central European *oppida*.

The present fragment is one of two, perhaps mounts for attaching to a wooden box, crude *repoussé* work but showing the same basic clean-shaven, crew-cut Celtic faces as illustrated elsewhere on this and the opposite page; it is another example of local 'folk' craftsmanship, and from Bohemia may be compared with one of several miniature bronze heads from Stradonice.[1]

KvsE, 114 ff. and Tab. CXXV:12; E. Šimek, *Poslední Keltové na Moravě=Opera Univ. Brunensis Facultas Philosophica* 53 (1958), Obr. 21:5; J. Meduna, *Staré Hradisko=Fontes Arch. Moravicae* II (1961), Taf. 1:10

[1] J. Píč (trans. J. Déchelette), *Le Hradischt de Stradonitz en Bohème* (1906), Pl. XX:13

208 Szárazd, Regöly, hoard I. Gold bead. D. c. 3·5 cm. I BC. Magyar Nem. Múz., Budapest. *J. Karàth.*

At the turn of the century two metal hoards were found

in the neighbourhood of Regöly in southern Hungary. In the first hoard were found five small biconical beads – one of which is illustrated here – one large bead and a series of miniature five-spoked wheels also in gold [see also notes to **209** and **224**].

Each bead has four clean-shaven faces round each half of the bead and the use both of mask decoration and of granulation or of separate strips of fine twisted gold wire reflects an era when Celtic and Illyrian traditions intermixed, the latter, as always, offering a medium for the preservation and transmission of techniques and styles from the Graeco-Italic world.

K. Hadaczek, *Arch. Értesitő* XXXI (1907), 166–71; W. von Jenny, *Keltische Metallarbeiten aus heidnischer und christl. Zeit* (1935), Taf. 18; I. Hunyady, 'Kelták a Kárpátmedencében', *Diss. Pannonicae* II ser., 18 (1942), T. XXXIX:7–9; (1944), 43 ff. and T. III; (ed.) E.-B. Thomas, *Archäologische Funde in Ungarn* (1956), 170 and ill. on p. 171

209a Gundestrup, Rævemosen, Aars. Reassembled silver gilt cauldron with inlay. As mounted: ht. 42 cm., d. 69 cm.; internal plates c. 40 × 20 cm., external plates c. 25 × 20 cm. ? Late II/early I BC. National Mus., Copenhagen. (L. Larsen.)

Probably no other surviving relic of prehistoric European craftsmanship – with the exception of Stonehenge – has occasioned so much publication and dispute as the silver cauldron of Gundestrup. This veritable toreutic treasure store of style, symbol and belief has been claimed as anything between second century BC and AD 300 in date; as to place of manufacture some consider it to be the work of Thracians in the east, others of Gallo-Romans in the west, with the views of Arbman, Reinecke and Klindt-Jensen following a middle path with emphasis on the relationship with the art of southern and central Gaul in the first centuries BC/AD.

The cauldron was found in north Jutland in 1891, the various dismounted plates and other pieces having been placed near a low mound and on the surface of a bog in the manner of the Dejbjerg carts [**203**]. The cauldron was both incomplete and obviously old when deposited. The remaining fragments, weighing nearly 9 kilogrammes, consisted of part only of the 'U' section rim, an iron hoop for holding the rim together, all five internal rectangular plates [**209b, c**] and seven out of the originally eight nearly square external plates [**Plate VI**]. The lower, undecorated bowl of the cauldron beaten out of a single sheet of silver with an added central medallion [**214**] bears the marks of differential oxidisation due to the manner in which the various component parts had been stacked – the small silver clips visible in the rim of the reassembled cauldron are modern; it has recently been suggested that the cauldron may in fact have been mocked up from pieces originally forming part of a shrine or box.

Since its first publication in 1892, it has been recognised that at least three different hands were responsible for decorating the main parts of the cauldron. The decoration was hammered up from the undersurface of each separate plate and then chased on the outer surface; both the inner circular plate [**214**] and the outer plates with their male and female torc-wearing busts [**Plate VI**] were originally covered with thin gold foil pressed

into the silver. The outer deities in certain cases still retain their red or blue glass inset eyes.

The range of exotic and almost heraldic animals – lions, griffons, elephants, panthers, eagles, a seahorse, a barbarian Hercules and his Nemean lion, and even a boy on a dolphin – can be explained as later borrowings from that Graeco-Etruscan or Hellenistic pool of motifs whose contributions to '*situla*' art [**24, 26**], to the early art of La Tène [**62, 64, 84**], and to Celtic coinage [**194e**] have already been noted. Such motifs also had their contribution to make to later Germanic animal art.[1] Other details indicate more basically Celtic or at least barbarian European cults and material equipment: the bull, stag, and boar, the stag-headed torc-holding god himself [**209b**] on the inner plates together with the typical Late La Tène equipment of the soldiers in the procession scene [**209c**] which offers the best dating evidence for the manufacture of the cauldron. On one outer plate, 'b', there even seems to be an animated version of a Late La Tène fire-dog [see notes to **278–279**]. On another plate a man grips a spoked wheel which, together with the isolated wheels on the inner plate with elephant figure, recalls those miniature wheels construed by some as latter-day sun symbols[2] and which have been found on several central European *oppida* sites as well as in Britain [see notes to **224**] and in one of the Regöly hoards [see **208**]; the Gundestrup wheel shares with Dejbjerg an allocation of fourteen spokes.

It is the details of the decorative technique which offer the best stylistic evidence for an eastern origin for Gundestrup – a view first put forward as long ago as 1915 and shared by the present writer. The use of ivy-leaf 'fill-ins', the punch dotted backgrounds, and the treatment of clothing and pelts of animals all find parallels on undoubted eastern fine metal-work as illustrated in the following pages. The mainly eastern concentration of natural silver supplies is reflected in the general division between native gold and silver coinage [**194**], although it was the northern-originating Cimbri whose gift to Augustus of their most sacred silver cauldron was recorded by Strabo,[3] and it would not be unreasonable to regard Gundestrup as a trophy of the northern tribes' southward forays in the late second century. The possible stylistic connection of Gundestrup with native coinage[4] and particularly that of east Celtic mints at Bratislava in Slovakia [**217a–b**] is strengthened by other classical accounts such as Athenaeus' account of the Scordistae of the middle Danube who prized silver above gold; and Scipio's victory over the Boii in 191 BC produced cauldrons as well as a great mass of silver by way of booty.[5]

The importance of ritual deposits in water or marshy areas has already been discussed in connection with the type site of La Tène [**179**]; to the treasure of the Boii may be added the discovery in 1893 at Tayac in southern France of some 400 gold coins and three torcs as well as the account of the treasure of the Volcae-Tectosages plundered by the Romans in 106 BC from a sacred grove at Tolosa, ancient Toulouse.[6] The importance of the cauldron in ancient European belief – perhaps first developed with the expansion of sheet metal working at the end of the Late Bronze Age – can be seen from other objects illustrated in these pages [**162, 222**], while there is also on Gundestrup itself the great figure at the left-hand end of the inner procession plate [**209a, c**] in the process of immersing a soldier in or removing him from a cauldron. The scene is much disputed but it is possible

131

that here is either a central or an east European version of the Celtic war-god Mars Teutates or the insular 'Dagda', the good god with his cauldron of plenty and immortality giving life again to a warrior slain on the field of battle.[7]

S. Müller, 'Det store sølvkar fra Gundestrup i Jylland', *Nordiske Fortidsminder* I (1892), 33–68 and Pls. VI–XIV; F. Drexel, *Jahrb. des Deutsch. Arch. Inst.* XXX (1915), 1–96; W. A. von Jenny, *Keltische Metallarbeiten* (1935), Taf. 20–27:1; H. Arbman, *Thor* I (1948), 109–16; O. Klindt-Jensen, *Acta Arch.* XX (1949), 119–59; P. Reinecke, *Praehist. Zeitschr.* 34–35 (1949–50), 361–72; H. Norling-Christensen, *Aarbøger f. Nordiske Oldk. og Hist.* (1954), 77–100; J. Gricourt, *Latomus* XIII (1954), 376–83; *WK*, Taf. 95–97; *KvsE*, 245, 322; *Celts* 154, 167–68; Klindt-Jensen, *Antiquity* XXXIII (1959), 161–69; id., *Analecta Romana Inst. Danici* I (1960), 45–66; J. Brønsted, *Danmarks Oltid* III (2 ed., 1960), 75–83 and ill.; Norling-Christensen in (ed.) H. Reykers, *Analecta Archaeologica: Festschr. Fritz Fremersdorf* (1960), 247 ff.; Klindt-Jensen, *Gundestrupkedelen* (1961); *CCH*, 92, 170, 176, Pls. XXIV–XXV; W. Holmqvist in *Atti del VI° Congr. Intern. delle Sci. Preist. e Protostoriche* I (1962), 337–49; R. Grosse, *Die Silberkessel von Gundestrup – ein Rätsel keltischer Kunst* (1963); S. Piggott, *Ancient Europe* (1965), 226 and Pl. XXXIX; *PreA*, 228 and ill. 230; *PCB*, 136 ff., 303 ff.; *PAE*, 253 ff. and Pls. 282–84; E. Nylén, *Tor* XII (1967–68), 133–73; H. R. Ellis-Davidson, *Pagan Scandinavia* (1967), 75 ff.; *EV*, 206, 225 and ill.; P. V. Glob, *The bog people* (1968), 171 ff. and ill. 65–70

[1] N. Fettich, *Acta Arch.* I (1930), 221–62
[2] *Manuel* IV, 804 f. and fig. 561–62; *KvsE*, Tab. CXXVII; 26, 28, 30; J. Břeň in *Epitymbion Roman Haken* (1958), 55–60
[3] Strabo IV, 2, 1
[4] C.-A. Moberg, *Några synpunkter* (1952), 362–71
[5] Scordistae: S. Piggott, *The Druids* (1968), 221; Boii: Livy, *Histories* XXXVI, 40
[6] Tayac: *KvsE*, 247–48; Tolosa: Strabo, IV, 1, 13
[7] W. Kimmig, *FbS* 17 (1965), 135 ff.

209b Gundestrup, Aars. Silver-gilt cauldron, detail of inner plate 'A'. Ht. of seated figure 16·5 cm. Late II/early I BC. National Mus., Copenhagen.

Attempts have often been made to identify several of the figures on the Gundestrup cauldron with individuals from the shadowy Celtic pantheon, a pantheon which can be reconstructed only with difficulty from our later source material. The goddess figures of the outer plate with their mortal victims, torcs, and bare breasts perhaps represent the eastern equivalents of the Teutonic Nerthus or 'Terra Mater' figure; the god with a helmeted attendant clutching a wheel, reminds one of Gallo-Roman or even provincial British representations of Jupiter Taranis.[1] Of these supposed deities the figure for whom most parallels have been cited is the cross-legged antlered god holding one twisted, buffer-terminalled torc in his hand and wearing another; these torcs are of the same type represented round the neck of the famous statue of the Dying Gaul in the Capitoline Museum[2] or, elsewhere in this book, in the Snettisham hoards [291]. The god is usually identified with 'Cernunnos' ('the horned one'), a type well-known from a number of

Gallo-Roman statues concentrated in central France. Antler-headed figures also appear in Britain where their distribution, mainly in the southern Belgic area, suggests a continental origin. It should be pointed out, though, that the use of the name of Cernunnos itself is based on a single inscription of the time of Tiberius found on an altar below Notre-Dame in Paris.[3] The Gundestrup figure with its animal attendants, stag, boar (top right) and, clutched firmly in the left hand, ram-headed serpent, is perhaps no more than a European Iron Age 'Lord of the animals', a figure first seen on the early 'Ticino' girdle-plaques [95–99]. Such figures in Gallo-Roman times were associated with local versions of Jupiter, Mars, or Mercury with an ambivalence of approach to the precise nature of their gods that was typical of the Celts.

The squatting posture of the antler god, to be seen certainly in later Gaulish sculpture and metal-work [212, 232] seems to be typical of the Celts, a practical posture for outside assemblies and one first encountered on the Waldalgesheim twin ?chariot mounts [118]; the holding of the torc as well as the general appearance of the figure has been already commented on in connection with coins from the Somme [194e]. The ram's-headed serpent is the subject of late Ha C bronze rings, while in the later Celtic world it is both a symbol of death and fertility and associated both with Mercury and Mars; a bracelet in this form comes from a late chariot burial at Snailwell in Cambridgeshire.[4] The stag is certainly not unimportant in Late La Tène Gaul although almost absent on coinage; it occurs in association with warriors and the hunt as early as the Strettweg ritual waggon [38]. On outer plate 'd' of the Gundestrup cauldron a bearded god holds up a pair of stags by the hind legs [**Plate VI**].[5] The boar, most ubiquitous of all Celtic cult animals [see also **223** ff.] is found from the north of England to Bulgaria.[6] It appears again as a warrior's crest ornament on the Gundestrup procession plate [**209c**]; pig bones are found in early as well as late Celtic burials and, where local skills were not available to make the necessary figures, the more than life-size products of neighbouring peoples were used [see notes to **170**].

Phyllis P. Bober, *Am. J. Arch.* LV (1955), 13–51; O. Klindt-Jensen, *Gundestrupkedelen* (1961), 10 ff., fig. 5; *PCB*, 127 ff., 136, 338 ff. and Pl. 42

[1] Klindt-Jensen, *op. cit.*, 12–13; *PCB*, 136, 196
[2] *WK*, Taf. 1; *Celts*, Pl. 3
[3] E. Thevenot, *Div. et sanct. de la Gaule* (1968), 144–49
[4] *PCB*, 344 ff.; F. Maier, FbS 16 (1962), 39 ff.; Snailwell: *PP*, 81, 111 ff. and Pl. 53b
[5] *PCB*, 333 ff.
[6] *PCB*, 308 ff.

209c Gundestrup, Aars. Silver-gilt cauldron, detail of inner plate 'E'. Ht. 25 cm. Late II/early I BC. National Mus. Copenhagen.

This detail comes from the centre of the rectangular inner plate clearly visible in the general view of the reassembled cauldron on the opposite page [**209a**]. The main figure of the scene, the god with his cauldron, has already been discussed and to the interpretations of the scene offered above may only be added the comments of a scholiast on Lucan writing on the custom of barbarians offering sacrifices to Mars Teutates on a ritual shaft. However, rather than consider the rope-like shaft or tree placed above the spears of the foot soldiers on the lower register as some cult object, it may be no more than a device to indicate a ground-line. The 'ivy leaves' or lotus buds sprouting from this 'ground-line' have their closest parallel on greaves from a fifth- or fourth-century tomb at Vratsa in Bulgaria; the greaves are inscribed with the same name 'Kotyos' as appears on the Agighiol finds.[1]

The spurs of the horse riders and the circular shield bosses of the infantry on the other hand indicate clearly a Celtic Late La Tène context or not before c. 100 BC. Most of the soldiers have ridged caps similar to a helmet from Lauterach in the Voralberg in Upper Austria.[2] The helmets with boar and bird crests look like the Negau type as depicted on the La Tène C–D fibulae illustrated overleaf [201] while the *phalerae* or discs on the horses' bridles remind one of the Manerbio silver mounts [204–205]; all the soldiers as well as the god and his 'victim' wear the short trousers or *braccae* of the Celts, a fashion which seems to have died out in western Europe with the coming of the Romans.[3] The ram-headed serpent makes another appearance here but the most striking feature in this detail of Gundestrup is the great vertical war-trumpets with bells decorated in the form of – once again – boars' heads. These are the *carnyx* of later Greek writers' descriptions of the second-century Galatians in battle [see notes to 170] and representations appear not only amongst the trophies carved at Pergamon but also on the triumphal arch at Orange probably erected during the reign of Tiberius. Depictions of the *carnyx* appear on both continental and insular Celtic coinage [306c] and an actual boar's head bell has survived from Scotland [272]; other fragments, probably once parts of such war-trumpets, come from south Germany and Romania.[4]

KvsE, 322 and obr. 92; *Celts*, fig. 33; O. Klindt-Jensen, *Gundestrupkedelen* (1961), 31, front cover and figs. 10–11, 34; W. Kimmig, *FbS* 17 (1965), 135–43

[1] I. Venedikov, *Arkheologia* (Sofia) VIII (1966), 17 ff.; E. Nylén, *Tor* XII (1967–68), 152 and fig. 7
[2] O. Menghin, *Österr. Kunsttopographie* 27 (1937), 17= no. 27
[3] J. P. Wild, *Bonner Jahrb.* 168 (1968), 181 ff., 230 ff.
[4] S. Piggott, *Antiq. J.* XXXIX (1959), 19–22 and Pl. VIIb; F. Fischer, 'Der spätlatènezeitl. Depot-Fund von Kappel', *Urkunden zur Vor- u. Frühg. aus Südwürtt.-Hohenzollern* I (1959), 21–22; J. V. S. Megaw in (ed.) J. M. Coles and D. D. A. Simpson, *Studies in Ancient Europe* (1968), 349–50

Plate VI Gundestrup, Aars. Silver-gilt cauldron. Detail showing outer plate 'd'. Total ht. c. 21 cm. I BC. National Mus. Copenhagen. *Archaeologie Bild Berlin.*

This outer plate shows clearly the remains of the gilding which originally covered all the decorated parts of the cauldron. The full beard and its outward curling ends follow the style not only of early prototypes like the Italic satyrs or presumed early pieces like the 'Tarasque' of Noves [76], but also of later provincial Roman forms. The stag, seen as a companion of a god on the inner plate [209b] is here a sacrificial victim. The eye insets are missing.

O. Klindt-Jensen, *Gundestrupkedelen* (1961), 23 and fig. 19

210 Boughton Aluph, near Ashford, Kent. Bronze ?bucket mount with traces of enamel. Ht. 16·2 cm. ?I BC/IAD. Maidstone Mus. *Ivor Morgan* (*courtesy Kent Arch. Soc.*).

This mount, with traces of red enamel still surviving in the ridged hair line, was ploughed up in 1957, and represents one of the examples of the horned god in the southern British Belgic area. In its general form it somewhat resembles the Aylesford bucket handle mounts [187] but is closer not only to the outer faces of Gundestrup but also to later continental objects, especially with regard to the eyes with provision again for insets [222, 239–240]. The notched eyes and dot-punched surface of the Boughton Aluph bronze recall much earlier continental pieces [48], while looking forward to pieces certainly contemporary with the beginnings of Roman rule in Britain [264]. The 'neck' of the Boughton Aluph head ends in a ram's-head and may be another association of the horned god and the ram's-head serpent.

Horned god bronze mounts continue into the Roman period; a ?bucket mount with knobbed horns [see notes to 274] comes from the Roman fort of Richborough on the Kentish coast.[1]

Elizabeth J. E. Pirie, *Arch. Cantiana* LXXII (1958), 212–14 and Pl. II; F. Jenkins, *Men of Kent before the Romans=Kent Arch. Soc. Occ. Paper* 3 (1962), 18 and Pl. V; *PRB*, Pl. 316; S. Piggott, *The Druids* (1968), Pl. 11

[1] J. P. Bushe-Fox, *Richborough III=Soc. Antiq. London Res. Rep.* X (1932), 79 and Pl. X:17

211 Ciumeşti, Maramureş. Iron helmet with bronze crest (beak and eye restored). Ht. 25 cm. III–II BC. Muz. regional, Baia Mare. *Institutul de Istorie şi Arheologie, Cluj.*

This helmet – of the same type as that depicted on the Pergamon reliefs and named after the Batina find with decorated scabbard [see notes to 180] – was discovered in 1961 as part of a disturbed warrior's grave on the edge of a La Tène cemetery. The cemetery included metal-finds of the LT Ic–II phases with cremations associated with local pottery. Other objects from the disturbed grave were a socketed spear, the remains of a chain-mail coat decorated with a bronze button with cast ornament closely paralleled by a bracelet from Montsaugeon, Haute Marne;[1] chain-mail may possibly be represented on the Gundestrup silver cauldron and certainly seems to be represented by one of the cross-legged figures from the sanctuary at Entremont[2] which match those from Roquepertuse [212]. A pair of Hellenistic greaves were also found in the helmet grave and it is probably from a Hellenistic source that the local and possibly non-Celtic craftsman got his inspiration for the bronze bird of prey with its movable wings which forms the fearsome crest of the helmet. Gundestrup also provides a good parallel to the bird helmet in that worn by the leading horseman on inner plate 'E' [209c] while two other birds with curved beaks and outstretched wings – ?eagles – hover either side of the 'goddess' on outer plate 'f'.[3] The Celtic chieftain of Ciumeşti, with eagle-crested helmet, chain-mail, casting spear like that of the Gundestrup horsemen, and greaves – the greaves the prize of some foray into the southern Balkans – could have belonged to one of those Celtic tribal groups whose ultimate eastern journeyings brought them to Asia Minor. It is this amalgamation of Celt and non-Celt in eastern Europe in the Middle La Tène period which laid the foundations for the eclectic art which gave rise to the style represented by the Gundestrup cauldron.

D. Berciu, *Romania before Burebista* (1967), 152 ff. and Pl. 73; *id., Inst. Arch. Univ. London Bull.* 6 (1966), 87 and fig. 3; Vl. Zirra, *Un cimitir Celtic în Nord-vestul României* (1967), 115 and Pl. XII; R. M. Rowlett, *Science* 161 (1968), 129 and fig. 7; C. Daicoviciu, *Archéologia* 28 (1969), ill. p. 61 above

[1] *ECA*, no. 250; see also notes to [175]
[2] O. Klindt-Jensen, *Gundestrupkedelen* (1961), 28 and fig. 29
[3] Klindt-Jensen, *op. cit.*, fig. 22

212 Roquepertuse, Velaux, Bouches-du-Rhône. Limestone statue. Ht. 1·05 m. ?IV–II BC. Mus. d'Archéologie, Château Borély, Marseilles. *Franceschi-Zodiaque.*

By the fourth century BC, La Tène Celts had penetrated to the Ligurian seaboard and the future Gallia Graeca as evidenced by such pieces as a typical early 'Ticino' class of belt-plaque from Ensérune [see notes to **95 ff.**]. As a result, there evolved a mixture of Italo-Greek style and Celtic iconography combined with some of the monumentality of classical architectural sculpture. The *oppidum* site of Roquepertuse had its own sanctuary with three stone pillars and a lintel with a row of low-relief horses' heads [**236**]. A number of niches in the pillars were once set with human skulls, all male and none over 40 years of age, recalling Livy's description of how the Boii sacrificed prisoners taken in the prime of life; also over the portico was a bird of prey and a Janus head [**235**].[1] In front of the portico were five figures, all once coloured. Shown here is one of two cross-legged figures, both apparently wearing breastplates in the manner of the Balzers figurine [**202**]. The right hand of each figure once held iron sceptres, or symbols of thunder proper to Mars Taranis, while the other outstretched hand may have held severed heads in the manner of the 'Tarasque' of Noves, or the similar cross-legged figures and associated fragments from Entremont.[2] Entremont, with its own sanctuary, was destroyed by the Romans in 124 BC, which gives at least a lower limit for the date of the Celto-Ligurian sculpture.

The cross-legged posture has already been commented on in connection with the Gundestrup 'Cernunnos'; it certainly need not be considered to show any oriental or orientalising influence. The incised step patterns and swastikas on the base of the Roquepertuse figure and the simple chequer pattern on its back belong to the old geometric – and certainly ultimately Graeco-Italian – element in early La Tène art [see **30**].

Espérandieu I (1907), no. 131; *ECA*, no. 4A; F. Benoit, *L'art primitif méditerranéen de la vallée du Rhone = Publ. des Ann. de la Faculté des Lettres Aix-en-Provence* 9 (1955), 42 ff., fig. 10 and Pl. XXXVI–XXXVII, XXXVIII:2, XXXIX:1, LVII:4; *ArtG*, 96, Pls. 21–23; *WK*, Taf. 54; M. Pobé and J. Roubier, *Art of Roman Gaul* (1961), Pls. 35–36; *CCH*, 155 and fig. 36; *PCB*, 65 ff.; *PAE*, 249 and Pl. 271; *EV*, 242 and ill.

[1] *ECA*, no. 1; Benoit, *op. cit.*, Pl. XXVII (=reconstruction)

[2] Benoit, *op. cit.*, 49 ff., figs. 11–12 and Pls. LV–LIX; see also notes to [76]

213 Hradiště, Stradonice, okr. Beroun. Bronze figurine. Ht. 4·5 cm. LT D1, I BC. Národní Muz., Prague.

The great *oppidum* of Stradonice is probably the best known of the central European tribal centres and was the first to attract the attention of western European scholars through the translation in 1906 of Jaroslav Píč's study made by France's greatest archaeological synthesiser, Joseph Déchelette.

The site, which Píč regarded as Marobudum, capital of the Teutonic Marcomani who overran the Bohemian lands in the last years of the first century BC, was discovered accidentally when in 1877 a hoard of some 200 gold coins was uncovered. The subsequent plundering of the area by enthusiastic amateur archaeologists did untold damage to the site which seems in fact to have had its heyday as a Celtic capital in the early first century BC with connections with such western *oppida* as Manching [see notes to **189**] and was probably destroyed – by Teutonic invaders – around 9 BC.

The little figure illustrated here is that of a ritually naked, and indeed ithyphallic, La Tène warrior brandishing his war-trumpet – not always recognised for what it is – a suitable talisman for a central European Celt and who may be compared with the contemporary dress-uniform trumpeters on the Gundestrup cauldron [**209a** and **c**].

J. Píč, 'Hradiště u Stradonic jako historické Marobudum', *Starožitnosti Země České* II:2 (1903), Tab. XX:33; *Manuel* IV, 686; W. and B. Forman and J. Poulík, *Prehistoric Art* (n.d.), 35 and ill. 138; *KvsE*, Tab. CXXV:7; A. Buchner, *Musical instruments through the ages* (n.d.), Pl. 15; E. and J. Neustupný, *Czechoslovakia before the Slavs* (1961), fig. 48; *CCH*, 178 and Pl. XXXV centre; J. V. S. Megaw in (ed.) J. M. Coles and D. D. A. Simpson, *Studies in Ancient Europe* (1968), 349–50 and Pl. XVIc; *EV*, 190 and ill.

214 Gundestrup, Aars. Silver-gilt basal disc from cauldron. D. 25·6 cm. Late II/early I BC. National Mus., Copenhagen.

The disc on the bottom of the Gundestrup cauldron [**209a**] is in many ways the most artistically satisfying of all the separate components of this most striking import in the prehistory of Denmark. It is also the piece around which most of the arguments concerning Gundestrup's eastern origin have revolved. Now, though only traces of its gilding survive – a technique generally absent in the Celtic West – and despite its lacking the horns which once would have been attached to the massive bull, the plate still has an awesome quality. The three hunting dogs, the upper one a fierce cousin of the Wallerheim 'terrier' [**Plate Va**], and the dismounted huntsman, spurs on shoes and longsword in hand, surround the massive bull, who may have been intended to be shown turning at bay and pawing the ground, the oddly twisted limbs being due to faulty perspective and to the artist's inability to place his composition fully within a circular border. Alternatively, the great Mithraic-looking bull may be in his last death throes and as such his stance is very close to later coinage of Massilia and the Black Sea as well as to native bronze coinage based on issues of Augustus.[1]

Close too and even more clearly based on coinage prototypes, is the bull on one of a number of small silver *phalerae* known only from a series of drawings recently discovered in the possession of the Society of Antiquaries of London.[2] These discs were found on the Island of Sark in the Channel Islands in 1718. The hoard of which they formed a part contained the following objects: (1) an urn typical of the later Iron Age pottery of north-western France but bound with an iron ring; this contained (2) 18 coins, 1 Roman republican *denarius* of c. 80 BC and the balance inscribed silver coinage of central and north Gaul, some as found on the site of Alesia [destroyed in 52 BC; see notes to **Plate IVe**], the latest dating to about 30–20 BC, (3) a saddle- or 'U' sectioned silver object with the *repoussé* representation of dolphins, (4) 2 large and 11 small silver *phalerae*, the larger examples clearly related to the type represented on this page by the Helden disc [215], the smaller discs having their decoration restricted to single figures, griffons, a unicorn, an elephant-and-castle reminding one of the elephants of Gundestrup but clearly closer to an actual model; the number of Sark discs is almost precisely that of the Manerbio find [204–205].

The style of the Sark *phalerae* will be briefly noted again below; to return to the Gundestrup disc, the 'ivy-leaf' background tends to relate this piece rather to earlier Dacian material than to the discs of the Helden-Sark type. The dogs certainly have more than an element of nomadic iconography and hark back to the hunting dogs or wolves of the Basse-Yutz handles [60–61]. One detail: in the centre of the forehead of the great bull is a curl executed as a triskel or 'yin-yang'.

As to the significance of the scene on the Gundestrup plate, a link with the Persian-originating Mithraic sacrifice of the bull has already been hinted at. On the other hand, such a sacrifice seems at variance with what can be deduced from archaeological material of the use of the bull as a symbol of virility and prowess in battle; perhaps in view of the many sources behind the iconography of Gundestrup – whatever its actual place of origin – one should not seek any too precise a cultic explanation.

J. Brønsted, *Danmarks Oltid* III (2 ed. 1960), colour pl. opp. p. 80; O. Klindt-Jensen, *Gundestrupkedelen* (1961) 38 ff. and fig. 15; *PAE*, 256 and Pl. 282; E. Nylén, *Tor* XII (1967–68), 124 and fig. 6

[1] Klindt-Jensen, *Acta Arch.* XX (1949), 142 ff.
[2] *Current Archaeology* 8 (1968), 205–07; D. F. Allen, *Numis. Chron.* VIII (1968), 37–54, here esp. 47 and fig. 5

215 Helden, Roermond. Silver disc. D. 17·5 cm. ?Late I BC. Rijksmus. van Oudheden, Leiden.

The stray find of a silver disc from Helden in the southern Dutch province of Limburg is, together with the 'new' Sark finds, the most westerly of some 15 locations of what are probably the latest in a series of harness mounts which begin with Hallstatt and the Hořovičky discs [30, 47] and run through to the Manerbio find [204–205]. The best dated of these discs, whose main concentration is around the Black Sea and whose westerly scatter may have been due to the movement of

Sarmatian and Thracian horsemen, especially those in the service of Rome, is one from the Roman fort of Oberaden, Westphalia, on the *limes* or frontier fortifications near Augsburg. Oberaden was deserted in 9 BC and thus the as yet little-known Oberaden disc is probably somewhat earlier than two discs from the Black Sea now in the Cabinet des Médailles of the Bibliothèque Nationale, Paris.[1] These are not identical, though both have a circular design of wild and mythical beasts like those which circle the Helden disc. The incomplete example of the Paris pair has a central elephant's head, positioned, like some hunter's trophy, in the centre of the disc. The complete disc has as its 'trophy' a single bull's head with 'Celtic' almond eyes like that on the lower margin of the Helden disc. The same Paris disc has a Greek inscription, a dedication by Mithridates VI Eupator (120–63 BC) to the shrine of the goddess Artemis, a dedication which reminds one of Appian's description of the Roman discovery of *phalerae* in an abandoned treasure at Talauri in Asia Minor.[2] Such a gift seems suitable in view of the 'sacred hunt' nature of the surviving *phalerae*; on the inscribed Paris disc a boar attacks a hind while around circle winged griffons and a Pegasus figure. The central group of figures on the Helden disc shows a barbarian Hercules struggling with a lion, like that on outer plate 'g' of the Gundestrup cauldron.[3] A similar but more classicising version of the same scene forms the centre piece of another disc found with two others, chain mail, a sword scabbard and late Hellenistic material in a tomb in 1965 at Stara Zagora in Bulgaria, the burial having been that of a warrior and his horse; a cruder plaque of about the third century comes from Letnitsa, also in Bulgaria.[4] Details of ornament link Helden to the other discs mentioned above; the dot background (instead of the leaves of Gundestrup although the treatment of pelts and clothing is similar to that on the cauldron figures), and the undulating border motif were produced by alternate blows of the punch either side of a median line. A group of Thracian shield mounts also demonstrates the continuity of classical influences in later native art in the Balkans.[5]

W. A. von Jenny, *Keltische Metallarbeiten* (1935), Taf. 28:1; O. Klindt-Jensen, *Aarbøger f. Nordiske Oldk. og Hist.* (1952), 209–11; S. J. De Laet, *The Low Countries* (1958), 161 and Pl. 57; *id.* and W. Glasbergen, *De voorgeschiedenis der Lage Landen* (1959), 184 and Pl. 43 above; Klindt-Jensen, *Gundestrupkedelen* (1961), 37–42 esp. fig. 59; E. Nylén, *Tor* XII (1967–68), 141 ff. and fig. 4a

[1] Klindt-Jensen, *Gundestrupkedelen*, figs. 56, 58; *EV*, 187 and ill.
[2] Appian, *De bello Mithrad.*, 115
[3] Klindt-Jensen, *op. cit.*, figs. 24 and 53
[4] I. Venedikov, *Stara Zagora: Art Ancien* (1965), 28–30, 33–35; Letnitsa: *id.*, *Bulgaria's treasures from the past* (1965), 17 ff. and ill.
[5] Ljuba Ognenova, in *Acta Antiqua Philippopolitana: Studia Archaeologica* (1963), 27–34

216 Trichtingen, Kr. Rottweil. Silver torc with iron core. Total d. 29·5 cm., l. of bulls' heads c. 6 cm. ?II BC. Württ. Landesmus., Stuttgart.

This great silver torc from Württemberg weighs over

6 kilogrammes and has been frequently associated with the eastern art of Gundestrup and the silver *phalerae*. The heads have a degree of realism unmatched by western Celtic representations of bulls' heads [160–162], although the large soulful eyes have a Celtic look and the twisted buffer terminalled torcs which each bull wears follow the form of several on the Gundestrup cauldron [209b]. The wavy ornamental backbone produced by alternate blows of the punch is similar to that around the edge of the Helden disc [215] whose bull's head with horizontally placed short horns is also a point of comparison. The zigzag pattern on the Trichtingen torc below the wavy mid-rib is compared by Jacobsthal to a late helmet from the river Neckar[1] but a not dissimilar patterned headband can be seen on the 'goddess' on outer plate 'f' of the Gundestrup cauldron, the plate with the hovering eagles [see notes to 211].

The concept of animal-headed torcs is not basically Celtic and an ultimate source may be found in Achaemenid art; a series of torcs from Hungary compared by Goessler to Trichtingen might be considered suitable intermediaries and the presence of Achaemenid influence in eastern Europe from the time of the Graeco-Persian wars of the fifth century is a point to bear in mind. All in all, a source for Trichtingen somewhere in the eastern culture contact zone of the Celtic world seems probable, though dating must rely on such details as the bull's own torcs, the type worn certainly by later central and eastern Celts, to judge from Mšecké Žehrovice [171] or the figure of the 'Dying Gaul'.[2]

P. Goessler, *IPEK* 5 (1929), 46–52; *id., Der Silberring von Trichtingen* (1929); F. J. Keller, *Germania* 16 (1932), 193–6; W. A. von Jenny, *Keltische Metallarbeiten* (1935), Taf. 19; *ECA*, P 162; *Celts*, Pls. 35–36; *WK*, Taf. 22 above; *VRD*, ill. 131; J. V. S. Megaw, *Antiq. J.* XLVII (1967), 211–12; *EV*, 197 and ill.

[1] *ECA*, P 161; *WK*, Taf. 42 below
[2] *Celts*, Pl. 3; *WK*, Taf. 1

217a Bratislava, Slovakia. Silver coin, reverse, D. c. 2·5 cm. c. 70–60 BC. Slovenské Národné Múz., Bratislava.

Bratislava in the first century BC was the site of a local Celtic *oppidum* and mint of the Boii whose territory at that period extended also into Pannonia where they remained until the invasion of the region by the Dacians under Burebista. The coinage of the Bratislava region, two examples of which are illustrated here, with the unusually heavy weight of c. 17 grammes, follows a long series of gold coins and comes as a sudden and short-lived phenomenon in the area. The inscriptions in Latin characters, presumably of local chieftains' names, are the first recorded for the region; as a whole the coins show strong influence from Roman issues. The present example has, reversed, the name 'Nonnos' while the most common name is 'Biatec' by which the whole group is now known. Coins of this type also occur in the Vienna area and the burial of hoards of 'Biatec' coins in south-west Slovakia may be a result of the wars between the Boii and the Dacians around 60 BC. The winged griffon shows the currency in the region of the mythical menagerie drawn upon by the artists of Gundestrup and of the silver *phalerae* and has been offered as one argument for the location of the craftsmen responsible for Gundestrup having been near this region.

R. Paulsen, *Die ostkeltischen Münzprägungen* (1933), no. 830; *KvsE*, 234 ff.; V. Ondrouch, *Keltské mince typu Biatec z Bratislavy* (1958), esp. Tab. 23:3

217b Bratislava, Slovakia. Silver coin, reverse. D. c. 2·9 cm. c. 70–60 BC. Slovenské Národné Múz., Bratislava.

This rare specimen (one of three) of a coin of the 'Biatec' type has the inscription 'Maccius', and, set against a dotted background in the manner of the silver *phalerae* [215], a wild beast from whose mouth dangles the hind quarters of his prey. The devouring beast first appears in Iron Age iconography in the 'art of the *situlae*' [24 ff.] and has its most famous example in the 'Tarasque' of Noves [76] but is common on first-century BC coins. It can also be seen in eastern silver work such as the pieces illustrated on this page, silver work whose development chronologically must have run more or less parallel with that of the southerly 'situla' art while drawing on the same classical and orientalising motifs.

KvsE, obr. 70:9; V. Ondrouch, *Keltské mince typu Biatec z Bratislavy* (1958), Tab. 3:2

218 Santon, Norfolk. Bronze disc brooch cover. D. 3·5 cm. Mid-I AD. Univ. Mus. of Archaeology and Ethnology, Cambridge.

This is one of three British brooch discs with heraldic beasts on them from late Iron Age contexts, the other two being from Lancing in Sussex – a stray find in the form of a seahorse [see notes to 194e] – and from Westhall in Suffolk where, like Santon, it is associated with enamel-decorated harness mounts.[1]

The Santon disc is clearly a griffon in the long-established pedigree of such beasts; in Britain griffons can also be found amongst other types on native coins of Cunobelin struck at his capital of Camulodunum (Colchester).[2] The spindly technique of drawing the limbs also follows the general tendency of the Celtic moneyer's art, as seen also on the Aylesford bucket [187].

The brooch cover was found by a labourer in 1897 in a cauldron together with a steel-yard, a two-link bridle bit of the same type as one found on the Polden Hills, Somerset,[3] a pair of enamelled harness mounts [**Plate VIIIa**], various tools and other fittings [299] and brooches of the so-called 'thistle' type common in Gaul during AD 25–50. Though the discovery in a cauldron may make one think of such presumably ritual deposits as the Duchcov find [see notes to 134], the presence of legionary armour suggests that the revolt of the Iceni under Boudica in AD 60 and the consequent effect on local travelling smiths were the reasons for the burial.

R. A. Smith, *Proc. Cambridgeshire Antiq. Soc.* XIII (1909), 146–63, esp. 154 and fig. 7; R. Rainbird Clarke, *Arch. J.* XCVI (1939), 69 ff. and 100; C. Fox, *Archaeology of the Cambridge Region* (reissue 1948), 106 and Pl. XVIII:9; *PP*, 81 and Pl. 37b; Rainbird Clarke, *East Anglia* (1960), 105 and fig. 27; J. M. C. Toynbee, *Art in Britain under the Romans* (1964), 23 and Pl. Ic

[1] E. T. Leeds, *Celtic ornament* (1933), 95 and fig. 30a; Rainbird Clarke, *Arch. J.* XCVI (1939), 65 ff. and fig. 12:1–2; *id., East Anglia*, fig. 28

[2] *PP*, Pl. 79:14; see also [306b]
[3] *PP*, Pl. 72d

219a Babadag, Agighiol, Dobrudja. Silver vase. Ht. c. 28 cm. V/IV BC. Muz. Naţional de Antichităţi, Bucarest. *Institutul de Arheologie, Bucarest.*

The most famous find of what has been termed 'Thraco-Getic' art but which might be given the more meaningful regional title of 'the Istro-Pontic style', and certainly on the evidence the oldest datable, is the treasure from a stone-built chamber tomb excavated near Agighiol in 1931. This tomb, which had been partially plundered before its excavation, with its carefully dressed stone construction and entrance passage or *dromos* recalls the Thracian *tholos* at Mezek [see notes to **170**]; Agighiol had a separate burial enclosure for three horses and their harness. Within the main chamber were two burials, one male and one female, the male having, in addition to various weapons, a pair of silver greaves each decorated with a human face and a serpent design, at least one helmet and the vase here illustrated as well as a crushed second vase; the dating for the burial is given by a number of Greek amphorae and other vessels which apparently included fifth-century Attic red-figure ware. The vase, whose pair, supposedly from the Iron Gates, is described in the following note, has on its base the name 'Kotys' similar to that on the greaves from the contemporary grave at Vratsa in Bulgaria [see notes to **209c**]. The running spiral or wave pattern forming the ground line is common in the Celtic west but it also has a long life in the east where it can be seen on the two-handled silver cups from a second–first century BC hoard at Sîncrăieni near Mureş, the cups incorporating the same ivy-leaves as appear on Gundestrup [**209**].[1] Indeed, the style of the bird of prey with its monstrous talon, of the fish, and of the caprids, the hind quarters of which can be made out on the right of the Agighiol vase, no less than the actual *repoussé* technique of rendering the various textures, strongly recalls the style and technique of Gundestrup. This suggests that the Gundestrup cauldron stands towards the end of the development of an individual eastern style at least as long-lasting as that of La Tène,[2] stretching from perhaps as early as the fifth century to at least the end of the second century BC.

I. Andrieşescu, *Revista de preistorie şi antichităţi naţionale* I:1 (1937), Pls. XIII–XXVII; E. Condurachi in (ed.) P. Demargne, *Le Rayonnement des civilisations grecque et romaine . . . =VIIIᵉ Congrès Intern. d'Arch. Classique* (1965), 323 ff., esp. 324 and Pl. 65; D. Berciu in *Din Istoria Dobrogei* I (1965), 114–19, figs. 27–30; *id.*, *Zorile Istoriei în Carpaţi şi Dunăre* (1966), 281 ff., and Pl. XXIV:2; *id.*, *Neue Forschungsergebnisse zur Vorg. Rumäniens*=*Antiquitas* Reihe 2:4 (1966), 58–59 and Taf. 19a–b; *id.*, *Inst. Arch. Univ. London Bull.* 6 (1966), 75 ff.; *PreA* 226 f. and Pl. 228; Berciu, *Romania before Burebista* (1967), 143–45, and Pls. 60–61; *PAE*, 231; E. Nylén, *Tor* XII (1967–68), 152 and figs. 10–11

[1] O. Popescu, *Dacia* II (1958), 157–206=no. 14; J. V. S. Megaw, *Helinium* I (1961), 236 ff.; *Inventaria Arch.: Roumanie* 3 (1967), R17f–j
[2] Berciu, *Dacia* XI (1967), 331–37

219b ?'Iron Gates.' Silver vase. Ht. c. 28 cm. V/IV BC.

Metropolitan Mus. of Art, New York. (Rogers Fund, 1947.)

This and the helmet illustrated below [**220**], after a recent adventurous life in the sale room, can be identified with objects supposedly dredged up in 1913–14 from the Danube by the Iron Gates. The cup is as near a twin of those definitely from Agighiol [**219a**] as is possible with a hand-made object and the views shown here are therefore complementary to that of the Romanian vase shown on the left. It is clear now that the latter's upper wave-like row of birds' heads grows out of the antlers of what, from the number of legs, must have been meant as not one but a pair of stags while the base is decorated, as Agighiol, with the motif of the devouring beast, a griffon in this case [see also **217b**]. The hoofs of the animals no less than the animals themselves perhaps offer a hint of the sources behind such Early La Tène pieces as Rodenbach and Erstfeld [**55, 84**].

As with the silver helmet, two possibilities arise: either that the 'Iron Gates' material comes from the plundering of the Agighiol grave – though it seems odd that one chieftain should have such a double set – or that it represents the work of the master silversmith responsible for Agighiol and lost on its way to a more westerly customer. An inscription on the base in Greek characters is a meaningless later addition.

M. I. Rostovtsev, *Skythien und der Bosporus* I (1931), 534; V. Griessmaier, *Wiener Beiträge zur Kunst u. Kulturges. Asiens* IX (1935), 49–60; *ECA*, 36 and Pls. 226–27a; B. Goldman, *Bull. Detroit Inst. of Arts* 42 (1963), 67 ff.; S. Piggott, *Ancient Europe* (1965), 226; Goldman, *IPEK* 22 (1966–69), 68 ff. and fig. 4 a–c

220 ?'Iron Gates.' Silver helmet. Total ht. 24 cm., w. of cheek-flap c. 6 cm. V/IV BC. Detroit Institute of Arts.

The silver helmet from the Iron Gates find now in Detroit is clearly by the same hand as the twin vases illustrated above, as can be seen by the combination of fish and bird of prey; on the other flap is a caprid. A stylised ear is moulded either side of the head while on the brow of the domed helmet cap are a pair of staring eyes with great scrolling eyebrows. It is instructive to contrast the scallop design or tongue pattern with that on a more or less contemporary but very different Celtic piece such as the helmet from Umbria [**108**]. The stylisation of the eyes on the 'Iron Gates' helmet cap would, however, be familiar to a La Tène craftsman [e.g. **48**]. The former is a motif borrowed from the classical artist's pattern book, the latter exhibits the apotropaic effect of the human features common in barbarian art.

The helmet from the Agighiol grave[1] is not so similar to the present piece as a quick comparison between the two vases might lead one to expect, though the basic shape and layout are fairly alike; the right-hand cheek-piece here has a warrior on horseback in very Greek dress reminding one that the slightly asymmetrical form of both helmets with deep side-pieces is basically that of the classical Greek helmet.

B. Schröder, *Jahrb. d. Deutsch. Arch. Inst.* 27 (1912), 316–44; B. Goldman, *Bull. Detroit Inst. of Arts* 42 (1963), 63–72; S. Piggott, *Ancient Europe* (1965), 226 and Pl. XLb; E. Nylén, *Tor* XII (1967–68), 152 ff. and fig. 12; Goldman, *IPEK* 22 (1966–69), 67–76, esp. Taf. 43–45

[1] I. Andrieşescu, *Revista de preistorie şi antichităţi naţionale* I:1 (1937), Pl. XIII; D. Berciu, *Din istorie Dobrogei* I (1965), fig. 27; Nylén, *op. cit.*, fig. 11a

221 Coţofăneşti, Poiana–Vărbilău. Gold helmet. Ht. c. 24 cm. ?V/IV BC. Muz. Naţional de Antichităţi, Bucarest. *Institutul de Arheologie, Bucarest.*

This helmet of 20 carat gold weighing some 750 gm., is clearly related in style to those from Agighiol and the Iron Gates. It was discovered unassociated in 1929 but in the general area of an occupation or burial site as indicated by sherds of local grey wheel-made pottery.

The element of sacrifice which seems a key feature in the iconography of this Istro-Pontic art appears here as a warrior sacrificing a caprid. The apotropaic eyes are present, while at the rear of the helmet (in this view only dimly visible from the wrong side as the reverse image of the goldsmith's hammer), are a facing pair of winged griffons with hind quarters protruding from their mouths. Here it is not only the art of the *situla* which is evoked but also the incised 'Alice-through-the-looking-glass' figures of the Stupava plaque [64] – perhaps now to be seen as a local addition to this Rhineland-made piece by its Slovak owner, though stylistically this does not seem very likely. The hooves of the caprid are very similar to those of the 'orientalising' Rodenbach armlet goats [55].

The non-figural decoration of the helmet is more ornate than that of the other pieces on this page, in keeping with the more skilful detailing of the main scenes; for the simple running wave pattern of the vases is substituted a series of again not un-Celtic-looking linked 'S' coils.

PreA, 228 and ill. 229; S. Piggott, *Ancient Europe* (1965), 226 and Pl. XLa; D. Berciu, *Zorile Istoriei în Carpaţi şi Dunăre* (1966), 282–83 and Pl. XXIV, XXXI–XXXII; *id.*, *Romania before Burebista* (1967), 145–46 and Pl. 57; E. Nylén, *Tor* XII (1967–68), 156 and fig. 13

222 Rynkeby, Illemose, Funen. Bronze fragments from cauldron. Total d. c. 70 cm.; [a] 42×19 cm., [b] ht. c. 20 cm. I BC/I AD. National Mus., Copenhagen.

Illustrated here are two of three separate fragments of a cauldron deposited, like Gundestrup [209], in a bog, the third fragment being part of a boar figure associated with an inner plate like [222a]. The construction of the cauldron out of separate sheets of metal is not so much in the tradition of eastern Europe, however, as part of the general tinkering techniques established in north and western Europe in the later Bronze Age. The large domed rivets with twin washers are finely scored on the inner surface to take enamel in the manner of the ornamental nails on the Dejbjerg waggon [203] and their parallels in the central European *oppida*.[1]

On the outside fragment [b] the central face, with its broad planes and staring eyes once set with glass or enamel insets, may be compared with not so much the Gundestrup 'gods' and 'goddesses' as with early Gallo-Roman bronze work [232, 239–240] or the hard-to-date Euffigneix boar god on the opposite page [226] – complete like Rynkeby with buffer-terminal torc. The flanking bulls have their almost comical front legs raised in an attitude otherwise reserved for humans as on not only Gundestrup [Plate VI] but also, much earlier, on the Waldalgesheim 'chariot mount' [118]. Other Danish bull mounts, stray bog finds from Sophienborg, North Zealand, and elsewhere[2] continue the tradition for bull cauldron mounts first established in northern Europe by the imported Brå finds [162]. One should not consider that the long hair of the human face indicates a woman's head; indeed the presence of those powerful male symbols, the bulls, argues the opposite.

The rectangular inner sheet [a], once fastened by rivets to the inside curve of the main cauldron, could well be by a different hand in the way in which the varying components of Gundestrup may also be claimed to have been made by several craftsmen. The central feature of this Rynkeby plaque is a triskel or yin-yang. No less than the antithetical wild beast supporters, it recalls the less assured work of the upper band on the Aylesford bucket [187] and it is the inside plate of Rynkeby as much as the outer faces which suggests the affinity of the Danish find with the putative central Gaulish 'school' of Aylesford-Marlborough-Levroux.[3] As to identification of the animals, that on the left is clearly a boar; for the right-hand figure a wolf has been proposed, though a hunting dog or, perhaps even more likely, a second boar in the emaciated drawn-out manner of the original Witham, Lincolnshire, shield mount [252][4] are equal possibilities. Although comparisons with coinage in the present state of our ignorance about other late pre-Roman metal-work in Gaul are made rather on the principle of an iconographic lucky dip, the triskel[5] is not the only feature of Rynkeby which may be cited on north Gaulish coins; the flower fronds are similar to the vines on coins of the Aulerci Eburovices of Normandy and of the Arverni.[6]

H. Petersen, *Vognfundene i Dejbjerg Præstegardsmose* (1882), 38; S. Müller, 'Det store sølvkar fra Gundestrup i Jylland', *Nordiske Fortidsminder* I:2 (1892), 59 and fig. 123; H. Arbman, *Tor* I (1948), 109 ff.; O. Klindt-Jensen, *Acta Arch.* XX (1949), 109–19, figs. 68 a–b; J. Brønsted, *Danmarks Oltid* (2 ed. 1960), 83–84; W. Holmqvist in *Atti del VI° Congr. Intern. delle Sci. Preist. e Protostoriche* I (1962), 349–51; *PreA*, 223–25 and ill. 223; H. R. Ellis-Davidson, *Pagan Scandinavia* (1967), 76; *PAE*, 252 ff., and Pls. 281, 285

[1] E. Nylén, *Tor* XII (1967–68), 133 ff.
[2] Klindt-Jensen, *op. cit.*, 112 f. and figs. 69, 70a–c; Ellis-Davidson, *op. cit.*, Pl. 35
[3] J. V. S. Megaw, *Gallia* XXVI (1968), 37 ff., esp. fig. 4
[4] *PP*, Pl. 15a
[5] J. A. Blanchet, *Traité des monnaies gauloises* II (1905), fig. 230 (Lexovii)
[6] Blanchet, *op. cit.*, fig. 20 (Aulerci); figs. 459–60 (Arverni)

223 Kraghede, cremation grave A and pit 1, Hjøring. Detail of incised pot. Total ht. c. 20 cm., l. of left-hand animal c. 6 cm. ?I BC. National Mus., Copenhagen.

In 1905 on the site of a combined cemetery and settlement, a pair of pits were discovered beside a grave. The grave contained human remains as well as joints of meat

Fig. 11 [223] Kraghede, Denmark, grave A–1. Expanded view of decoration on pot. Scale c. 1:6
After Müller

and some pottery and toilet objects. The pits contained the bones of at least two horses, and a pair of pigs or sheep as well as the fire-damaged fittings for a four-wheeled waggon, a situation paralleled by the Dejbjerg deposit [see 203]. This detail comes from the punched-dot frieze decorating the middle of a squat, round-bellied, single-handled hand-made pot. The complete scene, as far as it can now be reconstructed, begins with the detail shown here, a boar or perhaps hunting dog attacking a backward-looking deer, a galloping ox, a horseman with spear, and a second pair of deer and dog. This amateurishly executed scene incorporates so many figures of the ancient ritual hunt or procession which in pottery we have noted on the Hallstatt Sopron urns and the La Tène Matzhausen flask [10, 27] and earlier in metal-work on the 'art of the *situla*' or the Strettweg cult model [24, 38], that it could have been specially made as a northern extension of the burial customs of the more southerly Celts.

A somewhat similar pot decorated with a frieze of six quadrupeds comes from Tendrup, Randers. The form of both pots is typical of the Danish pre-Roman Iron Age; brooches from the Kraghede pits are of the Middle La Tène type with the foot loosely clasping the centre of the bow, a type which in fact survives well into Late La Tène times in east and central Europe.

O. Klindt-Jensen, *Acta Arch.* XX (1949), 102–03, 157–58 fig. 102 and Appendix 'A' esp. pp. 202–05

224 Hounslow, Middlesex. Bronze boar figurine. L. 8 cm. I BC/I AD. British Mus., London. *J. V. S. Megaw.*

This little figure like other representations of boars in these pages well demonstrates Anne Ross's point that here is 'the cult animal *par excellence* of the Celts';[1] as a figure of death its common appearance in Celtic graves is readily explicable. Despite its comparative lack of iconographic importance in the pre-Iron Age periods, some twenty boar figurines have been discovered in Britain, the majority in the south of England. The Hounslow boar was found with a companion piece, each originally with a great openwork crest like that on the continental boar illustrated on the right. Two elongated dogs and a model wheel were also associated with the boars. Fox considered the boar figures rather improbably to be helmet mounts like that found at Belzers [see notes to 202] though the fore-trotters do have peg-like ends which suggest attachment to something. The wheel, like the boars, represents an insular and contemporary extension of the little models found on the central European *oppida* sites [see notes to 209a]. Model spoked wheels also appear in Romano-British contexts such as the Felmingham, Norfolk, cult deposit of probably third century AD date.[2]

As to the artistic quality represented by the Hounslow boar, it may not be great art but it seems fairer to consider it as 'a brilliant short-hand statement of the face and form of the animal' than to agree with an eminent authority on Anglo-Saxon material culture that it 'is at best a very sorry hog'! The Hounslow animals, like the best products of essentially folk craftworkers today, are made to a formula but a formula which is based on a careful distillation of the essential elements of nature.

A. W. Franks, *Proc. Soc. Antiq.*, 2 ser., III (1864–67), 90–92; E. T. Leeds, *Celtic ornament* (1933), 95; T. D. Kendrick, *Anglo-Saxon Art to A D 900* (1938), 7; *ABA*, Pl. 66; *LPA*, 70 and Pl. XXII:1; *PP*, 76 and Pl. 53a; *PRB*, Pl. 313; J. M. C. Toynbee, *Art in Britain under the Romans* (1964), 24

[1] *PCB*, 308 ff.; M. Dobs, *Rev. Celtique* XLIII (1936), 277–342
[2] J. W. Brailsford, *Antiquities of Roman Britain in the British Mus.* (2 ed. 1958), 60 and Pl. XXIV:2

225 Luncani, Romania. Bronze boar. L. c. 10·5 cm. I BC. Mus. Cluj.

In the continental European *oppida* boar figurines are common, particularly at such comparatively eastern sites as Stradonice [see also notes to 213]. The boar figure shown here is the easternmost so far known but with its great openwork crest is presumably a Celtic piece. The sacred boar hunt seems to be a frequent feature in European beliefs, both classical and barbarian [37], and the boar appears not only on coinage [194g] but also as a common sword stamp [see notes to 181] and even as large free-standing figures both on the continent [238] and Britain.[1]

I. Hunyady, 'Kelták a Kárpátmedencében', *Diss. Pannonicae*, ser. II:18 (1942), T. XXXVIII:2; (1944), 106; *KvsE*, obr. 91:5; *PreA*, ill. 262

[1] *KvsE*, 244–45 and obr. 91–92; S. Piggott, *Antiq. J.* XXXIX (1959), 28; J. V. S. Megaw, *Antiq. J.* XLIII (1963), 32 f.; *PCB*, 308–21

226 Euffigneix, Haute-Marne. Sandstone pillar-statue. Total ht. c. 30 cm., w. 18 cm. ?I BC. Mus. des Antiquités nat., St-Germain-en-Laye. *Jean Roubier, Paris.*

With its rigid block-like form like the undoubtedly earlier Waldenbuch stone [142], the little and much restored Euffigneix figure looks like a copy in stone of a wooden figure such as those from the fascinating and recent find at the head-waters of the Seine [see 233]. The lower third now restored in plaster was presumably intended to be buried below ground surface. The features of the buffer-torc-wearing head – now sadly scalped – the large protruding eyes but the, on the whole, well-modelled facial features remind one of late sculpture both continental and insular in which the influence of provincial Roman art is beginning to be felt [243].

The boar figure, with its great upstanding crest like that on the Rynkeby flagon [222a] or the free-standing figure from Neuvy-en-Sullias [238], has suggested to some authorities that this figure may be intended as a representation of the Gallo-Roman boar god variously known as 'Baco' and 'Moccus'; a very archaic feature, however, is the boar's 'shoulder curl' [see notes on **186**]. Largely hidden in the present illustration, and on the left side of the pillar, like the boar parallel with the long axis, is a great staring eye. The iconography of the apotropaic eye can be traced in the west back to the comma-leaf elements of the Ostheim brooch and its early La Tène parallels [**69**], and may be seen reappearing in the insular 'trumpet-scroll' or 'bird-comma' [**254**].

Various dates ranging from the third century BC have been suggested for the Euffigneix stone but in view of the careful delineation of the eye feature and the style of the boar, a date closer to the Roman occupation of Gaul would seem more likely.

Espérandieu XI (1938), no. 7702; *ArtG*, p. 96, Pls. 6–7; *WK*, Taf. 63; *Celts*, Pl. 67; M. Pobé and J. Roubier, *Art of Roman Gaul* (1961), Pls. 6–7; H.-P. Eydoux, *La France antique* (1962), ill. 354; *PAE*, 249–50 and Pls. 272–73; *EV*, 238–39 and ill.

227 Hohensalzburg, Salzburg. Stone head. Total ht. of block c. 50 cm., ht. of head c. 17 cm. ?I AD. Burgmus., Salzburg. *Salzburger Mus. C.A.*

This gnome-like head of local Untersberg marble commonly known as the 'Romerkopf' was until 1956 built into the Rosspforte of Salzburg Castle.

It is difficult to decide whether this head is to be dated before or after the occupation of Noricum by the Romans in 16 BC. The 'permanent wave' effect in the hair and the general set of the head may be compared with heads from the cult centre of Entremont destroyed by the Romans in 126 BC,[1] or with what can now be seen of the coiffure of Euffigneix [**226**]. A new and cruder head found in 1957 in the region of the great late La Tène *oppidum* of Závist south of Prague, another Janus pillar from Beaucaire, Bouches-du-Rhône, and the Roquepertuse Janus heads illustrated below [**235**][2] may be compared with the twisted 'omega'-shaped mouth; the Závist piece, though, may quite possibly be even later than the Salzburg head. Archaic features are certainly discernible; the dot-pupils in the neat almond-shaped eyes appear on such early La Tène masterpieces as the Dürrnberg flagon from the first chariot grave, now preserved in Salzburg in the new Museum Carolino Augusteum below the Castle [**72**]. The hair style also matches the strange 'caps' of figures on the Gundestrup cauldron [**209**]. No early Celtic figure, however, has such a well executed nose; indeed to most Celtic artists the human nose seems the most insignificant part of the human physiognomy, fit only for caricature rather than for copying.

All in all, there seems no stylistic reason why the Salzburg head should not date from the Roman period but still exhibit many features of native pre-Roman sculpture.

K. Willvonseder, *Archaeology* 13 (1960), 251–52; *id.*, in (ed.) R. von Uslar, *Studien aus Alteuropa* II=*Bonner Jahrb*. Beiheft 10 (1965), 129–34 and Taf. 15–160 *PreA*, 231–32 and ill. 233

[1] *ArtG*, 96, Pls. 31–32; *PreA*, ill. 234
[2] Závist: L. Jansová, *Arch. roz.* XVIII (1966), 261 ff. esp. obr. 88; Beaucaire: F. Benoit, *L'art primitif méditerranéen de la vallée du Rhône*=*Publ. des Ann. de*

la Faculté des Lettres Aix-en-Provence 9 (1955), Pl. XXIX

228 'Les Jacquematres', Salon, Aube. Details of hilt of bronze-coated iron sword. Total l. 46·5 cm., w. across arms c. 4·5 cm. LT II, II BC. British Mus., London. *J. V. S. Megaw.*

This short sword, of which two details are shown here, is amongst the earliest La Tène swords with true anthropoid hilts although antecedents can be found in the anthropoid-hilted daggers of Ha D [see notes to **17** ff.] and the pseudo-anthropoid hilts of some early La Tène swords such as that found with the Kyšice brooch [**68**]. The Salon sword – like all later anthropoid-hilted swords, a dirk rather than a true sword – was formerly in the Morel collection and comes from an inhumation grave discovered in 1875 and associated with a normal Middle La Tène longsword. The only other anthropoid-hilted sword of this type with association – Hawkes's class 'E' with single central knob on the hand grip – comes from a cremation grave at Malnate, Varese, in northern Italy near Lake Como[1] where it was found with an iron chain belt and part of a glass armlet, characteristic of later Middle La Tène graves in central Europe.

The Salon hilt head with its heavy ridged hair, large eyes, and gloomy turned-down mouth, is not far from the class 'E' anthropoid sword found with its scabbard from the River Zihl at Gampelen, Kt. Bern, which has been compared here with the Manerbio silver mounts [see **206**]. The class 'F' sword from Châtenay-Macheron, Haute-Marne, from an inhumation grave, again with a regular La Tène II longsword, is also similar.[2] In both these cases, however, the head is more sophisticatedly modelled and the knobbed 'hands' curve out rather than stretch straight at an angle of 45° as with Salon. The appearance of anthropoid-hilted swords in Switzerland and northern Italy has been explained as an introduction by the Cimbri and Teutones in the later part of the second century; however, if this is so then they must simply have transferred them from central and northern France where is their greatest concentration.

In many ways the Salon sword face is earliest in its stylistic features of all the recognisably human-headed swords; it is not very far from the glum pairs of the Courtisols buffer-terminalled torc [**119**]. One detail: on the reverse side of the Salon head a single pigtail can clearly be seen, not double as in the base coinage of the Somme which has somewhat similar glum-faced characters [**194g**]. Such pigtails recall the Celtic habit of using lime wash as a stiffener[3] and single pigtails occur not only on a Hungarian 'Janus head' from Badacsony-Lábdi but also on east and west Gaulish coinage, particularly on one of the Armorican issues showing an anthropomorphic sword being gripped by a naked warrior.[4]

L. Morel, *La Champagne souterraine* (1898), 145–46, 177 and Pl. XXXIII:1; *Manuel* IV, 647 and fig. 474; C. F. C. Hawkes, *PPS* XXI (1955), 201–27, esp. 209–11, 224–25 and Pl. XXV:6=no. 35

[1] P. Castelfranco, *Riv. arch. di Como* (1907), 101 ff. and Pl. II:6; Hawkes, *op. cit.*, no. 17
[2] Hawkes, *op. cit.*, no. 27

[3] M.-L. Sjoestedt, *Études Celtiques* I (1938), 21 ff.; see also notes to [88]

[4] M. Szabó, *Arch. Értesítő* 90 (1963), 69–74

229 Ballyshannon Bay, off Co. Donegal. Detail of bronze anthropoid hilt from sword. Total l. of sword 49 cm., ht. of head c. 2·5 cm. LT III, I BC. National Mus. of Ireland, Dublin.

The contrast between the human features of this sword hilt, which, with its triangular iron blade, was dredged up by fishermen in 1916, and that from Salon hardly needs emphasising. The complete hilt with its short arms and 'legs' and projecting head is of Hawkes's class 'G', well-dated to La Tène III in France though usually with rather a different style of head [241–42]. Armorican coins and especially those of the Redones [see notes to **194e**] do show anthropoid-hilted short swords though none with clearly human heads, perhaps owing to nothing more than the scale of the dies used.[1] Despite the typically Celtic vertical ridging of the hair, the finely modelled ears – which Jacobsthal seems to have mistaken for a vestigial 'leaf crown' – nose, and mouth have a distinctly Gallo-Roman look and may be compared with the Bouray sheet-bronze figure [232] rather than with the earlier class 'E' swords [228], though whether the Ballyshannon sword hilt could ever have been made in Britain, as has also been suggested, is quite another matter. A continental piece which has certain features of resemblance is the Duchcov, Lahošt' finger ring [88] – perhaps, after all, a much later piece than has often been thought.

At least one other imported late anthropoid-hilted sword is known from Britain, a short sword from a warrior's inhumation burial from North Grimston, in the East Riding of Yorkshire, found with a long sword, fragments of an iron sword belt and jet ornaments and a pig's skeleton. This is more likely to be evidence of second- than of first-century contact with the continent;[2] the head of the Yorkshire sword is related to that from Châtenay-Macheron cited in connection with Salon [see notes to **228**].

ECA, 14, n. 4; C. F. C. Hawkes, *PPS* XXI (1955), 215 and Pl. XXVII:5=no. 50

[1] H. de la Tour, *Atlas des monnaies gauloises de la Bibliothèque Nationale* (1892), Pl. XX, no. 6941; J. A. Blanchet, *Traité des monnaies gauloises* I (1905), fig. 12
[2] Hawkes, *op. cit.*, no. 44

230 Welwyn, Hertfordshire, grave 'A'. Bronze mounts. Ht. of largest 3·3 cm. Second half I BC. British Mus., London. *J. V. S. Megaw.*

In this area of Hertfordshire there are a number of richly furnished cremation graves of the later, Belgic, Iron Age, the grave goods being contained within a chamber or lined burial vault. These follow at long range the old central European custom of burial chambers under barrow mounds though in the present case there is no such conspicuous marking of the burial spot. These are burials of what has recently been termed the 'Welwyn' type after a pair discovered in the early years of this century.

Grave 'A' contained two native vessels including one of the characteristic wheel-turned pedestalled form as found at Aylesford [see notes to **187**], a pair of iron fire-dogs [see notes to **278–279**] and a bronze bowl with two handles. Apart from this last import there was an amphora of the so-called Dressel type I as found at Baldock [see **187**] and bearing a stamp 'S O S'; a third import was the handle of a north Italian bronze jug of the 'Ornavasso' type, a form to be dated after rather than before 50 BC.

The three cast bronze masks are only slightly dished on the reverse side and give no clue as to how they were attached or to what. Two have clearly delineated pupils, the hollows being perhaps to take enamel, and all have the vertical brushed hair, ridged eyelids and long moustaches of much earlier continental pieces, while on the other hand not being far from the Dejbjerg cart mounts. Later Celts seem on the whole to be shown more often clean-shaven than either bearded or moustached – perhaps here is the influence of Rome – though the coins of Cunobelin show that there were at least some Belgic chieftains who followed the old styles [306b]. In the comparative absence of obvious figural art in the later British Iron Age it is difficult to decide whether the Welwyn heads, a triad of Celtic gods or Belgic chief-tains, are of continental or local workmanship; there is clearly a general affinity with the anthropomorphic sword hilts.

There is one other comparable bronze mount from Britain. This is a little head found in 1883 on the site of a Roman villa at Chiddingfold in Surrey with coins indicating a first- or second-century AD date.[1] Here though the hair and ridged eyes are close to the Welwyn heads, there is a wavy beard somewhat in the manner of the 'gods' of the Gundestrup outer panels [209, **Plate XIII**].

One detail of the Welwyn heads not here visible is that under the chin is a slightly raised double oval moulding of the type illustrated on the Besseringen torc [56] but also on early native British work [249; see also **245**, fig. 12].

R. A. Smith, *Archaeologia* LXIII (1911–12), 1–30; *ABA*, Pl. 70; *LPA*, 70 and Pl. XXII:2; *PP*, 65, 72 and Pl. 33b; J. M. C. Toynbee, *Art in Britain under the Romans* (1964), 23 and Pl. If; Ann Birchall, *PPS* XXXI (1965), 305, 266; I. M. Stead, *Archaeologia* CI (1967), 1–62, esp. 57

[1] Joan P. Alcock, *Surrey Arch. Coll.* LX (1963), 45–49 and Pl. VIb

231 Salleneuve, Touget, Gers. Stone statue. Ht. 74·5 cm. I–II AD. Mus. des Antiquités nationales, St-Germain-en-Laye. *J. V. S. Megaw.*

This figure, discovered in a quarry, shows an almost complete Romanisation of Celtic style; the general com-position, with the dog trying to get at the hare, and details such as the cloak, the sword scabbard behind the hare's ears, the treatment of the hunter's ears, nose and mouth, all suggest a provincial Roman stonemason. On the other hand, the almost rigid stance of the man, his dumpy proportions and the heavily stylised hair betray its native origins.

That the hare has here any symbolic significance is unlikely, though hares appear early in Celtic art intro-duced via the '*situla*' style [29], and in Britain, together with the goose and cock, seem to have been considered important cult animals;[1] Boudica released a hare before setting out on a campaign.[2]

Espérandieu II (1908), no. 1054; *ArtG*, 96, Pls. 63–64; H.-P. Eydoux, *La France Antique* (1962), 292 and ill. 353

[1] *PCB*, 349–50
[2] *Dio Cassius* LXII, 2

232 Bouray, nr. La Ferlé-Alais, Seine-et-Oise. Sheet-bronze and cast figure with white-and-blue glass inlaid eye. Ht. 42 cm. ?I BC. Mus. des Antiquités nat., St-Germain-en-Laye. *Belzeaux-Zodiaque.*

This figure, dredged from the River Juine in 1845, is made in six separate pieces, a feature which, together with the general appearance of the head, recalls the work of the sheet-bronze workers responsible for such pieces as the Marlborough bucket [188] and the Rynkeby fragments [222].

The head is cast in two sections, the body is sheet-bronze. The cross-legged stance reminds one of Roquepertuse [212], Gundestrup [209b] and, before them, Waldalgesheim [118]. Indeed here the feet end in deer-like hooves, perhaps a variant on the normal attributes of the antler-god. Despite the head's similarity also to pieces which must undoubtedly date to the period of the Roman occupation of Gaul [239–240], the hair style, ridged treatment of the eyes and a typical Celtic disregard of essential details – note the arms reduced to mere amputated stumps – suggest a date around the beginning of our era for a piece which has been placed anywhere between the second century BC and the third century AD.

A somewhat similar bronze bust with glass-inlaid eyes and, like Bouray, with something of the spirit of an early medieval reliquary about it, comes from the area of Lyons[1] but this bust seems without doubt to belong to the Roman period. More comparable is the bronze mask-bust from Garacières-en-Bauce, Eure-et-Loir, with even more formalised vertically divided hair.[2]

R. Lantier, *Mon. Piot* 34 (1934), 35–58; *ArtG*, 96, Pls. 42–43; 304, Pl. 18; *WK*, Taf. 62; M. Pobé and J. Roubier, *Art of Roman Gaul* (1961), Pls. 11–12; R. Joffroy in *Die Welt der Kelten=Kunst der Welt* (1964), 129 and ill. on p. 131; *PAE*, 251 and ill. on front cover; *EV*, 242–43 and ill.,; F. Braemer, *Rev. Arch.* (1969:2), 86–88 and figs. 43–45

[1] G. Rodenwalt, *Kunst um Augustus* (2 ed. 1943), 29 and Abb. 17
[2] *ArtG*, colour pl. opp. p. 145, 96, Pl. 61; *WK*, Taf. 65; Pobé and Roubier, *op. cit.*, Pl. 55; *CCH*, 163 and fig. 46; Braemer, *op. cit.*, 81 ff.

233 St-Germain-Sources-Seine, Côte d'Or. Wooden oak carving. Total ht. 72 cm., ht. of individual heads c. 13 cm. I AD. Mus. Archéologique, Dijon. *R. Rémy, Dijon.*

Wooden statuary is known in Europe from Mesolithic times on, but, as a rule, the perishable nature of the material has limited discoveries to single finds [280–282]. Later classical writers such as Caesar and Lucan make reference to gloomy *simulacra* carved from logs and placed in woodland sanctuaries,[1] and in 1861 a number of figures were found in a well within a sanctuary at Montbouy, Loiret, dated between the Augustan and Constantinian periods. A somewhat earlier discovery more fully excavated in 1968 is the site at the spring of Les Roches, Chamalières (Puy-de-Dôme), dated by associated pottery to the first half of the first century AD.[2] There is nothing, however, to match the discoveries made during 1963–66 some 35 kilometres north-west of Dijon. Here, nearly 200 carved objects of oak were dredged out of what had been considered a ritual bathing pool attached to the Gallo-Roman sanctuary of Sequana, goddess of the Seine and patron deity of the Sequani, and which had been first excavated in the nineteenth century. Taken together with Roman pottery indicating a date not after about the middle of the first century AD, it looks as if all the various wooden pieces had been deposited more or less at one time as a *favissa* or dedication at the period when the earliest Gallo-Roman square shrine was being built, thereby probably destroying an earlier primitive native shrine.

Several different styles are represented by the sculptures, mixtures of both the classical and native artistic traditions. As at Les Roches, a large number of model anatomical parts represent ex-votos or gifts to the goddess in hopeful anticipation of cures, while imitation fruit and particularly apples (sacred to Sequana) may have represented thank-offerings. Of the figural sculpture, some pieces again, like carvings from Les Roches, show the influence of such major pieces of contemporary Gallo-Roman bronze and metal-work as are illustrated on this and the following pages. Another category extends the old Celtic tradition of hieratic pillar-statues ranging from Holzgerlingen [14] to Euffigneix [226] and here seen in the basic wooden tree-trunk form which must have been the origin of the stone figures.

From the headwaters of the Seine are some 16 figures comprising two or more heads carved from a single block. There must surely be a link here with the tradition of the cult of the 'severed heads', the display of victims' heads on poles seen at its most gruesome in the Roquepertuse 'skull rack' [see notes to 212 and 235] and also in the carved pillars with low relief heads in groups of three from such sites as Nîmes, Entremont, and St Rémy (the site of the *oppidum* of Glanum).[3]

Gallia XXII (1964), 302–06, esp. fig. 16; R. Martin, *Rev. Arch. de l'Est et du Centre-Est* XIV (1963), 1–19, esp. Pl. VII; *id., Antiquity* XXXIX (1965), 247–52, esp. Pl. LIa; Simone Deyts, *Ex voto de bois . . . du sanctuaire des Sources de la Seine: Art celte et gallo-romain* (1966), no. 17; *id., Rev. Arch. de l'Est et du Centre-Est* XVII (1966), 198–211; M. Dillon and Nora K. Chadwick, *The Celtic realms* (1967), 297–99; E. Thevenot, *Divinités et Sanctuaires de la Gaule* (1968), 216 ff.; S. Piggott, *The Druids* (1968), Pl. 9

[1] Piggott, *op. cit.*, 85
[2] Montbouy: *Espérandieu* IV (1911), no. 2970; *PCB*, 35; *EV*, 234 and ill.; Les Roches: Cl. Vatin, *Rev. Arch.* (1969:1), 103–14
[3] F. Benoit, *L'art primitif méditerranéen de la vallée du Rhône=Ann. de la Faculté des Lettres Aix-en-Provence* 9 (1955), Pl. XXII ff.

234 St-Germain-Sources-Seine, Côte d'Or. Bull figure in oak. Total ht. 38 cm., l. of head 12·5 cm. I AD. Mus. Archéologique, Dijon. *R. Rémy, Dijon.*

This fine head of a bull is a far cry from the careful stylisations of pre-Roman Celtic artists but is less 'bullish' than the little Mâcon mount of the third century BC. [161]. The style is comparable with the presumably considerably earlier frieze of horses from Roquepertuse where, as here, the sculptor seems as concerned with pure line as with representation.

Gallia XXII (1964), fig. 18; R. Martin, *Antiquity* XXXIX (1965), Pl. XLV; Simone Deyts, *Ex voto de bois . . . du sanctuaire des Sources de la Seine: Art celte et gallo-romain* (1966), no. 81

235 Roquepertuse, Bouches-du-Rhône. Limestone double head. Total l. 34 cm. ?III–II BC. Mus. d'Archéologie, Château Borély, Marseilles. *Institut Pédagogique nationale, Paris.*

This Janus group from the post-World War I excavations of the Roquepertuse sanctuary north of the ancient town of Massalia [see notes to **212**], is divided, not by a horned crown as has been suggested, but by the down-curving beak of a bird of prey. This is a continuation of the struggle between man and the unidentified powers of evil first given visual expression in the Erstfeld gold rings [84] – or in more heraldic vein as on the Reinheim gold [79–80], and the 'Ticino' belt-plaques [95–99]; a separate bird figure, perhaps a goose, perches above the portico. The 'Janus' head has also a long life in La Tène art, whether one looks at actual sculpture like the Leichlingen head [85], at double-sided brooches like that from the first Weiskirchen grave [67] or, as here with two separate heads, the Zemplín iron knife handle [199]; separated 'Janus' heads occur also in eastern Europe[1] and there is in fact a considerable literature on double heads.[2]

Roquepertuse has features other than its basic iconography which indicate its Celtic background: for example the outlined almond-shaped eyes and the brows and nose executed in one smooth curve. Jacobsthal indeed considered it the work of a Celtic sculptor who had studied in Massalia. The bow-shaped mouth of the right-hand head is not unlike the later Salzburg face [227].

H. de Géran-Ricard, *Études de Centénaire de la Soc. de Statist., d'Hist., et d'Arch. Marseilles* (1927), 3–35, esp. p. 16; *Espérandieu* X (1928), no. 7616; *ECA*, no. 3; F. Benoit, *L'art primitif méditerranéen de la vallée du Rhône=Ann. de la Faculté des Lettres Aix-en-Provence* 9 (1955), 40 and Pl. XXXIV:1, XXXV; M. Pobé and J. Roubier, *Art of Roman Gaul* (1961), Pls. 14–15; H. P. Eydoux, *La France antique* (1962), ill. on p. 21; P.-M. Duval, *Art de France* IV (1964), ill. on p. 23 top; M. Szabó, *Acta Arch. Hung.* XVII (1965), 236 f. and fig. 3; *ArtG*, Col. Pl. opp. p. 64, 96, Pls. 10–11; *WK*, Taf. 55; *PreA*, 231 and Pl. 232; *PAE*, 248–49 and Pl. 270; *EV*, 230 ff. and ill. on p. 241

[1] J. Csemegi, *Arch. Értesítő* 88 (1961), 52–67; Szabó, *Arch. Értesítő* 90 (1963), 69–74; id., *Acta Arch. Hung.* XVIII, 233 ff.

[2] P. Lambrechts, *L'exaltation de la tête dans la pensée et dans l'art des Celtes=Diss. Arch. Gandenses* II (1954), 81–83

236 Roquepertuse, Bouches-du-Rhône. Fragment of lime-

stone frieze with traces of paint. L. 63 cm. ?III–II BC. Mus. d'Archéologie, Chateau Borély, Marseilles. *J. Roubier, Paris.*

Like the other pieces of sculpture from Roquepertuse illustrated here [**212, 235**], this block is carved from local Coudoux limestone and, with its original painted surface fresh, would have presented as strange a sight to modern eyes as would the Parthenon frieze could one view it in all its original technicolor glory.

This frieze of horses' heads may have been intended to have cultic significance since the horse is not only a figure associated with Epona, but in association with the goose, a figure of which was set above the portico, it is a familiar of the Celtic Mars.

ECA, no. 1; F. Benoit, *L'art primitif méditerranéen de la vallée du Rhône=Ann. de la Faculté des Lettres Aix-en-Provence* 9 (1955), 31–32 and Pl. XIII; *ArtG*, 96, Pl. 13; *WK*, Taf. 50; M. Pobé and J. Roubier, *Art of Roman Gaul* (1961), Pl. 13; *PCB*, 66, 271 and fig. 29

237 Neuvy-en-Sullias. Loiret. Bronze female figurine. Ht. 14 cm. I BC. Mus. Historique d'Orléanais, Orléans. *Belzeaux-Zodiaque.*

A hoard of bronze figures, possibly buried at the time of the Roman conquest, was found at Neuvy-en-Sullias which is positioned on the left bank of the Loire just opposite the Celtic sanctuary of Fleury, St Benoit-sur-Loire (Roman *Floriacum*). The figure, which bears a stamped name, presumably the maker's, 'S(C)UTO', and its nude male companion,[1] caught by the bronze worker in the attitude of some sacred dance, have a feeling of movement, a studied informality of pose which is quite different from the planned asymmetries of true pre-Roman Celtic art. Whether this is an attempt to represent a new 'fashionable' aspect in Gallo-Roman art, or whether this is the unconscious influence of Graeco-Roman culture is not a matter of great moment one way or the other. This is a delightful example of small scale art but definitely one which looks stylistically forward rather than back.

A similar dancing figure was found in 1865 at St-Laurent-des-Bois (Loir-et-Cher).[2]

S. Reinach, *Bronzes figurés de la Gaule romaine* (1895), 241–61; *Espérandieu* IV (1911), no. 2984; *ArtG* 96, Pls. 45–46; *WK*, Taf. 67; M. Pobé and J. Roubier, *Art of Roman Gaul* (1961), Pl. 47; H.-P. Eydoux, *La France antique* (1962), 238–41 and ill. 274–75; *PAE*, 251–52 and Pl. 280; *EV*, 244 and ill. on p. 226

[1] Pobé and Roubier, *op. cit.*, Pls. 49–50
[2] *Ibid.*, Pl. 51

238 Neuvy-en-Sullias, Loiret. Bronze boar. Ht. c. 68 cm. ?I BC. Mus. Historique d'Orléanais, Orleans. *Jean Roubier, Paris.*

Amongst the bronzes from Neuvy-en-Sullias – which include a bronze horn with well-shaped mouthpiece[1] – are three nearly life-sized boars; one, a fairly realistic figure in cast metal,[2] a second, illustrated here, of sheet-metal. The highly stylised crest and long lean lines with the tusks economically indicated in a few *repoussé* indentations make this a much more 'Celtic' piece than the two dancers. The crest can be compared with that of boars on coins both continental and British [306b] and the face with the Deskford horn mount [272] while the whole form is close both to the Rynkeby and Euffigneix boars [222a, 226].

ArtG, 96 and Pls. 47–48; *WK*, Taf. 68 below; M. Pobé and J. Roubier, *Art in Roman Gaul* (1961), Pl. 8; *PAE*, 251 and Pl. 277; *EV*, ill. on p. 227; F. Braemer, *Rev. Arch.* (1969:1), 88–91, esp. fig. 46

[1] F. Behn, *Musikleben in Altertum und frühen Mittelalter* (1954), 144 and Abb. 186
[2] *WK*, Taf. 68 above; M. Mulon, *Archéologia* (Paris), 24 (1968), ill. on p. 36

239 La Croix-St-Ouen, Forêt de Compiègne, Oise. Bronze head. Ht. c. 18 cm. I/II AD. Mus. des Antiquités nat., St-Germain-en-Laye. *J. V. S. Megaw.*

In 1873 seven similar cast bronze heads were found in the Forest of Compiègne, all with hollow eyes so as to take inlay and all hollowed at the back as if, mask-like, the faces were intended to be attached to wooden lay-figures or *simulacra*. All appear to be provided with torcs like the (also cast) head of the Bouray figure [232] or the Rynkeby outer cauldron fragment [222] where, however, the torc is more definitely modelled.

The formalised curls, the general appearance of the face and the ear-pendants do not necessarily mean that the present figure is intended as a female; indeed, in view of the similarity with the sword mounts illustrated below as well as a group of similar masks on both sides of the English Channel, some considered to be of Julio-Claudian date, the head is more likely to be male. There is little need to dispute the classical influence behind the modelling of the head, though it is still Celtic in the manner in which the face, for all its classicism, is reduced to a number of formal shapes.

S. Müller, *Nordiske Fortidsminder* I:2 (1892), 58 and fig. 9; R. Lantier, *Mon. Piot* 34 (1934), 52 and figs. 18–19; S. Piggott, *Antiq. J.* XLIII (1963), 117 f.; R. Duruin, *Celticum* XV=suppl. à *Ogam—Trad. Celtique* 106 (1966), 136–37 and Pl. 64, fig. 2:7; F. Braemer, *Rev. Arch.* (1969:1), 81 ff.

240 ?England. Bronze head. Ht. 12·8 cm. I/II AD. National Mus., Copenhagen.

This cast head, purchased in London in 1913 with the information that it had been found 'somewhere in England', is very similar to the group of Gaulish heads from the Forest of Compiègne [239] and their parallels. If anything, it is even more Celtic, since, though it has no torc – unless one so interprets the raised strip around the edge of the neck-flange – the eyes are ridged in the manner of the Welwyn mounts [230] and their parallels such as the heads on the Manerbio discs [204–205] ranging back into time to such masterpieces of early La Tène art as the cast figures on the Reinheim flagon [73].

The width of the flange certainly suggests that, if not used for adorning a wooden statue, this head could have formed part of a composite bronze figure like Bouray [232]. Again, like Compiègne, this head of what is clearly

a god rather than a mortal is more likely to be male than female.

Despite the parallels which have been made between Gallo-Belgic workmanship on both sides of the Channel both before and after the Roman conquest of England, on balance it seems more likely that this head is of continental manufacture even though there is little reason to doubt an English find-spot.

O. Klindt-Jensen, *Acta Arch.* XX (1949), 118–19, n. 315; S. Piggott, *Antiq. J.* XLIII (1963), 116–18; J. M. C. Toynbee, *Art in Britain under the Romans* (1964), 110, n. 2

241 Châtillon-sur-Indre, Indre. Details of bronze sword hilt and upper part of scabbard. Ht. of handle c. 14 cm., ht. of head c. 2·5 cm. LT III, Mid-I BC. Mus. Dobrée d'Archéologie, Nantes.

In 1886 what seems to have been a rich warrior's grave similar to southern British graves of the 'Welwyn' type [see notes to **230**], was uncovered on the right bank of the River Indre. Apart from the present short sword and its scabbard (broken at the tip) and fragments of a second long iron sword, were found a bronze basin and long-handled *patella* or skillet and part of a bronze jug of the so-called 'Kelheim' type, the skillet certainly an import from Italy. Seven amphorae also attested to the continuance of the significance not only of the Otherworld feast but of the wine trade between the classical south and barbarian north; boar's tusks were also found and two bronze rings may have formed part of a leather sword belt. The imports suggest a date around the middle of the first century BC for the grave.

The front of the anthropoid sword scabbard has a late La Tène saltire pattern – not visible here – while a circular plaque from the grave is decorated in a spindly-armed whirligig[1] not unlike that on the Aylesford bucket [187]. The suspension loop on the rear of the scabbard has a very classical-looking cockle design closely matched by another anthropoid sword which could easily be from the same swordsmith's workshop, that from Tesson, Saintes, Charante–Maritime.[2] The swords are of Hawkes's Class 'G' type which also include the sword from Ballyshannon Bay with a head of very different type [229]. Here the head of the Châtillon-sur-Indre sword, like the cast bronze faces illustrated above [239–240], clearly reflects the growing influence of Roman provincial art; the purpose of decorating a sword hilt with a human head continues, whatever its purpose may have been – apotropaic, talismanic, sympathetic magic or whatever one's fancy might dictate – and only the style changes.

C. F. C. Hawkes, *PPS* XXI (1955), 213–15, fig. 6:2 and Pl. XXVI:4–5=no. 28

[1] P. Coussin, *Rev. Arch.* II (1926), 32–63; Hawkes, *op. cit.*, Pl. XXVI:8
[2] Tesson: Hawkes, *op. cit.*, no. 36

242 Staré Hradisko, Prostějov. Bronze mount from sword hilt. Ht. 2·6 cm. LT III, I BC. Muz. města Boskovice. Aú ČSAV, Brno.

Since the days of Déchelette, the evidence for commercial and cultural contacts between the *oppida* of west Europe and their central European counterparts has been generally recognised. There was such a late Celtic 'common market' that in fact it becomes quite difficult to separate a random selection of iron, glass, and painted pottery into constituent regional groups. Occasionally, however, clear imports can be established such as the specialist brooch types found at Manching [see notes to **201**] or the present terminal from a class 'G' anthropoid-hilted sword. Like a very similar head from the Stradonice *oppidum*,[1] this head from the most easterly of the Late La Tène 'common market' sites to be under present investigation [see also notes to **207**] has the formalised classical features of the French swords and, on the evidence of the precisely parallel mount from the *oppidum* of Corent in the Puy-de-Dôme,[2] must be an import from central France. One detail only of Celtic stylisation remains: the manner in which the eyebrows with their upturned, almost scrolling, ends form a single unit with the bridge of the nose.

E. Šimek, *Poslední Keltové na Moravě* (1958), obr. 21:3, 23:10; *KvsE*, Tab. CXXX:17 left; J. Meduna, *Staré Hradisko=Fontes Arch. Moravicae* II (1961), Taf. 1:9

[1] C. F. C. Hawkes, *PPS* XXI (1955), 214 and fig. 6:3= no. 16; *KvsE*, Tab. CXXVII:21; see also notes to [**213**]
[2] Hawkes, *op. cit.*, no. 29

243 Northgate Street, Gloucester. Stone head. Ht. 20 cm. Mid-I AD. Gloucester City and Folk Mus.

This head, found during the construction of Bon Marché in 1934 within the Roman site of Glevum, is made of local oolitic limestone and may once have been heightened with paint; the flat rear to the head suggests that this may have been part of an architectural setting or possibly the crowning feature of a pillar-monument.

As has been justly commented, such a head could never have been conceived without at least some knowledge of imported Julio-Claudian portrait-sculpture. In the same way, Roman influence can be seen in some of the wooden heads from the sanctuary of Sequana at the old source of the Seine, when they are compared with such famous pieces of provincial bronze sculpture as the heads from Bordeaux and Prilly, Ct. Vaud[1] – the second being the nearest thing to a portrait of a Celt which survives from the early period of the Roman empire. 'Portrait', however, is not a term one should apply too readily to the Gloucester head, which stylistically is a pastiche; the hair style is Julio-Claudian, the brow and skull certainly in the tradition of Graeco-Roman sculpture, but the huge staring eyes, sharp nose and small mouth are pre-Roman Celtic and the ears as formalised as those of Mšecké Žehrovice [**171**]. It may even be that the Gloucester head represents a male Celtic god in Roman guise.

The Gloucester head demonstrates as clearly as any native work of art of the Roman period the tenacity of archaic stylistic elements even in the face of a foreign culture which for all its insidiously penetrating nature and powers of regional adaptability was unable completely to submerge the traditions of half a millennium of Celtic creative expression.

J. M. C. Toynbee, *Art in Roman Britain* (1962), Pl. 8= no. 7; *id.*, *Art in Britain under the Romans* (1964), 56–57 and Pl. VIII a; J. F. Rhodes, *Cat. of Romano-British Sculptures in the Gloucester City Mus.* (1964), no. 3; *PreA*, 232 and ill. 235; *PCB*, 88 and Pl. 32a; S. Piggott, *The Druids* (1968), Pl. 10; *EV*, ill. on p. 248

[1] *CCH*, 165 and Pl. XXI; Simone Deyts, *Rev. Arch. de l'Est et du Centre-Est* XVII (1966), 206 ff. and figs. 17–18

244 Torrs Farm, Kelton, Kirkcudbrightshire. Detail of sheet-bronze 'chamfrein' or pony cap. Total l. c. 31 cm., ht. at semi-circular end c. 8·7 cm., l. of 'bird's head' spiral c. 3 cm. ?II BC. National Mus. of Antiquities of Scotland, Edinburgh. *M. J. M. Murray*.

Some time before 1829 the bronze cap and twin (now fixed) horns known as the 'Torrs chamfrein' were found in a peat bog and came into the possession of James Train, a local excise man who acted as an agent for the collection of antiquities by Sir Walter Scott, antiquarian as well as poet and novelist; the same parish has also produced a first-century BC buffer-terminalled bronze torc.[1] The chamfrein remained in the possession of the Scott family at their near-by house of Abbotsford from 1829 until 1921.

The actual cap, squared off and semicircular in section at one end and half-domed at the other, is made of two sheets of bronze c. 0·65 mm. thick, riveted together along a central overlapping transverse joint. Two large circular openings low down on the sides are original, but the cap has been much repaired both in antiquity and in the recent past; the two circular openings on the crown of the cap (where the twin tubular horns [**245**] are now fixed) at least in their present form are not original. The main design is in *repoussé*, hammered up from the inner surface. A separately riveted edging strip has a tooled border pattern which looks as if it were produced by alternately angled blows of the metalsmith's punch. The *repoussé* pattern is balanced about the centre line and consists of two linked units based on an open-looped pelta motif [see also **250**], each unit ending on either side with an incurving comma spiral 'trumpet' or pseudo-'bird's head'. These last, as illustrated here, have a general affinity to the patterns on the Newnham Croft armlet [**131**]. Piggott in his stylistic analysis of what he termed in general the 'Torrs-Wandsworth' group,[2] comprising objects largely found in isolated contexts often suggestive of ritual deposition, considered that there was an early 'Newnham-Torrs' sub-group including other pieces such as the Turoe stone [**129**] with affinities to the late fourth-century 'Waldalgesheim' style. A supposedly later, more three-dimensional, 'Witham-Wandsworth' sub-group consists of many of the pieces illustrated on the following pages. This division, developed some fifteen years ago, may be more apparent than real, especially when it is realised that so-called 'Waldalgesheim' elements have a very long life and can no longer be used with any certainty to establish a mid-third-century date for the beginning of the 'Torrs-Wandsworth' group as a whole.

That certain similarities can also be seen, for example, between the Maloměřice griffon openwork mounts or Middle La Tène scabbards[3] and the Torrs 'birds' head' terminals is in essence true but again this can be of no chronological value in trying to establish the beginnings of true British insular art, an art which, like the 'Early Style' of Jacobsthal's continental La Tène material,

K

seems largely to appear without any well-defined genesis. It certainly is not made any clearer through the presence of a few undoubted imports such as the Clonmacnoise torc [174]. Although the 'bossy' or bird-terminal features of Torrs do have close points of similarity with the asymmetric jungle of Turoe, the closest parallel is with almost strictly balanced designs such as the mounting of the Lough-na-Shade trumpet [246]. Though, in view of much that has been written on Torrs, it may seem a provocative statement, it is the present writer's view that nothing in Piggott's Torrs-Wandsworth group need be earlier than mid-second century BC in date; earlier dates certainly seem unproven. One last detail of the Torrs cap decoration may be cited in support of this statement; the ball-like terminals of the larger 'bird's-head' features at the domed end of the cap with their 'S' spirals are precisely in the manner of the quadrupeds' fore-'hooves' on the sheet-bronze fragments from Levroux, Indre,[4] compared in these pages with the decoration of the Aylesford, Marlborough and Rynkeby vessels [187–188, 222].

As to the exact purpose of the 'pony cap', despite some continuing discussion as to the actual relationship of the twin horns [see 245] to the cap, it is now recognised that the sheet-bronze ornament with the two circular openings fitting over the animal's ears and the bordered semi-circular margin of the cap to the rear would have well fitted a Celtic pony of some 11 hands.

J. Train in W. Mackenzie, *History of Galloway* II (1841), Appendix, 70–71; Mary Monica Maxwell Scott, *Abbotsford: the personal relics and antiquarian treasures of Sir Walter Scott* (1893), 39 and Pl. XVI top; W. A. von Jenny, *Keltische Metallarbeiten* (1935), Taf. 33; R. J. C. Atkinson and S. Piggott, *Archaeologia* XCVI (1955), 197–235, esp. Pl. LXXXI; *PP*, 22–24 and Pl. 19; *PRB*, Pl. 248; *PreA*, 234 and ill. 239–40; R. B. K. Stevenson in (ed.) A. L. F. Rivet, *Iron Age in Northern Britain* (1966), 24 and Pl. I; *PAE*, 260–61, fig. 99 and Pl. 286

[1] Stevenson, *loc. cit.*
[2] Atkinson and Piggott, *op. cit.*, 197 ff.
[3] Maloměřice: *KvsE*, tab. LXXVII:4; see also notes to [159]; scabbards: ECA, no. 107 ('La Tène') – this scabbard, which in fact is the same as that listed by Jacobsthal as his no. 109, is from Port, Kt. Bern [see also notes to 190]
[4] *Manuel* IV, fig. 657; J. V. S. Megaw, *Gallia* XXVI (1968), 38 and figs. 1–2

245 Torrs Farm, Kelton, Kirkcudbrightshire. Detail of bronze horn 'A'. Total l. c. 25 cm., ht. of head c. 1·1 cm. ?II BC. National Mus. of Antiquities of Scotland, Edinburgh. *J. V. S. Megaw*.

The two horns, now attached to the top of the Torrs 'cap', are each formed of two half-shells hammered up from sheet-bronze which tapers at the broader end from 1 mm. to 0·7 mm. in thickness at the narrow end. Both horns taper and each is turned sharply back on itself; the horn not illustrated here ends in the head of a long-billed bird perhaps intended to represent a Shoveller Duck. This bird originally had large inset eyes and is not unlike the bird handle on the presumably somewhat later Keshcarrigan bowl [273]. It is also a more realistic version of the terminal comma-birds of the Torrs 'cap'

[244]. The two halves of each horn meet at a butt joint and were originally held together by a riveted strip running along the inside edge. The decoration – filled in white in modern times – is incised, the outer lines being executed by the rocked tracer technique, the straight-edged engraver's burin or chisel which was held at an angle of 45° and pushed forward with a rocking movement. This method of producing a tremolo line starts on the continent in later Hallstatt times and is first illustrated in these pages by the decoration of the Hallstatt sword scabbard [30]. Rocked tracer work seems to have been introduced early in the Iron Age of the British Isles. Already in the fourth century, a workshop in the Lower Thames Valley which must have been founded by immigrant La Tène craftsmen was producing daggers with sheaths decorated with rocked tracer work; the technique, however, had a long life in Britain as on the continent [see also 262, 266–7].

The asymmetric loose, disjointed tendril design which differs on both horns is probably the nearest thing to the conception of the engraved ornament of the Swiss sword-makers who also made occasional use of the rocked tracer [183].

Fig. 12 [245] Torrs Farm, Kircudbrightshire, Scotland. Incised decoration on horn 'A'. Scale c. 2:3
After Piggott and Atkinson

The mature continental sword 'style' (of no earlier than the second) has often been considered to be an important factor in insular British art or what has been termed 'style IV' of the Iron Age sequence of 'Early', 'Waldalgesheim', 'Plastic-and-sword' styles.[1] Certainly, asymmetry apart, there are details of the decoration of the Torrs horns which recall third/second-century continental work. On horn 'A' just on the left of the central head is a vertical break in the design like that, perhaps imitating a binding strip, on a sword from Bölcske, Hungary, with straggling asymmetric tendril pattern.[2] The tiny human head itself, one of the few really clear manifestations of the human form in British Iron Age art, with its flanking foliage is in essence a descendant of the Italic Cheshire cats peeping out of the classical undergrowth which gave rise to the cheerful faces on the helmet from Umbria [108] or the formal pairs on the Waldalgesheim gold bracelets [124–125]; the Torrs head could also be considered to have some affinities with the semi-circular sword stamps [191]. On the other hand the use of tight 'snail' or 'hair-spring' spirals to fill in individual leaves of the engraved design is a feature shared by several other British pieces illustrated here which, though it is not possible to ascribe them with certainty to precise regional 'schools', seem to be drawing upon a common vocabulary of engraving motifs and have been found largely in the area of eastern

England between the Thames and the Wash [247–248, 252, 255]. One piece not illustrated here, which also incorporates the system of 'infilling' the lobes of a loose tendril design with incised spirals, is a sword scabbard from Sutton Reach on the River Trent in Lincolnshire.[3] This sword has a basic pattern of horizontal incised ladder decoration which again offers a link with material of the continental sword 'style' but material which is probably not earlier than the first half of the second century BC.[4]

Two other details: pairs of pointed ovals meeting at an angle as found on the Torrs horns, as well as the punch-dotted background pattern, are both features to be noted on swords of undoubtedly insular character [see 249].

It has been suggested that the actual original use of the horns was as mounts for a pair of native drinking horns in the manner of the Klein Aspergle gold fittings [44], although in view of the 'one-sided' nature of their decoration the horns could also have decorated a helmet [see notes to 294]. Technical examination of the Torrs cap, as at present assembled, strongly suggests 'reconstruction' between the original discovery and the arrival of the cap at Abbotsford. In view of the different technique, if nevertheless generally related style, of the horns and cap it is not even necessary to regard the objects as having been made at one and the same place and time.

R. J. C. Atkinson and S. Piggott, *Archaeologia* XCVI (1955), esp. 202 ff., 219–22 and Pl. LXXXIIa; *PP*, 24–25 and Pl. 20; *Celts*, Pls. 39–41; *Problems*, 78 and 89; *PRB*, Pls. 249–50; *PAE*, 262 and fig. 100

[1] J. M. de Navarro in (ed.) M. Charlesworth, *Heritage of early Britain* (1952), 74 ff.
[2] *ECA*, no. 116; *Problems*, 77 and Pl. VIb
[3] *PP*, 32 and Pl. 21
[4] De Navarro in (ed.) R. Degen *et al.*, *Helvetia Antiqua: Festschr. Emil Vogt* (1967), 148, 150

246 Lough-na-Shade, Co. Antrim. Bronze mount from horn bell. D. 20·3 cm. ?II/I BC. National Mus. of Ireland, Dublin.

This disc from the end of a long curved horn found with three other horns in a peat bog in 1794 has its *repoussé* decoration arranged within an annular space but in a very different manner from that on the complete Witham shield [252] with which it has been related. It is closer to the Torrs pony cap [244] both in its balanced layout and in the 'trumpet' or pseudo-bird's-head terminals to the main pelta designs; it also shares a similar division into four units about a main horizontal and vertical axis. The 'bossy' look of the ornament, however, relates the Lough-na-Shade disc to pieces considered here to be late in the sequence of insular art [see 131] and the layout of the design is not unlike parts of the Battersea shield [253].

Such is the catholicity of earlier British Iron Age metalwork that it is foolhardy to be too dogmatic in the ascription of pieces as imports or local products; none the less the similarity of the Lough-na-Shade horn disc to Torrs makes it more plausible to regard it as an object from across the Irish Sea than, for example, the group of decorated sword scabbards from Northern Ireland, two of which are illustrated overleaf [248–249].

The Lough-na-Shade 'trumpets', as they are usually incorrectly termed in view of their conical bore, like most fine bronzes of the period come from a context which once more must be regarded as ritual, like that of the Irish later Bronze Age horns before them. The construction of the main curved tube of the Lough-na-Shade horn is the same as that of the twin mounts from Torrs [245] – two halves meet at a butt joint originally joined with an interior riveted strip. A small ridged ring is placed about half way down the tube and, together with a simple rolled rim mouthpiece, offers a parallel for fragments of an undecorated horn in the Llyn Cerrig Bach, Anglesey, find – not that this is sufficient grounds to argue as Fox did for an Irish origin for both horns,[1] although it may indirectly suggest a lateish date for the Irish piece.

Musically, Lough-na-Shade can have offered little; the only other surviving Irish ?Iron Age horn from Co. Down is at present capable of producing three very impure notes; Lough-na-Shade will not present a sound owing to the slackness of the joints – but then archaeological evidence for music as such in the Celtic world is strictly limited and, where positive, only martial or ritual[2] [see also notes to 209c, 213].

R. MacAdam, *Ulster J. Arch.* VIII (1860), 103; F. Henry, *Irish Art* (1940), Pl. 7a; J. Raftery, *Prehistoric Ireland* (1951), fig. 267; R. J. C. Atkinson and S. Piggott, *Archaeologia* XCVI (1955), 216 and Pl. LXXXVa; *Celts*, Pl. 44

[1] C. Fox, *A find of the Early Iron Age from Llyn Cerrig Bach, Anglesey* (1947), 45, 87 and Pl. XIIa (left)
[2] J. V. S. Megaw in (ed.) J. M. Coles and D. D. A. Simpson, *Studies in ancient Europe: Essays presented to Stuart Piggott* (1968), 349–50

247 River Thames at Wandsworth, Middlesex. Detail of bronze shield boss 1. D. 33 cm., l. of incised ornament c. 7·5 cm. ?II/I BC. British Mus., London. *J. V. S. Megaw.*

Two shield bosses of different form were found together in the Thames in the last century [see also 255]. The boss of which a detail is shown here has a central spherical dome just large enough to fit a hand inside and must be considered as the centre piece attached by rivets to what would otherwise have been a wooden shield. The basic shape of the boss is a decorative variant on the typical continental La Tène III bosses as shown on the Gundestrup cauldron [209a, c]; in Britain circular bosses are found more commonly in the north of England.

The decoration of the circular shield boss from Wandsworth combines both the *repoussé* and the incised elements of the Torrs cap and horns [244–245]. What appears at first to be an asymmetrical pattern is in fact balanced in mirror image about a transverse line. The most obvious feature is a pair of great birds shown in flight with outstretched wings and long tail feathers, the asymmetry being mostly due to the artist's laudable but not entirely successful attempt to build up his basic motif from the difficult perspective view of a natural object observed in half profile. As has been recently commented, these 'obsessive birds were hatched from a Hallstatt egg in the central La Tène province' and the rocked tracer 'fill-in' motifs include split-palmettes which once more make one think of the incised ornament of Swiss swords [180–181] or of the Bölcske scabbard cited above [see notes to **245**]. Otherwise the detailed comparisons are all with such companion pieces as the Torrs horns and the Witham shield [**252**].

The number of Iron Age objects found in the vicinity of Wandsworth has suggested that this, rather than Brentford [see notes to **130**], might have been the site of an important river crossing;[1] alternatively it may have been a local votive deposit.

J. M. Kemble, *Horae Ferales* (1863), Pl. XVI:1; W. A. von Jenny, *Keltische Metallarbeiten* (1935), Taf. 32:2; P. Jacobsthal, *Burlington Mag.* 75 (1939), 28–29 and Pls. B and D; *LPA*, 70 and Pl. XX:1; *PP*, 25–26 and Pl. 13; *PRB*, Pls. 254–56; *PreA*, 234 and ill. 238; *PAE*, 261 ff. and Pl. 289

[1] C. E. Stevens, *Antiquity* XXI (1947), 6

248 Lisnacrogher, Co. Antrim. Bronze sword scabbard no. 2. Total l. c. 56 cm., w. 4·2 cm. ?II BC. British Mus., London. *Belzeaux-Zodiaque.*

Over the years some ten decorated sword scabbards have been found – without their swords which just possibly might have been lost through cathodic reduction of the iron – in fairly close proximity to each other in the district to the north of Lough Neagh in Northern Ireland. Of these the present example and two others survive out of seven or eight found allegedly in the area of a *crannog* or circular timber settlement in a bog area. Since the other three scabbards have been found in or near the River Bann, all in a seemingly fresh condition like so much else from similar contexts in Britain, this suggests once more something other than chance deposition in time of trouble.

One of two general types of incised design appears on all the scabbards: either a running spiral or, as here, a poorer loose, tendril pattern, generally but not precisely balanced despite occasional use of a compass. As a group the northern Irish scabbards look like products of one single workshop tradition but just how this tradition was established and what sort of time span may be represented by the surviving scabbards is a very difficult matter to decide. Once again much has been made of the influence of the continental sword 'style' without there ever being any concrete suggestion as to how such an influence might have been transmitted. Certain features of these scabbards may be matched on the Continent; the use of the rocked tracer as with both examples illustrated here, a central mid-rib and bow-shaped scabbard mouth, a clinging chape – early La Tène II on the continent and thus not before 200 BC – and a steep-waved edging pattern. The general all-over decoration is, however, unusual amongst swords of the Middle La Tène period[1] and no one has yet suggested that earlier scabbards like those from Weiskirchen barrow I [**109**] or Filottrano grave 22 [**137**] can have any claim to an influence on Irish swordsmiths of probably no earlier than the second century BC.

Against the supposed continental evidence, which may be summed up as no more than the presence of a series of archaic elements such as are commonly found in insular art, one may put the 'hair-spring' spirals and dot-infilling as well as the common use of paired ovals and even the same simple step pattern as decorates the base of the Turoe stone [**129**] as well as the rim of another circular shield boss, that from Grimthorpe in York-

shire.[2] The third Lisnacrogher scabbard has gridded basketry, a technique only common in southern Britain in the first century BC [see notes to **257** ff.].[3] The most comparable scabbard to the present example is Lisnacrogher 1 where the loose tendril design runs unimpeded by a mid-rib and 'hair-spring' spirals are much in evidence.

Dates for the northern Irish swords have varied from the third to mid-first century BC and their form has been supposed to demonstrate a link with English sword-smiths in Yorkshire. There is no evidence in Ireland, however, of such early specialised smithing as that of the continental settlers of the Thames valley who from the fourth century were producing fine short swords and daggers.[4] There can be no doubt, though, that people as well as ideas must have moved across from England to Ireland and back again during the course of the pre-Roman Iron Age; in such a context the lack of well-defined regional styles is hardly surprising.

The two bowl-shaped settings at the mouth of the scabbard presumably originally held enamel inlay, on the whole rare amongst presumed early insular metal-work.

R. Munro, *Lake dwellings of Europe* (1890), 383–84 and fig. 124:28–30; J. Romilly Allen, *Celtic art in pagan and pre-Christian times* (1904), Pl. opp. p. 148; J. B. Ward Perkins, *PPS* V (1939), 182; S. Piggott, *PPS* XVI (1950), 14 ff. and Pl. III; E. M. Jope, *Ulster J. Arch.* 17 (1954), 81–91, esp. 86 and fig. 1c; *LPA*, 60 and fig. 23:2; *Problems*, 79 ff.; Françoise Henry, *Irish art in the Early Christian period (to A D 800)* (1965), 10 f. and Pl. 5; *PAE*, 266 ff. and fig. 101a

[1] Compare *ECA*, nos. 105, 108
[2] *PP*, 35 and Pl. 23c; I. M. Stead, *PPS* XXXIV (1968), fig. 12
[3] Jope, *op. cit.*, 86, 90
[4] Jope, *PPS* XXVII (1961), 307–43

249 River Bann at Coleraine, Co. Antrim. Detail of bronze sword scabbard. Total l. c. 48 cm., w. c. 3·8 cm. ?II BC. National Mus. of Ireland, Dublin.

This and a second scabbard in private hands form a group with a scabbard from Toome also on the River Bann.[1] The second Coleraine scabbard and Toome share with Lisnacrogher 1 the profusion of tight 'hair-spring' spirals. Toome has the archaic joined pointed ovals, and the second Coleraine scabbard the Turoe 'step pattern'. In this context the Coleraine scabbard illustrated here looks a very poor piece; the artist, or perhaps it should be rather 'apprentice', has intended a series of alternately facing units somewhat in the manner again of the Toome scabbard with its echoes of contemporary 'folk art' in south-west England.[2] Instead the design has collapsed into a series of separated uneven spirals ending in comma-leaves with, in between each main unit, an isolated comma-spiral, the whole unevenly executed free-hand with a rocked tracer. A faint background pattern is produced by a series of lightly scored hyphens running across the diagonals in both directions; at each edge of the scabbard is a line of round punch marks.

J. Raftery, *Prehistoric Ireland* (1951), 186–87, 191 esp. fig. 216A; E. M. Jope, *Ulster Arch. J.* 17 (1954), 86–87

[1] Jope, *op. cit.*, 81 ff.; *PP*, 43 and Pl. 73b ('Lisnacroghera'); *Problems*, 79 and fig. 25

[2] *PP*, Pl. 76:1–2; see also [295]

250 River Thames at Standlake, Oxfordshire. Bronze scabbard mount. W. 5 cm. ?Early II century BC. Ashmolean Mus., Oxford.

The sword mount illustrated here forms the upper decorative plaque for the mouth of a wrought iron scabbard of what at first sight looks a typical early Middle La Tène sword complete with 'bird bridge' [see notes to **166**]. A lower and much worn plate covers the tip of the scabbard and is decorated in a low-relief writhing 'tail' or running tendril somewhat in the manner of the 'Waldalgesheim' decoration on the bows of 'Münsingen'-type brooches [**134–136**] but with the same irregular cross-hatching and scalloped or 'peaked wave' edging as the upper mount. The main feature of the upper mount is the *repoussé* looped 'pelta' such as forms the lower feature of the main Torrs pony cap decoration to which it was compared by Piggott, though he was convinced of Standlake's continental origin.

The Standlake pelta, almost face-like when viewed with the mouth down, ends in low-relief swelling tendrils in the manner of the lower plate. It has been suggested that the upper plate, almost in mint condition in comparison, may in fact be a later imitation of the lower part; it is certainly possible that *both* plaques may not have been part of the original design. The cross-hatching is executed with a rocked tracer and together with that of the Cerrig-y-Drudion bowl fragments [**114**] and the Lisnacrogher 3 scabbard may certainly be regarded as ancestral to the true regular basketry of the southern mirrors and related pieces [**260**]. The wavy edging is an element in the incised decoration of the other two Lisnacrogher scabbards [see **248**], but the pelta here also has an edging – a fine tremolo line executed again with a rocked tracer as in the outlining on the Tal-y-llyn material [**262, 267**].

To compare the swirling tip plate ornament or the swelling lobes of the upper Standlake mount with such pieces as the Filottrano grave 22 scabbard [**137**] – as has been done – is no more helpful than to cite later continental versions of the same tendril pattern such as that running down the backs of the Brå owls [**164**]. The seemingly 'early' openwork chape of Standlake, which is like that assumed by Jope for the Toome scabbard, has comma-leaf elements while the bird-bridge has a version of the hair-spring spiral; this type of chape, however, also occurs on some Middle La Tène swords including one from La Tène with a Type III dragon-lyre [see **179**].[1] Once again there seems, on analysis, to be little beyond the basic form of sword and scabbard which may be definitely regarded as continental – and if it is continental then it is right at the end rather than the beginning of the third century BC. Insular British art, like the early art of the continental Celts, is an interpretation, rather than a series of copies, of many varied sources and while it may still be possible to regard Standlake as in the forefront of this interpretative process, it is impossible to be precise in placing such work in respect of the other 'early' British pieces so far discussed; the dating suggested here for Standlake is a purely personal guess.

H. J. Case, *Rep. Oxford Arch. Soc.* LXXXVII (1949), 7–8; S. Piggott, *PPS* XVI (1950), 4 and Pl. II top centre; R. J. C. Atkinson and S. Piggott, *Archaeologia* XCVI (1955), 228, 231; *PP*, 13–14 and Pl. 22a; J. M. de

Navarro, *40. Ber. R-GK 1959* (1960), 91 and n. 25; *Problems*, 76–77 and Pl. Va, c; E. M. Jope, *PPS* XXVII (1961), 312 ff. esp. 320 and fig. 6

[1] *ECA*, no. 125

251 River Witham, near Lincoln. ?Gilt bronze sword scabbard mount L. 13 cm. ?II/I BC. Coll. Duke of Northumberland, Alnwick Castle. *Kenneth Graham, Alnwick.*

This sword and mount for a sheath, which was presumably originally of leather and no longer survives, is only one of several Iron Age objects recovered from the River Witham [see also **252** and notes to **272**]. This locket with its consciously asymmetric pattern imitating the decorative layout of the upper part of all-bronze continental scabbards,[1] like the first Wandsworth boss [**247**], combines fine line engraving with low-relief ornament. The chape, now lost, seems to have been derived from the tight clinging Middle La Tène pattern, but is close to the 'split-lipped' form of Bugthorpe [**259**].

The basic pattern, a combination of partial or split-palmette forms in which one may see a chance for a 'bilingual' reading – is it a plant or the leg and wing of a bird? – is very close to details of the Wandsworth boss and must be regarded as a product of the same workshop, if not indeed craftsman. In view of the early concentrations of La Tène metal-workers in the Thames valley [see notes to **248**], it would seem reasonable to centre the workshop of the 'Wandsworth-Witham master' in the latter region rather than in Lincolnshire or further to the north.

Proc. Soc. Antiq. I ser., II (1849–53), 199; J. M. Kemble, *Horae Ferales* (1863), 194 and Pl. XVIII:10; P. Jacobsthal, *Burlington Mag.* 75 (1939), 28 ff.; T. D. Kendrick, *Antiq. J.* XIX (1939), 194–95 and Pl. XLV; F. Saxl and R. Wittkower, *British Art and the Mediterranean* (1948), Pl. 2:5; S. Piggott, *PPS* XVI (1950), 4; *ABA*, Pl. 46; *PP*, 25 ff. and Pl. 22b; *PAE*, 262–63 and Pl. 287

[1] *ECA*, nos. 105, 115–16

252 and Plate VII River Witham near Washingborough, Lincolnshire. Bronze shield with enamel or glass inlay. Present l. 1·13 m., d. of lower roundel c. 14 cm. ?II BC. British Mus., London. (Black-and-white detail of central boss) *R-GK* (E. Neuffer); (all other views) *courtesy Trustees of the British Museum.*

The parade shield found, like the sword [**251**], in 1826, was of some antiquity when disposed of by its Celtic owners since it had been extensively remodelled during its use. It consists of two sheets of bronze; the longitudinal join between the sheets is now covered by the central spine. The bronze had been mounted on a wooden backing, slightly bevelled and bound with a U-strip along the edge; part only of the strip survives. Around a central boss a long emaciated figure of a boar had once been fixed with rivets. The 'ghost' of the boar with its head facing left can just be made out in the general view. The shield was subsequently dismantled and slightly cut down by trimming the inner margins of the two halves. After hammering the sheets all over, a long cast mid-rib with central high domed boss to allow for a rear hand grip was added; a tooling mark runs round the outer margin of the mid-rib, a guide line to the sheet metal worker responsible for trimming the original shield to fit the new casting. Three glass studs have been added to the central boss, while carefully laid out, though not strictly symmetrical, incised ornament has been used in the area of the two terminal discs.

In general layout the spine of the Witham shield is close to the second Wandsworth mount, a detail of which is shown below [255].[1] Artistically Witham is a rag-bag of motifs. To commence with the terminal discs – which look as if at some stage the smith has seen a classical mirror – their internal incised decoration is a transference of the motifs of the Irish sword scabbards from a long rectangular frieze to a circular area; 'hair-spring' spirals and split palmettes abound. Below the nose of the animal supporter an asymmetric panel combining low relief and incision forms almost a twin for the layout of the Witham sword locket [251]. Indeed, nothing about the shield is as symmetrical as it looks at first sight. The central boss is placed above the mid-point of the shield and the upper roundel is smaller than the lower as if to compensate for the effects of parallax in the eyes of a chieftain holding the shield and looking down its length. Only the central boss itself has a genuine fold-over symmetry like that of the first Wandsworth boss [247]. A detail concerning the engraved decoration: many motifs, particularly the palmettes and split-palmettes end with an enlarged dot, a trick which is as archaic as the split palmette itself. The technique can be seen on the Basse-Yutz flagons [60–61] and, more apposite here, on the Cerrig-y-Drudion bowl fragments [114]. As to the (possibly) horse's rather than bull's head supporters with their wing-like ears, these clearly demonstrate the animal-face-constructed-from-a-lyre-palmette which, complete with dot ending, can really be seen behind much more naturalistic heads like the little bull from Mâcon [161]. The wing-like fill-ins, which can also be seen on the central boss, also have a continental air; the motif occurs on the Waldalgesheim gold torc [127] and later on cast armlets,[2] while in Britain it can be seen in a rather freer form on the tubular electrum torc found in Hoard 'A' of the Snettisham group[3] and related to Frasnes-lez-Buissenal [see notes to 173].

Another particularly significant detail, for which insular no less than continental parallels may be quoted, is the triple division of the 'eyes' of the horses and of the glass inlays. These, particularly the moulded pattern on the central glass boss with its three central circles, may be matched not only with the Tarn bracelet [175], but with the ornament on the spring-end discs of the Newnham Croft brooch, whose basic form cannot be earlier than Middle La Tène on the continent.[4]

The Witham shield lacks the obvious bird features of the first Wandsworth boss but the swelling lyre forms flanking the central coral roundel and the fat double comma features above each horse head are certainly as duck-like as the pseudo-birds on earlier continental material [106–107]. The wavy crimped surround of the terminal 'roundels', as well as these pseudo-birds, is another point of similarity with the two Wandsworth shield mounts. The edging ornament of the Witham mount, produced by alternate blows of the punch, is similar to the Torrs cap [244], a piece which is usually, but without particularly good reason, considered earlier in date than Witham. The 'rosettes' on the large Witham

boss have an affinity with those on what should be a later piece, the boss from Peterborough.[5]

As to the use to which Witham may have been put, it can hardly have been defensive since even with a wooden backing the thickness of the shield cannot have exceeded 0·5 cm. The shape of the shield is similar to those shown on the Gundestrup cauldron or to early first century AD representations such as the triumphal arch at Orange, erected probably in either AD 21 or 26/27 after suppression of the Gaulish revolt[6] and which provides good models for the later Battersea shield illustrated on the following page [253]. The boar crest of the first stage of Witham's construction is yet another example of the importance of this cultic totem animal, whose elongated limbs and curly tail recall the Rynkeby figures [222a].

J. M. Kemble *Horae Ferales* (1863), Pl. XIV:1; W. A. von Jenny, *Keltische Metallarbeiten* (1935), Taf. 34–35; F. Saxl and R. Wittkower, *British Art and the Mediterranean* (1948), Pl. 4:1; *ABA*, Pl. 56; *LPA*, Pl. XIX:1; *Besançon*, 10 and Abb. 4; *PP*, 26–27, Frontispiece and pl. 15; *Problems*, 77 ff.; *PRB*, Pls. 252–53; *PreA*, 236 and ill. 241–42; *PAE*, 203, Frontispiece and Pls. 290–91

[1] *PP*, Pl. 14b
[2] *ArtG*, 240, Pl. 36
[3] R. Rainbird Clarke, *PPS* XX (1954), 35 ff. and fig. 4; *PP*, fig. 35; see also notes to [291]
[4] *PP*, 11 and fig. 6b; see also [131]
[5] *LPA*, 66 and fig. 25:2; *Problems*, 82, n. 87
[6] *Celts*, Pls. 50–51; R. Amy *et al.*, 'L'Arc d'Orange' = XVᵉ suppl. *Gallia* (1962), esp. 107–40 and Pls. 75–82

253 River Thames at Battersea, Middlesex. Bronze shield with glass inlays. L. 77·5 cm., w. of 'horns' in detail c. 5 cm. I AD. British Mus., London. (General view): *courtesy Trustees of the British Museum*; (detail) *J. V. S. Megaw*.

This shield, recovered from the Thames in 1857, is made up of four separate sheets of bronze only 0·1 to 0·3 mm. thick and originally bound and riveted to a wood or leather backing. Three discs with central bosses and red glass inlay are cast and riveted on to the main surface. At the rear of the main boss an openwork bronze plaque found with the shield must have formed the handle grip; it has provision for thirteen small rivets and is decorated with a series of dot-filled curved triangles. Voids in the design form paired ovals and linked trumpets at the centre of each side, a motif common only in later British art [see 272]. The dotted background is a feature of much of later British metal-work, while the actual relief ornament on recent examination proves to be made by press-moulding, a technique followed by a late group of so-called 'casket ornament' strips [see notes to 299].[1]

Despite a general similarity in form between the Witham shield [252] and Battersea, the latter is immediately set apart from Witham and objects associated with it by its rigid symmetry. The whole shield, with its markedly waisted form, owes more to Roman military equipment as seen, for example, on Trajan's column and to provincial bronzes of the Augustan period than to the planned disorganisation of the presumed 'early' British material; even the employment of variants on the trumpet spiral on the Battersea shield have perfectly good analogies amongst provincial Roman material.[2]

Like Witham, however, is the provision of animalistic supporters; here they look outward, or so it might seem at first glance. The detail view shows the upper face seen from the end of the shield as it would have appeared to the wearer of the shield. From this angle one has a monstrous being with bulbous nose, eyes formed by two rivets and a great crown or curling horns in the manner of the Aylesford bucket heads [187]. When viewed the 'correct' way up, the same detail gives us a great gaping-mouthed creature with out-curling whiskers to be compared with the rear 'face' of the large Maloměřice mount [160] or the first/second century AD Culbin Sands armlet [302]. Two other reversible and even more elusive 'faces' can be made out above and below the central roundel. Here in a much less explicit version of the Dürkheim 'funny faces' [59] two 'eyes' formed by a closely placed pair of glass-filled roundels meet either side of a thin spine. From one aspect one may see a nose with tiny glum mouth very much in the manner of the surviving face of the second Wandsworth mount [255], from the other aspect a thin pencil moustache, the spindly tendrils curling up to the sides being a last version of the old leaf-crown motif. Here the bird symbolism of Witham and the Wandsworth mounts has been replaced by man, albeit in shadowy form. The Celtic belief in the personality within individual weapons may be behind these strange faces no less than behind such things as the human-head sword stamps of the continent [191–193]. Birds' heads may also be read into the outer spirals of the smaller roundels – a pair of open-mouthed ducks, the actual heads formed by in-filled roundels.

The basic shape and method of manufacture of each of the originally 25 red glass-decorated roundels is similar. Recent studies in the British Museum's Research Laboratory have shown that the glass was first pressed, when in a semi-molten state, against the swastika-shaped and domed openwork bronze, the whole when cool being fixed into dished hollows coated with pitch or bituminous cement (as can be seen in the empty area on the left of the detailed illustration), each piece being held by a central pin. A similar technique was followed in assembling the glass-decorated discs found in two Belgic graves of the first century AD, the Lexden 'royal barrow' outside Colchester containing the remains of a Romanised Celtic chieftain associated with a great boar figure and a medallion of Augustus, and a burial of the Welwyn type of c. AD 40 on Hertford Heath, with imported amphorae.[3] The 'swastika' or 'paddle-arm' form of the fretting has a close parallel on a horn' cap' from the Llyn Cerrig Bach deposit,[4] related in shape to that from Brentford [130]. On analysis the glass – not strictly an enamel – seems to have a very similar chemical composition not only to the Lexden and Hertford studs but to the inlay on two helmets illustrated here [294, 300] as well as to some of the harness mounts decorated in the post-conquest period [see **Plate VIIIa**]. The material, a cupric glass with high lead content, to judge from the evidence of a block found at Tara in Ireland, seems to have been imported in bulk form from Italy or perhaps even from the Near East, a process which could well have made use of the established trade routes of the early Roman empire and which recalls late accounts of the skill of 'the barbarians who live by the Ocean'.[5]

Despite earlier accounts, there is no evidence that the

Battersea shield was ever gilded. A sword scabbard of Piggott's I AD Group IV class also comes from the same reach of the Thames.[6] All in all, it now seems best to regard the Battersea shield as a late piece made under strong Roman influence.

R. A. Smith, *Early Iron Age Antiquities in the British Museum* (2 ed., 1925), 106; E. T. Leeds, *Celtic Ornament* (1933), 23; W. A. von Jenny, *Keltische Metallarbeiten* (1935), Taf. 34:2; *ABA*, Pl. 55; J. W. Brailsford *Actas IV sesion Congr. Intern. de Ciencias prehist. y protohist.* (1954), 759–60; *LPA*, Pl. XX:2; *PP*, 27 ff. and Pls. 14a, 16–17; *Problems*, 82; *PRB*, Pl. 251; *PreA*, 236 and ill. 246; *PAE*, 264 and Pl. 292; *EV*, 220, ill. p. 221

[1] J. V. S. Megaw, *Antiq. J.* XLIII (1963), 30
[2] W. A. von Jenny, *IPEK* (1935), 31–48
[3] Lexden: P. G. Laver, *Archaeologia* LXXVI (1926–27), Pl. LX:1; see also Françoise Henry, *Préhistoire* II:1 (1933), 81 and fig. 7:2–6; Hertford Heath: J. Holmes and W. M. C. Frend, *East Herts. Arch. Soc.* XIV (1955–57), 1–19, esp. Pl. 2
[4] *PP*, 28 and fig. 15; see also notes on [254]
[5] Philostratus, *Iconographia* I, 1, XXVIII
[6] *PP*, 117 and fig. 73:6

254 Llyn Cerrig Bach, Anglesey. Detail of bronze disc with eccentric circular opening. Total d. 18·3 cm., d. of central decorated area 6·7 cm. ?Early I BC. National Mus. of Wales, Cardiff.

This is a detail of what may have been part of the decoration of a chariot pole at the point where the pole meets the body of the chariot. The disc comes from a find which might be termed the British counterpart of the site of La Tène.

In 1942–43, during the construction of Valley Aerodrome near Holyhead on the Isle of Anglesey, off the north-western tip of Wales, some 150 objects were recovered from a peat-bog. The objects seem to span in date the period from the later second century BC to the first century AD. They probably originated from three main areas, south-west England, south-east England and Ireland, and comprised various parts for chariots and waggons, shield mounts, some eleven swords, harness fittings and domestic objects such as box mounts [see 299]; there was also a slave chain with forged steel links. In the general area of the deposit were quantities of pig, ox and goat or sheep bones. It seems probable that here was another area for ritual depositions,[1] the last stages of which may be related to the events of AD 60–61 when Suetonius Paulinus led his legions against the Druid-controlled stronghold of Mona (Anglesey).[2]

The Llyn Cerrig plaque stands as a key piece for the later mainstream of British Iron Age art in which a simplification of the 'pseudo-birds' heads' and 'snail spirals' of Torrs and Witham are translated into a series of designs which often incorporate low relief cast or *repoussé* (as here) comma-leaf or lobed elements ending in a concave facet like a simple horn or trumpet. Such 'Llyn Cerrig' spirals may be seen as descendants of motifs as early as the fourth century comma-eyes on such objects as the 'Janus' brooch from Weiskirchen [67] and in its purest insular form is illustrated here by a horse-bit from the Thames at Old Windsor [258]. On the present plaque we have an elaboration of the old triskel pattern, a motif of great importance and, perhaps, magical potency in later insular art which must be related to the two-dimensional engraved patterns on the contentious Tal-y-llyn finds [266].

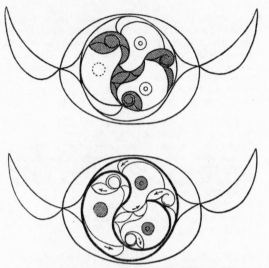

Fig. 13 [254] Llyn Cerrig Bach, Anglesey. Two readings of decoration on bronze disc; (above) triskel and (below) *yin-yang*. Scale c. 2:5 *After Duval*

Two other features may be noted about this later mainstream art. First, it is usually asymmetric despite careful layout often clearly making use of a compass-drawn sketch [see 256]. Second is the equal importance to the over-all design offered by the blanks or voids often as here represented by curved-sided triangles. Voids are particularly important in the development of the layout of the mirror series of the Belgic south-east [260–261], and related to the Celtic 'yin-yang' or tightly clinging double-comma motif. Two examples of a similar use of voids may be quoted: an openwork plaque from the Oxford region and a disc from the Yorkshire Grimthorpe warrior's grave.[3]

It is difficult to suggest an area for the development of the 'Llyn Cerrig' spiral; Fox favoured central or north-eastern England and since the former sees a fair concentration of objects of the presumed earlier Torrs Wandsworth style, this may be a reasonable guess though the concept of fixed 'regions' may cloak the true peripatetic nature of Iron Age skilled craftsmen, even if the Tal-y-llyn find suggests craftsmen working in Wales – and the actual Llyn Cerrig hoard contains smith's tongs.

C. Fox, *A find of the Early Iron Age from Llyn Cerrig Bach, Anglesey* (1947), esp. 46 ff. and Pls. I, XXXII=no. 75; *ABA*, Pl. 42; *PP*, 33, fig. 18, and Pl. 23a; L. Alcock in (ed.) E. Davies, *Celtic Studies in Wales: a survey* (1963), 23 ff. and Pl. IV below; P.-M. Duval, *Art de France* IV (1964), illus. on p. 26; *PRB*, Pl. 273; H. N. Savory, *Early Iron Age Art in Wales* (1969), 20 and fig. 15

[1] *PCB*, 24 ff.
[2] Tacitus, *Annals* XIV, 30
[3] Oxfordshire: *PP*, 121–22, fig. 75 below and Pl. 69a;

Grimthorpe: *PP*, 33, 35 and Pl. 23b; I. M. Stead, *PPS* XXXIV (1968), 169 and fig. 13:1

255 River Thames at Wandsworth, Middlesex. Detail of bronze shield mount 2. Total surviving l. 38 cm., w. across top of 'head' c. 5 cm. ?II/I BC. British Mus., London. *J. V. S. Megaw.*

The long mid-rib with central boss raised from a single sheet with subsequent engraved detailing was found with the first shield boss [247] during dredging operations in 1849. Illustrated here is the one surviving end of the mid-rib, the other end having broken off, though rivets still in place (which indicate a total thickness for the shield of c. 1 cm.) suggest that the shield may have been deposited with some of the wooden backing remaining. The decoration of the central boss is a fold-over design. The main feature is a pair of birds' heads with great down-curving beaks which spring from one corner of a pair of triangles at opposite ends of the boss, while from another corner of the same triangle depends a lobed leaf with engraved hair-spring spirals; the two opposing triangles are linked by a wavy or crimped line. Many details are matched by the first Wandsworth boss and both pieces must have come from the same crafts centre. The recent discovery of a I BC/AD workshop at South Cadbury includes a related shield-boss.[1]

As to the head shown here, the bulbous nose and tiny mouth look forward to the faces and pseudo-faces of Battersea [253]; the great eyes were originally constructed of a spiralling dome forming a unit with the nose whose nostrils are formed by tiny 'hair-spring' spirals. A rare piece of detailing appears in the much worn 'teeth' on the face's lip. Here, it seems clear, the representation is basically that of man rather than beast.

J. Kemble, *Horae Ferales* (1863), Pl. XVI:2; *LPA*, Pl. XX:2; *PP*, 26 and Pl. 14b; *PAE*, 261–62 and Pl. 288

[1] L. Alcock, *Antiquity* XLIV (1970), 46 ff.; M. G. Spratling, *Current Arch.* 18 (1970), 188 ff.

256 Lough Crew, Cairn 'H', Co. Meath. Two bone 'trial pieces'. L. of larger piece c. 14 cm. ?Late I BC/I AD. National Mus. of Ireland, Dublin. *Belzeaux-Zodiaque.*

Cairn 'H' is one of the complex of Neolithic passage graves at Lough Crew in the bend of the River Boyne. Within the cairn and interpreted by all save the most recent excavator – whose full report is still awaited – as a later Iron Age re-occupation, was a mass of glass and amber with iron debris as well as a group of thin slivers of decorated bone of which two are illustrated here. In advance of the final analysis of the site it seems not unlikely that Cairn 'H' contains a unique archaeological find; the remains of a temporary workshop belonging to a local Celtic craftsman [see also notes to 255].

The plaques – which include in two cases what appear to be parts of weaving combs – have parts of or complete ornamental units carefully scribed on them. All the patterns save one are carefully compass-drawn curvilinear designs, the exception being a fragmentary plaque with a crude drawing of a stag followed by another animal, though even here the stag's single eye is a compass-drawn circle. The larger plaque here is a careful exercise in geometric construction since from the compass points it is possible to reconstruct that the

152

design has been laid out on the basis of a drawn grid perhaps first sketched out and then transferred to the surface of the bone; the basic pattern with its Celtic 'yin-yangs' resembles features of the southern mirrors and related objects [257, 259–260] or, more closely, such late harness mounts as those from Santon in Norfolk

Fig. 14 [256] Bone trial piece. Squared framework for determining centres for main arcs and construction of incised design. Scale c. 2:1
After Henry

[Plate VIIIa]. This latter parallel is perhaps the better since the second plaque illustrated here incorporates a broken-backed coil, a motif which is generally not in evidence until about the mid-first century AD.[1] Yet other plaques from Lough Crew have dot-infilled patterns matched not only by details of the Battersea shield but by an actual comb with slight but carefully compass-drawn ornament found with an early penannular brooch at Langbank Crannog, Renfrewshire, datable also to the first century AD.

The careful laying out of geometric designs on the Lough Crew 'trial pieces' prior presumably to their transfer on to metal objects – perhaps neck-rings like the great Broighter torc [289] – predates the similar geometric concern of the illuminators of the Hiberno-Scottish gospels, let alone the smith responsible for making the hero Cú Chulainn's shield, who was instructed by a god laying out the design with compasses.

E. A. Conwell, *The Tomb of Ollamh Fodhla* (1873), 54; Margaret Stokes, *Archaeologia* XLVII (1883), 478 and Pl. XXIV; H. S. Crawford, *J. Roy. Soc. Antiq. Ireland* XLIV (1914), 161–63; *ibid.*, LV (1925), 15–29; H. G.

Tempest, *Man* XLIV (1949), 13–16; J. Raftery, *Prehistoric Ireland* (1951), 106 n., 206; J. M. de Navarro in (ed.) M. Charlesworth, *Heritage of Early Britain* (1952), 77 and figs, VI–VII; S. P. Ó Ríordáin and G. E. Daniel, *New Grange and the Bend of the Boyne* (1964), 122–24; Françoise Henry, *Irish Art (to AD 800)* (1966), 15, 218 ff., fig. 31 and Pl. 8; *PAE*, 257 ff.

[1] *PP*, 107 and Pl. 29a; Morna Simpson in (ed.) J. M. Coles and D. D. A. Simpson, *Studies in Ancient Europe: essays presented to Stuart Piggott* (1968), 248 ff.

257 River Thames at Datchet, Berkshire. Iron spear with bronze attachments. Total l. c. 30 cm., l. of right-hand bronze ornament 9 cm. Later I BC/early I AD. British Mus., London. *J. V. S. Megaw.*

The assured asymmetry of the bronze plates of the Datchet spear has been compared with the layout of objects of the Torrs-Wandsworth 'school' – a design which looks as if it should have fold-over balance but hasn't. None the less, the incised decoration of the four bronze plates, fixed to both sides of the spear with bronze rivets filed flush with the surface, is as carefully laid out as that on the Lough Crew 'trial pieces'. The more accomplished side is shown here.

If the asymmetry should recall earlier supposedly central or north-eastern work, the setting off of a pattern of circles and curved-sided triangles by a series of areas of true 'matting' is a characteristic of southern England and particularly of such pieces as the Mayer mirror [260]. This matting, which may possibly imitate contemporary weaving techniques, is produced by interrupted rather than rocked tracer lines and consists of groups of parallel incisions set at right angles to each other, a technique which Fox regards as peculiar to the south-west but which occurs on the Lisnacrogher 3 scabbard.[1] From the south-west it can be noted on a mirror from a woman's grave in a cemetery at Trelan Bahow, St Keverne, Cornwall, and a scabbard found in a peat bog on Meare Heath, Somerset, in 1928,[2] one of Piggott's group III scabbards[3] comparable with that from Bugthorpe illustrated on the right [259]. Another scabbard of this group closer in its decoration to Datchet is that from the Hunsbury hill-fort in Northamptonshire, and another mirror which tends to support Fox's ultimate choice of an eastern, indeed local Thames origin for Datchet is the engraved one of a pair from Billericay, Essex.[4]

J. B. Ward Perkins, *PPS* V (1939), 189–90 and Pl. XX; *ABA*, Pl. 47; *LPA*, fig. 21:6; *PP*, 49, 52–53 and Pl. 39a

[1] E. M. Jope, *Ulster J. Arch.* 17 (1954), 84–86 and Pl. VII
[2] Trelan Bahow: *PP*, 98, and Pl. 7a; A. Fox, *South West England* (1964), Pl. 76; Meare: *PP*, 40–41 and fig. 24:3; Fox, *op. cit.*, 133 and fig. 41
[3] S. Piggott, *PPS* XVI (1950), fig. 3
[4] Hunsbury: *PP*, 40–41 and fig. 24:1; Billericay: *PP*, 97–98, fig. 61 and Pl. 56f.; *PAE*, 268 and fig. 102

258 River Thames at Old Windsor, Berkshire. Detail of link and side-ring of bronze bit. Total l. 10·6 cm., d. of actual ring 1·2 cm. ?Earlier I BC. London Mus.

The horse bit of which this is a detail was found in

1897 and is one of four bits found in or close to the Thames. It belongs to a group of first-century decorated bits, designated class IIb in a series which begins in the late Yorkshire chariot graves now dated to late in the second century. Such bits are only generally related to the bit types of the continental Early La Tène graves.[1]

This bit, like others of its class, consists of a central figure-of-eight link with pronounced central moulding flanked by two side-links and two side-rings, not quite true circles and cast in one solid piece with the link heads. Each side-ring has provision for enamel-filled studs – vestigial stop-knobs copied from those bits in which the rings move freely on the links. Decoration survives on the heads of both side-links. On the detail shown here, within a scribed double bowed border is a fine example of a plastic 'Llyn Cerrig' comma or trumpet spiral given even more of an eye-like aspect by the setting for a now missing enamel or glass stud. The double bow border follows the style of the Datchet spear. On the reverse, not visible here, is a curved-sided triangle or void with tailing-out spiral somewhat in the manner of the smaller Lough Crew plaque [256] with its foretaste of the broken-backed spiral motif.

On the other link-head of the Old Windsor bit is a series of four scribed circles. The largest of these circles is on the upper surface and is hollowed out for inlay and, like the vestigial stop-knobs, has the pin fastening still visible. There is a small area of rough matting design, as on Datchet produced by interrupted taps of the tracer. Matting also occurs on other horse bits presumed to be contemporary. One from Walthamstow in Essex has the design enclosed between a bordering line, matting on ends of side-links, and ridged centre knob all offering similarities with Old Windsor and suggesting a common workshop. Bits from Ulceby in Lincolnshire also have some comparable features but cannot be considered as real companion pieces.[2]

Some doubt has been voiced by the present writer amongst others that such small bits as Old Windsor with immovable side-links could ever have been more than show pieces; instead they may have been awards given for prowess in chariot racing as one reads of in the old Irish hero tales. The decoration is certainly concentrated on one side only of the bits; though, making allowance for the smaller Celtic ponies of the pre-Roman Iron Age, standing some 11 hands, it would in fact be possible actually to use the horse bits;[3] after all, not every piece of insular fine metal-work must necessarily have served a ritual purpose.

J. Barber and J. V. S. Megaw, *PPS* XXIX (1963), 206–13; I. M. Stead, *La Tène Cultures of Eastern Yorkshire* (1965), 37–42, esp. p. 43

[1] J. B. Ward Perkins, *PPS* V (1939), 175–92; C. Fox, *A find of the Early Iron Age from Llyn Cerrig Bach, Anglesey* (1947), 27–34; E. M. Jope, *Ulster J. Arch.* 13 (1950), 57–60; 18 (1955), 37–44
[2] Ward Perkins, *op. cit.*, 181, figs. 3, 6 and Pl. XVIII
[3] R. B. K. Stevenson in (ed.) A. L. F. Rivet, *Iron Age in Northern Britain* (1966), 42, n. 82

259 Bugthorpe, East Riding, Yorkshire. Detail of bronze and iron scabbard with fragmentary iron blade. Total

l. 61·5 cm., maximum w. 4·5 cm. Later I BC. British Mus., London. (*Courtesy Trustees of the British Museum.*)

This example of one of Piggott's group III scabbards with its great cast lipped chape was found with bronze discs and studs, originally with enamel rather than coral settings, and probably came from a grave rather than from a ritual deposit.

Most decorated of all British scabbards, which unlike most of the continental Middle La Tène examples are decorated all over from mouth to chape, Bugthorpe may be contrasted rather than compared with the Ulster scabbards [248–249]. Circular settings, two as on Lisnacrogher 3 below the mouth, and the two visible here must have held inlay, but the incised pattern which also occurs on the more mirror-like decoration of the Meare and Hunsbury group III scabbards is like Datchet [see 257] in that no two sections of the pattern quite match; each unit of the design encloses a curved-sided triangle. The Bugthorpe scabbard is close in form to that from a warrior's grave with shield and spear from near a hill-fort at Grimthorpe, also in the East Riding. On the Grimthorpe scabbard 'bird bridge' bindings are replaced by comma-leaves with cross-hatching.[1]

Noting the matting hatching one might consider Bugthorpe a product of refugee craftsmen from the south-east following the pressures applied from about 100 BC by the Belgic settlement, although in view of the association of the 'mirror style' with Belgic sites this seems unlikely [see notes to 260 ff.]. Certainly the cast tailed 'trumpets' on the chape match closely those on torcs of the East Anglian Snettisham-Ipswich group [291–292] while the surviving horse bit fragment from Ulceby combines some matting with the spindly trumpets for which the Llyn Cerrig plaque is considered the prototype. One strange allusion of form – or is it illusion? – of the Bugthorpe chape can be observed if the scabbard is viewed sideways: the lips of the chape become the great pouting mouth of a fish, perhaps a carp, one tailed trumpet here actually becoming an eye. Fish, though rare in Iron Age art save for the eastern antecedents of Gundestrup [219–220], are known in Britain from one other piece [276].

It seems unnecessary to separate Datchet and Bugthorpe chronologically; indeed the latter's stylistic schizophrenia is probably due to nothing more than the exchange of motifs between two travelling groups of craftsmen.

S. Piggott, *PPS* XVI (1950), 12 ff. and fig. 2:5; *LPA*, fig. 23:3; *PP*, 41–42 and figs. 26–27; I. M. Stead, *La Tène Cultures of Eastern Yorkshire* (1965), 60 ff.; *PAE*, 266 and fig. 101 right

[1] *PP*, 35 and fig. 20:1; Stead, *PPS* XXXIV (1968), 170, 179 and figs. 14–15; see also notes to [248, 254]

260 ?South-east England. The 'Mayer' engraved bronze mirror. Over-all ht. 22·5 cm. Later I BC. City of Liverpool Mus.

Mention has been made briefly in these pages of mirrors found in continental early La Tène contexts [see notes to 73]; occasional mirrors with human handles in the classical manner do occur but in fact Celtic mirrors of any type are rare on the continent after the fourth century BC,[1] though an even later find, the mirror from Hochheim, has a face handle, compared sometimes with the Nauheim pendant [197].[2]

The earliest mirror in Britain is that from the 'Lady's Barrow' at Arras in Yorkshire; however, if continental parallels must be sought for this probably second-century BC piece, the closest come from east European nomad contexts![3]

Until now the study of some eighteen surviving decorated British mirrors has been based almost entirely on the work of the late Sir Cyril Fox;[4] Fox maintained that the tradition of decorating mirrors on one surface developed over a fairly short period of time between about 50 BC and the mid-first century AD, probably in the territory of the Dobuni around the Bristol Channel at the southern end of the Jurassic limestone ridge which acts as a natural link between the south-west and north-east Yorkshire. In fact, though there is little need to quarrel with the suggested dating, the distribution of mirrors is mainly in the south-east where most come from elderly women's graves which in several cases may be associated with the Belgic overlords of southern England. In the south-east, most of the mirrors are kidney-shaped rather than circular and most may well have been made by non-Belgic craftsmen working for members of the dynasty of the Catuvellauni with their tribal capital at Colchester. Outside Colchester a woman's grave yielded up a kidney-shaped mirror with lyre-based design whose layout is a rationalisation in three units of the loose flowing ornament as seen on the Torrs pony-cap [see 244]. Colchester,[5] with no matting ornament but parallel tremolo lines executed at a date in the last decades of the first century BC, may be as early as any of the south-eastern mirrors.

Basically the British mirrors are variations on a triple unit, a lyre with flanking scrolls. In later mirrors, together with a greater complexity of the separately cast handles, the main motif either breaks down into a complex disunity or, in contrast, is over-formalised perhaps under the influence of Augustan or early Julio-Claudian provincial art.

The Mayer mirror, given to Liverpool Corporation in 1867 by Joseph Mayer, son of a tanner from Newcastle-under-Lyme, is supposed to have come from the Thames. Under a carefully constructed exercise in geometric draftsmanship can just be made out the freehand sketch lines; the pattern itself as observed here is an inverted lyre with three separate variations on, ultimately, 'Llyn Cerrig' themes [254]. Such seemingly dissimilar pieces as the Datchet spear [257] look like work from the same master engraver; amongst mirrors the Trelan Bahow and Billericay mirrors, cited already in connection with Datchet, are closest. The matting on Mayer is produced by simple engraved lines and not rocked tracer work as has been recently stated.

PP, 85 ff., fig. 25 and Pls. 55–56a; *PRB*, pl. 274; *PreA*, 243 and ill. 249; *PAE*, 268 and Pl. 303; H. N. Savory, *Early Iron Age art in Wales* (1968), 21 and fig. 18

[1] J. Břeň, *Třísov: a Celtic oppidum* (1966), 120 and n. 97
[2] *ECA*, no. 324

[3] *PP*, 7 and Pl. 7a; I. M. Stead, *La Tène Cultures of Eastern Yorkshire* (1965), 55–56 and fig. 31
[4] C. Fox, *Arch. Cambrensis* XCVIII (1944–45), 199–220; *id.*, *Arch. Cambrensis* C (1948–49), 24–44; Fox and M. R. Hull, *Antiq. J.* XXVIII (1948), 123–37; *PP*, 84–105
[5] Fox and Hull, *Antiq. J.* XXVIII, *loc. cit.*, *PP*, 88 ff. and fig. 51; see also notes to [223]

261 Great Chesterford, Essex. Detail of top right corner of engraved bronze mirror. Over-all ht. 23·5 cm., ht. of detail c. 4 cm. Early I AD. University Mus. of Archaeology and Ethnology, Cambridge.

Fig. 15 [**261**] Great Chesterford, England. Engraved bronze mirror. Layout of decoration on back (small dots indicate calculated centres for drawing main arcs). Scale 3 : 7   *After Fox*

This detail of the most recently found of the south-east kidney-shaped mirrors shows a much more roughly executed design carefully laid out nonetheless on an eccentric axis which runs top left to bottom right and which is based, like Mayer, on three units with much use of the curved-sided triangle. The detail shown here illustrates well the near-abandon with which the incised ornament has been executed. Two other mirrors, that from Old Warden in Bedfordshire and the so-called 'Disney' mirror[1] exhibit the same loose asymmetry in which the design can be seen almost falling apart before one's eyes; the starting point is again the Billericay mirror. The hatched decoration runs under the complex moulded handle in the same way as the hatching on the Colchester mirror, also with complex moulded handle; such handles recall the central mouldings of horse-bits like that from Old Windsor [258]. The circumstances of the Great Chesterford find suggest that the mirror may have formed part of a bucket burial [see notes to 187].

Sir Cyril Fox, *Antiquity* XXXIV (1960), 207–10

[1] Old Warden: *PP*, 94–95 and Pl. 60; 'Disney': *PP*, Pl. 56g

262 Tal-y-llyn, Merioneth. Detail of bronze shield mount no. 1. D. of decorated area c. 8·5 cm. ?Early I BC. National Mus. of Wales, Cardiff. (*Courtesy Idris Table Waters Ltd.*)

In 1963 a hoard of bronze and brass fragments was found under a boulder at a height of about 230 metres above sea-level on the western slopes of Nant Cader [see also 266–267]. The present detail is from one of a pair of pelta-shaped mounts reconstructed as part of a shield with central mid-rib like that found at Moel Hiraddug [see 268]; a central boss from the same Tal-y-llyn shield is illustrated below [267].

The basic triskel design laid out on the basis of lightly scored grid lines, as is the whole roundel, has echoes of the Llyn Cerrig plaque – a central knob or rivet head now missing has worn down the centre point of the design which is executed with a rocked tracer throughout. A subsidiary outer pattern of triple 'wave curls' – an archaic note this, since it can be traced back to such fourth-century La Tène pieces as the Želkovice plaque [71] – forms the outer margin of a second triskel formed by the undecorated void. The surround of triangles can be paralleled on, once more, the Trelan Bahow mirror [see notes to 257], as well as the other two surviving Tal-y-llyn shield no. 1 mounts. Another Welsh shield mount with rocked-tracer decoration, rough outlining and similar playing on the voids comes from the Llyn Cerrig Bach deposit[1] while the trumpet repair strip from the same find shows rather cruder tracer work.[2]

There has been much discussion concerning the date of the Tal-y-llyn material, the original publisher favouring a date not later than the third century BC. If valid, on the dating here favoured for British material, the Tal-y-llyn find would contain the oldest insular art in Iron Age Britain. Whatever the date of the oldest finds in the hoard, which has all the appearance of a tinker's collection of scrap, the date of deposition must be in the first century AD since it includes a Roman lock plate.[3] Rocked-tracer technique is no chronological guide since, though used on Early La Tène derived daggers from the Thames valley,[4] it can also be seen on the first-century Old Warden mirror [see notes to 261]. The triskel is certainly a motif of great antiquity but, given the derivatives on the Llyn Cerrig shield boss which Fox relates to Bugthorpe [259], can be brought down to at least the second century BC and lasts well into the Roman period as evidenced by a compass-drawn triskel on a plaque from Kyngadle, Carmarthenshire, and an openwork piece from Coygan Camp.[5] The use of thin plating and copper-zinc or brass alloys for other pieces of the Tal-y-llyn hoard may suggest a latish date since copper-zinc alloying is usually considered as a Roman introduction to native metallurgy; however, in our present lack of detailed knowledge of later prehistoric British technology, this cannot be used as so firm an argument for a late date for the *whole* hoard. Nonetheless, though the Tal-y-llyn hoard certainly emphasises the importance of the west of Britain at an early stage in the development of insular Iron Age art, to date this stage to the third century seems as yet largely unfounded, all the more since shield bosses of the type found at Tal-y-llyn were not evolved on the continent until LT II.

H. N. Savory, *Bull. Board Celtic Studies*, 20 (1964), 449–75, esp. 455 ff., figs. 1–3, and Pl. III; *id.*, *Antiquity* XXXVIII (1964), 20–23 and Pl. VII; *PRB*, Pl. 276; *PreA*, 240 and ill. 247; Savory, *Early Iron Age Art in Wales* (1968), fig. 8; *PAE*, 268 and n. 25; I. M. Stead, *PPS* XXXIV (1968), 176 and fig. 18

[1] *PP*, 43–44 and figs. 28–29
[2] C. Fox, *An Early Iron Age find from Llyn Cerrig Bach, Anglesey* (1947), no. 74; Savory, *Early Iron Age Art in Wales*, fig. 14
[3] M. G. Spratling, *Antiquity* XL (1966), 229–30; *contra*, Savory, *Antiquity* XL, 305
[4] E. M. Jope, *PPS* XXVII (1961), 316–17
[5] Kyngadle: H.-J. Eggers, *JR-GZM*, 13 (1966), 3–4, 103 and Abb 47=no. 12; Coygan: G. J. Wainwright, *Coygan Camp* (1967), 85–86 and fig. 22:3; Savory, *Early Iron Age Art in Wales*, fig. 29

263 Nijmegen, Gelderland. Detail of inlaid bronze mirror handle. Total w. 29·3 cm., w. of handle mount c. 9 cm. Later I AD. Rijksmus. G. M. Kam, Nijmegen. (*Courtesy Trustees of the British Museum.*)

This is one of two later Iron Age exports from Britain to the continent [see also 277]; originally repaired with a bone or wooden handle, it was found in the Roman legionary centre of Numaga in 1926–7, allegedly in a grave with a glass vessel with 'M'-shaped handles and with Gallo-Belgic ware of first-century AD date, of a type exported to southern English sites including the tribal capital of the Dobuni at Bagendon in Gloucestershire.[1] The mirror is the largest and also one of the latest of the British mirrors. The incised design with its matting is an open palmette with disjointed segments or peltas in a broken-down but symmetrical version of the tight symmetry of such pieces as the Colchester mirror; similar peltas can be seen in a West Country find, the ?shield mount from St Mawgan-in-Pydar fort in Cornwall.[2] The heavy cast handle mount which covers a small area of punched matting has three 'buttons' of grey paste, while the broken handle still retains part of its red enamel inlay. The handle proper is more in the style of the post-Roman harness mounts[3] than the other lighter cast handles, and the layout of the central rosette and the high ridges of the main setting may be matched not only with Battersea [253] but, much closer, with the Meyrick collection helmet [300], the over-all design of the Elmswell plaque [303] or the presumably somewhat earlier Aldborough terret [264]. The rosette of the Nijmegen handle which appears first on the Witham shield [252] also occurs on a bronze panel found with Flavian material at the Roman fort of Newstead in Peeblesshire.[4]

It is possible that the mirror may have been brought to the Low Countries by a returning Batavian auxiliary.

G. C. Dunning, *Arch. J.* LXXXV (1928), 67–79; Françoise Henry, *Préhistoire* II:1 (1933), 94 and fig.15:3; H.J.H. van Buchem, *Numaga* Gedenknummer (1955), 21 and Afb. 11; *PP*, 97, 101 and fig. 66:5; J. V. S. Megaw in *Atti del VI Congr. Intern. delle Sci. Preist. e Protostoriche* III (1966), 146 and Tav. CXXXVIII:2

[1] E. Clifford, *Bagendon, a Celtic oppidum* (1961), 12
[2] *PP*, 115 and Pl. 67b
[3] Henry, *op. cit.*, 84 and fig. 11:4; E. T. Leeds, *Celtic ornament* (1933), 52 and Pl. II:3; see also **Plate VIIIa**
[4] J. Curle, *A Roman frontier post and its people: the fort of Newstead* (1911), 303 and Pl. LXXV:5; see also notes to [268]

264 Aldborough, West Riding, Yorkshire. Bronze coated iron terret. Ht. 12·8 cm., w. across 'horns' 10·1 cm. I AD. Yorkshire Mus., York.

Originally the horns of this terret or rein-ring from Roman Aldborough (Isurium Brigantum) would have formed double rings, the forepart of the mount being curved to fit the edge of a chariot rail.

In Brigantia, a feeling for plastic modelling seems to have survived at a time when linear art was dominant in most of southern Britain. The key features are the use of raised ridges and the effects of light and shade consequent thereupon. The treatment of the originally inlaid eyes of this great jutting-jawed horned face recalls the frontal faces on the Marlborough bucket [188] or the horns of the Boughton Aluph 'Cernunnos' [210]. Here, however, the face is not only more formalised but almost ambiguous. The Nijmegen-like lyre which forms a scarf round the neck of the Aldborough head, almost meeting below the chin and then curling back to end in circular inlay settings on the shoulders, could also be intended to do duty as arms or, with the Rynkeby bulls in mind [222b], legs. It is unfortunate that the nasal area has suffered damage or one might have wondered whether there was not meant to be something bull-like in the face's make-up; note the 'ears' below the horns. One archaic detail is the little bud between the creature's brows, last seen on the Champagne buffer-terminalled torc [120].

As to date, the similarity with the face plaques from Stanwick and the general type represented by this 'skirted' terret indicate the first century AD, though the coating of iron with bronze is an old northern trick used for the earliest native horse-bits [see notes to 258]. A lower limit is offered by the Roman campaign in north Britain of AD 71–74.

I. A. Richmond, *J. Roman Studies* XLIV (1954), 49–50 and Pl. II:2; *PP*, 73 and Pl. 43a; S. Piggott, *Antiq. J.* XXXIX (1959), 31 and Pl. XI:b; J. M. C. Toynbee, *Art in Britain under the Romans* (1964), 24; *PCB*, 93 and Pl. 34a

265 Melsonby near Stanwick, North Riding, Yorkshire. Bronze mount. Ht. 10·1 cm. I AD. British Mus., London. *J. V. S. Megaw.*

About AD 70–74 Petilius Cerialis led a campaign against

Venutius, estranged husband of Cartimandua, queen of the stock-rearing Brigantes who had betrayed Caratacus to the Romans when he had fled from southern Britain to seek asylum in the north.[1] One consequence of the Roman reprisals was the sacking of the Brigantian *oppidum* sited in the area of the little village of Stanwick.[2] Some time before 1846 a number of associated finds of metal-work, in particular harness mounts and horse-bits, were unearthed in the vicinity of the old Brigantian stronghold, most probably buried during the threat of Roman attack; many pieces were decorated with glass matching the composition of the Battersea insets [253].

The present ?chariot mount is one of a pair in *repoussé* technique; the face with its eyes originally inlaid is in a similar style to Aldborough [264], a similarity which would have been even closer if the nose were not damaged. Here there seems no doubt as to the face's human nature; the great curling moustache – or is it a forked beard in the style not only of Gundestrup [209] but also of contemporary Roman *terra sigillata*?[3] – may be matched with the shoulder curls of the Aldborough lyre, the Battersea shield and a tankard-hold-fast from the second, Welwyn 'B' grave, found with two imported wine amphorae,[4] and even the tight curls of the Irish offering bowls [see 269]. Again, like Aldborough, the style, particularly of the eyes, is close to the Marlborough bucket faces. As to the purpose of the plaques one can only assume, like the Waldalgesheim mounts of more than three centuries earlier [118], that the Stanwick faces performed some apotropaic role. The presence of refugees in Brigantia may well explain the 'foreign' elements in certain pieces of the Stanwick finds.

LPA, 62 and Pl. XII:4; *PP*, 73 and Pl. 43b; S. Piggott, *Antiq. J.* XXXIX (1959), 31 and Pl. XIa; Morna MacGregor (=Simpson), *PPS* XXVIII (1962), 27, fig. 13 and Pl. V below=nos. 103–04

[1] Tacitus, *Annals* XXII, 32 ff.; *Histories* III, 43
[2] R. E. M. Wheeler, *The Stanwick fortifications=Soc. Antiq. London Res. Report* XVII (1954)
[3] O. Klindt-Jensen, *Acta Arch.* XX (1949), 121 ff. and fig. 79b–c; *id., Gundestrupkedelen* (1961), 28 and fig. 26–27
[4] J. X. W. P. Corcoran, *PPS* XVIII (1952), Pl. X:2

266 Tal-y-llyn, Merionethshire. Detail of trapezoid bronze ?shield mount. Max. w. 10·4 cm. ?late I BC/early AD. National Mus. of Wales, Cardiff. (*Courtesy Idris Table Waters Ltd.*)

The pair of mounts from the Tal-y-llyn hoard [see also 262], of which one is shown here, are really without parallel. A central stem ends in matching clean-shaven faces and the hair is *en brosse*; these disembodied heads look like twin impaled victims of battle. Certainly if the two trapezoid plaques did decorate a shield and not another chariot, such severed heads would be a visual reminder of the fate in store for a vanquished foe; evidence of heads placed on the ramparts of hill-forts come from several British sites. Surrounding the human-headed dumb-bells is a loose tendril pattern recalling that on the Aylesford bucket while, truncated at the bottom of the illustration, are two duck-like comma features to be matched with those on a first-century

AD collar from Pen-coed-foel hill-fort in Cardiganshire.[1] The separate lobes and the general clumsiness of the vegetable motifs indeed look like a poor local attempt to imitate provincial Roman harness mounts such as were found in the Seven Sisters, Glamorganshire hoard [see also 301][2] or such native masterpieces as the Aesica brooch [305]. The edging of the *repoussé* design with a rocked tracer is, however, a technique followed also by the Tal-y-llyn shield no. 1 boss illustrated on the next page [267]. All in all, a puzzling piece but one which, if anything, tends to support a late-ish date for at least part of the hoard.

H. N. Savory, *Bull. Board Celtic Studies*, 20 (1964), 461–63, fig. 6 and Pl. V; *id.*, *Antiquity* XXXVIII (1964), 24 and Pls. I–II; *id.*, *Celticum* XII=suppl. *Ogam— Tradition Celtique*, 98 (1965), 172–74 and Pl. 107; *id.*, *Early Iron Age Art in Wales* (1968), 19 and fig. 4

[1] *PP*, 106 ff. and Pl. 12d; Savory, *Early Iron Age art in Wales*, fig. 16
[2] *PP*, 127–29 and fig. 78:12

267 Tal-y-llyn, Merioneth. Bronze boss from shield no. 1. Max. w. c. 11·5 cm. ?I BC. National Mus. of Wales, Cardiff. (*Courtesy Idris Table Waters Ltd.*)

The bronze boss illustrated here has been reasonably reconstructed as the central decorative feature of a shield, a second mount from which is illustrated above [262]. The shield has been reconstructed as similar to one from Moel Hiraddug [see 268], and the Stanfordbury 'A' 'Welwyn type' burial chamber also contained such a boss which may have been of related form.[1] The main design of the Tal-y-llyn boss is, like the incised plaque, a triskel, here in *repoussé* but with provision for a central stud and with the main curves of the pattern outlined with a rocked tracer as on the trapezoid plaques [266]. There is a series of rocked-tracer triangles on the outside perimeter of the designs not visible in this illustration.

Here, though the triskel is 'broken-backed', the comma tails of each arm droop sharply from an angled break. Such broken-backed elements, seen more clearly in the next illustration, are a feature of native, post-conquest material such as on a series of brooch covers – which, on the latest evidence, should date from the first century AD[2] – a lost tankard mount from Elvedon in Suffolk, and another possible chariot mount from Melsonby.[3]

H. N. Savory, *Bull. Board Celtic Studies*, 20 (1964), 452 ff., fig. 2 and Pls. I:2, II:1; *id.*, *Antiquity* XXXVIII (1964), Pl. III; *id.*, *Early Iron Age Art in Wales* (1968), figs. 5–7

[1] I. M. Stead, *Archaeologia* CI (1967), 47
[2] E. T. Leeds, *Celtic ornament* (1933), 139–40 and fig. 36a
[3] Elvedon: *PP*, 109 and Pl. 54b; *PAE*, 268, n. 25; Melsonby: Morna MacGregor (=Simpson), *PPS* XXVIII (1962), 35 and fig. 15=no. 106

268 Moel Hiraddug, Dyserth, Flintshire. Tin-plated bronze plaque. L. of side 15·3 cm. I AD. Formerly Powysland Museum, Welshpool. *National Mus. of Wales, Cardiff.*

This plaque, unfortunately since stolen, was found in 1872 with a number of other objects including shield mounts related closely to those from Tal-y-llyn [262, 267]. The actual find spot was in a ditch of a triple rampart hill-fort. The shield mounts and plaque may have been lost during an attack on the fort but in view of the association with a quantity of iron ore and sword fragments and of the fact that the whole was sealed under the collapsed rampart, it could be that the Moel Hiraddug finds represent a tinker's hoard like Tal-y-llyn.[1]

Fox, considering the piece as an import from the north of England, interprets the design of the plaque, with its triple broken-backed scroll, conjoined trumpets, high central ridges for each arm and concentric boss, as hammered out on a metal mould cast from a wooden original [see notes to 299]. The features just listed are all to be found on material of not earlier than first-century AD date, some of which is illustrated on the following pages [269, 272, 298, 303]. Comparable also is a northern import to Ireland, a disc brooch from Lambay Island, Co. Dublin, found with a Roman first-century fibula, and a bronze strip found with Flavian pottery at the Roman fort of Newstead in Peeblesshire.[2] Concentric raised circles appear on the torc fragment from Shaw Hill [290] while the setting out of a tripartite design within a square reappears later, a feature of the early Christian illuminated gospels.

W. J. Hemp, *Arch. Cambrensis* LXXXIII (1928), 253–84, esp. fig. 16; E. T. Leeds, *Celtic ornament* (1933), 56–57 and fig. 22; W. F. Grimes, *Prehistory of Wales* (1951), 119–21 and Pl. XVIII=no. 700; *PP*, 75, 117 and Pl. 45b; L. Alcock in (ed.) E. Davies, *Celtic Studies in Wales: a survey* (1963), 14, 23 and Pl. III; Françoise Henry, *Irish art in the Early Christian period (to AD 800)* (1965), 214, 220 and fig. 30d; H. N. Savory, *Early Iron Age art in Wales* (1968), 23 and fig. 19

[1] C. M. Holder, *Publ. Flints. Historical Soc.*, 19 (1961), 1–20, esp. 18 ff.
[2] Lambay Island: Leeds, *op. cit.*, 59–60 and fig. 24a–b; Newstead: J. Curle, *A Roman frontier post and its people: the fort of Newstead* (1911), 303 and Pl. LXXV: 5; Morna Simpson in (ed.) J. M. Coles and D. D. A. Simpson, *Studies in Ancient Europe: Essays presented to Stuart Piggott* (1968), 243 ff. and fig. 63:n

269 ?Ireland. Bronze disc. D. 27·2 cm. I/II AD. British Mus., London. *R-GK* (*E. Neuffer*).

This is one of three discs or so-called 'offering bowls' in the British Museum[1] which belong to a group of these objects of unknown use, all unfortunately unassociated or unprovenanced finds, no less than six of which come from the one discovery at Monasterevan, Co. Kildare.[2]

The *repoussé* pattern with the two spirals at the top looks for all the world like a grotesque face with large staring eyes and as such may be compared with the Deskford *carnyx* mount [272] and the Culbin Sands armlet [302]. The otherwise undecorated areas are hatched with short stabbed tooling marks save for the actual dished 'bowl'. The conjoined trumpet feature can be compared with Deskford or with the Melsonby faces [265]; the fat spirals of the 'eyes' are similar to the spirals of Aldborough 'arms' [264]. Both these features indicate a post-conquest date, though there is no reason to consider the discs as even particularly late in the second century. From their general distribution it seems likely that they represent local products and perhaps are all variations on one craftsman's theme. The development of what has been termed the 'ultimate La Tène style' must at least indirectly be influenced by contemporary provincial Roman metal-work.

W. A. von Jenny, *IPEK* (1935), 42 and Taf. 10:7; *id.*, *Keltische Metallarbeiten* (1935), Taf. 30:1; J. Raftery, *Prehistoric Ireland* (1951), 195 and fig. 232; *LPA*, 70 and Pl. XXIII:2; S. Piggott, *Antiq. J.* XXXIX (1959), 31 and Pl. XIc; Françoise Henry, *Irish Art in the Early Christian period (to AD 800)* (1965), 10 and Pl. 10 above; *EV*, ill. on p. 224

[1] *ABA*, Pls. 48–49
[2] E. C. Armstrong, *J. Roy. Soc. Antiq. Ireland* LIII (1923), 22 and Pl. V

270 Ireland. Detail of the 'Petrie Crown'. Total ht. c. 15 cm., d. of disc 6 cm. I/II AD. National Mus. of Ireland, Dublin. *Belzeaux-Zodiaque.*

This detail of a cone, the surviving one of a pair attached to one of two flat sheets with slightly dished discs mounted front and rear, was formerly in the possession of the nineteenth-century Irish antiquary George Petrie. Whatever its original use, it can hardly, owing to its small size, have been used as any normal head-gear, though holes in the edges of the backing sheets suggest attachment to something.

A comparison with the group of three similarly decorated horns in Cork Public Museum – clearly work by the same hand as the Petrie Crown[1] – shows that most of the decoration was tooled down from an original thickness of 0·7 mm. to 0·5 mm. This process seems to have followed the basic assembly since the rivets holding the horn together by means of an internal strip in the manner of the Torrs horns [245] are cut into by the engraving tool; some *repoussé* work was also carried out.

The design of the disc is not unlike that of the Irish 'offering bowls' [269]. Here with the addition of provision for inlay, lipped or conjoined slender trumpets abound while, on the plates behind the disc and more clearly on the horns, are the heads of great crested birds, tufted ducks or teal perhaps. These birds' heads mark a late stage in the animation of a tight spiral design which begins with the Middle La Tène decorated sword scabbards such as Drna and Cernon-sur-Coole [182–183] and which continues in the second-century AD Romano-British 'dragonesque' and Aesica-type brooches [305],[2] and Irish Early Christian metal-work,[3] all constructions based on the broken-backed scroll whose birds' heads are remarkably close to those on the Torrs cap. The general spindly layout of the Petrie Crown recalls the pseudo-birds' heads supporting the central triskel of the Aylesford bucket [187].

Margaret Stokes, *Archaeologia* XLVI (1883), 473–80; E. T. Leeds, *Celtic ornament* (1930), fig. 38a; J. Raftery, *Prehistoric Ireland* (1951), 106n, 120, 206 and fig. 254; M. J. O'Kelly, *J. Cork Hist. and Arch. Soc.* LXVI

(1961), 9–10 and Pl. V; Françoise Henry, *Irish Art in the Early Christian period (to AD 800)* (1965), 67, 71, 207 and Pl. 11; *EV*, 222–23 and ill.

[1] O'Kelly, *op. cit.*, 1–8 and Pls. I–IV
[2] *PP*, 107 and Pl. 41b; R. B. K. Stevenson in (ed.) A. L. F. Rivet, *The Iron Age in Northern Britain* (1966) 31; R. W. Feachem, *Antiq. J.* XLVIII (1968), 100–02; Morna Simpson in (ed.) J. M. Coles and D. D. A. Simpson, *Studies in Ancient Europe: Essays presented to Stuart Piggott* (1968), 248 ff. and fig. 63:1-m.
[3] Máire and L. de Paor, *Early Christian Ireland* (3 ed., 1961), Pl. 5; Henry, *op. cit.*, Pl. 13 above

271 Longban Island, River Bann, Co. Antrim. Bronze disc. D. 10·5 cm. I/II AD. Ulster Museum, Belfast.

Dredged from the River Bann near Coleraine in 1939 [see also **249**], this slightly domed disc seems to be a product of the same craftsman as the Petrie 'crown' and the Cork horns. Provision for three suspension rings, one only now surviving, placed equidistantly suggests the disc's use as a *phalera* or ornamental breastplate like that in the Newnham Croft burial,[1]

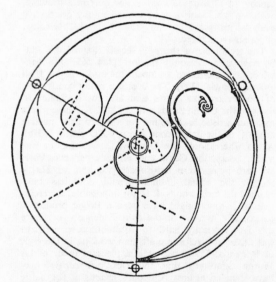

Fig. 16 [**271**] Longban Island, R. Bann, N. Ireland. Construction of design on bronze disc. Scale 7 : 10   *After Henry*

although it may have been a steel-yard pan like that found in the Santon hoard [see notes to **218, 299**].

The decoration, based on a triskel joining a central spiral which itself contains a triskel, incorporates three individual crested duck heads at the centre of each spiral, the whole, like the southern Irish finds, being tooled down to its present form, with a maximum thickness 0·26 cm. The construction of the pattern consists of laying out from the centre three equidistant radii which are then further divided, each into three segments, a careful exercise in geometry hardly less skilful than the setting out of the Lough Crew 'trial pieces' [**256**].

J. Raftery, *Ulster J. Arch.*, 3 (1940), 27–30; E. M.

Jope and B. C. S. Wilson, *Ulster J. Arch.*, 20 (1957), 95–102; M. J. O'Kelly, *J. Cork Hist. and Arch. Soc.* LXVI (1961), 10–12 and Pl. VI; Françoise Henry, *Irish Art in the Early Christian Period (to AD 800)* (1965), 55, 66 ff., 218 ff., fig. 30a-c and Pl. I

[1] *PP*, fig. 6e

272 Deskford, Banffshire. Bronze *carnyx* or horn terminal. L. 21·5 cm. Mid I AD. Banff County Council, Keith. *National Mus. of Antiquities of Scotland, Edinburgh* (*courtesy Banff Town Council*).

This curious sheet-metal boar's head was discovered in about 1816 during peat digging at a depth of about two metres. At the time of finding, it was still fitted with a movable wooden tongue. Its purpose has remained unknown until recent comparison with another of the finds from the River Witham in Lincolnshire. This last was a war-horn or *carnyx* similar to those on the Gundestrup cauldron [209c] or, in the British context, the horns represented on coins of Eppillus and Tasciovanus [306c]. The Witham horn, probably originally also with a boar's head terminal, was discovered at the Tattershall Bridge crossing near Lincoln in 1768 but is known now only in a drawing, owing to what can only be termed totally destructive analysis instigated by Sir Joseph Banks, scientist, imperialist and explorer.

The treatment of the eyes recalls that of the Aldborough and Melsonby mounts [264–265], the conjoined and elongated trumpets the style of the Irish 'offering bowls' [269]. The eyes are really constructed of slender trumpet forms and are not dissimilar to those of the Culbin Sands armlet [302]. All these pieces form an artistic background for the Scottish 'massive armlets' of the first–second century AD [Plate VIIIb]. As to whereabouts the Deskford *carnyx* mount was made, boars, the Celtic cult animals *par excellence*, are rare in northern British art [see note to 224] – though the actual animals would doubtless have roamed the local woods. It is not impossible, therefore, that the *carnyx* might have been a Belgic product – particularly in view of the coin evidence – or, since this is stylistically hard to substantiate, it perhaps was made by a refugee craftsman working in the style of Brigantia. Either way it is a pleasant fancy of Dr Morna Simpson's that the Deskford *carnyx* may have sounded against Agricola's legions at the battle of Mons Graupius which one argument at least places not far from Deskford.[1]

ABA, Pl. 61; S. Piggott, *Antiq. J.* XXXIX (1959), 24–32; J. V. S. Megaw, *Antiq. J.* XLIII (1963), 32 and Pl. XIVa; R. B. K. Stevenson in (ed.) A. L. F. Rivet, *Iron Age in Northern Britain* (1966), 32 and Pl. 4; Morna Simpson in (ed.) J. M. Coles and D. D. A. Simpson, *Studies in Ancient Europe: Essays presented to Stuart Piggott* (1968), 243 ff.

[1] O. G. S. Crawford, *Topography of Roman Scotland* (1949), 130–32

273 River Shannon at Keshcarrigan, Co. Leitrim. Bronze bowl. D. 14·2 cm., late I BC/early I AD. National Mus. of Ireland, Dublin. *A. E. P. Collins (courtesy Archaeological Survey, Ministry of Finance, N. Ireland)*.

Unlike the Northern Ireland decorated scabbards [248–249], there can be little doubt that with the present piece one is dealing with an import. It forms one of a group of bowls or, more probably in several cases, drinking cups made in southern England at the same period as the production of the incised mirrors [260–261, 263].

Like the majority of the mirrors, the bowls have been regarded as being made in the west rather than the east, though again the general distribution of find spots does not completely support this.[1] The method of production seems to have been not so much to spin them on a lathe – a technique probably introduced into Britain by the Romans – but to roughly beat up the main shape and 'lathe-clean' or 'spin-finish' the resultant shape by pressing the bowl while turning into a prepared wooden mould or former; certainly several of the southern bowls have central chuck marks in their bases.

The bowls have occasionally been found in isolated peat bogs but they also seem to have been particularly favoured by local Belgic chieftains, or rather by their women-folk. One was found in the Colchester mirror burial[2] [see notes to 260] with pottery dated during AD 10–25. A second came from a warrior's burial at Snailwell in Cambridgeshire dated to c. AD 43[3] together with a bracelet in the form of a ram's-headed serpent [see also 209b]. A third bowl from Birdlip in Gloucestershire,[4] an inhumation and not a cremation burial and therefore probably the grave of a woman of the local Dobuni, was associated with a fine mirror, a knife with handle in the form of a knob-horned bull [see 274] and a silver-gilt brooch with two strange semi-human masks, probably partially imitating a provincial Roman form.

On the bow of the Birdlip brooch is a sinuous ridge; a similar, more angular backbone appears on the Snailwell armlet and this is a common feature on several of the southern kinds. It was produced by alternate blows of an engraver's chisel or stamp and is to be seen both on the rim of Keshcarrigan and on the distributional odd-man-out illustrated on the opposite page [277]. The separately cast handle of Keshcarrigan is one of a handful of British bronzes in what might be termed the insular 'Plastic style'; the little bull from Ham Hill illustrated below [274] is another. The Keshcarrigan duck, a shoveller or more likely a shelduck, with its great eye prepared for enamel inlay, was first compared with the surviving terminal of the Torrs ?drinking horn mounts [see 245] which, if a valid parallel, would be another argument for a later date for the Scottish pieces. Similar big-lipped – or rather beaked – ducks go back to the continental Early La Tène period;[5] and a mirror handle of certainly not earlier than first-century AD date from Ballymoney, Co. Antrim,[6] has lipped joints – not unlike that on the Mâcon bull handle ring [161] – which give more or less the same bird-like impression as the Keshcarrigan handle.

The presence of Colchester-Keshcarrigan-type bowls and their relatives in burials continues the practice of specially constructed funerary drinking vessels which on the continent goes back to Late Bronze Age times.[7] In Belgic Britain such local vessels must have been made to complement or even act as substitutes for the special adjuncts of the funerary symposium supplied from provincial Roman sources.

R. J. C. Atkinson and S. Piggott, *Archaeologia* XCVI (1955), 223 and Pl. LXXXIII; E. M. Jope, *Ulster J. Arch.*, 17 (1954), 92–96, fig. 2:1 and Pl. VIII; *PreA*, 243 and ill. 250

[1] (Lady) Aileen Fox, *Antiq. J.* XLI (1961), 186–98; see also [277]
[2] C. F. C. Hawkes and M. R. Hull, *Antiq. J.* XXVIII (1948), 136 and fig. 8
[3] T. C. Lethbridge, *Proc. Cambridge Antiq. Soc.* XLVIII (1953), 30–31; *PP*, Pl. 53b; J. V. S. Megaw, *Antiq. J.* XLIII (1963), 29 ff. and Pl. XVc; *PCB*, 345 and Pls. 82c, 83a
[4] C. H. Green, *PPS* XV (1949), 188–90; *PP*, fig. 59b
[5] E.g. *ECA*, no. 289 (=Schwabsburg)
[6] Jope, *op. cit.*, fig. 2:2
[7] Piggott, *Antiquity* XXXIII (1959), 122–23

274 Ham Hill, Somerset. Bronze vessel mount. Ht. c. 4 cm. I AD. Somerset County Mus., Taunton.

Knobbed horned bulls' heads have a long life in Iron Age symbolism. A continental Late La Tène example has already been illustrated from Manching [189]; those on fire dogs are noted below [279]. Some authorities consider such knobs to have a ritual if not phallic significance. In the old Irish legends 'golden apples' were used to decorate objects in supernatural contexts.[1] The Birdlip knife handle head [mentioned in note to **273** above][2] has knobbed horns and indeed a link between the burial and the Ham Hill hill-fort, where the present mount was discovered, is suggested by the finding at the fort of a brooch[3] with twin grotesques closely comparable to that found at the Gloucestershire site. Knobs on horns may, of course, reflect nothing more than local stock-breeding practice. Certainly with or without knobs, there is a fairly extensive series of late British Iron Age bucket mounts in the form of bulls extending the tradition first met in these pages in the Hallstatt period [36] and which last right through the Roman period.[4] A bucket mount, which dated to the second century AD by association with Roman imports from Welshpool in Shropshire still has typical lentoid and ridged Celtic eyes, and a local bowl related to the Colchester-Keshcarrigan type from Rose Ash in Devon has a much simplified bull mount.[5]

Basically the Ham Hill head is an extension of the head constructed from an 'hour-glass' or palmette-lyre which can be seen in the Frasnes-lez-Buissenal rams [173] or in Britain on the Witham shield [252] or, a piece not illustrated here, from the Melsonby, Stanswick, finds – a plaque in the form of a cheerful horse-head.[6] The Ham Hill mount, with its scrolled nostrils very much in the northern metal-working tradition [see **264–265**] – there is no reason why craftsmen or their products should not have moved south as well as north – is a fair sample of the British late 'Plastic style'; it can be contrasted with the little third-century BC Mâcon bull [161]. The surviving knob of Ham Hill is incised with a triangle within a circle [see also notes to **252**].

Free-standing bulls in something of the same manner are also known from both sides of the continent; an unprovenanced bull formerly in the collection of the nineteenth-century Wiltshire antiquary, Sir Richard Colt Hoare, and now in the Ashmolean Museum may be matched with a probably La Tène III figure from Weltenburg, Kr. Kelheim.[7]

F. Haverfield in *Victoria County History of Somerset* I (1906), fig. 63:12; *PP*, 73 and Pl. 48b; *PRB*, Pl. 315; J. M. C. Toynbee, *Art in Britain under the Romans* (1964), 21 and Pl. 1a; *PCB*, 304 and fig. 167

[1] O. Jansé, *IPEK* 10 (1935), 66–72; *PCB*, 130
[2] R. A. Smith, *Archaeologia* LXI (1909), 332 and fig. 2; *PRB*, Pl. 303
[3] Smith, *op. cit.*, 341–42 and fig. 9; *PP*, fig. 59c
[4] C. F. C. Hawkes in (ed.) W. F. Grimes, *Aspects of archaeology in Britain and beyond* (1951), 191–99, esp. 192; J. V. S. Megaw, *Proc. Soc. Antiq. Scotland* XCI (1957–58), 179–82
[5] Welshpool: G. C. Boon, *Antiq. J.* XLI (1961), 25–26, fig. 4 and Pl. X; H.-J. Eggers, *JR-GZM*, 13 (1966), 88=no. 16; Rose Ash: Aileen Fox, *Antiq. J.* XLI (1961), 186–98
[6] *PP*, 76, 120 and Pl. 52b; Morna MacGregor (= Simpson), *PPS* XXVIII (1962), 26–27 and Pl. V=no. 102; Toynbee, *op. cit.*, 22 and Pl. Ib; see notes to [265]
[7] Ashmolean Mus.: E. T. Leeds, *Celtic ornament* (1933), fig. 29; Weltenburg: W. Krämer, *Germania* XXVIII (1944–50), 210–13; W. Torbrügge and H.P. Uenze, *Bilder zur Vorg. Bayerns* (1968), ill. 272; *EV*, ill. on p. 231 right

275 Harpenden, Hertfordshire. Bronze ram's head mount. L. c. 8 cm. Early I AD. Museum and Art Gallery, Luton.

This one of a pair of cast mounts originally with enamel inlay illustrating, as Leeds states, 'the hot fierceness of a lean, old, fighting pasha of the flock', was recovered from a grave in 1867. Other objects included two heavy rings and fragments of a stave bucket – like those from Aylesford and Marlborough [187–188] – to the rim of which the rams would have been fixed. Three carefully turned pedestalled pots manufactured from Dorset kimmeridge shale match one found with the decorated mirror at Old Warden in Bedfordshire[1] related to the Great Chesterford mirror [261]. There was also an imported provincial Roman handled bowl like that found with the British export to Poland illustrated on the opposite page [277]. Originally the rams' heads had red enamel in the nostrils – in the same position as the enamel on the ram's-headed-serpent armlet from Snailwell whose ridged horns are not dissimilar;[2] blue and possibly white enamel filled the eye-sockets, such use of polychrome being a feature of Roman-influenced work, though it is yet to be proved that the introduction of polychromy was first due to Roman models.

Rams separated from humans are not particularly common in Iron Age iconography until the later period, though a series of continental clay fire-dogs[3] suggests their association with the hearth and feasting. A crude ram's head decorates a bronze bowl of the Colchester-Keshcarrigan type from Youlton in Cornwall;[4] this ram's mount's horns have something of the great crests of the Aylesford helmeted heads, and the ram was a common attribute of the Celtic Mars.

The style of the Harpenden mounts is in contrast with the more assured caricature of the Ham Hill mount [**274**]; perhaps Roman rigidity is creeping in.

L

T. W. Bagshaw, *Antiq. J.* VIII (1928), 520–22 and Pls. LXXXII–LXXXIII; E. T. Leeds, *Celtic ornament* (1933), 93 and fig. 28; *PP*, 76 ff., fig. 47 and Pl. 50; H.-J. Eggers, *JR-GZM*, 13 (1966), 69–70 and Abb. 6=no. 32

[1] *LPA*, 71 and Pl. XXIII:3
[2] *PP*, 81 and Pl. 53b; see also notes to [273]
[3] *Manuel* IV, 905–13
[4] *PP*, 79 and Pl. 51

276 Felmersham-on-Ouse, Bedfordshire. Bronze spout. L. c. 11 cm. I AD. Bedford Mus. (*Courtesy Trustees of the British Museum.*)

This heavy casting was found in gravel near Felmersham Bridge together with bronze fittings for a bucket – a swing handle and a delightful if naïve pair of cow and bull mounts – as well as with fragments of at least one bowl of the Colchester-Keshcarrigan type probably marking the remains of a grave like that from Harpenden [275]. This spout, with its 'essence of fishiness', is a true example of what has been called here the later British 'Plastic style'. The eyes probably held inlay and, despite the mounting requiring a rim at least 1 cm. thick, could well have been fitted to a bucket or large bowl instead of being a permanent fixture at a local spring, as has also been stated.

Fishes are otherwise unknown in British Iron Age art, unless one accepts the Bugthorpe 'carp' [259]. The enamelled 'S' spiral tail follows the principle of enamelled harness mounts from southern England [see **Plate VIIIa**]. Where the idea of animal spouts came from is difficult to decide though another contemporary example is illustrated below [277]. Roman examples in pottery, some with built-in strainers, are of the second-third centuries AD and thus too late to offer much evidence of classical influence. A bowl of the first half of the second century from St Martin's-le-Grand, London, has a spout in the form of a boar's head[1] and mention will be made below of the dish with sieve from Welwyn Garden City [see notes to 277]. Further finds made at the time of the original discovery, including part of a shale bracelet, have recently come to light.[2]

W. Watson, *Antiq. J.* XXIX (1949), 37 ff. esp. 41, 50–51, figs. 3, 4, 8 and Pl. Va–b; *PP*, 80, fig. 49 and Pl. 46; J. V. S. Megaw, *Antiq. J.* XLIII (1963), 31–32 and Pl. XIVa

[1] (Sir) R. E. M. Wheeler, *London in Roman times*= *London Mus. Cat.*, 3 (1946), 148 and fig. 55:2
[2] F. W. Kuhlicke, *Bedfordshire Arch. J.* IV (1969), 81–87

277 Łęg Piekarski, Turek, grave 1. Detail of spout of bronze bowl with enamel inlay. Total d. 25·5 cm., l. of surviving spout c. 7·5 cm. Mid I AD. Państwowe Muz. Archeologiczne, Warsaw. *T. Biniewski.*

This British Belgic bowl comes from 'Free Germany' or that area beyond Roman control north of the Rhine. From here in the second century BC and later a series of folk movements came south. These movements included the Cimbri who not only defeated the Romans in the eastern Alps but also displaced some of the central European Boii and probably also con-

tributed to the pressures which resulted in the early stages of the Belgic settlement of south-east England; it may have been just such a wandering group of Cimbri who brought the Gundestrup cauldron back to Jutland [209].

Such contacts with not only the more southerly Celts but also with the classical world can be seen in the contents of three stone-lined inhumation graves – a contrast with the usual Teutonic rite of cremation – found above the River Warta about half-way between Łódź and Poznań in central Poland. These graves belong to a group of rich burials, usually with Roman imports, termed the 'Lübsow' (Lubieszewo) type,[1] grave 1 at Łęg Piekarski containing Roman bowls of first–second century AD date. The Lübsow graves are the north European counterpart of Belgic graves of the Welwyn type [see notes to 230] and both contain imports such as the broad flat skillets or *patellae* found also at Aylesford [187]. Certain features of the Lübsow graves – mortuary chamber construction, absence of weapons, inhumation instead of cremation, frequent finds of shears and sometimes of ceremonial staffs – have suggested that these might be the last resting places of members of a Celticised if not Celtic priestly caste. More likely these represent the local *nouveaux riches* living on the northern fringes of the Roman empire, such pieces as the present bowl or the Nijmegen mirror [263] being bartered from southern Britain along the same trade routes as brought the luxury imports essential for feasting in both this and the Otherworld to southern England; a bronze found in the River Weser, recently published as another late Iron Age British import, seems better taken with contemporary continental material like that from Manching [see notes to 189].[2]

Though the Łęg Piekarski bowl has lost some of its main body, the rim and the two red-enamelled and separately riveted spout and iron handle mounts are intact. The bowl belongs in fact to the Colchester-Keshcarrigan group of southern British bowls [273], a key feature being the sinuous punch-decorated rim following the pattern on not only other bowls of the group but the Snailwell armlet which also, like the Polish find, makes use of closely spaced punched dots as fill-ins.[3]

Both the front and the rear mounts and the nose of the spout animal have areas of champlevé enamel filling a loose palmette or lyre pattern not unlike that incised on the Nijmegen mirror, or, even closer, one of two mirrors from Stamford Hill in Devon.[4] Both the technique and the pattern closely match one of a number of quadrilobe harness mounts from the Polden Hills, Somerset, hoard which should date to c. AD 50.[5]

The animal spout of Łęg Piekarski which covers a sieve, presumably to strain out some of the additives such as lumps of resin which northern barbarians no less than Greeks considered an essential part of civilised drinking, must represent a boar with great brows and upstanding crest – now broken short. The eyes once contained inlay and the fixing pin holes are clearly visible. A related animal is that on the silver-gilt *Augenfibel* from the Birdlip burial.[6] Animal spouts are rare in the Celtic world but one fourth-century BC example has already been illustrated [163], and a bronze bowl with a spout and separate strainer was found in the Belgic 'Welwyn'-type grave at Welwyn Garden City, an import probably embellished by a local craftsman.[7]

Inventaria Arch.: Pologne V (1961), PL 32; J. V. S. Megaw, *Antiq. J.* XLIII (1963), 27–37 esp. Pl. XIIb; K. Jażdżewski, *Poland* (1965), 157 and fig. 26; Megaw, *Atti del VI Congr. Intern. delle Sci. Preist. e Protostoriche* III (1966), 144–47

[1] H.-J. Eggers, *Praehist. Zeitschr.* XXXIV–V:2 (1949–50), 58–111; R. E. M. Wheeler, *Rome beyond the Imperial frontiers* (1955), 49–63
[2] W. H. Zimmermann, *Neue Ausgrabungen und Forschungen in Niedersachsen*, 4 (1969), 123–30
[3] *PP*, Pl. 53b; see also [304]
[4] *PP*, 97 and fig. 60
[5] *PP*, Pl. 72c; Megaw, *Antiq. J.* XLIII, Pl. XVa; see also **Plate VIIIa**
[6] C. H. Green, PPS XV (1949), 188–90 and fig. 16; see also notes to [273, 304]
[7] I. M. Stead, *Archaeologia*, CI (1967), 23 ff. esp. fig. 12 and Pl. V; see also notes to [230]

Plate VIIIa Santon, Norfolk. Two enamel-decorated harness mounts. Max. ht. 8 and 7 cm. AD 40–60. University Mus. of Archaeology and Ethnology, Cambridge. *L. P. Morley.*

Mention has already been made of the hoard of objects including scrap, repaired pieces and brand-new products supposedly found in 1897 in a cauldron and often inaccurately assigned to Santon Downham in Suffolk [see 218, 299]. The hoard is dated on the basis of its association with Roman thistle brooches to the period around just before the uprising of Boudica – now more reliably set at AD 60.[1] Amongst these objects were the two finely preserved quadrilobe mounts illustrated here, each with strap tags on the under surface suggesting their use as part of the rich caparison of a pair of chariot ponies. A similar mount has been found at Polden Hills in a hoard which includes, like Santon, horse bits as well as three shield bosses, one of which has a thin version of linked 'S' curves with Llyn Cerrig-like bird commas[2] such as can be found in a group of late and predominantly south-western neck-rings [see notes to 297]. The Polden Hills find makes use of imported cupric glass [see notes to 253] and should date to the middle of the first century AD. The presence in the West Country of what seem to be particularly eastern pieces may be due to exchanges for such things as Colchester-Keshcarrigan bowls or south-eastern mirrors, or the gradual Belgicisation of the Dobunic area'

A Suffolk find, that from Westhall with a similar disc brooch cover to Santon [see 218] contains eight enamelled terrets, a matching pair of quadrilobe harness mounts with green, white, blue and red inlay, and a fragmentary lugged bronze furnished with escutcheons. A pear-shaped Roman lamp has been considered evidence of deposition somewhat after the uprising of the Iceni, but the lamp was not actually associated with the hoard and cannot be more closely dated than to within the first two centuries AD.[3] The most decorative though least well preserved quadrilobe mount comes from the London area where yellow is added to red enamel; a seventh quadrilobe mount comes from Norton in Suffolk.[4]

The design of the larger Santon mount is a characteristically 'bilingual' one; the eye moves from the brilliance of the enamel design to the lightly incised and carefully, geometrically, laid-out pattern of voids incorporating curved-sided triangles, *yin-yang* scrolls, and two-dimensional 'Llyn Cerrig' scrolls as fine as that in the round on the Old Windsor bit [258]. Such a pattern is very close to the basic style of the Datchet spear [257], differences being probably due as much to the differences between individual craftsmen as to differences in time; the similarity also to the larger of the Lough Crew trial pieces illustrated here [256], particularly in the use of the *yin-yang*, demonstrates the mobility of motifs as well as craftsmen in the later British Iron Age. A terret in the Ashmolean Museum probably also from Suffolk and possibly from Lakenheath has the same combination of incision and inlay though this is in two colours.[5]

The smaller Santon mount has a much less carefully laid-out pattern and punched dot ornament which relates it to the dissected appearance of the Polden Hills piece which has already been compared to the Łeg Piekarski bowl [277].

The distribution of enamelled mounts over three separate native tribal areas, those of the Iceni, the Dobuni and the Belgic settlers of the Thames valley, makes a decision as to the actual background of the craftsmen concerned difficult to make; the patterns on the whole do not match those of the finer mirrors and a source in East Anglia and at least outside the Belgic south-east seems likely.

H. Harrod, *Arch. J.* XII (1855), 276; R. A. Smith, *Proc. Cambridgeshire Antiq. Soc.* XIII (1909), 149–50 and figs. 1–2; Françoise Henry, *Préhistoire* II:1 (1933), 84 ff.; C. Fox, *Archaeology of the Cambridge Region* (reissue 1948), 104 ff. and cover ill.; *PP*, 125 and Pl. 72e; Morna MacGregor (=Simpson), *PPS* XXVIII (1962), 33 ff.

[1] Sir Ronald Syme, *Tacitus* (1958) I, 391 II, 762 ff.; D. R. Dudley and G. Webster, *The Rebellion of Boudicca* (1962), esp. Chap. 6 and Appendix III
[2] C. J. Harford, *Archaeologia* XIV (1803), 90–93 and Pls. XXI–XXII; *PP*, 116, fig. 72 and Pl. 72c; *LBA*, 62 and Pl. XIII:8
[3] R. Rainbird Clarke, *Arch. J.* XCVI (1939), 68–69 and Pl. XVI
[4] London: J. M. Kemble, *Horae Forales* (1863), Pl. XIX:2; E. T. Leeds, *Celtic ornament* (1933), 41; Henry, *op. cit.*, fig. 13:1; Norton: Kemble, *op. cit.*, Pl. XIX:4; Henry, *op. cit.*, fig. 20:4
[5] Leeds, *op. cit.*, 40 and Pl. I:3

278 Niederursel, Frankfurt. Wrought iron fire-dog, l. 95 cm., ht. 69 cm. LTD, I BC/I AD. Formerly Mus. f. Vor- u. Frühg., Frankfurt/Main.

This fine example of late Celtic iron smithing, unfortunately lost in World War II, came from a Roman villa excavated in 1929. It belongs to a group of late La Tène fire-dogs found on both sides of the English Channel. The dozen or so continental examples, in contrast to the British, are not usually found in graves and stretch across the whole *oppidum* 'common market'[1] from France to the Hradiště at Stradonice, and can be made out on the side of the Gundestrup cauldron;[2] the fire-dog distribution matches that of such accessories of the feast as cauldrons and their chains. Low iron fire-dogs are known in eighth-century BC Greece during the Geometric period from whence they were introduced into Etruscan Italy which may have been the source of a pair from a Hallstatt cemetery at Beilngries in Bavaria[3] as well as the pair now surviving from the early La Tène grave at Hořovičky in Bohemia.[4] The Senones were using low Etruscan-type fire-dogs in fourth-century BC graves at Montefortino.

The finest series of fire-dogs on the continent is that from the bog find at Kappel near Stuttgart associated with waggon fittings, part of a *carnyx*, and one of the so-called 'Kelheim' jugs. The Kappel fire-dogs have terminals in the shape of an eagle's head as well as oxen with knobbed horns.[5]

K. Woelcke, *Mus. f. heimische Vor- u. Frühg.*, 2 (1938), 34 ff. and Abb. 33; H. Schönberger, *Saalburg-Jahrb.* XI (1952), 81 and Abb. 4; S. Piggott, *Ancient Europe* (1965), 247, fig. 139 and Pl. XLVIIIa

[1] *Manuel* IV, 913–18; D. Drost, *Ethnog.-Arch. Forsch.* 2 (1954), 100–158; S. Piggott, *The Druids* (1968), fig. 3; O.-H. Frey, *R-GF* 31 (1968), 87
[2] Stradonice: *KvsE*, Tab. CXXVIII:27; see also notes to [213]; Gundestrup: O. Klindt-Jensen, *Gundestrup-kedelen* (1961), fig. 21; see also notes to [209a]
[3] W. Torbrügge and H.P. Uenze, *Bilder zur Vorg. Bayerns* (1968), ill. 84; see also notes to [10]
[4] *KvsE*, 159; see also notes to [47]
[5] F. Fischer, 'Der spätlatènezeitl. Depot-Fund von Kappel', *Urkunden zur Vor- u. Frühg. aus Südwürtt.-Hohenzollern* I (1959), 26–29, Abb. 4 and Taf. 10–11; *PreA*, ill. 255–56

279 Lord's Bridge, Barton, Cambridgeshire. Wrought iron fire-dog. Ht. 71 cm., late I BC/early I AD. University Mus. of Archaeology and Ethnology, Cambridge.

Even classical writers were aware of the Celts' concern for appropriate goods for the dead;[1] in the Celtic world debts could be contracted which were payable after death. To the frequent presence, in Belgic graves of south-eastern England, of drinking sets, joints of meat, and amphorae, each containing up to the equivalent of seven dozen bottles of wine, suitable for those who had all eternity before them, may be added more than a dozen iron fire-dogs frequently decorated with ox- or bull's heads sometimes knobbed as here [see also notes to 189]. The technical skill for the production of such fire-dogs was probably introduced into Britain by craftsmen coming from the continent in the wake of the second-century BC Belgic incursions.[2] Subsequently important iron smithy centres sprang up; the west also became an important centre for later prehistoric smithing to judge from the large number of iron sword-shaped ingots or 'currency bars' found there.[3]

The fire-dog from Lord's Bridge was found in 1817 near the barrow of Hay Hill and was possibly associated with a slave gang-chain like that found at Llyn Cerrig Bach [see notes to 254]. Both Welwyn graves also contained fire-dogs [see notes to 230] as did the recent Baldock discovery associated with a poor copy of an Aylesford-type bucket.[4] Here the Catuvellaunian ruling classes must have been using the products of local smiths working in a common tradition to produce the adjuncts for a belief in the importance of a domestic complex centred on the open hearth; there was a need to observe the customs due to family status and hospitality and debts due to the dead as represented by these standard and symbolic grave goods.

C. Fox, *Antiq. J.* XIX (1939), 447; id., *Archaeology of the Cambridge Region* (reissue 1948), 100; S. Piggott, *Antiquity* XXII (1948), 21–28; *ABA*, Pl. 50; *PP*, 75 and Pl. 47; J. M. C. Toynbee, *Art in Britain under the Romans* (1964), 22; *PRB*, Pl. 306 right; *PreA*, ill. 254; I. M. Stead, *Archaeologia* CI (1967), 44 ff.; *PAE*, 272 and Pl. 304

[1] Pomponius Mela, *De situ orbis* II
[2] C. F. C. Hawkes, *Antiquity* XLII (1968), 6 ff.
[3] D. F. Allen, *PPS* XXXIII (1967), 307–35
[4] Stead, *Antiq. J.* XLVIII (1968), 306 and Pl. LXXVII; see also notes to [187]

280 Ralaghan, Co. Cavan. Figure of bog oak. Ht. c. 1·14 m. ?I/II AD. National Mus. of Ireland, Dublin.

Though the British Isles has not as yet yielded up a find so archaeologically exciting or artistically developed as the figures from the source of the Seine [233–234], a scattered group of chance discoveries has given at least some circumstantial evidence for the Celtic veneration of trees – a possible reason for the importance of the early 'leaf crowns'? – and for the setting up of figures in local open-air shrines. The present figure has been considered by some to be male but the neatly drilled hole in what appears otherwise to be a well-defined vulva surely does not prevent a female interpretation. If male, it may have been intended for a detachable penis as with several other figures like that from Dagenham, Essex.[1] Definitely female is the now much shrunken oak figure with pebble eyes and roughly carved hands – an unusual feature since limbs are usually vestigial in the manner of the Bouray bronze [232] – found in peat in 1880 at Ballachuillish, Argyllshire.[2] Other, distinctly phallic, wooden figures come from the West Country[3] but the distribution must represent chance preservation rather than a true picture of what was doubtless a very widespread phenomenon in later prehistoric Britain.

In the absence of radio-carbon analysis of any of these figures dating must be purely notional, the upper limit being set by the resemblances to the miniature figures associated with the Roos Carr boat with its supposedly late Bronze Age shields [284]. The face of Ralaghan is, however, not unlike several of the simple Seine heads[4] and a post-conquest date is far from impossible, especially in view of the dating usually given to the north European figures [281–282].

R. A. S. Macalister, *Ancient Ireland* (1935), fig. 22; *ABA*, Pl. 31 ('Shercock, Co. Cavan'); *PCB*, 4, 35, fig. 5 and Pl. 11b; S. Piggott, *The Druids* (1968), 84–87 and fig. 31a, Pl. 12

[1] *ABA*, Pl. 32; *PRB*, Pl. 317
[2] Sir Robert Christison, *Proc. Soc. Antiq. Scot.* XV (1880–81), 158–78 esp. 162 and fig. 1; *ABA*, Pl. 33; *PRB*, Pl. 318; Piggott, *op. cit.*, fig. 31c
[3] (Lady) Aileen Fox, *South West England* (1964), Pls. 79–80
[4] Simone Deyts, *Ex voto . . . du sanctuaire des Sources de la Seine: Art celte et gallo-romain* (1966), nos. 25, 38–39; see also notes to [233–34]

281 Broddenbjerg mose, Viborg, Jutland. Wooden figure. Ht. c. 88 cm. II–I BC. National Mus., Copenhagen. *L. Larsen.*

This figure, about whose sex, like that of the Stradonice trumpeter [213], there can be no doubt, was found in 1880 with a number of local Early Iron Age pots amongst a pile of stones. The figure, which appears to be bearded, was hewn out of a forked oak trunk. Bronze Age finds from the same bog suggest its use as a cult place over some considerable time while other crude figures associated with offering places are known; both sexes are also represented. For example, a stick-like 'Nerthus' figure three metres long from Foerlev Nymølle was found wrapped in cloth by a cooking place with four plates, a wooden dipper or club and two wooden, ski-shaped, objects.[1] At this, just one of several offering places in the neighbourhood, there were the remains of cattle, sheep, goat, horse, hare and dog. Both a human shoulder blade and a bundle of flax give some additional idea of the nature of the sacrifices which may have been made no less than in Celtic lands in the Teutonic north where the goddess Nerthus was all-important.[2]

A. Feddersen, *Aarbøger* (1881), 269–74; P. Riismøller, *Kuml* (1952), 119–32, and fig. 2; O. Klindt-Jensen, *Denmark* (1957), 90 and Pl. 47; J. Brønsted, *Danmarks Oldtid* III (2ed, 1960), 117 and ill.; Marianne Bro-Jørgensen, *Billeder af Viborgs amts forhistorie*, Historisk Samfund, Viborg (1966), 118 and ill. p. 119; P. V. Glob, *The bog people: Iron-Age man preserved* (1969), 182 ff. and ill. 74–75

[1] H. Andersen, *Skalk* (1961:1), 7–11; Glob, *op. cit.*, 180 f. and ill. 71
[2] Tacitus, *Germania*, 40; H. R. Ellis-Davidson, *Pagan Scandinavia* (1967), 74

282 Aukamper Moor, Braak, Kr. Eutin. Details of two wooden figures. (a) Total ht. 2·4 m., ht. of face c. 20 cm.; (b) total ht. 2·7 m., ht. of face 20 cm. After I BC. Schleswig-Holstein. Landesmus. für Vor- u. Frühg., Schleswig.

These details are of two tall slender figures, like that from Broddenbjerg cut from forked branches, the fork forming the legs; (a), the female of the pair, has a neat topknot like some of the bog people of late Bronze and Iron Age times. Sockets for arms exist as well as for eyes, perhaps for pebble insets like the figures in the Roos Carr boat [284]. Some 70 metres distant from the spot where the figures were found in 1947 was a wooden gable and a number of local late La Tène swords while in the immediate vicinity of the find spot was a hearth with coals and ash, charred stones and fragments of pottery.

Despite what appears to be evidence for a very similar cult offering place to those just described from Denmark [see 281], recent pollen analysis suggests that the Braak figures could be Slavic and as late as the eighth or ninth centuries AD; the simple carving style of the pair of naked figures is hardly an indication of age one way or the other. Roman Iron Age lake-side cult places are certainly known from north-west Thuringia of at least third-century AD date.[1]

H. Jankuhn in (ed.) O. Klose, *Geschichte Schleswig-Holsteins* 3 (1957), 133 and Taf. VII–VIII; id., *Denkmäler der Vorzeit zwischen Nord- u. Ostsee* (1957), 50, Taf. 59–61; E. Oxenstierna, *Die Nordgermanen* (1957), Taf. 36; Jankuhn in (ed.) W. Krämer, *Neue Ausgrabungen in Deutschland* (1958), 252 and Abb. 5; H. Hingst, *Offa* 24 (1967), 108–14; H. R. Ellis-Davidson, *Pagan Scandinavia* (1967), 82 and Pl. 34; *PAE*, 208 and fig. 82; H. Geisslinger in *Schleswig-Haithabu-Sylt=Führer zu Vor- u. Frühg. Denkmälern* 9 (1968), 138 f.

[1] G. Behm-Blancke, *Ausgrabungen u. Funde* 3 (1958), 263–66, 378 ff. and id., *Ausgrabungen u. Funde* 5 (1960), 232 ff.

283 Caerwent, Monmouthshire. Sandstone head. Ht. 23 cm. I/II AD. Newport Mus. and Art Gallery. *Dept. of Archaeology, University College of South Wales and Monmouthshire (courtesy Newport Mus.).*

The finest piece of Celtic sculpture so far known from Britain has already been illustrated [243]; however, the head from Gloucester already shows the modifying influence of Roman art. In contrast, the stone heads on these two pages seem to modern eyes almost entirely bereft of artistic worth, the products of folk-artists on the fringes of occupied Britain carving the essential adjuncts of their own head-dominated religion.

In recent years, thanks largely to the work of Dr Anne Ross, a considerable quantity of presumed native sculpture has been recognised mainly in the north and west of the British Isles. In the absence of a complete corpus and detailed stylistic analysis and – usually – any dateable associations, it must be admitted that it remains often a matter of personal whim as to the dating of individual 'Celtic' heads. Some seem not earlier than the nineteenth century AD, to judge from details like carved caps and pipes; other heads in Ireland can be argued on stylistic grounds to be no earlier than the introduction of Romanesque architecture into Britain.[1]

There is little doubt about the general period to which the present head should be ascribed. It was found on the floor of a room, probably a shrine, at the top of a flight of three granite steps in the Roman town of Venta Silurum and may be compared with another head from a Roman context, from Corbridge, the base camp of Corstopitum at the eastern end of Hadrian's Wall.[2] The low relief features of the Caerwent head, with the eyebrows carved in one with the nose, also recall the faces on a triple-headed stone from Corleck, Co. Cavan[3] [see also 286], while the deep slots in place of ears must be for detachable ears; Dr Ross suggests stag's or horse's ears. There would certainly be nothing untoward in this juxtaposition of native beliefs and customs with the everyday life of a provincial Roman town since religious intolerance was, with one or two exceptions, not a Roman vice.

T. Ashby, Jnr. *et al.*, *Archaeologia* LVIII (1902), 148–50 and fig. 7; V. E. Nash-Williams, *Bull. Board of Celtic Studies* XV (1952–54), 81–98 and Pl. V; Anne Ross, *Proc. Soc. Antiq. Scot.* XCI (1957–58), 24=no. 24; L. Alcock in (ed.) E. Davies, *Celtic studies in Wales: a survey* (1963), 37 and Frontispiece; J. V. S.

Megaw, *Arch. Cambrensis* CXV (1966), 97 and Pl. VII; *PCB*, 88, 310 and Pl. 31a

[1] E. Rynne in *North Munster Studies: Essays in commemoration of Monsignor Michael Moloney* (1967), 146–65
[2] *PCB*, Pl. 28a
[3] Ross, *op. cit.*, Pl. IV below; *PCB*, fig. 45

284 Roos Carr, Holderness, East Riding, Yorkshire. Detail of pinewood figure with quartz pebble eyes. Ht. of head c. 5 cm. ?VII BC – I AD. Kingston-upon-Hull Museums. *S. E. Thomas.*

This is a detail of one of five wooden figures, four now being assembled with a simple wooden boat model, found in 1836 in the Humber estuary. Dates for what must originally have been more than one group of figures have varied from the later Bronze Age to the Viking period. The prow of the boat, some 51 cm. long, has an animal- or perhaps snake-head with quartz pebble eyes. This, together with the round shields and presumably weapons which must once have been carried in the outstretched hands of each figure, certainly invites comparison with the well-known Nordic rock carvings of ships and with the little helmeted figures from Faardal in Denmark as well as those from Loshult in Sweden,[1] no less than the Strettweg cult model [38]; there is certainly plenty of archaeological evidence for contact between Britain and northern Europe in later Bronze Age times. On the other hand little is known of simpler shield types of the Iron Age in the north of Britain and the figures are very like those from Ralaghan and Dagenham [see **280**], considered on equally inconsequential arguments to be of at least Iron Age date.

The Roos Carr men have neatly drilled holes above the scrotum, like the larger Ralaghan figure.

G. Poulson, *History and antiquities of Holderness* II (1840), 100; Sir Robert Christison, *Proc. Soc. Antiq. Scot.* XV (1880–81), 175 ff. and figs. 4–5; E. Sprockhoff, *Zur Handelgeschichte der Germanisches Bronzezeit = Vorg. Forsch.*, 7 (1930), 30–31 and Taf. 7b; F. and H. W. Elgee, *Archaeology of Yorkshire* (1933), 202–03 and Pl. X; S. Lindqvist, *Acta Arch.* XIII (1942), 235–42; *ABA*, Pl. 30; *PRB*, Pls. 319–20; *PAE*, 208; *EV*, 148 ff. and ill. on p. 149

[1] P. V. Glob, *Kuml* (1961), 9–18; *PAE*, 204 and fig. 79

285 Tanderagee, Co. Armagh. Stone figure. Ht. c. 60 cm. ?I/II AD. Chapter House, Armagh Protestant Cathedral. *Dr Françoise Henry.*

The hill on which now stands the Protestant Cathedral of Armagh was the site of a pre-Christian shrine long before the coming of Patrick. This horrific figure apparently in the process of devouring an arm in the manner of the 'Tarasque' of Noves [76], has a helmet or cap and appears also to have vestigial horns. Either here is a helmet of the Waterloo type [see **294**] or a local antler god to be compared with a northern British figure, the head from Netherby near Carlisle.[1]

Some similarity has also been claimed with the Holzgerlingen pillar-statue [14]; closer in fact is a sandstone statue from Raibreitenbach, Kr. Starkenburg,

considered, however, by Jacobsthal to be Slav in date.[2] A stone figure with its paws resting on human heads from Tonregan, Co. Cavan may also be pre-Christian in date or at least associated with pagan rites.[3] Whatever its precise dating, the Tanderagee figure stands as a reminder of all that is dark and brutish in pagan Celtic belief and which is not even hidden by the glitter of gold [see **84**].

A. Kingsley Porter, *Burlington Mag.*, 70 (1934), 227; R. A. S. Macalister, *J. Roy. Soc. Antiq. Ireland* XLV (1935), 156–58; E. Rynne in *Ber. V. Intern. Kongr. f. Vor- u. Frühg.* (1961), 707; Françoise Henry, *Irish Art in the Early Christian period (to A D 800)* (1965), Pl. 3

[1] *PCB*, 81, 155–56 and Pl. 21a
[2] E. Anthes, *Germania* 4 (1920), 37; *id.*, *Germania* 5 (1921), 9; F. Behn, *Urg. von Starkenburg* (1936), 26 and Taf. 41c; *ECA*, 10, n. 3
[3] K. M. Dickie, *J. Roy. Soc. Antiq. Ireland* XCIII (1963), 198–99

286 ?Sutherlandshire. Granite *tricephalos*. Ht. 12 cm. ?III–I BC. National Mus. of Antiquities of Scotland. *M. J. M. Murray.*

Purchased in Glasgow before World War I and supposedly from Eastern Scotland, this head is not made from local stone but has a near match with some continental sources including Norway.

The triple element is a common factor in the symbolism of native beliefs within the western part of the Roman empire and is particularly strong in Irish and Welsh tradition – three faces, three horns on figures of cattle and so on. In pre-Roman contexts two examples of triple heads have already been illustrated [**85–86**] while several stone heads with triple faces are now known from Britain,[1] that first compared with the Sutherland head being from Corleck, Co. Cavan, already mentioned in connection with the Caerwent piece illustrated on the opposite page [**283**]. An interesting example of triple conjoined profile heads – a Romanised version of the Dürkheim 'trick' faces [see **59**] – has recently been found in dredging outside the west gate of the old Roman town of Caistor St Edmund (Venta Icenorum).[2] This is an iron finger-ring with engraved jasper intaglio; an inscription 'CEN' may be an abbreviation of the tribal name. Triple heads themselves occur both on coins of Armorica and on those of the Iceni; here the heads have pigtails [see **194g, 228**]. The Sutherland head with its drooping moustaches and general rounded form, matches two unpublished heads in the British Museum, a *tricephalos* from Bron-y-Garth, Shropshire and a 'Janus' head from Ross-on-Wye, Gloucestershire. The *locus* or 6 cm-deep libation hollow on the top of the Sutherland stone suggests, together with the general style, whatever the significance of the simple cross incised between two of the three aspects, a date around the time of the Roman conquest. If the stone really is imported it may have come with Belgic settlement [see notes to **306**].

Anne Ross, *Proc. Soc. Antiq. Scot.* XCI (1957–58), 10–11, 13 and Pl. XCI; *PCB*, 71 ff. and Pl. 17

[1] Ross, *Antiquity* XLI (1967), 53–56
[2] Ross, *Norfolk Arch.*, 34 (1968), 263–71

287 Bexbach, Kr. Homburg, 'Steinerne Mann' II. Stone head. Ht. 23·5 cm. ? I BC. Turmmus. Bexbach. *Staatl. Denkmalpflege, Saarland.*

The forested area near Bexbach on the line of an old road was marked as a cult place of some importance in Roman times by a 'Jupiter pillar'[1] with base showing four deities. Already in 1564 the site was named 'Der Steinerne Mann' and the head illustrated here seems to have been employed as part of the boundary marker. The face with its great eyes, fine up-sweeping moustaches and hollowed top has been compared, not very convincingly, with the late Hallstatt figure from Stockach [13]; it is in fact very close to the triple heads from Sutherland [286] and, with its flattened rear indicating its having been fixed in some permanent position, probably marks the area's first use as a sanctuary site, a wooded setting being particularly suitable for a Celtic cult place.

Mitt. Hist. Ver. f.d. Pfalz 23 (1889), 259f.; A. Kolling, *Saarland. Beiträge zur Arch. u. Kunstgeschichte*, 12 (1965), 45–50, Abb. 2c and Taf. 3–4

288 Aastrup, Glejbjerg, Jutland. Detail of granite carving. Ht. c. 30 cm. ? I/IV AD. *Pastor K. Høgsbro Østergaard.*

This stone triple head is one of two in the area, the present example having been discovered in 1880. It is mounted on a sloping shouldered block which itself has two low-relief heads, one in the centre of both of the long sides.

Triple heads seem also to have played an important role in the beliefs of the non-Celtic Cimbri; the similarity of the features of the Danish *tricephaloi* to the general run of British pieces demonstrates not so much a common artistic basis but rather the difficulty of ascribing either a firm chronology or a cultural background for such simple expressions of native beliefs.

K. Høgsbro Østergaard, *Kuml* (1954), 55–77; *PCB*, 117–18 and Pl. 41a

289 Broighter, Linvady, Co. Londonderry. Gold torc. External d. 19·5 cm., d. of tube 3 cm. Late I BC. National Mus. of Ireland, Dublin.

The find conditions of this, one of the finest of all pieces of later Iron Age gold work, are distressingly uncertain. The torc is supposed to have been found under an old umbrella in 1895 together with a model gold boat complete with oars, a gold 'hanging bowl', two gold chains, one with complex linked strands and fastening catch of a type which has Roman parallels, and two twisted torcs with simple hook-and-eye fastenings which have fairly close analogies amongst the Snettisham finds [see 291].

The torc is now in two separate sections but originally had been made of a single sheet of gold which, after being decorated with the main incised and *repoussé* design, was soldered along the inner margin, filled with pitch or resin, carefully curved to shape and finally soldered to the separately made buffer terminals. It is this general method of manufacture and in particular the terminals with their rotating heads allowing the

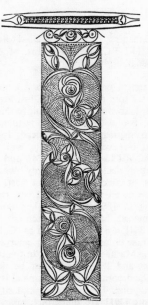

Fig. 17 [289] Broighter, N. Ireland. Rolled out decoration on hoop of gold torc. Scale 1 : 3
After Evans

locking of a tap-shaped tennon into a slot which invite close comparison with the Frasnes-lez-Buissenal torc and its cousins in Snettisham hoard 'A' [see 173].

Although the form is that of the imported Snettisham rings, the decoration, restricted to the outer surface of the ring, is definitely insular, or indeed basically Irish. The carefully drawn mesh of radiating lines set out by compasses from a number of centres, slender trumpet joints and free-moving swirling lines, is work which could be expected of those responsible for the Lough Crew trial pieces [256] or for the British Museum 'offering bowl' with its tight-hatched background [269]; comparable with the latter are the separately pinned-on tight spirals of the Broighter torc. It is of course possible that Broighter may have been made in Ireland by an itinerant British goldsmith – definitely British objects of the period such as the Keshcarrigan bowl did find their way to Ireland [see 273] – but in fact detailed comparison with products of the eastern Snettisham - Ipswich 'school' does not reveal anything more than a general similarity. Equally, no continental material of the first century BC can be cited to argue that Broighter was a European import, though it is not impossible that foreign terminals might have been married on to a locally made ring; classical references refer to the import of torcs to Britain in the reign of Augustus.[1]

A. J. Evans, *Archaeologia* LV (1897), 391–408, esp. fig. 7 and Pl. XXII; E. C. R. Armstrong, *Catalogue of Irish gold ornaments in the National Mus. of Ireland* (1920), no. 129; E. T. Leeds, *Celtic ornament* (1933), 132 and fig. 35b; W. A. von Jenny, *Keltische Metallarbeiten* (1935), Taf. 44:1; H. H. Maryon, *Proc. Roy. Irish Academy*, 44 C7 (1938), 210–11; R. L. Praeger, *J. Roy. Soc. Antiq. of Ireland* LXXII (1942), 29–32; *ABA*, Pl. 45; R. Rainbird Clarke, *PPS* XX (1954), 41–42 and Pls. III–IV; *PP*, 45 ff.; *EV*, ill. p. 210

[1] Strabo, *Geography* IV, 53

290 Shaw Hill, Netherurd, Peeblesshire. Gold torc terminal. D. 5·5 cm. Mid-I BC. National Mus. of Antiquities of Scotland, Edinburgh.

In 1806 a shepherd boy came across a hoard of gold consisting of the torc terminal here illustrated – better but incorrectly known as the Cairnmuir terminal – three twisted torcs, two with single-ring terminals similar to those from Snettisham and Belstead, Ipswich [see **291**–**292**] and one with a spatulate end somewhat like that found at Clonmacnoise [**174**], and a number of bullet-shaped electrum coins, only two of which showed signs of much wear. These last, of which about 40 were noted when the find was reported by the landowner in 1808 to Sir Walter Scott, whose antiquarian interests have already been commented on [see notes to **244**], are a type known as 'Gallo-Roman XB' coins. These coins, in effect an emergency issue, come from the Marne–Aisne region, in the territory of the Suessiones and Remi, and must be dated to c. 75–50 BC.[1] The decoration of the terminal is limited to one side of the ring. The points of similarity with the Snettisham torc [**291**] are numerous; apart from the general layout of slender ridged curls, one can match a concentric stack of circles, tiny raised knobs with three punch dots, dotted lines bordering a scribed line and rough matting produced by alternate lines of a blunt graver.

The composition of the terminal, once variously interpreted as a sceptre head or a terret, is 85 per cent. gold and 9 per cent. silver with 3·5 per cent. copper, 2·5 per cent. iron and a trace of tin. The decoration is quite fresh and the terminal shows no sign of having been wrenched forcibly off a main ring – a point which may indicate the separate origin of torc and terminals suggested by the Broighter collar. However this may be, comparison with the complete Snettisham hoard 'E' torc shows that Netherurd is in fact the most northerly example of a group of rings found in East Anglia, the products of local craftsmen making use perhaps of the native gold of south-west Scotland which would offer an explanation of the terminal's presence so far north.

Arch. Scotica IV:2 (1857), 217–19 and Pl. IV; J. D. Cowen, *Proc. Soc. Antiq. Scot.* LXIX (1935), 455–59; W. A. von Jenny, *Keltische Metallarbeiten* (1935), Taf. 41:2; R. Rainbird Clarke, *PPS* XX (1954), 49, 64 and Pl. XVII:1–2; *PP*, 48, 56 and Pl. 29a; R. W. Feachem, *Proc. Soc. Antiq. Scot.* XCI (1957–58), 112–16; S. Piggott and R. B. K. Stevenson in (ed.) A. L. F. Rivet, *The Iron Age in Northern Britain* (1966), 10, 12, 22, 31

[1] *Problems*, 104, 170

291 Ken Hill, Snettisham, Norfolk, hoard 'E'. Electrum torc. D. c. 20 cm. Mid-I BC. British Mus., London. (*Courtesy Trustees of the British Museum.*)

Dio Cassius' description of Boudica, queen of the Iceni, as she rode into battle, tells how 'she wore a great twisted golden necklace'.[1] Between 1948 and 1968 a large number of gold rings and some coins have been found on Ken Hill Farm in north-west Norfolk in the course of ploughing. Snettisham hoard 'E', apart from the present twisted-wire ring-terminal torc, con-

sisted of a hollow gold bracelet with rather stringy tendril ornament including areas of matting generally similar to the design on the surviving Ulceby bit [**293**], and an electrum torc of two twisted rods found threaded through one of the larger torc's terminals. Only one plain expanded hoof-shaped terminal survives on the smaller torc; all the Snettisham hoards give the impression of containing a certain amount of scrap as well as complete objects. Hoards 'B' and 'C', for example, contain both parts of and complete single-loop-terminalled torcs related to those found at Broighter [see **289**] and Netherurd [**290**].

The big ring-terminalled torc, though mainly gold, contains some 38 per cent. silver and less than 3 per cent. copper with some zinc, tin, and iron. A hoop of eight separate strands, each of eight twisted wires, some 0·19 cm. in diameter, has been soldered into the separate hollow cast and chased terminals, one of which contained a worn quarter-stater of the Gallo-Belgic Dc type, the so-called 'Atrebatic' form with a continental distribution based on Arras and a time span of c. 90–50 BC contemporary with the native British 'B' series of coins.[2]

Comparison with the ?unfinished Belstead, Ipswich, torcs [see **292**] shows how the decoration's main layout of symmetrically balanced zones, limited, as Netherurd, to one face of each ring, was cast probably as the *cire perdue* or non-repetitive 'lost wax' process, the detailed chasing and punched ornament being added subsequently. Points of comparison have already been made with Netherurd; an isolated ring terminal torc found in 1962 two miles away at Sedgeford[3] is also close. Snettisham also makes use of the raised sinuous design as found on the Snailwell armlet and discussed in connection with its appearance on the rims of bowls of the ?south-eastern Colchester-Keshcarrigan group [see **273**]; the pattern also appears on another, though crude, outlier of the Snettisham-Ipswich group, a torc from Needwood Forest in Staffordshire with its hoop made of six strands, each of three twisted wires.[4] What might be termed the hall-mark of the Snettisham-Ipswich 'master' – it is difficult not to consider at least some of the torcs as the product of a single individual – is the tiny indentations on the miniature raised knobs which, usually in pairs, decorate matting-filled hollow-sided triangles; this feature also appears on the bracelet from hoard 'E'.

The date of deposition of the Snettisham workshop hoards is suggested not so much by the worn Gallo-Belgic coin contained in the hoard 'E' torc terminal or by other Belgic coins of the Atrebatic or Bellovacian type [see also notes to **306a**] but rather by a number of local so-called 'tin' or *speculum* coins which had a circulation of about a century from 50 BC and which were clearly old when buried.[5] These coins, perhaps the workshop's 'take' from successful sales – although barter in this period must have still been a staple method of payment – were buried probably not before 25 BC and it is not impossible that the Snettisham-Ipswich workshop based on north-west Norfolk, or at least its products, were still going concerns at the time of the Roman conquest. The presence of a continental Belgic coin, a type which is known elsewhere in southern England, is more likely to be due to the handing down of an old import associated with the earlier Belgic incursions, but the coins from Netherurd demonstrate how contacts with the continent were maintained by the native communities of south-eastern England – one must also recall the Frasnes-type torcs in Snettisham hoard 'A' [see notes to **173**].

R. Rainbird Clarke and R. M. Dolley, *PPS* XX (1954), 27–86, esp. 31, 59–67 and Pls. XV–XVI, XVIII; *Celts*, Pls. 42–43; *PP*, 45 and 48, and figs. 33–34; *LPA*, 66, 68, Frontispiece and Pl. XVII; Rainbird Clarke, *East Anglia* (1960), 104 and Pl. 25; *PRB*, Pl. 268; *PAE*, 265 and Pl. 296; *EV*, ill. p. 211

[1] Epitome to *History of Rome* LXII, 3, 4
[2] Rainbird Clarke, *PPS* XX, 59 and Pl. XIV:14; *Problems*, 122–23, 160; R. P. Mack, *Coinage of Ancient Britain* (2 ed., 1964), 1 ff.
[3] Elizabeth J. Owles, *Antiquity* XLIII (1969), Pl. XXXIc
[4] Rainbird Clarke, *PPS* XX, 65; *PP*, 37 and Pl. 25a
[5] *Problems*, 111, 122–23

292 Belstead Estate, Ipswich, Suffolk. Gold torc no. 2. Max. d. 20 cm. Mid-I BC. British Mus., London. (*Courtesy Trustees of the British Museum.*)

In October 1968 a bulldozer driver found a group of five gold torcs on a building site near Ipswich. The hoard consisted of four decorated loop-terminalled and one ring-terminalled torcs, of which the hoops all consisted, like the example illustrated here, of just two large twisted strands of slightly faceted cross-section.

The fascinating feature of what otherwise might be just another group of neck-rings to add to the series of Snettisham finds, is that the four loop-terminalled torcs are all different, so that what one has at Belstead is a unique find, the remains of a Celtic craftsman's style in progress. Though the construction of the Belstead torcs is slightly different from that of the other ring-terminalled torcs previously found – the separately cast and hollow rings are carefully joined by a simple casting-on process and hammered flush with the surface of the loops – various motifs are common to both Snettisham and Belstead. There is, of course, the basic curved-ridge layout; like Netherurd [**290**] the two more finished torcs have notched or cable ridging while the present example is the only torc not to have the tell-tale tiny bosses, possibly to be worked up in a final stage of manufacture.

In fact, torc no. 2 from Belstead (which weighs 1,044 gm.) may mark the second phase of construction, when the rough-cast terminals have just been fixed to the main hoop which is still fairly widely expanded to give the craftsman full access to the terminals for the subsequent chasing. Faint scribed guide-lines can be made out and the basic curved-sided voids can clearly be seen; the left-hand terminal in particular can be compared to the decoration on the Old Windsor bit [**258**], 'Llyn Cerrig' commas and all. The 'matting' also still awaits adding, mating which may either imitate the southern mirror style of fill-in decoration or the rough hatching on the Thames helmet [**294**].

One other possibly unfinished example of what now may justly be termed the Snettisham-Ipswich 'school' is that from North Creake, Norfolk; a silver terminal from Hengistbury Head fort, Hampshire, found with Roman coins of a date later than A D 60, is either a later piece or a local copy of the same style.[1]

Elizabeth J. Owles and J. W. Brailsford, *Antiquity* XLIII (1969), 208–12, esp. no. 2, Pl. XXXb; *Current Archaeology* 17 (1969), 169

[1] R. Rainbird Clarke, *PPS* XX (1954), 64 and Pl. XVII: 3–4, 7–8

293 Ulceby-on-Humber, Lincolnshire. Bronze sheathed iron side-ring from horse bit. Max. d. 8·8 cm. Later I BC. City of Liverpool Mus.

Found some time before 1859, this ring, once part of the Mayer collection [see **260**], is all that remains of a pair of decorated horse bits found with an ?electrum bracelet and three twisted loop-terminal torcs, of which two only survive in the Ashmolean Museum, Oxford. These loop-terminal torcs are similar to those from Hoards 'B', 'C' and 'D' at Snettisham [see notes to **291**]. The missing bit had areas of matting on its link head which relate it to the Waterloo helmet illustrated below [**294**], rather than to the Walthamstow and Old Windsor bits [see notes to **258**]; in relief against the matting background, conjoined Llyn Cerrig trumpets formed a fine pseudo-face. Matting is also present on the ring illustrated here though it is worn, and it fills curved-sided triangles similar to those on the bits; one triangle has a Snettisham-Ipswich double knob pair. Fox has observed how the loose-linked design, in which curved-sided voids play an important part in providing a subsidiary pattern, is related to a spherical surface – in contrast to the expansion of a similar layout into what, rolled out, is really an elongated rectangle. Fox's comparison of the 'open' tendril design to such pieces as the Grimthorpe disc,[1] which he considered a product, like Ulceby, of a north-eastern or central English workshop, seems to run against Ulceby's association with the Snettisham-Ipswich rings. Grimthorpe certainly may be compared to the Llyn Cerrig plaque [**254**], but then so many pieces can be related to this archetypal piece which, one should remember, in the chronology usually advanced for it, may be earlier by only a few decades than the group of objects illustrated on this and the previous pages.

Not clear in this view of Ulceby is the crimped or filled outer margin of the bronze sheath of the ring split by the oxidisation of the core. This frilling is the same motif as the Snettisham hoard 'E' or the Needwood Forest torcs [see **291**]. The rosette-like stop-knobs cannot be compared precisely with the Snettisham-Ipswich rings although the outer ring is formed of the hall-mark of the group, tiny dot-impressed knobs; the rosette is also an element of importance amongst material which can without doubt be associated with the period of the Boudiccan revolt [see **299**]. The horse bits from Ringstead in Norfolk[2] show the disintegration of the Snettisham-Ipswich layout applied to a sphere, and must be regarded as a poor, but not necessarily later, attempt to produce an Ulceby type of decoration.

H. Syer Cuming, *J. British Arch. Ass.* 15 (1859), 225–28 and Pls. 20–22; E. T. Leeds, *Antiq. J.* XIII (1933), 466–68; J. B. Ward Perkins, *PPS* V (1939), 181 ff. and fig. 6; R. Rainbird Clarke, *PPS* XX (1954), 49 ff.; *PP*, 35–36, fig. 21a and Pl. 24; J. Barber and J. V. S. Megaw, *PPS* XXIX (1963), 212–13

[1] *PP*, 33 f., fig. 19:1 and Pl. 23b; I. M. Stead, *PPS* XXXIV (1968), 169, 179 and fig. 13:1

[2] *PP*, 44–45 and Pl. 28; Rainbird Clarke, *East Anglia* (1960), 103–04 and Pl. 24

WK, Taf. 100; *PP*, 49, fig. 36 and Pl. 27b; *LPA*, 68 and Pl. XVIII:1; *PAE*, 264–66 and Pl. 293

[1] *Manuel* IV, 1057 ff. and figs. 491, 716–18

294 River Thames at Waterloo Bridge, London. Bronze helmet with enamel inlay. Ht. of cap 16 cm., w. between horns 42·5 cm. Later I BC. British Mus., London (Thames Conservancy loan). *J. V. S. Megaw.*

Found by Waterloo Bridge in 1868, the cap of this helmet is formed from two pieces of sheet-bronze decorated in *repoussé* on both sides, the better preserved of which is here visible. Below what is usually termed the front part is a third crescent-shaped sheet, all three sheets being riveted together, the joints being masked by narrow bronze strips fastened in turn by countersunk rivets, of which the large visible cast rivet heads are almost entirely decorative. The twin horns are made of conical sheets also riveted and with outer strips; the knobbed terminals are separate castings. Originally six discs scored to take red enamel, or rather cupric glass identical to that used on the Battersea shield [253], decorated the front and the back; one is now missing. A 'U'-sectioned binding strip fastened by riveted clips strengthens the edge of the cap round which a series of irregular holes may have been for stitching a cloth lining.

The 'stringiness' of the design masks at first its relationship to the Snettisham-Ipswich group of torcs [290–292]. Much has been made by certain authorities of the asymmetry of the layout but in fact this is limited to the points at the apex of each main plate; such asymmetry is present also in details of the torcs' decoration. More important are the points of similarity: the long slender curved ridges, the punched matting within curved-sided triangles and the tiny raised knobs with central punch marks. Indeed, instead of placing the Waterloo helmet in a separate Thames 'school', it would seem more reasonable to regard it as the not-too-successful excursion into decorating large, more or less flat areas by a craftsman of the Snettisham-Ipswich group, a craftsman more accustomed to restricting his skill to the limited area of a torc terminal. In view of the distribution of the actual torcs, to expect that craftsmen from the general territory of the Iceni should have moved between the Wash and the Thames is hardly expecting too much when actual products of the same school certainly travelled much greater distances.

One final detail: the cross-ridged circular backing for the enamel settings follows the pattern of similar decorated areas on helmets and other objects found in late La Tène continental contexts such as the *oppida* of Bibracte (Mount Beauvray) and the Hradiště at Stradonice.[1]

The small size and comparatively thin nature of the Waterloo helmet have suggested that, like the Battersea shield, here may be a parade piece perhaps, with Tanderagee in mind [285], for decorating a wooden statue in some Thames-side shrine.

A. W. Franks, *Proc. Soc. Antiq.* II ser. III (1864–67), 342–44; C. E. Vulliamy, *Archaeology of Middlesex and London* (1930), 127–28; E. T. Leeds, *Celtic ornament* (1933), 24 ff.; Françoise Henry, *Préhistoire* II: 1 (1933), 81–82 and fig. 8:7; W. A. von Jenny, *Keltische Metallarbeiten aus heidnischer und christl. Zeit* (1935), Taf. 37; *ABA*, Pl. 53; J. W. Brailsford in *Actas IV sesion Congr. Intern. de Ciencias prehist. y protohist.* (1954), 760–61;

295 Meare West, Somerset. Three incised pots: (a) storage jar from site XVB; ht. 35·5 cm.; (b) open bowl from site XXXIV; d. 23 cm.; (c) lid (=P 75), d. 17 cm. II/I BC. Somerset County Mus., Taunton. *S. E. Thomas.*

These examples of what Sir Cyril Fox termed 'peasant art' of the later Iron Age belonging to a local group variously referred to as the 'Third South-western B' or more simply 'Glastonbury' culture, come from one of the two large complexes of occupation sites discovered in the low-lying peat of the Somerset Levels to the north-west of Glastonbury Tor. In the area of the twin 'villages' of Meare, subject to periodic flooding by the freshwater River Brue, recent investigations[1] have tended to challenge the interpretation of the sites as a series of huts placed on artificial 'islands' in the middle of shallow lakes, there being a strong possibility that the timber substructures first uncovered at Meare in 1910 may belong to an earlier prehistoric period. Notwithstanding, the mass of Iron Age finds recovered from the areas of clay dumped on the surface of the peat rivals those of the continental *oppida* and gives a so far unique picture of domestic life in Iron Age Britain; there is not only the remarkably elegant wheel-turned decorated pottery illustrated here and with a distribution extending throughout the south-west, but also much plain domestic wares, fine turned woodwork, bronze and iron (including the easternmost of a type of brooch derived from the LT III 'Nauheim' form), glass armlets [see note to **Plate VIIa**], as well as the evidence for the carding and weaving of wool. The wider connections of these local communities of the last centuries of independence are marked by the find of a coin of the Coriosolites of north-western France [see notes to **194f**] as well as the trade for Kimmeridge shale from Dorset. Following a final period of flooding and presumed abandonment the 'villages' were reoccupied in Roman times (c. III/IV AD).

The recent petrological examination of Glastonbury ware suggests production outside the main settlements and subsequent trade by regional specialist potters.[2] The decoration of the pots, incised before firing, included the use of compasses and areas of 'matting', as can be seen on both (b) the bowl and (c) the lid. This recalls not only the layout of the engraved bronze mirrors, some of which certainly may be of south-western origin [see notes to **260**], but also the Broighter torc [**289**] and the Ulster sword scabbards [**249**]. Another link with Ireland, this time with the Lough Crew trial plaques [**256**] are the straight-line breaks in the otherwise curvilinear patterns of the large storage jar (a) which otherwise forms a continuous 'S' scroll. Such links between the west of Britain and Ireland are well established throughout the prehistory of the British Isles. Previous theories of links with Breton decorated and stamped wares [see notes to **156–157**], the result of trade or even settlement from the latter area, cannot be ruled out, but local development is preferable in view of the early date of the French presumed prototypes.[3]

The decorated pots from Meare and Glastonbury represent simply one of several regional styles of what might be termed large-scale folk industry craft potting;

other important centres, which recent analysis of the actual composition of the individual fabrics is doing much to elucidate, are in the Midlands and in south-east England. Certain archaisms creep in, including versions of the insular Waldalgesheim domed tendril design, which might well be compared with the Newnham Croft armlet [131].

The triple setting of holes on the Meare jar here illustrated marks the position where binding was inserted to repair an old crack.

A. Bulleid and H. St G. Gray, *Glastonbury Lake Village* II (1917), 505–12; *id., The Meare Lake Village* I (1948), 17, 21, 59, figs. 4, 8 and Pl. VII; W. F. Grimes, *PPS* XVIII (1952), 160–75; *PP*, 135–36, figs. 80–81 and Pl. 76:3–6; *PRB*, Pls. 238–39

[1] M. Avery, *Proc. Somerset Arch. and Nat. Hist. Soc.*, 112 (1968), 21 ff. esp. 31–37
[2] D. P. S. Peacock, *Antiq. J.* XLIX (1969), 41–61
[3] Peacock, *op. cit.*, 52 ff.; F. Schwappach in *Festschr. Dehn*, 272 ff.

296 Trawsfynydd, Merionethshire. Yew stave tankard with bronze covering and handle. Ht. 14·3 cm., d. 18·3 cm. Late I AD. City of Liverpool Mus.

This is the most elegant of surviving pieces of the later British Iron Age, with its cast handle, like a balustrade by Charles Rennie Mackintosh, a fine example of pre-Christian Celtic 'art nouveau'. In construction, with upright staves cased in sheet-bronze and a turned wooden base with central bronze knob, the tankard follows the pattern of the Aylesford and Marlborough buckets [187–188], though the elegantly curved profile is unique. On the base a double circle of undulating bronze wire is hammered into the wood while the handle is riveted at its centre point and held fast at the rim by a turned-over strip rather in the manner of the 'U'-shaped strips on the Waterloo helmet [294].

Metal-covered tankards or copies in pottery are a feature peculiar to the later Iron Age of the south of England [see also 301] with a concentration in the Belgic area, though a tankard from Shapwick Heath in Somerset[1] gives the clearest parallel to the turned base of Trawsfynydd. Pottery versions, probably created owing to the lack of skilled wood-turners and metal-smiths, came from first–second century AD contexts at Gloucester (Glevum), Cirencester (Corinium Dobunorum) and the Durotrigan hill-fort of Maiden Castle, Dorset, destroyed by Vespasian and his Augustan legion in AD 43–45.

Fox considered that the Trawsfynydd tankard had been made in the south-west, in the territory of the Dobuni, and compared it with the openwork handle of the mirror from the Birdlip, Gloucestershire, woman's grave,[2] but the broken-backed scroll of the main pointed oval invites comparison with more northern and easterly objects such as an openwork finger ring from Mildenhall, Suffolk, and another ring from the Lambay Island, Co. Dublin, 'trading station'.[3] Another comparison is the relief decoration on the chape plate of a sword scabbard of Piggott's group IV 'Brigantian' swords from Mortonhall, Midlothian.[4] Add to this the 'dragonesque' fibulae and the presence on continental provincial Roman work[5] of not only the broken-back scroll but the triskel as seen in the four knobbed roundels

of the Trawsfynydd handle, and the sources for many elements of what in many ways is not an ultimate La Tène style but indeed a new art become clear.

R. E. M. Wheeler, *Prehistoric and Roman Wales* (1925), 210–11 and fig. 85; E. T. Leeds, *Celtic ornament* (1933), 53–54 and fig. 20a; *ABA*, Pl. 73; J. X. W. P. Corcoran, *PPS* XVIII (1952), 85–102, esp. 97–98, fig. 1 and Pl. XII; *PP*, 109–10 and Pls. 65–66; G. C. Boon, *Bull. Board Celtic Studies* XIX (1962), 347–48; *PreA*, 226 and ill. 227; H. N. Savory, *Early Iron Age art in Wales* (1968), 21 and fig. 19

[1] *PP*, Pl. 63a
[2] *PP*, Pl. 57b
[3] Mildenhall: R. Rainbird Clarke, *Arch. J.* XCVI (1939), Pl. XIX:5; Lambay Island: R. A. S. Macalister, *Proc. Roy. Irish Acad.* 38 C9 (1928–29), Pl. XXIV:5; see also notes to [262, 297]
[4] S. Piggott, *PPS* XVI (1950), 18 and fig. 9:3; Morna Simpson in (ed.) J. M. Coles and D. D. A. Simpson, *Studies in Ancient Europe: Essays presented to Stuart Piggott* (1968), 248 and fig. 63q
[5] W. A. von Jenny, *IPEK* (1935), Taf. 8–9; Simpson, *op. cit.*, 246; see also notes to [270]

297 Birdcombe Court, Wraxall, Somerset. Cast bronze collar with provision for insets. Internal d. 12·5 cm. I AD. City Mus., Bristol. *S. E. Thomas.*

Found without association at the Tower House, Birdcombe Court in 1837, this heavy (1268 gm.) necklace, with a hinged and riveted swivel joint at the rear and a hooked tenon-catch or 'joggle joint' at the front, is the finest of a group of collars from the south-west of England. All, as here, have provision for inlay and where inlay survives, it is glass; enamel seems to be a technique little practised in the west. The Wraxall collar has 15 circular settings on each half; a neat nineteenth-century copper-plate inscription runs round the inner surface of the ring recording its discovery.

The decoration, a basic pattern of interlocking 'S' curves and trumpet spirals which mark the last stages of the Llyn Cerrig 'commas' [see 254], incorporates the tendency to enlarge the trumpet endings which has been noted on the Deskford *carnyx* mount, while the actual jointing of the 'S's may be compared with the so-called 'casket ornament' strips [see 299]. A half-collar – the form is provincial Roman rather than Celtic – from the hill-fort of Pen-coed-foel, Llandyssul, Cardiganshire,[1] has a rather more pointed version of the running 'S' and five large raised bosses separately riveted to the main plate in the insets. A circular shield boss from the Polden Hills hoard has a more ornithological version of the same pattern.[2] Llandyssul may be contrasted rather than compared with the ring from Lochar Moss, Dumfriesshire,[3] which also has raised bosses, set this time into broken-backed 'S' scrolls. Lochar Moss, which has been placed in a group of mainly first-century AD 'beaded torcs', some at least of Brigantian manufacture and one of which comes from Lambay Island, Co. Dublin, a site with imports of undoubtedly Brigantian origin.[4] Lochar Moss shares with Wraxall a toothed or simple cable edging decoration. The running scrolls of both Wraxall and Llandyssul may also be compared with motifs on the south-western decorated pottery.[5]

Wraxall, with its strict symmetry of balanced layout,

171

stands as a good example of the tenacity of certain old motifs here competently executed in a period when regional workshops untouched by Roman provincial influence were on the wane and only in certain areas like the extreme north and south-west did a certain provincial archaism prevail.

E. Ellacombe, *Archaeologia* XXX (1844), 521 and Pl. 61a; A. W. Franks, *Archaeologia* LIV (1895), 495–96 and Pl. XLVII; W. A. von Jenny, *Keltische Metallarbeiten* (1935), Taf. 41:1; *PP*, 106, Pl. 61a; Aileen Fox, *South West England* (1964), 134 and Pl. 77; *PRB*, Pl. 271

[1] *PP*, 106 ff., 150 and Pl. 12d
[2] *PP*, 116 and fig. 72
[3] *PP*, 107 and Pl. 29b; Morna Simpson in (ed.) J. M. Coles and D. D. A. Simpson, *Studies in Ancient Europe: Essays presented to Stuart Piggott* (1968), 248 f.
[4] R. B. K. Stevenson, *Proc. Soc. Antiq. Scot.* LXXXII (1947–48), 293–95; *id.*, in (ed.) A. L. F. Rivet, *The Iron Age in Northern Britain* (1966), 26 ff.
[5] W. F. Grimes, *PPS* XVIII (1941), 166–67 and fig. 6; see also [295]

298 Stichill (or Stichel), Roxburghshire. Bronze neck-ring with pin fastening. Outer d. 19 cm. Late I AD. National Mus. of Antiquities of Scotland, Edinburgh. (General view) *M. J. M. Murray.*

The Stichill collar, found in digging a well in 1747, was probably associated with a pair of 'massive armlets' of a particular late Scottish type [see notes to **Plate VIIIb**] Although in outline it is not too unlike some of the south-western collars [see **297**], the decoration is in complete contrast. The separately riveted-on *repoussé* front panels, like those on an armlet from Plunton Castle, Kirkcudbrightshire, exhibit a variation of what Leeds termed the 'swash N' which, like other motifs found in Roman finds in the north of England, is a variation on the trumpet scroll version of the classical acanthus which in Britain starts with the Torrs horns [**245**] and runs through to the post-conquest 'casket ornaments' [**299**]. The Stichill swash N's have their closest parallels in a series of enamelled seal boxes, as found at Chester and Lincoln, one from Castle Hill, Nottinghamshire, having a firm Flavian date.[1] The tooled decoration on the remainder of the horizontal surface and at the rear of the Stichill collar is quite different from that on the riveted panels. The spindly spirals and slender trumpet features contrast with any known southern motif; rather they compare with the Petrie crown and Bann disc's tooled decoration [**270–271**] and their basic form and layout may owe something to the spacers for Roman multi-strand necklaces like that from the Greatchesters (Aesica) 'hoard'.[2]

D. Wilson, *Archaeology and Prehistoric Annals of Scotland* 2 ed. (1863), 451; J. Anderson, *Scotland in Pagan Times* I (1883), 135–37; E. T. Leeds, *Celtic ornament* (1933), 110 f.; W. A. von Jenny, *IPEK* (1935), 41 and Taf. 10:4; *id.*, *Keltische Metallarbeiten* (1935), Taf. 42:1; R. J. C. Atkinson and S. Piggott, *Archaeologia* XCVI (1955), 232–33 and Pl. LXXXVb; *PP*, 106 and Pl. 62b; *PRB*, Pl. 272; Piggott and R. B. K. Stevenson in

(ed.) A. L. F. Rivet, *The Iron Age in Northern Britain* (1966), 10–11, 32 and Pl. 6; Morna Simpson in (ed.) J. M. Coles and D. D. A. Simpson, *Studies in Ancient Europe: Essays presented to Stuart Piggott* (1968), 238 ff.

[1] F. Oswald, *Nottingham Castle: City of Nottingham Art Gallery and Mus.* (1927), 28, fig. 2 and Pl. VI:7
[2] T. Hodgkin, *Proc. Soc. Antiq. Newcastle-upon-Tyne* VI (1893–94), 24 and ill.; see also notes to [305]

299 Santon, Norfolk. Detail of embossed bronze strip. Total l. 22 cm., w. c. 3 cm. Later I AD. University Mus. of Archaeology and Ethnology, Cambridge.

This detail is of one of three press-moulded strips from the Santon tinker's hoard [see also notes to **218** and **Plate VIIIa**]. Such strips belong to a general class of so-called 'casket ornaments' of which some 40 are known mainly from south of the Severn–Wash line; these are dated to the first two centuries AD.[1] Though such strips were sometimes clearly used for the decoration of containers of various sorts, disc brooch covers are also decorated with similar motifs and a press-mould for one such disc comes from the Santon hoard.[2] An iron press-mould found at Roman Wroxeter (Viroconium) has a similar layout to the Santon strips, while from Lochlee in Ayrshire is an ash wood block relief carved with a triskel on one face and a ring-and-dot and simplified lyre pattern on the other; the Lochlee mould was associated with brooches of the first half of the second century AD.[3]

The basic motif behind such pieces as the Santon strip is an acanthus scroll; the transition into a separated series of units comprising broken-backed commas (compare the Moel Hiraddug plaque [**268**]), berried rosettes (with perhaps such features as the Ulceby stop knobs as a starting point [**293**]), and raised half-moons can be seen more clearly in the finest of all 'casket ornaments', the plaque from Elmswell [**303**]. Fragments from Rodborough Common near Stroud, Gloucestershire, and others found with the remains of an oak box from the second, Stanfordbury 'B', Bedfordshire, 'Welwyn'-type grave associated with Roman imports and local fire-dogs [see **279**], are also close.[4]

Not only the general layout but also the concept of decorating furnishings with sheet-bronze is probably due to Roman influence.

R. A. Smith, *Proc. Cambridge Antiq. Soc.* XIII (1908–09), 153 and Pl. XVI:1; P. Corder and C. F. C. Hawkes, *Antiq. J.* XX (1940), 346 and fig. 2; *PP*, 105 and Pl. 67c

[1] C. Fox, *A find of the Early Iron Age from Llyn Cerrig Bach, Anglesey* (1947), 89
[2] Smith, *op. cit.*, 149–50 and fig. 3; see also E. T. Leeds, *Celtic ornament* (1933), fig. 36a; G. C. Boon, *Med. Arch.* 3 (1959), 85 n. 16; *Current Arch.* 18 (1970), 190, fig. 4
[3] Wroxeter: D. Atkinson, *Report on excavations at Wroxeter 1923-27* (1942), 52, 216–18 and Pl. 52:1–2; Lochlee: R. Munro, *Ancient Scottish Lake Dwellings* (1883), 133–34 and figs. 149–50
[4] Rodborough: Smith, *Guide to Early Iron Age Antiquities in the British Museum* (2 ed., 1925), 146 and fig. 169; Stanfordbury: Fox, *Archaeology of the Cambridge Region* (reissue 1948), 100, 105 and Pl. XVIII:4

300 ? Northern England. Detail of neck-guard of bronze helmet. Total ht. 16·5 cm., max. w. of neck-guard 8·9 cm. Late I AD. British Mus., London. (*Courtesy Trustees of the British Museum.*)

The actual helmet from the Meyrick collection, of which this is a detail, is a conical cap, possibly spun finished from a single sheet, with the addition of the neck-guard with its *repoussé* decoration; fragmentary side-pieces also have *repoussé* ornament. There is provision for a central top-knot. A couple of strokes like a Roman 'II' are incised on the outer margin of the helmet.

Basically the form of the helmet is that of a Roman auxiliary; indeed, Fox considers it the property of 'a Celtic noble in Roman service'. Very similar, though undecorated, is a Roman helmet from the River Walbrook in the City of London.[1] Similar also is the helmet from the AD 60–65 debris at Colchester (Camulodunum);[2] legionary helmets and native copies are also known from the Rhineland.[3]

The neck-guard decoration with its open lyre pattern matches the upper part of the Nijmegen mirror handle [263]. The half-moons, and knobs hatched in late La Tène style as if for enamelling, have a general similarity to the Elmswell plaque. The side-panels not visible here are decorated also in the general manner of the run of 'casket ornament' with a kind of shorthand version of the Llyn Cerrig triskel [see 254]. If the northern collection from which this helmet came is a true indication of its provenance it could have been brought north by a native auxiliary fighting with the Romans against the Brigantes in the campaigns of AD 71–74 [see notes to 265].

R. A. Smith, *Guide to the Early Iron Age antiquities in the British Museum* (2 ed., 1925), 107; W. A. von Jenny, *Keltische Metallarbeiten* (1935), Taf. 36:2; *ABA*, Pl. 54; *LPA*, 68 and Pl. XVIII:2; *PP*, 119 and Pl. 62c

[1] J. W. Brailsford, *Antiquities of Roman Britain in the British Museum* (2ed., 1958), 67 and Pl. XXVI:5
[2] C. F. C. Hawkes and M. R. Hull, *Camulodunum=Soc. Antiq. London Res. Rep.* XIV (1947), 33 ff. and fig. 62
[3] Brailsford, *British Mus. Q.* XVI (1951–2), 17–19

301 Upper Dylais, Neath, Glamorganshire. Bronze tankard-handle no. IV with traces of enamel (reconstructed). L. 12 cm. Later I AD. National Mus. of Wales, Cardiff.

Around 1875 a group of children came across the find better known as the 'Seven Sisters' hoard in a mountain stream bed on the south-east side of Nant-y-Cafn. From the worn nature of many of the objects which included both native enamelled harness fittings and a number of provincial Roman military fittings and pendants which can be dated to the later first-century Roman advances north and west,[1] it seems that this was a scrap-metal collection.

The tankard hold-fast – of which there are five – has in fact only one surviving scored setting for enamel but otherwise is closely comparable to the decoration on the neck-guard of the Meyrick collection helmet, again a late version of the Llyn Cerrig 'comma' with characteristic high ridged 'S' curves. It is perhaps not so definite that the Seven Sisters hold-fasts are all imports into the territory of the Silures from that of the Dobuni or Durotriges in the south and west as has been suggested since, though comparisons may be made with a handle from Hod Hill in Dorset, one could also cite that from the Welwyn 'B' grave [see also notes to 230].[2]

J. Romilly Allen, *Arch. Cambrensis* LX (1905), 127–46, esp. 137 and fig. 12; W. F. Grimes, *Prehistory of Wales* (1951), 123 and fig. 40=no. 694; J. X. W. P. Corcoran, *PPS* XVIII (1952), 100 and Pl. XIII below right: *PP*, 28, 110, fig. 78:9 and Pl. 66a–b

[1] G. Webster, *Arch. J.* CXV (1958), 69 ff.
[2] Hod Hill: Corcoran, *op. cit.*, Pl. X:1; *LPA*, 70 and Pl. XXII:5; J. W. Brailsford, *Antiquities from Hod Hill in the Durden Collection=Hod Hill I* (1962), 15 ff., and fig. 14=I 6; Welwyn 'B': Corcoran, *op. cit.*, Pl. X:2

302 Culbin Sands, Morayshire. Cast bronze armlet. W. c. 11 cm., d. c. 8 cm. ? I AD. National Mus. of Antiquities of Scotland, Edinburgh.

This unique armlet, which offers a humanised version of the ram's-headed snake as met with in the Snailwell, Cambridgeshire, armring,[1] offers a visual grammar for many of the motifs of the late period of British Iron Age art which have been seen on the previous pages. It can also be regarded as standing *in loco parentis* to the Scottish series of 'massive armlets' [see below notes to **Plate VIIIb**].

The terminal heads have round settings for enamels in place of mouths and may be compared with one reading of the heads of the contemporary Battersea shield [253]. The slender trumpets or broken-backed spiral commas which form the eyes with their blue glass pupils and the neatly set hair in the old Celtic manner hark back to the formula used on the 'Janus' heads of the early La Tène Weiskirchen I fibula [67]. But such spirals may also be compared with the three-legged motif of the Tal-y-llyn shield boss no. 2 and the Moel Hiraddug plaque [267–268], just as the tight spirals on the 'back' of the armlet – suggesting another, more elusive, pair of faces – remind one of the Broighter torc [289]. The Mortonhall, Midlothian, group IV scabbard cited in connection with the Trawsfynydd tankard [see notes to 296], is perhaps a nearer companion and one which suggests the area from which the Culbin Sands armlet may have come – Brigantia at the time of the Roman reprisals of AD 71–74. Here too must be mentioned the Melsonby masks [265] and the Deskford *carnyx*, again with the 'slender trumpet' much in evidence [272].

R. Lauder, *Arch. Scotica* III (1831), 99–102; J. A. Smith, *Proc. Soc. Antiq. Scot.* XV (1880–81), 344–48; R. B. K. Stevenson in (ed.) A. L. F. Rivet, *The Iron Age in Northern Britain* (1966), 32 and Pl. 5a; Morna Simpson in (ed.) J. M. Coles and D. D. A. Simpson, *Studies in Ancient Europe: Essays presented to Stuart Piggott* (1968), 243 ff. and fig. 62

[1] *PP*, Pl. 53b; see also notes to [273]

Plate VIIIb Pitkelloney, Muthill, Perthshire. Pair of massive armlets with red and yellow enamel inlay. Max. internal d. 10·9 and 11·4 cm.; w. 8·3 cm. I/II AD. British Mus., London. (*Courtesy Trustees of the British Museum.*)

Some twenty examples of the so-called massive armlets

173

are known, all probably originally with complex enamel *cloisonné* settings, and mainly from north-east Scotland but with an outlier from Newry, Co. Down.

All are castings made by the *cire perdue* method and no two are absolutely identical. Some at least seem to have been cast flat and then annealed or hammered into shape. The motifs employed include many common to Brigantian material: slender trumpets, sinuous saltires and broken-backed 'S's. The same motifs also can be found on the Lough Crew 'trial pieces' [see **256**] and here one may recall not just the Newry 'massive armlet' but that from Lambay Island, Co. Dublin, come scabbard mounts, 'casket ornament' fragments and a beaded torc related to that found at Lochar Moss [see notes to **297**]. All these are Brigantian forms[1] which indicate a common market in objects as well as motifs particularly in the troubled years of the immediate post-conquest period. The dual colour enamel settings of Pitkelloney match the use of red and yellow enamels on the native harness mounts from the 'Seven Sisters' hoard and are closest to terrets from an Icenian hoard at Saham Toney, Norfolk.[2]

The Scottish distribution of massive armlets lies in an area which from the late third century AD may be called Pictish; however, as to dating, the analogies of such putative artistic predecessors as the Culbin Sands bracelet suggest a beginning in the mid-first century AD. The massive armlets found near Castle Newe, Aberdeenshire, in a *souterrain* or 'earth house', one of which retains the only other surviving enamel setting, were associated with a coin of Nerva (AD 96–98); others have been found in contexts which include Roman sherds of the first century or later. The lower limit for the massive armlets is not likely to be later than the second century, and they probably owe their development to the same refugee movements which brought both the Deskford *carnyx* mount and the Lochar Moss collar into southern Scotland.

R. A. Smith, *Guide to the Early Iron Age Antiquities in the British Museum* (2 ed., 1925), 155–56 and fig. 186; *PreA*, 244 and ill. 245 ('Castle Newe'); Morna Simpson in (ed.) J. M. Coles and D. D. A. Simpson, *Studies in Ancient Europe: Essays presented to Stuart Piggott* (1968), 233–54, esp. 235 ff., figs. 61a–b, 63j and Pls. IX below, X

[1] R. A. S. Macalister, *Proc. Roy. Irish Acad.* 38 C 9 (1928–29), 240–46 and Pl. XXIV; Máire and L. de Paor, *Early Christian Ireland* (1958), 26
[2] Seven Sisters: E. T. Leeds, *Celtic ornament* (1933), 103 and Pl. II:1–5; *PP*, fig. 78:1–4; Saham Toney: G. Clinch in *Victoria County History of Norfolk* I (1901), Pl. opp. p. 273; Françoise Henry, *Préhistoire* II:1 (1933), figs. 19, 21; R. Rainbird Clarke, *Arch. J.* XCVI (1939), 70

303 Elmswell, East Riding, Yorkshire. Bronze casket mount on iron base with champlevé red and blue-green enamel. W. 24 cm. Late I AD. Kingston-upon-Hull Museums. (*Courtesy Trustees of the British Museum.*)

Found unassociated in 1938, but in the area of a settlement established by the native Parisii and subsequently occupied by the Romans from the Flavian period to the end of the occupation, this mount has been described by Fox as emblematic of 'the end of a style as well as a

culture. The Elmswell plaque looks both to the past and to the present; both the duck terminals in the bottom corners of the design – only one of which survives – and the basic lyre-palmette or pelta-loop design go right back to the Torrs 'chamfrein' [**244–245**]. On the other hand the berried rosettes and half-moon spirals compare with the Santon strips [**299**] while the later history of the lyre can be seen on the neck-guard of the Meyrick Collection helmet [**300**]; with the Culbin Sands armlet beside one [**302**], it almost seems as if the central element is a last elusive mocking Celtic face peering out from under truly Augustan foliage. A fragment from Great Tower Street in the City of London also shows the use of the lyre palmette but as part of a running pattern,[1] while a related northern piece is the mirror handle from Balmacellan, Kirkcudbrightshire. This was found with a bronze crescentic plaque and other objects carefully wrapped in cloth and placed in a peat bog.[2] The Balmacellan crescentic plaque combines 'mirror style' matting in a loose spiral design but has a central square with a linear version of the Stichill terminal plates [**298**]. The mirror handle on the other hand has another version of the lyre-with-rosettes, a good example of the interchange of artistic ideas between north and south.

The inlaid bar at the top of the Elmswell plaque is closely related to Augustan vine scrolls as found on *terra sigillata* from northern England; the ends of the vine tendril are trumpet spirals – an indication of just how late this motif may be [see **129**].

P. Corder and C. F. C. Hawkes, *Antiq. J.* XX (1940), 338–57, esp. fig. 1 and Pl. LII; *PP*, 99, 105–06 and fig. 69; J. M. C. Toynbee, *Art in Roman Britain* (1962), no. 123; *id.*, *Art in Britain under the Romans* (1964), 333 and 404

[1] Corder and Hawkes, *op. cit.*, Pl. LIII; *PP*, fig. 53:5
[2] Corder and Hawkes, *op. cit.*, 348 ff. and Pl. LIVa–b; C. Fox, *Arch. Cambrensis* C (1949), 28–29, fig. 4 and Pl. 11; *PP*, 99, 116, fig. 65 and Pl. 61b; R. W. Feachem, *The North Britons* (1965), 223, 228, fig. 19 and Pl. 10a

304 Tre'r Ceiri. Caernarvonshire. Gilt-bronze brooch. W. 3 cm. Later I AD. National Mus. of Wales, Cardiff.

This brooch was excavated in 1904 at a height of 500 metres above sea level within hut 10 of a hill-fort with evidence of occupation running through the fourth century AD. There was a blue glass 'melon bead' of a type found at the Meare and Glastonbury lake-villages. The cast brooch with its gilt covering looks like the 'Aesica' brooch illustrated on this page [**305**], and must represent a local copy of the so-called Romano-Belgic 'fan-tail' type which during AD 60–100 developed out of 'X' or 'thistle' brooches imported from Roman Gaul during the Julio-Claudian period and found at such sites as Santon and Lambay Island [see notes to **218** and **Plate VIIIa**].

The pseudo-face of the Tre'r Ceiri brooch with its rosette-comma 'eyes' and angled trumpet 'eyebrows' may be matched with the Elmswell casket ornament [**303**]. The layout is also not unlike that of the silver-gilt Birdlip, Gloucestershire, *Augenfibel* which also copies Roman forms,[1] while the dotted fill-in of the curved-sided triangle on the 'crest' or tail of the Welsh brooch matches Birdlip and occurs on the slender trumpets of the Battersea shield [253]. Comparable also are the dot-infilled lobes on top of the escutcheon animal's head of the Rose Ash, Colchester-Kesh-carrigan bowl.[2] Since there is not only the association with the glass bead but also a somewhat similar local fan-tail brooch from Camerton, Somerset,[3] it seems likely that the Tre'r Ceiri brooch was an import, perhaps an heirloom, from the south if not to say south-west of England, a local craftsman's attempt to translate a foreign object into his own familiar local artistic vocabulary.

It should also be noted that fragments of a beaded torc [see notes to 297] were found in another hut.

S. Baring Gould and R. Burnard, *Arch. Cambrensis* LIX (1904), 1–16, esp. 9 and fig. 6; P. Corder and C. F. C. Hawkes, *Antiq. J.* XX (1940), 349 f. and fig. 4; *PP*, 107–08, fig. 70 and Pl. 41d; A. H. A. Hogg, *Arch. J.* CXVII (1960), 10 ff., esp. pp. 16–17; H. N. Savory, *Early Iron Age art in Wales* (1968), 25 and fig. 28

[1] R. A. Smith, *Archaeologia* LXI (1909), 341–42 and fig. 9; *PP*, fig. 59; see also notes to 277

[2] (Lady) Aileen Fox, *Antiq. J.* XLI (1961), 186 ff. and fig. 5

305 Greatchesters, Northumberland. Gilt-bronze brooch. L. 11·5 cm. Late I AD. Museum of Antiquities, University of Newcastle upon Tyne and Society of Antiquaries of Newcastle upon Tyne.

This famous and luxuriously ornamented cast brooch was found in the Hadrian's Wall fort of Greatchesters (Aesica) from which it has come to be known as the 'Aesica brooch'. It was found in 1894 during uncontrolled excavation of the western guard chamber by the south gate. As it was contained in tumble from the roof of the tunnel into the chamber, all associations must be doubtful and thus dating must rely on stylistic comparisons.

Even more clearly than the crude Tre'r Ceiri brooch, Aesica shows the influence of the southern fan-tail type of the second half of the first century.[1] Although there are southern elements in the basic form, the style of the brooch has several northern quirks; the great down-pointing ivy-leaf on the high arched bow and the long-billed pseudo-birds which can be made out, 'Cheshire' style, on the fan and the circular plate to which the bow is joined may be matched by the much less flamboyant – one might say less Celtic – Elmswell plaque [303]. On the other hand, though what has been termed the 'swag-and-drop' motif, composed of slender elements depending from a central point, is a feature of northern Britain, it can be seen on much southern 'casket' work; the version of the slender trumpet which can be seen on Aesica is just that which appears on the 'dragonesque' brooch from Lakenheath, Suffolk. But closest of all to the individual trumpets which can be seen most clearly on the spring plate of the Aesica brooch is the layout of the Wraxall collar – another non-Celtic form translated into the Celtic 'art nouveau' style and sharing with Aesica a simple beaded or cable edging ornament. Though usually considered as a northern product, there is nothing against considering this masterly piece an import from the south, a piece which should give the lie to the implication that the coming of the Romans brought an immediate end to the long life of Celtic art

tradition – even if in the north from about the end of the second century this tradition became submerged for some three or four centuries. As Professor Toynbee has written, 'Roman influence, far from drowning local art, was a liberating, fertilising and conserving force.'[2]

The suspension rings on Aesica, a large central one and two smaller flanking ones, for a chain or chains, indicates, as recent work on provincial Roman brooches has shown,[3] that the brooch must have been worn with the fan upwards. Normally this type of brooch would have had a pair; alas, no such pair for Aesica has yet come to light.

J. P. Gidson, *Arch. Aeliana* n.s. XXIV (1903), 19–64, esp. 22 and ill. p. 25; R. G. Collingwood, *Archaeologia* LXXX (1930), 37–42 and Pl. XI; E. T. Leeds, *Celtic ornament* (1933), 109 and fig. 20c; W. A. von Jenny, *Keltische Metallarbeiten* (1935), Taf. 36:1; P. Corder and C. F. C. Hawkes, *Antiq. J.* XX (1940), 350 ff. and Pl. LIVc; *PP*, 108 and Pl. 41c; Dorothy Charlesworth, *Arch. Aeliana* ser. 4, XXXIX (1961), 6, 22, 35; J. M. C. Toynbee, *Art in Roman Britain* (1962), no. 130; *id.*, *Art in Britain under the Romans* (1964), 341; Morna Simpson in (ed.) J. M. Coles and D. D. A. Simpson, *Studies in Ancient Europe: Essays presented to Stuart Piggott* (1968), 246 ff. and fig. 63k; R. G. Collingwood and I. A. Richmond, *Archaeology of Roman Britain* (rev. ed. 1969), 294–95='group X'

[1] Collingwood, *op. cit.*, 39–40

[2] Toynbee, *Art in Britain under the Romans*, 25

[3] J. P. Wild, *Latomus*, XXIV (1965), 610–13

306 Britain. Various coins.

In a lecture delivered in 1849, ten years before the publication of Charles Darwin's *Origin of Species*, John Evans, father of Sir Arthur Evans, propounded a typological series based on the principles of evolution and natural selection. His raw materials were what were already recognised as the early uninscribed series of British coins and his demonstration[1] of how a progressive series of devolutionary stages could be traced from an archetype in the gold staters of Philip II of Macedon [see 194] has become a landmark in modern archaeological theory. The publication of Evans's *Coinage of the Ancient Britons* and the subsequent gift by his son of his father's coin collection to the British Museum, was a key-point in the study of Celtic coinage in the British Isles, which had begun in the eighteenth century with the antiquarian notes of William Stukeley.

The question of the date of the earliest British coinage, both the first imported coins and the earliest locally minted series, has really only been resolved in recent years. Two important factors are involved, one a general theory based on a combination of archaeological and historical evidence and the second a chance series of finds. First was the realisation that Belgic settlement of south-eastern England from the north of France and Belgium was not to be ascribed to any single event but to a general period of migration responsible for introducing not only coinage but such other incidentals of continental Late La Tène culture as anthropoid daggers [228 ff.] and fire-dogs [278–279].[2] From the coinage some six groups may be discerned commencing about the middle of the second century BC and running down to c. 80 BC, the original impetus probably being pressure from southward-moving non-Celtic tribes living north of the Rhine. The second factor was the discovery in 1957 of one of the largest of a number of coin hoards found at Le Catillon, Jersey, in the Channel Islands.[3] The presence of six silver coins of the Durotriges of Dorset with coins of various tribes of north-western France (*Gallia Armorica*), in particular a large number of issues of the Coriosolites [see **194f**] must be referred to the troubled events of 56 BC when Caesar's troops were crushing the entire native forces of Armorica led by the Veneti who appealed to their non-Belgic British cousins for assistance. The Durotriges, then, were issuing their own silver coinage even before the middle of the first century BC, which suggests that the first native British issues were being struck within a few years of the arrival of the last major wave of Belgic settlers – or at least their coins. The Catillon hoard also contained a gold coin struck in Britain of the so-called British 'B' type which was worn and thus even earlier in date than the silver issues.

The following four illustrations demonstrate that with Celtic coinage one can make the transition from a free pre-Roman Iron Age to what is already the first stage of a wholly dependent province of the Roman empire. Although non-Belgic tribes such as the Brigantes, Iceni and Durotriges, issued their own but uninscribed coinage, the small selection shown here is limited to coins from the south-east where the transition from Celtic to Roman Britain is most obvious. As with the notes to continental coins illustrated above [**194** and **Plate IV**], a few basic references are appended at the outset.

(Sir) John Evans, *The Coins of the Ancient Britons* (1864), suppl. (1890); D. F. Allen, *Archaeologia* XC (1944), 1–46; *PP*, 136–40 and Pls. 78–80; Allen, *PPS* XXIV (1958), 43–63; *Problems*, 97–308; *O.S. Map of Southern Britain in the Iron Age* (1962), 19–32; R. P. Mack, *The Coinage of Ancient Britain* (2 ed. 1954); J. M. C. Toynbee, *Art in Britain under the Romans* (1964), 29–37 and Pl. II; S. S. Frere, *Britannia* (1967), 20 ff. and Pls. 1–3; L. R. Laing, *Coins and Archaeology* (1969), esp. 173 ff.

[1] Evans, *Numis. Chronicle* XII (1850), 127–37, esp. Pl. on p. 126
[2] C. F. C. Hawkes, *Antiquity* XLII (1968), 6–16
[3] J.-B. Colbert de Beaulieu, *PPS* XXIV (1958), esp. Pl. XXXII:1–5

306a Gallo-Belgic AB1. Gold coin, obverse. D. 2·7 cm. Second quarter II BC. Nicholson Mus. of Antiquities, University of Sydney.

The earliest uninscribed Gallo-Belgic coinage of Britain is the Gallo-Belgic 'A' type; the present coin is a variant on this type commonly associated with the Atrebates although its continental distribution in the Somme valley around Amiens puts it rather in the territory of the Ambiani [see also notes to **Plate IVb**]. The head shown here may be compared with issues of the Parisii [**Plate IVc**] as a far-developed Celticised version of the fourth-century BC Macedonian Apollo head with influence from variations on issues of Tarentum; the die engraver is clearly more interested in the curvilinear variations which may be played on the hair, laurel wreath and even individual facial features such as the ears than in the face itself. Non-Belgic tribes followed

the same type in ever more widely abstracted form – for example the Durotrigan issue as found at Le Catillon.

The British distribution of Gallo-Belgic AB1 coins is limited to the primary settlement area of Kent and the home counties. The surviving specimens are much worn, indicating considerable circulation before deposition.

Problems, 100 ff. and Pl. VII:2, Mack *op. cit.*, no. 3

306b South-east England, 'Catuvellauni'. Bronze coin, obverse and reverse. D. 1·4 cm. c. AD 5–40. British Mus., London (*courtesy of the Trustees of the British Museum*).

The inscribed Belgic coinage of south-eastern England is an invaluable aid in sorting out the complexities of the various local dynasties. Cunobelin, the 'Cymbeline' of Shakespeare's play, was a chieftain of the Trinovantes and Catuvellauni. During Caesar's reconnoitring campaigns of 55–54 BC the Catuvellauni had their tribal centre in the vicinity of St Albans in Hertfordshire (later to become Roman Verulamium), and here Tasciovanus issued coins. By the reign of Cunobelin (probably by c. AD 6), the old tribal centre of the neighbouring Trinovantes at Colchester in Essex (Camulodunum) had been occupied and Cunobelin issued coins from both centres with, as here, the mint mark 'CAMV' on the reverse. A few blanks and coin moulds similar to those from continental *oppida* [see notes to **194**] found in the excavations of Roman Colchester and, more recently, St Albans, have suggested the actual location of the Belgic mints.[1]

The present coin, often illustrated but in fact a rare type, is definitely in the Celtic mould. Not based on any classical prototype, the face on the obverse with its full moustaches, pointed oval eyes and wild hair, is as much a standard Celtic representation of a typical Celt as the heads on the Dejbjerg cart [**203**] or, more apposite here, the frontal heads on the Marlborough bucket [**188**]. Full face views are not, however, common on continental coins any more than on British though they do occur on such coins as those of the Redones [see **194e**]. On the reverse under a palm frond or, more likely, a sheaf of corn symbolic of the extensive pastoral interests of the Belgae, the boar makes an appearance yet again [see **224**]. Here his tail has turned into that other longest surviving of Celtic animalistic symbols, the bird's head, in a representation closely matched by the heads in the bottom corners of the Elmswell plaque [**303**].

The area finally controlled by Cunobelin extended into mid-Oxfordshire and bordered on Gloucestershire, the territory of the Dobuni, a factor which doubtless contributed to the distribution of such objects as the engraved mirror series [see **260** ff.] and the Colchester-Keshcarringan bowls [see **273**].

ABA, Pl. 72; *PP*, 138 and Pl. 79:13; Mack, *op. cit.*, no. 223; Toynbee, *op. cit.*, Pl. IIk; *PreA*, 256 and ill. 263

306c South-east England, 'Catuvellauni'. Gold coin, reverse. D. 1·65 cm. c. 20 BC–AD 5. British Mus., London (*courtesy Trustees of the British Museum*).

Although the name of Tasciovanus is unknown in historical sources it is clear from the coin legends that he was the father of Cunobelin [see also **306d**] and chief or king of the Catuvellauni. It was in his reign that the first British inscribed series were issued. Coins of Tasciovanus and the Verulamium (St Albans) mint form the bulk of inscribed coins in the central area of the period from the last quarter of the first century BC to the early first century AD. The main issues were minted at the tribal capital at St Albans though one coin suggests that in 17 BC Tasciovanus may have temporarily occupied Colchester (Camulodunum), at that time the capital of the Trinovantes.

The obverse of the present coin bears not a 'portrait' head but the inscription 'TASCIO' within a curved-sided tablet – perhaps in imitation of Roman inscription plaques. Tasciovanus also used the inscription 'RICON' ('Great King'), possibly a Celtic version of 'rex'. The reverse shown here also has an inscription 'SEGO', of unknown significance, possibly the name of a second son of Tasciovanus. The warrior brandishing a boar's head war-horn or *carnyx* [see notes to **209c** and **272**] follows the general pattern of continental Celtic coin representations such as on coins of the Remi, though on the continent horn players are never, as here, shown on horseback; a Roman republican *denarius* of Scaurus (?92–118 BC) shows what might be Bituitos, chief of the Arverni [see also **Plate IVe**], riding naked in a chariot complete with *carnyx*.[1]

Details to be noted on what is certainly a much more precisely detailed representation than many continental coins of the same period, are the somewhat displaced bridle bit and ring [compare **258**], the dot-in-circle above the horse's head, the typical ridged coiffure of the rider and the separate 'Jupiter wheel' symbol, here surely more than the vestigial remains of the chariot on the earlier coin prototypes [see notes to **209a, 224**].

Allen, *PPS* XXIV, 44–46 and Pl. I:2; Mack, *op. cit.*, no. 194

[1] S. Piggott, *Antiquity* XXVI (1952), 87 and Pl. I top left; *id.*, *Antiq. J.* XXXIX (1959), 22

306d South-east England, 'Catuvellauni'. Bronze coin, reverse. D. 1·7 cm. Before AD 40. British Mus., London. (*Courtesy Trustees of the British Museum.*)

In contrast to early coins of the reign of Cunobelin [**306b**], coins struck in his later period show the strong influence of Roman iconography and include such un-Celtic figures as lyre players, sphinxes, and throned emperors, although beyond general similarities with certain issues of Augustan *denarii*, it is generally difficult to provide precise sources. The obverse of the present coin has the inscription 'CVNOB' with a naked horseman with throwing spear and typical Celtic shield. The reverse shown here has the inscription 'TASCIIO-VANTIS', an untutored version of 'TASCIOVANI(I)(F)', '(son) of Tasciovanus'. The inscription is not the only feature to show the stranglehold of Rome over many aspects of Belgic culture; the standing soldier is himself a Roman *cap à pied* save for one detail – the baggy trousers or *braccae*, the Celtic trews worn not only on the continent [see **30, 209**] but by Celtic warriors in Britain in the face of foreign attack for at least two thousand years from the abortive invasion of Julius Caesar until the Scottish regiments of the modern British Army.

Allen, *PPS* XXIV, 53 and Pl. V:38; Mack, *op. cit.*, no. 244; Toynbee, *op. cit.*, 30

CATALOGUE TO THE PLATES

Comparative chronology of the Central European Iron Age

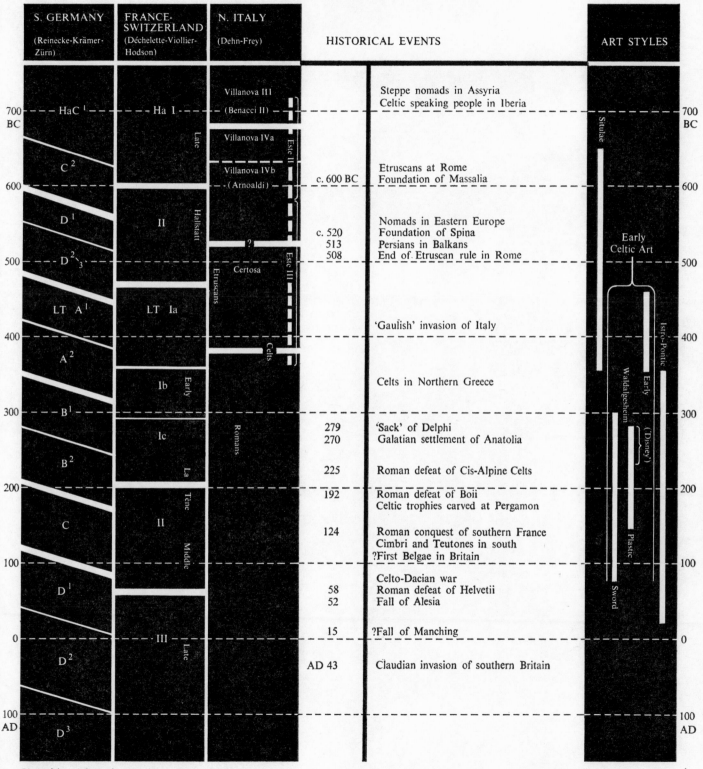

Diagonal bars indicate the approximate range
of dating offered for these phases

INDEX

Figures in bold type refer to entries and illustrations in the catalogue section.

I 'Burrenhof', Kr. Nürtlingen, Germany.
Painted pot. *Ht*. 22 cm. Late VII/early
VI BC (see notes on p. 46-7)

1-2 Valcamonica, N. Italy. Rock engravings.
L. (**1**) c. 50 cm., (**2**) c. 65 cm. ?VII BC

3 Bad Cannstatt, Stuttgart, Germany.
Gold bowl. *D.* 16·5 cm.
Late VI/early V BC

4 Altstetten, Zürich, Switzerland.
Gold bowl. *D.* 25 cm. Late VI BC

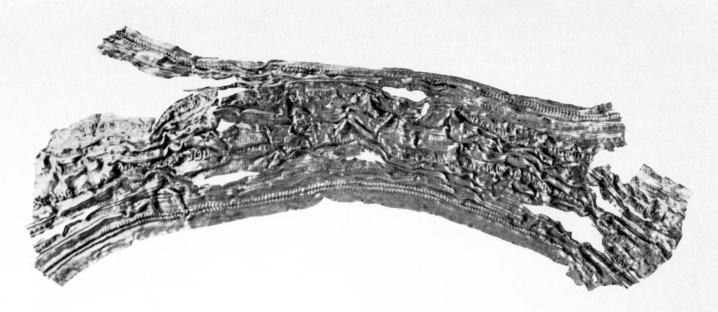

5 ?'Brittany', France.
Sheet gold ring, fragment. *W.* c. 4 cm.,
ht. of heads c. 2 mm. VI BC

6 Kaltbrunn, Germany. Bronze belt plate. *Ht.* of detail c. 15 cm. Early VI BC

7

9 Gomadingen, Germany. Incised and painted pot. *D.* 55 cm., *ht.* c. 9 cm. Early VII BC

8

7 'Hohmichele', Hundersingen, Germany. Textile fragment. *L.* 11 cm. Early VI BC

8 Hradenín, Czechoslovakia. Wooden horse-yoke. *L.* 1·20 m. VII BC

10 Sopron-Várhely, Hungary. Incised pot. *Ht.* c. 38 cm. Late VII BC

11 Gomadingen, Germany. Iron sword hilt with gold and ivory inlay. *W.* of pommel c. 8·6 cm. VIII/VII BC

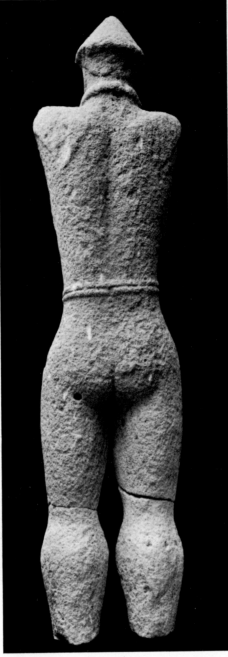

12 Hirschlanden, Germany. Stone statue. *Ht.* 1·5 m. Late VI/early V BC

13 Stockach, Germany. Stone *stele. Ht.* 75 cm. Early VII BC

14 Holzgerlingen, Germany. Stone *stele.*
Ht. without horns (*right*) 2·3 m. ?VI/V BC

15 'Kröllkogel', Kleinklein, Austria.
Bronze mask. *W.* 23 cm. VI BC

18

16

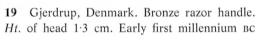

16   Wijchen, Netherlands. Bronze linch-pin.
L. c. 8 cm. Early VII BC

17   Hallstatt, Austria. Bronze axe with rider figure.
L. 10·9 cm. c. 600 BC

18   Hallstatt, Austria. Bronze figurine. *Ht.* 2·9 cm. VI BC

19   Gjerdrup, Denmark. Bronze razor handle.
Ht. of head 1·3 cm. Early first millennium BC

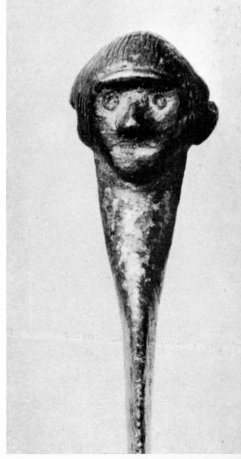

17   19

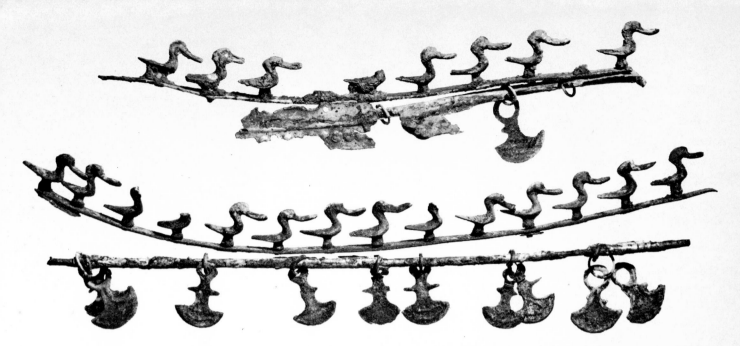

20 Lezoux, Puy-de-Dôme, France. Bronze cauldron rims and rattle plates. *L.* (above) 28·5 cm., (below) 35·5 cm. VIII BC

21 Hallstatt, Austria. Bronze pail. *Ht.* 30·5 cm. VII/VI BC

22 Hallstatt, Austria. Bronze container and stand. *Ht.* 36 cm. VII/VI BC

23 Dunaverney Bog, Co. Antrim, N. Ireland. Bronze 'flesh-hook'. *L.* 60·7 cm. ?VI BC

24 Bologna, N. Italy. Bronze *situla*.
Total *ht.* 32·7 cm., *ht.* of panels c. 7 cm.
Early V BC

25 Vače, Jugoslavia. Bronze belt-hook.
L. 28·5 cm. V BC

27 Matzhausen, Germany. Pottery flask:
detail. *L.* of stag c. 9 cm. Early IV BC

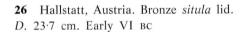

26 Hallstatt, Austria. Bronze *situla* lid.
D. 23·7 cm. Early VI BC

28 Stična, Jugoslavia. Bronze earring.
W. 2 cm. V/IV BC

29 Libkovice, Duchcov, Czechoslovakia.
Stamped pottery fragment.
c. 4·5 × 5 cm., *l.* of hares c. 2 cm.
Early IV BC

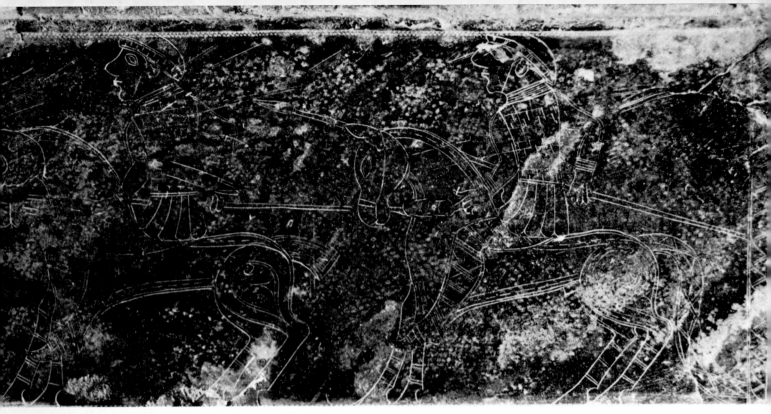

30 Hallstatt, Austria. Iron and bronze sword scabbard with
remains of coral studs. *L.* 68 cm., *w.* c. 5 cm. c. 400 BC

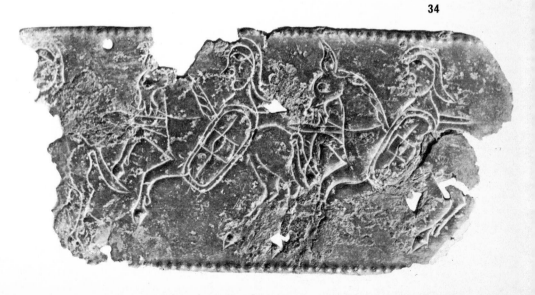

31 Manětín-Hrádek, Czechoslovakia. Bronze brooch. *L.* 8·8 cm. V/IV BC

32 Dürrnberg, Austria. Bronze brooch. *L.* 2·7 cm. c. 400 BC

33 Kärlich, Germany. Bronze appliqué figure. *L.* 5 cm. Early V BC

34 Este, N. Italy. Bronze plaque. *L.* 16·7 cm. IV/III BC

35 Býčí Skála, Czechoslovakia. Bronze bull with iron inlay. *Ht.* 11·4 cm. ?VI BC

36 Hallstatt, Austria. Bronze bowl: detail of handle. *L.* of cow 14·4 cm. VI BC

37 Mérida, Spain. Bronze cult model.
L. c. 25 cm., *ht.* of horse 13 cm. ?II/I BC

38 Strettweg, Austria. Bronze cult model.
Base 35 × 18 cm., *ht.* of central figure
22·6 cm. VII BC

39 Schwarzenbach, Germany.
Gold open-work on bronze backing.
D. 12·6 cm. Later V BC

41 Klein Aspergle, Germany.
Attic cup with gold embellishment.
W. 22 cm. Date of cup c. 450 BC

40 Eigenbilzen, Belgium. Gold band.
L. 22 cm. c. 400 BC

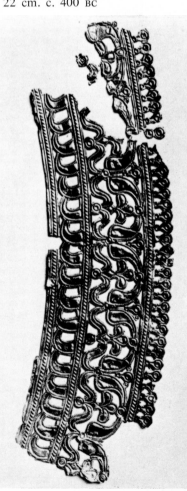

II (a) Weiskirchen, Kr. Merzig-Waldern.
Germany. Gold covered plaque.
W. 8 cm. Early IV BC (see notes to **46**)
(b) Želkovice, Okr. Beroun,
Czechoslovakia. Bronze belt
plaque. *L*. 7·3 cm. c. 400 BC (see
notes to **71**)

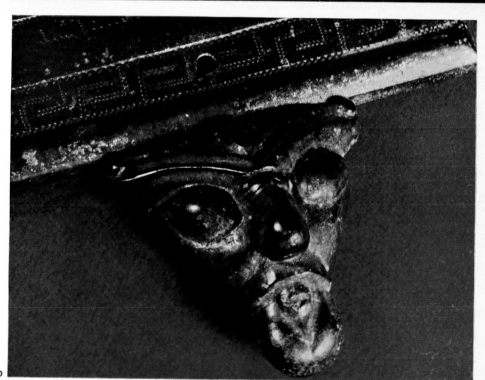

42　Auvers-sur-Oise, France.
Gold sheet over two bronze discs.
D. 10 cm. V/IV BC

43　Klein Aspergle, Germany.
Gold open-work on iron plate.
W. 6·8 cm. Mid V BC

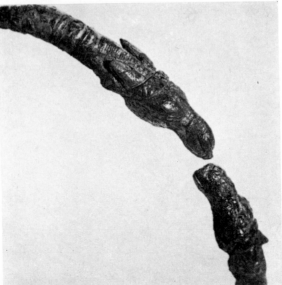

44 Klein Aspergle, Germany. Gold
drinking-horn mounts: details.
L. of lower head 1·8 cm. Mid V BC

45 Vieille Toulouse, France. Bronze torc:
detail. *L*. of heads c. 2·5 cm.
Late V/early IV BC

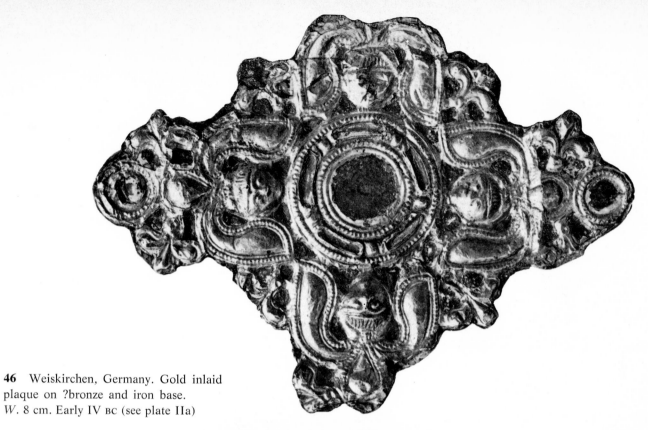

46 Weiskirchen, Germany. Gold inlaid
plaque on ?bronze and iron base.
W. 8 cm. Early IV BC (see plate IIa)

47 Hořovičky, Czechoslovakia.
Bronze *phalera. D.* 12 cm.
Late V/early IV BC

48 Dürrnberg, Austria. Bronze mount for wooden flagon. *Ht.* 8·3 cm. c. 400 BC

49 Heidelberg, Germany.
Stone head. *Ht.* 31 cm. Late V/early IV BC

50 Klein Aspergle, Germany.
Bronze flagon. Total *ht.* 37 cm., *ht.* of handle
base c. 7 cm. Mid V BC

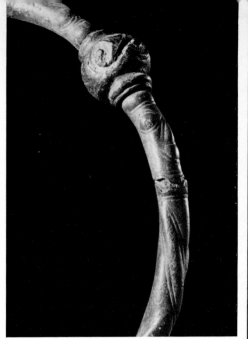

▲
51
53►

51   Andernach, Germany. Bronze neck-ring: detail. *Ht.* of face 2 cm. IV BC

52   Spiez-Schönegg, Switzerland. Bronze torc: detail. *Ht.* of face c. 1·5 cm. IV BC

53   Schwarzenbach, Germany. Gold armring: detail. *L.* of pair of faces c. 2·5 cm. Mid V BC

54   Bad Dürkheim, Germany. Gold armring: detail. *L.* of pair of faces c. 2·8 cm. Late V/early IV BC

◄**52**
54
▼

55 Rodenbach, Germany. Gold armring. *D.* 6·7 cm. Later V BC

57 Ferschweiler, Germany. Gold leaf
mount. *Ht.* 4 cm. Later V BC

58 Rodenbach, Germany. Gold finger-ring.
D. 2·1 cm. Later V BC

56 Besseringen, Germany. Gold neck-ring: detail. *W.* of central feature 3·9 cm. V BC
59 Bad Dürkheim, Germany. Gold open-work fragment. *Ht.* of face c. 1·7 cm.
Late V/early IV BC

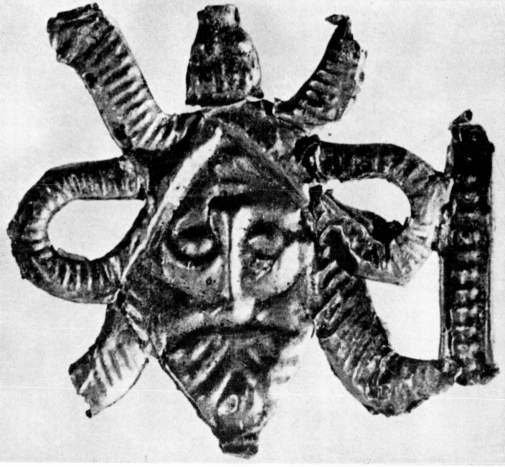

III Basse-Yutz, Moselle, France. Details of coral inlaid bronze flagons, *above* handle and *below* throat. Max. *w.* of. throat panel 3·25 cm., *w.* of face 3·6 cm. Late V/early IV BC (see notes to **60-61**)

60-61 Basse-Yutz, France. Bronze flagons with ?coral and enamel inlay. *Ht.* (**60**) 39·4 cm., (**61**) 40·4 cm., *w.* at shoulders c. 19 cm. Late V/early IV BC (see plate III)

62 Weiskirchen, Germany. Bronze belt-plaque with coral inlay. *W.* 6·6 cm. Late V BC

63 Parsberg, Germany. Bronze brooch. L. 8·8 cm. c. 400 BC

64 Stupava, Czechoslovakia. Bronze plaque. 6·6 × 3·3 cm. c. 400 BC

65 Panenský Týnec, Czechoslovakia. Bronze brooch. Total *l.* 10·2 cm., *l.* of sheep's head c. 1·3 cm. V BC

66 Borsch, Germany. Bronze flagon (reconstructed). *Ht.* of handle 17 cm. Late V BC

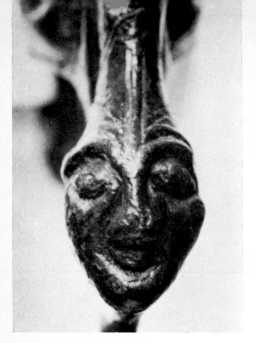

67 Weiskirchen, Germany. Bronze brooch with ?coral inlay: details. Total *l.* 4 cm., *l.* of faces; (left) c. 1 cm., (right) c. 1·5 cm. Early IV BC

68 Kyšice, Czechoslovakia. Bronze brooch. *L.* 5·6 cm. Early IV BC

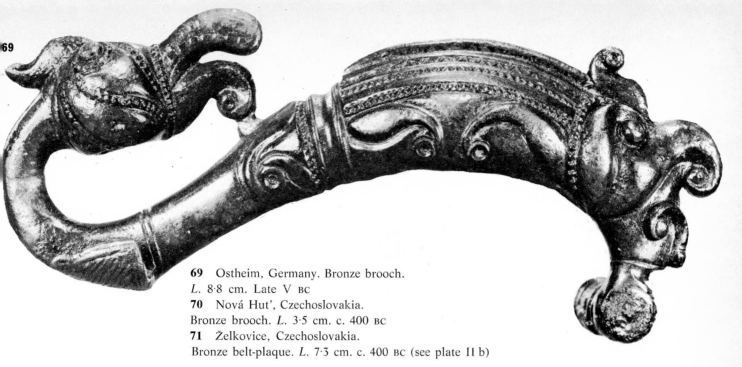

69 Ostheim, Germany. Bronze brooch.
L. 8·8 cm. Late V BC
70 Nová Hut', Czechoslovakia.
Bronze brooch. *L.* 3·5 cm. c. 400 BC
71 Želkovice, Czechoslovakia.
Bronze belt-plaque. *L.* 7·3 cm. c. 400 BC (see plate II b)

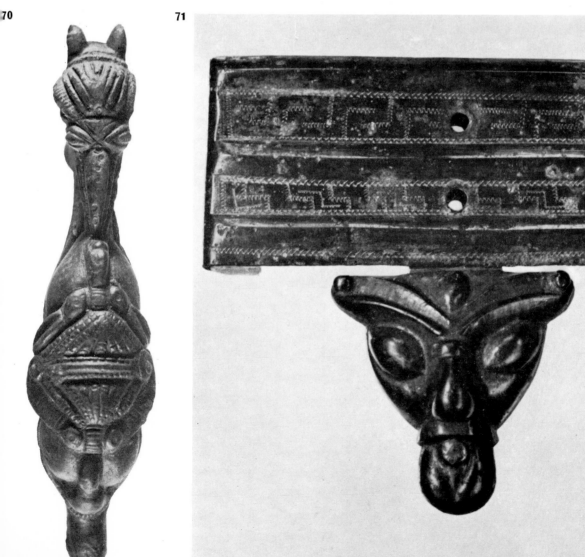

72 Dürrnberg, Austria. Bronze flagon.
Ht. 46·7 cm., *w.* at shoulder 18 cm.,
ht. of neck 12·2 cm. Late V/early IV BC

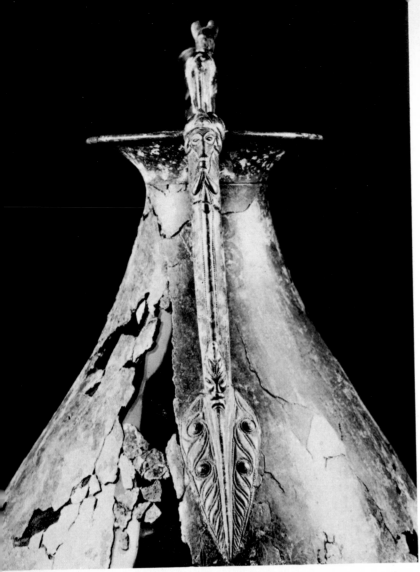

73 Reinheim, Germany. Gilt-bronze flagon. *Ht.* 50·4 cm., max. *d.* 23·2 cm. First half IV BC

74 Bad Dürkheim, Germany. Iron and bronze chariot fitting. *Ht.* 3·5 cm.
Late V/early IV BC

75 Pfalzfeld, Germany. Carved sandstone pillar. *Ht.* 1·48 m. Late V/early IV BC

77   ?Mâcon, France. Silver torc.
D. 15·2 cm., *ht.* of heads c. 1·7 cm.
First half IV BC

78 Waldalgesheim, Germany.
Bronze spouted flagon. Total *ht*. 35 cm.,
l. of lid animal 4·9 cm., *ht*. of head at base
of handle with beard c. 4 cm. First half IV BC

79-83 Reinheim, Germany. Gold rings. On left (**79**) torc d. 17·2 cm.; (**80-81**) armrings, d. (lower) 8·1 cm. and (upper) 6·7 cm.; (**82-83**) finger-rings, d. (left) 2·0 and (right) 2·1 cm. Details of torc and larger armring below and opposite. V/early IV BC

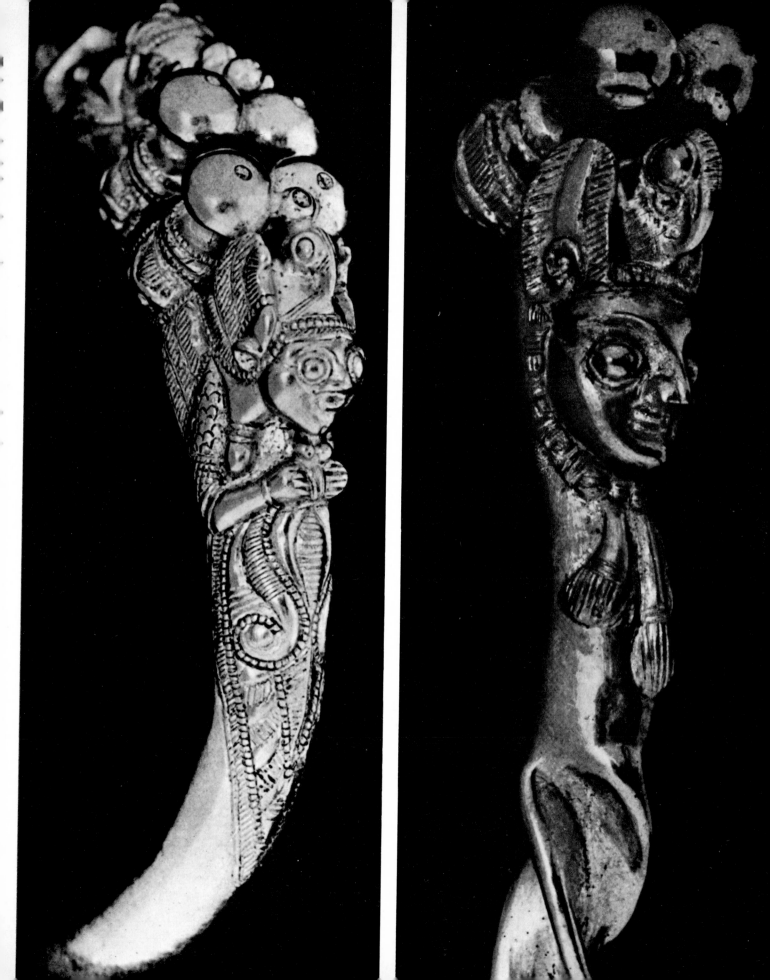

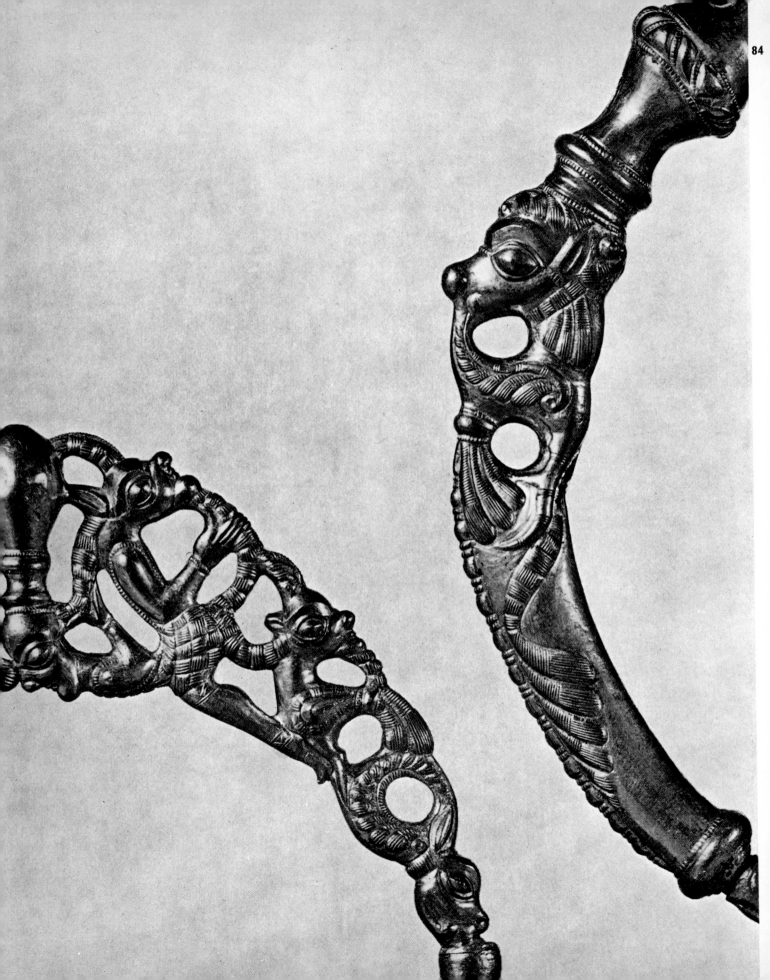

84 Erstfeld, Switzerland. Two gold neck-rings: detail. Total *d.* (left) 14·5 cm.; (right) 15·5 cm., *l.* of right hand animal face c. 2 cm. V/early IV BC

85 Leichlingen, Germany. Stone 'Janus' head. *Ht.* 12 cm. ?IV BC

86 Marson, France. Bronze sword scabbard mount. *Ht.* 4·5 cm. Late V BC

87 Glauberg, Germany. Bronze torc: detail. *Ht.* of heads c. 1·5 cm. Late V/early IV BC

89 Schwieberdingen, Germany. Bronze brooch with coral inlay: details. Total *l.* 4·5 cm. Late V/early IV BC

88 Lahošt', Czechoslovakia. Bronze finger-ring. *D.* 2·2 cm. ?IV/III BC

90 Chýnovský Háj, Czechoslovakia. Bronze brooch with coral inlay. *L.* 7 cm. Late V/early IV BC

92 Oberwittighausen, Germany.
Bronze brooch. *L.* 4·4 cm. Late V/early IV BC

91 Oberwittighausen, Germany. Bronze brooch: detail.
Ht. of head c. 1·2 cm. Late V/early IV BC

93 Dürrnberg, Austria. Silver-bronze brooch.
L. 4 cm. Late V/early IV BC

94 'Kleiner Gleichberg', Steinsburg, Germany.
Bronze brooch. *L.* 3 cm. Late V/early IV BC

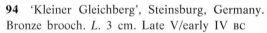

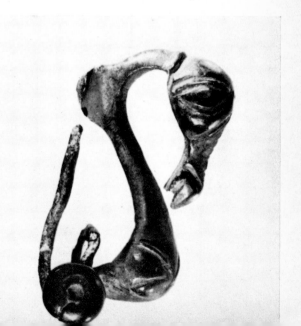

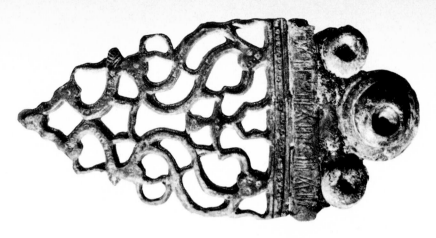

97   Castaneda, Switzerland. Bronze belt-hook. *L.* 11·2 cm. Early IV BC

95   Hölzelsau, Austria. Bronze belt-hook.
L. 16·2 cm. Early IV BC

98   Este, N. Italy. Bronze belt-hook. *L.* 11 cm. Early IV BC

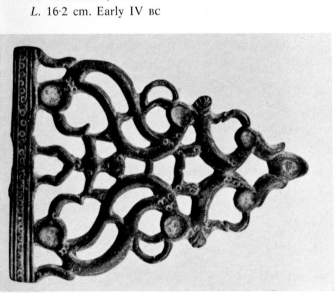

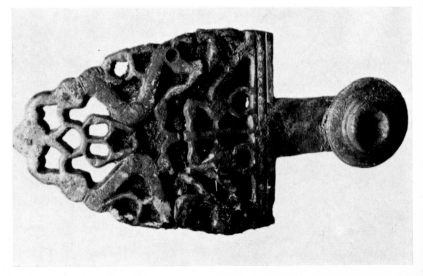

96   S. Polo d'Enza, N. Italy. Bronze belt-hook.
L. 8·1 cm. Early IV BC

99   Giubiasco, Switzerland. Bronze belt-hook. *L.* 11·7 cm. Early IV BC

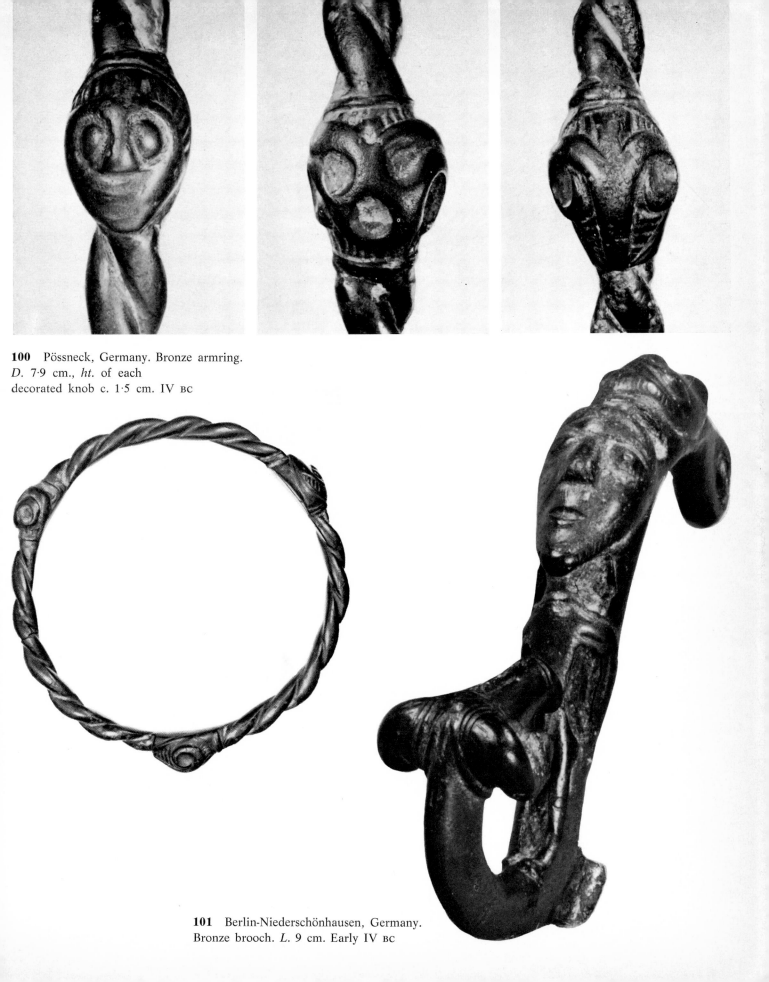

100 Pössneck, Germany. Bronze armring.
D. 7·9 cm., *ht.* of each
decorated knob c. 1·5 cm. IV BC

101 Berlin-Niederschönhausen, Germany.
Bronze brooch. *L.* 9 cm. Early IV BC

102 Padua, N. Italy.
Grave *stele* 79 × 69 cm. IV/III BC

103 N.E. France, 'Remi'. Bronze coin,
reverse. *D.* 1·5 cm. Mid I BC

104 Kšice, Stříbro, Czechoslovakia.
Fragment of bronze brooch.
Ht. c. 1·5 cm. Mid IV BC

IV Iron Age coinage (see notes on p. 122)

(a) ?Transylvania. Silver coin obverse and reverse *D.* 2·5 cm. III BC

(b) Belgium, 'Ambiani'. Gold coin: obverse and reverse. *D.* 1·5 cm. ?Late III BC

(c) Seine basin, 'Parisii'. Gold coin: obverse and reverse. *D.* 2·5 cm. I BC

(d) Brittany, 'Namnetes'. Gold coin: reverse. *D.* 1·2 cm., II/I BC

(e) 'Poinsat' hoard, 'Arverni'. Gold coin: obverse. *D.* 1·8 cm. Mid I BC

a

d

c

b

e

106

107

105 Canosa di Puglia, S. Italy.
Iron helmet with bronze and coral decoration.
Ht. 25 cm. *d.* 23·3 cm. Second half IV BC

106-7 Gottolengo, N. Italy.
Bronze helmet cheek-piece (**106**),
ht. 13 cm.; bronze helmet mount (**107**),
ht. 10·5 cm. Later IV BC

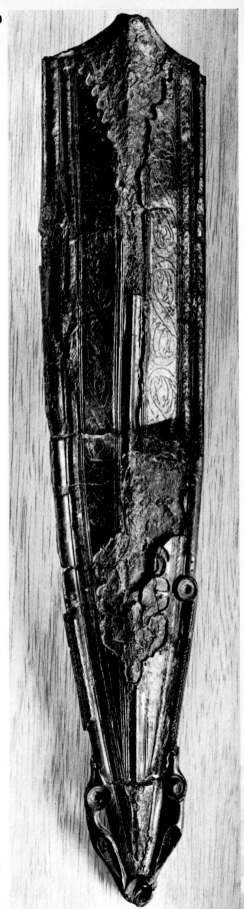

108

108 'Umbria', N. Italy. Iron helmet
with bronze covering. *Ht*. of cap 19·5 cm.,
ht. of cheek-pieces 13 cm. Late IV BC

109 Weiskirchen, Germany. Iron sword
in bronze scabbard with coral inlay.
L. of scabbard 32·5 cm. Later IV BC

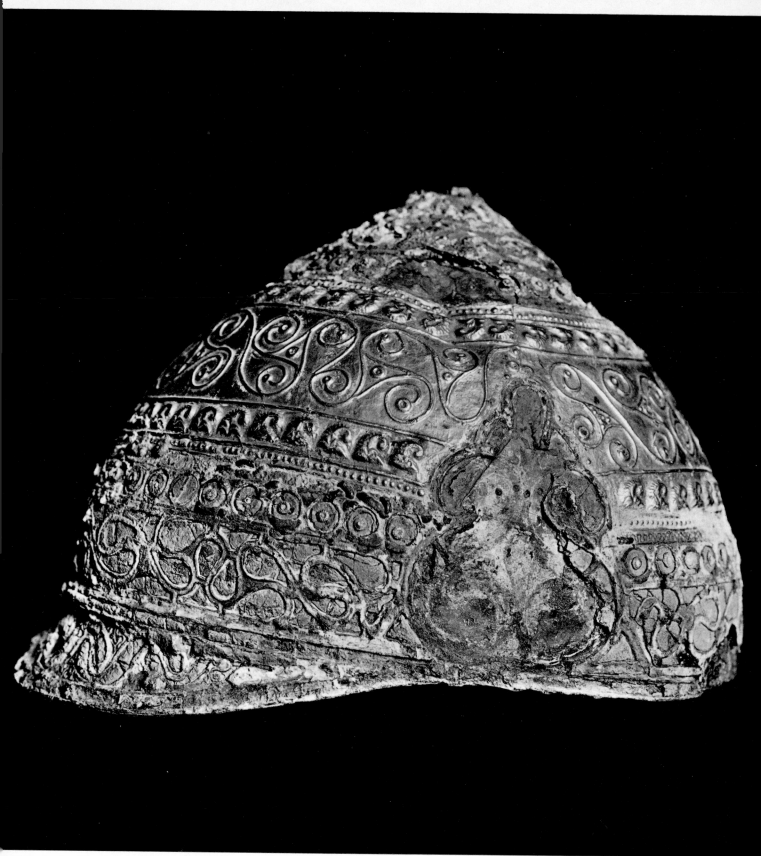

110 Amfreville, France. Bronze and iron
helmet decorated with gold and enamel.
Ht. 17·5 cm., *d.* 23 cm. Later IV BC

111

111 Somme-Bionne,
Marne, France.
Bronze disc. *D.* 6·9 cm.
Late IV BC

112 'La Bouvandeau',
Marne, France. Bronze
open-work harness
mount: detail.
Ht. c. 2 cm. Late V BC

113 Unprovenanced.
Decorated bronze jug:
detail. *D.* of circular
motif c. 6·5 cm.
First half IV BC

114 Cerrig-y-Drudion,
Wales. Fragment of
bronze bowl rim.
W. of fragment 3 cm.
?IV/III BC

112

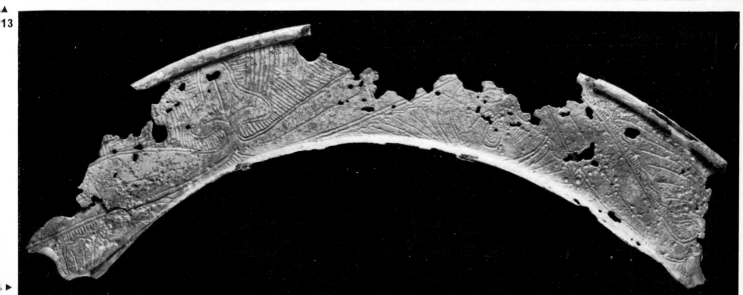

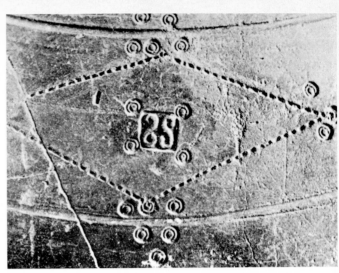

115 Alsópél, Hungary. Ornamented pot: detail. *Ht.* c. 2 cm. Late IV BC

116 Komjatice, Czechoslovakia. Ornamented pot: detail. *L.* of lozenge stamp c. 10 cm. Late IV/early III BC

117 ?Comacchio, N. Italy. Bronze mount. *L.* 12·5 cm. Late IV BC

118 Waldalgesheim, Germany. Bronze ?chariot mount. *Ht.* 8·9 cm. Late IV BC

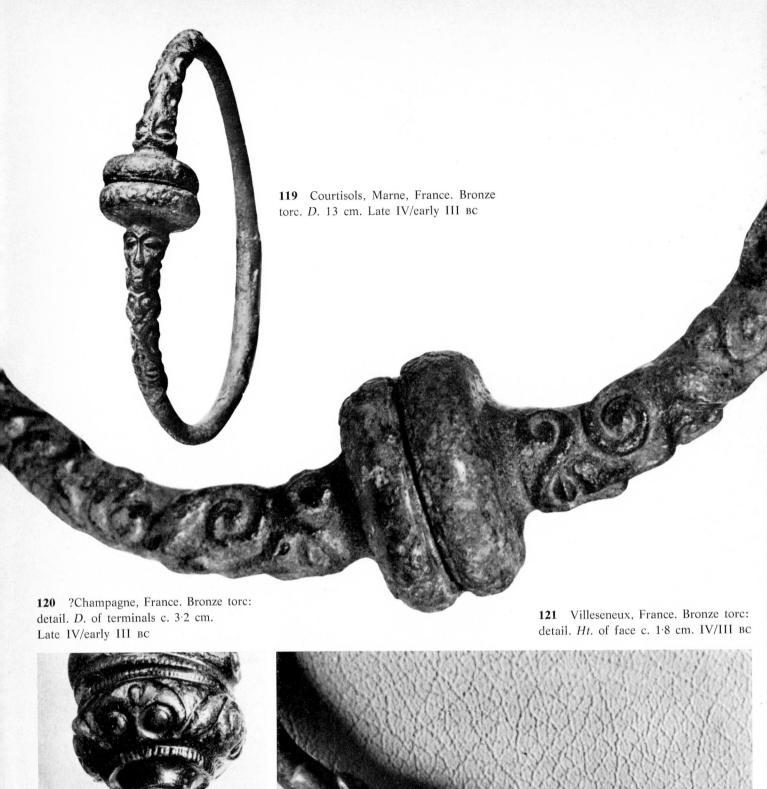

119 Courtisols, Marne, France. Bronze
torc. *D.* 13 cm. Late IV/early III BC

120 ?Champagne, France. Bronze torc:
detail. *D.* of terminals c. 3·2 cm.
Late IV/early III BC

121 Villeseneux, France. Bronze torc:
detail. *Ht.* of face c. 1·8 cm. IV/III BC

123 Criesbach, Germany.
Bronze brooch: detail.
L. 4·7 cm. Early IV BC

122 Avon-Fontenay, France. Bronze torc: detail.
D. 13 cm. IV/III BC

124-125 Waldalgesheim, Germany.
Pair of hollow gold bracelets. D. 6·5 cm. Late IV BC

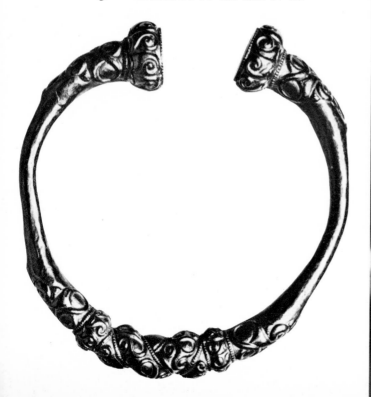

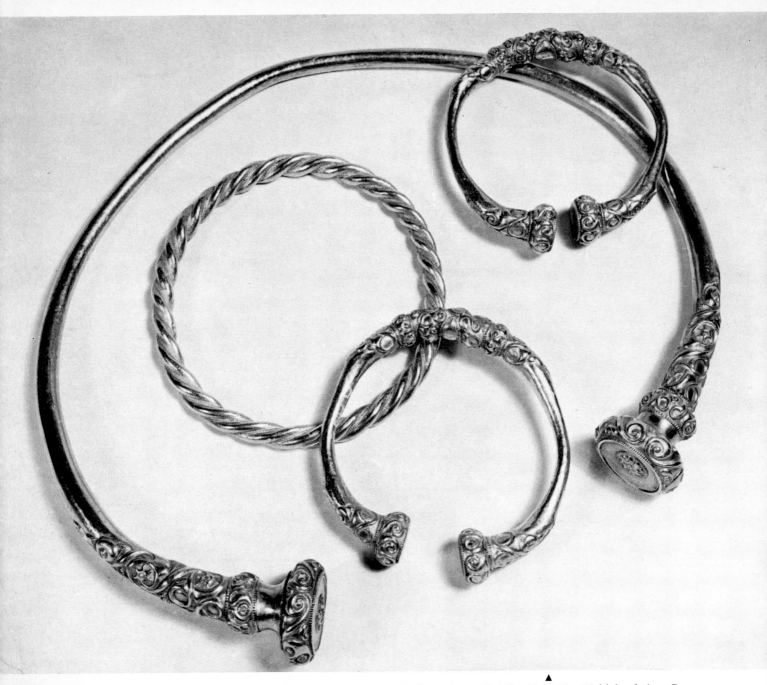

124-127 Waldalgesheim, Germany. Gold rings. **124-5** pair of hollow bracelets. *D.* 6·5 cm.; **126** wrought armring with twisted effect. *D.* 8·2 cm.; 127 Torc. *D.* 19·9 cm. Late IV BC

128 Filottrano, Italy. Gold torc: detail. *D.* of terminals c. 2·5 cm. Late IV BC

129 Turoe, Galway, Ireland. Carved granite boulder. *Ht.* 1·20 m. ?III/I BC

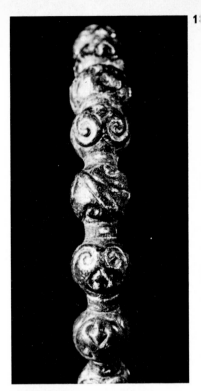

130 Brentford, England (R. Thames). Bronze chariot 'horn' with enamel inlay. *D.* 7·3 cm. ?I BC/I AD

131 Newnham Croft, England. Bronze armring: detail. Total *d.* 7·9 cm., *w.* 0·8 cm. ?II/I BC

132 Waldalgesheim, Germany. Bronze bracelet. *W.* c. 0·7 cm. Late IV BC

133 Sopron, Hungary. Decorated detail. *Ht.* of lozenges c. 1·5 cm. Late IV BC

134 Duchcov spring, Czechoslovakia.
Bronze brooch. *L.* c. 6·4 cm. Late IV BC

135 Rickenbach, Switzerland.
Bronze brooch with coral inlay.
L. 9·2 cm. Late IV BC

136 Schosshalde, Switzerland.
Silver brooch. *L.* 6·3 cm. Late IV BC

134   **135**   **136**

137 Filottrano, N. Italy. Fragment of
bronze and iron scabbard.
L. c. 20 cm. Late IV BC

138 Dürrnberg, Austria. Gold finger-ring.
D. c. 2·4 cm. Late IV BC

139 Deisswil, Switzerland.
Silver finger-ring. *D.* 2·4 cm. Late IV BC

140 La Charme, France. Bronze armring and detail. External *d*. 5·7 cm. ?Early III BC

141 Křinec, Czechoslovakia. Bronze bracelet. *D*. 8 cm. III BC

142 Waldenbuch, Germany. Stone pillar-statue. *Ht.* 1·25 m. IV/III BC

143 Barbuise, France.
Bronze neck-ring and detail.
Internal *d*. 12·7 cm. Late IV/early III BC

144 Eschersheim, Germany.
Bronze brooch with coral inlay.
L. 7·3 cm. III BC

V (a)   Wallertheim, Kr. Alzey, Germany.
Glass dog. *L.* 2·1 cm. Late I BC
(see note on p. 121)
(b)   Basle, Gasworks site, Switzerland.
Painted pot. *Ht.* 37 cm. I BC
(see note on p. 128)

a

b

145 Andelfingen, Switzerland.
Bronze torc with enamel inlay.
D. 14·7 cm. III BC

146 Nebringen, Germany.
Bronze neck-ring with enamel inlay and
mounts. *D.* 15·2 cm. III BC

147 Michelbach, Germany.
Bronze neck-ring with enamel inlay.
D. 12·5 cm. III BC

148 Dammelberg, Germany.
Bronze torc and armlet.
D. of torc 14 cm. III BC

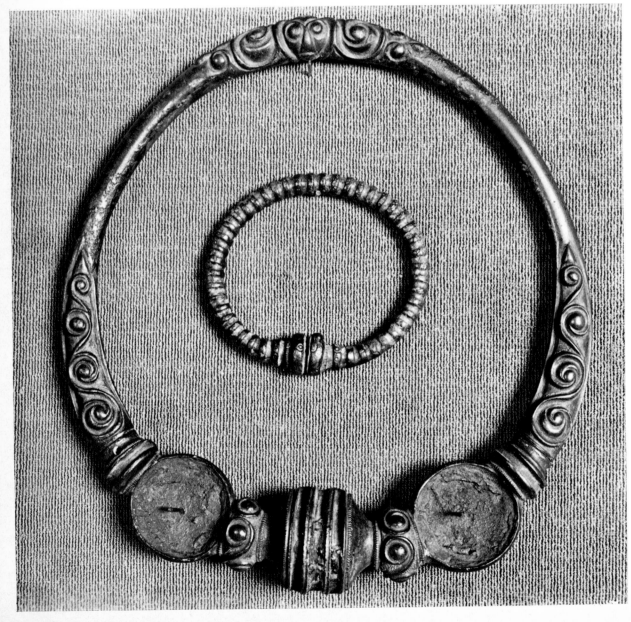

149 La Courte, Belgium. Iron linch-pin with bronze head: detail. *W.* of head 5 cm. IV BC

150 Urach, Germany. Iron and bronze linch-pin: detail. *L.* 11·1 cm. ?IV/II BC

151 Gašić, Jugoslavia. Gold torc. *D.* 10 cm. III BC   152 Fenouillet, France. Gold torc. *D.* 13.5 cm. III BC
153 Aurillac, France. Gold armlet. *Ht.* 3 cm. III BC

154 Prunay, France. Painted pot. *Ht.* 31 cm. IV/III BC

155 Prunay, France. Painted pot. *Ht.* 19 cm. IV/III BC

156 Plouhinec, Brittany. Pot with stamped decoration. *Ht.* 31 cm. IV BC

157 St Pol-de-Léon, France. Pot with incised and stamped decoration. *Ht.* 26 cm. IV BC

154

155

156

157

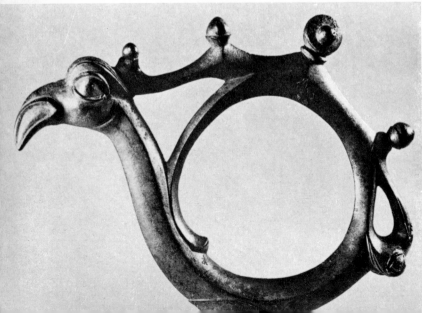

158 Maloměřice, Czechoslovakia. Bronze mount fragments: (upper) 5 × 4·4 cm.; (lower) 6·2 × 3 cm. Early III BC

159 Maloměřice, Czechoslovakia. Bronze handle mount. D. 11·8 cm. Early III BC

160

161

160 Maloměřice, Czechoslovakia. Bronze mount. *Ht.* of central animal head 6 cm. Early III· BC

161 ?Mâcon, France. Bronze ?cup handle. *L.* 7·1 cm. III BC

162 Brå, Denmark. Bronze mount from cauldron. *W.* between horns c. 5·2 cm. Early III BC

163 Dürrnberg, Austria. Bronze spout: detail. *L.* of head c. 4 cm. IV BC

164 Brå, Denmark. Bronze handle mount from cauldron. *W*. c. 4·2 cm. Early III BC

165 Maloměřice, Czechoslovakia. Bronze mount. *L*. 10·5 cm., *w*. 4·6 cm. Early III BC

166 ?Paris, France. Bronze and iron linch-pin.
W. 8·5 cm. III BC

167 ?Paris, France. Bronze terret ring
with iron core. *Ht.* 8·5 cm. III BC

168 ?Paris, France. Bronze ring with
iron core. *D.* c. 7 cm. III BC

169 ?Sardinia. Gold finger-ring. *D.* 2·5 cm. III BC
170 Mezek, Bulgaria. Bronze and iron terret.
W. 7·5 cm. III BC

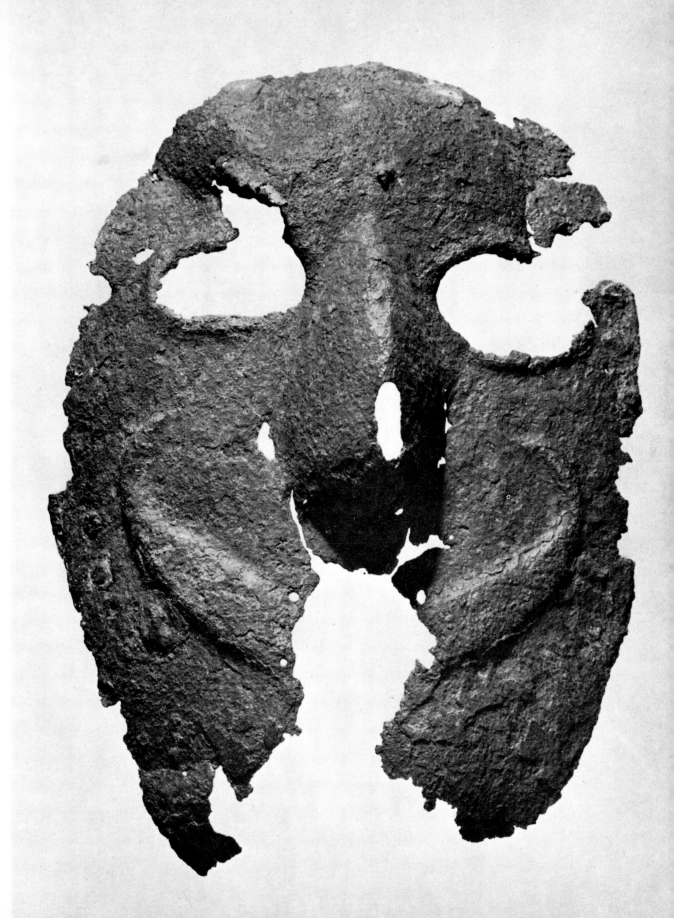

171 Mšecké
Žehrovice,
Czechoslovakia.
Stone head.
Ht. 23·5 cm.
?III/II BC

172 Kamenné
Žehrovice,
Czechoslovakia.
Iron mask.
Ht. 22 cm.
?II BC

173 Frasnes-lez-Buissenal, Belgium. Gold torc. Max. *d.* 20·3 cm., *d.* of tube 2·7 cm. ?II/I BC

175 R. Tarn, France. Bronze ?bracelet. Internal *d.* 5 cm. III BC

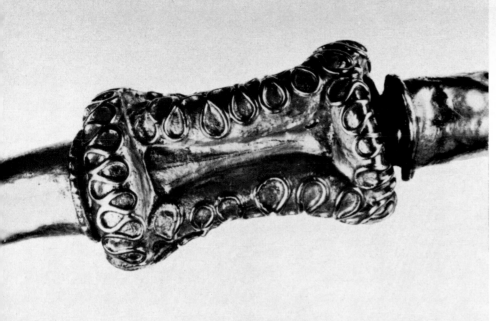

174 Clonmacnoise, Ireland. Gold torc: details. Total *d.* 13 cm., *d.* of terminals 3·8 cm. III BC

176 Klettham, Germany. Bronze hinged anklet. *D.* 13·5 cm. Later III BC

177

178

179

180

181

182

177 La Cheppe, France.
Decorated pot: detail.
D. at rim 20 cm. ?IV BC

178 Kelheim, Germany.
Bronze ?box mount.
Ht. 6·1 cm. II/I BC

179 La Tène, Switzerland.
Iron sword scabbard:
detail. *W.* 5·1 cm. II BC

180 Groitzsch, Germany.
Fragmentary sword
scabbard: detail.
W. 5·3 cm. III/II BC

181 Dickenhof,
Switzerland. Iron sword
scabbard: detail.
W. 5·2 cm. II BC

182 Drňa, Czechoslovakia.
Iron sword scabbard: detail.
W. c. 5 cm. III/II BC

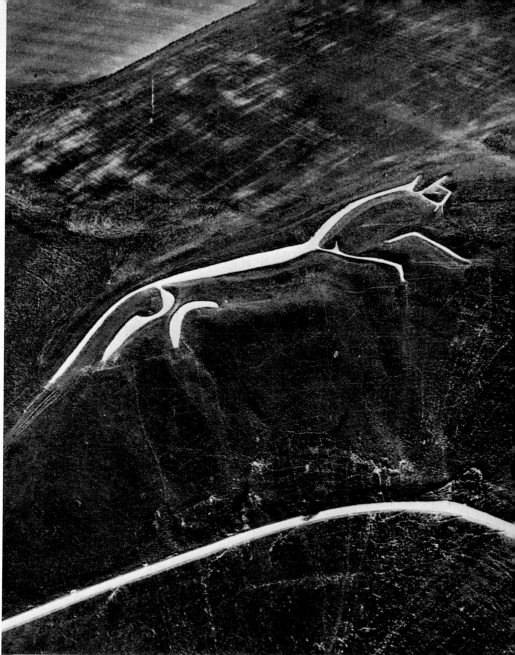

183 Cernon-sur-Coole, France.
Iron sword scabbard: detail.
W. c. 5·2 cm. III/II BC

184 Uffington, England. White
horse cut in hillside. *L.* c. 1·10 m.
?AD I-VI

185 Valcamonica, N. Italy.
Rock engraving.
L. c. 20 cm. ?IV BC

186 Marlborough, England. Bronze sheet
covering for wooden bucket: detail.
L. 18·5 cm. ?I BC/I AD

185

186

187 Aylesford, England. Bronze covered wooden bucket: details.
D. 26·7 cm., *ht.* of head c. 4 cm. I BC

188   Marlborough, England.
Reconstructed bronze-covered wooden
bucket. *Ht.* 52 cm., *d.* 60 cm. ?I BC/AD

189   Manching, Germany.
Bronze ?rein-ring. *Ht.* 9 cm. II/I BC

188

189

190   Port, Switzerland. Sword stamp.
L. of inscription and stamp 2·7 cm. I BC

191   Heiligenstein, Germany.
Sword stamp. *W.* of stamp 0·9 cm. II BC

192   La Tène, Switzerland. Sword stamp.
W. of stamp c. 1 cm. II BC

191

190

192

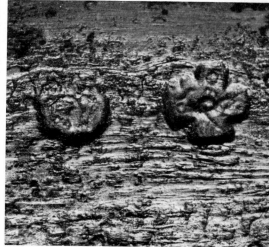

193   Ilbesheim, Germany. Sword stamps.
D. of left stamp c. 0·8 cm. II BC

194 Continental Iron Age coins
(a) Scărişoara, Romania. Silver coin:
obverse and reverse. *D.* 2·6 cm. IV BC

(b) N.W. France, 'Redones'.
'Billon stater': obverse. *D.* 2·3 cm. II/I BC

(c) N. Italy. Silver coin, reverse.
D. 1·5 cm. ?III BC

(d) Lower Danube. Silver coin, reverse.
D. c. 2·8 cm. III BC

(e) Brittany, 'Redones'. Gold coin, reverse.
D. 2·2 cm. II/I BC

(f) Brittany. 'Coriosolites'. 'Billon stater', obverse and reverse.
D. 2 cm. I BC

(g) Somme basin.
'Potin' coins, obverse and reverse.
D. 2 cm. I BC

(h) Mardorf, Germany. Gold coins, obverse.
D. c. 1·8 cm. I BC

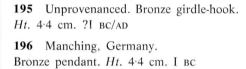

195 Unprovenanced. Bronze girdle-hook. *Ht.* 4·4 cm. ?I BC/AD

196 Manching, Germany. Bronze pendant. *Ht.* 4·4 cm. I BC

197 Bad Nauheim, Germany. Bronze pendant. *Ht.* 5·3 cm. I BC

198 Basle, Switzerland. Bronze knife: detail. *L.* of handle c. 7·5 cm. I BC/A

199 Zemplín, Czechoslovakia. Iron knife: detail. *Ht.* of head c. 1·8 cm. I

198

199

202 Balzers, Liechtenstein.
Bronze figurine. *Ht.* 12·7 cm. ?II/I BC

200-201 Giubiasco, Switzerland. Bronze
brooches *L.* (**200**) of head 1 cm.; (**201**) 11·4 cm. II BC

203 Dejbjerg, Denmark. Ritual waggon and details of hand-grips. *D.* of wheels c. 95 cm.; masks on hand-grips 6·5 × 7·6 cm. I BC

204

205

204-206 Manerbio sul Mella, N. Italy.
Silver discs and fragment.
D. (**204**) 19·2 cm.; (**205**) 9 cm.;
l. (**206**) 10·2 cm. ?III/II BC

206

207 Staré Hradisko, Czechoslovakia.
Bronze fragment. 6·3 × 7·7 cm. I BC

208 Szárazd, Hungary. Gold bead.
D. c. 3·5 cm. I BC

209

210 Boughton Aluph, England.
Bronze bucket mount. *Ht.* 16·2 cm. ?I BC/AD

211 Ciumeşti, Romania. Iron helmet
with bronze crest. *Ht.* 25 cm. III/II BC

209 Gundestrup, Denmark. Silver-gilt
cauldron. (left) *Ht.* 42 cm. *d.* 69 cm.;
(upper right) detail of inner plate 'A'.
Ht. of seated figure 16·5 cm.;
(lower right) detail of inner plate 'E'.
Ht. 25 cm. Late II/early I BC
(see plate VI)

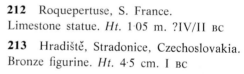

212 Roquepertuse, S. France.
Limestone statue. *Ht.* 1·05 m. ?IV/II BC

212

213 Hradiště, Stradonice, Czechoslovakia.
Bronze figurine. *Ht.* 4·5 cm. I BC

213

214 Gundestrup, Denmark. Base plate from silver-gilt cauldron. *D.* 25·6 cm. Late II/early I BC

215 Helden, Netherlands. Silver disc. *D.* 17·5 cm. ?Late I BC

216 Trichtingen, Germany. Silver torc: detail. *L.* of bulls' heads c. 6 cm. ?II BC
▼

VI Gundestrup, Denmark. Outer plate
'd' of silver-gilt cauldron. *Ht.* 21 cm.
Late II BC (see note to **209** and p. 133)

221

17   Bratislava, Czechoslovakia.
Silver coins. (a) *D.* c. 2·5 cm.;
(b) *D.* c. 2·9 cm. c. 70-60 BC

18   Santon, England. Bronze disc brooch
cover. *D.* 3·5 cm. Mid I AD

▲
220   ?'Iron Gates'. Silver helmet
Ht. 24 cm. V/IV BC

221   Coţofăneşti, Romania. Gold helmet.
Ht. c. 24 cm. ?V/IV BC

219a   Agighiol, Romania. Silver vase.
Ht. c. 28 cm. V/IV BC

219b   ?'Iron Gates'. Silver vase and
detail of base. *Ht.* c. 28 cm. V/IV BC

219 a   **219 b**

222 Rynkeby, Denmark. Bronze cauldron fragments. (a) 42 × 19 cm.; (b) *ht.* c. 20 cm. I BC/AD

223 Kraghede, Denmark. Detail of pot. L. of left-hand animal c. 6 cm. ?I BC

225 Luncani, Romania. Bronze boar. *L.* c. 10·5 cm. I BC

224 Hounslow, England. Bronze boar. *L.* 8 cm. I BC/AD

226 Euffigneix, France. Sandstone pillar-statue. Total *ht.* c. 30 cm., *w.* 18 cm. ?I BC

227 Hohensalzburg, Austria. Stone head. *Ht.* of head c. 17 cm. ?I AD

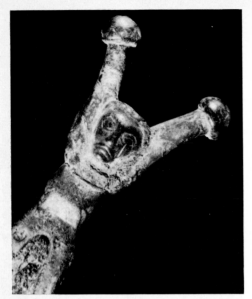

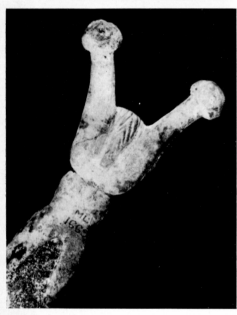

228

229

228 Salon, France. Bronze and iron sword hilt: detail. *W.* across arms c. 4 5 cm. II BC

229 Ballyshannon Bay, Ireland. Bronze anthropoid sword hilt: detail. *Ht.* of head c. 2·5 cm. I BC

230 Welwyn, England. Bronze mounts. *Ht.* of largest 3·3 cm. Second half I BC

230

232

231 Touget, France.
Stone statue.
Ht. 74·5 cm. I/II AD

232 Bouray, France.
Bronze figure.
Ht. 42 cm. ?I BC

233 St-Germain-
Sources-Seine, France.
Oak carving.
Ht. of heads c. 13 cm. I AD

233

234 St-Germain-Sources-Seine, France. Wooden bull. *L.* of head 12·5 cm. I AD

235 Roquepertuse, France. Limestone double head. Total *l.* 34 cm. ?III/II BC

236 Roquepertuse, France. Fragment of limestone frieze. *L.* 63 cm. ?III/II BC

237 Neuvy-en-Sullias, France.
Bronze dancing figurine. *Ht*. 14 cm. I BC

238 Neuvy-en-Sullias, France.
Bronze boar. *Ht*. c. 68 cm. ?I BC

239   Forêt de Compiègne, France.
Bronze head. *Ht.* c. 18 cm. I/II AD

240   ?England. Bronze head.
Ht. 12·8 cm. I/II AD

241   Châtillon-sur-Indre, France.
Bronze sword hilt and scabbard: detail.
Ht. of handle 14 cm., *ht.* of head c. 2·5 cm.
Mid I BC

242   Staré Hradisko, Czechoslovakia.
Bronze sword hilt mount. *Ht.* 2·6 cm. I BC

243   Gloucester, England.
Stone head. *Ht.* 20 cm. Mid I AD

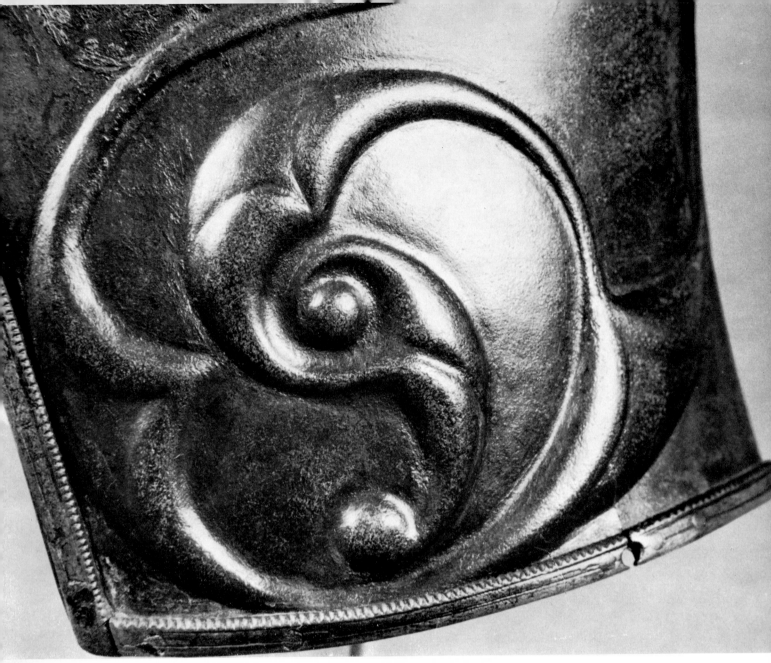

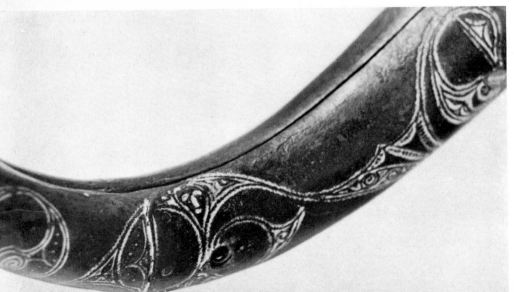

244-5 Torrs Farm, Kirkcudbrightshire, Scotland. (**244**) Bronze pony cap: detail. *L.* of bird's head spiral c. 3 cm. (**245**) Bronze horn: detail. *Ht.* of head c. 1·1 cm. ?II BC

245

246 Lough-na-Shade, N. Ireland. Bronze horn mount. *D.* 20·3 cm. ?II/I BC

247 Wandsworth, England (R. Thames). Bronze shield boss: detail. *D.* 33 cm. ?II/I BC

248 Lisnacrogher,
N. Ireland. Bronze sword
scabbard. Total *l.* c. 56 cm.,
w. 4·2 cm. ?II BC

249 Coleraine, N. Ireland.
Bronze sword scabbard:
detail. Total *l.* c. 48 cm.,
w. c. 3·8 cm. ?II BC

250

250 Standlake, England (R. Thames). Bronze scabbard mount. *W.* 5 cm. ?early II BC

252 R. Witham, England. Bronze shield. *L.* 1·13 m. ?II BC (see plate VII)

252

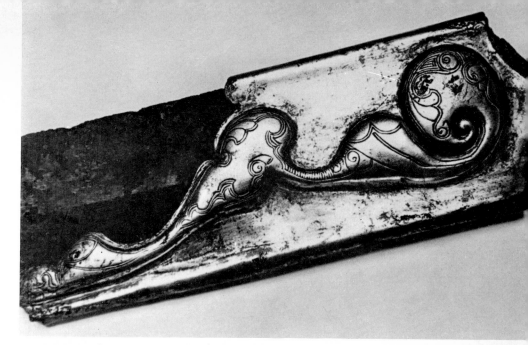

251 R. Witham, England.
Sword scabbard mount. *L.* 13 cm. ?II BC

252

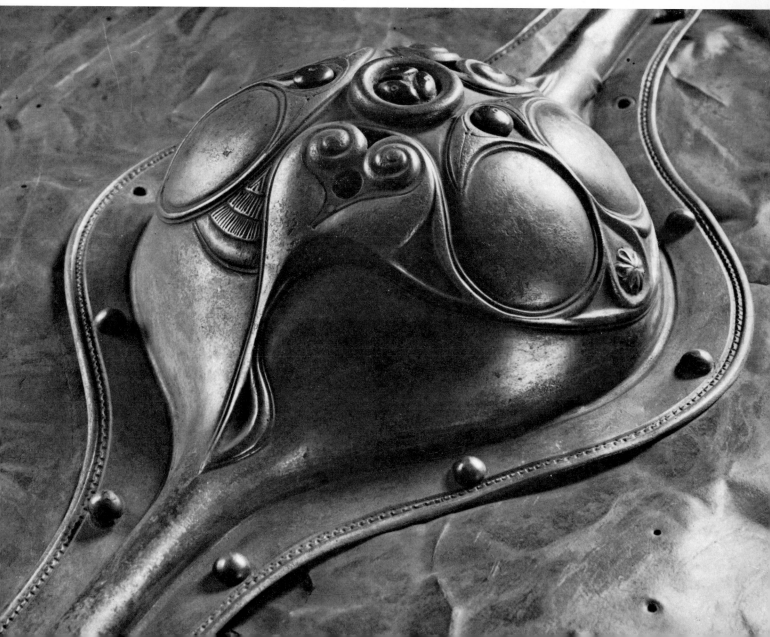

253 Battersea, England (R. Thames).
Bronze and glass inlaid shield.
L. 77·5 cm., *w.* of 'horns' (detail) c. 5 cm. I AD

VII River Witham, Nr. Washingborough.
Detail of bronze shield with glass inlay.
W. 15·7 cm. ?II BC (see notes to **252**)

254 Llyn Cerrig Bach, Anglesey. Bronze
disc: detail. *D.* of central area 6·7 cm. ?Early I BC

255 Wandsworth, England (R. Thames).
Bronze shield mount: detail.
W. across top of 'head', c. 5 cm. ?II/I BC

256 Lough Crew, Ireland.
Bone 'trial pieces'.
L. of larger piece 14 cm. ?late I BC/AD

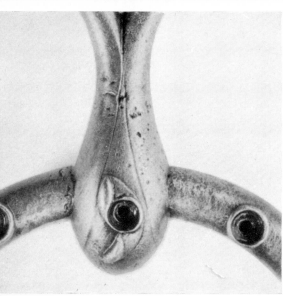

257 Datchet, England
(R. Thames). Iron spear with
bronze mounts. Total *l.* c. 30 cm.
Later I BC/early I AD

258 Windsor, England
(R. Thames). Bronze horse bit:
detail. *D.* of ring 1·2 cm.
?Earlier I BC

259 Bugthorpe, England.
Bronze and iron scabbard: detail.
Max. *w.* 4·5 cm. Later I BC

258   **259**

260 ?South-east England. Engraved
bronze mirror. *Ht.* 22·5 cm. Later I BC

261 Great Chesterford, England.
Engraved bronze mirror: detail. *Ht.* c. 4 cm.
Early I AD

262 Tal-y-llyn, Wales. Bronze shield
mount: detail.
D. of decorated area c. 8·5 cm. ?early I BC

263 Nijmegen, Netherlands.
Bronze mirror handle: detail.
W. of handle mount c. 9 cm. I AD

264 Aldborough, England.
Bronze-coated iron terret (rein-ring).
Ht. 12·8 cm. I AD

265 Melsonby, England. Bronze mount.
Ht. 10·1 cm. I AD

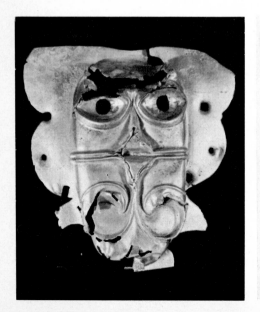

266 Tal-y-llyn, Wales.
Bronze ?shield
mount. Max. *w.* 10·4 cm.
?late I BC/early I AD

267 Tal-y-llyn, Wales. Bronze shield boss. Max. *w.* c. 11·5 cm. ?I BC

268 Moel Hiraddug, Wales. Bronze plaque. *L.* 15·3 cm. I AD

269 ?Ireland. Bronze disc. *D.* 27·2 cm. I/II AD

267

268

269

270 Ireland. 'Petrie crown': detail.
D. of disc 6 cm. I/II AD

271 Longban Is., N. Ireland (R. Bann),
Bronze disc. *D.* 10·5 cm. I/II AD

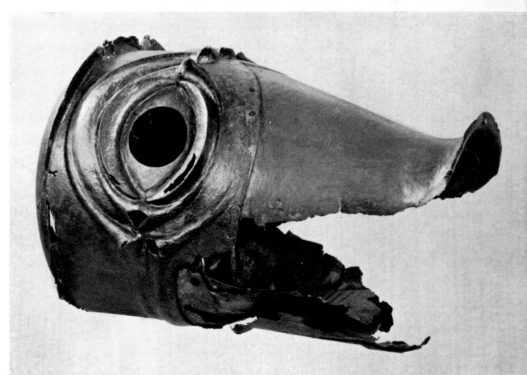

272 Deskford, Scotland. Bronze horn
terminal. *L.* 21·5 cm. Mid I AD

273 Keshcarrigan, Ireland (R. Shannon). Bronze bowl. *D.* 14·2 cm. Late I BC/early I AD

274 Ham Hill, England. Bronze vessel mount. *Ht.* c. 4 cm. I AD

275 Harpenden, England. Bronze ram's head mount. *L.* c. 8 cm. Early I AD

273

274

275

276 Felmersham-on-Ouse, England. Bronze spout. *L.* c. 11 cm. I AD

277 Łęg Piekarski, Poland. Bronze bowl: detail of spout. *L.* c. 7·5 cm. Mid I AD

278

279

278 Niederursel, Germany. Wrought iron fire-dog. *Ht.* 69 cm. I BC/AD

279 Lord's Bridge, England. Wrought iron fire-dog. *Ht.* 71 cm. Late I BC/early I AD

280 Ralaghan, Ireland. Carved oak figure. *Ht.* c. 1·14 m. ?I/II AD

281 Broddenbjerg, Denmark. Carved
wooden figure. *Ht.* c. 88 cm. II/IBC

282 Braak, Germany. Pair of carved
wooden figures: details.
Ht. of faces c. 20 cm. After I BC

283 Caerwent, Wales.
Sandstone head. *Ht.* 23 cm. I/II AD

284 Roos Carr, England. Carved
pinewood figure: detail.
Ht. of head c. 5 cm. ?VII BC/I AD

285 Tanderagee, N. Ireland.
Stone figure. *Ht.* c. 60 cm. ?I/II AD

284

286

286 ?Sutherlandshire, Scotland.
Granite *tricephalos*. *Ht.* 12 cm. ?III/I BC

287 Bexbach, Germany.
Stone head. *Ht.* 23·5 cm. ?I BC

288 Glejbjerg, Denmark. Granite
carving: detail. *Ht.* c. 30 cm. ?I/IV AD

288

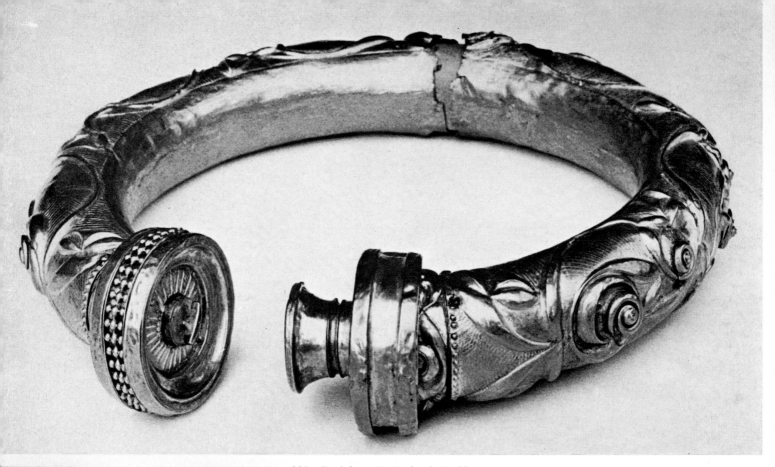

289 Broighter, N. Ireland. Gold torc.
D. of torc 19·5 cm., *d.* of tube 3 cm.
Late I BC

290 Netherurd, Scotland. Gold torc
terminal. *D.* 5·5 cm. Mid I BC

VIII (a) Santon, Norfolk. Two bronze
harness mounts with enamel inlay.
Ht. 7·9 cm. and 6·8 cm. Mid I AD
(see note on p. 163)
(b) Pitkelloney, Perthshire. Pair of
bronze armlets with red and yellow
enamel inlay. *W.* 8·3 cm. I/II AD
(see note on p. 173-4)

a

b

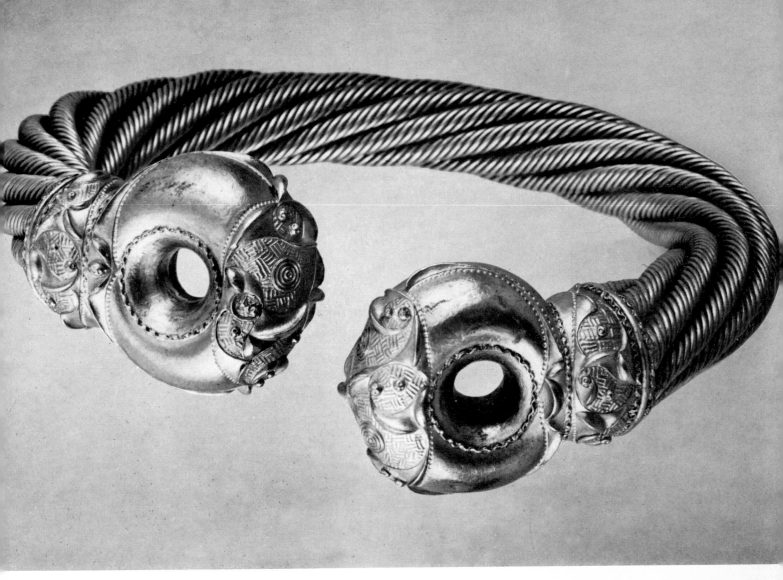

291 Snettisham, England.
Electrum torc. *D.* c. 20 cm. Mid I BC
292 Ipswich, England.
Gold torc. Max. *d.* 20 cm. Mid I BC

293 Ulceby, England. Bronze and iron biting. Max. *d.* 8·8 cm. Later I BC

294 R. Thames at Waterloo Bridge, England. Bronze helmet. *Ht.* of cap 16 cm., *w.* between horns 42·5 cm. Later I BC

295 Meare West, England. Three incised pots.
(a) upper left; storage jar. *Ht.* 35·5 cm.
(b) right; open bowl. *D.* 23 cm.
(c) lower left; lid. *D.* 17 cm. II/I BC

296 Trawsfynydd, Wales.
Wooden tankard with bronze fittings.
Ht. 14·3 cm., *d.* 18·3 cm. Late I AD

297 Birdcombe Court, Wraxall, England.
Cast bronze collar.
Internal *d.* 12·5 cm. I AD

298

298 Stichill, Scotland. Bronze neck-ring.
Outer *d.* 19 cm. Late I AD

301 'Seven Sisters' hoard, Upper Dylais, Wales. Bronze tankard-handle. *L.* 12 cm. Later I AD

302 Culbin Sands, Scotland. Cast bronze armlet. *W.* c. 11 cm., *d.* c. 8 cm. ?I AD

299 Santon, England. Bronze embossed strip: detail. *W.* c. 3 cm. Late I AD

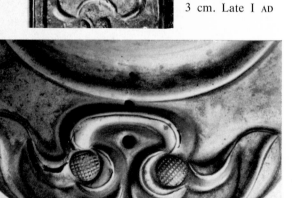

300 ?Northern England. Bronze helmet: detail of neck-guard. *W.* 8·9 cm. Late I AD

303 Elmswell, England. Bronze casket mount on iron base. *W.* 24 cm. Late I AD

304 Tre'r Ceiri, Wales. Gilt-bronze brooch. *W.* 3 cm. Later I AD

305 Greatchesters, England. Gilt-bronze brooch. *L.* 11·5 cm. Late I AD

306 Britain. Coins.

(a) Gallo-Belgic gold coin, obverse.
D. 2·7 cm. II BC

(b) 'Catuvellauni'. Bronze coin, obverse
and reverse. *D.* 1·4 cm. c. AD 5-40

(c) 'Catuvellauni'. Gold coin, reverse.
D. 1·65 cm. c. 20 BC-AD 5

(d) 'Catuvellauni'. Bronze coin, reverse.
D. 1·7 cm. Before AD 40

a

b

c

d

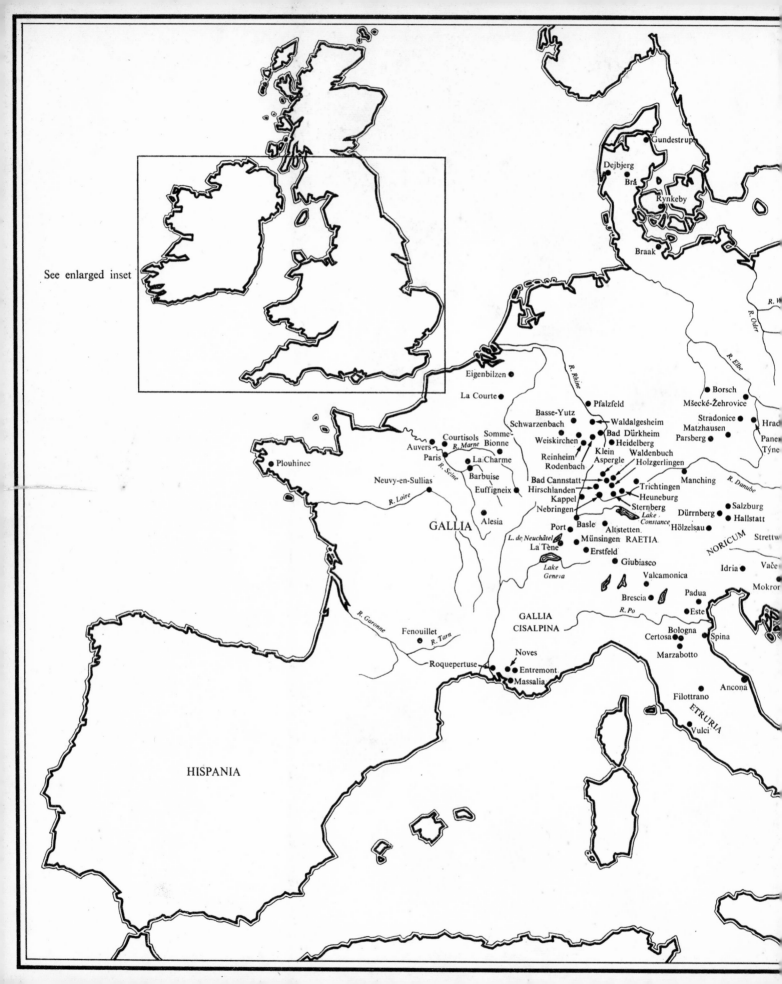